Colour Library Books

· *STEP BY STEP* ·

MICROWAVE
COOK BOOK

Colour Library Books

CLB2239
This edition published 1989 by
Colour Library Books Ltd
Godalming Business Centre, Catteshall Lane,
Godalming, Surrey GU7 1XW

Prepared by Marshall Cavendish Books Ltd
58 Old Compton Street, London W1V 5PA

ISBN 0 86283 752 9

Typeset by ABM Typographics Ltd., Hull
Printed in Italy

CONTENTS

Microwave cookers and safety

Microwave cookers are safe to use provided all recommendations and instructions are followed. Every cooker undergoes stringent tests by the manufacturer to detect possible leakage, so that thawing, reheating and cooking of foods can be carried out safely.

Microwave cookers are also tested for electrical safety at the Electricity Council's Appliance Testing Laboratories to the requirements of the British Standard. They should carry the familiar British Electrotechnical Approvals Board (BEAB) label.

There is no possible way that microwaves can be present when the door is opened. As soon as the door catch moves the microwaves stop.

Remember the following precautions:
★ Always follow cooker and food manufacturers' instructions carefully
★ Never tamper with door seals and locks
★ If you suspect your cooker might be leaking, have it tested by a qualified microwave engineer
★ Check that all frozen foods are thoroughly thawed before they are cooked
★ Cook food to a high enough temperature. Remember to turn, stir or re-arrange food during cooking time
★ Never cut down on Standing Time which is an important part of the cooking process and is necessary to ensure food is cooked through
★ Follow recipes carefully
★ Read the Watchpoints on page 11

INTRODUCTION

Microwave cookers now play an important role in the kitchens of today. Bringing with them a new approach to cooking, they have led to faster, healthier and more economical meal preparation.

The *Step-by-step Microwave Cookbook* provides a valuable source of information and inspiration for anyone using a microwave. Whether you live alone and find the microwave cooker the best solution to the problems of cooking for one, or have to rush home from work to start preparing a family meal, you will find this book packed full of helpful tips, time-saving ideas and hundreds of delicious recipes to choose from.

Throughout the book, the emphasis is on speed and simplicity. Every recipe is written in a clear step-by-step format, and cooking and standing times are given so that you can tell at a glance how long a recipe will take. Many techniques are illustrated with series of step-by-step colour photographs, making doubly sure you won't go wrong, while the opening section of the book includes a Glossary and more detailed advice on using the recipes.

The first recipe chapter, Microwave Basics, shows you how to microwave basic recipes that you will use over and over again. The microwave is ideal for preparing meals in a hurry and you will find plenty to choose from in the Quick and Easy Snacks chapter.

If you want to put together something more formal for a family meal, the following chapters cover Fish and Seafood, Meat and Poultry, Vegetables and Fruit, and Desserts and Baking, so you will have no difficulty in selecting the perfect menu for the occasion. The final chapter on Entertaining is a collection of complete menus ranging from an easy weekend lunch to an elegant dinner or a summer buffet party. Every menu is accompanied by vital countdown information so you can be sure of perfect timing.

All in all, this bumper volume provides everything you need to accompany your microwave cooker. You will be sure to turn to it again and again – for advice on techniques, for a quick and easy snack for the kids, or to select an impressive menu for a special occasion.

GLOSSARY

Arcing This visible sparking effect is the result of microwaves bouncing off foil, gold or silver trim on crockery, or other metallic substances in the cooker. Slight arcing does not damage the cooker but, if allowed to continue, can damage the magnetron and the cooker walls.

Arranging Positioning food correctly is important for even cooking or thawing. Always place thicker or denser parts to the outside and thinner, more easily cooked parts to the centre, where they receive less microwave energy. Arrange individual items in a circle for even cooking.

Breaking up When thawing food in a microwave, break it up into pieces as soon as possible, and stir to expose different areas to microwaves. (Made-up dishes which cannot be stirred or broken up should be thawed more slowly, then be allowed to stand until thawed right through.)

Browning agent As the microwave usually imparts no colour to food during cooking, browning agents such as soy sauce, paprika, breadcrumbs and commercial browning powders or liquids can be used to make foods look appetizing.

Browning dish The base of a browning dish contains a substance which, like food, becomes hot during microwaving. Always follow the manufacturer's instructions for pre-heating, prior to searing and browning foods. Apart

from browning dishes, empty dishes must never be placed in an operating microwave cooker.

Browning element Some cookers are fitted with an element, very similar to a conventional grill. This cooks by direct heat and gives an appetizing colour and crispness to microwaved foods.

Combination cooker These cookers combine microwave and conventional cooking in one model, giving the advantage of speed by microwave and good appearance through convection cooking.

Covering Most foods are covered as this speeds up cooking. Use loosely fitting lids, vented cling film, absorbent paper and greaseproof paper; a new type of cling film is now available, made without plasticizers and suitable for microwaving. Do not cover foods to be kept dry.

Hot and cold spots These are areas in the cooker which, because of microwave patterns receive either too much or too little microwave energy. Although rotating antennae, stirrer fans and turntables reduce this problem, stirring and rearranging is generally recommended for even cooking.

Magnetron This device converts electrical energy to microwaves.

Memory Some cookers have the facility to store two or more microwave cooking times and power levels. This is useful if you cook

the same dish often or do not wish to supervise the cooking.

Microwave This is a wave of electro-magnetic energy which penetrates food, agitating the molecules of which it is composed, thus creating heat.

Microwave meat thermometers These specially designed thermometers can be inserted into joints of meat and used to check internal temperature throughout cooking. (Conventional thermometers must not be used in the microwave — although they can be used to check temperatures once meat has been removed from the cooker.)

Microwave-safe Containers used in the microwave must not have metal trims or handles. Test crockery for safety by placing a glass, half-filled with water in the cooker with the dish. Microwave at 100% (High) for 2-3 minutes. The water, not the dish, should be hot. If the dish is hot, it should not be used. Lead crystal and certain plastics and earthenware are not microwave-safe.

Piercing Always pierce foods with a skin or soft shell (eg unpeeled potatoes, egg yolks or scallops) before microwaving. Never microwave eggs in shells, as they will explode. Pierce roasting bags and vent cling film covers to allow steam to escape.

Raising in the cooker Microwaves reach the top of food first, so this part cooks more quickly. This can be a problem with some deep dishes. To help cook the base, food can be raised off the floor of the cooker by standing it on an inverted saucer or plate. This is particularly necessary when cooking deep cakes and breads.

Rearrange To change the position of food during microwaving to ensure more even cooking. Turn over and rearrange individual portions and rotate and rearrange individual dishes to bring the less cooked parts to the outside.

Resting time When microwaving joints of meat, a resting time is needed, in addition to standing time. This allows the fibres of the meat to settle and reabsorb the meat juices for easy carving.

Roasting bags These cooking bags encourage browning when roasting meat or poultry. Tie bags loosely with a non-metallic tie and pierce to allow steam to escape.

Roasting racks These are specially designed to raise meats above their juices during cooking.

Rotating Because microwave energy cooks unevenly, it is necessary to turn dishes occasionally during cooking. In cookers with fitted

turntables, rotating is not always necessary.

Rotating antennae This is a system built into the floor of the cooker, found in some cookers without turntables. The waves are deflected from base of cooker to encourage even cooking.

Runaway cooking Foods being thawed in the microwave can start to cook before they are completely thawed. To avoid runaway cooking, stir and break up thawing foods regularly or reduce the power setting and thaw more slowly.

Sensor control A device in the machine which senses when food is sufficiently cooked and switches the cooker off automatically.

Shelves Some cookers are fitted with a shelf which enables cooking to be carried out on two levels. This is very useful if you want to cook two dishes at once.

Shielding When microwaving foods of irregular thickness or in dishes with corners, shielding may be necessary. The thinner, quicker-cooking areas are covered with foil and, because microwaves cannot pass through the foil, the cooking of these areas is slowed down. Use only small, smooth pieces of foil for shielding, making sure that they are well secured and cannot touch any part of the cooker during microwaving.

Sparking See Arcing.

Standing time Food cooked by microwave continues to cook after the machine has been switched off, so most food is removed from the cooker when slightly underdone,

and is left to finish cooking during standing time.

Stirrer fan This is a fan or paddle situated in the roof of some cookers. It rotates, distributing the microwaves more evenly.

Stirring As microwaves penetrate from the outside, foods like soups, vegetables and stews benefit from stirring during cooking. Stir from the centre to the outside, drawing less cooked parts to the outside of the dish.

Tenting This is the loose covering of foods which have reached the end of microwaving, but which need to stand before they are fully cooked (such as joints of meat). Use foil, shiny side in, to keep the heat in, and cover loosely but so as to prevent cold air from reaching the food.

Temperature probe A temperature probe can be attached to some cookers. It enables you to control microwave cooking by internal temperature, rather than by time. It is inserted into the thickest part of the joints of meat or large, dense pieces of food and the desired temperature selected. On reaching this temperature, the cooker either switches off automatically or reduces to a low setting to keep the food warm.

Turntable A built-in device found in some microwave cookers which rotates food automatically during microwaving. The advantage is that cooking is more even.

Variable power Many models of microwave cooker can be set to cook at different powers. The higher the power, the faster the rate of cooking. Certain foods benefit from slower cooking at a reduced power setting.

Venting Tight coverings and cooking bags must be pierced or have a vent through which steam can escape. If steam builds up, the pressure can burst the bag or covering during microwaving.

Wave deflector See Stirrer fan.

9

Factors affecting microwaving

Various factors affect how microwaves cook food, the most important is the wattage in combination with the size of the cooker cavity. For this reason, all timings can only be a guideline.

Density of food
The speed of cooking is affected by the density of the food — light, aerated foods such as sponge cakes cook more quickly than dense, heavy ones such as meat.

To cook evenly, food should, where appropriate, be chopped or divided into evenly-sized pieces, so that microwave penetration is uniform between the pieces.

Composition of food
High-sugar and high fat dishes cook more quickly than others. For this reason, the reducing of quantities of such recipes is not recommended, as the food may burn while it is being microwaved.

Liquids attract microwave energy, so it is important to drain away the meat juices which gather when cooking a whole joint, as these attract microwaves from the meat, altering cooking time.

Quantity of food
The more food you cook at once in the microwave, the longer it will take. Small quantities cook very quickly because of overlapping microwaves which penetrate from all sides. (In larger quantities, conducted heat from the outside cooks the inside.) Care should be taken to prevent burning.

Cooking containers
Cooking is quicker in microwave-safe plastics than in pottery — plastics absorb less microwave energy, leaving more for the food.

Depth and volume of dishes affect the speed of cooking — shallow, spread-out foods cook more quickly than thick masses.

The shape of the cooking dish is important. Round dishes are best for even cooking — the corners of square or rectangular dishes need shielding to prevent overcooking. Cakes are most successful in ring moulds, as these allow microwaves to penetrate all around from the centre as well.

Size of cooker
The size of the cavity of the cooker affects the speed of cooking; in a small cooker, waves are stronger because they have less distance to travel, and therefore cook more quickly.

Power of cooker
The power output of the cooker affects the cooking time — a high-wattage microwave will cook more quickly than 650, 600 or 500 watt models.

Position of food in the cooker
Thin parts of food cook more quickly than thick parts. Even-shaped portions should be arranged, thickest parts to the outside, where the microwave energy is strongest.

Individual dishes or portions of food cook more uniformly if arranged, evenly spaced in a circle, so microwaves can penetrate from all sides. Fast-cooking foods, such as cakes and biscuits, have less time in which to cook evenly; for best results, they may be placed on an upturned dish in the centre of the cooker to raise them above the floor or turntable.

Stirring of food
Microwaves cook from the outside. For even cooking, foods should, where possible, be stirred regularly to move the uncooked parts from the centre to the outside and vice versa.

To achieve even cooking, larger pieces of food need to be turned over because in most cookers, waves are distributed from the top of the cavity, making the top of the food more likely to cook first. This is particularly evident when pieces of food reach almost to the top of the cooker.

Covering of food
Cooking results vary if covering instructions are not followed. To retain moisture in the dish, use vented cling film or a lid. If liquid formed by microwaving has to be removed, use absorbent paper. To stop splashing, cover with greaseproof paper.

Temperature of food
Chilled or cold food from the refrigerator takes longer to microwave than food which is warm or at room temperature, as time is needed for heating too.

COOKING TIMES

Cooking times may need to be extended if cooking on a lower wattage model. If it is necessary to adjust recipes for a **600 watt** model, *as a guide* add 20 seconds per minute to the cooking time by using the chart (right). But, always check food at the end of the cooking time given in the recipe, and always check manufacturer's instructions as individual cookers may vary. For **500 watt** models, follow the guidelines above and, if necessary, add more time, but only after checking the food in the cooker.
Note: When reheating pastry and other fatty and/or sugary food, **do not** increase the cooking time and **do not** leave food in the microwave unattended.

MICROWAVE COOKING TIME CONVERSIONS			
650/700W	Equivalent time on a 600 watt model	650/700W	Equivalent time on a 600 watt model
10 secs	13 secs	7 mins	9 mins 20 secs
15 secs	20 secs	8 mins	10 mins 40 secs
30 secs	40 secs	9 mins	12 mins
45 secs	1 min	10 mins	13 mins 20 secs
1 min	1 min 20 secs	20 mins	26 mins 40 secs
2 mins	2 mins 40 secs	30 mins	40 mins
3 mins	4 mins	40 mins	53 mins 20 secs
4 mins	5 mins 20 secs	50 mins	66 mins 40 secs
5 mins	6 mins 40 secs	1 hour	80 mins
6 mins	8 mins	1½ hours	2 hours

Watchpoints

To get the best from your cooker, be aware of the following points:

● **Don't** use metal utensils/dishes, metal ties, cooking tags, lead crystal or foil lined packages (see also **Foil,** below). Check that plastics are microwave-safe before using. Avoid dishes with metal decorations. Don't use conventional meat or sugar thermometers.

● **Alcohol:** heating alcohol alone in the microwave is not recommended, as it can ignite.

● **Eggs:** never attempt to cook eggs in their shells – they will burst on heating up or when cracked open.

● **Oil:** never attempt to deep-fry in the microwave – keep to small quantities of oil in cooking.

● **Maintaining the cooker:** never tamper with door locks or use a damaged cooker.

● **Browning dishes:** always check with your manufacturer's handbook. Never pre-heat the dish for longer than the recommended time as this can damage the glass turntable or glass plate cooker base. Some manufacturers recommend placing the browning dish on an upturned heatproof glass plate or special microwave trivet to protect the cooker base.

● **Foil:** always check the manufacturer's instructions to ensure foil can be used. Use small, smooth pieces of foil, securely fastened. Do not allow foil to touch walls, roof or door inside cooker.

● **Following recipes:** it is essential to follow microwave recipes and instructions carefully. The balance of ingredients is crucial to the success of a recipe. (For example, if you reduce the amount of food, the microwaving time will not be correct.)

● **High sugar and/or fatty foods:** do not leave such foods unattended in the cooker, as they heat up very quickly and burn easily. Do not reduce recipe quantities for cooking or reheating.

● **Reducing 'starchy' recipes:** if cutting quantities, make sure that ingredients like pasta and rice, are still covered with liquid.

● **Small quantities:** when microwaving very small quantities of food, such as reheating baby food or browning nuts, place a glass of water in the cooker to ensure a sufficient load.

● **Clothes:** never attempt to dry wet clothing or papers in the microwave.

● **Inadvertent switching on:** this can damage the magnetron. As a safeguard, keep a cup of water in the cooker when it is not in use.

Using the recipes in this book

All recipes have been tested on **650/700 watt** models but can be used for 500 and 600 watt microwaves by making adjustments to cooking times (see chart opposite).

Individual cookers may vary, so microwaving times given in recipes are a guide only.

Total cooking time At the top of each recipe, the number in the box gives the total microwaving time for 650/700 watt models. If there are two or more stages of cooking, this number will be the sum of those times. If the recipe gives timings per kilo/pound or a range of times, then the number in the box refers to the lower weight and shorter microwaving time. These timings are for microwaving only – not preparation or standing time.

Don't forget Food can overcook in seconds in a microwave, so it is always better to undercook it. You can always cook it for just a little longer.

Smaller quantities If you use smaller amounts of food than the recipe specifies, reduce the microwaving time accordingly.

Equipment The size, shape and capacity of your cooking dishes will affect how the food cooks in your microwave. Recipes are therefore specific about containers.

Power settings These are given in percentages – 100%, 70%, 50%, 30% and 20% – and also as descriptions – High, Medium High, Medium, Low, Defrost. These terms may not be the same on your model. Check with your manufacturer's operating instructions.

Using foil Do not use large pieces of foil or foil dishes to cook, heat or thaw food in the microwave unless specifically recommended in your manufacturer's operating instructions.

Small pieces of foil may be used for shielding, but ensure foil is smooth, well secured and cannot touch the walls, roof or door of the cooker.

Ingredients
Weights and measures: both metric and imperial measurements are given. Work from one set only.

Measuring spoons should be used. Level the ingredients across lightly.

Sugar is granulated unless specified.

Vegetables and fruits are medium-sized and peeled unless otherwise specified.

Eggs are medium unless specified – weight 50g / 2oz (EEC size 4).

All recipes have been tested using ingredients at room temperature.

11

CHAPTER ONE

MICROWAVE BASICS

Once you have mastered the techniques of microwave cooking you will feel confident enough to use your cooker for any number of tasks. This chapter illustrates just how flexible the microwave can be, giving recipes for many of the basic items you would normally cook on your conventional cooker, such as sauces, rice and pasta.

As well as basic cooking instructions, each section includes a number of delicious recipes using a particular ingredient, giving you plenty of choice. The section on rice, for example, includes both main courses and side dishes that can be made using rice, hot or cold. There are also tips on how to freeze rice and then thaw and reheat it in your microwave.

A number of recipes for both sweet and savoury sauces are provided – everything from classic Béchamel to a Boozy Coffee Sauce to serve with ice cream, soufflés, mousses or crêpes. However, if the sauce you need is not here, instructions are given for adapting your own conventional sauce recipes for cooking in the microwave. Similarly, a basic recipe is given for Asparagus quiche, but this can easily be used to adapt any of your favourite conventional quiche recipes so you can cook them more quickly in your microwave.

Other sections in this chapter show you how to cook food in parcels in the microwave cooker (ideal for single portions) and how to make the best use of herbs and spices in microwaved dishes. There are also helpful sections on using marinades to give food extra flavour and tenderness, and on the use of aspic, which is marvellously easy to microwave. Finally the chapter closes with invaluable advice on how to use a variety of sweet and savoury toppings, or to add decorative touches that ensure your microwaved food looks as good as it tastes.

Adapting a recipe: sauces

Sauces are an essential part of any cook's repertoire. Follow the step-by-step instructions and see how to adapt your favourite sauces for cooking in the microwave.

The simple touch of a good sauce can 'make' a dish. Most sauces, even when made conventionally, are not difficult, but made in the microwave cooker they are even easier. Sauces demonstrate the advantages of microwaving beautifully. For a start, many of them can be measured, mixed and microwaved in the same container.

While different types of sauces vary in the amount of stirring needed, none of them need constant stirring as they do conventionally. And sauces like the egg-based ones that you may have regarded as a bit more tricky are made quickly and simply.

The following recipes show how basic and traditional sauces can be converted for cooking successfully in a microwave cooker. The step-by-step information shows how easy it is to convert your own favourite recipes for microwaving.

When making milk-based sauces always use a large, deep container as the sauces rise to almost double their volume when boiling. A straight-sided container will heat liquid quicker than an angled one. If adding sugar, add it at the initial blending stage.

NOTE: Milk may be replaced with half milk and half well-flavoured stock in savoury sauces.

Points to note

Stirring frequently ensures sauce is smooth and shiny. A small balloon whisk is ideal for stirring as it is the quickest and most effective way of ensuring the sauce is evenly blended.

Reheating flour-based sauces made in advance, will take about 2 minutes for 275ml / ½pt of thin (or sweet) sauce and about 3 minutes for the same quantity of thick sauce. Stir well to serve. (Sugar heats quickly in a microwave oven therefore sweet sauces will heat quicker than unsweetened ones.)

Advantages of microwaved sauces

- *No risk of congealed or burned saucepans to wash up!*
- *Less washing up as the sauce can be made in a serving jug ready to take straight to the table.*
- *Microwave sauces are so quick they do not have to be made in advance but may be simply prepared when everything else is ready.*

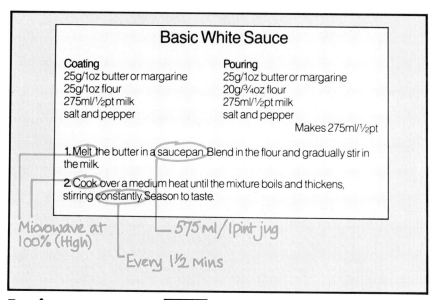

Basic White Sauce

Coating
25g/1oz butter or margarine
25g/1oz flour
275ml/½pt milk
salt and pepper

Pouring
25g/1oz butter or margarine
20g/¾oz flour
275ml/½pt milk
salt and pepper

Makes 275ml/½pt

1. Melt the butter in a saucepan. Blend in the flour and gradually stir in the milk.

2. Cook over a medium heat until the mixture boils and thickens, stirring constantly. Season to taste.

Microwave at 100% (High)

575ml/1pint jug

Every 1½ Mins

How to microwave Basic white sauce

Measure *out the butter or margarine and place in a 575ml / 1pt jug. Cover with vented cling film as it will spatter during melting.*

Basic white sauce

5½ mins

Standing time: none

Follow the method below for making either a coating sauce or a slightly thinner pouring sauce.

COATING
25g / 1oz butter or margarine
30ml / 2tbls plain flour
275ml / ½pt milk
salt and pepper

POURING
25g / 1oz butter or margarine
22.5ml / 1½tbls plain flour
275ml / ½pt milk
salt and pepper

MAKES 275ml / ½pt

1 Place the butter in a 575ml / 1pt jug. Microwave at 100% (High) for about 30 seconds until the butter has just melted.
2 Stir in the flour and then blend in the milk until smooth.
3 Microwave at 100% (High) for about 5 minutes, stirring every 1½ minutes, until sauce is thick and smooth. Season to taste.

VARIATIONS
Cheese: Add 75g / 3oz grated Cheddar cheese at the end of cooking time. If necessary, return sauce to cooker for a few seconds to complete melting.
Parsley: Add 30-45ml / 2-3tbls chopped parsley to the sauce.

Prawn: Stir 50g / 2oz peeled prawns, 5ml / 1tsp lemon juice and 5ml / 1tsp tomato purée into the sauce 1 minute before end of cooking time.
Mushroom: Microwave 50g / 2oz sliced mushrooms with 15g / ½oz butter for 2 minutes at 100% (High). Stir into sauce 2 minutes before the end of cooking time.
Caper: Add 15ml / 1tbls drained, finely chopped capers to sauce 1 minute before the end of cooking.
Onion: Add 1 chopped onion to the melted butter in a jug and microwave at 100% (High) for 2-3 minutes, or until softened.

ENRICHING A BASIC WHITE SAUCE
A little butter, cream or egg yolk added to a white sauce (or any of the flavour variations) gives extra richness and makes it especially good to eat.
Adding butter: Stir 15g / ½oz butter into 275ml / ½pt hot sauce before serving.
Adding egg: Beat 1 egg yolk in a bowl and gradually stir 275ml / ½pt hot sauce into the beaten egg. Microwave at 100% (High) for 1 minute, stirring twice during cooking. Do not allow to boil.
  Adding the egg by this method makes it more stable and the sauce less likely to separate.
Adding cream: Stir 50ml / 3tbls double or single cream into 275ml / ½pt warm coating sauce. Microwave at 100% (High) for about 1 minute. Stir well. Do not allow to boil.

Microwave *at 100% (High) for 30 seconds until the butter has melted, stir in the flour and slowly pour in the milk, mixing with a wooden spoon until smooth. Microwave for 5 minutes.*

Stir *sauce every 1½ minutes during the microwaving time until it is thick and either coats the back of a spoon or pours from the spoon in a thin stream, depending on your requirement.*

Hollandaise Sauce

2 egg yolks (size 2)
30ml/2 tbls lemon juice or vinegar
15ml/1tbls water

large pinch salt
pinch cayenne pepper
100g/4oz butter, cut into pieces
Makes 150ml/¼pt

1. Combine the egg yolks, lemon juice or vinegar, water, salt and cayenne pepper in the top of a double boiler, beat with a wire whisk.

2. Add ⅓ butter to the egg yolk mixture and cook over hot, not boiling, water, stirring constantly until the butter melts.

3. Repeat with another ⅓ of butter. Repeat with the remaining butter, beating until the mixture thickens. Remove from the heat.

[handwritten] Melt all the butter and whisk into yolk mixture

[handwritten] small bowl

[handwritten] Microwave at 50% (medium) stirring every 15 seconds

Microtips

Egg sauces can separate if overcooked. To prevent this happening, stir sauce frequently during cooking, particularly around edge of bowl, and remove sauce from cooker when slightly underdone. The final cooking can then be completed in standing time.

If the sauce is at the correct consistency when removed from the cooker, stand bowl in cold water to prevent further cooking.

Hollandaise sauce

1¼ mins

Standing time: 1-2 mins

2 egg yolks (large)
30ml / 2tbls lemon juice or vinegar
15ml / 1tbls water
large pinch of salt
pinch of cayenne pepper
100g / 4oz butter, cut into pieces

MAKES ABOUT 150ml / ¼pt

1 Beat the egg yolks in a bowl with the lemon juice or vinegar, water, salt and cayenne pepper.
2 Place the butter in a jug and microwave at 100% (High) for about 45 seconds until melted.
3 Whisk the butter into the egg mixture with a wire whisk. Microwave at 50% (Medium) for 15 seconds, then stir and check consistency. Microwave again for 15 second bursts until sauce resembles lightly whipped cream.
4 Let stand for 1-2 minutes, whisking several times during this time.

Cook's notes

Should the Hollandaise sauce start to separate, immediately stir in 15ml / 1tbls cold water to cool it down quickly.

If the sauce should separate, don't worry, it can be simply rectified: measure 10ml / 2tsp vinegar or lemon juice into a bowl and, while stirring vigorously with a wire whisk, add the separated sauce, little by little.

If the sauce is too thick, stir in 15ml / 1tbls warm water.

16

Savoury sauces

With the microwave cooker, sauce-making has never been so easy. If making Brown sauce has always seemed like too much trouble and Béarnaise sauce too difficult, branch out now and discover a recipe for success.

For easy preparation and perfect results when making sauces, choose your microwave cooker every time. Flour or cornflour thickened sauces are lump free and need less constant attention during cooking. Cream sauces and egg-enriched sauces are less likely to separate or curdle.

A well made sauce can transform a dish using everyday ingredients into something special. Many of the sauces here can be made in 10 minutes or less. This means you can cook the sauce while the food it is to accompany is standing. If you want to get ahead, make the sauce in advance and lay cling film on the surface to stop a skin forming. Reheat sauce in the microwave just before serving.

A sauce does not have to be fancy, or complicated to be successful, but it should complement and enhance the food. See the serving suggestions chart overleaf for food that each sauce will accompany particularly well.

Cream Sauce

17

Chunky tomato sauce

23 mins

Standing time: none

A tasty tomato sauce will perk up all sorts of family fare.

1 carrot, finely chopped
1 large onion, finely chopped
15ml / 1tbls olive oil
397g / 14oz can chopped tomatoes
6 black olives, stoned, chopped
60ml / 4tbls dry white wine or
    vegetable stock
1 bay leaf
large pinch dried thyme
salt and pepper

MAKES 425ml / ¾pt

How to microwave Chunky tomato sauce

RAY DUNS

Place *the carrot, onion and oil in a bowl. Cover and microwave at 100% (High) for 8 minutes. Stir once.*

Stir *in all the remaining ingredients. Cover and microwave at 100% (High) for 7 minutes until boiling.*

Stir, *then reduce to 50% (Medium). Microwave uncovered, for 8-10 minutes until thickened. Stir once.*

How to serve classic sauces

SAUCE	DESCRIPTION	SERVE WITH
Béarnaise	Rich, classic French sauce	Prime steaks, fish, tongue, vegetables
Béchamel	French classic white sauce	Poultry, pasta, vegetables, eggs
Anchovy	Variation of Béchamel	Fish
Egg	Variation of Béchamel	Fish or cold chicken
Mornay	Cheesy variation of Béchamel	Eggs, fish, vegetables, gratins
Mustard	Variation of Béchamel	Smoked or white fish, vegetables, pork
Tarragon	Variation of Béchamel	Chicken, white fish, vegetables
Brown	Dark, rich gravy	All kinds of meat and game. Use for reheating meat.
Cider	Light, fruity sauce	Ham, gammon steaks or pork chops
Cream	Rich, creamy sauce	Vegetables, chicken or white fish
Egg and lemon	Egg-enriched pouring sauce	Game birds or meat
Lemon	Tangy, clear sauce	Chicken, ham, meatballs
Rosé	Herb-flavoured wine sauce	Chicken, turkey, pork or gammon
Savoury soured cream	Tangy sauce with mushrooms	Veal escalopes, pork chops, gammon, game
Tomato	Chunky, spooning sauce	Pasta, pizzas, gammon, fish, poultry, barbecued food or sausages

18

Cream sauce

6½ mins

Standing time: none

40g / 1½oz butter
45ml / 3tbls plain flour
250ml / 9fl oz vegetable stock
150ml / ¼pt single cream
15ml / 1tbls chopped parsley
salt and pepper

MAKES 275-425ml / ½-¾pt

1 Melt the butter in a covered bowl for 30-45 seconds at 100% (High).
2 Stir in the flour and cook at 50% (Medium) for 2 minutes.
3 Blend in vegetable stock. Cook at 50% (Medium) for 2 minutes.
4 Stir in the cream and parsley and season to taste. Microwave at 50% (Medium) for 2-3 minutes until the sauce is hot and smoothly blended. Stir once or twice.

Brown sauce

20½ mins

Standing time: none

25g / 1oz butter
225g / 8oz mushrooms, very
 finely chopped
30ml / 2tbls plain flour
375ml / 13fl oz red wine or half
 red wine and half stock
large pinch dried thyme
1 bay leaf
salt and pepper
45ml / 3tbls single cream

MAKES 425ml / ¾pt

1 Microwave the butter and mushrooms in a covered bowl at 100% (High) for 8-10 minutes, or until the mushrooms are softened.
2 Stir in the flour and microwave for 30 seconds at 100% (High).
3 Gradually blend in the wine, mixing until smooth. Add the thyme, bay leaf and season to taste.
4 Microwave at 70% (Medium-High) for 10-12 minutes, until thick. Stir every 3 minutes.
5 Stir in the cream and microwave at 50% (Medium) for 2 minutes. Strain if wished, before serving.

Brown Sauce

Golden rules for perfect sauces

● *Use a bowl and not a dish with sharp corners (such as a soufflé dish). This prevents any flour overcooking at the edges.*

● *Use a wire whisk to mix and stir a cream or smooth sauce. This ensures a good sheen and a smooth, lump-free consistency.*

● *If using flour or cornflour, make sure that it is well cooked to avoid a starchy-tasting sauce.*

● *Stir the sauce frequently during cooking to even out the heat distribution and to prevent it sticking to the bowl. Always follow instructions and timings carefully.*

● *If adding single, double or soured cream, cook the sauce at 50% (Medium) to prevent it curdling and separating.*

● *Stir frequently when reheating sauces.*

Savoury soured cream sauce

10¾ mins

Standing time: none

Serve this sauce with roast meat and game and add the meat juices for extra flavour.

25g / 1oz butter
100g / 4oz mushrooms, sliced
45ml / 3tbls plain flour
60ml / 4tbls dry sherry
150ml / ¼pt soured cream
150ml / ¼pt chicken stock
salt and pepper

MAKES 275ml / ½pt

Left: *Savoury Soured Cream Sauce*
Right: *Lemon sauce*

1 Melt the butter for 15-30 seconds at 100% (High) in a covered bowl. Add the mushrooms to the butter, cover and microwave for 3 minutes at 100% (High).
2 Stir in the flour and cook, uncovered, for 30 seconds.
3 Gradually blend in the sherry, soured cream and stock. Mix thoroughly until smooth. Season to taste.
4 Microwave at 50% (Medium) for 7-9 minutes, or until thickened. Stir twice and watch carefully to make sure the sauce does not boil or the cream will separate.

Lemon sauce

5 mins

Standing time: none

15ml / 3tsp cornflour
60ml / 4tbls lemon juice
finely grated zest of 1 lemon
275ml / ½pt chicken stock
salt and pepper

MAKES 275ml / ½pt

1 Blend the cornflour, lemon juice and zest until smooth. Stir in the stock and season to taste.
2 Microwave at 100% (High) for 5 minutes, or until thickened. Stir halfway through and on removal.

20

Rosé sauce

14½ mins

Standing time: none

25g / 1oz butter
1 onion, finely chopped
1 green pepper, seeded and chopped
1 celery stalk, sliced
30ml / 2tbls plain flour
150ml / ¼pt chicken stock
150ml / ¼pt rosé wine
10ml / 2tsp tomato purée or paste
1.5ml / ¼tsp dried parsley
1.5ml / ¼tsp dried sage
1.5ml / ¼tsp dried tarragon
salt and pepper

MAKES 275ml / ½pt

1 Put the butter, onion, pepper and celery into a bowl. Cover and microwave at 100% (High) for 8-10 minutes until softened.
2 Stir in the flour and microwave for 30 seconds at 100% (High).
3 Blend in the stock, rosé wine and tomato purée until smooth; add herbs and seasoning to taste.
4 Cook at 100% (High) for 6-8 minutes, until the sauce has thickened. Stir every 2 minutes.

Cider sauce

24 mins

Standing time: none

1 onion, finely chopped
1 dessert apple, finely chopped
90ml / 6tbls chicken stock
275ml / ½pt dry cider
salt and pepper
30ml / 6tsp cornflour
15-30ml / 1-2tbls water

MAKES 425ml / ¾pt

1 Place the onion, apple and chicken stock in a bowl. Microwave covered, at 70% (Medium-High) for 15 minutes, until the onion and apple are quite soft.
2 Stir in the cider and salt and pepper to taste. Microwave, covered, at 100% (High) for 5 minutes.
3 Blend the cornflour with the water, then stir it into the sauce.
4 Microwave at 100% (High) for 4-5 minutes, or until the sauce has thickened. Stir twice.

Blender Béarnaise sauce

1¾ mins

Standing time: none

If you do not have a food processor or blender, an alternative recipe for Béarnaise sauce can be found on page 183.

3 egg yolks
7.5ml / ½tbls white wine vinegar
7.5ml / ½tbls dry white wine
large pinch fresh or dried tarragon
salt and pepper
75g / 3oz butter
15ml / 1tbls minced or very finely chopped onion

MAKES 150ml / ¼pt

1 Combine the egg yolks, vinegar, wine, tarragon and salt and pepper to taste in a food processor or blender. Blend for about 5 seconds or until smooth.
2 Place the butter and onion in a jug and microwave, covered, at 100% (High) for ¾-1¼ minutes, until the butter is bubbling.
3 Pour the butter and onion mixture on to the egg yolk mixture in a steady stream, blending at low speed until the sauce thickens.
4 Pour the sauce into a serving dish and microwave at 50% (Medium) for 1-2 minutes or until the sauce is thick and creamy. Stir every 30 seconds.

VARIATION
If a thinner sauce is required, do not reheat in the microwave after blending and serve in a sauce boat.

Egg and lemon sauce

8 mins

Standing time: none

15ml / 1tbls made English mustard
275ml / ½pt single cream
45ml / 3tbls lemon juice
salt and pepper
120ml / 8tbls milk
1 egg yolk

MAKES 425ml / ¾pt

1 Put the mustard into a bowl and

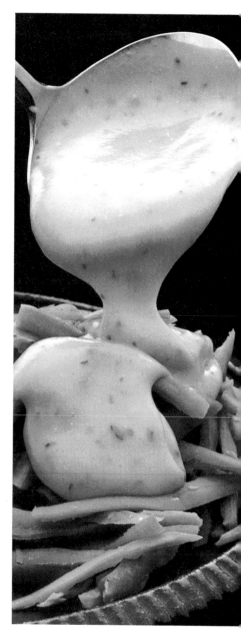

Blender Béarnaise Sauce

very carefully blend in the single cream with a wooden spoon. Add the lemon juice and salt and pepper to taste and stir until thoroughly blended.
2 Cover the bowl and microwave at 50% (Medium) for 5 minutes or until hot.
3 Beat the milk and egg yolk together, then beat in a little of the hot sauce.
4 Whisk the mixture back into the remaining sauce, then microwave at 50% (Medium) for 3-4 minutes until the sauce is slightly thickened. Stir the mixture twice during cooking.

Béchamel sauce

8 mins

Standing time: none

The onion and bay leaf give a subtle flavour to this white sauce.

25g / 1oz butter
1 small onion, minced
45ml / 3tbls plain flour
salt and pepper
275ml / ½pt single cream
1 small bay leaf

MAKES 275ml / ½pt

1 Microwave the butter and onion in a bowl at 100% (High) for 1-2 minutes, or until the onion is tender.
2 Stir in the flour and salt and pepper to taste. Microwave at 50% (Medium) for 1 minute.
3 Gradually blend in the cream, then add the bay leaf and microwave at 50% (Medium) for 6-8 minutes, or until the sauce thickens. Stir the mixture three times

Above: *Mornay Sauce*
Left: *Béchamel Sauce*

during cooking. Strain the sauce and serve.

VARIATIONS
● For **Anchovy sauce,** stir 15-30ml / 1-2tbls anchovy essence or sauce and a little lemon juice into the strained sauce.
● For **Egg Sauce,** add 1 chopped hard-boiled egg and 10ml / 2tsp snipped chives to the strained sauce.
● For **Mornay sauce,** add 60-90ml /4-6tbls mixed grated Parmesan and Gruyère cheese and 2.5ml / ½tsp French mustard after straining and stir until the cheese has melted.
● For **Tarragon sauce,** add 15ml / 1tbls freshly chopped tarragon after straining the sauce.
● For **Mustard Sauce,** stir 5ml / 1tsp made English mustard, 5ml / 1tsp white wine vinegar and 5ml / 1tsp caster sugar into the strained sauce.

22

Sweet dessert sauces

Microwave a sweet dessert sauce in a matter of minutes, and use to jazz up weekday puds or add the finishing touch to glamorous dinner party desserts.

Everyday desserts can easily be made that extra bit special by adding a microwaved sauce. Make puds extra luscious by serving with a truly wicked chocolate or butterscotch sauce, or 'cut' the richness of an indulgent dessert with a light and fruity sauce.

Cooking sauces in the microwave avoids the problem of hard-to-clean sticky pans, and there is less danger of the sauce catching

Topping Choc Sauce

and burning on the base of the pan. However, because they have a high sugar content, sweet sauces should be watched carefully and whisked or stirred regularly to avoid any danger of the sauce overheating and burning. For easy pouring, choose a large microwave jug; otherwise, use a deep heatproof bowl.

Protect your hands with oven gloves, if necessary, when handling the jug or bowl.

Many of the sauces here are good hot or cold. Remember that jam, chocolate and other sugary ingredients become very hot indeed when microwaved, so allow the sauces to cool slightly before serving. If the sauce has been thickened with a starchy ingredient (such as flour, cornflour or arrowroot), lay a piece of stretch wrap directly on the surface before leaving it to cool — this prevents a skin forming. All the fruit sauces here can be made up to 2 days ahead; refrigerate.

Topping choc sauce

2 mins

Standing time: none

100g / 4oz plain dessert chocolate, broken into pieces
30ml / 2tbls golden syrup
15ml / 1tbls chicory and coffee essence
15ml / 1tbls milk

SERVES 4

How to microwave Topping choc sauce

Combine *the chocolate pieces, golden syrup, coffee essence and milk in a 575ml / 1pt microwave jug or bowl. Cover the jug loosely with vented cling film.*

Microwave *at 100% (High) for 1½-2 minutes, or until the chocolate is soft but still holds its shape; stir thoroughly halfway through the microwaving time. Take care to avoid overheating.*

Beat *the chocolate mixture vigorously until smooth and shiny. Microwave, covered, at 100% (High) for 30 seconds more, or until bubbling. Serve hot.*

Tangy lemon sauce

6 mins

Standing time: none

30ml / 6tsp cornflour
45ml / 3tbls caster sugar
1 lemon
25g / 1oz unsalted butter

SERVES 4

1 Place the cornflour and sugar in a 575ml / 1pt bowl.
2 To encourage the lemon to yield the maximum amount of juice, microwave it at 20-30% (Defrost) for 1 minute. Finely grate the lemon zest and add to the cornflour and sugar.
3 Squeeze the juice from the lemon and make up to 275ml / ½pt with water. Gradually whisk into the cornflour mixture, mak-

ing sure the mixture is smooth.
4 Microwave, uncovered, at 100% (High) for 5 minutes, or until smooth and thickened, stirring every minute during microwaving. Serve hot or cold. If serving cold, lay stretch wrap on the surface to prevent a skin forming and store in the refrigerator until needed; whisk well before serving.

Microtips

Care must always be taken when microwaving mixtures with a high sugar content, as they attract the microwaves and can easily overheat and burn. Use a deep, heatproof jug or bowl and watch carefully during cooking.

Tangy Lemon Sauce

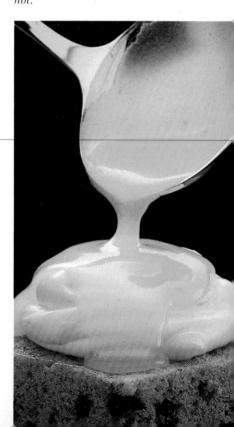

24

Quick berry sauce

| **5** mins |

Standing time: none

425g / 15oz can strawberries in syrup
30ml / 6tsp arrowroot

SERVES 4

1 Drain the strawberries and reserve the juice. Purée the strawberries very briefly in a blender, or mash them with a fork. Place in a 575ml / 1pt jug.
2 Blend the arrowroot with a little of the reserved juice then stir into the crushed fruit with the remaining juice.
3 Microwave, uncovered, at 100% (High) for 5 minutes, or until hot and thickened, stirring every minute. Serve hot or cover the surface and leave until cold.

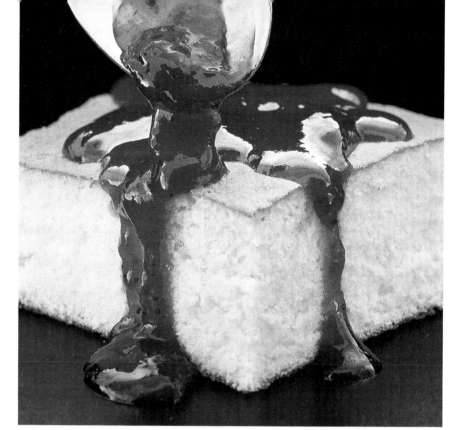

Quick Berry Sauce

Boozy coffee sauce

| **4** mins |

Standing time: none

150ml / ¼pt strong black coffee
30ml / 2tbls soft brown sugar
45ml / 9tsp coffee liqueur
15ml / 3tsp cornflour
45ml / 3tbls double cream

SERVES 4

1 Place the coffee and sugar in a 575ml / 1pt jug. Blend together the cornflour and liqueur and stir into the coffee mixture.
2 Microwave, uncovered, at 100% (High) for 4 minutes until thickened and piping hot, stirring every minute.
3 Gradually stir in the cream. Serve immediately. (Do not reheat or it will curdle.)

Fruity sauce

| **7** mins |

Standing time: 4-5 mins

This colourful sauce with a tangy flavour, brightens up any pud!

225g / 8oz frozen raspberries
30ml / 2tbls icing sugar
finely grated zest and juice of 1 large orange
30ml / 6tsp cornflour

SERVES 4

1 Place the raspberries in a bowl and cover loosely. Microwave at 20-30% (Defrost) for 2-3 minutes, or until thawed, gently rearranging the fruit twice. Stand for 4-5 minutes.
2 Purée the raspberries in a food processor or blender for a few seconds or press through a sieve with the back of a wooden spoon. Transfer to a 1.1L / 2pt bowl and stir in the sugar.
3 Add the orange zest, then blend the juice with the cornflour and stir into the fruit mixture.
4 Microwave, uncovered, at 100% (High) for 5-6 minutes, or until thickened, stirring every minute. Allow to cool for a few seconds before serving.

How to serve sweet dessert sauces

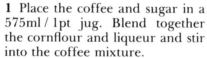

SAUCE	DESCRIPTION	SERVE WITH
Boozy coffee	Liqueur-laced, creamy pouring sauce.	Ice cream, mousses soufflés or crêpes.
Butterscotch	A dark, toffee coloured sauce; very sweet.	Sponge desserts, waffles, baked fruit and ice cream.
Fruity	Raspberry/orange flavoured sauce.	Baked sponge puddings, meringues or pancakes.
Passion fruit	Light and fruity, with an 'exotic' flavour.	Sorbets and ice creams; pancakes.
Quick berry	Thick strawberry sauce.	Crêpes and sponge puddings.
Tangy lemon	Translucent, pouring sauce.	Fruit pies and puddings; cheesecakes.
Topping choc	A richly flavoured pouring sauce.	Ice cream, poached fruit and crêpes.

Butterscotch sauce

4 mins

Standing time: none

15g / ½oz butter
30ml / 2tbls golden syrup
60ml / 4tbls soft dark brown
   sugar
15ml / 3tsp cornflour
170g / 6oz can evaporated milk

SERVES 4

1 Place the butter, syrup and sugar in a 575ml / 1pt microwave jug or bowl.
2 Microwave at 100% (High) for 2-3 minutes, or until the butter melts and the mixture is bubbling, stirring twice.
3 Blend the cornflour with a little evaporated milk until smooth.

Gradually stir the evaporated milk and cornflour mixture into the buttery sauce.
4 Microwave at 100% (High) for 2 minutes, until thickened, stirring once. Serve hot.

VARIATION
For a lighter coloured sauce, use a soft light brown sugar.

Microtips

Butterscotch and Topping Choc Sauce may become too solid to pour if allowed to cool too much. Pop them back into the cooker and microwave at 100% (High) for ½-1 minute, until hot and runny.

Butterscotch Sauce

PAUL GRATER

Passion fruit sauce

2½ mins

Standing time: none

This aromatic fruit gives a delicate sauce, with an exotic taste.

30ml / 6tsp cornflour
275ml / ½pt unsweetened orange
   juice
6 passion fruits, cut in half, pulp
   scooped out
30ml / 2tbls redcurrant jelly

SERVES 6

1 In a 1.1L / 2pt jug or bowl, mix the cornflour to a smooth paste with a little of the orange juice. Gradually stir in the remaining juice.
2 Mix in the passion fruit pulp and redcurrant jelly. Microwave, uncovered, at 100% (High) for 2½-3 minutes, or until boiling, stirring every minute.
3 If wished, press the sauce through a nylon sieve to remove the pips. Serve hot.

VARIATIONS
If wished, fold this sauce into whipped double cream or thick Greek yoghurt for a deliciously creamy fool dessert.

Passion Fruit Sauce

Adapting a recipe: quiches

If quiche is a favourite in your family, see how easy they are to make in your microwave. Super quick pastry with a variety of fillings will give you deliciously attractive end results.

Making quiches in your conventional oven can be time-consuming. A half baked pastry case to begin with will take the best part of 20 minutes cooking. When you make a quiche in the microwave the pastry still has to be cooked in advance but it takes only 5-6 minutes.

Microwaved pastry has to be completely cooked before adding a custard filling or it will absorb too much moisture before the custard sets and becomes soggy.

It is also easier and safer to partially cook the custard filling before adding it to the pastry case. In this way you can stir the custard while it is thickening slightly and be sure of a smooth and even-textured filling. Because eggs and cream are delicate foods, cook the custard separately and in the pastry case on 50% (Medium).

Rotate the quiche dish a quarter turn 4 times during cooking to ensure an even set.

Quiches are always popular, served both at family meal-times and at more formal occasions. Serve for a light luncheon with a crisp green salad or try them piping hot with a baked potato and a winter salad for those colder evenings. However you serve quiches, the microwave will make your life easier in preparing them.

Asparagus Quiche

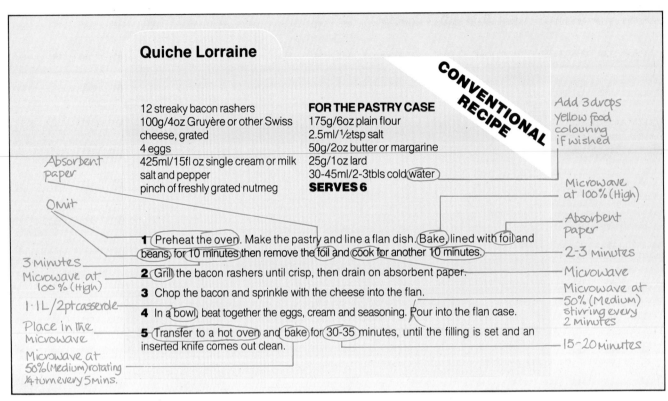

Quiche Lorraine

CONVENTIONAL RECIPE

12 streaky bacon rashers
100g/4oz Gruyère or other Swiss cheese, grated
4 eggs
425ml/15fl oz single cream or milk
salt and pepper
pinch of freshly grated nutmeg

FOR THE PASTRY CASE
175g/6oz plain flour
2.5ml/½tsp salt
50g/2oz butter or margarine
25g/1oz lard
30-45ml/2-3tbls cold water
SERVES 6

(handwritten annotations:)
Add 3 drops yellow food colouring if wished
Absorbent paper
Omit
Microwave at 100% (High)
Absorbent paper
3 minutes Microwave at 100% (High)
2-3 minutes
1.1L/2pt casserole
Microwave
Place in the microwave
Microwave at 50% (Medium) stirring every 2 minutes
Microwave at 50% (Medium) rotating ¼ turn every 5 mins.
15-20 minutes

1 Preheat the oven. Make the pastry and line a flan dish. Bake, lined with foil and beans, for 10 minutes then remove the foil and cook for another 10 minutes.

2 Grill the bacon rashers until crisp, then drain on absorbent paper.

3 Chop the bacon and sprinkle with the cheese into the flan.

4 In a bowl, beat together the eggs, cream and seasoning. Pour into the flan case.

5 Transfer to a hot oven and bake for 30-35 minutes, until the filling is set and an inserted knife comes out clean.

Quiche Lorraine

32 mins

Standing time: 13 mins

12 streaky bacon rashers
100g / 4oz Gruyère cheese, grated
4 eggs
425ml / 15fl oz single cream or milk
salt and pepper
pinch of freshly grated nutmeg

PASTRY CASE
175g / 6oz plain flour
2.5ml / ½tsp salt
50g / 2oz butter or margarine
25g / 1oz lard or white vegetable fat
30-45ml / 2-3tbls cold water combined with 3 drops yellow food colouring optional

SERVES 6

1 First make the pastry case. Sift together the flour and salt, then cut in the butter and lard until the mixture resembles fine breadcrumbs.

2 Add the water, a little at a time, stirring with a fork until the mixture starts to cling together.

3 Form the pastry into a ball then roll out on a floured surface to a circle 5cm / 2in larger than the top of a 23cm / 9in flan dish.

4 Transfer the pastry to the dish then leave to relax in a cool place or in the refrigerator for 10 minutes. Trim the pastry overhang to 12mm / ½in to allow for a high rim.

5 Place the left index finger inside the rim and the right thumb and index on the outside of the rim. Push the pastry into a 'V' shape every 12mm / ½in. Pinch to make a sharp edge.

6 Prick the pastry case with a fork all around the bend of the dish, across the base and around the edge. Line the pastry base with a double layer of absorbent paper and Microwave at 100% (High) for 3 minutes, rotating the dish ¼ turn every minute.

7 Remove the absorbent paper and cook on 100% (High) for a further 2-3 minutes. The pastry is cooked when the base is dry and opaque. If the sides of the pastry case should collapse during cooking it will be pliable enough to push them back into shape.

8 To prepare the quiche filling: place 6 rashers of bacon on 3 layers of absorbent paper; cover with absorbent paper and place remaining rashers on top. Cover with more absorbent paper. Microwave at 100% (High) for 7-9 minutes, or until the bacon is cooked, but looks slightly underdone. Remove from the absorbent paper and stand for 3-5 minutes.

9 Chop the bacon and sprinkle, with the cheese, over pastry case.

10 Meanwhile, beat the eggs with milk or cream and seasonings in a 1.1L / 2pt casserole. Microwave, uncovered, at 50% (Medium) for 5-8 minutes, until thoroughly heated. Stir every 2 minutes.

11 Stir the custard mixture once more and pour into the flan case. Microwave at 50% (Medium) for 15-20 minutes, or until set. Rotate the dish ¼ turn every 5 minutes. The quiche is set when an inserted knife comes out clean. Let stand, for 10 minutes. Decorate with tomato slices sprinkled with cheese. Grill to brown.

Microtips

Take great care when you are microwaving the custard filling in the jug. It needs to be thickened enough to aid the set when it is transferred to the quiche, but if you cook it too much it will turn to scrambled egg.

28

How to make Quiche Lorraine

Line *a 23cm / 9in flan dish with pastry. Using your fingers push the pastry into a 'V' shape every 12mm / ¹/₂in. Pinch to make sharp edges.*

Prick *the pastry at the bend of the dish with a fork. Prick the base and also around the sides. Line the base with a double layer of absorbent paper.*

Microwave *at 100% (High) for 3 minutes; rotate ¹/₄ turn every minute. Remove the absorbent paper and microwave for 2-3 minutes.*

Beat *together the eggs, cream or milk and seasonings. Microwave, uncovered, at 50% (Medium) for 5-8 minutes, stirring every 2 minutes.*

Sprinkle *the chopped, cooked bacon and grated cheese over the base of the flan case and pour in the hot, partially cooked custard filling.*

Microwave *at 50% (Medium) for 15-20 minutes; rotate the dish ¹/₄ turn every 5 minutes. Leave to stand, uncovered, for 10 minutes.*

RAY DUNS

Asparagus quiche

29 mins

Standing time: 10 mins

Use fresh asparagus instead of canned when in season. Arrange in one layer in a shallow dish. Add a little water and microwave at 100% (High) for 6-7 minutes. Drain and use as for canned.

23cm / 9in cooked pastry case (see page 28)
175g / 6oz lean cooked ham
225ml / 8fl oz single cream
175ml / 6fl oz milk
6 eggs
50g / 2oz Cheddar cheese, grated
salt
large pinch of white pepper
12 canned or fresh asparagus spears

SERVES 6

1 Cut 12 thin slices from the ham for the garnish; chop the rest.
2 Sprinkle the chopped ham into the pastry case and set aside.
3 Combine the cream, milk, eggs, grated cheese, salt and pepper in a medium-sized bowl and beat well.
4 Cover and microwave at 50% (Medium) for 4-5 minutes, or until thoroughly heated, stirring every minute. Stir again, then pour over the ham in the pastry case.
5 Microwave at 50% (Medium) for 15-20 minutes rotating the dish ¼ turn every 5 minutes. 5 minutes before the quiche is cooked remove and arrange the asparagus spears, pointed ends towards the centre, like the spokes of a wheel. Arrange a strip of ham between each asparagus spear.
6 Return to the cooker for 5 minutes or until cooked. Leave to stand, uncovered, for 10 minutes.

Microtips

To reheat an individual slice of leftover quiche, place the slice on absorbent paper on a plate, cover and microwave at 100% (High) for 30-60 seconds, or until warm and the quiche transfers heat to the bottom of the plate.

Crab quiche

26 mins

Standing time: 10 mins

23cm / 9in cooked pastry case (see page 28)
½ green pepper, chopped
1 onion, chopped
170g / 6oz can crab meat, drained
113g / 4oz can peeled prawns, drained
75g / 3oz Cheddar cheese, grated
3 eggs
150ml / ¼pt milk
salt and pepper

SERVES 6

1 Place the pepper and onion in a medium-sized bowl, cover, and microwave at 100% (High) for 2-3 minutes.

Crab Quiche

2 Spread the onion and pepper mixture over the pastry base and top with the mixed crab and prawns. Sprinkle with grated cheese.
3 Beat together the eggs and milk and season to taste.
4 Heat the custard mixture, uncovered, at 50% (Medium) for 3-4 minutes or until hot. Stir every minute and at the end of the cooking time.
5 Pour the custard into the pastry case. Microwave at 50% (Medium) for 16-18 minutes or until set, rotating the dish ¼ turn every 5 minutes. The quiche is cooked when a knife inserted halfway between the edge and the centre comes out clean. Stand, uncovered, for 10 minutes.

30

Microwaving pasta

If your pasta sticks and clogs when you cook it conventionally, try it in the microwave. You can avoid starchy, sticky saucepans and the pasta is less likely to turn mushy.

Pasta should always be cooked in a large quantity of boiling water — keeping the large amount of water at simmering point makes the cooking rather long compared with other foods. But if you use a shallow baking dish rather than a deep bowl you can cut the water heating time to a minimum. Cover the dish with cling film to hold in the steam and help the water boil more quickly. Alternatively boil the water in an electric kettle before you start.

Always make sure added salt has dissolved and the water is really boiling before you add the pasta, then the water will stay fully hot throughout the cooking. Use a large dish that allows plenty of room for water and pasta shapes, remembering that you will want to stir during cooking. Use a long, flat dish for long shapes. If the spaghetti is fractionally long for the dish, break off the ends. As in

Clockwise from top: *Crab sauce served on green and white pasta spirals, pasta shells and vermicelli.*

conventional cooking, a little oil added to the water is an additional precaution against sticking.

Different shapes and thicknesses of pasta take different times — thin ribbons of tagliatelle cook more quickly than thicker macaroni. Use the chart as a guide but remember that different brands vary too, so test frequently to avoid overcooking. When cooking larger quantities of pasta, increase the volume of water and the size of the dish — the time for the pasta to cook will be the same. You may find it easier to cook larger quantities of pasta conventionally.

Cook pasta until it is just *al dente* — tender but slightly crisp to the

bite. If you overcook it, it will be unpleasantly soft. If you can just cut through a piece with your thumbnail, it is ready to eat.

When the pasta is cooked, tip it into a colander or sieve to drain thoroughly and rinse it under running water. Use hot water if the dish is to be served hot, cold for salad. This rinsing removes any excess starch which might make the pieces stick together. Let all the water drain away then, for serving hot, return it to the hot bowl and toss it in a little oil or butter until it glistens, and season with plenty of coarsely-ground black pepper. Pasta that is to be stuffed, such as cannelloni or

lasagne, should be even more thoroughly drained by placing on a clean tea towel or several layers of absorbent paper until you are ready to use it.

Cooked pasta reheats well, whether in sauce or alone. Reheat two servings in a greased bowl with a knob of butter in a dish covered with cling film rolled back at one edge. Microwave at 100% (High) for about 2-2½ minutes or until hot, stirring very gently, if possible. Leftover pasta can also be frozen and then thawed and reheated by microwave. This avoids waste, but does not save on time — it takes as long to thaw and reheat as to cook from fresh.

How to microwave pasta

Combine *the water, salt and vegetable or olive oil in suitable dish (see chart). Cover with cling film and microwave at 100% (High) until the water comes to the boil.*

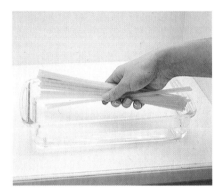

Add *the pasta to the dish and microwave, uncovered, at 100% (High) for the time directed in the chart, until* al dente — *tender but still firm.*

Leave *to stand, covered, for 5 minutes then rinse under hot or cold water. Drain thoroughly. Place pasta to be stuffed on absorbent paper or a tea towel to dry thoroughly.*

Microwaving times for pasta

PASTA	AMOUNT	DISH SIZE	WATER	SALT	TIME ON 100% (HIGH)
Cannelloni	25-100g / 1-4oz 2-8 tubes	25 × 20cm / 10 × 8in	700ml / 1¼pt	2.5ml / ½tsp	10-12 minutes
Lasagne	3-12 sheets	25 × 20cm / 10 × 8in	700ml / 1¼pt	2.5ml / ½tsp	7-10 minutes
Macaroni Shells Jumbo shells	25-100g / 1-4oz 25-100g / 1-4oz 25-100g / 1-4oz	2.3L / 4 pt 2.3L / 4pt 2.3L / 4pt	700ml / 1¼pt 700ml / 1¼pt 700ml / 1¼pt	2.5ml / ½tsp 2.5ml / ½tsp 2.5ml / ½tsp	8-10 minutes 9-11 minutes 10-12 minutes
Rigatoni	50-100g / 2-4oz	2.3L / 4pt	700ml / 1¼pt	2.5ml / ½tsp	9-11 minutes
Spaghetti	25-100g / 1-4oz	25 × 20cm / 10 × 8in	700ml / 1¼pt	2.5ml / ½tsp	7-10 minutes
Tagliatelle	25-100g / 1-4oz	2.3L / 4pt	700ml / 1¼pt	2.5ml / ½tsp	6-8 minutes
Vermicelli	25-100g / 1-4oz	2.3L / 4pt	700ml / 1¼pt	2.5ml / ½tsp	2-3 minutes

Cheesy cannelloni

17 mins

Standing time: 8 mins

The smooth sauce and rich, creamy filling used in cannelloni, can be microwaved in minutes.

4 cannelloni tubes
parsley, to garnish

FILLING
100g / 4oz cottage cheese, well drained
50g / 2oz Mozzarella cheese, grated
45ml / 3tbls Parmesan cheese, grated
1 egg, lightly beaten
2.5ml / ½tsp dried basil
good pinch of salt
pepper

SAUCE
10ml / 2tsp cornflour
175ml / 6fl oz tomato juice
10ml / 2tsp olive oil
2.5ml / ½tsp dried basil
2.5ml / ½tsp sugar
pepper
45ml / 3tbls milk
15ml / 1tbls red wine or port

SERVES 2

1 Cook the cannelloni as directed in the chart. Drain, rinse and drain again, then place on absorbent paper or a clean tea towel.
2 Combine all the filling ingredients and beat with a wooden spoon until well blended.
3 Fill each cannelloni tube with the mixture and place in a small, shallow casserole or dish.
4 Place the cornflour in an 850ml /1½pt bowl, add a small amount of tomato juice. Stir until smooth.
5 Mix in the remaining tomato juice, olive oil, basil, sugar and pepper, to taste.
6 Microwave at 100% (High) for 2-3 minutes or until slightly thickened, stirring every minute.
7 Blend in milk and wine or port. Pour over stuffed cannelloni.
8 Reduce the power to 50% (Medium), cover and microwave for 5-9 minutes or until hot. Leave to stand for 3 minutes. Garnish with parsley.

PAUL WEBSTER

Vermicelli with crab sauce

9 mins

Standing time: 5 mins

Serve this delicious pasta dish as an appetizer for two people for a special occasion meal. It also makes an excellent quick supper for one person.

50g / 2oz vermicelli
½ onion, finely chopped
25g / 1oz butter
15ml / 1tbls olive oil
good pinch of garlic powder
15ml / 1tbls plain flour
15ml / 1tbls chopped parsley
good pinch of salt and pepper
169g / 5.6oz can crab, juice reserved
30ml / 2tbls milk
30ml / 2tbls tomato purée
grated Parmesan cheese for sprinkling
lemon twists and parsley, to garnish

SERVES 2

1 Cook the vermicelli as directed in the chart, drain and set aside.
2 In a 1.4L / 2½pt bowl, combine the onion, butter, olive oil and garlic powder. Cover and microwave at 100% (High) for 4 minutes or until the butter melts and the onion is tender.
3 Blend in the flour. Stir in the parsley, salt, pepper, crab and juice, milk and tomato purée. Microwave at 100% (High) for 2-3 minutes or until thickened, stirring once or twice.
4 Rinse the vermicelli, then drain again. Pour the sauce over the hot vermicelli and microwave at 100% (High) for 1-2 minutes.
5 Sprinkle with Parmesan cheese, if wished. Garnish with lemon twists and flat-leaved parsley.

VARIATION
This tasty sauce will go well with all types of pasta. Simply follow the directions in the chart and combine the sauce with your favourite pasta shape.

33

Microwaving rice

Gone are the days of sticky rice and messy saucepans! Cooking rice in the microwave gives you separate fluffy grains every time, whether cooked from scratch or reheated.

Rice cooked in the microwave may not be much quicker than cooking rice conventionally, but this method means less messy washing up. It is also simple to add tasty pieces of meat, vegetables, nuts and fruit to make a variety of delicious main courses or side dishes.

Try freezing any of your rice dishes, then thawing and reheating them in the microwave as needed or just cook the day before, refrigerate and reheat. They will be a guaranteed success, tasting as though just freshly cooked.

Salad Rice Ring

How to microwave rice

Measure *the desired quantity of rice into a casserole, together with a knob of butter or margarine and corresponding amount of salt as directed in the chart below. Do not over-salt, as extra can be added after cooking.*

Stir *in the measured amount of boiling water; cover with cling film rolled back at one edge or a loose-fitting lid. Microwave at 100% (High) as directed below, then reduce power to 50% (Medium).*

Microwave *for the remaining time, stirring a couple of times during cooking. Leave to stand, still covered, for 5 minutes. Always fluff rice with a fork before serving to lift and separate the grains.*

Methods and microwave times for cooking rice

TYPE	BOILING WATER	SALT	METHOD
Long grain white rice 100g / 4oz 150g / 5oz 175g / 6oz 200g / 7oz 225g / 8oz 275g / 10oz	275ml / 10fl oz 350ml / 12fl oz 400ml / 14fl oz 450ml / 16fl oz 500ml / 18fl oz 575ml / 22fl oz	2.5ml / ½tsp 2.5ml / ½tsp 2.5ml / ½tsp 5ml / 1tsp 5ml / 1tsp 5ml / 1tsp	Combine the rice, boiling water and salt, together with a knob of butter or margarine, in a large casserole; cover with vented cling film or a loose-fitting lid. Microwave at 100% (High) for 3 minutes. Reduce power to 50% (Medium) and microwave for 12 minutes, stirring 2-3 times during the cooking time. Let stand, covered, for 5 minutes. Fluff with a fork before serving.
Long grain brown rice 100g / 4oz 150g / 5oz 175g / 6oz 200g / 7oz 225g / 8oz 275g / 10oz	275ml / 10fl oz 350ml / 12fl oz 400ml / 14fl oz 450ml / 16fl oz 500ml / 18fl oz 575ml / 22fl oz	2.5ml / ½tsp 2.5ml / ½tsp 2.5ml / ½tsp 5ml / 1tsp 5ml / 1tsp 5ml / 1tsp	Combine the rice, boiling water and salt, together with a knob of butter or margarine, in a large casserole; cover with vented cling film or a loose-fitting lid. Microwave at 100% (High) for 3 minutes. Reduce power to 50% (Medium) and microwave for 25 minutes, stirring 2-3 times during the cooking time. Let stand, covered, for 5 minutes. Fluff with a fork before serving.
Quick cook brown rice 100g / 4oz 150g / 5oz 175g / 6oz 200g / 7oz 225g / 8oz 275g / 10oz	225ml / 8fl oz 275ml / 10fl oz 350ml / 12fl oz 400ml / 14fl oz 450ml / 16fl oz 500ml / 20fl oz	2.5ml / ½tsp 2.5ml / ½tsp 2.5ml / ½tsp 5ml / 1tsp 5ml / 1tsp 5ml / 1tsp	Combine the rice, boiling water and salt, together with a knob of butter or margarine, in a large casserole; cover with vented cling film or loose-fitting lid. Microwave at 100% (High) for 3 minutes. Reduce power to 50% (Medium) and microwave for 8 minutes, stirring 2-3 times during the cooking time. Leave to stand, covered, for 5 minutes. Fluff with a fork before serving.

Curried rice

$15\frac{3}{4}$ mins

Standing time: 5 mins

1 celery stalk, chopped
knob of butter or margarine
275ml / 10fl oz boiling water
100g / 4oz long grain white
  rice
1.5ml / ¼tsp curry powder
1.5ml / ¼tsp salt
45ml / 3tbls raisins or sultanas

SERVES 2

1 Place the celery and butter in a 1.7L / 3pt casserole; cover. Microwave at 100% (High) for 45-60 seconds, until the celery is tender-crisp.
2 Add the remaining ingredients except the raisins; cover. Microwave at 100% (High) for 3 minutes, or until boiling. Stir.
3 Reduce the power to 50% (Medium). Microwave for 12 minutes, or until the rice is tender. Stir in the raisins and cover. Let stand 5 minutes. Fluff up.

Cheesy rice

15 mins

Standing time: 5 mins

100g / 4oz long grain rice
275ml / 10fl oz boiling water
2.5ml / ½tsp salt
knob of butter or margarine
45ml / 3tbls Cheddar cheese,
  grated
2.5ml / ½tsp dried parsley
paprika

SERVES 2

1 Cook rice, see chart page 35.
2 Stir in the cheese and parsley. Cover and let stand for 5 minutes.
3 Stir; sprinkle with paprika.

Freezer notes

To freeze one serving of Curried Rice or Cheesy Rice. Place in a freezer/microwave dish, cover, label and freeze for no longer than two weeks. To cook from frozen, microwave at 70% (Medium/High) for 3-5 minutes; stir once. Fluff up.

Savoury rice

15 mins

Standing time: 5 mins

500ml / 18fl oz boiling stock
225g / 8oz long grain white rice
knob of butter or margarine
5ml / 1tsp salt
250g / 8oz packet frozen mixed
  vegetables

SERVES 4

1 Combine ingredients in a 2.3L / 4pt casserole; cover. Microwave as directed in the chart on page 35, adding the frozen vegetables after 6 minutes. Let stand, covered, for 5 minutes. Fluff up.

Freezer notes

Freeze leftover rice in small portions. Place in freezer/microwave dishes, cover, label, and freeze for no longer than one month. To cook the rice from frozen, cover and microwave at 100% (High) as directed in table below, stirring once or twice during cooking.
1 serving   2-3 minutes
2 servings   4-6 minutes
4 servings   6-8 minutes

Seasoned brown rice

$28\frac{3}{4}$ mins

Standing time: 5 mins

2 spring onions, chopped
½ celery stalk, chopped
10ml / 2tsp chopped fresh parsley
knob of butter or margarine
275ml / 10fl oz boiling stock
100g / 4oz brown rice
2.5ml / ½tsp salt

SERVES 2

1 Place the vegetables, parsley and butter in a 2.3L / 4pt casserole; cover. Microwave at 100% (High) for 45-60 seconds, until the vegetables are tender. Stir.
2 Add the remaining ingredients; cover. Microwave at 100% (High) for 3 minutes. Reduce power to 50% (Medium) for 25 minutes; stir 2-3 times. Let stand 5 minutes.

Vegetable rice mix

24 mins

Standing time: 5 mins

Use this mix on its own or as a foundation for Fried Rice Medley or Oriental Rice.

150g / 5oz mushrooms, sliced
2 carrots, finely cubed
½ green pepper, chopped
2 celery stalks, chopped
½ small onion, chopped
1 garlic clove, crushed
25g / 1oz butter or margarine
275g / 10oz white or brown rice,
  cooked (see chart, page 35)
salt and pepper

SERVES 6-8

1 In a 2.3L / 4pt casserole, combine the vegetables, garlic and butter; cover. Microwave at 100% (High) for 5-7 minutes, or until vegetables are tender; stir once.
2 Stir in the rice, salt and pepper. Microwave, covered, at 100% (High) for 4-6 minutes. Fluff with a fork.

Brown rice

`28 mins`

Standing time: 5 mins

500ml / 18fl oz boiling water
225g / 8oz brown rice
knob of butter or margarine
5ml / 1tsp salt

SERVES 4

1 Put ingredients in a 2.3L / 4pt casserole, cover. Microwave at 100% (High) for 3 minutes.
2 Reduce power to 50% (Medium). Microwave for 25 minutes, stirring twice, until the rice is tender. Let stand for 5 minutes.

Microtips

Cook rice early and reheat before serving. Cover and microwave at 100% (High) as directed below.

1 serving	*1-2 minutes*
2 servings	*2-4 minutes*
4 servings	*4-6 minutes*

Fried rice medley

`29 mins`

Standing time: 5 mins

½ quantity Vegetable Rice Mix
  (see recipe opposite)
225g / 8oz cooked chicken, beef
  or pork, diced
2 eggs, slightly beaten
knob of butter or margarine
15ml / 1tbls soy sauce

SERVES 4-6

1 In a 1.7L / 3pt casserole, combine the Vegetable Rice Mix and meat; cover with cling film rolled back at one edge.
2 Microwave at 100% (High) for 4-7 minutes, or until heated, stirring once. Set aside.
3 Place the eggs and butter in small bowl or casserole. Microwave at 100% (High) for 1-1¾ minutes, or until the eggs are set, stirring after half the cooking time.
4 Chop up the eggs. Stir into the rice mixture. Add the soy sauce, tossing to coat the rice.

Oriental rice

`30 mins`

Standing time: 5 mins

1 small eating apple, peeled
  and chopped
15g / ½oz butter or margarine
½ quantity Vegetable Rice Mix
  (see recipe opposite)
15ml / 1tbls raisins
5ml / 1tsp curry powder
2.5ml / ½tsp sugar
25g / 1oz cashew nuts or
  peanuts

SERVES 4

1 Place the apple and butter in a small bowl. Cover and microwave at 100% (High) for 1½-3 minutes, or until the apple is tender.
2 In a 1.1L / 2pt casserole, mix together the Vegetable Rice Mix, apple, raisins, curry powder and sugar; cover.
3 Microwave at 100% (High) for 4½-7 minutes, or until the rice mixture is heated through, stir after half the time. Mix in the nuts and serve.

37

Salad rice ring

18 mins

Standing time: 5 mins

2 tomatoes, chopped and
   seeded
1 spring onion, thinly sliced
15ml / 1tbls chopped green
   pepper
5ml / 1tsp olive oil
30ml / 2tbls chopped fresh
   parsley
100g / 4oz long grain white rice,
   cooked (see chart, page 35)

SERVES 2

1 In a 1.1L / 2pt casserole, combine the vegetables and olive oil. Cover and microwave at 100% (High) for 1-2 minutes, or until the vegetables are tender.
2 Stir in the parsley. Stir the vegetable mixture into the rice. Spoon the rice mixture into a greased 18cm / 7in non-metallic ring mould. Press down gently.
3 Cover with greaseproof paper and microwave at 100% (High) for 2-3 minutes, or until heated through. Turn out onto a serving plate.

Wild rice and sausage

39 mins

Standing time: 5 mins

1.4kg / 3lb sausage meat
350g / 12oz mushrooms,
   sliced
100g / 4oz celery, chopped
15g / ½oz butter or margarine
400g / 14oz long grain and
   wild rice mix, cooked (see
   Microtips, below)
295g / 10.4oz can condensed
   cream of mushroom soup
125ml / 4fl oz hot water
30ml / 2tbls chopped parsley
1 chicken stock cube

SERVES 10-12

1 Crumble the sausage meat into a 2.3L / 4pt casserole. Microwave at 100% (High) for 11-15 minutes until no longer pink, stirring 2-3 times. Drain.
2 In a 3.4L / 6pt casserole, combine the mushrooms, celery and butter; cover. Microwave at 100% (High) for 5-8 minutes, or until celery is tender. Drain.
3 Stir in the sausage meat and remaining ingredients. Microwave at 100% (High) for 8-10 minutes. Fluff with a fork.

Microtips

To microwave 400g / 14oz long grain and wild rice mix, use 675ml / 24fl oz water, 5ml / 1tsp salt and a knob of butter or margarine. Microwave at 100% (High) for 3 minutes. Reduce power to 50% (Medium) and microwave for 12 minutes. Leave rice to stand, covered, for 5 minutes. Fluff up and adjust seasoning, if necessary.

Cooking in parcels

The microwave is not only excellent for making family meals; these elegant parcels will grace any dinner party table. Both sweet and savoury ingredients make delicious parcel food.

Parcel cookery or cooking *en papillote* (literally 'in an envelope') is a useful and flavoursome way of cooking small quantities of food in the microwave. The principle is to tightly enclose food sealing in all the goodness, juices and flavour.

Parcel cookery works very well in the microwave. It stops small pieces of food from drying out — and also solves the problem of the right-sized container. The parcels can be arranged on a plate, or simply placed in the microwave. If you do place them straight in the

microwave, make especially sure they are securely closed to avoid leaking.

Non-edible wrappings
With the obvious exception of foil, there are several choices of wrapping that all work well in the microwave. Greaseproof or non-stick baking paper are the first choice for attractive presentation but thick paper bags, boiling bags or oven or roasting bags can also be used.

If you are using a boiling bag, oven or roasting bag, pierce in

several places so that any build-up of hot air or steam can escape.

Edible wrappings
All types of large edible leaves can be used: spinach, different kinds of Chinese greens, lettuce, cabbage and spring greens. Select large, even-shaped leaves without blemishes, cut away centre core or stalk and microwave for a few minutes until pliable. Wrap around the filling and secure with a wooden cocktail stick or string.

Tarragon Salmon Parcels

39

Do

- Brush greaseproof paper shapes with melted butter or oil to stop food from sticking.
- Fold the edges down tightly or secure with string, rubber bands or adhesive tape.
- Cut the shapes at least three times larger than the food.

Don't

- Use metal ties to secure the parcels.
- Use foil as a wrapping.
- Over-cook leaves for wrapping, they should be just pliable enough to wrap around the filling without cracking.
- Grease edible wrappers.

Gingered figs

1½ mins

Standing time: none

Serve accompanied by a bowl of thick Greek yoghurt.

4 fresh green figs
maple syrup for brushing
15ml / 1tbls chopped flaked almonds
1 small piece of preserved ginger, finely chopped

SERVES 4

1 Make two cuts, in a cross shape, in the top of each fig. Squeeze the base gently so the fruit opens out like a flower.
2 Cut four 19cm / 7½in squares of greaseproof paper and lay them on the floor or turntable of the microwave. Place a fig in the centre of each square and brush the outside of each with a little syrup. Microwave, uncovered, at 100% (High) for 45 seconds.
3 Divide the almonds and ginger into four equal portions and sprinkle into the centre of the figs. Gather up the sides of the paper squares and twist the tops to form money bag shapes.
4 Microwave at 100% (High) for 45-60 seconds until the figs are softened and the juices start to run. Serve at once with yoghurt.

Gingered Figs

Step-by-step to parcel shapes

Semi-heart: *cut a heart shape and grease lightly. Place the food on one half. Fold other half over, giving edges double fold to seal.*

Turnover: *cut an oval shape and grease lightly. Place food on one half and fold the other half over. Fold the edges twice to seal.*

Money bag: *cut a square and grease lightly. Place food in centre and gently pull up edges. Twist or tie top like a money bag.*

40

Vegetables en papillote

Standing time: none

Offer individual servings of vegetables for guests to open at the table.

melted butter or oil for greasing
100g / 4oz bean sprouts
6 spring onions, chopped
1 small red pepper, seeded and sliced
100g / 4oz courgettes, sliced
15ml / 1tbls soy sauce
2.5ml / ½tsp chopped ginger

SERVES 4

1 Cut four squares of greaseproof paper and brush lightly with melted butter or oil.
2 Combine the prepared vegetables and seasonings, then pile a quarter of the vegetables in the middle of each paper square.
3 Either fold the paper over the vegetables or pull up the edges like a money bag. Microwave parcels at 100% (High) for 4-6 minutes, depending on how crisp you prefer your vegetables.

Cabbage and caraway parcels: remove the core from a white or green cabbage and very thinly slice 450g / 1lb. Combine with 5ml / 1tsp caraway seeds, 30ml / 2tbls sultanas and juice of ½ lemon. Proceed as above and serve with soured cream.

Mushroom medley: combine 100g / 4oz sliced mushrooms, 100g / 4oz sliced cherry tomatoes, 100g / 4oz small broccoli florets, 100g / 4oz very thinly sliced carrots and 15ml / 1tbls chopped mixed herbs. Proceed as above.

Cook's notes

When making mixed vegetable parcels, cut slow-cooking carrots or potatoes, into very thin slices or small pieces. This ensures they cook through in the same time as quick-cooking vegetables like peppers.

Tarragon salmon parcels

Standing time: none

4 salmon steaks, about 100g / 4oz each
melted butter or oil for greasing
8 sprigs fresh tarragon or 10ml / 2tsp dried
juice of ½ lemon
¼ cucumber, very thinly sliced

SERVES 4

1 Remove the bones and skin (if liked) from the salmon steaks. Cut four heart shapes out of non-stick baking or greaseproof paper and brush with melted butter or oil. Place a salmon steak in the centre of one half of each piece of paper.
2 Top each steak with two sprigs or a little dried tarragon, a squeeze of lemon juice and three cucumber slices. Enclose the salmon in the greaseproof paper hearts and

Vegetables en Papillote

fold down the edges, giving them a double fold to seal.
3 Place the parcels on a plate or in a shallow dish and microwave at 100% (High) for 5 minutes or until the salmon flesh flakes easily. Rearrange once during cooking. Serve hot or cold.

Tarragon salmon parcels for two: halve the ingredients and microwave the parcels for 2-2½ minutes.

Tarragon salmon parcel for one: cook one prepared salmon steak and garnish in a parcel for 1-1½ minutes.

Cook's notes

Removing the central bone is not essential, but it does reduce the tendency of the fish to 'pop' during cooking.

Shredded beef cabbage rolls

 20 mins

Standing time: 5 mins

These cabbage rolls make an unusual dinner party dish. Serve them with sliced potatoes in their skins or with boiled or fried rice, oriental-style.

1 white or green cabbage

FILLING
100g / 4oz mushrooms, sliced
1 small onion, chopped
1 large carrot, grated
1 garlic clove, chopped
225g / 8oz cooked beef, cut into thin strips
397g / 14oz can tomatoes, drained and chopped
2.5ml / $\frac{1}{2}$tsp dried basil
1.5ml / $\frac{1}{4}$tsp dried rosemary
salt and pepper

SAUCE
1 small onion, finely chopped
30ml / 2tbls olive oil
425ml / $\frac{3}{4}$pt tomato juice
30ml / 2tbls soft dark brown sugar
10ml / 2tsp beef or vegetable extract
10ml / 2tsp white wine or cider vinegar
2.5ml / $\frac{1}{2}$tsp dried basil

SERVES 4

1 Prepare the cabbage casing and filling following the steps opposite.
2 Fold in the sides of the leaves, then roll up and secure each cabbage parcel with a wooden cocktail stick. Place seam side down in a shallow baking dish.
3 Make the sauce: put the onion and olive oil into a bowl. Microwave, covered, at 100% (High) for 2-3 minutes, or until the onion is tender. Stir in the remaining sauce ingredients. Cover and microwave at 100% (High) for 8-12 minutes, or until slightly thickened, stirring three times.
4 Pour the sauce over the cabbage parcels, cover and microwave at 100% (High) for 4-5 minutes until the parcels and filling are hot, rotating the dish once. Stand for 5 minutes, then serve.

Oriental chicken rolls

7 mins

Standing time: none

Serve these crunchy lettuce-leaf rolls with cooked rice and extra sweet and sour sauce, if wished.

8 large, crisp lettuce leaves
380g / 13$\frac{1}{4}$oz can crushed pineapple, well drained
1 green pepper, seeded and chopped
4 spring onions, trimmed and chopped
2.5ml / $\frac{1}{2}$tsp five spice powder
350g / 12oz cooked chicken meat, diced
30ml / 2tbls sunflower seeds
15ml / 1tbls bottled sweet and sour sauce

SERVES 4

1 Place the lettuce leaves on a plate. Microwave at 100% (High) for 30-60 seconds or until slightly softened. Set aside to cool.
2 Mix the pineapple, green

Oriental Chicken Rolls

pepper and onions together in a bowl. Stir in the five spice powder. Microwave, covered, at 100% (High) for 4$\frac{1}{2}$-5$\frac{1}{2}$ minutes, or until the pepper and onion are tender. Drain off any liquid.
3 Stir in the chicken, sunflower seeds and sweet and sour sauce. Divide the mixture between the lettuce leaves, fold the leaves in at the side then roll around the filling and secure with wooden cocktail sticks.
4 Place the rolls in a shallow dish, cover and microwave at 100% (High) for 2-3 minutes, or until well heated through. Serve immediately with plain boiled or fried rice.

Slimmer's notes

These are tasty and succulent lunch time or supper snacks which have only 200 Cal / 840 kJ per portion. Serve with a crisp salad.

How to prepare and fill Shredded beef cabbage rolls

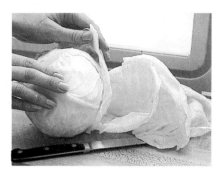

Cut *the hard centre core from the cabbage. Wrap the cabbage in cling film and microwave at 100% (High) for 1½-3½ minutes, or until eight outer leaves can be easily removed. Remove centre rib from each leaf.*

Shred *100g / 4oz of remaining cabbage. Microwave cabbage, mushrooms, onion, carrot and garlic in a large, covered bowl at 100% (High) for 3-6 minutes or until tender; stir once. Drain if necessary.*

Stir *in remaining filling ingredients. Put leaves on a microwave baking sheet, cover and microwave at 100% (High) for 1½-4½ minutes, until the leaves are pliable. Spoon the filling into the centre of each leaf.*

Banana boats

| 3 mins |

Standing time: none

Eat the bananas straight from the skins with a spoon.

**4 even-sized, ripe bananas
25g / 1oz butter, cut into small pieces
15ml / 1tbls demerara sugar**

SERVES 4

1 Make a slit down the length of each of the bananas, without cutting right through. Open them out a little.

2 Divide butter and sugar between bananas, pushing them right down into the cuts. Press the banana back into shape.

3 Place the bananas in a shallow dish with the slits uppermost. Microwave, uncovered, at 100% (High) for 3-4 minutes or until the skin starts to blacken and the banana flesh is soft and becoming translucent. Serve the bananas at once, in their skins, with cream if liked.

VARIATIONS
Other ingredients can be added to the filling, such as finely chopped nuts, dried fruit, honey, grated chocolate, or a sprinkling of alcohol and/or lemon juice. Do not over-fill the bananas or the skins might split open.

43

Cooking with marinades

Marinating makes a good meal memorable. An aromatic combination of herbs and spices mixed with olive oil, citrus juice or wine both flavours and tenderizes meat, poultry, fish and vegetables.

The purpose of marinating — soaking food in a mixture of liquids and flavourings before cooking — is to improve the flavour of the food and tenderize it, if necessary. All types of meat, poultry, firm white fish and even oily fish can be marinated, as well as vegetables, particularly those with an absorbent texture. Combined with microwaving, a marinade can be very effective.

Why marinate?
The speed of microwave cooking does not lend itself to tenderizing food. Although microwaving on a lower power does help, marinating is an even more effective answer, allowing the acid-based liquids to break down any tough fibres. Marinating also allows flavours to thoroughly blend; not always possible during brief microwaving.

Adding colour is another bonus. Using a colouring agent in the marinade, adds colour which microwaved food may otherwise lack. Finally, marinating is a handy prepare-ahead technique.

How to marinate
Usually the marinade ingredients are combined raw, but they can be microwaved before adding food.

Choose oil, wine vinegar, alcohol or citrus juice and combine with your favourite herbs and spices and — if you like — add vegetables for extra flavouring.

Cover the food and leave at very cool room temperature or refrigerate food in a hot climate or when marinating for over four hours. Allow to come to room temperature before microwaving. If food is not completely covered turn it occasionally to coat.

Take extra advantage of all the added goodness by serving the marinade as a sauce.

Minted Lamb Kebabs

Minted lamb kebabs

16 mins

Standing time: 3 mins

450g / 1lb neck fillets or boneless leg of lamb, cut into bite-sized cubes
6 button onions
6 small cherry tomatoes, or 3 tomatoes, halved
1 small green pepper, seeded and cut into bite-sized pieces
1 small yellow pepper, seeded and cut into bite-sized pieces

MINT MARINADE
125ml / 4fl oz cider or apple juice
20ml / 4tsp red wine vinegar
5ml / 1tsp grated lemon zest
10ml / 2tsp chopped fresh mint or 5ml / 1tsp dried
1 bay leaf
pepper

SERVES 4

1 Combine all the marinade ingredients, seasoning to taste with pepper. Place the lamb in a shallow dish and add the marinade. Stir well to make sure all the lamb is coated, cover and leave to marinate for ½-1 hour.
2 Place the onions in a bowl. Cover and microwave at 100% (High) for 2 minutes.
3 Remove the lamb from the marinade with a slotted spoon. Thread the lamb on to four large or eight small wooden or bamboo skewers, alternating the onions, tomatoes and green and yellow peppers decoratively.
4 Place the kebabs on a microwave roasting rack and baste liberally with the marinade. Cover loosely with greaseproof paper. Microwave at 50% (Medium) for 14-16 minutes or until the lamb is cooked according to taste. Turn the skewers four times during microwaving, and baste with the marinade. Leave to stand for 3 minutes before serving.

VARIATION
Use other seasonal fresh vegetables for the kebabs, such as slices of courgette, chunks of aubergine or whole button mushrooms or baby sweetcorns.

USEFUL MARINADES

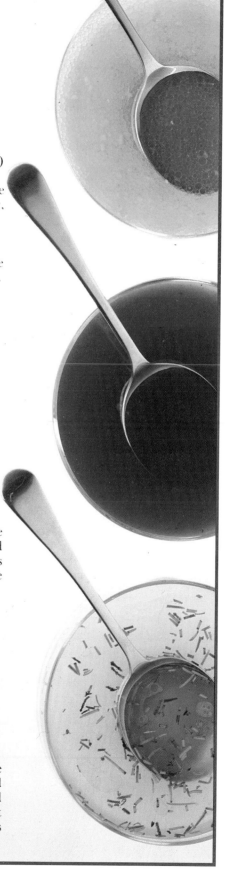

Spicy orange marinade

75ml / 5tbls dry sherry
60ml / 4tbls fresh orange juice
5ml / 1tsp grated orange zest
30ml / 2tbls wine vinegar
15ml / 1tbls vegetable oil
7.5ml / 1½tsp Worcestershire sauce
1 garlic clove, crushed (optional)

Beat together all the marinade ingredients and use with poultry, veal and pork.

VARIATION
Oriental Marinade: use soy sauce instead of orange juice; omit zest.

Chilli red wine marinade

30ml / 2tbls soft brown sugar
30ml / 2tbls wine or tarragon vinegar
150ml / ¼pt red wine
5ml / 1tsp celery salt
45ml / 3tbls tomato ketchup or purée
5ml / 1tsp chilli powder
few drops of Tabasco sauce (optional)

Beat together all the marinade ingredients and use with beef and lamb; also good with rich meats like venison and hare and game birds.

Herby cider marinade

30ml / 2tbls lemon juice
45ml / 3tbls cider vinegar
15ml / 1tbls vegetable oil
125ml / 4fl oz dry cider
5ml / 1tsp fresh rosemary or 2.5ml / ½tsp dried

Beat together all the marinade ingredients and use with white and oily fish, also chicken, veal and pork. For a richer marinade omit the herbs and add 15ml / 1tbls runny honey.

Marinated vegetables

14 mins

Standing time: none

1 large onion, chopped
225g / 8oz leeks, cut into
  5cm / 2in pieces and sliced
  lengthways
4 celery stalks, sliced diagonally
225g / 8oz button mushrooms
1 garlic clove, crushed
4 tomatoes, skinned, seeded and
  chopped
chopped parsley and lemon
  slices, to garnish

MARINADE
45ml / 3tbls olive oil
125ml / 4fl oz dry white wine
15ml / 1tbls tomato paste or purée
10ml / 2tsp chopped fresh thyme
  or 5ml / 1tsp dried
pepper

SERVES 4-6

1 Place the onion, leeks, celery, mushrooms and garlic in a large bowl and stir together well.
2 Mix the oil with the wine, tomato paste, thyme and pepper to taste. Pour over the vegetables and toss well to coat. Cover and leave to marinate for 1 hour, stirring twice.
3 Add the tomatoes, mixing well. Cover and microwave at 100% (High) for 14-16 minutes, or until tender, stirring twice.

Left: *Marinated Vegetables*
Below: *Tangy Chicken*

RAY DUNS

46

4 Allow to cool slightly, then serve warm, sprinkled with chopped parsley and garnished with lemon slices. Serve with French bread.

VARIATION
In this vegetable dish, fresh tomatoes are best for flavour; but for convenience, substitute 227g / 8oz can peeled tomatoes.

Tangy chicken

| 11 mins |

Standing time: none

4 small chicken breasts on the bone, skinned
4 orange slices
chopped parsley, to garnish

CITRUS MARINADE
45ml / 3tbls lemon juice
15ml / 1tbls soy sauce
60ml / 4tbls water
black pepper
pinch of garlic powder
5ml / 1tsp grated orange zest

SERVES 4

1 Microwave the marinade ingredients in a bowl at 100% (High) for 1-2 minutes, until hot.
2 Place the chicken in a shallow dish and pour over the hot marinade. Cover; chill for 1-2 hours.
3 Top the chicken breasts with the orange slices. Cover and microwave at 100% (High) for 10-15 minutes, or until the chicken is tender and no longer pink, rearranging and basting twice.

Mandarin beef

| 6 mins |

Standing time: none

225g / 8oz sirloin steak,
  2.5cm / 1in thick, in thin strips
230g / 8oz can sliced bamboo
  shoots, drained and cut into
  matchstick strips
1 green pepper, seeded and sliced
  into matchstick strips
2 small carrots, coarsely grated
½ bunch spring onions,
  sliced thickly diagonally

MARINADE
30ml / 2tbls soy sauce
1 garlic clove, crushed
2.5ml / ½tsp sugar
1.5-2.5ml / ¼-½tsp finely
  chopped dried red chillies
pinch of ground ginger

SERVES 3-4

1 Mix together all the marinade ingredients in a bowl and add the beef. Stir well to make sure the meat is well coated, cover and leave to marinate for 15 minutes.
2 Place the beef and marinade in a shallow 10 × 8in / 25 × 20cm casserole with the prepared vegetables and stir well.
3 Cover the dish and microwave at 100% (High) for 6-8 minutes, or until the beef is no longer pink and the vegetables are just tender but still slightly crisp. Stir once, halfway through microwaving time. Serve with egg noodles.

Microtips

Do not add salt to marinades as it draws the natural juices out of meat and vegetables. Use only pepper then season with salt after microwaving, if wished.

Cooking with spices

Add spice to your cooking! Whether whole or ground, spices pep up a dull dish and add interest to a familiar one; the microwave enhances their flavour — so just a little goes a long way.

Microwaving accentuates the flavour of all spices. Their flavours, whether subtle or fiery, add zest to a wide variety of dishes.

Buying and storing spices
It is best to buy spices in small quantities and use within one to two months to enjoy them at their best. Avoid buying spices that have been standing on a shelf for a long time in glass bottles, especially if they are ground, as they will have less aroma and flavour. For the finest results, buy whole spices from speciality shops and grind small quantities at a time, as needed, using an electric mill or pestle and mortar. They will have more flavour than ready ground.

Store spices in small airtight jars or tins in a cool dark place. Although spice racks look attractive on the kitchen wall, the spices in the jars soon deteriorate if exposed to bright light.

Microwave cooking with spices
Cooking brings out the flavour of spices — and this is especially true in the microwave. This is an

advantage because it means you can use less than normal. (Take care not to over-flavour food by being too heavy-handed.)

Experiment with different spices to see which combinations you like — some are hot, some aromatic — but just use a little of each to begin with. The same applies when using an unfamiliar spice for the first time — start off with a little and increase the amount if the flavour appeals.

To avoid spices tasting 'raw', it is a good idea to microwave them with a little oil for 1-2 minutes before adding the rest of the ingredients.

Curried Vegetables

Curried vegetables

| 11 mins |

Standing time: 3 mins

Use a mixture of seasonal vegetables — carrots, potatoes, green pepper, cauliflower, turnips and aubergine to make a good combination.

30ml / 2tbls vegetable oil
1 onion, finely chopped
2.5cm / 1in piece of ginger root, peeled and finely chopped
5ml / 1tsp black mustard seeds
1 green chilli, seeded and chopped
2 garlic cloves, crushed
7.5ml / 1½tsp turmeric
15ml / 1tbls ground coriander
700g / 1½lb fresh mixed vegetables, cut into small, even-sized pieces
30ml / 2tbls water
50g / 2oz creamed coconut, grated
salt and pepper

SERVES 4

1 Put the oil, onion, ginger root, mustard seeds, chilli, garlic, turmeric and coriander in a bowl and cover. Microwave at 100% (High) for 3-4 minutes, or until the onion is soft, stirring twice.
2 Add the vegetables and stir to coat with the spices. Add the water and coconut and stir well. Cover and microwave at 100% (High) for 8-12 minutes, until the vegetables are just tender. Stir, season to taste and stand, covered, for 3 minutes.

Five spice beef

| 8 mins |

Standing time: none

Chinese five spice powder (see chart) gives this oriental-style dish an unusual flavour.

30ml / 2tbls water
30ml / 2tbls dark soy sauce
5ml / 1tsp Worcestershire sauce (optional)
5ml / 1tsp Chinese five spice powder
15ml / 3tsp cornflour

pinch of garlic salt
450g / 1lb lean rump steak, thinly sliced across the grain
1 green pepper, cut in strips
2 tomatoes, quartered
4 spring onions, chopped

SERVES 4

1 In a large bowl, blend together the water, soy sauce, Worcestershire sauce, five spice powder, cornflour and garlic salt. Add the steak; stir until well coated. Stir in vegetables.
2 Microwave at 100% (High) for 8-10 minutes or until the meat and green pepper are tender, stirring two or three times.

Tropical dressed crab

| 6¼ mins |

Standing time: none

15ml / 1tbls vegetable oil
1 small onion, finely chopped
2 garlic cloves, crushed
15ml / 1tbls curry powder
5ml / 1tsp paprika
15ml / 1tbls plain flour
125ml / 4fl oz boiling chicken or fish stock
5ml / 1tsp lemon juice
2 pineapple rings in natural juice, drained and chopped
4 small, fresh cooked crabs, prepared with shells reserved (see page 148)
15ml / 1tbls natural yoghurt
salt
20ml / 4tsp browned breadcrumbs
10ml / 2tsp desiccated coconut

SERVES 4

1 Place oil, onion and garlic in a 1.7L / 3pt bowl. Microwave at 100% (High) for 1½ minutes, until softened, stirring once. Stir in the curry powder and paprika and continue microwaving for 45 seconds. Stir in flour and stock and microwave for a further 2-2½ minutes, or until boiling.
2 Mix in the lemon juice, pineapple pieces, crab meat, yoghurt and salt. Spoon into the crab shells and sprinkle with the breadcrumbs and coconut. Microwave at 100% (High) for 2-3 minutes, or until heated through.

Allspice   Cardamom

Chilli   Cinnamon

Cloves

Fennel   Coriander

Ginger

Mustard

Turmeric

Nutmeg

Saffron

Vanilla

SPICES/DESCRIPTION	USES
ALLSPICE Hard, dark brown berries also known as Jamaican pepper: whole or ground.	In both sweet and savoury dishes. Christmas cake, marinades, pickles.
CARAWAY Tiny curved seeds; very aromatic.	Popular in cabbage and pork dishes.
CARDAMOM Sold as whole pods, seeds, or ground.	Excellent in curries and pickles.
CAYENNE Hot pepper made from dried chillies.	Use sparingly. Good savoury garnish.
CHILLI Red or green chillies sold fresh, or dried, whole or ground in different strengths. Seeds are very hot.	Used in many curries and spicy meat dishes, especially Middle Eastern, South American and Spanish.
CINNAMON Sweet, spicy flavour and aroma.	In puddings, desserts, and hot drinks.
CLOVES The dried buds of a tropical tree. Whole or ground. Highly scented.	Good with sweet and savoury apple dishes. Used in pickling spices.
CORIANDER Delicate orange-y aroma and flavour. Sold as whole seeds or ground.	Good with pork, chicken and carrot dishes. Use in curries and Greek food.
CUMIN An aromatic seed. Also ground. Strong, distinctive flavour.	In Indian, Spanish and Mexican dishes. Often used in curry powders.
CHINESE FIVE SPICE POWDER Combination of star anise, cinnamon, Szechuan pepper, cloves and fennel.	Popular in Chinese cooking.
FENNEL Seeds of herb. Liquorice flavour.	Good with fish.
GINGER Knobby root of tropical plant. Sold fresh, dried or ground.	Gives subtly 'hot' flavour. Use in Oriental food, also cakes and breads.
MUSTARD Whole seeds, ground as powder or ready made. May be strong or mild.	Use sparingly to give hot flavour to sauces, dressings and relishes.
NUTMEG Best bought whole, and grated as needed. Ground nutmeg loses flavour.	Use in sweet and savoury dishes: also green vegetables, custards and cakes.
PAPRIKA Red pepper from dried sweet peppers. Flavour varies from hot to mild.	Adds colour and flavour, good garnish. Used in Hungarian goulash.
PEPPERCORNS Black peppers from dried, unripe berries; white from ripe berries. Green and pink peppercorns are pickled.	Black pepper is used in most savoury dishes. White pepper is best in pale sauces and creamy dishes.
SAFFRON The dried stamen of a type of crocus. Sold as threads or a powder. Very expensive. Threads need soaking first.	Use to flavour and colour savoury dishes, also cakes and sweet breads. In paella and bouillabaisse.
TURMERIC Hot flavour and bright colour.	Use to flavour and colour rice, chicken and seafood dishes.
VANILLA Available as dried pods, essence or synthetic flavouring.	Popular in ice cream, custards, sponge cake and milky puddings.

50

Mexican meatloaves

14½ mins

Standing time: 3 mins

If only small tortillas are available, use three for each dish, making two cuts in each tortilla.

1 small green pepper, seeded and chopped
1 onion, chopped
450g / 1lb lean minced beef
5ml / 1tsp ground cumin
5ml / 1tsp paprika
2.5ml / ½tsp ground cardamom (optional)
dash of Tabasco sauce
227g / 8oz can tomatoes, chopped
30ml / 2tbls tomato purée or paste
425g / 15oz can red kidney beans, drained
1 egg, beaten
salt and pepper
4 × 15cm / 6in corn tortillas or crêpes

TOPPING
25g / 1oz Cheddar cheese, grated
shredded lettuce
chopped tomato

SERVES 4

1 Combine the green pepper and onion in a bowl, cover and microwave at 100% (High) for 1½-2 minutes or until tender-crisp.
2 Add the beef, cumin, paprika, cardamom, Tabasco, the chopped tomatoes, tomato purée, kidney beans and beaten egg. Season.
3 If using tortillas, make four 5cm / 2in-deep slashes around the edge of each one. Place each tortilla in a 15cm / 6in diameter round serving dish. Overlap the edges to fit neatly. Crêpes are pliable and will not need cutting.
4 Fill each lined dish with a quarter of the meat mixture. Cover; microwave at 100% (High) for 13-15 minutes, until filling is firm.
5 Top each with a little grated cheese and leave to stand, covered for about 3 minutes to allow the cheese to melt. Garnish with chopped lettuce and tomato.

Devilled barbecue ribs

28 mins

Standing time: 6 mins

900g / 2lb Chinese pork ribs
vegetable oil for brushing

DEVILLED BARBECUE SAUCE
1 small onion, finely chopped
5ml / 1tsp vegetable oil
150ml / ¼pt tomato ketchup or sauce
30ml / 2tbls sweet chilli sauce

Mexican Meatloaves

30ml / 2tbls white wine vinegar
30ml / 2tbls demerara sugar
5ml / 1tsp made mustard
2.5ml / ½tsp garlic salt

SERVES 4

1 Combine the onion and oil for the sauce in a bowl and microwave at 100% (High) for 1-2 minutes, or until the onion is soft, stirring once. Stir in the remaining sauce ingredients and microwave at 100% (High) for a further 1-2 minutes; stir once. Set aside.
2 Arrange half the ribs on a roasting rack and brush with a little oil. Cover and microwave at 100% (High) for 7 minutes, rearranging once. Drain the ribs and transfer to a shallow dish. Repeat with the remaining ribs.
3 Brush enough sauce over the ribs to coat. Arrange half the ribs on the roasting rack, and microwave at 100% (High) for a further 6 minutes, turning over once and basting with the sauce once or twice. Transfer to a dish, cover with foil (shiny side in) and leave to stand for at least 3 minutes.
4 Brush the remaining ribs with sauce and cook as above. Cover with foil and leave to stand, then add to the serving dish.

51

Ginger chicken and greens

12½ mins

Standing time: none

30ml / 2tbls flaked almonds
15g / ½oz butter
350g / 12oz boneless chicken
 breasts, skinned and cut into
 12mm / ½in strips
100g / 4oz Pak Soi, coarsely
 shredded
1 carrot, very thinly sliced
6 spring onions, cut into
 12mm / ½in lengths
225g / 8oz can bamboo shoots,
 rinsed, drained and roughly
 chopped

SAUCE
150ml / ¼pt chicken stock
15ml / 1tbls dark soy sauce

Right: *Fruits in Spiced Syrup*
Below: *Ginger Chicken and Greens*

RAY DUNS

15ml / 1tbls dry sherry
10ml / 2tsp cornflour
2.5cm / 1in piece of ginger root,
 peeled and finely chopped
pinch of sugar
pinch of chilli powder
pinch of cayenne pepper

SERVES 4

1 Put the almonds and butter in a small bowl. Microwave, uncovered, at 100% (High) for 3½-4½ minutes, or until the almonds are just beginning to brown, stirring once. Set aside.
2 In a large bowl, combine the chicken, Pak Soi, carrot and onions. Cover and microwave at 100% (High) for 5-7 minutes or until the chicken is no longer pink, stirring twice. Stir in the bamboo shoots and set aside.
3 In another bowl, blend all the sauce ingredients together. Microwave, uncovered, at 100% (High) for 2-3 minutes, or until the mixture bubbles and thickens, stirring twice.
4 Stir the sauce into the chicken and vegetables, making sure they are thoroughly combined. Microwave, uncovered, at 100% (High) for 2-3 minutes or until piping hot. Serve, sprinkled with the almonds on a bed of boiled rice.

Fruits in spiced syrup

4 mins

Standing time: none

½ small honeydew melon,
 peeled, seeded and cubed
2 seedless oranges, peeled and
 segmented
2 bananas, sliced
1 red-skinned dessert apple,
 cored and cut into chunks
1 peach, stoned and diced
thick Greek yoghurt, to serve

SYRUP
150g / 5oz demerara sugar
275ml / ½pt water
juice of 1 lemon
few drops of vanilla flavouring
 or 1 vanilla pod, slit
1.5ml / ¼tsp ground cloves or
 3 whole cloves
1.5ml / ¼tsp grated nutmeg
1.5ml / ¼tsp ground allspice, or 6
 whole allspice berries

SERVES 4

1 Combine all the syrup ingredients in a deep, heatproof bowl.
2 Microwave at 100% (High) for 4-5 minutes to boil. Stir once.
3 Add the fruit and stir to coat. Cool a little before serving.

Aspics and savoury jellies

Aspic — clear savoury jelly — is marvellously easy to microwave. Use it to give meat, poultry and fish party pieces a sparkling finish or to make sophisticated savoury mousses and moulds.

Aspic is made from rich meat, poultry or fish stock, flavoured with vegetables and herbs. The stock is clarified to make it transparent and if needed, gelatine is added to help the set. It is more conveniently sold in powder form.

Gelatine or sweet jelly tablets can also be used to set and mould savoury ingredients. Jelly tablets come in a variety of different sizes. Divide them into cubes and place in a bowl with 150ml / ¼pt water. Microwave at 100% (High) for 2 minutes. Stir to dissolve, then make up with extra liquid, if necessary, according to the manufacturer's instructions.

Using aspic
Aspic powder is quickly and easily dissolved in the microwave cooker. Sprinkle over liquid, microwave until hot then just stir to dissolve. Chill the jelly until syrupy or the consistency of unbeaten egg white, and it is ready to use.

Aspic can be used to coat whole fish, such as salmon (see recipe), or individual portions and slices of chicken or meat. These are made even more attractive if a garnish is also set in aspic. Be creative with your choice of garnish here; wafer-thin slices of cucumber or radish, shapes cut from carrot or pepper or sprigs of fresh herbs. The jelly itself can be used as a garnish, see steps, page 54.

Whole boned and rolled joints can also be coated in aspic. A whole, stuffed chicken coated in chaudfroid sauce — a white sauce set with gelatine — looks stunning brushed with aspic.

Use aspic, too, to line a mould before filling with a savoury mousse mixture or finely chopped meat or poultry, vegetables, fish or seafood.

Boeuf à la Mode

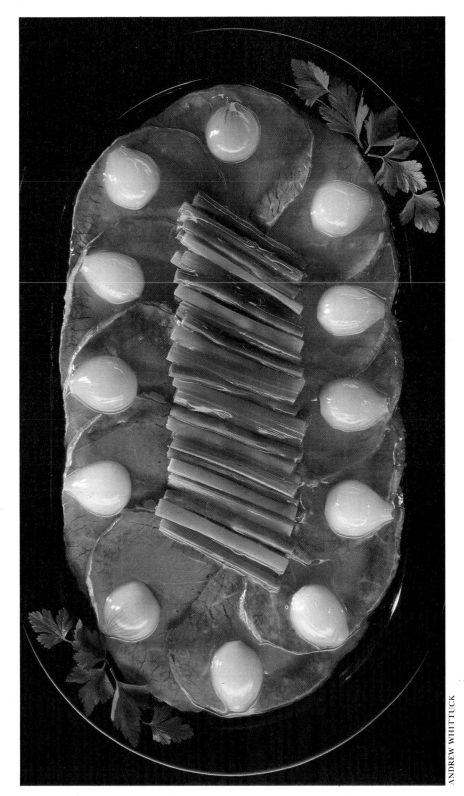

ANDREW WHITTUCK

53

How to dissolve and use aspic powder

Sprinkle *32.5ml / 6½tsp aspic powder over 150ml / ¼pt cold water or stock. Microwave at 100% (High) for 3½-4 minutes, until dissolved, stirring twice. Make up to 500ml / 18fl oz with water.*

Cool *the aspic jelly until syrupy — like unbeaten egg white. Place food to be coated on a rack or platter and brush or spoon over a thin layer of the jelly. Dip garnishes in the aspic and arrange on the food. Coat again and chill.*

Pour *aspic into a shallow dish and chill until set. Using a wet knife, cut the set aspic vertically and horizontally into even dice. Remove from the dish with a moistened metal spatula.*

To make *shapes, set the aspic in a shallow dish, then cut out small shapes using a wet knife or moistened canapé or petits fours cutter. Remove shapes with moistened spatula.*

flakes. Give the dish a half turn once and shield the head and tail with two small pieces of smooth foil. Uncover and cool.

4 Peel away the fish skin, leaving the head and tail intact.

5 Mix the mayonnaise with the dissolved gelatine and chill for 15 minutes, or until thickened. Place the salmon halves together on a serving platter and fill any gap with mayonnaise. Chill.

6 Chill the aspic jelly until syrupy. Spoon a thin layer over the surface of the fish.

7 Dip the radish slices into the aspic and arrange like scales on the fish. Dip five dill sprigs in aspic and set on top. Chill to set.

8 Discard any aspic from base of fish. Surround the fish with cucumber slices and sprigs of dill and garnish head with lemon slices and dill. Spoon remaining aspic jelly over fish and 'flood' the dish and cucumber with aspic. Chill for ½-1 hour, until set.

9 Pipe the remaining mayonnaise in a decorative border around the fish before serving.

Aspic-glazed salmon

| **18** mins |

Standing time: none

1.7kg / 3¾lb salmon, gutted, cleaned and halved
1 carrot, sliced
1 small onion, sliced
1 celery stalk, sliced
1 lemon, sliced
3-4 white peppercorns
45ml / 3tbls lemon juice
125ml / 4fl oz water

ASPIC GARNISH
150ml / ¼pt mayonnaise
5ml / 1tsp powdered gelatine dissolved in 30ml / 2tbls very hot water
500ml / 18fl oz aspic jelly, see steps above
100g / 4oz radishes, finely sliced
dill sprigs
½ cucumber, very thinly sliced
1 lemon slice, halved

SERVES 6-8

1 Prick the salmon skin in several places to prevent it bursting during cooking.

2 Place vegetables, flavourings and liquid in a shallow 30cm / 12in square dish. Cover and microwave at 100% (High) for 6 minutes.

3 Add the salmon, cover and microwave at 100% (High) for 12-18 minutes, until the fish just

Aspic-glazed Salmon

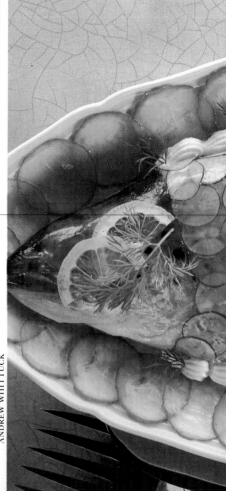

54

Moulded tomato savoury

2 mins

Standing time: none

350ml / 12fl oz tomato juice
1 beef stock cube dissolved in 90ml / 6tbls hot water
1 sachet or 17.5ml / $3\frac{1}{2}$tsp powdered gelatine
20ml / 4tsp lemon juice
grated zest of $\frac{1}{2}$ small lemon
2.5ml / $\frac{1}{2}$tsp Worcestershire sauce
pepper, to taste
6 drops Tabasco sauce
284g / $9\frac{1}{2}$oz can diced carrots, drained
$\frac{1}{2}$ green pepper, chopped
1 small onion, chopped

SERVES 6

1 Add sufficient tomato juice to the beef stock to make up to 250ml / 8fl oz. Sprinkle the powdered gelatine over this, cover and microwave at 100% (High) for 2-4 minutes. Stir briskly to dissolve.
2 Blend in remaining tomato juice, lemon juice and zest, Worcestershire, pepper and Tabasco.
3 Chill for 1-2 hours, until syrupy. Add carrots, pepper and onion.
4 Pour into a 1.1L / 2pt mould and chill overnight to set.
5 To serve, dip the mould or moulds briefly into hot water.

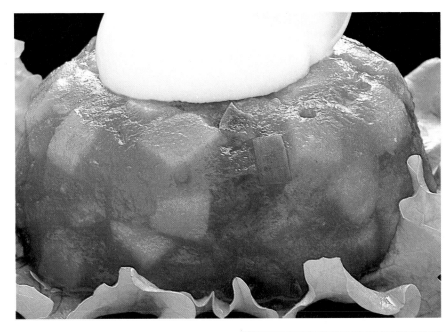

Cook's notes

To make unmoulding easier, rinse out the mould with cold water before adding the syrupy jelly mixture and dip mould in hot water to turn out.

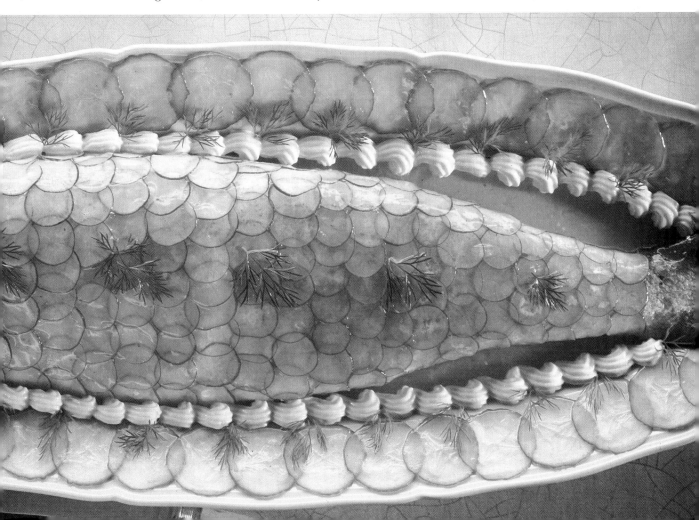

Boeuf à la mode

55 mins

Standing time: 20 mins

This elegant party dish of aspic coated beef and vegetables is a speciality of France.

1.4kg / 3lb boneless topside or silverside, tied to a neat compact shape
1 onion, sliced
1 celery stalk, sliced
2 bay leaves
few parsley sprigs
1 garlic clove, crushed (optional)
150ml / $\frac{1}{4}$pt red or white wine
salt and pepper
32.5ml / $6\frac{1}{2}$tsp aspic powder

VEGETABLE GARNISH
2 small carrots, cut into thin strips
6 button onions, halved
2 celery stalks, quartered and cut into thin strips
75g / 3oz French beans, topped and tailed

SERVES 6

1 Place the meat in a bowl with the onion, celery, bay leaves, parsley, garlic if used, and wine. Blend well. Cover and marinate for 2-4 hours, or overnight in the refrigerator, turning occasionally.

2 Remove the meat from the marinade and place in a large roasting or boiling bag. Strain the marinade into the bag and fasten it with a rubber band.

3 Microwave at 100% (High) for 8 minutes. Turn the beef in the bag over, reduce power to 50% (Medium) for 20 minutes, rotating the dish once. Open the bag.

4 Turn the meat over and add the vegetables for the garnish and season to taste. Re-fasten the bag and microwave at 50% (Medium) for 25 minutes, giving the dish two half turns during cooking. Leave to stand in the closed bag for 20 minutes.

5 Remove the meat and vegetables from the juices with a slotted spoon. Slice the meat and arrange around the edge of a platter with the onion halves, arrange the remaining vegetables in the centre. Leave to cool.

6 Strain the juices from the bag through a fine nylon sieve into a measuring jug and make up to 500ml / 18fl oz with water or wine, if necessary. Microwave at 100% (High) for 2-4 minutes until almost boiling. Sprinkle over the aspic powder and stir briskly to dissolve.

7 Cool the jelly until syrupy but still liquid, then spoon it carefully over the meat and vegetables until they are evenly coated. Chill for $\frac{1}{2}$-1 hour until set.

Microtips

If wished, dissolve aspic powder by microwaving 500ml / 18fl oz liquid at 100% (High) for 3-4 minutes, until very hot then sprinkle over powder and stir briskly with a fork until the powder has dissolved and the liquid is clear.

If jelly becomes unworkable when using as a coating, microwave at 100% (High) for 30-60 seconds to soften it. Chill again if necessary.

Bitter-sweet fruit mould

3 mins

Standing time: none

This colourful mousse can be served as an unusual accompaniment for roast poultry or as a tangy dessert.

275ml / ½pt unsweetened grape juice
175ml / 6fl oz red wine
125ml / 4fl oz water
2 sachets or 35ml / 7tsp powdered gelatine
175g / 6oz cranberry sauce
125ml / 4fl oz chilled whipped cream
40g / 1½oz chopped walnuts or pecans

SERVES 8

1 Place the grape juice, wine and water in a large bowl and sprinkle over the powdered gelatine. Microwave at 100% (High) for 3 minutes, then stir to dissolve.
2 Stir in the cranberry sauce then chill in the refrigerator for about 1 hour or until syrupy.
3 Fold in cream and nuts and pour into a 1.1L / 2pt mould. Chill for 3-4 hours, or until set. To unmould, dip briefly in hot water.

Hallowe'en jelly

3 mins

Standing time: none

425ml / ¾pt hot water
2 orange jelly tablets, cubed
425ml / ¾pt cold water
450g / 1lb carrots, grated
curly endive, stoned dates and celery stalk to garnish

SERVES 10-12

1 Place the hot water and jelly cubes in a bowl and microwave at 100% (High) for 3 minutes, stirring once, until dissolved.
2 Add the cold water and chill for about 1 hour, until syrupy. Assemble following steps right.

Left: *Bitter-Sweet Fruit Mould*
Right: *Hallowe'en Jelly*

How to assemble Hallowe'en jelly

Stir *in the carrots, mixing well. Pour into a 23cm / 9in round dish. Chill for 2-4 hours, until set. To unmould, dip the dish in hot water.*

Surround *with curly endive. Position dates on the top to form a pumpkin face and use the celery stick as a stem. Serve chilled, cut in wedges.*

Cooking with herbs

Herbs add a touch of magic to meat, salads or vegetables. Grow your own and use them freshly-cut, or buy the dried varieties — either way the microwave will retain all their delicious flavours.

For centuries herbs have been used to accentuate the flavour of food — and in really hard times to mask it! Now international cuisine is becoming more accessible to us all, the use of herbs is undergoing a revival.

In the microwave, both the flavour and colour of herbs remain quite distinct after cooking. Unlike many conventionally cooked dishes that retain little flavour of their herbs, a microwaved dish will be quite pungent. On this basis, it is a good idea to add fewer herbs than you would in conventional cooking — unless, of course, you prefer strong flavours.

Fresh herbs
For a ready supply of fresh herbs, grow your own. Many herbs make ideal pot or window box plants so you don't have to plant a herb garden. When using fresh herbs, only snip off as much as you need for a recipe. If you are given a few sprigs, keep them fresh in a jar of water.

Fresh herbs are increasingly available in small packs from

Lamb with Rosemary

58

supermarkets. Keep these in their original wrappings in a cool, dry place and use within a day or two of purchase.

Dried herbs

A vast assortment of dried herbs is now available. With the microwave, it is easy to dry fresh herbs yourself. Store them individually, in airtight containers and use within three months.

When herbs are dried their flavour is intensified. So, when using dried herbs instead of fresh reduce the quantity by about one third to a half. With a few exceptions, most herbs are available fresh and dried.

When adding dried herbs to a dish, rub them a little between your fingers to help release their flavour. Dried herbs are not suitable for garnishing as they need to be cooked in the dish to bring out their flavour.

Freezer notes

Frozen herbs have a fresher colour and flavour than dried. Some freezer centres and large supermarkets sell them in small cartons, but it is easy to freeze your own. Finely chop fresh herbs, pack loosely in small tubs, seal and freeze for up to 1 month. Use straight from frozen.

How to dry herbs in the microwave

Loosely *pack leaves in a measuring jug until you have about 275ml / ½pt. Transfer to a close mesh colander and rinse under cold water. Drain, then dry on a clean tea towel.*

Spread *the herbs in a single layer on absorbent paper in the microwave. Cover with more paper and place a glass of water in the microwave to ensure a sufficient load.*

Microwave *at 100% (High) for 7-9 minutes, until the leaves feel dry and lose their bright, green colour. Stir to re-distribute the layer of herbs every 2 minutes.*

Tip *herbs on to clean absorbent paper; spread out and leave until cool and dry. Rub between your fingers and transfer to an airtight container. Label and store for up to 3 months.*

Lamb with rosemary

| 35½ mins |

Standing time: 15 mins

This is a classic Mediterranean dish, the skin of the lamb is spiked with rosemary and garlic and their flavours permeate the whole roast during microwaving. Delicious!

1 boned shoulder of lamb, about 1.5kg / 3¼lb
10ml / 2tsp Worcestershire sauce
2-3 sprigs of rosemary
1 garlic clove, crushed

STUFFING
6 spring onions, finely chopped
1 celery stalk, finely chopped
25g / 1oz butter
50g / 2oz fresh breadcrumbs
5ml / 1tsp dried thyme
5ml / 1tsp grated lemon zest
50g / 2oz raisins
salt and pepper
1 egg, beaten

SERVES 4-6

1 Make the stuffing: place the spring onions, celery and butter in a bowl and microwave at 100% (High) for 3-4 minutes, or until tender, stirring once.
2 Remove from the microwave and stir in the breadcrumbs, thyme, lemon zest and raisins. Season to taste, then bind with the beaten egg.
3 Lay the lamb on a board and

brush with Worcestershire sauce. With the skin side down, spread the stuffing on the lamb. Roll up to enclose the stuffing and tie at 2.5cm / 1in intervals with string.
4 Make small slits in the skin of the lamb with a sharp knife. Remove the rosemary needles and tuck a few needles and a little garlic in each slit. Weigh the lamb and calculate the microwaving time, allowing 10-15 minutes per 450g / 1lb depending on preferred doneness.
5 Stand the lamb on a roasting rack or in a shallow dish, then place in a vented roasting bag. Tie loosely. Microwave for 5 minutes at 100% (High), then at 50% (Medium) for the remaining time. Stand for 15 minutes.

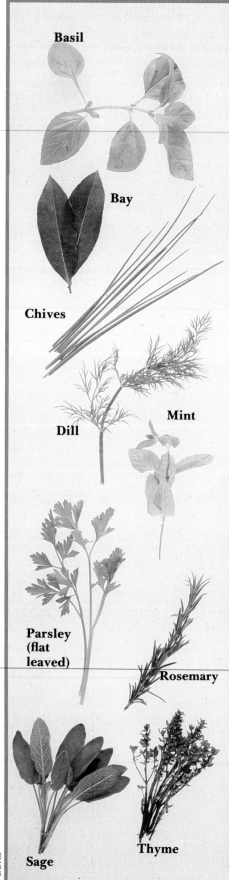

Basil

Bay

Chives

Dill

Mint

Parsley
(flat
leaved)

Rosemary

Sage

Thyme

HERB/DESCRIPTION	USES
BASIL A pungent flavour with a sweet aroma. The fresh leaves have a superior flavour.	Goes well with all Mediterranean dishes. A must for all tomato dishes. Excellent with lamb.
BAY LEAVES Very strong flavour, especially if whole leaves are torn or crushed. One ingredient of a classic bouquet garni. Available dried whole or ground, as well as fresh.	Use in meat and poultry dishes, especially soups, casseroles and stews. Also for fish and vegetable dishes, pickles and stuffings. Remove from a cooked dish before serving.
OREGANO Flavour and aroma similar to marjoram, but stronger.	Use in spicy Greek, Mexican and Italian dishes.
PARSLEY Two types — flat-leaved (French or Continental) or curly leaved. The stalks are included in a bouquet garni.	Popular herb which goes well with almost any dish, Parsley sauce is excellent with boiled ham or fish.
ROSEMARY Needle shaped leaves that need to be chopped before use. Tea-like aroma and bitter-sweet flavour.	In meat dishes, particularly lamb. Also stuffings and marinades.
SAGE Pungent, slightly bitter aroma. Flavour can be strong and over-powering if used in excess.	Use to flavour meat, particularly pork; and also bean and cheese dishes. Excellent with sausages and in stuffings.
TARRAGON Two varieties — the Russian is more common, the French has a superior flavour. A sweet, aromatic flavour, with an aniseed like tang.	Include in sauces, poultry, seafood, cheese and egg dishes. Also good with vegetables and in salad dressings, particularly with mayonnaise.
THYME Many varieties. The easiest and most successful herb to dry. Pungent and aromatic.	Add to meat and poultry dishes, also soups, stuffings and dressings. Excellent, with vegetables.
DILL Pretty, feathery leaves with a flavour similar to caraway. The dried herb is known as dillweed.	Use in meat dishes, particularly pork, also poultry, fish, cheese, egg, vegetable and Italian style dishes.
FENNEL The fern-like leaves have an aniseed flavour.	With lamb; potatoes and peas. Use also to garnish drinks and in cocktails.
MARJORAM Spicy, slightly bitter flavour.	Superb with fish and potato dishes.
MINT Many varieties. Strong, distinctively sweet and aromatic.	Use the fresh leaves to flavour and / or garnish fish and pâtés or soups.
CHERVIL Like a delicate parsley but with no smell. A faintly sweet flavour, similar to tarragon.	Used in French dishes, especially egg, cheese and chicken ones. Cook in soups, salads, sauces and stews.
CHIVES A member of the onion family. The spiky leaves are best snipped with scissors rather than chopped.	Excellent in salads or omelettes, and in any dishes where a subtle onion flavour is needed.
CORIANDER Scented aromatic leaves only available fresh. The seeds are sold as a spice.	Chop leaves into Indian dishes or use as garnish instead of parsley.

60

Stewed chicken with herbs

27 mins

Standing time: 5 mins

1.1-1.4kg / 2½-3lb chicken,
  cut into eight pieces, skinned
1 onion, thinly sliced
2 carrots, chopped
75g / 3oz mushrooms, sliced
75ml / 3fl oz white wine
15ml / 1tbls chopped parsley
1 thin lemon slice
5ml / 1tsp dried savory
1.5ml / ¼tsp dried thyme
pinch of pepper
2 garlic cloves, halved
½ × 425g / 15oz can cream of
  chicken soup
200ml / 7fl oz chicken stock

SERVES 4

1 Place the chicken (thickest parts to the outside) vegetables, herbs and flavourings in a 3.4L / 6pt casserole. Mix together the soup and stock, add to casserole.
2 Cover and microwave at 70% (Medium-High) for 27-33 minutes, or until the meat near the bone is no longer pink and the juices run clear. Turn and rearrange the chicken once. Stand for 5 minutes, then serve.

Chived potatoes

10 mins

Standing time: 5 mins

2 large baking potatoes,
  225g / 8oz each, scrubbed and
  pricked
75ml / 3fl oz warm milk
30ml / 2tbls salad cream or
  mayonnaise
15ml / 1tbls melted butter or
  margarine
salt and pepper
5ml / 1tsp chopped fresh chives
  or 2.5ml / ½tsp dried chives

SERVES 2

1 Microwave the potatoes at 100% (High) for 8-9 minutes, wrap in foil and stand for 5 minutes.
2 Slice each potato in half lengthways and scoop out the centres, taking care not to pierce the skins.

3 Mash the potato with the milk, mayonnaise, butter, and seasoning. Spoon the mixture into the potato shells and sprinkle the chives over the top.
4 Place the potatoes on a plate, cover and microwave at 100% (High) for 2-3 minutes, until hot.

VARIATION
To add piquancy to the baked potato filling combine crisply-cooked bacon with cottage cheese and a sprinkling of chives. Make a slit in the piping hot potatoes, fill and serve.

Stewed Chicken with Herbs

Vegetable salad

8¾ mins

Standing time: none

225g / 8oz frozen cauliflower
  florets
½ small onion, thinly sliced into
  rings
1 small green pepper, seeded and
  finely sliced
1 tomato, coarsely chopped

MARINADE
50ml / 2fl oz red wine vinegar
50ml / 2fl oz olive or vegetable oil
15ml / 1tbls soft brown sugar
10ml / 2tsp lemon juice
2.5ml / ½tsp dried basil
salt and pepper
pinch of mustard powder

SERVES 3-4

1 Combine all the marinade ingredients in a large bowl and microwave at 100% (High) for 45-60 seconds, or until the sugar has dissolved, stirring halfway through.
2 Add the cauliflower florets, cover and microwave at 100% (High) for 3-3½ minutes. Cut any large florets in half and microwave

Vegetable Salad

for a further 3-3½ minutes.
3 Stir in the onion and pepper, toss well to coat. Cover and microwave at 100% (High) for 2-3 minutes, until the vegetables are tender but still crisp, stirring once.
4 Stir in the tomato, cover and chill for at least an hour before serving.

Rosemary carrots

8 mins

Standing time: 3 mins

450g / 1lb carrots, thinly sliced
60ml / 4tbls hot strong chicken
  stock
15ml / 1tbls soft light brown
  sugar
2.5ml / ½tsp dried rosemary
5ml / 1tsp chopped fresh chives
pepper

SERVES 4

1 Place the carrots in a bowl or casserole. Mix together the stock, sugar, crushed rosemary, chives and pepper and pour over the carrots. Toss to coat.
2 Cover and microwave at 100% (High) for 8-10 minutes, or until the carrots are just tender, stirring twice during cooking. Stand for 3 minutes, then serve.

Herby tomato sauce

11 mins

Standing time: none

This chunky sauce can be served with fish, meat or poultry — or try it as a tasty pizza topping.

15ml / 3tsp cornflour
30ml / 2tbls water
4 tomatoes, peeled and chopped
1 green pepper, seeded and cut
  into thin strips
1 small onion, finely chopped
2.5ml / ½tsp dried basil
1.5ml / ¼tsp dried oregano
1.5ml / ¼tsp dried thyme
1.5ml / ¼tsp dried marjoram
pinch of powdered garlic
salt and black pepper

MAKES ABOUT 300ml / ½pt

1 Blend the cornflour and water together in a small bowl. Combine all the other ingredients in a large bowl or casserole and stir in the cornflour mixture.
2 Cover and microwave at 100% (High) for 5 minutes. Stir, re-cover and continue to microwave at 100% (High) for 6-10 minutes or until the onion and pepper are tender and the sauce has thickened, stirring once.

Making food look good

A sprinkling of herbs or spices on savoury dishes, or a dusting of icing sugar on sponge cakes are just two easy ways to add colour and interest to microwaved food.

The appearance of food after it has been cooked in the microwave can sometimes be rather pale and lacking in colour — but there are many quick and easy ways in which you can add surface colour and texture to food before or after cooking.

The short cooking time — and the fact that microwaves do not evaporate moisture to the same extent as a conventional cooker — both mean that microwaved food does not acquire a crisp, golden surface. There are, however, microwaving techniques for making sure that your food looks as good as it tastes.

Browned breadcrumb and cheese topping

Savoury toppings

For savoury food which is usually browned, try one of these topping ideas.

Packet potato crisps or chips can both be used for a golden topping: sprinkle on after cooking as they go soggy when microwaved.

Breadcrumbs can be browned in the microwave and used as a topping for casseroles, pasta and sauces. Microwave 50g / 2oz brown breadcrumbs with 25g / 1oz butter on 100% (High) for 4-5 minutes. Stir 3 times. Use browned breadcrumbs with grated cheese and pop the food back in the microwave to melt the cheese.

Alternatively, just pop microwaved food under the grill or into a conventional oven to brown and crisp the top.

Using bastes and dry seasonings

These special microwave bastes have been designed so that they add colour as well as flavour to meat and poultry cooked in the microwave. Brush onto food before and during microwaving.

The dry seasoning mixture, made with a combination of dried herbs, spices and flavourings, will also add texture. Store the mixture in an airtight container. Sprinkle the seasoning over meat and poultry and rub in lightly before microwaving.

Savoury baste

30 secs

Standing time: none

25g / 1oz butter or margarine
5ml / 1tsp dried parsley
1.5ml / ¼tsp paprika
pinch of dried mixed herbs
salt and pepper

1 Melt the butter in a covered bowl at 100% (High) for 30-45 seconds. Stir in remaining ingredients.

VARIATION
For a Soy-honey baste, stir 15ml / 1tbls honey into the melted butter until dissolved, then blend in 30ml / 2tbls soy sauce and 1.5ml / ¼tsp mustard powder.

Herb mix

30ml / 2tbls dry beef soup mix
5ml / 1tsp dried mixed herbs
5ml / 1tsp dried parsley
1.5ml / ¼tsp onion salt
1.5ml / ¼tsp pepper

1 Mix all the ingredients together and store in an airtight container.

VARIATION
You can use any combination of dried herbs and spices as a seasoning mix. Experiment with your favourites until you find the best combination.

How to make savoury food look good

Sprinkle *on fresh herbs such as parsley or chives to add colour and interest. A twist of lemon or cucumber looks fresh and appetizing.*

Dry *soup or stuffing mix can be used to coat meat before microwaving, for colour and texture. A variety of seasoned coating mixes can be used.*

Colourful *sauces will enhance pale food. Marinades, available as dry mixes, will add flavour and colour and can be made into sauces for serving.*

RAY DUNS

64

Attractive desserts

Because microwaving is a moist form of cooking, many baked desserts and cakes do not have an opportunity to develop their characteristic crisp, golden surfaces. Plain sponge cakes, for instance, may look a little bland so disguise this with icing or a sprinkling of sugar. Add colour to cakes, using dark ingredients like treacle, dark sugar or chocolate. Sweet sauces, whipped, thick cream and chopped nuts can all be used to make desserts look attractive.

Pastry secrets

Decorate *sweet pies with pastry cutouts (see right). Sprinkle the shapes with a little ground cinnamon or sugar before microwaving.*

Add *15ml / 1tbls sugar and 30ml / 2tbls cocoa to 100g / 4oz flour to make a chocolate crust for sweet pies or use wholewheat flour for a darker pastry.*

Making cakes and desserts look good

Toast *40g / 1½oz blanched almonds in a small bowl 2½-3 minutes at 100% (High), stirring. Stand for 5 minutes. Use with cakes and desserts.*

Chopped, blanched or toasted nuts *make an attractive topping for plain iced sponge cakes which do not form a crust during microwaving.*

Toast *100g / 4oz desiccated coconut for 3-5 minutes in a roasting bag at 100% (High). Shake bag every 20 seconds and rearrange to avoid overcooking.*

65

Microwaving stuffings

With the help of a microwave, stuffings can be made in minutes — fruit, herbs or sausagemeat all add moisture and flavour and can transform a simple roast joint or bird into a delectable dish.

Stuffings can serve several purposes: they add flavour and moisture to meat, help keep poultry or a boned joint in good shape, make a small bird or joint go further — and are a great family favourite. They really make a tasty addition to any meat.

Most stuffings use breadcrumbs, rice or sausagemeat as a base. A variety of herbs, vegetables, fruit and nuts can be added, while brown rice or wholemeal breadcrumbs provide extra texture and flavour.

Any stuffing can be made quickly and easily with the help of a microwave. Small quantities of onion and other vegetables are quickly softened in butter; sausagemeat or bacon is speedily cooked, and other ingredients can be added and cooked in the same bowl. Stuffing cooked separately in a dish or made into balls is ready in two minutes and all microwaved stuffings will remain moist and full of flavour.

Remove the stuffing from the meat and store separately in the refrigerator. Use within one or two days, heated for 1-2 minutes in the microwave or served cold with the cold meat.

Stuffed Guard of Honour

Stuffed guard of honour

62 mins

Standing time: none

This is a spectacular centrepiece for an elegant dinner party.

2 racks of lamb, each weighing about 1.1kg / 2½lb
400g / 14oz can apricots, to garnish (juice reserved)

STUFFING
1 small onion, chopped
50g / 2oz butter
100g / 4oz breadcrumbs
75g / 3oz dried apricots, chopped
50g / 2oz walnuts, chopped
grated zest and juice of ½ orange
salt and pepper
1 egg, beaten
15ml / 1tbls chopped parsley

BROWNING BASTE
30-45ml / 2-3tbls reserved apricot juice
10ml / 2tsp soy sauce

SERVES 6

VARIATION
Replace the apricots with apples, if wished, and use Brazil or chestnuts in place of the walnuts.

How to microwave Stuffed guard of honour

Prepare *guard of honour by cutting 4cm / 1½in of the meat from top of each rib and scraping the bone clean. Place racks facing each other with bones interlocking.*

Microwave *the onion and butter in a covered bowl at 100% (High) for 2-3 minutes, until soft. Stir in remaining ingredients and stuff the cavity in the centre of the lamb joints.*

Using *fine string, tie the joint around the rib bones and under the base, to keep the shape. Cover the top with cling film to protect any exposed stuffing. Place on a roasting rack.*

Allow *12-14 minutes per 450g / 1lb for rare meat, 13-16 minutes for medium. Mix browning baste and brush over lamb. Microwave at 100% (High) for the first 5 minutes.*

Reduce *power to 50% (Medium) for remaining calculated time. Halfway through the cooking time, drain the juices from the roasting dish and reserve for gravy, see Microtips, left.*

67

Stuffed crown roast of pork · 99 mins

Standing time: 10 mins

This is a perfect special-occasion meal or family celebration. Order the cut in advance from your butcher and ask him to prepare it for you. He will split the loin in two, stitch the edges together and secure with a piece of string around the outside.

1 loin of pork of 16 chops, weighing about 3kg / 6lb 10oz
8 cherry tomatoes to garnish

STUFFING
100g / 4oz sausagemeat
1 celery stalk, thinly sliced
1 small onion, chopped
100g / 4oz mushrooms, sliced
50g / 2oz rice, cooked
15ml / 1tbls chopped parsley
salt and pepper
2.5ml / ½tsp dried rosemary

SERVES 8

VARIATION
A stuffed Crown roast of lamb may be prepared and cooked in the same way, but allow 12-14 minutes per 450g / 1lb for rare meat and 13-16 minutes for medium. If wished, use the minced trimmings from the bone ends of the lamb in the stuffing instead of the sausagemeat.

Cook's notes

Using the microwave thermometer is the easiest way to judge accurately when the meat is cooked; however, it is possible to cook meat successfully without one.

Following the cooking times given in the recipe is important. At the end of the cooking time, pierce the thickest part of the pork with a sharp knife. There should be no sign of pink and the juices should also run clear, not pink or red.

Check again after standing time; if the meat is not quite done, return it to the cooker and microwave at 100% (High) for a few more minutes.

Chestnut stuffing · 6½ mins

Standing time: none

This rich stuffing is ideal for a traditional Christmas turkey. For timings for microwaving whole turkeys, with or without stuffing, see the chart on page 223.

6 streaky bacon rashers, rinds removed
225g / 8oz sausagemeat
1 small onion, chopped
450g / 1lb can whole unsweetened chestnuts, drained and roughly chopped
grated zest of ½ lemon
5ml / 1tsp mixed dried herbs
salt and pepper

FOR A 5.4kg / 12lb TURKEY

1 Place the bacon on a plate, cover with two sheets of absorbent paper

Stuffed Crown Roast of Pork

and microwave at 100% (High) for 3-3½ minutes, or until crisp. Transfer to fresh absorbent paper to drain, then crumble into small pieces.
2 Crumble the sausagemeat into a 1.1L / 2pt bowl. Microwave at 100% (High) for 2-3 minutes until the meat has lost its pinkness. Break up with a fork and drain on absorbent paper.
3 Clean the bowl and add the onion. Cover and microwave at 100% (High) for 1½-2 minutes until the onion is tender.
4 Add all the stuffing ingredients to the onion in the bowl and mix together thoroughly. Use to stuff the neck end of the turkey.

VARIATION
Add one peeled, cored and chopped dessert apple to the stuffing for extra fruity flavour.

68

How to microwave Stuffed crown roast of pork

For the stuffing: *microwave sausagemeat at 100% (High) for 2-3 minutes, then drain. Microwave celery, onion and mushrooms in a clean bowl at 100% (High) for 4-5 minutes. Combine all the stuffing ingredients.*

Insert *microwave thermometer between two ribs; place tip in meaty area on inside of crown, not touching fat or bone. Place crown on a rack, ends down. Calculate cooking time at 15-17 minutes per 450g / 1lb.*

Microwave *the crown roast at 100% (High) for the first 5 minutes of the calculated cooking time. Reduce the power to 50% (Medium) and continue to microwave for the first half of the calculated time.*

Drain *away any juices which have run out of the meat. Using two thickly folded pieces of absorbent paper, turn the crown roast over carefully so that it rests on its meaty base on the roasting rack.*

Microwave *at 50% (Medium) until 30 minutes before the end of the calculated cooking time. Drain off the cooking juices and replace the meat on the rack. Spoon the stuffing into the cavity.*

Cover *the crown roast with greaseproof paper or cling film and microwave for the rest of the cooking time, or until the internal temperature reaches 75°C / 170°F. Remove from the cooker.*

Tent *the crown roast loosely with foil and leave to stand for 10 minutes, or until the internal temperature of the meat reaches 80°C / 175°F. The meat will continue to cook during the standing time.*

Transfer *the crown roast to a serving dish, using a fish slice to support the stuffing in the centre. Pierce the skins of the tomatoes and microwave at 100% (High) for 1-2 minutes until hot.*

Garnish *the meat with the hot cherry tomatoes. Add paper frills on the tip of each chop for special occasions. To serve, carve down between the bones of the chops, and serve some stuffing with each chop.*

Fruity chicken

18¼ mins

Standing time: 10 mins

This is a deliciously light, summer-time stuffing, ideal for poultry or light meats.

15g / ½oz butter
5ml / 1tsp soy sauce
5ml / 1tsp microwave browning
1-1.5kg / 2¼-3¼lb oven-ready
  chicken

STUFFING
1 celery stalk, chopped
1 small red dessert apple, cored
  and cut into 12mm / ½in cubes
30ml / 2tbls raisins
2 slices of bread, cut into 12mm /
  ½in cubes
1 small onion, chopped
salt and pepper
1.5ml / ¼tsp dried thyme
grated zest of ½ orange

SERVES 4-6

1 Place the butter in a bowl, cover and microwave at 100% (High) for 10-20 seconds until melted. Stir in the soy sauce and microwave browning.
2 Combine all the stuffing ingredients, then use to stuff the neck cavity. Brush the chicken with half the soy sauce basting mixture. Place the chicken, breast side down, on a roasting rack in a shallow dish and cover loosely with a slit roasting bag. Calculate the cooking time, allowing 8-9 minutes per 450g / 1lb.
3 Microwave the chicken at 100% (High) for 5 minutes. Reduce the power to 50% (Medium) and microwave for the remaining first half of the calculated cooking time.
4 Turn the chicken breast side up and brush with the remaining soy sauce mixture. Replace the roasting bag and microwave for the remaining calculated time.
5 Remove the roasting bag. Cover the cooked chicken loosely with a tent of foil (shiny side in) and leave to stand for 10 minutes. Serve the chicken and stuffing with a salad and new potatoes.

Fruity Chicken

Sage and onion stuffing

2 mins

Standing time: none

A traditional stuffing which can be used to stuff poultry or served with roast pork. It is also excellent spread over pork chops before microwaving.

2 onions, chopped
50g / 2oz butter or margarine
30ml / 2tbls chopped fresh sage
100g / 4oz fresh brown breadcrumbs
grated zest of ½ lemon
1 egg, beaten
salt and pepper

FOR A 5.4kg / 12lb TURKEY

1 Place the onion and butter or margarine in a bowl. Cover and microwave at 100% (High) for 2-3 minutes until the onion is soft, stirring once to rearrange.
2 Add the sage, breadcrumbs, lemon zest and egg and mix together thoroughly. Season to taste with salt and pepper before using as a stuffing or coating.

Cook's notes

Stuffings must always be cooled completely before being used, and should not be placed in a bird or joint until just before it goes into the cooker. This reduces the risk of bacteria forming inside the stuffed meat.

Do not pack the stuffing too tightly as it absorbs the meat juices and expands during cooking. Microwave excess stuffing separately for 2 minutes if required.

Microtips

Check poultry is cooked after standing time. To do this pierce the thickest part of the thigh; the juices should run clear. If they are pink, cook the bird for a little longer. Also check that the drumsticks move easily at the joint as an extra test for doneness.

Celery and nut stuffed chicken

21¼ mins

Standing time: 10 mins

Serve this dish with buttered carrots, plain boiled rice and the cooking juices from the chicken.

15g / ½oz butter
15ml / 1tbls brown sauce
1kg / 2¼lb oven-ready chicken

STUFFING
1 celery stalk, sliced
1 small onion, chopped
50g / 2oz butter or margarine
50g / 2oz hazelnut kernels, chopped
75g / 3oz fresh brown breadcrumbs
grated zest and juice of ½ orange
salt and pepper

SERVES 2-4

1 Melt the butter in a covered bowl at 100% (High) for 10-20 seconds. Stir in the brown sauce and set aside.
2 For the stuffing, place the celery, onion and butter or margarine in a bowl. Cover and microwave at 100% (High) for 3-3½ minutes, until the vegetables are tender. Add the nuts, breadcrumbs, orange zest and juice and salt and pepper and mix the stuffing thoroughly.
3 Stuff the neck end of the chicken with this mixture, then brush with half the soy browning mixture. Place, breast side down, on a roasting rack in a shallow dish. Cover loosely with a slit roasting bag. Calculate the cooking time at 8-9 minutes per 450g / 1lb.
4 Microwave the chicken at 100% (High) for the first 15 minutes. Reduce to 50% (Medium) and microwave for the remaining first half of the calculated cooking time.
5 Turn the chicken breast side up and brush with the remaining browning mixture. Replace the roasting bag. Microwave for the remaining calculated time.
6 Remove the roasting bag. Cover with foil (shiny side in) and leave to stand for 10 minutes before serving.

Celery and Nut Stuffed Chicken

Cook's notes

Stuff only the neck end of poultry and not the whole body cavity. Too much stuffing hinders heat conduction and cooking of the bird will be affected.

To help a stuffed bird keep its shape, truss it and secure loose neck skin with wooden cocktail stick.

71

CHAPTER TWO
QUICK AND EASY SNACKS

The microwave cooker really comes into its own when it is used to prepare delicious light meals quickly and easily. Most of the recipes in this chapter make perfect lunch and supper dishes and many will keep the chidren (and their friends) happy at lunchtime or 'high tea'.

Meals that are prepared as a quick snack can be just as nutritious and satisfying as main meals that have been planned and prepared in advance. The recipes in this chapter make use of wholesome ingredients, such as cheese, eggs, bread and fresh vegetables to make delicious snacks that are good for you as well as enjoyable. The soups in the first section may use corner-cutting ingredients, such as stock cubes and condensed canned soups, for speed, but they combine them with fresh vegetables and flavoursome herbs to make soups, such as Minestrone and Garden Vegetable, which can be served with crusty wholemeal rolls for a complete meal.

Eggs and cheese make the perfect snack food. Eggs can be made into savoury omelettes, French Toast, Sausagemeat Bake, or simply scrambled and served on toast. Eggs should be thoroughly cooked, but not overcooked in the microwave. The clear instructions given in this chapter will help you cook them exactly to your liking.

All types of bread and rolls can be used to make delicious and nutritious snacks. You will find plenty to choose from in this chapter, including filled pitta breads, burgers of all sorts, muffins topped with tuna fish, and a variety of filled rolls.

Finally, the section on fun snacks has been specially written so that the children can help to prepare their own quick meals. The novelty recipes, such as Cheesy Popcorn or Fun Burgers, will be sure to hold their interest and might even encourage them to cook more of their own meals in the future.

Snack soups

Vegetables, imagination and a little microwave magic — that's all you need to create a satisfying snack in its own right, or the ideal starter to a light meal.

Soups are quick to make in the microwave cooker, especially if you use stock cubes or condensed canned soups for the base. Stir the soup both during cooking and on removal from the cooker.

Cover the soup when pre-cooking vegetables to keep in maximum moisture and quicken the cooking, but generally leave uncovered once the liquid is added. Soups can be stored, covered, for up to 2 days only. Reheat 1-2 portions in individual bowls; for more, use one large container. Serve with croûtons or grated cheese.

Minestrone Soup

74

Egg drop soup

10 mins

Standing time: none

1 spring onion, chopped
2 chicken stock cubes, crumbled
15ml / 1tbls light soy sauce
850ml / 1½pt hot water
2 eggs, lightly beaten

SERVES 4

1 In a 2.3L / 4pt casserole, combine the onion, stock cubes, soy sauce and water.
2 Microwave at 100% (High) for 10-12 minutes, uncovered, or until soup is boiling.
3 Stir the soup, pour the eggs in a thin circular stream over the boiling soup. The egg will start to cook in the heat of the soup and will set in soft strands.
4 Serve immediately.

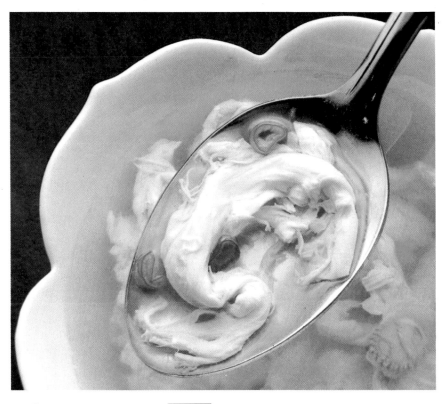

Minestrone soup

30 mins

Standing time: none

2 celery stalks, thinly sliced
2 carrots, thinly sliced
2 garlic cloves, crushed (optional)
1 large potato, cut into 12mm / ½in cubes
397g / 14oz can chopped tomatoes
2 courgettes, thinly sliced
175g / 6oz green beans, cut into pieces (see Microtips)
25g / 1oz spaghetti, broken up
850ml / 1½pt hot water
1 beef stock cube, crumbled
5ml / 1tsp dried basil
15ml / 1tbls parsley flakes

SERVES 6

1 In a 2.3-2.8 / 4-5pt casserole, mix all ingredients, then cover.
2 Microwave at 100% (High) for 30-35 minutes or until vegetables are tender. Stir once or twice.

Microtips

If using frozen green beans, thaw in a bowl, covered, at 100% (High) for 3 minutes.

Spicy tomato soup

10 mins

Standing time: none

850ml / 1½pt tomato juice
1 beef stock cube, crumbled
5ml / 1tsp Worcestershire sauce
large pinch of dried basil
pinch of dried thyme
5ml / 1tsp dried parsley
pinch of sugar
lemon slices and celery leaves

SERVES 4

1 Combine all the ingredients (except lemon and celery) in a 1.1L /2pt casserole, cover.
2 Microwave at 100% (High) for 10-12 minutes or until the soup is thoroughly heated.
3 Pour the soup into 4 serving bowls or mugs and garnish with lemon slices and celery leaves.

Above: *Egg Drop Soup*
Below: *Spicy Tomato Soup*

Garden vegetable soup

11 mins

Standing time: none

295g / 10.4oz can condensed
  cream of chicken soup diluted
  with 2 × cans hot water
10ml / 2tsp soy sauce
pinch of dried thyme
pinch of dried basil
small pinch of dried onion
  powder
175g / 6oz broccoli
2 carrots
6 lettuce leaves

SERVES 4

1 In a 2.3L / 4pt casserole combine the soup, water, soy sauce,
thyme, basil and onion powder.
2 Microwave at 100% (High) for
5-7 minutes or until just boiling.
3 Cut the broccoli stems into thin
slices, and florets into small pieces.
cut the carrots into long thin
strips.
4 When the soup boils, add the
broccoli and carrots. Microwave,
uncovered, for 6-9 minutes or until the vegetables are just tender

Microtip

*If cooking Garden Vegetable Soup
in advance, do not add the lettuce
until just before serving or it will
become very soft.*

and still crisp.
5 Just before serving, shred the
lettuce and stir into the hot soup.

VARIATION
**Garden vegetable soup for
two:**
295g / 10.4oz can condensed
  cream of chicken soup diluted
  with 1 can of hot water
5ml / 1tsp soy sauce
small pinch of dried thyme
small pinch of dried basil
small pinch of dried onion
  powder
100g / 4oz fresh broccoli
1 carrot
3 lettuce leaves

Follow instructions given, left; but
microwave in Step 2 for 3-5 minutes and in Step 4 for 4½-7 minutes at 100% (High).

Reheating time for two portions
in separate bowls is 4-6 minutes,
uncovered, at 100% (High). Stir
after half the cooking time.

Cream of mushroom soup

18 mins

Standing time: none

This recipe gives a quick and easy
method for making a classic cream
soup. This sauce-type method can
be used to make all manner of
vegetable soups, which can be
puréed in a blender and reheated
if liked.

Garden Vegetable Soup

225g / 8oz mushrooms, sliced
1 onion, chopped
50g / 2oz butter
75ml / 5tbls plain flour
850ml / 1½pt hot water
1 chicken stock cube, crumbled
75g / 3oz Emmental cheese,
  grated
salt and pepper
60ml / 4tbls double cream
15ml / 1tbls white wine

SERVES 4

1 In a 2.3L / 4pt casserole, combine the sliced mushrooms, chopped onion and the butter.
2 Cover and microwave at 100%
(High) for 6-8 minutes or until the
onion is tender, stirring after half
the cooking time.
3 Blend in the flour, then gradually stir in the water and add the
chicken stock cube.
4 Microwave at 100% (High) for
10-15 minutes or until slightly
thickened, stirring two-three times
during cooking.
5 Blend in the cheese, salt and
pepper, double cream and wine.
Microwave at 100% (High) for 2-3
minutes until the cheese melts.

VARIATION
**Cream of mushroom soup
for two:**
Halve the ingredient amounts as
above and follow the sauce
method, but microwave at 100%
(High) for half the specified times.

Cream of asparagus soup

22 mins

Standing time: 5 mins

2 celery stalks, finely chopped
1 small onion, finely chopped
25g / 1oz butter
450g / 1lb fresh asparagus,
 trimmed and chopped
295g / 10.4oz can cream of
 chicken soup
275ml / ½pt milk or single cream
salt and pepper

SERVES 4

1 Combine the celery, onion and butter in a 1.1L / 2pt casserole. Cover and microwave at 100% (High) for 5-7 minutes or until tender, stirring once.
2 Add the asparagus and cover.
3 Microwave at 100% (High) for 10-13 minutes or until tender, stirring once. Stand for 5 minutes. Purée in a blender.
4 Return to casserole, blend in the remaining ingredients and reduce power to 50% (Medium). Microwave, uncovered, for 7-11 minutes, stirring every 3 minutes.

Cream of cauliflower soup

22 mins

Standing time: 5 mins

2 celery stalks, finely chopped
1 small onion, finely chopped
25g / 1oz butter
1 cauliflower, divided into florets
295g / 10.4oz can condensed
 cream of chicken or celery soup
275ml / ½pt milk or single cream
100g / 4oz Cheddar cheese, grated
salt and pepper

SERVES 4

Follow the instructions above substituting cauliflower for asparagus and adding grated cheese with the milk at Step 4.

VARIATION
Cream of cauliflower soup for two: Halve ingredients; follow instructions for Cream of asparagus soup, microwaving as follows: Step 1: 3-5 minutes; Step 3: 6-9 minutes; Step 4: 6-10 minutes.

Fresh tomato soup

20 mins

Standing time: none

6 tomatoes, cut into 8 pieces
1 onion, finely chopped
2 celery stalks, finely chopped
25g / 1oz butter
5ml / 1tsp sugar
salt and pepper
60ml / 4tbls plain flour
700ml / 1¼pt hot water
1 chicken stock cube, crumbled
parsley or watercress, to garnish

SERVES 4

1 In a 2.3L / 4pt casserole, combine the tomatoes, onion, celery, butter, sugar, salt and pepper.
2 In a small bowl, mix the flour with 150ml / ¼pt water until smooth.

Cream of Cauliflower Soup

3 Stir the remaining hot water into the flour.
4 Pour the flour and water into the casserole, add the stock cube and stir to mix. Cover.
5 Microwave at 100% (High) for 15-20 minutes or until the tomatoes are tender. Stir every 5 minutes.
6 Purée the soup or pass through a wire sieve. Heat for 5 minutes at 100% (High) before serving. Garnish with parsley or watercress.

VARIATIONS
Fresh tomato soup for one:
Refrigerate one portion for up to 2 days. To reheat, microwave the soup at 100% (High) for 3-5 minutes, uncovered. Stir after half the cooking time. Blend in 60ml / 4tbls double cream if wished.

77

Speedy supper dishes

When you need to dish up an appetizing family supper in double-quick time, the clever cook uses the microwave together with items from the store-cupboard, fridge or freezer.

Many tasty dishes can be created at only a few moments' notice, with the help of the microwave, a well stocked larder, fridge and freezer and a little imagination.

Let's face it, we're almost spoilt for choice with the vast range of excellent convenience foods now available — in cans or packets; fresh, chilled or frozen, and including exotic items as well as basics. Convenience foods are invaluable when it comes to easy preparation and the microwave ensures successful speedy results. Put the two together and you are able to produce a wide range of delicious dishes.

Red Bean Beef Pot

Red bean beef pot

| 20 mins |

Standing time: 5 mins

3 celery stalks, chopped
1 onion, thinly sliced
225g / 8oz lean minced beef
300g / 10.6oz can cream of tomato
  soup
425g / 15oz can red kidney beans
15ml / 1tbls chilli sauce
5ml / 1tsp Worcestershire sauce
good pinch of cayenne pepper
2.5ml / ½tsp brown sugar
salt and pepper

SERVES 4

How to microwave Red bean beef pot

Mix *the celery, onion, and beef together in a casserole. Microwave at 100% (High) for 11-12 minutes, stirring several times until the vegetables are tender. Drain off fat and stir well to break up the meat.*

Stir *in the soup, drained kidney beans, sauces, cayenne, sugar and seasoning. Cover and microwave at 70% (Medium-High) for 9-10 minutes. Let stand for 5 minutes. Serve with crackers or crusty bread, if liked.*

Hasty Ham and Broccoli Rolls

Hasty ham and broccoli rolls

| 13 mins |

Standing time: none

22g / ¾oz packet onion sauce mix
300ml / ½pt milk
25g / 1oz butter or margarine
5ml / 1tsp lemon juice
salt and pepper
225g / 8oz packet frozen broccoli
  spears
8 slices processed cheese
16 thin, square slices ham

SERVES 4

1 Put the sauce mix into a bowl and whisk in the milk. Microwave at 100% (High) for 4-5 minutes, whisking several times, until cooked. Gradually whisk in the fat, then add lemon juice and seasoning. Cover and set aside.
2 Pierce the packet of broccoli and microwave at 100% (High) for 3-3½ minutes until spears can be separated easily. Drain well.
3 Sandwich a slice of cheese between two slices of ham. Place two broccoli spears at one end of each ham and cheese 'sandwich' and roll up neatly. Repeat with the remaining cheese, ham and broccoli to make eight rolls in total. Arrange in a 30 x 20cm / 12 x 8in dish. Cover and microwave at 100% (High) for 3-4 minutes; rotate dish once until cheese melts.
4 Pour over sauce and microwave at 70% (Medium-High) for 3-4 minutes until heated through. Serve with hot buttered toast.

Freezer notes

You may prefer to buy frozen broccoli, in economy packs, in which case, simply place the amount required (225g / 8oz) in a bowl and add 60ml / 4tbls water. Cover with vented cling film and microwave at 100% (High) for 3-3½ minutes. Separate the spears, then drain well and follow instructions given from step 3 onwards. The broccoli liquid can be reserved, to use when making soups and gravies.

Prawn Creole

13½ mins

Standing time: none

40g / 1½oz butter or margarine
45ml / 3tbls plain flour
1 onion, finely chopped
3 spring onions, chopped
2 celery stalks, chopped
½ green pepper, chopped
1 garlic clove, crushed
60ml / 4tbls tomato purée
425g / 15oz can tomatoes
5ml / 1tsp lemon juice
5ml / 1tsp Worcestershire sauce
1.5ml / ¼tsp cayenne pepper

2 bay leaves
salt and pepper
375g / 12oz peeled prawns
450g / 1lb boiled rice, cooked
  conventionally, to serve

SERVES 4

1 Put butter in a bowl, cover and microwave at 100% (High) for 30-60 seconds until melted. Mix in the flour, onion, spring onion, celery, pepper and garlic. Cover and microwave at 100% (High) for 3 minutes, stirring once.

2 Add the remaining ingredients, except prawns and rice. Cover and microwave at 100% (High) for 2 minutes. Reduce power to 70%

Prawn Creole

(Medium-High) for 7-8 minutes, stirring several times until thickened. Remove bay leaves.

3 Stir in the prawns and microwave at 100% (High) for 1-2 minutes. Serve with boiled rice.

Freezer notes

If using frozen prawns, thaw at 30% (Low) for 5-6 minutes. Drain well on absorbent paper before adding to the sauce and following instructions in step 3.

80

Snappy tuna macaroni

7 mins

Standing time: none

2 hard-boiled eggs
100g / 4 oz quick cooking macaroni
198g / 7oz can tuna, drained
290g / 10.2oz can cream of chicken soup
150ml / 5fl oz evaporated milk
1 onion, finely chopped
15ml / 1tbls malt vinegar
30ml / 2tbls chopped parsley
salt and pepper

SERVES 4

1 Shell and slice the eggs; reserve a few slices for the garnish and chop the remainder. In a large casserole, mix together the chopped eggs, macaroni, tuna, soup, milk, onion, vinegar, parsley and seasoning.
2 Microwave, uncovered, at 100% (High) for 7-8 minutes, stirring two or three times. Garnish with the reserved egg slices and serve hot with crusty bread and a mixed salad.

Snappy tuna macaroni for two: halve quantities of ingredients. To save using only half a can of tuna and soup, omit the evaporated milk and use a full can of soup and a small 99g / 3½oz can of tuna. Microwave at 100% (High) for 4-5 minutes, stirring twice.

Crab toasts

5½ mins

Standing time: none

40g / 1½oz butter or margarine
45ml / 3tbls plain flour
275ml / ½pt single cream
45ml / 3tbls dry white wine
10ml / 2tsp lemon juice
salt and pepper
2 egg yolks, lightly beaten
175g / 6oz can crabmeat, rinsed and drained
50g / 2oz Cheddar cheese, grated
8 small slices wholemeal bread, toasted and cut in triangles

SERVES 4

1 Put butter in a bowl, cover and microwave at 100% (High) for 30-60 seconds until melted. Stir in the flour, then gradually whisk in the cream. Microwave at 100% (High) for 3-3½ minutes, whisking every minute until thickened.
2 Whisk in the wine, lemon juice and seasoning. Whisk the egg yolks in a bowl and whisk in a little of the hot sauce, then return egg mixture to sauce mixture and whisk thoroughly. Microwave at 100% (High) for 1½-2 minutes, whisking every 30 seconds until smooth.
3 Stir in crabmeat and check the seasoning. Microwave at 100% (High) for 30-45 seconds until hot. Add the cheese and stir until melted. Serve at once with the toast.

Crab toasts for two: halve the quantities and microwave at 100% (High) for 2-2½ minutes until cooked and thickened. When egg yolk is added, microwave at 100% (High) for 45-60 seconds.

Slimmer's notes

Use half single cream and half milk instead of all cream for a less rich dish. This gives you only 455 Calories / 1910kJ per portion.

Snappy Tuna Macaroni

Speedy sausage rice

8¼ mins

Standing time: none

15g / ½oz butter or margarine
295g / 10.4oz can condensed
  cream of mushroom soup
295g / 10.4oz can condensed
  cream of celery soup
150-300ml / 5-10fl oz chicken
  stock
2 × 277g / 10oz cans ready-
  cooked 3-minute rice
10ml / 2tsp German mustard
450g / 1lb frankfurters, quartered

SERVES 5-6

1 Put butter in a casserole, cover and microwave at 100% (High) for 15-30 seconds until melted.
2 Stir in the soups, 150ml /5fl oz of the stock and the rice. Cover and microwave at 100% (High) for 4-5 minutes, stirring twice.
3 Stir in the mustard and frank-furters and a little extra stock if liked. Cover and microwave at 100% (High) for 4-5 minutes.

Right: *Quick Ham Medley*

Quick ham medley

28 mins

Standing time: none

225g / 8oz can ham, cut into small
  cubes
2 x 295g / 10.4oz cans of cream of
  chicken soup
228g / 8oz can water
  chestnuts, drained and sliced
  (optional)
75g / 3oz small pasta shells
3 celery stalks, finely chopped
1 onion, finely chopped
50g / 2oz frozen peas
45ml / 3tbls flaked almonds
213g / 7½oz can mushrooms,
  drained and sliced
5ml / 1tsp dried parsley
10ml / 2tsp chutney
150ml / ¼pt water
¼ chicken stock cube
75g / 3oz packet potato crisps,
  coarsely crushed

SERVES 4

How to microwave Quick ham medley

Place *the ham, soup, water chestnuts if using, pasta shells and celery in a large casserole. Add the onion, peas, almonds, mushrooms, parsley, chutney, water and crumbled stock cube. Mix all ingredients together lightly until thoroughly combined.*

Cover *dish very tightly with vented cling film and a lid to produce plenty of steam. Microwave at 100% (High) for 3 minutes. Stir well, re-cover and cook at 70% (Medium-High) for 25-27 minutes, stirring several times until pasta is tender. Sprinkle with crisps.*

Quick and easy eggs

Fast food need not be junk food. When you need a good meal quickly, rustling up an egg dish can be a gourmet experience. Full of protein, eggs can form a main meal or light snack.

Your microwave will cook most egg dishes just as successfully as a conventional cooker — and you will find that microwaved omelettes and other egg recipes are much creamier.

Just as when they are cooked over direct heat, eggs are particularly sensitive to over-cooking, so for best results err on the side of caution when establishing the cooking time. You can always leave the eggs to stand for a minute or two after microwaving.

You can produce a deliciously light fluffy soufflé omelette easily and quickly in the microwave. The soufflé omelette is an interesting variation on the traditional dish which takes superbly to the microwave. To enjoy it at its best, eat as soon as it comes out of the cooker.

An omelette is best cooked at 50% (Medium); if cooked at 100% (High) the edges may be done before the centre and become leathery by the time the whole omelette is done.

Combined with meat, eggs can make a substantial, filling meal. The Sausagemeat Bake on page 86 can be served as a lunch or supper dish. If wished, the dish can be browned on top by sprinkling over grated cheese and placing under the conventional grill for a few minutes before serving.

Eggs are also useful for those times when you feel a bit peckish and could do with a quick snack.

Pepper Soufflé Omelette

83

Pepper soufflé omelette

| 5½ mins |

Standing time: none

Serve your omelette plain or with one of the fillings. Keep the ingredients in the storecupboard or refrigerator and you'll always be able to produce a quick meal for unexpected guests.

4 large eggs
60ml / 4tbls milk
salt
pepper
15g / ½oz butter or margarine

FILLING
¼ green pepper, diced
¼ red pepper, diced
2 spring onions, finely chopped
50g / 2oz cheese, grated

SERVES 2

VARIATIONS
Use one or more of the following fillings instead of or as well as the pepper filling:
Ham soufflé omelette: add 50g / 2oz chopped ham to the omelette before folding.
Herb soufflé omelette: fold finely chopped fresh herbs into the omelette mixture before microwaving. Alternatively, sprinkle over the omelette before serving.
Bacon soufflé omelette: place 4 rashers of bacon in microwave on double layer of absorbent paper. Cover with single layer of absorbent paper. Microwave at 100% (High) for 4 minutes or until crisp. Chop and add bacon to omelette before folding and serve immediately.
Mushroom soufflé omelette: wipe and slice 100g / 4oz mushrooms. Place in a bowl with 15g / ½oz butter or margarine. Cover with a lid or cling film rolled back at one edge. Microwave at 100% (High) for about 3 minutes or until tender. Add to omelette before folding and serving.

How to microwave a soufflé omelette

Separate *the eggs, taking care not to allow any yolk to mix with the whites or they will not beat stiffly. Place the whites in a 1.1L / 2pt mixing bowl and the yolks in a separate bowl about the same size.*

Beat *the eggs whites together until they are stiff but not dry. The mixture should form soft peaks. In the other bowl, blend the egg yolks with the milk, salt and pepper until they are well incorporated.*

Stir *15ml / 1tbls of the beaten egg whites into the yolk mixture, then very gently fold in the rest of the whites, using a metal spoon. Take care not to overmix or the omelette will not rise to its full extent.*

Place *the butter in a 25cm / 10in shallow pie dish; microwave at 100% (High) for 30-45 seconds until melted. Pour in the eggs. Microwave at 50% (Medium) for 3-5 minutes until the mixture is partially set.*

Lift *the edges of the partially cooked omelette with the spatula so that the uncooked portion spreads evenly. Microwave for a further 2-3 minutes until the centre is set. It does not require standing time.*

Sprinkle *the filling of your choice over half the omelette. Loosen the omelette from the bottom of the dish with the spatula and fold carefully in half without breaking it. Gently slide on to a serving plate.*

Sweet French toast

| 5½ |
| mins |

Standing time: none

15g / ½oz butter
1 egg
15ml / 1tbls milk
2.5ml / ½tsp icing sugar
pinch of ground cinnamon
pinch of salt
2 x 2.5cm / 1in-thick slices of
    French bread

SERVES 1

1 Place the butter in a small bowl and microwave at 100% (High) for 30-60 seconds or until melted.
2 In a larger bowl, beat together the egg, milk, sugar, cinnamon and salt. Beat in the butter.
3 Pre-heat a browning dish at 100% (High) for 4 minutes. Soak the bread in the egg mixture.
4 Arrange the bread slices in the heated browning dish, gently pressing down with a spatula. Microwave at 100% (High) for 30 seconds.
5 Turn and rearrange the bread slices. Microwave for a further 30-45 seconds or until light brown and set. Serve with warm syrup.

French toast for two: Double all ingredients. Prepare as above up to Step 5. Turn and rearrange the bread slices and microwave for 30-60 seconds.

Broccoli omelette

| 6½ |
| mins |

Standing time: none

1 soufflé omelette
75g / 3oz cooked broccoli,
    chopped
25g / 1oz Gruyère or Mozzarella
    cheese, thinly sliced

SERVES 2

1 Prepare a soufflé omelette according to the step-by-step instructions on the opposite page.
2 Arrange the chopped broccoli as evenly as possible on the omelette and top with the strips of cheese, placed one next to the other, roughly evenly spaced.
3 Microwave at 100% (High) for 1 minute or until the cheese melts. Serve immediately so the omelette does not have time to sink.

Sausagemeat bake

18 mins

Standing time: 5 mins

350g / 12oz sausagemeat
1 green pepper, chopped
1 onion, chopped
8 eggs
150ml / $\frac{1}{4}$pt milk
1.5ml / $\frac{1}{4}$tsp salt
pepper
75g / 3oz Cheddar cheese, grated
SERVES 4

1 Put the sausagemeat in a large bowl and stir in the pepper and onion.
2 Microwave at 100% (High) for 3-6 minutes, or until the meat is no longer pink, stirring well after half the cooking time.
3 Break up the sausagemeat with a fork and pour off any excess fat. Spread in a 20 x 20cm / 8 x 8in baking dish. Set aside.
4 Beat together the eggs, milk, salt and pepper in a 2.3L / 4pt bowl. Microwave at 50% (Medium) for 5-9 minutes, until eggs are set but moist, stirring every 2 minutes.
5 Stir in the cheese and pour over the sausagemeat. Cover with cling film rolled back at one edge.
6 Place on an inverted saucer in the microwave cooker and microwave at 50% (Medium) for 10-12 minutes or until the centre is set but slightly moist on top, rotating $\frac{1}{4}$ turn every 3 minutes. Leave to stand, covered, for 5 minutes.

Quick egg supper

5 mins

Standing time: 2-3 mins

1 egg
2.5ml / $\frac{1}{2}$tsp plain flour
30ml / 2tbls milk
50g / 2oz Cheddar cheese, grated
1 small slice ham, chopped
salt
1.5ml / $\frac{1}{4}$tsp chilli powder
$\frac{1}{2}$ tomato, sliced
SERVES 1

1 Beat the egg and add the flour, milk, cheese, ham and seasonings, blending well. Pour into a greased individual shallow dish and place in the microwave cooker.
2 Microwave at 50% (Medium) for 4 minutes. Arrange the tomato slices on top and microwave for a further 1-2 minutes or until almost set. Leave to stand for 2-3 minutes to finish cooking. Serve hot with a salad, if liked.

Quick egg supper for two
Double all the ingredients. Prepare according to the instructions given above but use two individual dishes. Microwave at 50% (Medium) for a total of 9-13 minutes. Leave to stand for 2-3 minutes.

Quick cheese dishes

Toasted or melted cheese — the easiest thing in the world for a snack. Using a microwave cooker, substantial cheese dishes can be just as quick to make as conventional cheese on toast.

Cheese is the good anytime fast food — nutritious and filling. The warming tang of toasted cheese is a pleasure that has been appreciated for centuries. In less than 10 minutes, the microwave can turn it into a simple main course when combined with macaroni, or into a lunch or supper-time snack as a grilled cheese sandwich. If you are only making one or two it isn't even necessary to put the sandwiches into the microwave once the browning dish has reached maximum heat.

Cheesy French bread

3
mins

Standing time: none

1 38cm / 15in French loaf
3 slices processed Cheddar cheese, cut diagonally into 4 triangles
3 slices Emmental cheese (each weighing about 20g / $\frac{3}{4}$oz), cut diagonally into 4 triangles.

SERVES 6-8

1 Cut loaf in half. Make six straight cuts at intervals to within 12mm / $\frac{1}{2}$in of bottom crust.
2 Insert a triangle of each type of cheese between bread slices. Wrap each half in absorbent paper.
3 Microwave both together at 50% (Medium) for 3-3½ minutes.

Cheesy French bread for two: use half French loaf and one slice of each cheese, cut into three pieces. Make three cuts in bread. Microwave at 50% (Medium) for 2-2½ minutes.

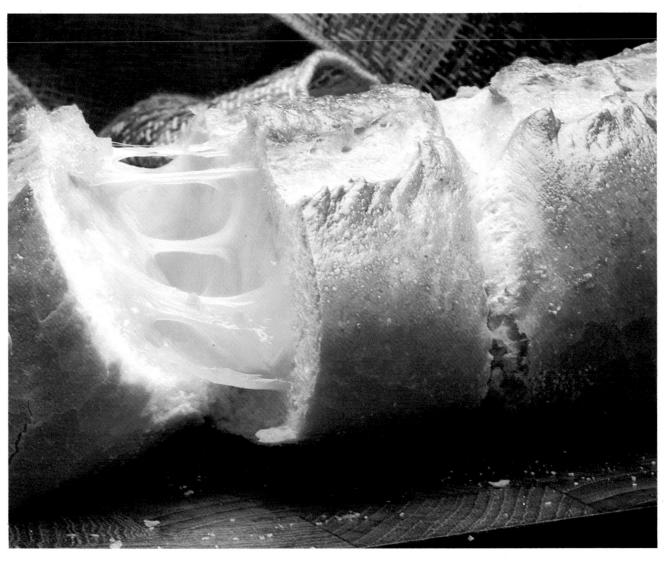

3 Mix the cheese and flour together and gradually stir into the beer mixture.
4 Reduce power to 50% (Medium) and cook for 1-2 minutes or until cheese melts and the mixture is smooth, whisking vigorously after each minute.
5 Meanwhile, toast the muffin. Pour over the cheese mixture and serve at once.

Potato and cheese soufflé | 4½ mins

Standing time: none

30ml / 2tbls grated Parmesan cheese
150g / 5oz cooked mashed potato
2 eggs, separated
75ml / 5tbls milk
100g / 4oz Cheddar cheese, grated
salt and cayenne pepper

SERVES 4

1 Butter 4 ramekin dishes and coat the inside with grated Parmesan cheese.
2 Beat the potato, egg yolks and milk together until smooth. Stir in the Cheddar cheese and seasoning. Whisk the egg white and fold into the cheese mixture.
3 Spoon into the ramekins in equal quantities. Microwave at 100% (High) for 4½ minutes. Serve immediately.

VARIATION
For 2 people, use 15ml / 1tbls grated Parmesan cheese, 65g / 2½oz cooked mashed potato, 1 egg, 45ml / 3tbls milk, 50g / 2oz grated Cheddar cheese and seasoning. Butter 2 ramekin dishes and microwave for only 2½ minutes at 100% (High).

Bacon-cheese stuffed potatoes | 22 mins

Standing time: 5 mins

4 225g / 8oz potatoes, scrubbed
6 bacon rashers
150ml / ¼pt milk
40g / 1½oz butter or margarine
1.5ml / ¼tsp salt
2.5ml / ½tsp dry mustard
large pinch of ground pepper
75g / 3oz grated Cheddar cheese
5ml / 1tsp chopped chives

SERVES 4

1 Prick the potatoes twice. Place 2.5cm / 1in apart in the cooker and microwave at 100% (High) for 7½ minutes.
2 Rearrange the potatoes and turn over and microwave at 100% (High) for 7½ minutes. Wrap in foil and leave to stand for at least 5 minutes to complete cooking.
3 Put the bacon on a plate, cover with absorbent paper and microwave at 100% (High) for 4-4½ minutes until slightly underdone.
4 Cut a slice from each potato and scoop out the centres. Add milk, butter and seasonings to the potato and mash well. Stir in cheese. Crumble the bacon and add two-thirds to the potato mixture. Spoon into the potato shells.
5 Sprinkle with the remaining bacon and chives. Arrange on a plate and microwave at 100% (High) for 3-4 minutes, rotating once.

Muffin rarebit | 3 mins

Standing time: none

50ml / 2fl oz beer
knob of butter or margarine
2.5ml / ½tsp Worcestershire sauce
large pinch of mustard powder
100g / 4oz grated Cheddar cheese
7.5ml / 1½tsp plain flour
1 muffin, split

SERVES 1

1 Mix the beer, butter, Worcestershire sauce and mustard powder together in a 600ml / 1pt casserole.
2 Microwave at 100% (High) for 2 minutes or until the mixture boils and the butter melts.

Cook's notes

Use 40g / 1½oz instant mashed potato granules mixed with 150ml / ¼pt water to make up 150g / 5oz cooked mashed potato.

How to microwave Macaroni cheese

Microwave *macaroni (see recipe) or cook conventionally and microwave sauce while it is cooking.*

Swiss fondue

9
mins

Standing time: none

1 garlic clove
225g / 8oz Cheddar cheese, grated
225g / 8oz Gruyère or Emmental cheese, grated
45ml / 3tbls plain flour
large pinch of grated nutmeg
225ml / 8fl oz dry white wine
cubes of crusty French bread

SERVES 4

1 Rub a 2.3L / 4pt casserole with the cut garlic clove.
2 Shake the cheeses, flour and nutmeg together in a polythene bag until well combined.
3 Pour the wine into a large bowl and microwave at 50% (Medium) for 3-4 minutes; do not boil.
4 Stir in the cheese and flour mixture and microwave at 50% (Medium) for 6-8 minutes. Stir every 2 minutes. Serve hot with the cubes of French bread.

VARIATION
Add a good pinch each of cayenne pepper and mustard powder to the cheese and flour mixture.

Macaroni cheese

25½
mins

Standing time: none

225g / 8oz short cut macaroni
1.7L / 3pt water
40g / 1½oz butter or margarine
22.5ml / 1½tbls flour
salt and pepper
2.5ml / ½tsp mustard powder
350ml / 12fl oz milk
175g / 6oz grated Cheddar cheese

SERVES 6

1 Put the macaroni in a large casserole and add the water. Cover and microwave at 100% (High) for 5 minutes, then reduce the power to 50% (Medium) and microwave for 12 minutes. Drain; set aside.
2 Melt the butter in a 2.3L / 4pt casserole at 100% (High) for 40 seconds. Stir in the flour and seasonings.
3 Microwave at 100% (High) for 30 seconds, then blend in the milk; microwave for 4½ minutes, stirring every minute until thickened.
4 Mix in the grated cheese then stir in the macaroni. Microwave for 3 minutes to heat through, stirring once. Serve immediately.

Blend *the milk into the flour and butter; microwave, stirring every minute as the sauce cooks and thickens.*

Stir *in the grated cheese, making sure it is all melted. If necessary, microwave for 15–20 seconds.*

89

Crispy cheese sandwiches

4½ mins

Standing time: none

The heat from the browning dish browns the bread and melts the cheese. To prepare several sandwiches, microwave each for 15-20 seconds after browning.

**2 slices bread
butter or margarine for spreading
50g / 2oz Cheddar cheese, sliced**

MAKES 1 SANDWICH

1 Heat the browning dish (see steps). Butter the slices and sandwich together with cheese.
2 Place on the browning dish. Leave for 15-20 seconds. Turn over and repeat.

How to microwave Crispy cheese sandwiches

Preheat *a browning dish for 4-5 minutes in the microwave cooker at 100% (High) or heat according to the manufacturer's instructions.*

Place *cheese between bread. Butter outside of sandwich on both sides. Place on the dish for 15-20 seconds. Turn over and repeat.*

THEO BERGSTRÖM

90

Bready snacks

When you need a quick but satisfying bite, a bread-based snack is the obvious answer. But you don't have to limit yourself to beans on toast. It's time for a change — using your microwave.

Bread is a wholesome, staple food that is a pleasure to eat — full of flavour and nourishment. It comes in an endless variety of shapes and types, sizes and textures, so be adventurous and try different local bakers for regional specialities and encourage them to produce the good product bread should be.

It is a versatile base for a filling snack or light meal. Hot snacks, open sandwiches, rolls and filled pittas make lunch, teatime or supper time treats for the whole family. You can make clever use of leftovers, making small amounts go further in hot, satisfying snacks. The microwave is the ideal way to cook them quickly with no fuss.

To extend sandwiches into a light meal, serve them with a salad, crisps or French fries.

Picnic pitta snacks

$3\frac{3}{4}$ mins

Standing time: none

4 oval wholewheat pittas, halved
50g / 2oz Cheddar cheese, grated
$\frac{1}{2}$ crisp lettuce, shredded
2-3 tomatoes, sliced
120ml / 8tbls alfalfa sprouts
$\frac{1}{2}$ green pepper, seeded and
  chopped

FILLING
1 onion, chopped
30ml / 2tbls chopped parsley
30ml / 2tbls sesame seeds
15ml / 1tbls vegetable oil
2.5ml / $\frac{1}{2}$tsp dried oregano
2.5ml / $\frac{1}{2}$tsp dried mint
2.5ml / $\frac{1}{2}$tsp paprika
pinch each of garlic powder,
  allspice and cayenne
425g / 15oz can chick peas, rinsed
  and drained
60ml / 4tbls natural yoghurt

SERVES 4

1 For the filling, mix onion, parsley, sesame seeds, oil, oregano, mint, paprika, garlic powder, allspice and cayenne in a 1.1L / 2pt bowl. Cover and microwave at 100% (High) for 3-4 minutes, or until onion is almost tender, stirring once. Cool slightly.
2 Place mixture in food processor or blender. Add chick peas and yoghurt and purée until smooth.
3 Spoon 45ml / 3tbls filling and 15ml / 1tbls cheese into each pitta half. Place on absorbent paper and microwave at 100% (High) for 45-60 seconds, or until cheese melts.
4 Divide salad ingredients between pitta halves and serve.

Picnic Pitta Snacks

Barbecue beef toasties

$7\frac{1}{2}$ mins

Standing time: none

Turn the remains of a roast into this richly flavoured snack. The sauce prevents the meat from drying out during microwaving.

8 slices bread, toasted, and cut diagonally in half
450g / 1lb cooked beef, sliced

BARBECUE SAUCE
120ml / 8tbls tomato ketchup or sauce
225g / 8oz can sliced button mushrooms, drained
30ml / 2tbls brown sugar
10ml / 2tsp malt vinegar
pinch of chilli powder
pinch of ground cloves

SERVES 4

1 Combine ketchup, mushrooms, brown sugar, vinegar and spices in a 575ml / 1pt bowl. Microwave at 100% (High) for $3\frac{1}{2}$-4 minutes, or until hot, stirring twice.
2 Meanwhile, arrange the beef slices on toast.
3 Spoon the sauce over the meat. Place four toasties on a plate and microwave at 100% (High) for 1-$1\frac{1}{2}$ minutes, or until heated through. Repeat with the remaining toasties in three batches.

Barbecue beef toasties for two:
Halve the ingredients. Microwave the sauce for 2-3 minutes and the topped toast, four pieces at a time, for 1-$1\frac{1}{2}$ minutes.

Barbecue Beef Toasties

Freezer notes

To use frozen beefburgers for Beef 'n' Bacon Burgers, arrange 4 × 100g / 4oz beefburgers in a ring on absorbent paper. Microwave, uncovered, at 20-30% (Defrost) for 10-12 minutes, turning over and rearranging burgers three times. Stand for 2-3 minutes. To test whether the beefburgers are thawed, press; they should be soft all over.

Beef 'n' bacon burgers

$7\frac{1}{4}$ mins

Standing time: 1-2 mins

450g / 1lb minced beef
75ml / 5tbls chopped spring onions
5ml / 1tsp Worcestershire Sauce (optional)
4 bacon rashers, rinded and halved
4 slices cheese
4 hamburger buns, to serve

SERVES 4

1 Mix together the mince, onions and sauce. Shape into four 12mm / $\frac{1}{2}$in-thick burgers.
2 Arrange burgers on a plate lined with absorbent paper, or place on a roasting rack and microwave at 100% (High) for 3-4 minutes. Turn burgers over and microwave for a further 2-3 minutes, or until done to your liking. Cover and stand 1-2 minutes.
3 Place the bacon rashers on a plate lined with absorbent paper. Cover with more absorbent paper and microwave at 100% (High) for $1\frac{1}{2}$-2 minutes, or until cooked.
4 Place bacon on top of the burgers and cover each with a slice of cheese. Cover and microwave at 100% (High) for 45-60 seconds, to melt cheese. Serve in the buns.

92

Saucy turkey toasts

6 mins

Standing time: 5 mins

4 rashers streaky bacon, rinded
$\frac{1}{2} \times 40g$ / $1\frac{1}{2}oz$ packet cheese sauce mix
150ml / $\frac{1}{4}$pt milk
2 slices bread, toasted and cut diagonally in half
4 slices cooked turkey breast
50g / 2oz Cheddar cheese, grated

SERVES 2

1 Place bacon on a roasting rack. Cover with absorbent paper and microwave at 100% (High) for $2\frac{1}{2}$-3 minutes. Stand 5 minutes.
2 Blend sauce mix with milk. Microwave at 100% (High) for $2\frac{1}{2}$-3 minutes, or until thick; stirring twice.
3 Halve bacon rashers. Put two halves on each piece of toast. Top with one slice of turkey and sauce. Sprinkle with grated cheese.
4 Arrange on a plate and microwave at 100% (High) for 1-$1\frac{1}{2}$ minutes to heat through.

Microtips

To ensure even cooking, arrange toast triangles on absorbent paper with the cut edge to the outside.

Above: *Beef 'n' Bacon Burgers*
Right: *Saucy Turkey Toasts*

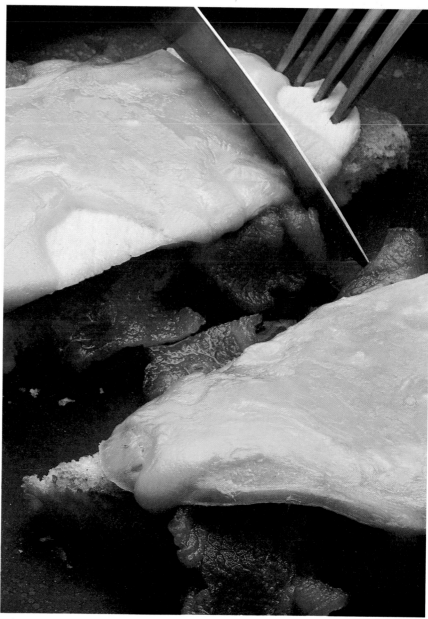

93

Beefy pittas

5 mins

Standing time: none

450g / 1lb minced beef
2 rashers streaky bacon, rinded
  and cut into 12mm / ½in pieces
1 onion, chopped
1 garlic clove, crushed
2.5ml / ½tsp dried mixed herbs
salt and pepper
4 tomatoes, chopped
175g / 6oz cucumber, chopped
30ml / 2tbls chopped parsley
2 large oval pitta breads, cut in
  half

SERVES 4

1 Mix beef, bacon, onion, garlic, herbs and seasoning in a 2.3L / 4pt casserole. Microwave at 100% (High) for 5-7 minutes, stirring twice. Drain.
2 Stir in tomatoes, parsley and cucumber. Spoon into the pitta 'pockets' and serve.

Hot ham and cheese roll

30 secs

Standing time: none

1 poppy seed roll, split and
  lightly toasted
butter for spreading
3 slices ham
1 slice yellow processed cheese
1 slice white processed cheese
English mustard to serve

SERVES 1

1 Butter the roll. Top the bottom half with alternate slices of ham and cheese.
2 Microwave at 100% (High) for 30-60 seconds, until cheese melts.
3 Spread with mustard, replace the top of the roll and serve.

Freezer notes

Freeze unmicrowaved rolls for 2 weeks. To thaw one roll, microwave at 100% (High) for 1½-2 minutes; serve hot.

Beefy Pittas

94

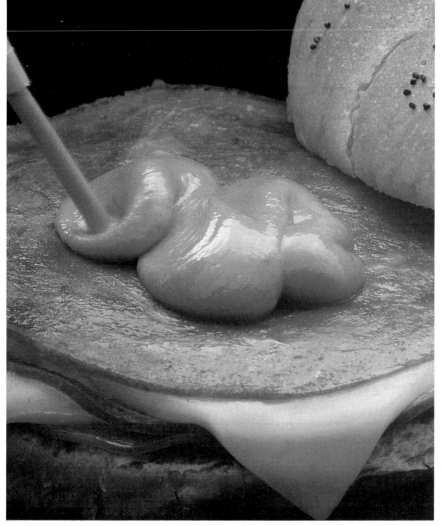

Tuna muffins

4 mins

Standing time: none

200g / 7oz can tuna, drained
2 hard-boiled eggs, chopped
45ml / 3tbls mayonnaise
½ onion, finely chopped
30ml / 2tbls cucumber relish
30ml / 2tbls chopped stuffed
  olives, capers or celery
2.5ml / ½tsp made mustard
salt and pepper
4 muffins, split and toasted
2 tomatoes, sliced
50g / 2oz Cheddar cheese, grated

SERVES 4

1 Combine tuna, eggs, mayonnaise, onion, relish, olives and mustard in a bowl. Season to taste and mix well. Divide mixture between the muffin halves. Top each half with tomato and 15ml / 1tbls cheese.
2 Place four muffin halves on a large plate lined with two layers of absorbent paper. Microwave at 100% (High) for 2-3 minutes, or until cheese melts, rotating once. Repeat with remaining muffins.

Above: *Tuna Muffins*
Left: *Hot Ham and Cheese Roll*

95

Hey presto pizzas

Pizzas are so speedy to prepare with the help of your microwave. Make your own creations using your favourite toppings — as many as you want — then serve with a simple salad for a quick family meal.

Microwaved pizzas are a great success, since the cheese bubbles and melts in mere minutes, to leave both base and filling still deliciously moist. Combine your microwave's speed with the convenience of ready-made pizza products for fast family meals — a simple salad is the only extra needed.

Most supermarkets now stock ready-prepared pizza toppings in cans or jars — and in several varieties. This not only saves time but also the trouble of cooking thin tomato sauces until they are good and thick. However, if you can't find a supermarket topping, flavour a can of chopped tomatoes (they're thicker than the ordinary whole ones) with herbs, seasoning, grated onion and a little sugar, for

Quick Pepper Pizza

an equally successful alternative.

Large supermarkets also stock ready-prepared pizza bread bases, usually several to a pack. Freeze any that you don't need for another time. Lighter French bread makes a tasty shortcut base too, and is preferred by many to the slightly heavier dough bases. Simply halve French sticks lengthways and spread the cut sides lavishly with pizza topping. Sprinkle with grated cheese and microwave until cheese melts to make a quick and easy snack.

As a further time saver, ready-assembled pizzas freeze perfectly.

Quick pepper pizza | 6 mins

Standing time: 3 mins

50g / 1.75oz can anchovies, drained
170g / 6oz jar pizza topping
25cm / 10in ready-prepared white pizza base
½ small red pepper, seeded and sliced into rings
175g / 6oz Mozzarella cheese, grated
8 black olives, halved
15ml / 1tbls grated Parmesan

SERVES 2

1 Chop the anchovies and mix with the pizza topping. Spread over the pizza base.
2 Cover with the pepper rings and microwave at 100% (High) for 2 minutes.
3 Sprinkle over the Mozzarella cheese. Press the olives into the cheese and sprinkle with the grated Parmesan.
4 Microwave at 100% (High) for 4-5 minutes, until heated through and the cheese has melted. Leave to stand for 3 minutes.

Cook's notes

If pizza topping is unavailable, use canned chopped tomatoes mixed with any fresh or dried herbs you choose. Oregano adds a specially authentic Italian flavour, or try fresh basil, if it is in season.

Zingy pizza pie | 16 mins

Standing time: none

1 microwaved pie case (see page 28)
1 green pepper, seeded and cut into strips
100g / 4oz button mushrooms, sliced
30ml / 2tbls tomato ketchup or sauce
30ml / 2tbls tomato purée or paste
225g / 8oz smoked pork sausages, cut into 12mm / ½in slices
large pinch of chilli powder
large pinch of ground cumin
large pinch of dried oregano
30ml / 2tbls black olives, stoned and sliced
50g / 2oz Mozzarella, grated

Zingy Pizza Pie

50g / 2oz Cheddar cheese, grated
SERVES 2

1 Combine the green pepper and mushrooms in a small bowl, cover with cling film and microwave at 100% (High) for 5 minutes, or until tender. Drain well.
2 In a 1.1L / 2pt casserole, combine the tomato ketchup or sauce, the tomato purée and all the seasonings. Microwave, uncovered, at 100% (High) for 2 minutes.
3 Stir in the sliced sausages, green pepper, mushrooms and olives and pour into the prepared pie case. Sprinkle over the grated cheese and microwave for 1-2 minutes, until the cheese has melted and the pie is very hot; serve at once.

97

Deep-dish pizzas

12½ mins

Standing time: 5 mins

Pizza is a favourite snack at any time, with any age group. Cut into wedges, these pizzas make a quick suppertime or party nibble.

280g / 10oz packet white bread mix
67.5ml / 4½tbls dry breadcrumbs
15ml / 1tbls poppy seeds
15g / ½oz butter, melted

TOPPING
450g / 1lb lean minced pork
1 small onion, chopped
2 garlic cloves, crushed
5ml / 1tsp soy sauce
1 small green pepper, seeded and chopped
5ml / 1tsp oregano
5ml / 1tsp caster sugar
5ml / 1tsp dried basil
500g / 18oz carton creamed tomatoes
salt and pepper
100g / 4oz Mozzarella or Cheddar cheese, grated
15ml / 1tbls chopped fresh parsley
grated Parmesan cheese to finish

EACH SERVES 8

VARIATIONS
If cartons of creamed tomatoes are not available, use canned chopped tomatoes. You can enhance the tomato flavour by adding 15ml / 1tbls of tomato paste.

How to microwave Deep-dish pizzas

Put *the bread mix in a bowl and add water according to the packet directions. Mix to form a soft dough and knead for about 5 minutes, until the dough is smooth and elastic.*

Combine *breadcrumbs and poppy seeds. Brush two 25cm / 10in pie plates with half the melted butter. Sprinkle in the poppy seed mixture, tilting plates to coat evenly.*

Freezer notes

Prepare the pizza filling and leave to cool. Spread it over the pizza base, but do not add the cheese. Wrap, label and freeze for up to 3 months.

To thaw, unwrap the pizza and cover with absorbent paper. Stand on upturned plate and turn every 2 minutes. Microwave at 30% (Defrost) for 10-12 minutes, leave to stand for 4-5 minutes, then sprinkle with cheese. Microwave at 100% (High) for 8-9 minutes, until very hot. Stand, covered, 1-2 minutes.

Place *pork, onion, garlic and soy sauce in a large bowl. Microwave at 100% (High) for 2½-3 minutes, until the pork crumbles easily, stirring halfway through.*

Stir *in green pepper, oregano, basil, sugar, tomatoes and seasoning. Cover and microwave at 100% (High) for 4-5 minutes, stirring once, until mixture is cooked through.*

98

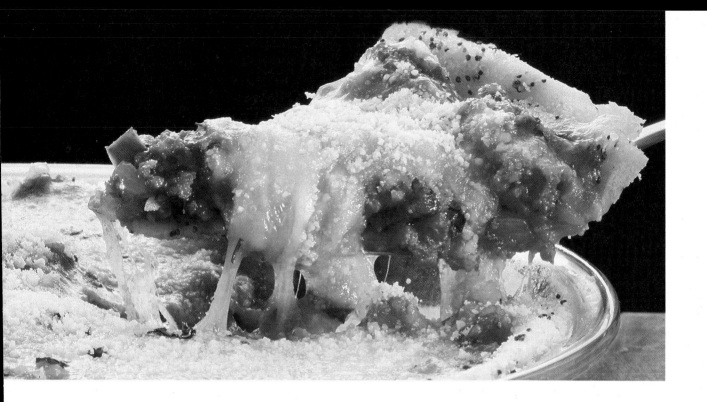

Halve *the dough; roll out each half to a 26cm / 10½in circle and press well into the plates. Brush with remaining butter; sprinkle over the remaining crumb mixture.*

Cover *the plates with cling film and leave to rise in a warm place for about 30 minutes. Remove the cling film and prick the bases thoroughly with a fork to prevent them from rising.*

Microwave *the pizza bases one at a time, at 100% (High) for 3½-4 minutes, or until the bread feels dry and springs back when pressed. Give the dish a quarter turn three times.*

Divide *the mixture between the bread cases. Sprinkle evenly with Mozzarella or Cheddar cheese (50g / 2oz for each case), then scatter over a layer of chopped parsley.*

Microwave *the pizzas, one at a time, at 100% (High) for 2½-3 minutes, until cheese melts and pizza is hot. Sprinkle with Parmesan and stand for 5 minutes.*

Microtips

Make use of your microwave to prove the dough, particularly if your kitchen is very cool. Place one pizza base, covered with cling film, in the microwave and cook at 100% (High) for 15 seconds. Leave to stand for 7-10 minutes. Repeat the cooking and standing twice more, until the dough has doubled in bulk. You can alternate the two pizza bases, cooking one while the other is standing to save time. Microwave bases (see Step 5) and either use immediately or freeze.

99

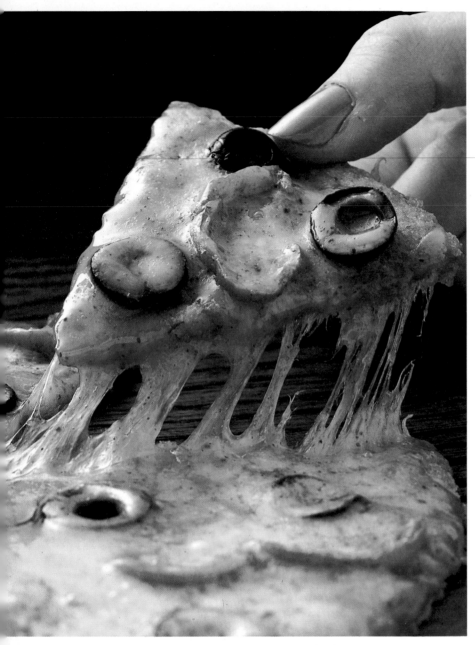

5 Microwave, uncovered, one pizza at a time, at 100% (High) for 2½-3 minutes, until the cheese has melted. Cut into wedges and microwave for 1 more minute, if you like the cheese really 'stringy'.
6 Cook second pizza and serve.

Cook's notes

For a more substantial 'main meal' version, arrange a layer of cooked ham or salami over the onion layer before sprinkling with the cheese, and allow an extra 30 seconds cooking for each pizza.

Spicy sausage pizza

11 mins

Standing time: 5 mins

1 onion, chopped
450g / 1lb pork or beef
    sausagemeat
15ml / 1tbls Worcestershire sauce
salt and pepper
90ml / 6tbls mild chilli relish
230g / 8oz can chopped tomatoes
30ml / 2tbls chopped parsley
5ml / 1tsp fennel seeds
25cm / 10in pizza base
75g / 3oz Cheddar cheese, grated

SERVES 6

1 Place the onion in a large shallow dish together with the sausagemeat, Worcestershire sauce and salt and pepper to taste.
2 Microwave, uncovered, at 100% (High) for 7-8 minutes, until the meat is cooked through. Turn dish and mash the mixture with a fork three times during cooking.
3 Mix together the chilli relish, chopped tomatoes, half the chopped parsley and the fennel seeds. Spread half this mixture over the pizza base.
4 Mix the remaining tomato mixture with sausagemeat and spread over the pizza. Sprinkle with remaining parsley then the cheese.
5 Microwave at 100% (High) for 4-5 minutes, until heated through and the cheese has melted. Leave to stand for 5 minutes.

Spicy Sausage Pizza

Olive pizzas

9¾ mins

Standing time: none

25g / 1oz butter
1 onion, finely chopped
2 garlic cloves, crushed
2 × 18cm / 7in ready-prepared
    wholemeal pizza bases
225g / 8oz Emmental or Gruyère
    cheese, grated
2.5ml / ½tsp paprika
8 stoned black olives, sliced
8 stoned green olives, sliced

EACH SERVES 4-6

Olive Pizza

1 Place the butter in a small bowl, cover and microwave at 100% (High) for 45 seconds, until melted.
2 Stir in the onion and garlic. Cover with cling film rolled back at one edge and microwave at 100% (High) for 4-5 minutes, until tender, stirring once. Spread over the pizza bases.
3 Combine the grated cheese and paprika and sprinkle two-thirds evenly over the onion.
4 Top with sliced olives, then sprinkle over the remaining cheese.

Easy omelettes

Get cracking with eggs — with the help of your microwave and the simplest of ingredients you can make omelettes that are plain or puffy, savoury or sweet — perfect for easy, informal eating.

Microwaved omelettes are quick to make and easy too, provided you follow the instructions and timings given in the recipes. Bear in mind that because a microwaved omelette is cooked in a glass dish and not a conventional frying pan it does not brown in the usual way.

You can microwave all sorts of tasty omelettes — savoury for a main course, or sweet for a dessert — in a matter of minutes. The tra-ditional French omelette is quite flat and either folded over, or rolled up with a filling. Puffy omelettes are made by folding the beaten egg yolks into the whisked egg whites. During microwaving the mixture separates to give a smooth eggy base under a light, fluffy top layer. A puffy omelette is cut in half to serve.

The Italian Frittata is quite different. The eggs are cooked together with the filling and this gives a thick, substantial result. Cut it in half, or into wedges and serve straight from the dish. Whichever type of omelette you make, rotate the dish a quarter turn, three times during cooking, to ensure even cooking. This is particularly important when making any of the puffy omelettes given here as it helps produce an even rise.

Puffy Savoury Omelette

102

Types of omelette

Puffy Omelette: *lightly fold the egg yolk mixture into the stiffly whisked egg whites. Microwave as directed in the recipes for Puffy Savoury or Puffy Fruit Omelette (right, and page 104).*

French Jam Omelette: *pour the lightly beaten eggs into the melted butter in pie dish and cook, following instructions given in recipe (right). Add the filling and fold in half.*

Italian Frittata: *microwave the vegetables in the oil until tender-crisp, then mix in the lightly beaten eggs. Cook following instructions given in the recipe (right).*

Puffy savoury omelette

8¼ mins

Standing time: none

4 eggs, separated
30ml / 2tbls milk
salt and pepper
large knob of butter

FILLING
4 rashers streaky bacon, chopped
1 large tomato, chopped
½ green pepper, seeded and chopped
100g / 4oz Cheddar cheese, grated

SERVES 2

1 Prepare the filling: put the bacon, tomato and all but 15ml / 1tbls green pepper in a bowl. Cover with absorbent paper and microwave at 100% (High) for 3-4 minutes, stirring once. Set aside, covered.
2 In a small bowl, mix the egg yolks, milk and seasoning together. Put the butter in a shallow 20cm / 8in heatproof glass pie dish. Cover and microwave at 100% (High) for 15-30 seconds until melted. Swirl the butter over the base and sides of dish to prevent omelette sticking.
3 Whisk the egg whites in a large grease-free bowl until stiff. Stir 15ml / 1tbls of whisked egg white into the yolks to lighten the consistency. Lightly fold the egg yolk mixture into the egg whites. Gently pour the mixture into the dish and microwave at 50% (Medium) for 4-6 minutes until the mixture is partially set. Rotate the dish a quarter turn three times during cooking.
4 Spoon the cooked filling over half the omelette and sprinkle with half the cheese. Loosen omelette with a spatula and fold in half. Top with the remaining grated cheese and green pepper. Microwave at 50% (Medium) for 1-2 minutes until the cheese melts and centre of omelette is set. Cut in half and serve at once.

VARIATIONS
Replace the chopped green pepper with red pepper, or 4 sliced spring onions, if preferred.

Italian frittata

6 mins

Standing time: none

15ml / 1tbls olive oil
1 potato, cooked and chopped
1 courgette, cut into thin slices
½ green pepper, seeded and chopped
salt and pepper
3 eggs, lightly beaten

SERVES 2-3

1 Put the oil, potato, courgette and green pepper in a shallow 20cm / 8in heatproof glass pie dish. Cook at 100% (High) for 3 minutes or until the vegetables are tender-crisp.
2 Season the lightly beaten eggs, then pour over mixture in dish. Microwave at 50% (Medium) for 3-4 minutes until cooked through. Rotate dish a quarter turn three times during cooking. Cut in half, or into three wedges, and serve.

French jam omelette

3½ mins

Standing time: none

30ml / 2tbls raspberry jam
large knob of butter
3 eggs, lightly beaten
15ml / 1tbls icing sugar, sifted

SERVES 2

1 Put the jam in a small bowl and microwave at 100% (High) for 15-25 seconds until heated through.
2 Put butter in a shallow 20cm / 8in heatproof glass pie dish, cover and cook at 100% (High) for 15-30 seconds until melted. Swirl butter over base and sides of dish.
3 Pour in the lightly beaten eggs and microwave at 50% (Medium) for 3-4 minutes until cooked through. Rotate dish a quarter turn three times during cooking.
4 Spoon the warmed jam over half the omelette. Fold over the other half; sprinkle with icing sugar, cut in half and serve.

VARIATIONS
Use apricot jam mixed with 15ml / 1tbls toasted flaked almonds.

103

Puffy fruit omelette

9¼ mins

Standing time: none

4 eggs, separated
30ml / 2tbls milk
2.5ml / ½tsp caster sugar
large knob of butter

FILLING
10ml / 2tsp cornflour
312g / 11oz canned mandarin
  segments, drained and juice
  reserved
100g / 4oz strawberries, halved
icing sugar for dusting

SERVES 2

1 Prepare the filling: in a bowl, blend the cornflour with a little of the reserved mandarin juice until smooth, then add the remaining juice. Microwave at 100% (High) for 2-3 minutes or until clear and thickened, stirring every minute. Stir in the mandarins and strawberries and cook for a further 2 minutes, stirring once. Cover tightly with cling film to retain the heat and reserve while preparing and making the omelette.

2 Blend together the egg yolks, milk and sugar in a small bowl. Put the butter in a shallow 20cm / 8in heatproof glass pie dish. Cover and microwave at 100% (High) for 15-30 seconds until melted. Swirl the butter over the base and sides of the dish to prevent the omelette sticking.

3 Meanwhile, whisk the egg whites in a grease-free bowl until stiff. Stir 15ml / 1tbls of the whisked egg whites into the yolks to lighten the consistency. Lightly fold egg yolk mixture into whisked egg whites.

4 Gently pour the mixture into the dish and cook at 50% (Medium) for 5-7 minutes until the centre of the omelette is set. Rotate the dish a quarter turn three times during cooking.

5 Spoon half the filling over half the omelette. Loosen omelette with a spatula and carefully fold in half. Spoon the remaining filling over the top. Sift icing sugar over the omelette. Cut in half and serve.

Puffy Fruit Omelette

VARIATION
Black cherry omelette: smoothly blend 15ml / 3tsp cornflour with 30ml / 2tbls kirsch. Stir in a 425g / 15oz can stoned black cherries. Cook at 100% (High) for 6-8 minutes, stirring every 2 minutes. Make omelette as directed in recipe but fill and top with the cherry mixture.

Cook's notes

If you prefer to use oil instead of butter for greasing, brush the base and sides of the dish with oil and microwave at 100% (High) for 15-30 seconds before adding the eggs. Microwave the omelette following the instructions given in the particular recipes.

104

Harlequin omelette

5¼ mins

Standing time: none

4 eggs
30ml / 2tbls milk
salt and pepper
large knob of butter

FILLING
¼ green pepper, seeded and chopped
¼ red pepper, seeded and chopped
½ small onion, chopped

SERVES 2

Cook's notes

If you prefer a cooked filling, put the chopped peppers and onion in a small bowl, then cover and cook at 100% (High) for 3 minutes, stirring once.

How to microwave Harlequin omelette

Separate *the eggs, placing the whites in a large grease-free bowl and the yolks in a small bowl.*

Whisk *the whites until stiff. Add the milk and seasoning to the egg yolks and blend together.*

Gently *fold the egg yolk mixture into the egg whites, using a rubber spatula or a large metal spoon.*

Melt *butter in a covered, shallow 20cm / 8in heatproof glass pie dish at 100% (High) for 15-20 seconds. Pour in egg mixture. Cook at 50% (Medium) for 3-5 minutes.*

Lift *edges of omelette with a spatula to allow any uncooked egg mixture underneath to run over base of dish. Microwave for a further 2-3 minutes until the centre is set.*

Sprinkle *two-thirds of the filling over half the omelette. Loosen edges of omelette and fold in half. Sprinkle remaining filling ingredients over the top. Cut in half and serve.*

105

Spiced yoghurt omelette

4¼ mins

Standing time: none

4 eggs, separated
large knob of butter
150ml / 5fl oz natural yoghurt
1.5ml / ¼tsp ground nutmeg
5ml / 1tsp caster sugar

SERVES 2

1 In a small bowl, mix the egg yolks together lightly. Put the butter in a shallow 20cm / 8in heatproof glass pie dish. Cover and microwave at 100% (High) for 15-30 seconds until melted, then swirl the butter over the base and sides of the dish.
2 Whisk egg whites in a large grease-free bowl until stiff. Stir 15ml / 1tbls of the whisked egg whites into the egg yolks. Lightly fold the egg yolk mixture into the egg whites. Gently pour the mixture into the dish. Microwave at 50% (Medium) for 3-5 minutes or until partially set, then lift the edges to allow any uncooked egg mixture to run over the base of the dish.
3 Mix together the yoghurt, nutmeg and sugar, pour over the omelette and cook for a further 1 minute. Serve at once.

Omelette Arnold Bennett

9¾ mins

Standing time: none

100g / 4oz smoked haddock
150ml / 5fl oz double cream
4 eggs, separated
pepper
large knob of butter
25g / 1oz Leicester cheese, grated
30ml / 2tbls chopped parsley

SERVES 2

1 Put the haddock on a plate, cover and microwave at 100% (High) for 2½-3 minutes or until the flesh flakes easily. Discard skin and bones and flake the fish fairly finely, then mix with 30ml / 2tbls of the cream. Leave to cool, then

Omelette Arnold Bennett

mix in the egg yolks and pepper to taste.
2 Put the butter in a shallow 20cm / 8in heatproof glass pie dish. Cover and microwave at 100% (High) for 15-30 seconds until melted. Swirl butter over the base and sides of the dish to prevent the omelette sticking.
3 Whisk the egg whites in a large grease-free bowl until stiff, then lightly fold in the fish and egg yolk mixture. Gently pour the mixture into the dish and cook at 50% (Medium) for 6-8 minutes until the centre is almost set. Rotate dish a quarter turn three times during cooking to ensure omelette rises evenly.
4 Pour the remaining cream over the omelette and sprinkle with the cheese. Cook at 50% (Medium) for a further 1-2 minutes or until the cheese melts and omelette is set. Sprinkle the omelette with the chopped parsley, cut in half and serve at once, accompanied by a tomato salad and crusty bread.

Speedy sandwich snacks

With the help of your microwave cooker, a range of delicious sandwich snacks can be ready in just a few minutes, with the minimum of fuss.

Be creative with the sandwich bases as well as the filling or toppings and make the most of the selection of interesting breads now available: white or wholemeal Greek pittas, for example, make ideal 'containers' for juicy fillings.

Remember that overheating in the microwave toughens and dries bread, so timings really are critical. Slices of toast or day-old bread make perfect bases since they do not become soggy as easily as fresh bread and rolls, (day-old bread freshens during heating).

Courgette pittas

2¾ mins

Standing time: none

1 courgette, cut in strips
50g / 2oz mushrooms, sliced
4 tomatoes, chopped
2.5ml / ½tsp dried basil
1.5ml / ¼tsp garlic powder
30ml / 2tbls grated Parmesan cheese
4 pittas

SERVES 4

1 Combine the courgette and mushrooms in a bowl. Cover and microwave at 100% (High) for 2-2½ minutes until tender. Drain off liquid.
2 Stir in the tomatoes, basil, garlic and cheese. Split open one side of pittas and spoon in filling, dividing it between the four.
3 Place the filled pittas on a plate lined with 2 layers of absorbent paper and microwave at 100% (High) for 45-60 seconds until hot. Garnish with watercress.

Courgette Pittas

RAY DUNS

Baked cheese sandwiches | 7 mins

Standing time: none

8 slices white bread
4 slices processed Cheddar
  cheese
2 eggs, lightly beaten
250ml / 9fl oz milk
15ml / 1tbls dried minced onion
5ml / 1tsp made English mustard
5ml / 1tsp dried parsley
1.5ml / ¼tsp paprika

SERVES 4

1 Arrange 4 slices bread in a 20cm / 8in square baking dish. Top each with a slice of cheese and cover with the remaining bread.
2 Blend together the remaining ingredients, pour over sandwiches; let soak until liquid is absorbed.
3 Microwave, uncovered, at 50% (Medium) for 7-8 minutes until sandwiches are set. Garnish with tomato and watercress; serve hot.

Salad specials | 2 mins

Standing time: none

15ml / 1tbls mayonnaise
2.5ml / ½tsp made English
  mustard
2 slices bread, toasted
2 thin slices red onion
2 thin slices tomato
25g / 1oz alfalfa (or bean) sprouts
1 slice processed Cheddar cheese,
  cut into 8 strips

SERVES 2

1 In a bowl, combine the mayonnaise with mustard and spread over toast. Top each with a slice of onion and tomato. Cover with the alfalfa or bean sprouts and arrange cheese strips on top.
2 Place on a plate lined with 2 layers of absorbent paper. Microwave at 50% (Medium) for 2-2½ minutes or until the cheese melts, turning once during cooking. Serve at once.

Baked Cheese Sandwiches, Salad Specials, Cheesy Prawn Sandwiches

Cheesy prawn sandwiches | ¾ min

Standing time: none

Vary if liked by substituting flaked crab or tuna for prawns.

25g / 1oz Emmental cheese,
  grated
1 small onion, chopped
30ml / 2tbls chopped celery
100g / 4oz peeled prawns
salt and pepper
16 thin slices cucumber
4 slices buttered toast

SERVES 4

1 Place the cheese, onion and celery in a small bowl. Microwave at 50% (Medium) for 45-60 seconds until the cheese softens. Add the prawns and seasoning.
2 Place cucumber on slices of toast and top with the prawn mixture.

108

Mexican pizza sandwich

4 mins

Standing time: none

2 tomatoes, chopped
1 onion, chopped
15ml / 1tbls green chillies,
    seeded and chopped
1.5ml / ¼tsp garlic powder
2.5ml / ½tsp dried mixed herbs
salt and pepper
2 slices buttered toast
50g / 2oz Mozzarella cheese,
    grated

SERVES 2

1 In an 850ml / 1½pt casserole, combine the tomatoes, onion and chillies. Microwave at 100% (High) for 3-4 minutes, or until the onions are tender, stirring once. Drain, then add the seasonings.
2 Arrange toast on a serving plate lined with 2 layers of absorbent paper. Cover with the tomato mixture and top with the cheese.
3 Microwave at 100% (High) for 1-2 minutes until cheese melts, turning once.

Taco hot dogs

6 mins

Standing time: none

These make a filling and substantial snack — perfect for a teenage party treat.

8 hot dogs or frankfurters
8 hot dog rolls
205g / 7¼oz can beef taco filling
100g / 4oz Cheddar cheese, grated
25g / 1oz crushed corn or tortilla
    chips
shredded lettuce and chopped
    tomatoes, to garnish (optional)

SERVES 4-8

1 Place 4 hot dogs or frankfurters in 4 rolls. Arrange cut side uppermost in a 30 × 20cm / 12 × 8in baking dish, lined with 2 layers of absorbent paper. Spoon one half of the taco filling over hot dogs or frankfurters. Sprinkle with half the cheese and crushed chips.
2 Microwave at 100% (High) for 3

Above: *Mexican Pizza Sandwich*
Right: *Taco Hot Dogs*

minutes, or until the cheese is melted and rolls are hot to the touch, rotating after half the time.
3 Sprinkle with shredded lettuce and chopped tomatoes, if desired. Repeat with remaining hot dogs or frankfurters.

VARIATIONS
Chilli cheese dogs: Top hot dogs with 425g / 15oz can drained chilli beans and 4 slices processed Cheddar cheese, halved. Microwave at 100% (High) for 3 minutes.
German-style dogs: Top hot dogs or frankfurters with a mixture of 175g / 6oz drained sauerkraut and 50g / 2oz sweet pickle. Microwave at 100% (High) for 2 minutes, covered with greaseproof paper.
Bacon and cheese dogs: Mix 100g / 4oz cheese spread with 30ml / 2tbls cooked chopped bacon. Divide between hot dogs or frankfurters and microwave at 100% (High) for 2 minutes.

109

Savoury fun snacks

For a quick bite after school or a spur of the moment nibble, microwaving is child's play — so why not let the family join in and help cook their own super, speedy snacks?

With your microwave you can prepare quick and easy titbits for the whole family or, better still, let them prepare their own.

Cooking with a microwave is safer than conventional cooking, and children appreciate instant microwave results. However, before you let them loose in the kitchen, make sure that anyone unfamiliar with microwaving is aware of a few safety precautions.

Sailor's Spuds (recipe page 114)

Microwave reminders

● Always use oven gloves when taking food out of the microwave. Heat is transferred from the food to the containers and these can sometimes get very hot.

● Always remove covers and cling film with oven gloves. When using cling film, start removing it from the side furthest away and pull it towards you.

● Never use metal containers or utensils in the microwave.

● If using greaseproof or absorbent paper to cover food, remove it after microwaving or it may stick to the food.

● Whole potatoes, apples, sausages and so on — anything cooked in a skin, casing or plastic bag — must be pricked all over to prevent it bursting.

Fun burgers

7½ mins

Standing time: 3-4 mins

1 onion, chopped
1 carrot, grated
1 garlic clove, crushed
450g / 1lb minced beef
2 egg whites
50g / 2oz rolled oats
30ml / 2tbls tomato ketchup or sauce
2.5ml / ½tsp chilli powder
1.5ml / ¼tsp mustard powder
1.5ml / ¼tsp paprika
pinch of cayenne
10 wooden skewers or sticks

COATING
17g / ¾oz cornflakes, crushed
pinch of paprika
pinch of cayenne

MUSTARD DIP
100g / 4oz cottage cheese
30ml / 2tbls natural yoghurt
15ml / 1tbls made mustard
5ml / 1tsp chopped parsley
MAKES 10

Cook's notes

Try using minced turkey for the beef in Fun Burgers, and serve them with cranberry jelly or sweet and sour sauce.

Microtips

To ensure even cooking in the microwave, thicker portions of meat are placed towards the outside of the dish.

How to microwave Fun burgers

Combine *onion, carrot and garlic in a 1.1L / 2pt bowl. Cover and microwave at 100% (High) for 1½-2½ minutes, or until just tender.*

Add *mince, egg whites, oats, ketchup or sauce and spices. Mix well and divide into 10 equal portions. Shape into 7.5cm / 3in oval patties.*

Insert *a wooden skewer into each burger. Mix crushed cornflakes, paprika and cayenne and spread on a sheet of greaseproof paper.*

Roll *each burger in the cornflake mixture and coat both sides evenly. Arrange on a roasting rack with skewers towards the centre.*

Microwave *at 100% (High) for 6-8 minutes, or until burgers are firm and cooked through. Rotate rack once. Stand for 3-4 minutes.*

Blend *cottage cheese and yoghurt in a processor or blender until smooth. Add mustard and parsley. Serve the burgers with the dip.*

Cheesy popcorn

1 min

Standing time: none

75g / 3oz raw popcorn, popped
100g / 4oz Cheddar cheese, grated
50g / 2oz Parmesan cheese, grated
salt to taste

SERVES 4

1 Mix popcorn with cheeses in a large bowl and toss together well.
2 Microwave popcorn at 100% (High) for 1-1½ minutes, or until warmed through. Stir well halfway through cooking time.
3 Season to taste and serve warm.

Cook's notes

You can pop the corn in the microwave – but only if you have a special microwave corn popper to avoid damaging the magnetron.

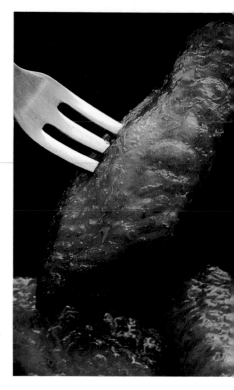

Tangy chicken with slaw dip

10 mins

Standing time: 3 mins

900g / 2lb chicken wings
30ml / 2tbls muscovado sugar
15ml / 1tbls cider vinegar
30ml / 2tbls soy sauce
60ml / 4tbls tomato ketchup or sauce

DIP
225g / 8oz coleslaw
30ml / 2tbls natural yoghurt
salt and pepper

SERVES 6-8

1 Cut off wing tips and halve wings at joints. Arrange in a single layer in a large shallow dish.
2 Mix together the sugar, vinegar, soy sauce and tomato ketchup. Spoon mixture over wings.
3 Microwave at 100% (High) for 10-12 minutes. Turn and brush with marinade. Stand 3 minutes.
4 Purée coleslaw, yoghurt and seasoning in a blender until smooth. Pour into a bowl and place on a large plate. Arrange chicken around bowl. Serve hot.

Above: *Tangy Chicken*
Left: *Cheesy Popcorn*

Sausage slices

13½ mins

Standing time: 2-3 mins

225g / 8oz sausagemeat
4 eggs
1 onion, finely chopped
45ml / 3tbls milk
45-60ml / 3-4tbls mayonnaise
salt and pepper
100g / 4oz red Leicester or
    Cheddar cheese, grated
10ml / 2tsp chopped chives

SERVES 4

1 Press sausagemeat over base of a 23cm / 9in round dish. Microwave at 100% (High) for 3 minutes. Break meat up with a fork, stir well and microwave for 1 minute at 100% (High), or use a browning dish (see Microtips).
2 Combine eggs, onion, milk, mayonnaise and seasoning. Pour on to sausagemeat and mix well. Microwave at 50% (Medium) for 4 minutes; stir from outside to centre, then microwave at 50% (Medium) for 4-4½ minutes, until almost set.
3 Mix grated cheese with chives and sprinkle over sausagemeat mixture. Microwave at 50% (Medium) for 1½-2 minutes, or until cheese melts.
4 Stand for 2-3 minutes. Serve.

Sausage slices for two: halve the ingredients. Divide sausagemeat between two plates. Microwave together for 2½ minutes. Break up meat and microwave for a further 1 minute. Divide other ingredients, mix well and microwave at 50% (Medium) for 2½-3 minutes. Stir and microwave for a further 3-3½ minutes. Sprinkle with grated cheese and microwave for 1½-2 minutes. Stand 2 minutes.

Microtips

Pre-heat browning dish for 5 minutes or as directed. Brown meat for 4 minutes at 100% (High). Stir once. Drain; transfer to 23cm / 9in round dish and continue from Stage 2.

Quickie kebabs

4 mins

Standing time: none

½ green pepper, seeded and cut
    into eight chunks
8 button mushrooms
8 cherry tomatoes
2 courgettes, cut into eight
    chunks
150ml / ¼pt stock
45ml / 3tbls cider vinegar
salt and pepper to taste
1.5ml / ¼tsp dried thyme
1.5ml / ¼tsp dried marjoram
bay leaf
8 wooden skewers

SERVES 4

1 Thread the green pepper, mushrooms, tomatoes and courgettes on to wooden skewers.
2 Combine stock, vinegar, seasoning and herbs and pour into a large, shallow dish. Arrange kebabs in dish.
3 Cover and microwave at 100% (High) for 4-6 minutes, or until vegetables are just tender; turn kebabs over once.
4 Serve with hot pitta bread.

Above: *Sausage Slices*
Right: *Quickie Kebabs*

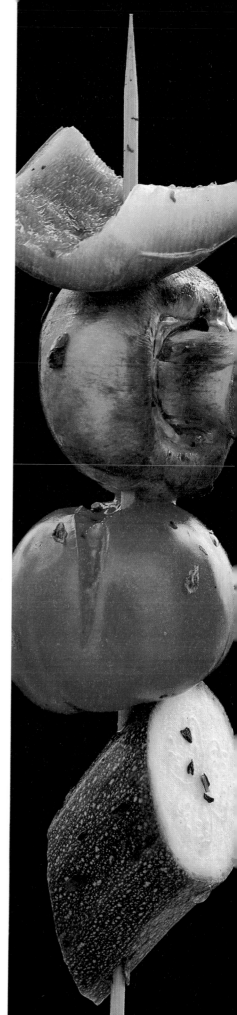

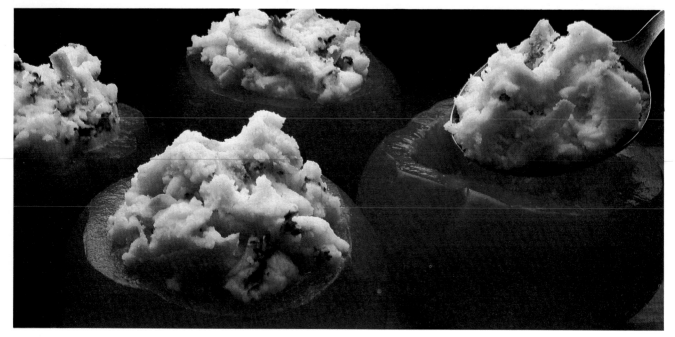

Stuffed tomatoes

<table><tr><td>11
mins</td></tr></table>

Standing time: none

4 large tomatoes (weighing about
    100g / 4oz each)
2-3 small potatoes (weighing
    350g / 12oz), thinly sliced
1 small onion, finely chopped
30ml / 2tbls water
225g / 8oz cottage cheese, sieved
45ml / 3tbls milk
15ml / 1tbls chopped parsley
1.5ml / ¼tsp dried basil
salt and pepper
1 carrot, grated

SERVES 4

1 Slice off the top of each tomato,
12mm / ½in from the stem end.
Scoop out pulp and leave the
shells upside down, to drain.
2 Mix together potatoes, onion
and water in a 1.1L / 2pt bowl.
Cover and microwave at 100%
(High) for 7-10 minutes, or until
potatoes are tender.
3 Add cottage cheese, milk, herbs,
seasoning and carrot to potato and
onion mixture and mix well.
4 Turn tomato shells over and fill
with cheese and potato mixture.
Arrange tomatoes in a ring
around the edge of a large plate.
Microwave at 100% (High) for 4-6
minutes, or until heated through.
Rearrange tomatoes once.

Sailor's spuds

<table><tr><td>16
mins</td></tr></table>

Standing time: 5 mins

4 × 225g / 8oz oval-shaped baking
    potatoes, scrubbed and pricked
25g / 1oz butter
50g / 2oz frozen petit pois
50g / 2oz frozen sweetcorn
50g / 2oz mature Cheddar cheese,
    grated
salt and pepper
4 slices processed cheese
8 cocktail sticks

MAKES 8

1 Arrange the potatoes on a sheet
of absorbent paper in the cooker.
Microwave at 100% (High) for 10-
15 minutes, turning them over
and rearranging them halfway
through cooking. Wrap in foil and
stand for 5 minutes.
2 Cut potatoes in half lengthways
and scoop out the flesh. Reserve
the shells.
3 Mash potato flesh with butter.
Add petit pois, sweetcorn and
cheese and season to taste. Microwave at 100% (High) for 2-3
minutes. Stir once during cooking
and again at end of time.
4 Fill potato shells with vegetable
and cheese mixture. Arrange in a
ring on a large plate and microwave at 100% (High) for 4-4½
minutes, or until heated through.

Stuffed Tomatoes

5 Cut processed cheese squares
into triangles. Fix each triangle to
a cocktail stick to form a sail.
6 Place one sail on each potato
'boat' and serve.

Tasty toasties

<table><tr><td>9
mins</td></tr></table>

Standing time: none

4 rashers streaky bacon, chopped
4 tomatoes, chopped
1 onion, chopped
1 green pepper, seeded and
    chopped
1 garlic clove, crushed
2.5ml / ½tsp dried oregano
2.5ml / ½tsp dried basil
4 slices bread, toasted and
    buttered
100g / 4oz Cheddar cheese, grated

SERVES 4

1 Place bacon, tomatoes, onion,
green pepper, garlic and herbs in
a bowl. Cover and microwave at
100% (High) for 7-8 minutes, or
until onion is softened. Drain well.
2 Lay toast on a double sheet of
absorbent paper and divide tomato mixture between each slice.
3 Sprinkle cheese evenly over
toast and microwave at 100%
(High) for 2-2½ minutes, or until
cheese melts, turning once.

114

Super snacks for kids

Use your microwave to rustle up great snacks and drinks for children. From substantial hamburgers to frothy hot chocolate, your versatile microwave will produce kids' snacks in moments.

Microwaving is an ideal way to conjure up quick snacks for your children, with the minimum of time, effort and mess. Whatever the time of day, when the kids come home ravennous and expecting to be fed then and there, you can oblige with the help of your microwave cooker and produce the hot drinks and nibbles they love, literally in a few seconds.

All the recipes here use ingredients which you would normally have in your store cupboard, refrigerator or freezer and they require little preparation — older children will find them easy to make by themselves.

Children adore the warming Hot Chocolate and deliciously refreshing Home-made Lemonade. They will be amazed at how quickly you can rustle up tasty Pizza Crackers for them to nibble while you cook these perennial favourites, Hot Dogs and Hamburgers. For a variation, why not try adding a slice of Cheddar cheese or some finely sliced onion rings before assembling the hamburger? For a really substantial snack, serve the burgers or Hot Dogs with the piquant Potato Salad; you can save chilling time by serving this warm — make it with salad dressing instead of mayonnaise in this case.

No pudding in the house? What child could resist a gooey Mini Mallow Nibble instead? You may find this becomes a regular teatime treat!

THEO BERGSTROM

Home-made lemonade

2 mins

Standing time: none

juice of 2 lemons
grated zest of 1 lemon
100g / 4oz sugar
30ml / 2tbls water
lemon slices, to serve (optional)

SERVES 4-6

1 Combine all the ingredients in a large jug and mix well. Microwave at 100% (High) for 2 minutes, stirring twice during cooking.
2 Cool the mixture, then chill in the refrigerator until very cold.
3 To serve, dilute 50ml / 2fl oz of the lemonade with 275ml / ½pt iced water. Decorate with lemon slices, if wished.

VARIATION
Substitute 15-30ml / 1-2 tbls clear honey for the sugar.

115

Hot chocolate

1¼ mins

Standing time: none

200ml / 7fl oz milk
10ml / 2tsp drinking chocolate

SERVES 1

1 Place the milk in a mug; blend in the chocolate. Microwave at 100% (High) for 1¼-2¼ minutes or until hot (76°C / 170°F).
2 If desired, top with chocolate chips or whipped cream.

Pizza crackers

30 secs

Standing time: none

4 large cracker biscuits
30ml / 2tbls bottled pizza or spaghetti sauce
1 slice Mozzarella cheese, quartered
4 thin slices pepperoni sausage

SERVES 1

1 Spread the crackers with the pizza or spaghetti sauce and top each with a cheese quarter and a slice of pepperoni.
2 Place on a paper plate and microwave at 50% (Medium) for 30-60 seconds, or until the cheese melts, rotating the plate ½ turn after half the cooking time.

Potato salad

2½ mins

Standing time: none

1 potato weighing 175-225g / 6-8oz
15ml / 1tbls water
30ml / 2tbls mayonnaise or salad dressing
1 celery stalk, chopped
1.5ml / ¼tsp mustard powder
salt and pepper
chopped fresh chives (optional)

SERVES 1

1 Peel the potato and cut it into 2cm / ¾in cubes. Place in a small bowl and sprinkle over the water. Cover with cling film rolled back at one edge.
2 Microwave at 100% (High) for 2½-4 minutes, or until the potato cubes feel tender when pierced with a fork, stirring gently after half the cooking time. Set aside and allow to cool.
3 In a small bowl, mix together the mayonnaise, celery, mustard, salt, pepper and chives, if using. Spoon over the potatoes and toss to coat thoroughly.

Mini mallow nibbles

1 min

Standing time: 1 min

2 digestive or wheatmeal biscuits
1 square of milk chocolate or 6 chocolate chips
1 large marshmallow, chopped

SERVES 1

1 Place one biscuit on absorbent paper. Top with the chocolate and microwave at 100% (High) for 45 seconds.
2 Add the marshmallow and microwave at 100% (High) for 15-30 seconds, until the marshmallow puffs up. Top with the other biscuit and leave to stand for 1 minute.

116

Hamburger

$1\frac{1}{2}$ mins

Standing time: 1-2 mins

100g / 4oz hamburger
1 hamburger bun

slices of pickled dill cucumber,
tomato, fresh cucumber or
lettuce leaves, or any
combination of these
tomato ketchup, mustard or
mayonnaise

SERVES 1

1 Place the hamburger on a microwave roasting rack. Cover with some absorbent paper and microwave at 100% (High) for 1 minute.
2 Turn over and re-cover. Microwave for a further 30 seconds-$1\frac{1}{2}$ minutes, or until the meat is no longer pink. Leave to stand for 1-2 minutes.
3 Split the bun and place the hamburger on the bottom half. Spread tomato ketchup and / or mustard or mayonnaise over the hamburger. Arrange the slices of pickled dill cucumber and any other salad, if using, on top of this. Spoon a little mayonnaise over the salad if wished and top with the other half of the bun.

For two hamburgers: prepare as above but microwave the first side for $1\frac{1}{2}$ minutes; turn. Microwave the second side for $1\frac{1}{2}$-2 minutes.

Hot dog

30 secs

Standing time: none

1 hot dog sausage
1 bun the same size as the hot dog
tomato ketchup or mustard

SERVES 1

1 Place the hot dog in the bun and wrap in absorbent paper.
2 Microwave at 100% (High) for 30-45 seconds or until the bun is warm to the touch, turning over after half the cooking time. Serve with tomato ketchup or mustard.

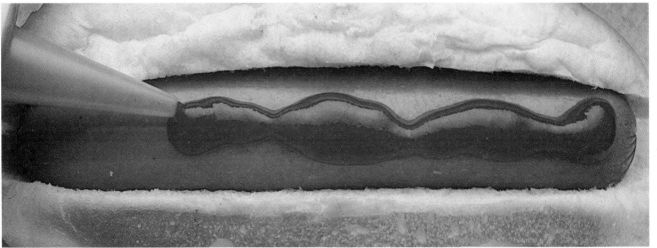

117

CHAPTER THREE
FISH AND SEAFOOD

Fish is one of the foods that benefits most from microwave cooking as the fast cooking conserves its fresh flavour and nutritive goodness. Microwaved fish should be flaky and moist so it is important to avoid overcooking. Always cook for only the minimum time given before checking.

All types and cuts of fish can be cooked in the microwave. This chapter includes sections on microwaving whole fish as well as fillets, cutlets and steaks. Fish can be stuffed, cooked 'en papillote' or combined in a casserole with other ingredients to make a filling and highly nutritious meal. Crisp or crumbly toppings bring added texture and flavour to fish dishes and can be made from a variety of ingredients, including breadcrumbs, nuts, cheese and oatmeal.

Shellfish is surprisingly versatile. A packet of frozen prawns in the freezer can provide a delicious meal in minutes. Thaw prawns quickly in the microwave, then use them in a number of tasty dishes, such as Prawn and Rice Medley or Prawns in Butter Sauce. When it comes to entertaining, a seafood starter often provides the perfect contrast to a main course meat dish. The recipes in this chapter use mussels, clams and scallops amongst other varieties of seafood.

Fish and seafood can also make surprising ingredients for a salad to serve as a light supper or appetizer. The recipes here combine seafood with crisp, fresh salad vegetables or creamy pasta mixtures to make unusual and interesting salads. Serve them as part of a buffet, or with hot garlic or herb bread as a lunch or supper dish.

Microwaving fish fillets

Fish fillets are easy to microwave and the family will let you know how easy they are to eat! Try fillets with an Italian or tropical flavour for a new approach to an old favourite.

With the microwave to conserve their fresh flavour, fish fillets are a treat to eat — even when presented in the most simple fashion. If there is time to add a sauce or topping (which take only a few minutes in the microwave), or to cook the fish in combination with fresh, colourful vegetables, they really are extra tempting. Also, microwaving with a sauce is a sure way to keep the fish moist and succulent.

Microwaving fish fillets

Fresh fish is perishable and should be cooked on the day of purchase. Always arrange fillets with the thickest parts to the outside of the dish and overlap the tail ends in the centre, or tuck them under, to avoid overcooking. Turn thick fillets over halfway through microwaving, but only rearrange the overlapping areas of thin or fragile fillets.

Oily fish, which has a higher fat content, should be microwaved at 50% (Medium). A higher power may cause heat to build up in fatty areas and result in popping. Some popping may occur anyway, so cover the dish to avoid splatters.

Different types of fillets within the white or oily categories can be interchanged. Choose fillets that are roughly the same thickness for similar cooking times and check frequently for doneness, testing a minute before the minimum time.

Testing for doneness

The flavour of fish is at its best when the flesh is just cooked through; the danger is that it can easily be overcooked. Always check fish after the minimum microwaving time: if the juices have started to run, this is a good indication it is cooked. Flake the fish carefully at the thinnest section: it should be opaque. After the standing time, the fillet should have completed cooking and be opaque at the thickest part too. If not, pop the fish back in the microwave for a minute or two, watching carefully to make sure it does not begin to overcook.

Tropical Fillets

120

Tropical fillets

| 8½ mins |

Standing time: 3 mins

450g / 1lb haddock fillets, about 12mm / ½in thick, skinned and cut into four serving portions
30ml / 2tbls flaked coconut, toasted, to garnish

BASTE
50g / 2oz butter or margarine
45ml / 3tbls unsweetened pineapple juice
5ml / 1tsp soft light brown sugar
5ml / 1tsp finely grated orange zest
1.5ml / ¼tsp ground cinnamon
dash of cayenne pepper

SERVES 4

1 Combine all the ingredients for the baste in a small bowl. Cover and microwave at 100% (High) for 1½-2½ minutes, or until the butter melts, the sugar dissolves and the mixture begins to boil. Stir every 30 seconds. Cool slightly.
2 Place the haddock fillets in a 23cm / 9in square baking dish with thicker portions to the outside.
3 Pour the baste over the fish and microwave at 100% (High) for 7-8 minutes, or until the fish just flakes easily. Rotate the dish a quarter turn twice. Stand for 3 minutes, then sprinkle with the toasted coconut and serve.

Fruity skewered cod

| 6¼ mins |

Standing time: none

350g / 12oz cod fillets, about 12mm / ½in thick, skinned

FRUITY SAUCE
15g / ½oz butter
15ml / 1tbls finely chopped spring onion
5ml / 1tsp chopped parsley
5ml / 1tsp shredded orange zest
15ml / 1tbls plain flour
salt, to taste
pinch of dry mustard
150ml / ¼pt half cream
15ml / 1tbls orange juice

SERVES 4

1 Cut the cod fillets, lengthways,

Fruity Skewered Cod

into 12mm / ½in strips about 10cm / 4in long. Thread the strips, accordion-style, on to small wooden skewers.
2 To make the sauce, combine the butter, spring onion, parsley and orange zest in a 1.1L / 2pt bowl. Microwave at 100% (High) for ¾-1¼ minutes to melt.
3 Stir in the flour, salt and mustard, then blend in the cream. Microwave at 100% (High) for 3-4½ minutes, or until the mixture thickens and bubbles, stirring every minute. Stir in the juice.
4 Place the fish in a baking dish and cover. Microwave at 100% (High) for 2½-3 minutes, until fish just flakes. Spoon over the fruity sauce to serve.

Microtips

Always place the thinnest part of fish fillets in the centre of the dish. Do not turn thin fillets over; instead, rearrange any areas that are overlapping.

Microwave times for 450g / 1lb fish fillets

TYPE OF FISH	TIME	PROCEDURE
White Cod	6-8 mins	Arrange in shallow dish, thickest parts to outside, tails or thin parts overlapping. Cover. Microwave at 100% (High); turn over halfway through and rotate dish a quarter turn twice. Stand for 3 minutes.
Haddock	6-8 mins	As above
Plaice	6-8 mins	As above
Turbot	6-8 mins	As above
Lemon sole	4-5 mins	As above, but do not turn over; instead reverse overlapping areas.
Dover sole	4-5 mins	As above, but do not turn over; instead reverse overlapping areas.
Oily Herring	6-6½ mins	Arrange in shallow dish, thickest parts to outside, tails or thin parts overlapping. Cover. Microwave at 50% (Medium). Turn over halfway through. Rotate dish a quarter turn twice. Stand 3 minutes.
Mackerel	6-6½ mins	As above
Salmon	6½-7 mins	As above
Trout	6-6½ mins	As above

To avoid overcooking, microwave fillets for the minimum time, then test thinner, opaque-looking areas with a fork — if the flesh flakes easily it is ready to be taken out of the cooker. After standing, the fish should look opaque and will be perfectly cooked.

Italian cod

7½ mins

Standing time: 3 mins

450g / 1lb cod fillets, about 2cm / ¾in thick, skinned and cut into four serving portions
½ × 425g / 15oz can spaghetti sauce
1.5ml / ¼tsp each dried basil, dried oregano and garlic powder
pepper, to taste
100g / 4oz Mozzarella cheese, thinly sliced
15ml / 1tbls grated Parmesan cheese

SERVES 4

1 Arrange the cod fillets in a 23cm / 9in square baking dish with the thickest parts to the outside.
2 In a 1.1L / 2pt bowl, combine the spaghetti sauce, basil, oregano, garlic and pepper. Cover and microwave at 100% (High) for 1½-2 minutes, or until the mixture boils, stirring once.
3 Spoon the sauce over the fish, then top with the Mozzarella and sprinkle with the Parmesan cheese. Cover with vented cling film and microwave at 70% (Medium-High) for 6-8 minutes, or until the fish just flakes easily with a fork. Rotate the dish every 2 minutes. Stand for 3 minutes then serve.

Swiss cheese sole

14 mins

Standing time: 3 mins

Mix the delicate flavour of sole with a rich Gruyère cheese sauce for an unusual fish dish.

1 small courgette, halved lengthways and chopped
2 celery stalks, chopped
350g / 12oz sole fillets, about 2cm / ¾in thick, skinned and cut into serving portions

CHEESE SAUCE
25g / 1oz butter or margarine
2 spring onions, sliced

Ginger-lime haddock

4½ mins

Standing time: 3 mins

450g / 1lb haddock fillets, about 2cm / ¾in thick, skinned and cut into four serving portions
50g / 2oz butter or margarine
2.5ml / ½tsp grated lime zest
salt
1.5ml / ¼tsp finely chopped peeled root ginger
1.5ml / ¼tsp paprika
4 thin lime slices, quartered, to garnish

SERVES 4

1 Arrange the haddock pieces in a 23cm / 9in square baking dish with the thickest portions towards the outside.
2 In a small bowl combine the butter, lime zest, salt, ginger and paprika and cover. Microwave at 100% (High) for 1-1½ minutes, or until the butter melts and the mixture begins to boil, stirring once halfway through.
3 Pour the butter over the fish and top with the lime slices. Cover with vented cling film and microwave at 100% (High) for 3½-4 minutes, or until the fish flakes easily. Rotate the dish a half turn once and spoon the buttery juices over the fish frequently during microwaving. Stand for 3 minutes, then serve, transferring the fish carefully with a fish slice.

Smoky fish casserole

16 mins

Standing time: 5 mins

25g / 1oz butter
½ onion, chopped
30ml / 2tbls chopped parsley
10ml / 2tsp plain flour
275ml / ½pt milk
2 potatoes, cut into 12mm / ½in cubes
450g / 1lb smoked haddock fillet, skinned and cut into 2.5cm / 1in cubes
salt and pepper, to taste
dash of ground nutmeg

SERVES 4

10ml / 2tsp chopped parsley
salt and pepper
1.5ml / ¼tsp dried marjoram
30ml / 2tbls plain flour
275ml / ½pt milk
100g / 4oz Gruyère cheese, grated

SERVES 4-6

1 Place the courgette and celery in a 1.1L / 2pt bowl, cover and microwave at 100% (High) for 3-4 minutes, or until tender-crisp; stir once. Set aside.
2 Combine the butter, onions, parsley, seasoning and marjoram for the sauce in a 1.1L / 2pt bowl. Cover and microwave at 100% (High) for 1-1¼ minutes, or until the butter melts. Stir in the flour, then whisk in the milk.

Swiss Cheese Sole

3 Microwave, uncovered, at 100% (High) for 3-4½ minutes, or until the mixture thickens and bubbles, whisking three times. Stir in the cheese until it melts.
4 Arrange the sole fillets in a 23cm / 9in baking dish with the thickest parts to the outside, and the thin tail ends overlapping in the centre of the dish. Spoon over the vegetables, then top with the cheese sauce. Microwave at 100% (High) for 7-11 minutes, or until the fish just flakes; carefully rearrange the overlapping tail pieces halfway through microwaving. Stand for 3 minutes, then serve with boiled new potatoes.

1 Combine the butter, onion and parsley in a 2.3L / 4pt casserole. Cover and microwave at 100% (High) for 3-4 minutes, until onion is tender. Stir once.

2 Stir in the flour, then blend in the milk. Add the potatoes, fish, seasoning and nutmeg. Stir well. Cover and microwave at 100% (High) for 13-15 minutes, or until the potatoes are tender, stirring twice. Stand for 5 minutes.

Saucy summer sole

11 mins

Standing time: none

1 cucumber, peeled, seeded and cut into 6mm / ¼in matchsticks
1 tomato, seeded and chopped
50g / 2oz mushrooms, sliced
5ml / 1tsp dried tarragon
450g / 1lb sole fillets, skinned and cut into serving portions
15ml / 1tbls chopped parsley

WINE SAUCE
25g / 1oz butter
30ml / 2tbls plain flour
salt and pepper
125ml / 4fl oz milk
125ml / 4fl oz white wine

SERVES 4

1 Combine the cucumber, tomato, mushrooms and tarragon in a 23cm / 9in baking dish. Cover and microwave at 100% (High) for 3-4 minutes, until tender. Stir once.

2 Top with the sole fillets, re-cover and microwave at 100% (High) for 4-5 minutes, or until the fish just flakes easily.

3 Drain off the juices and reserve 45ml / 3tbls. Transfer the vegetables and fish to a microwave-safe serving platter and cover.

4 Melt the butter for the sauce in a 1.1L / 2pt bowl at 100% (High) for 30-45 seconds. Stir in the flour and seasoning, reserved cooking liquid and milk. Microwave at 100% (High) for 3-4½ minutes, or until the sauce thickens, stirring every minute. Stir in the wine.

5 Pour the sauce over the sole and vegetables and microwave for 30-45 seconds, to heat through. Sprinkle with the chopped parsley to garnish, and serve.

124

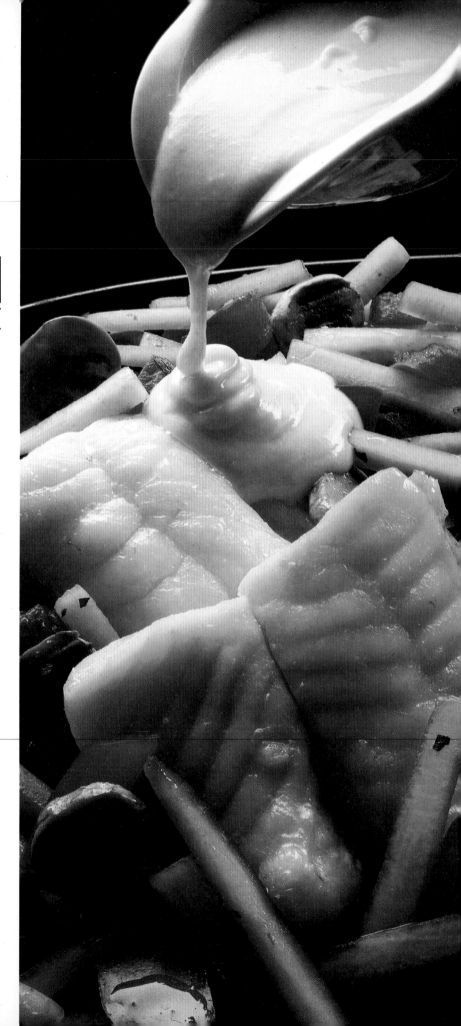

Microwaving whole fish

For delicious, succulent fish, cooking by microwave is an absolute winner. Fish is flaky and moist every time, provided you just follow the simple secrets of timing.

Fish is a delicate food to prepare and adapts extremely well to microwaving. Microwaved fish is flaky and moist and its full flavour really comes into its own. Since fish has no tough tissues, it cooks very quickly, so you can prepare a meal for several people in almost no time at all.

Always cook fish in a covered dish so that all the steam and moisture will be retained. Only cook it until the flesh flakes easily with a fork and leave it to stand for a few minutes after cooking so that the thicker centre part is cooked through.

Almost any kind of whole fish can be substituted for another in a recipe. As long as you follow the golden rule and do not overcook the fish, you will have perfect, moist results every time.

If you are preparing an entire meal in your microwave, always try to cook the fish last. Fish does not reheat as well as other foods and may easily become overdone during reheating. If you do need to reheat it, cover the dish to prevent dehydration.

Crab-stuffed Mullet

125

How to microwave — poach fish

Combine *the vegetables, lemon slices, herbs, seasoning and water in a large, shallow dish. Cover with cling film rolled back at one edge. Microwave at 100% (High) for 8-10 minutes.*

Arrange *the whole cleaned fish on top of the poaching ingredients. Cover tightly with cling film, rolled back at one edge to form a steam vent during microwaving.*

Microwave *the fish at 100% (High) for 4-6 minutes per 450g / 1lb or until the flesh flakes easily when tested with a fork, rotating the dish after half the cooking time.*

Poached fish

12 mins

Standing time: 5 mins

If preferred, use several small fish such as herring or mackerel, in place of one large one.

1 carrot, sliced
1 small onion, thinly sliced
1 celery stalk, sliced
3 lemon slices
1 bay leaf
10ml / 2tsp chopped fresh parsley
2 white peppercorns
large pinch of salt
150ml / 5fl oz water
1 whole fish, 450-900g / 1-2lb, cleaned

SERVES 4-8

1 Combine all the ingredients except the fish in a large, shallow dish. Cover with cling film rolled back at one edge and microwave at 100% (High) for 8-10 minutes.
2 Lay the fish on top of the poaching ingredients in the dish and cover again.
3 Microwave at 100% (High), allowing 4-6 minutes per 450g / 1lb, or until the fish flakes easily with a fork and the flesh becomes opaque. Rotate the dish after half the cooking time. Leave to stand for 5 minutes before serving.
4 Serve the poached fish on a bed of lettuce and garnish with tomato wedges and lemon slices.

Crab-stuffed mullet

11 mins

Standing time: 5 mins

4 red or grey mullet, 175-225g / 6-8oz each, cleaned and scaled
2 tomatoes, peeled, seeded and chopped
1 celery stalk, chopped
½ green pepper, chopped
1 small onion, finely chopped
15ml / 1tbls chopped parsley
75g / 3oz mild Cheddar cheese, grated
180g / 6½oz can crabmeat, drained
5ml / 1tsp chilli sauce
5ml / 1tsp lemon juice
1.5ml / ¼tsp ground coriander pepper

SERVES 4

1 Combine the tomatoes, celery, green pepper, onion and parsley in a casserole. Cover and microwave at 100% (High) for 3-4 minutes, or until tender, stirring after half the cooking time. Drain.
2 Stir in all the remaining ingredients except the fish. Spoon the mixture into cavity of each fish.
3 Arrange the fish in a large, shallow dish, cover with cling film and microwave at 100% (High) for 8-10 minutes, until the flesh flakes easily with a fork. Rotate the dish ½ turn every 2 minutes. Leave to stand for 5 minutes.

Microtips

Microwave a whole fish until it just begins to flake when tested with a fork. Do not overcook.

Broccoli-stuffed trout

5½ mins

Standing time: 3 mins

1 trout, about 175g / 6oz, cleaned
75g / 3oz broccoli, chopped
2 spring onions, finely chopped
15ml /1tbls butter or margarine
15ml / 1tbls chopped or flaked almonds
salt and pepper
2.5ml / ½tsp lemon juice
1 lemon slice cut into 3 pieces and a red pepper strip, to garnish (optional)

SERVES 1

1 Combine the broccoli, onions and butter in a casserole. Cover and microwave at 100% (High) for 1½-2 minutes, or until tender. Mix in the almonds; season.
2 Place the trout in a shallow dish. Spoon three-quarters of the broccoli mixture into the cavity of the trout. Arrange the remaining mixture around the fish. Sprinkle the trout with lemon juice.
3 Cover the dish with cling film and microwave at 100% (High) for 4-6 minutes, or until the fish flakes easily with a fork, rotating the dish once during cooking. Let stand for 3 minutes.
4 Garnish with the lemon and red pepper strip, if using, and serve.

Broccoli-stuffed trout for two. Double the ingredients. Prepare as above, but microwave the broccoli and onion for 2-3 minutes and the trout for 6-8 minutes, rotating dish ½ turn every 2 minutes.

Freezer notes

This dish can be made with frozen trout and frozen broccoli. Place the fish in a shallow dish, cover and microwave at 50% (Medium) for 1-1½ minutes, or until thawed, turning over halfway. Rinse in cold water until the cavity is no longer icy. Pat dry with absorbent paper, then use as above.

Microwave the broccoli at 100% (High) for 1-2 minutes, or until thawed. Stir, then use as above.

127

Stuffed trout

8 mins

Standing time: 5 mins

4 fresh trout, each about 225g / 8oz, cleaned
50g / 2oz butter or margarine
1 celery stalk, sliced
2 spring onions, chopped
50g / 2oz mushrooms, sliced
30ml / 2tbls finely chopped fresh parsley
5ml / 1tsp grated lemon zest
1.5ml / $\frac{1}{4}$tsp salt
large pinch dried basil
pepper
2 slices white bread, cut into 6mm / $\frac{1}{4}$in cubes
225g / 8oz peeled prawns, thawed

SERVES 4

1 In a medium bowl, combine the butter, celery and spring onions. Cover and microwave at 100% (High) for 4-6 minutes, or until the celery is tender.

2 Stir in the mushrooms, parsley, lemon zest, salt, basil and pepper, then add the bread cubes and toss until thoroughly coated with the vegetable mixture. Chop the prawns into small pieces; mix into the stuffing.

3 Spoon one-quarter of the stuffing into each trout. Place in a shallow dish, cover with cling film and microwave at 100% (High) for 4-6 minutes, turning the fish once during cooking. Leave to stand for 5 minutes before serving.

Freezer Notes

Unwrap 4 frozen trout and place on a baking tray or roasting rack. Cover, then microwave at 20-30% (Defrost) for 10 minutes. Spoon the stuffing into the trout; re-cover and microwave at 70% (Medium) for 20-25 minutes, or until the flesh near the backbone flakes easily with a fork. Rearrange trout once or twice during cooking.

The cooked stuffed trout can also be frozen; open freeze until firm, then wrap and freeze for not more than 2 months.

Microwaving fish steaks

Plump, juicy fish steaks cook to perfection in the microwave. Casserole them with spiced vegetables, cook them in a parcel, or give them a tasty topping for some super supper dishes.

Fish steaks are the nearest thing to a natural convenience food. They take only a few minutes' microwaving to cook and are packed full of goodness.

At different times of year, the fishmonger will have a different selection of fish cuts; cod is the most widely available. Choose cuts that are the same weight and of a similar thickness.

Ready-packaged blocks of boneless, skinned fish, usually sold as 'steaks' or 'portions', are also available frozen; they can be thawed (see Microtips, page 130) and substituted for fresh steaks — but allow a little less cooking time, as they are a bit smaller.

Testing for doneness

Test fish to see if it is cooked after the minimum microwaving time but before the standing time. Insert the point of a sharp knife into the thickest steak, at the meatiest section nearest the bone. If cooked, the flesh should flake easily but be slightly transparent near the bone. If it is not quite cooked, microwave for a further 30 seconds and test again. It is easy to spoil fish by overcooking, so it is better to undercook first. Check again after the standing time and microwave for another minute if still not cooked.

Mayonnaise-topped Cod

Microwaved fish steaks make ideal quick family meals. Serve with lightly cooked fresh vegetables and garnish with lemon wedges.

Cook's notes

Steaks are cut from the tail end of the fish and are solid circles of flesh. Cutlets are taken from further up towards the head, where the body cavity leaves a U- or V-shaped hole in the flesh. Pin the tips of cutlets together with a wooden cocktail stick to prevent these thinner parts from drying out during microwaving.

129

Mayonnaise-topped cod

4 mins

Standing time: 1½-3 mins

2 onion slices
1 celery stalk, sliced
4 × 100g / 4oz cod steaks
175ml / 6fl oz milk
10ml / 2tsp chopped parsley

GARLIC MAYONNAISE
150ml / ¼pt mayonnaise
5ml / 1tsp chopped parsley
1.5ml / ¼tsp onion powder
1 small garlic clove, minced

pinch of dried dillweed
pinch of pepper

SERVES 4

1 Combine all the ingredients for the garlic mayonnaise in a bowl. Mix well and chill.
2 In a shallow dish, combine the onion and celery. Arrange the steaks on top in a single layer. Pour over the milk, then sprinkle with the parsley.
3 Cover with vented cling film and microwave at 100% (High) for 4-5 minutes, or until the fish flakes easily, turning halfway through. Stand for 1½-3 minutes.

4 Transfer the fish to serving plates with a slotted spoon. Top each steak with a generous helping of garlic mayonnaise. Serve with broccoli and baby new potatoes, or grilled tomatoes and a salad.

Microtips

To thaw frozen steaks: pierce packs and space out on a plate. Microwave at 20-30% (Defrost) for 1½-2 minutes for one 92g / 3.25oz pack or 5-5½ for four. Stand 1-2 minutes (3-4 for four) and drain.

How to microwave fish steaks

Wash *the steaks and pat dry on absorbent paper. Arrange them in a ring in a shallow, square or round dish.*

Sprinkle *over 10ml / 2tsp lemon juice, water or white wine. Cover with vented cling film.*

Microwave *according to the chart below, until fish flakes but is opaque near the bone. Stand, covered, 1½-3 minutes.*

Microwaving times for fish steaks

TYPE OF FISH	AMOUNT	TIME	PROCEDURE
Cod	4 × 100g / 4oz 4 × 175g / 6oz	4-5 mins 7-9 mins	Add liquid (see Step 2). Microwave at 100% (High). Turn over and baste halfway through. Stand 1½-3 minutes.
Haddock	4 × 100g / 4oz 4 × 175g / 6oz	4-5 mins 7-9 mins	Add liquid (see Step 2). Microwave at 100% (High). Turn over and baste halfway through. Stand 1½-3 minutes.
Halibut	4 × 100g / 4oz 4 × 175g / 6oz	4-5 mins 7½-9 mins	Add liquid (see Step 2.) Microwave at 100% (High). Turn over and around, so that the opposite end points to the centre, and baste halfway through. Stand 1½-3 minutes.
Salmon	4 × 100g / 4oz 4 × 175g / 6oz	6½-7 mins 10-11 mins	Add liquid (see Step 2). Microwave at 50% (Medium). Turn over and baste halfway through. Stand 1½-3 minutes.

Chunky cod bake

11 mins

Standing time: 2-3 mins

1 garlic clove, crushed
1 onion, thinly sliced
1 green pepper, seeded and thinly
    sliced
15ml / 1tbls olive oil
4 tomatoes, chopped
2 courgettes, sliced
4 × 175g / 6oz cod steaks
5ml / 1tsp dried oregano
30ml / 2tbls white wine or lemon
    juice
salt and pepper

SERVES 4

1 Place the garlic, onion, green pepper and oil in a shallow dish, large enough to take the steaks in a single layer. Cover and microwave at 100% (High) for 3 minutes, or until tender.
2 Stir, then top with the tomatoes, courgettes and cod steaks. Sprinkle over the oregano and wine or lemon juice and season with salt and pepper.
3 Cover and microwave at 100% (High) for 8-10 minutes, or until the cod flakes easily, turning the fish over halfway through. Leave to stand for 2-3 minutes. Serve with boiled potatoes.

Chunky cod bake for two: halve all the ingredients. Microwave the garlic, onion, pepper and oil at 100% (High) for 1½-2 minutes in Stage 1; microwave the assembled dish for 4-5 minutes in Stage 3. Stand for 1½-2 minutes.

Fish 'n' fennel parcels

8 mins

Standing time: 2-3 mins

4 × 175g / 6oz haddock steaks
1 small fennel bulb, trimmed and
    finely sliced
8 sprigs of fennel
60ml / 4tbls Pernod
salt and pepper

SERVES 4

1 Cut four squares of greaseproof paper or baking parchment, large enough to enclose the individual fish steaks in a 'money bag' parcel. Brush one side of each parchment square lightly with a little vegetable oil.
2 Place a fish steak in the centre of each square and add a quarter of the fennel slices and two fennel sprigs. Gather up the sides of one paper square and spoon 15ml / 1tbls Pernod over the haddock. Season. Gather together the sides of the square and tie the top with a plastic tie, like a money bag. Repeat with each of the remaining parcels.
3 Place the parcels in a shallow dish and microwave at 100% (High) for 8-10 minutes, or until the fish is cooked, rearranging the parcels halfway through microwaving. Leave to stand for 2-3 minutes, before cutting open or untying the parcels to serve. Serve with a large salad and hunks of French bread to mop up the juices.

Fish 'n' Fennel Parcels

PAUL GRATER

131

Fruity fish steaks

$14\frac{1}{2}$ mins

Standing time: 1½-3 mins

4 × 100-175g / 4-6oz salmon
steaks or cutlets

TOPPING
100g / 4oz butter or margarine
40g / 1½oz slivered almonds
2.5ml / ½tsp dried marjoram
2.5ml / ½tsp finely grated orange
zest
1.5ml / ¼tsp garlic salt
1 small red eating apple, cored
and thinly sliced
1 small pear, cored and thinly
sliced
30ml / 2tbls apple jelly

SERVES 4

1 Combine the butter, almonds, marjoram, orange zest and garlic salt for the topping in a 1.1L / 2pt bowl.
2 Cover and microwave at 100% (High) for 3½-4½ minutes, or until the almonds are brown, stirring every minute.
3 Drain off and reserve the butter then stir the apple and pear slices and the apple jelly into the almonds. Re-cover and microwave at 100% (High) for 4-5 minutes, or until the fruit is tender, stirring gently once. Set aside.
4 Microwave the salmon steaks or cutlets following the step-by-step instructions on page 130 but replacing the lemon juice, water or wine with the reserved butter. Stand for 1½-3 minutes.

Fruity Fish Steaks

5 Meanwhile, reheat the fruit topping at 100% (High)for 30-60 seconds. Spoon a little of the topping over each piece of salmon. Serve with rice.

Spicy halibut bake

$10\frac{1}{2}$ mins

Standing time: 1½-3 mins

200g / 7oz tomatoes
½ green pepper, seeded and
sliced
½ red pepper, seeded and sliced
1 small onion, thinly sliced
4 × 175g / 6oz halibut steaks

MARINADE
30ml / 2tbls brown sauce
15ml / 1tbls soft brown sugar
15ml / 1tbls olive oil
15ml / 1tbls wine vinegar
2.5ml / ½tsp chilli powder
pinch each of garlic powder,
ground cloves and cayenne

SERVES 4

1 In a shallow dish large enough to take the halibut steaks in a single layer, combine all the marinade ingredients. Add the vegetables and microwave at 100% (High) for 3-4 minutes or until the peppers and onion are tender but still crisp.
2 Cool slightly, then add the halibut steaks and turn to coat well. Cover and marinate in the refrigerator for 4 hours, turning the fish over several times.
3 In the covered dish, microwave the fish and marinade at 100% (High) for 7½-9 minutes, or until the fish flakes easily. Turn the fish around and over and baste halfway through cooking. Stand for 1½-3 minutes. Serve with the vegetables and marinade juices.

Salmon with tarragon sauce

$13\frac{1}{2}$ mins

Standing time: 1½-2 mins

4 × 100-175g / 4-6oz salmon
steaks or cutlets

SAUCE
30ml / 2tbls butter or margarine

Above: *Spicy Halibut Bake*
Right: *Salmon with Tarragon*

½ **onion, finely chopped**
salt
2.5ml / ½tsp finely grated lemon
  zest
1.5ml / ¼tsp dried tarragon
30ml / 2tbls plain flour
275ml / ½pt milk
4-6 drops hot pepper sauce
1 egg yolk, beaten

SERVES 4

1 Combine the butter, onion, salt, lemon zest and tarragon in a 575ml / 1pt bowl. Cover and microwave at 100% (High) for 2-2½ minutes, or until the onion is soft, stirring once.

2 Stir in the flour, then blend in the milk and hot pepper sauce. Microwave, uncovered, at 100% (High) for 3½-5½ minutes, or until the mixture begins to boil, stirring every minute.

3 Blend a little of the hot sauce into the egg yolk, then whisk back into the rest of the sauce. Microwave at 50% (Medium) for 1-1½ minutes, or until just thickened, stirring twice. Lay a round of greaseproof paper or cling film on the surface of the sauce and set aside.

4 Microwave the salmon following the step-by-step instructions on page 130. Leave to stand for 1½-3 minutes.

5 Meanwhile, reheat the sauce at 50% (Medium) for 30-60 seconds, stirring once. Serve spooned over the salmon.

133

Stuffed fish

For family fillers and dinner party dazzlers, stuffed fish fits the bill! Wrap delicate fillets around mouthwatering fillings, or serve whole stuffed fish that look as good as they taste.

Stuffed fish can be special or simple: just right for the family or for a spectacular dinner party centre-piece. Round or flat fish are suitable for stuffing; or try squid for a truly Mediterranean flavour. Rice or breadcrumbs make a good base for a stuffing: and the variety of vegetables and herb and spice flavourings that can be added is endless.

Types of fish for stuffing

Round fish: the belly cavity of a gutted round fish makes a natural pocket for stuffings.

To gut round fish, make a slit in the belly from the gills along two-thirds of the body. Scrape out the inside of the belly and any black skin, then rub the cavity with salt and rinse. Cut away the gill covers and fins. Most fishmongers will perform these tasks for you if you ask.

To make extra room in the belly cavity for the stuffing, and to make the dish easier to eat, remove the backbone. Open out the fish, cut side down, and press down along the backbone. Turn the fish over and cut through the bone at the head end. Ease the bone away and cut it loose at the tail end.

Fish fillets are ideal: either roll one around a stuffing, or use two large fillets to sandwich a stuffing.

Flat fish: make a pocket in a whole flat fish, by running a knife down the backbone and easing the flesh away from the bones. A stuffing can then be carefully spooned in to give a deliciously plump appearance.

Seafood: the body cavity of squid makes an ideal container for stuffing. Remove the tentacles, then clean the inner cavity (see steps page 136); the tentacles can be chopped finely and included in the stuffing if wished.

Trout with Nut Stuffing

Serving

Stuffed fish can make an impressive dish to serve at a dinner party. Serve with plain boiled or steamed vegetables, rice or salad.

Trout with nut stuffing

15 mins

Standing time: 2-3 mins

2 × 175-225g / 6-8oz trout, cleaned and heads removed

STUFFING
30ml / 2tbls butter or margarine
1 celery stalk, finely chopped
3 spring onions, sliced
15ml / 1tbls chopped parsley
25g / 1oz chopped walnuts
45ml / 3tbls stock or water
salt
1.5ml / ¼tsp lemon pepper seasoning or lemon zest
pinch of dried marjoram

HERBY CROUTONS
4 slices thick white bread, crusts removed, diced
25g / 1oz butter
5ml / 1tsp mixed herbs

SERVES 2

1 Put the butter, celery, onions and parsley in a 1.1L / 2pt casserole. Cover and microwave at 100% (High) for 2-3 minutes, or until slightly tender. Stir in the remaining stuffing ingredients.
2 For the croutons: mix all of the ingredients in a large bowl and microwave at 100% (High) for 4-5 minutes, stirring every minute. Mix the croutons with the stuffing.
3 Arrange the trout in a 25cm / 10in square casserole with the backbone to the outside. Spoon stuffing into belly of each trout.
4 Cover and microwave at 70% (Medium-High) for 9-14 minutes, or until the fish flakes easily. Leave to stand for 2-3 minutes.

Horseradish mackerel

24 mins

Standing time: 3 mins

2 × 450g / 1lb mackerel, cleaned

STUFFING
3 spring onions, chopped
15ml / 1tbls vegetable oil
30ml / 2tbls rice
150ml / ¼pt water
salt and pepper
2 courgettes, grated
½ small red pepper, seeded and finely chopped
30ml / 2tbls creamed horseradish

SERVES 2

1 Put the spring onions and oil in a 1.7L / 3pt bowl, cover and microwave at 100% (High) for 2 minutes, until onions are tender.
2 Add the rice, water and seasoning to taste, re-cover and microwave at 100% (High) for 12 minutes, or until nearly all the water is absorbed, stirring twice.
3 Stir in the courgettes, red pepper and horseradish. Cover and microwave at 100% (High) for 3 minutes.
4 Spoon half the stuffing into each mackerel and wrap each fish in cling film. Pierce the film to allow the steam to escape, and microwave at 50% (Medium) for 7 minutes or until the fish just flakes easily, turning over halfway through. Stand for 3 minutes, then cut open the cling film and serve fish with steamed vegetables.

Cook's notes

Choose mackerel with bright eyes and red gills. A firm skin, that does not leave a finger mark when pressed, is also a good sign of freshness.

Saucy stuffed squid

18 mins

Standing time: none

Cleaned and prepared squid are now available from some supermarkets and fishmongers.

450g / 1lb squid

STUFFING
30ml / 2tbls olive oil
1 onion, chopped
2 garlic cloves, crushed
3 smoked back bacon rashers, rind removed and chopped
30ml / 2tbls dry white wine
150ml / ¼pt water
100g / 4oz fresh breadcrumbs
45ml / 3tbls chopped parsley
salt and pepper

SAUCE
30ml / 2tbls olive oil
1 onion, chopped
1 red chilli, seeded and chopped
150ml / ¼pt dry white wine
400g / 14oz can chopped tomatoes
10ml / 2tsp tomato purée or paste
5ml / 1tsp oregano or marjoram
1 small bay leaf
90ml / 6tbls mayonnaise

SERVES 4

1 Prepare the squid following steps 1 and 2. Put the oil, onion, garlic and bacon for the stuffing into a 1.1L / 2pt bowl. Cover and microwave at 100% (High) for 3 minutes, or until the onion and bacon are tender.

2 Stir in the remaining stuffing ingredients and season to taste. Spoon the stuffing into the squid bodies (see step 3). Lay the stuffed squid side by side in a lightly greased baking dish.

3 For the sauce, put the oil, onion and chilli into a large bowl, cover and microwave at 100% (High) for 3 minutes, or until the onion is tender. Stir in the reserved squid tentacles, wine, tomatoes, tomato purée or paste, oregano and bay leaf.

4 Pour the sauce over the squid, cover and microwave at 70% (Medium-High) for 12 minutes, rotating the dish a quarter turn twice during cooking.

5 Using a slotted spoon, transfer the squid to a warm serving dish. Discard the bay leaf from the sauce and stir in the mayonnaise, until evenly blended. Pour over the squid and serve with boiled rice and steamed courgettes or broccoli heads.

How to prepare Saucy stuffed squid

Cut *head from body of the squid. Cut off tentacles just below the eyes; chop them finely and reserve.*

Remove *stomach sac and discard. Pull quill out of body and discard. Peel off the thin mottled skin. Wash body.*

Stuff *each body two-thirds full with stuffing (allowing for expansion). Sew up the opening with needle and thread.*

136

Sole turban

21 mins

Standing time: 5 mins

225g / 8oz French beans, trimmed
225g / 8oz fresh asparagus, peeled
75ml / 3fl oz water
11 × 150g / 5oz lemon sole fillets, skinned
2 egg whites
150ml / $\frac{1}{4}$pt double cream
salt and pepper
275g / 10oz pasta twists, cooked conventionally
15g / $\frac{1}{2}$oz butter
dill to garnish

SERVES 8

1 Put the beans and asparagus in a large bowl and add the water. Cover and microwave at 100% (High) for 5 minutes, until tender-crisp. Rinse in cold water to cool, then drain. Line the mould as in steps 1 and 2 (right).

2 Put the remaining two fish fillets in a food processor or blender with the egg whites. Process for 1 minute, adding the cream in a thin stream while the processor is running. Season with salt and pepper.

3 Trim 5cm / 2in of the asparagus tips and reserve. Proceed as in step 3.

4 Fold the loose ends of the fish over the filling and cover with cling film. Microwave at 70% (Medium-High) for 15-17 minutes until the fish is cooked and the filling set when pierced with a skewer. Leave to stand for 5 minutes.

5 Drain the pasta spirals and combine with the asparagus tips and butter in a large bowl. Microwave at 100% (High) for 1-1$\frac{1}{2}$ minutes, until hot, stirring once.

6 Remove the cling film from the ring mould and place a large serving platter over the top of the mould. Turn the turban out, garnish and fill the centre with the pasta and asparagus.

How to assemble Sole turban

Lightly grease *a 20cm / 8in ring mould. Lay nine of the fillets, skinned side up, into the mould with head and tail ends overlapping the mould edges.*

Lay *the green beans side by side across the base of the mould, then stack them up the sides, to cover the fish completely.*

Spread *half the filling into the mould then lay four of the asparagus stems end to end on top of the filling. Spread in the remaining filling.*

PAUL GRATER

137

Plaice whirls

12½ mins

Standing time: 6 mins

700g / 1½lb plaice fillets (about 8 fillets), skinned

STUFFING
175g / 6oz frozen chopped spinach
175g / 6oz button mushrooms, chopped
15ml / 1tbls butter
1 onion, chopped
1 garlic clove, crushed
salt and pepper

SAUCE
125ml / 4fl oz dry white wine
2 shallots, chopped
15ml / 3tsp cornflour
15ml / 1tbls water
75ml / 5tbls double cream
50g / 2oz button mushrooms, sliced

SERVES 4

1 Put the frozen spinach in a bowl, cover and microwave at 100% (High) for 2½ minutes. Put the spinach in a fine sieve and press out the excess water.
2 Place the mushrooms, butter, onion, garlic and a pinch of salt and pepper for the stuffing in a bowl. Cover and microwave at 100% (High) for 2 minutes, or until softened. Stand for 3 minutes. Stir in the spinach.
3 Lay the fillets skinned side up, and place a spoonful of the stuffing on each. Roll the fillets tightly and arrange seam side down in a 20cm / 8in shallow dish.
4 Pour over the wine and sprinkle with the shallots. Cover and microwave at 100% (High) for 5 minutes, until the juices from the fish begin to run.
5 Transfer the fillets with a slotted spoon to a warm serving dish and

Plaice Whirls

allow to stand for 3 minutes.
6 Mix the cornflour and water together and stir into the cream. Stir the cream into the cooking liquid and add the sliced mushrooms. Cover and microwave at 100% (High) for 3 minutes, until thickened, stirring twice. Season with salt and pepper to taste, then pour over the fish. Serve with buttered new potatoes.

Moroccan grey mullet

17 mins

Standing time: 9 mins

1 × 750g / 1lb 10oz grey mullet, cleaned

STUFFING
1 onion, chopped
30ml / 2tbls olive oil
50g / 2oz couscous
75ml / 3fl oz water
juice and grated zest of ½ lemon
2.5ml / ½tsp dried thyme
salt and pepper

SERVES 2

1 Put the onion and olive oil in a 1.7L / 3pt bowl, cover and microwave at 100% (High) for 2 minutes or until tender.
2 Stir in the remaining stuffing ingredients and season to taste. Cover and microwave at 100% (High) for 3 minutes. Stand for 4 minutes, until all the liquid has been absorbed by the couscous. Stir well to mix.
3 Spoon the stuffing into the belly of the fish, then secure the opening with wooden cocktail sticks or sew up using needle and thread.
4 Place the fish on its side in a baking dish, cover and microwave at 100% (High) for 12 minutes, or until the flesh just flakes easily. Stand the fish, covered, for 5 minutes, then serve.

Cook's notes

To skin a fish fillet, place skin side down and work a knife between the flesh and skin at the tail end. Holding the skin with one hand, work knife down to remove flesh.

RAY DUNS

138

Fish casseroles

Fish casseroles are delicious, nutritious and very easy to prepare. Results are even more successful when fish are quickly cooked in the microwave.

Perhaps more than other food, fish benefits enormously from being cooked in the microwave. It retains its flavour and texture and can be made into a filling and highly nutritious meal when combined in a casserole with other ingredients.

These protein packed meals for family and friends can be made as plain or as spicy as you wish; simply adjust the spices to taste.

All the recipes given here are quite suitable for freezing; make a large casserole such as Bosun's Stew and freeze half of it for later use. Microwave at 20-30% (Defrost) until thawed but still icy in the centre, then reheat at 50% (Medium) until hot.

Remember that all fish cooks very quickly in the microwave, so it is important not to overcook any of the casseroles, or they will lose their lovely delicate flavour. Make the most of the many varieties of fish and experiment with different types of white fish.

Pineapple Fish Stew

Bosun's stew

21 mins

Standing time: 5 mins

2 streaky bacon rashers
15ml / 1tbls vegetable oil
1 onion, chopped
1 garlic clove, crushed
450g / 1lb potatoes, cut into
    12mm / ½in dice
400g / 14oz can chopped tomatoes
½ chicken stock cube, crumbled
30ml / 2tbls finely chopped
    parsley
1 bay leaf
5ml / 1tsp paprika
10ml / 2tsp capers
salt and pepper
700g / 1½lb cod fillets, skinned
    and cut into 2.5cm / 1in cubes
100g / 4oz cooked peeled prawns
chopped parsley, to garnish
paprika, to garnish
bay leaf, to garnish

SERVES 6

How to microwave Bosun's stew

Lay *the bacon between sheets of absorbent paper and microwave at 100% (High) for 1-2 minutes, until crisp. Leave to stand for 2 minutes.*

Crumble *the bacon into a large casserole. Add oil, onion and garlic, cover and microwave at 100% (High) for 3-4 minutes, until onion is tender.*

Add *the potatoes, stir well, then cover the casserole with cling film or a lid and cook for a further 3 minutes at 100% (High).*

Stir *in tomatoes, stock cube, parsley, bay leaf, paprika, capers. Season. Cover, microwave at 100% (High) for 10 minutes, until potatoes are tender.*

Carefully *stir in the fish and prawns then cover and microwave at 100% (High) for 4-5 minutes, stirring once, until the fish is cooked.*

Leave, *covered, to stand for 3 minutes. Garnish with chopped parsley and paprika and add the finishing touch with a bay leaf.*

RAY DUNS

140

Pineapple fish stew

7 mins

Standing time: none

250g / 9oz white fish, skinned, boned, cut in bite-sized pieces
30ml / 2tbls olive oil
2 spring onions, chopped
2 large garlic cloves, chopped
250g / 9oz cooked, peeled prawns
salt and pepper
1.5ml / $\frac{1}{4}$tsp ground aniseed
1.5ml / $\frac{1}{4}$tsp ground turmeric
1 bay leaf
10ml / 2tsp grated orange zest
2.5ml / $\frac{1}{2}$tsp cayenne pepper
275ml / $\frac{1}{2}$pt boiling water
30ml / 6tsp cornflour
45ml / 3tbls dry sherry
30ml / 2tbls soy sauce
250g / 9oz fresh or canned unsweetened pineapple chunks, drained
boiled rice, to serve

SERVES 4

1 Combine the fish, oil, spring onions and garlic in a large casserole. Cover and microwave at 100% (High) for 2 minutes.
2 Stir in the prawns, salt, pepper, aniseed, turmeric, bay leaf, orange zest and cayenne. Stir in the boiling water. Cover and microwave at 100% (High) for 2 minutes.
3 Dissolve the cornflour in the sherry and soy sauce. Stir into the casserole. Microwave at 100% (High) for 2-3 minutes, stirring every minute, until the sauce thickens. Stir in the pineapple, cover and microwave at 100% (High) for 1-2 minutes, until the pineapple is hot. Serve with rice.

Spicy standby casserole

17 mins

Standing time: 5 mins

2 onions finely chopped
1 large garlic clove, crushed
15ml / 1tbls olive oil
30ml / 2tbls tomato purée
10ml / 2tsp ground cinnamon
4 bay leaves
salt and pepper
700g / 1$\frac{1}{2}$lb frozen white fish fillets

SU JORGENSSEN

SERVES 6

1 Combine the onions, garlic and olive oil in a large, shallow dish. Microwave at 100% (High) for 3-4 minutes, until onions are soft.
2 Stir in the tomato purée and cinnamon. Add the bay leaves and 225ml / 8fl oz water; season to taste. Microwave, uncovered, at 100% (High) for 5 minutes, until

Spicy Standby Casserole

the sauce is thick.
3 Lay the frozen fish fillets in 2 or 3 layers in the dish. Spoon over the sauce to cover the fish, cover the dish and microwave at 100% (High) for 9-10 minutes, until the fish flakes easily. Turn the fillets over and rearrange every 3 minutes. Stand for 5 minutes.

141

Topping fish

Fresh, flaky fish with a crisp or crumbly topping — what could be more delicious? Bring a little variety to family suppers with these tasty dishes — so quick and easy to make in the microwave.

Fish always makes a quick, yet nourishing, meal and you can make the most of any fish or shellfish by adding a tasty topping. Just before the end of the microwaving time, adding a quick topping is the work of a moment. For extra crispness, flash the dish under a hot grill for a minute or two (provided that the dish is flameproof).

Most of the toppings suggested in the recipes and in the Topping ideas box will complement popular white fish and simple seafood dishes — but be careful not to use too powerful a flavour in a topping for a delicate fish. Mixed fish dishes — such as Cajun Prawns — need a plain topping, or the variety of flavours is too great.

Fish facts
Remember to protect the thinner ends of fillets and cutlets by tucking tails underneath, or overlapping them, and always placing thinner ends towards the centre of the dish. Whenever possible, use equal-sized pieces of fish to ensure even cooking. Cover the fish during cooking and keep it covered to retain the heat if you need to set it aside while making a sauce or accompaniment.

Test fish for doneness after the minimum microwaving time but before any standing time. Insert the point of a sharp knife into the thickest piece, at the meatiest section. If cooked, the flesh should flake easily but still be slightly translucent near the bone. If it is not quite cooked, microwave for a further 30 seconds and test again. It is easy to spoil fish by overcooking so it is better to undercook it first. Check it again after any standing time and return it to the microwave for another 30 seconds if it is still not cooked.

Crumb-coated Cod Bake

Tasty toppings
Toppings for fish can be made from a wide range of ingredients — including leftover bits of cheese, bread or cereal. Experiment with mix-and-match toppings to find your favourites. Most toppings can either be cooked with the fish or added at the last minute, depending on how much you want the cooking juices to soak into the topping. Cheese, however, should always be added shortly before the end of the cooking time, the power reduced to 50% (Medium) and the whole dish cooked just until the cheese melts; this is because cheese microwaved at 100% (High) tends to become tough. The Topping ideas chart shows how much of each topping you will need to cover the dish of the size stated. To ring the changes, add any of the following per 25g / 1oz topping used: 15-30ml / 1-2tbls chopped herbs or 7.5-15ml / ½-1tbls dried; 15ml / 1tbls grated Parmesan cheese; 2.5ml / ½tsp (or to taste) ground spice, such as nutmeg or allspice.

Serving
Remember that a topping can turn a simple fish dish into something more substantial. Serve with salads or steamed vegetables.

Crumb-coated cod bake | 13¼ mins

Standing time: 2-3 mins

175g / 6oz broccoli, broken into florets
2 carrots, peeled and cut into thin strips
1 potato, thinly sliced
4 × 100g / 4oz cod fillets, about 20mm / ¾in thick

Topping ideas

TOPPING	SIZE OF DISH		
Ingredient	7.5cm / 3in ramekin	15cm / 6in square	20cm / 8in round
Almonds, flaked	7g / ¼oz	45g / 1¾oz	80g / 3¼oz
Bran flakes or cornflakes	15g / ½oz	75g / 3oz	150g / 5oz
Breadcrumbs, dried	15g / ½oz	40g / 1½oz	75g /3oz
Breadcrumbs, fresh	15g / ½oz	65g / 2½oz	80g / 3¼oz
Bulgar wheat (unsoaked weight)	7g / ¼oz	65g / 2½oz	90g / 3½oz
Cheddar cheese, grated	25g / 1oz	80g / 3¼oz	100g / 4oz
Cream crackers, crushed	15g / ½oz	50g / 2oz	75g / 3oz
Oatmeal (medium)	15g / ½oz	65g / 2½oz	75g / 3oz
Pine nuts, chopped	15g / ½oz	65g / 2½oz	90g / 3½oz
Pistachios, chopped	15g / ½oz	65g / 2½oz	90g /3½oz
Stilton cheese, crumbled	30g / 1¼oz	115g / 4½oz	165g / 5½oz

75g / 3oz Cheddar cheese
  crackers, crushed
65g / 2½oz butter or margarine
15ml / 1tbls chopped parsley
pinch of garlic powder
pinch of pepper

SERVES 4

1 Place the broccoli, carrots and potato in a 23cm / 9in square dish and cover. Microwave at 100% (High) for 5½-6½ minutes, or until the vegetables are tender but still firm, stirring once.

2 Arrange the cod, tails overlapping and towards the centre of the dish, on top of the vegetables. Press the crushed crackers onto the fillets. Set aside.

3 Combine the remaining ingredients in a small bowl. Microwave, uncovered, at 100% (High) for 45-90 seconds, or until the butter melts and begins to bubble. Stir halfway through the cooking time.

4 Drizzle the butter mixture over the cod and vegetables and cover the dish with greaseproof paper. Microwave at 70% (Medium-High) for 7-10 minutes, or until the fish flakes easily, giving the dish a quarter turn every 3 minutes.

Cheesy scallop gratin

8¼ mins

Standing time: none

350g / 12oz scallops, sliced into
  discs
90ml / 6tbls dry white wine
50g / 2oz mushrooms, sliced
salt and pepper
3 black peppercorns
1 bay leaf
2 parsley sprigs
1 shallot, finely chopped
30ml / 2tbls water
700g / 1½lb potatoes, cooked,
  creamed and seasoned
25g / 1oz Gruyère cheese, grated
lemon slices and parsley sprigs,
  to garnish

SAUCE
40g / 1½oz butter
15ml / 1tbls plain flour
90ml / 6tbls milk
1 egg yolk
60ml / 4tbls double cream
salt and pepper
few drops of lemon juice

SERVES 4

PAUL GRATER

1 Mix the white part of the scallops with the wine, mushrooms, salt and pepper, peppercorns, bay leaf, parsley, shallot and water in a 800ml / 1½pt bowl. Cover and microwave at 50% (Medium) for 4 minutes, or until almost tender, stirring once.

2 Add the coral (orange flesh) from the scallops and microwave, covered, at 50% (Medium) for 1-2 minutes, or until hot, stirring once.

3 Strain off the cooking juices and reserve. Divide the scallops and mushrooms among four small scallop shells or ramekins. Cover tightly and set aside.

4 To make the sauce: place the butter in a 1.1L / 2pt bowl, cover and microwave at 100% (High) for 45-60 seconds, or until it melts. Stir in the flour, milk and some of the reserved cooking liquid. Microwave at 100% (High) for 1½-2 minutes, or until smooth and thick,

JAMES JACKSON

Above: *Golden Fish Gratin*
Left: *Cheesy Scallop Gratin*

whisking twice. Add the remaining sauce ingredients and microwave at 50% (Medium) for 1-1½ minutes, or until heated through, whisking once. If the sauce is too thick, add a little more of the cooking liquid.

5 Pour the sauce over the scallops. Pipe the creamed potatoes around the edges of each dish and sprinkle the centre of each dish with grated cheese. Brown briefly under a hot grill. Serve garnished with lemon slices and parsley.

Golden fish gratin

12 mins

Standing time: none

450g / 1lb smoked haddock fillets, skinned and cut into even-sized pieces
75g / 3oz Cheddar cheese, grated
65g / 2½oz canned or frozen sweetcorn
30ml / 2tbls capers
salt and pepper

SAUCE
60ml / 4tbls plain flour
275ml / ½pt milk
25g / 1oz butter

TOPPING
175g / 6oz tomatoes, sliced
2 hard-boiled eggs, shelled and sliced
50g / 2oz wholewheat breadcrumbs
30ml / 2tbls chopped parsley

SERVES 4-6

1 To make the sauce: place the flour in a large bowl and gradually whisk in the milk. Add the butter and microwave at 100% (High) for 4-5 minutes, until smooth and thick, whisking once.
2 Whisk the sauce again and add the haddock pieces. Cover and microwave at 100% (High) for 3 minutes, or until the fish is warmed through.
3 Stir in the cheese, sweetcorn and capers, season and turn the mixture into a 1.7L / 3pt gratin dish. Arrange the sliced tomatoes and eggs on top, cover and microwave at 100% (High) for 5 minutes or until the tomatoes are heated through.
4 Mix together the breadcrumbs and parsley and spoon in a stripe down the centre of the dish. Brown under a hot grill, until the breadcrumb topping is crisp.

Crunchy-topped sole rolls

17 mins

Standing time: none

grated zest of 1 lemon
450g / 1lb lemon sole fillets
100g / 4oz mushrooms, sliced

SAUCE
1 small onion, finely chopped
25g / 1oz butter
60ml / 4tbls plain flour
10ml / 2tsp chopped tarragon or 5ml / 1tsp dried
150ml / ¼pt water
125ml / 4fl oz dry white wine
30ml / 2tbls single cream
salt and pepper

TOPPING
100g / 4oz fresh white breadcrumbs

50g / 2oz Cheddar cheese, grated
40g / 1½oz walnuts, chopped

SERVES 4

1 To make the sauce: place the onion and butter in a large bowl, cover and microwave at 100% (High) for 5 minutes, or until the onion is tender, stirring twice.
2 Stir in the flour and tarragon. Whisk in the water and wine and microwave at 100% (High) for 2 minutes, or until smooth and thick, whisking once. Whisk again, adding the cream, and season.
3 Sprinkle the lemon zest over the skinned sole fillets, season lightly and roll up. Place the rolls in a 1.4L / 2½pt dish and scatter the mushrooms over the top.
4 Pour over the sauce, cover and microwave at 100% (High) for 10 minutes, or until the fish is cooked through, giving the dish a half turn after 5 minutes.
5 To make the topping: mix all the ingredients together in a small bowl. Spoon the mixture over the fish and brown under a hot grill, until crisp.

Crunchy-topped Sole Rolls

PAUL GRATER

145

Cajun prawns

12½ mins

Standing time: none

This spicy prawn dish comes from the American south.

1 small green pepper, seeded and chopped
3 spring onions, chopped
1 garlic clove, crushed
1.5ml / ¼tsp each dry mustard and chilli powder
pinch of dried thyme
200g / 7oz can tomato sauce
100g / 4oz fresh scallops, cut in half
1.5ml / ¼tsp salt
1.5ml / ¼tsp sugar
225g / 8oz cooked, peeled prawns

TOPPING
15ml / 1tbls butter or margarine
25g / 1oz wholewheat breadcrumbs
pinch of pepper
pinch of cayenne pepper

SERVES 4

1 To make the topping: place the butter or margarine in a small bowl and microwave, covered, at 100% (High) for 30-60 seconds, or until the butter has melted. Stir in the remaining topping ingredients and set aside.
2 Mix the green pepper, spring onions, garlic, mustard, chilli powder and thyme in a 1.1L / 2pt casserole. Cover and microwave at 100% (High) for 2-4 minutes, or until the onion is tender, stirring once.

3 Stir in the tomato sauce, scallops, salt and sugar. Microwave at 70% (Medium-High) for 6-8 minutes, or until the scallops are opaque, stirring twice.
4 Add the prawns, stir and spoon the mixture into four individual serving dishes. Microwave for 4 minutes, or until the prawns are heated through, rearranging once. Add the crumb topping and brown briefly under a hot grill.

Ritzy fish crumble

6 mins

Standing time: 3-4 mins

1 onion, chopped
1 stalk celery, chopped
15ml / 1tbls butter or margarine
1 garlic clove, minced
30ml / 2tbls red wine
pinch each of dried rosemary, dried marjoram and pepper
350g / 12oz white fish fillets, about 12mm / ½in thick, cut into 4 even-sized pieces
25g / 1oz mushrooms, sliced

TOPPING
50g / 2oz fresh wholewheat breadcrumbs
25g / 1oz Cheddar cheese, grated
15ml / 1tbls chopped parsley

SERVES 4

1 Combine the onion, celery, butter or margarine and garlic in a 23cm / 9in square dish. Cover and microwave at 100% (High) for 2-3 minutes, or until the onion is tender, stirring twice. Stir in the wine, herbs and pepper.
2 Arrange the fish fillets on top with the thinner ends towards the centre of the dish and spoon over the vegetable and wine mixture. Add the mushrooms.
3 Make the topping: mix all the ingredients together and sprinkle evenly over the fish. Cover and microwave at 100% (High) for 4-6 minutes, or until the fish flakes with a fork, giving the dish a half turn after 2 minutes. Brown briefly under a hot grill, if liked. Leave to stand for 3-4 minutes before serving.

Cajun Prawns

Microwaving crab

Crab has a deliciously subtle flavour that gives a taste of luxury to all sorts of recipes. Whether in a starring role or used to complement other food, it turns a meal into a feast.

Of all shellfish, crab is perhaps the most versatile — and also arguably the most tasty. Though superb cold in salads and sandwiches, it can also be served in a range of hot dishes, in soups, in a simple sauce or used to stuff vegetables or fish.

Cooked fresh crabs are available all year round from fishmongers and increasingly from fish counters in supermarkets. A crab can weigh up to 3.6kg / 8lb, but the most widely sold and the tastiest are the smaller ones, weighing 400-700g / 14oz-1½lb each. This will provide between 100-225g / 4-8oz crabmeat, depending on how handy you are with pliers and skewer!

Test for freshness by holding it and shaking it gently. The crab should have a pleasant smell, feel heavy for its size with no sound of water or loose meat inside.

Most of the meat in a crab is in the shell itself and in the two large claws. Flesh from the claws and

Crab Creole

147

legs is customarily removed using a lobster cracker (similar to a nut cracker) and a long thin lobster pick. However pliers, a hammer or a rolling pin and a long skewer work equally well. There is also a technique for breaking into the shell (see steps, right). Always discard the grey gills (dead man's fingers) from under the body as these are inedible.

Since the crab is already cooked, hot dishes need only be microwaved for a few minutes. This will heat the food, without overcooking it and ruining the flavour.

Crab creole

$7\frac{3}{4}$ mins

Standing time: 3 mins

$4 \times 700g$ / $1\frac{1}{2}$lb fresh cooked crabs, prepared, shells reserved
25g / 1oz butter
$\frac{1}{2}$ small onion, chopped
25g / 1oz mushrooms, sliced
15ml / 1tbls plain flour
125ml / 4fl oz dry white wine
pinch of saffron
1.5ml / $\frac{1}{4}$tsp curry paste
30ml / 2tbls chilli relish
$\frac{1}{2} \times 200g$ / 7oz can pimientos, drained and sliced
45ml / 3tbls double cream
salt and pepper
50g / 2oz Gruyère cheese
endive, to garnish

SERVES 4

How to prepare fresh crab

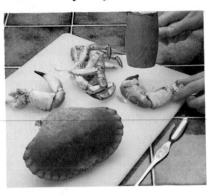

Place *cooked crab on board; twist off legs and claws. Crack with hammer or rolling pin. Remove flesh; use a skewer to remove meat from crevices and legs. Reserve small legs for decoration. Place meat in bowl.*

Turn *the crab on its back. Hold tail and gently pull away body and tail from outer shell. Discard mouth and stomach sac. Scrape out brown meat and any coral from inside shell; place in separate bowl.*

Pull off *and discard the grey gills (dead man's fingers) from body of crab. Cut body in two, scoop out white meat from leg sockets and central sections with skewer.*

Using *a hammer or rolling pin, gently tap out the thin ridge of shell back to natural dark line near scalloped edge. Wash and dry shell thoroughly for using in recipe.*

How to microwave Crab creole

Microwave *butter in covered bowl at 100% (High) for 15-30 seconds until melted. Add onion and mushrooms, cover and microwave for a further 2 minutes, stirring once. Stir in flour; blend in wine until smooth.*

Add *saffron, curry paste and chilli relish; microwave at 100% (High) for 2 minutes, until thickened; stir once. Add pimientos and cream; season. Divide brown and white crabmeat between shells. Grate cheese.*

Cover *crabmeat with sauce; sprinkle over cheese. Arrange on a dish; microwave at 100% (High) for $3\frac{1}{2}$-4 minutes, until bubbling and hot. Cover loosely with foil, stand for 3 minutes. Garnish with crab legs and endive.*

148

Seafood bisque

7 mins

Standing time: none

299g / 10.4oz can condensed
  cream of smoked salmon soup
  or crab bisque
150ml / ¼pt single cream
30ml / 2tbls brandy or sherry
30ml / 2tbls tomato purée or paste
salt and pepper
10ml / 2tsp lemon juice
175g / 6oz crabmeat (see Cook's
  notes, page 151), lightly flaked
mustard and cress, to garnish

SERVES 4-6

1 Make up soup with water, following directions on can.
2 Stir in single cream, brandy or sherry, tomato purée, seasoning and lemon juice.

3 Cover with vented cling film and microwave at 100% (High) for 4 minutes, until just warm, stirring the soup gently once or twice during cooking.
4 Stir in the crabmeat, cover and microwave for a further 3 minutes, stirring once.
5 Serve the bisque immediately, garnished with a sprinkling of mustard and cress leaves.

Freezer notes

To thaw 225g / 8oz crabmeat, remove from container but leave in polythene wrapping. Microwave at 20-30% (Defrost) for 3½-4 minutes. Stand for 2 minutes. Flake lightly before using.

Seafood Bisque

Crab-stuffed tomatoes

3½ mins

Standing time: none

These make a tasty and simple starter. Prepare ahead and heat through (see step 5) before serving. Or serve cold — they are delicious either way.

2 spring onions, finely chopped
¼ small green pepper, chopped
5ml / 1tsp oil
170g / 6oz can crabmeat, drained
  and lightly flaked
5ml / 1tsp chopped parsley
1.5ml / ¼tsp dried dillweed
5ml / 1tsp lemon juice
30ml / 2tbls mayonnaise
45ml / 3tbls dried breadcrumbs
salt and pepper
8 tomatoes

SERVES 4

1 Place onions, green pepper and oil in a bowl, cover and microwave at 100% (High) for 1 minute, stirring once, until vegetables have softened.
2 Stir in crabmeat, parsley, dill, lemon juice, mayonnaise, breadcrumbs and seasoning.
3 Cut a 6mm / ¼in slice from the top of each tomato. Chop this finely and add to crab mixture. Scoop out middle of tomatoes and season the insides with a little salt and pepper.
4 Fill scooped out tomatoes with crab mixture.
5 Arrange tomatoes in a circle on a plate and microwave at 100% (High) for 2½-3 minutes until heated through.

Microtips

To make the tomatoes more stable and prevent them from falling over during cooking, cut a very thin slice off the base before filling the centres with the crab mixture. Chop this finely and add to filling.

The insides of the scooped-out tomatoes can be reserved for use in another dish, such as stew or soup. Refrigerate the pulp and use it within two days.

149

Crab-stuffed sole

<table><tr><td>17½
mins</td></tr></table>

Standing time: 5 mins

½ onion, chopped
½ green pepper, chopped
15ml / 1tbls olive oil
170g / 6oz can white crabmeat
  lightly flaked
30ml / 2tbls fresh breadcrumbs
10ml / 2tsp chopped parsley
15ml / 1tbls lemon juice
salt and pepper
2 sole or flounder fillets, about
  225g / 8oz each, skinned
150ml / ¼pt tomato juice
1.5ml / ¼tsp dried oregano
5ml / 1tsp chopped fresh basil
  or 1.5ml / ¼tsp dried
1.5ml / ¼tsp caster sugar
2-3 lemon slices, halved

SERVES 4

How to microwave Crab-stuffed sole

Mix *onion, pepper and oil in a large bowl. Cover and microwave at 100% (High) for 3½-4 minutes, until tender, stirring once.*

Add *the crabmeat, breadcrumbs, chopped parsley, 5ml / 1tsp of the lemon juice and seasoning and stir to mix thoroughly.*

Arrange *one sole fillet on a microwave roasting rack. Spoon the crab mixture over the fish and place the second sole fillet on top.*

Mix *tomato juice, oregano, basil, remaining lemon juice, sugar and seasoning in a bowl. Microwave at 100% (High) for 5 minutes until bubbling and slightly thickened.*

Spoon *a little of the sauce over the stuffed sole and top with lemon slices. Cover with buttered greaseproof paper and microwave at 50% (Medium) for 4-5 minutes.*

Turn *dish and cook for a further 4-5 minutes, until sole flakes easily. Stand, covered, for 5 minutes. Meanwhile, reheat sauce for 1 minute. Slice fish and serve.*

150

Baked eggs with crab

5 mins

Standing time: 2-3 mins

175g / 6oz crabmeat, flaked
3 slices processed cheese
4 eggs
paprika

SERVES 4

Cook's notes

Although fresh crab is best, canned and frozen crab both make excellent and simple alternatives.

Some fishmongers sell crabmeat which has been prepared, returned to the shell, then frozen. Use this type if making Crab Creole, where the crab shell is required for serving.

How to microwave Baked eggs with crab

Reserve *one-quarter of flaked crabmeat. Divide rest between four lightly-oiled ramekins. Cut two cheese slices into four pieces; place two pieces in each dish.*

Break *an egg into each dish; sprinkle over reserved crabmeat. Cut third cheese slice into eight strips. Arrange on top of eggs. Sprinkle with paprika.*

Cover *dishes with cling film. Microwave at 50% (Medium) for 5-6 minutes for soft eggs or for 6-7 minutes if you prefer them more firmly cooked.*

Allow *to stand for 2-3 minutes, until eggs are soft or firmly set. Baked eggs with crab make a stylish starter or lunch. Serve with buttered brown bread.*

151

Using frozen prawns

A packet of frozen prawns in the freezer can give you a delicious meal in minutes. Thaw them in your microwave, then combine with simple ingredients for tasty dishes.

Prawns inhabit inshore waters throughout the world and are grey or almost transparent before cooking and acquire their familiar pink colour only when cooked.

A cooked prawn is a healthy pink colour, as seen on the fishmonger's slab (a few top fishmongers, freezer centres and Chinese supermarkets do sell raw prawns).

Top quality prawns are frozen in the shell, which helps to keep the flesh moist and particularly delicious to eat. (The heads and shells can be used to flavour sauces and soups.) However, ready-peeled prawns are far more convenient to use, and in many dishes the difference is not noticeable.

Always thaw prawns, then microwave immediately. You will find hardly any fishy smell escapes during cooking. For hot dishes, microwaving times will depend on the recipe; beware not to overcook, as this will make prawns tough.

Saucy Prawns

152

How to thaw prawns

To thaw *less than 450g / 1lb frozen prawns: arrange in a single layer in a shallow dish, cover with cling film rolled back at one edge and microwave at 20-30% (Defrost) for 1-2 minutes.*

To thaw *450g / 1lb prawns in a plastic pack: Leave prawns in the pack (provided it is not made of foil) and roll back the corner of the lid. Microwave at 20-30% (Defrost) for 3 minutes.*

Break *up any frozen lumps as soon as possible and stir prawns gently, pushing the outside prawns to the centre of the dish, and those in the centre to the outside of the dish.*

Microwave *at 20-30% (Defrost) for 1-2 minutes for less than 450 / 1lb; 3 minutes for 450 / 1lb. Prawns should be soft in centre but still cold.*

Drain *the prawns well on absorbent paper and cook them immediatetly (see recipes) or serve them quickly, if eating cold. Peel if necessary.*

Microtips

You can freeze prawns which have been cooked in their shells. You may have been lucky enough to catch your own or simply have bought in bulk from the fishmonger. Provided they have been well drained before freezing, whole prawns should remain loose when frozen. Microwave at 20-30% (Defrost) for 3-4 minutes, rearranging the prawns once to bring inside prawns to the outside. Stand for 2-3 minutes.

RAY DUNS

Prawns in butter sauce

8½ mins

Standing time: none

50g / 2oz butter
75ml / 3fl oz white wine
30ml / 2tbls lemon juice
15ml / 1tbls sugar
15ml / 1tbls cornflour
5ml / 1tsp snipped chives
450g / 1lb frozen peeled prawns, thawed (see above)

SERVES 4

1 In a 1.4L / 2½pt casserole, melt the butter at 100% (High) for 30-60 seconds. Stir in all the ingredients except the prawns. Cook for 2 minutes at 100% (High).
2 Stir in the prawns, cover with absorbent paper and microwave at 100% (High) for 6 minutes. Stir after 3 minutes. Serve with rice.

153

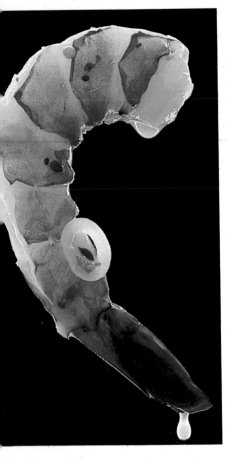

Prawns and spinach

43½ mins

Standing time: 5 mins

100g / 4oz Cheddar cheese, grated
150g / 5oz button mushrooms,
  cooked and sliced
45ml / 3tbls dry sherry
salt and pepper
450g / 1lb frozen peeled prawns,
  thawed (see page 153)
15g / ½oz butter
45ml / 3tbls seasoned fresh
  breadcrumbs
10ml / 2tsp dried parsley
pinch of paprika
900g / 2lb packet frozen chopped
  spinach

WHITE SAUCE
25g / 1oz butter or margarine
25g / 1oz plain flour
275ml / ½pt milk

SERVES 4-6

1 First prepare the white sauce. Put the butter in a 575ml / 1pt jug and microwave at 100% (High) for 20 seconds until just melted. Stir in the flour and then blend in the milk until smooth. Microwave at 100% (High) for about 5 minutes, stirring every 1½ minutes until sauce is thick and smooth. Season to taste with salt and pepper.
2 In a medium-sized bowl, mix together the white sauce, cheese, mushrooms, sherry, salt, pepper and prawns.
3 Place the butter in a small bowl and microwave at 100% (High) for 15-30 seconds. Stir in the breadcrumbs, parsley and paprika.
4 Make a small hole in the packet of frozen spinach and place in the cooker. Microwave at 100% (High) for about 12 minutes or until warm. Shake the packet once or twice during heating. Drain the liquid from the spinach, pressing well.
5 Turn the prawn mixture into a casserole and cover with cling film rolled back at one edge. Microwave at 30% (Low) for 12-16 minutes. Stir gently every 5 minutes.
6 Spread the spinach over the base of a shallow 25 × 20cm / 10 × 8in dish. Spoon the prawn mixture evenly over the top and cover with cling film rolled back at one edge. Microwave at 100% (High) for 5 minutes.
7 Gently rearrange the prawns, re-cover and microwave at 50% (Medium) for 9-12 minutes, or until the prawns are heated through. Cover and leave to stand for 5 minutes before serving.

Pickled prawns

6 mins

Standing time: none

150ml / ¼pt beer
1 bay leaf
7.5ml / 1½tsp whole pickling
  spice
1 small onion, thinly sliced
2.5ml / ½tsp salt
225g / 8oz frozen peeled prawns,
  thawed (see page 153)

SERVES 2

1 Combine all the ingredients except the prawns in a 1.4L / 2½pt casserole. Cover with cling film, rolled back at one edge.
2 Microwave at 100% (High) for 3-4 minutes or until boiling.
3 Stir in the prawns, cover and microwave at 50% (Medium) for 3-4 minutes. Stir after 2 minutes. Cool then chill before serving. Discard the pickling spice and serve with crusty bread.

Above: *Pickled Prawns*
Right: *Prawns and Spinach*

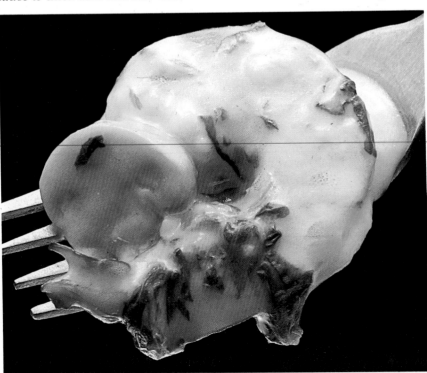

Prawn and rice medley

27¼ mins

Standing time: 5 mins

This delicious concoction would make an excellent quick and easy informal party dish.

25g / 1oz butter
25g / 1oz fresh brown breadcrumbs
275g / 10oz packet frozen rice with peas and mushrooms
170g / 6oz packet long-grain rice with wild rice
298g / 10½oz can crab bisque
575ml / 1pt hot water
350g / 12oz frozen peeled prawns, thawed (see page 153)

SERVES 4

1 Place the butter in a small bowl and microwave at 100% (High) for 15-30 seconds or until melted. Stir in the breadcrumbs and set aside.
2 Make a small hole in the frozen rice packet and microwave at 100% (High) for 3-4 minutes, or until warm.
3 Combine the long-grain and wild rice, soup and water in a 1.7L / 3pt casserole. Cover and microwave at 100% (High) for 10 minutes.
4 Stir in the heated rice, then cover and microwave at 100% (High) for 10 minutes. Stir in the prawns, re-cover and microwave for a further 4 minutes at 100% (High).
5 Stand for 5 minutes. Serve sprinkled with reserved breadcrumbs.

Microtips

If you have a quantity of left-over cooked rice, use it in place of the bag of vegetable rice. Use 200g / 7oz rice to 75g / 3oz cooked diced mixed vegetables. Mix them together in an 850ml / 1½pt casserole with 15ml / 1tbls water. Cover with cling film rolled back at one edge, and microwave at 70% (Medium-High) for 2½-3 minutes or until heated through. Use this rice for the recipe in the same way as the frozen rice with vegetables.

Saucy prawns

7 mins

Standing time: none

1 small green pepper, seeded and chopped
1 small onion, chopped
225g / 8oz jar Italian-style tomato sauce
large pinch of garlic salt
450g / 1lb frozen peeled prawns, thawed (see page 153)
boiled rice, to serve
lemon twists, to garnish

SERVES 4

1 Mix the pepper and onion in a 1.7L 3pt casserole and microwave at 100% (High) for 2 minutes, until slightly softened.
2 Add the tomato sauce, garlic salt and prawns. Cover with cling film rolled back at one edge. Microwave at 100% (High) for 5-7 minutes, stirring once during cooking and on removal from the cooker, to ensure the heat has been evenly distributed. Garnish and serve with boiled rice.

Seafood starters

Make appetizers the highlight of the meal with these tempting fishy treats. From a grand seafood platter to an informal hot dip, these recipes set the scene for happy entertaining.

Choose seafood for an interesting variety of appetizers. For the right balance in a special menu, these tasty appetizers fit the bill.

Menu planning
Menu planning usually begins by choosing the main course; a decision on the appetizer can be taken in the light of this. With a particularly heavy meat main course, one of the lighter appetizers such as Orange Shrimp Kebabs will be a good choice. Or try building an unusual seafood menu around the starter. Choose a fairly substantial dish, such as the Crab Quiches or Mushroom and Scallop Bites, to precede a lighter fish main course. If liked, ring the changes by serving the appetizer with pre-dinner drinks — a dip is ideal for an informal occasion.

Preparing and microwaving

The preparation of these appetizers ranges from the very simple to the slightly more time consuming, depending on the ingredients. Using canned or cooked, frozen fish ensures speedy — and delicious — results. Fresh seafood may require a little extra preparation, but the results give a real sense of luxury to the meal.

Seafood should be served on the day it is bought: make sure shells are well scrubbed and rinsed to remove sand and grit. When mic-rowaving, take care not to over-cook or what should be plump and juicy will be tough and disappointing. A gentle 50% (Medium) is often the answer for heating through an assembled dish, just before serving.

Appetizer Platter

Appetizer platter

11½ mins

Standing time: 5½ mins

14 cooked Mediterranean prawns, peeled but with tails left on
450g / 1lb small finger carrots
100ml / 3½fl oz water
100g / 4oz broccoli florets
225g / 8oz mussels in their shells, scrubbed
lemon wedges, to garnish

MARINADE
15ml / 1tbls white wine vinegar
15ml / 1tbls light soy sauce
15ml / 1tbls tomato ketchup

BUTTER SAUCE
100g / 4oz butter
juice and zest of 1 lemon
1 garlic clove, crushed
15ml / 1tbls chopped parsley

SERVES 6-8

1 Mix together the marinade ingredients in a shallow dish. Curl the head end of each prawn to the tail and secure with a cocktail stick; place in the marinade, cover and chill for at least 2 hours.

2 Place the carrots in a 1.1L / 2pt bowl with 30ml / 2tbls water, cover and microwave at 100% (High) for 4-4½ minutes, or until just tender but still quite crisp, stirring once. Stand, covered, for 5½ minutes.
3 Place the broccoli in an 850ml / 1½pt bowl with 15ml / 1tbls water. Cover and microwave at 100% (High) for 1½-2 minutes, or until tender crisp, rearranging once. Stand, covered for 4 minutes.
4 Tap any open mussel shells: if they do not close immediately, discard them. Place in a 1.7L / 3pt bowl with the remaining water; cover and microwave at 100% (High) for 2-3 minutes, stirring once. At the end of cooking all the shells should be open; discard any mussels that remain closed.
5 Place all the sauce ingredients in a 1.1L / 2pt sauceboat. Cover and microwave at 100% (High) for 2 minutes, or until melted and warmed through.
6 Drain the carrots, broccoli and mussels and arrange on a large platter. Remove the cocktail sticks from the prawns and add the prawns to the platter. Pour a little of the butter sauce over the vegetables and seafood so that they are lightly glazed.
7 Microwave the platter, covered with cling film, at 50% (Medium) for 2-2½ minutes, until hot through, rotating the dish once. Serve garnished with lemon wedges, with the remaining butter sauce handed separately.

How to choose and prepare fresh mussels

When buying *fresh mussels (or other bivalves), check shells are shut tight, or shut as soon as tapped. Discard any open ones.*

Scrub *shells under cold running water; scrape off barnacles and snip away beards. Soak for 1-2 hours in fresh water, then lift out and use.*

157

Mushroom and scallop bites

9¾ mins

Standing time: none

12 thawed shelled Queen
  scallops (total weight about
  225g / 8oz), see Freezer notes,
  page 160
12 large button mushrooms,
  stalks removed

MARINADE
125ml / 4fl oz sherry
15ml / 1tbls olive oil
2 spring onions, sliced
1 garlic clove, crushed

TOPPING
25g / 1oz butter
**65g / 2½oz seasoned fresh white
  breadcrumbs**
15ml / 1tbls chopped parsley

MAKES 12

1 Combine the marinade ingredients in a shallow dish. Cover and
microwave at 100% (High) for
1½-2 minutes, or until boiling.
Cool slightly, then add the scallops; toss to coat, then cover and
chill for at least 2 hours.
2 Place the butter for the topping
in a small bowl. Cover and microwave at 100% (High) for 20-30
seconds, or until it melts. Stir in
the breadcrumbs and parsley.
3 Drain the scallops and place one
scallop in each mushroom cap.
Sprinkle over the topping and
press down lightly.
4 Arrange half of the stuffed
mushrooms in a ring around the
edge of a large plate lined with
absorbent paper. Cover with absorbent paper and microwave at
50% (Medium) for 4-5 minutes, or
until the scallops are firm and
opaque, rotating the plate every
minute. Repeat with the remaining mushrooms.

Clams royale

12½ mins

Standing time: none

**6 medium-sized clams in their
  shells, scrubbed**
1.1L / 2pt water
50g / 2oz butter
15ml / 1tbls chopped parsley
10ml / 2tsp lemon juice
2.5ml / ½tsp paprika
1.5ml / ¼tsp dried thyme
salt and pepper to taste
50g / 2oz cooked ham, chopped
50g / 2oz fresh breadcrumbs
thyme to garnish

SERVES 6

1 Discard any clams with broken
or open shells. Rinse under running water to remove any sand.
2 Microwave the water in a 3.4L /

Clams Royale

6pt casserole at 100% (High) for
4½-5 minutes, or until boiling.
Add the clams, cover and microwave at 100% (High) for 4-5½
minutes, or until the shells open.
Use a slotted spoon to lift the
clams out of the casserole as they
open. Discard any closed clams.
3 Remove the clams from the
shells and reserve six shell halves
for serving. Mince the clams.
4 Combine the butter, parsley,
lemon juice, paprika, thyme and
seasoning in a small bowl. Cover
and microwave at 100% (High) for
1-1½ minutes, until bubbling.
5 Stir in the ham, breadcrumbs
and minced clams. Divide the mixture equally amongst the reserved
shells. Arrange in a ring on a plate
and microwave at 50% (Medium)
for 3-4 minutes, until hot.

Cook's notes

*Queen scallops are a smaller variety
of scallop, and they have a small
pink shell. They are ideal for using
whole in stuffings, and are also
available frozen.*

158

Scallop pockets

3 mins

Standing time: 2 mins

12 frozen scallops, thawed (see Freezer notes, page 160)
6 slices Danish salami, halved

CRUMB TOPPING
15ml / 1tbls grated Parmesan cheese
5ml / 1tsp chopped parsley
pepper
30ml / 2tbls fresh breadcrumbs

SERVES 4

1 Cut a slit lengthways down the centre of each scallop, but do not cut right through. Stuff each scallop with a piece of salami.
2 Arrange the scallops in a circle on a plate lined with absorbent paper. Set aside.
3 Combine the topping ingredients in a small bowl and mix well. Sprinkle the topping equally over the scallops.
4 Microwave at 50% (Medium) for 3-3½ minutes, or until the scallops are firm and opaque, rotating the plate a half turn once. Stand for 2 minutes; serve hot.

Right: *Mushroom and Scallop Bites*
Below: *Scallop Pockets*

159

Salmon canapés 5 mins

Standing time: none

Serve these tasty toasts as an informal appetizer with drinks, before sitting down to eat.

**8-10 crisp rye bread wafers
cucumber twists, to garnish**

TOPPING
**50g / 2oz mushrooms, chopped
½ green pepper, seeded and
   finely chopped
1 small onion, chopped
213g / 7½oz can red salmon,
   drained and flaked
10cm / 4in piece of cucumber,
   coarsely grated
50g / 2oz ricotta or cottage cheese
45ml / 3tbls grated Parmesan
   cheese
2.5ml / ½tsp Worcestershire
   sauce
1.5ml / ¼tsp dillweed
salt and pepper**

SERVES 4-6

1 Combine the mushrooms, green pepper and onion in a 1.7L / 3pt bowl. Cover and microwave at 100% (High) for 3-4 minutes, or until the onion is tender, stirring once.
2 Beat in all the remaining topping ingredients, seasoning to taste. Spread the mixture thickly on the rye bread wafers.
3 Cut each wafer into quarters across the width and arrange half the slices on a plate lined with absorbent paper.
4 Microwave at 50% (Medium) for 1-2 minutes, or until hot, rotating the dish a half turn once. Repeat with remaining canapés. Garnish with cucumber twists.

Hot shrimp dip 6½ mins

Standing time: 5 mins

**1 celery stalk, chopped
2 spring onions, sliced
1 garlic clove, crushed
15g / ½oz butter or margarine
2.5ml / ½tsp ground cumin
75g / 3oz full-fat soft cheese
150g / 5oz natural yoghurt
15ml / 1tbls tomato ketchup
215g / 7½oz can shrimps, drained
4 ocean sticks (total weight about
   65g / 2½oz), chopped
salt and pepper
75g / 3oz Cheddar cheese, grated
bread sticks, for dipping**

SERVES 4

Hot Shrimp Dip

1 Combine the celery, onions, garlic, butter or margarine and cumin in a 1.1L / 2pt mixing bowl. Cover and microwave at 100% (High) for 2-3 minutes, or until the vegetables are tender.
2 Put the full-fat soft cheese in a small bowl. Cover and microwave at 50% (Medium) for 30-45 seconds, or until softened. Beat into the vegetables.
3 Blend in the yoghurt and ketchup, shrimps and ocean sticks. Season to taste and sprinkle with the grated cheese.
4 Microwave at 50% (Medium) for 4-5 minutes, or until the cheese melts and the dip is hot, stirring three times. Stand for 5 minutes, then serve while still hot.

Freezer notes

To thaw 225g / 8oz scallops, place in a single layer in a shallow dish, cover and microwave at 30% (Low) for 3-4 minutes, turning them over halfway through; drain and stand for 5 minutes to complete thawing before cooking.

Clam-stuffed mushrooms

12 mins

Standing time: none

3 bacon rashers, rinds removed,
  chopped
225g / 8oz mushrooms
1 small onion, finely chopped
1.5ml / ¼tsp dried marjoram
1.5ml /¼tsp rubbed sage leaves
salt and pepper
45ml / 3tbls seasoned fresh white
  breadcrumbs
15ml / 1tbls chopped parsley
190g / 6½oz can minced clams,
  drained

SERVES 4-6

1 Place bacon in a bowl. Cover with absorbent paper and microwave at 100% (High) for 2½-3½ minutes, until crisp. Stir once. Drain.
2 Remove the mushroom stalks and chop finely. Mix them in another bowl with the onion, herbs and seasoning. Cover and microwave at 100% (High) for 2½-3 minutes, until tender. Stir once.
3 Stir in the bacon, breadcrumbs, parsley and clams. Spoon into the mushroom caps. Arrange half of the mushrooms in a ring around the edge of a plate lined with absorbent paper.
4 Microwave at 100% (High) for 3½-4 minutes or until hot, rotating the plate once. Repeat.

Orange shrimp kebabs

5 mins

Standing time: none

6 Mediterranean prawns, peeled
  but with tails left on
12 button mushrooms
12 spring onion tassels
1 small orange cut into six
  wedges

MARINADE
45ml / 3tbls olive oil
15ml / 1tbls orange juice
1 garlic clove, crushed

SERVES 6

1 Combine the marinade ingredients in a shallow bowl and add the prawns. Turn to coat, then cover and chill for two hours.
2 Assemble the kebabs on six 15cm / 6in wooden skewers: thread a mushroom, then a spring onion, prawn, orange wedge, spring onion and mushroom on each skewer.
3 Arrange the skewers on a roasting rack and baste with marinade. Cover with vented film and microwave at 50% (Medium) for 5-6 minutes, or until the prawns are opaque. Turn the skewers over halfway through and baste with more marinade.

Crab scallops

7 mins

Standing time: 5 mins

170g / 6oz can crab meat, drained
1 large carrot, grated
75g / 3oz Cheddar cheese, grated
2 spring onions, sliced
15ml / 1tbls plain flour
1.5ml / ¼tsp ground nutmeg
salt and pepper

150ml / ¼pt single cream
1 egg
paprika, to sprinkle

SERVES 4

1 Mix together the crab meat, carrot, cheese, onions, flour, nutmeg and seasoning. Divide the mixture equally between four scallop shells or ramekin dishes. Arrange in a circle on a large, round platter.
2 In a small bowl, beat the cream and egg together and season to taste with salt and pepper. Spoon about 30ml / 2tbls of this mixture over each shell or dish.
3 Sprinkle with paprika, then cover with cling film and microwave at 50% (Medium) for 6 minutes, rotating the shells a quarter turn three times. Remove the cling film and microwave for a further 1-2 minutes, or until just set in the centre. Stand for 5 minutes, then serve as a substantial starter or light lunch with salad.

Crab Scallops

161

Fish and seafood salads

For simply sensational salads that look as good as they taste, fish and seafood salads are hard to beat. From light suppers to extravagant appetizers, these recipes are sure to please.

Fish and seafood combined with crisp, fresh salad vegetables or creamy pasta mixtures are delicious and nutritious. What's more, they take just a few minutes to plan and prepare when you have the microwave to help. As an added bonus, both fish and seafood are particularly succulent when cooked in the microwave, while vegetables remain crisp and colourful.

Conveniently, many fish and seafood are available frozen, and it is a good idea to keep a varied

stock in the freezer for last minute meals — especially as they take only a few minutes to thaw in the microwave. Always check the bag for the manufacturer's recommended storage times.

If seafood is scarce or too expensive, choose alternatives. Ocean sticks can be used instead of lobster or crab, for instance, or use canned crab meat instead. A firm, meaty white fish can be used to replace scallops. Use a well-flavoured firm, white fish such as cod or haddock which also holds its shape well.

Serving

If possible, make these salads in advance and chill them well before serving to allow the flavours to blend. Minty new potatoes go well with crisp fish salads, while hot herb, garlic or onion bread is especially good with seafood and pasta salads. They make delicious informal summer lunches served with a crisp green salad.

Seafood special

4 mins

Standing time: 5 mins

450g / 1lb scallops (see Freezer notes, page 167)
700g / 1½lb large, cooked prawns in their shells
1 Cos lettuce, separated into leaves
100-175g / 4-6oz cooked lobster meat, shredded
1 hard-boiled egg, shelled and quartered
2 large tomatoes, cut into wedges
black olives, to serve
lemon twists, to garnish

DRESSING
150ml / ¼pt thick mayonnaise
30ml / 2tbls tomato ketchup or sauce
15ml / 1tbls double cream
squeeze lemon juice

SERVES 4-6

1 Place the scallops in a dish, cover with dampened absorbent paper and microwave at 100% (High) for 4-5 minutes, or until creamy in colour. Allow to stand for 5 minutes, then drain. Remove and reserve the pink corals. Slice the scallops and cool.
2 Shell the prawns, leaving the tail shell, if wished.
3 Arrange the lettuce leaves on a large serving platter and top with the scallops, prawns and lobster in separate piles. Add the egg, tomatoes and black olives. Garnish with lemon twists.
4 Combine all the dressing ingredients. Finely chop the reserved corals and stir in. Serve with the seafood platter.

VARIATIONS
For a more economical version use ocean sticks instead of lobster meat and white fish instead of the scallops. Microwave 175g / 6oz frozen ocean sticks at 30% (Low) for 2½-3 minutes, turning them over once. Stand for 5 minutes, then shred. Microwave 175g / 6oz skinned cod fillet in a covered dish at 100% (High) for 2-2½ minutes or until it flakes. Stand for 5 minutes, then flake coarsely.

163

PAUL GRATER

Scallop surprise

4 mins

Standing time: 5 mins

4 scallops in their shells
30ml / 2tbls white wine
1 large celery stalk, thinly
   sliced
4 pimiento stuffed olives, sliced
20g / ¾oz pine kernels
1 spring onion, thinly sliced
salt and pepper

DRESSING
30ml / 2tbls thick mayonnaise
15ml / 1tbls French dressing

TO SERVE
4 lettuce leaves
4 lemon wedges

SERVES 4

Cook's notes

*If you get scallops in hinged shells,
they should be closed. Insert a knife
just above the hinge of the shell and
prise it open. Run the blade across
the roof of the shell to sever the
internal muscle.*

How to microwave Scallop surprise

Sever *the outer rim of flesh attaching
the meat of the scallops to the shell.
Carefully remove the white muscle and
pink coral.*

Place *scallops and wine in a dish.
Cover; microwave at 100% (High) for
4-5 minutes, or until creamy. Stand for
5 minutes, then drain and slice.*

Put *scallops and remaining salad
ingredients in a bowl, and season. Mix
mayonnaise and dressing, pour over
salad and toss.*

Line *four individual serving dishes
with a lettuce leaf. Divide the scallop
salad between the dishes. Serve with
lemon wedges.*

164

Prawn and pasta salad

14 mins

Standing time: 20 mins

This is a lovely summer supper dish; also delicious for buffets.

350g / 12oz frozen cooked peeled prawns
100g / 4oz small pasta shells
575ml / 1pt boiling water
5ml / 1tsp salt
15ml / 1tbls vegetable oil
7.5cm / 3in piece cucumber, peeled, seeded and diced
40g / 1½oz black olives, stoned and thinly sliced
½ small green pepper, seeded and finely chopped

DRESSING
50ml / 2fl oz mayonnaise
50ml / 2fl oz soured cream
5ml / 1tsp lemon juice
1 spring onion, finely chopped
pinch of dillweed
salt and pepper to taste

SERVES 4-6

1 Place the frozen prawns in a large shallow dish. Cover and microwave at 30% (Low) for 4-5 minutes, or until thawed, stirring twice. Stand for 10 minutes, then rinse, drain and reserve.
2 Place the pasta shells, boiling water, salt and oil in a 2.3L / 4pt casserole. Cover and microwave at 100% (High) for 10-12 minutes, or until just tender. Allow to stand for 10 minutes, then rinse with cold water and drain thoroughly.
3 Place the prawns in a salad bowl and stir in the pasta, cucumber, olives and green pepper.
4 Combine all the dressing ingredients in a screw top jar, cover tightly and shake well to mix. Pour over the prawn and pasta salad and mix well. Chill for 2 hours.

Freezer notes

Rinse the thawed prawns under cold water to remove any remaining ice crystals from the surface. Drain well, then pat them dry with absorbent paper if necessary.

Golden rice salad

14½ mins

Standing time: none

225g / 8oz long grain rice
575ml / 1pt boiling fish stock
2.5ml / ½tsp turmeric
225g / 8oz haddock tail fillet, cut into bite-sized pieces
100g / 4oz peeled, cooked prawns
½ green pepper, seeded and sliced
½ red pepper, seeded and sliced
6 pimiento stuffed olives, sliced
90ml / 6tbls garlic salad dressing
salt and pepper

SERVES 4

1 Place the rice and stock in a 1.7L / 3pt bowl and stir in the turmeric. Cover and microwave at 100% (High) for 4 minutes, stir

Prawn and Pasta Salad

and reduce to 70% (Medium-High) for 10-12 minutes or until the liquid is absorbed. Stir twice. Set aside until cold.
2 Place the haddock in a small shallow dish. Cover and microwave at 100% (High) for 2-3 minutes or until the juices run and the fish just flakes. Cool then drain. Stir into the rice.
3 Place the red and green pepper strips in a small bowl and microwave at 100% (High) for 1-1½ minutes until just tender-crisp. Stir into the rice with the stuffed olive slices.
4 Season the salad to taste, then add the dressing and toss carefully to coat. Transfer to the refrigerator and chill for at least 30 minutes before serving with a crisp green salad.

Tangy cod and vegetables

9½ mins

Standing time: none

350g / 12oz cod fillets, skinned
salt and pepper
50ml / 2fl oz dry white wine
1 small onion, thinly sliced
1 garlic clove, crushed
45ml / 3tbls vegetable oil
1.5ml / ¼tsp dried fennel seeds, crushed
large pinch of cayenne pepper
225g / 8oz frozen special mixed vegetables
225g / 8oz spinach or 1 large Cos lettuce, leaves trimmed and torn into bite-size pieces
30ml / 2tbls white wine vinegar

SERVES 4

1 Cut the fish lengthways into 2.5cm / 1in strips and lay them in a rectangular dish large enough to take them in a single layer. Season lightly. Add the wine, then cover and microwave at 100% (High) for

Above: *Crunchy Seafood Salad*
Below: *Tangy Cod and Vegetables*

3½-4 minutes, or until the fish flakes easily, rearranging the pieces once. Set aside.
2 In a 1.7L / 3pt casserole, combine the onion, garlic, oil, fennel and cayenne pepper. Cover and microwave at 100% (High) for 2-3 minutes, or until the onion is tender, stirring once or twice.
3 Stir in the mixed vegetables, recover and microwave at 100% (High) for 4-5 minutes or until heated through; stir once. Cool.
4 Drain and flake the cod. Combine with the vegetables and spinach or lettuce leaves in a large salad bowl. Sprinkle with vinegar and toss to coat. Chill for at least 1 hour before serving.

Slimmer's notes

Tangy Cod and Vegetable Mix is a well-flavoured and substantial supper dish for a summer's evening, yet has only 230 Cal / 965 kJ per portion.

Crunchy seafood salad

16½ mins

Standing time: 17 mins

1 small carrot, cut into 6mm / ¼in slices
50g / 2oz frozen peas
1 garlic clove, crushed (optional)
60ml / 4tbls French dressing
100g / 4oz frozen prawns
100g / 4oz scallops, cut into pieces (see Freezer notes)
1.5ml / ¼tsp dried basil
50g / 2oz mushrooms, sliced
1 courgette, cut into 5cm / 2in long matchstick strips
175g / 6oz pasta twists
850ml / 1½pt boiling water
5ml / 1tsp salt
15ml / 1tbls vegetable oil
salt and pepper

SERVES 6-8

1 In a 1.1L / 2pt casserole, combine the carrot, peas, garlic if used and 45ml / 3tbls of the dressing. Cover and microwave at 100% (High) for 2 minutes, stirring once. Set aside.
2 Place the prawns in a small dish,

cover and microwave at 30% (Low) for 1½-2 minutes, or until thawed, stirring once. Allow to stand for 5 minutes, then rinse and drain.

3 Place the scallops in a shallow dish and sprinkle with basil. Cover with dampened absorbent paper and microwave at 100% (High) for 1-1½ minutes, or until the scallops are opaque. Allow to stand for 2 minutes, then drain.

4 Stir the scallops and prawns into the carrot mixture along with the mushrooms and courgette. Cover and chill for 1 hour.

5 Place the pasta, boiling water, salt and oil in a 2.3L / 4pt casserole. Cover and microwave at 100% (High) for 12-13 minutes, or until tender. Stand for 10 minutes. Rinse with cold water and drain well.

6 Place the pasta in a serving bowl and mix in the seafood and vegetables. Blend the remaining dressing with salt and pepper to taste, pour over the salad and toss to coat. Cover and chill for at least 2 hours before serving.

Curried prawn medley salad

10½ mins

Standing time: 10 mins

Serve this dish with rice salad for a substantial supper.

225g / 8oz broccoli florets
1 small carrot, grated
1 small onion, thinly sliced
1 garlic clove, crushed
30ml / 2tbls vegetable oil
15ml / 1tbls honey
2.5ml / ½tsp curry powder
1.5ml / ¼tsp caraway seeds
salt
good pinch of cayenne pepper
450g / 1lb large frozen cooked peeled prawns
50g / 2oz salted peanuts
lettuce leaves, to serve

SERVES 4-6

1 In a 2.3L / 4pt casserole, combine the broccoli, carrot, onion and garlic. Mix together the oil, honey, curry powder, caraway, salt and cayenne. Pour over the vegetables. Cover and microwave at 100% (High) for 4½-5 minutes or until the vegetables are tender-crisp, stirring halfway through.

2 Place the prawns in a large shallow dish. Cover and microwave at 30% (Low) for 6-7 minutes, or until thawed but icy, stirring twice during microwaving. Allow to stand for 10 minutes, then rinse and drain.

3 Stir the prawns into the vegetables. Cover and chill for 3-4 hours, stirring once or twice.

4 Stir the peanuts into the salad. Arrange lettuce leaves on a serving platter and spoon the salad mixture on top.

VARIATION
Use flaked almonds or cashew nuts instead of the peanuts.

Curried Prawn Medley Salad

Freezer notes

Fresh scallops are subject to seasonal availability. When they are unavailable use frozen scallops instead.

To thaw 100g / 4oz scallops, place in a single layer in a shallow dish, cover and microwave at 30% (Low) for 3-4 minutes, turning them over halfway through; drain and stand for 5 minutes before cooking. For 450g / 1lb frozen scallops, microwave for 8-10 minutes. Drain and stand for 5 minutes.

167

CHAPTER FOUR
MEAT AND POULTRY

Microwaved meat and poultry can be as succulent and tender as when they are cooked by slower traditional methods, and your Sunday roast beef or chicken can be ready in half the time. All you need is a little information about the best way to cook different meats in the microwave, and some advice on using browning dishes, browning agents and glazes to give your meat a lovely brown finish.

You will find all you need to know in this chapter, together with a host of recipes for everything from mince to whole stuffed turkey. The chapter covers beef, pork, lamb, veal, turkey and chicken and includes a wide range of recipes for weekday meals for the family (mince, pork chops, drumsticks), Sunday lunches (roast beef, chicken, turkey) and formal entertaining (steaks, pork tenderloin, poultry rolls). Freezing, thawing and reheating instructions are also given, so you don't have to panic if you suddenly discover you have forgotten to thaw the joint.

Casseroles are popular, both for entertaining and for family meals. They are ideal if you prefer your meat to look brown when cooked because any lack of browning is concealed by delicious gravy. A marinade can help brown, tenderize and flavour meat or poultry, before and during cooking in the microwave. Use of marinades is dealt with in detail in Chapter One (page 44) and you will find other suggestions here. Glazes, too, help to improve the appearance of some microwaved meat.

Many of the recipes in this chapter will make perfect dinner-party dishes, while others will be useful for family meals or informal occasions. The meat dish is often the most important part of the meal so you will want to be sure of getting it right. The clear instructions, helpful advice and step-by-step photographs given in this chapter will guarantee you success every time.

Roasting beef

Whether it's for Sunday lunch or a quick but appetizing midweek meal, a joint of beef roasts beautifully in the microwave. Gravy is quick and easy too.

Always cook meat from room temperature — so remove from refrigerator about one hour before cooking (unless you live in a hot climate). Joints of 1.4kg / 3lb and over will brown quite successfully in a microwave, but to increase colouring simply brush meat before cooking with a browning agent, such as a mixture of tomato sauce and brown sugar. Place in a roasting bag to further encourage browning.

Stand the joint on a microwave roasting rack or upturned plate in a roasting bag so that the meat cooks away from it juices, which can be used for gravy. Cooking times vary according to the density of the joint. The chart on page 171 gives rough guides to timings for smaller joints.

For joints over 1.4kg / 3 lb a microwave thermometer or meat probe inserted into the meatiest part of the joint will give more accurate results. Decide on doneness required and cook until the temperature reaches that in the chart. Turn the joint once halfway though the cooking time. Stand for 20 minutes after cooking, covered loosely with foil, shiny side inside.

Rib of Beef on the Bone

170

How to roast beef

Choose *red-coloured beef with creamy-coloured fat. Remove from refrigerator and stand at room temperature for 1 hour before cooking.*

Place *joint, fat side down, on a roasting rack or on an upturned tea plate so the juices can drain away. Place in a roasting bag.*

Place *on a roasting tray and fasten the roasting bag loosely with an elastic band or plastic clip, allowing room for steam to escape.*

Insert *a microwave thermometer or probe through the bag into the meatiest part of the joint to ensure the joint cooks to the desired doneness.*

Microwave *as recommended in chart. Remove when joint reaches correct finishing temperature for required doneness. Turn joint over once.*

Cover *cooked joint loosely with foil, shiny side in, and leave to stand for 20 minutes to tenderize the meat and make it easier to carve.*

Microwave times for roasting beef

CUT OF BEEF	REQUIRED DONENESS	TOTAL COOKING TIME	TIME AT 100% (HIGH)	TIME AT 50% (MEDIUM)	REMOVE AT
Rib (on the bone)	Rare	7-8 mins per lb	5 mins	Rest of calculated time	44°C / 112°F
	Medium	13-14 mins per lb	5 mins	As above	50°C / 122°F
	Well done	15 mins per lb	5 mins	As above	62°C / 144°F
Rib (boned and rolled)	Rare	11-12 mins per lb	5 mins	Rest of calculated time	40°C / 104°F
	Medium	13-14 mins per lb	5 mins	As above	50°C / 122°F
	Well Done	15-16 mins per lb	5 mins	As above	64°C / 148°F
Sirloin (boned and rolled)	Rare	8-9 mins per lb	5 mins	Rest of calculated time	40°C / 104°F
	Medium	11-12 mins per lb	5 mins	As above	52°C / 126°F
	Well Done	15-16 mins per lb	5 mins	As above	62°C / 144°F

Garlic beef

33 mins

Standing time: 20 mins

The recipe timing is for medium cooked meat.

1.4kg / 3lb sirloin of boned, rolled beef
25g / 1oz blanched almonds, halved lengthways

MARINADE
2-3 cloves garlic, crushed
10ml / 2tsp soy sauce
15ml / 1tbls tomato purée
30ml / 2tbls corn oil
15ml / 1tbls chopped parsley
15ml / 1tbls whole grain mustard

SERVES 6

1 Calculate cooking time according to chart on page 171.
2 Make small incisions in fat of joint. Insert $\frac{1}{2}$ almonds into each.
3 Combine marinade ingredients, and brush over joint. Cover and stand for 2 hours.
4 Prepare the meat for microwaving (see steps 2-4, page 171).
5 Microwave at 100% (High) for 5 minutes, then at 50% (Medium) for remainder of time. Brush joint with marinade halfway through cooking time, and turn over.
6 Stand, covered, for 20 minutes.

Gravy for roast beef

4 mins

Standing time: none

40g / 1½oz beef dripping or butter
15ml / 1tbls plain flour
salt and pepper
435ml / ¾pt warm beef stock
30ml / 2tbls red wine
150ml / ¼pt meat juices

SERVES 6

1 Place dripping into 1L / 1¾pt jug and microwave at 100% (High) for 1 minute or until very hot.
2 Stir in flour and seasoning then beef stock and wine. Microwave, uncovered, at 100% (High) for 3-4 minutes, beating every minute.
3 Stir in meat juices and serve.

172

DON LAST

Braising beef

Topside and silverside joints of beef cooked in a small amount of liquid in the microwave will be every bit as tender and juicy as when cooked in a conventional oven.

For a lean, reasonably tender cut such as topside or silverside, microwave-braising or pot roasting are the perfect cooking methods.

If you have a cooker with variable power controls, this is where it comes into its own; the slower you can cook it, the better the finished dish will be. You also need less added liquid than for conventional methods of braising, because there is little evaporation, so the juices in the finished dish will taste really meaty. As with conventional cooking, these cuts can also benefit from preliminary marinating in oil, wine and spices.

Topside and silverside of beef cannot be dry roasted in a microwave as they will not tenderize in the short cooking time. They have little marbling of fat to break up the long fibres and need added liquid and slow cooking to make them tender.

Braising beef
Braise joints in a roasting bag or casserole dish, covered with a lid or with cling film rolled back at one edge. Microwaved at 50% (Medium), these joints will be tender and juicy. However, the slower the cooking the more tender the meat will be; microwave at 30% (Low) for longer if you prefer.

The most accurate way to determine when a joint is cooked is to use a microwave thermometer, or a probe if your microwave has one. These register the internal temperature of the meat while it is in the microwave cooker.

A microwave thermometer can be left inside the meat in a roasting bag or casserole as long as there is room. If using a probe, make a slit in a roasting bag or cling film covering and insert the probe through the slit; it is not possible to use a probe in a dish with a lid.

Alternatively, if you do not have a microwave thermometer or probe, you can use a conventional meat thermometer. The meat must be removed from the microwave cooker first though, as microwaves are affected by the mercury in a conventional thermometer.

Standing time
The standing time specified in the following recipes is essential. It completes the cooking and tenderizing, allows flavours to blend and gives the juices time to settle, which makes carving easier.

How to braise beef joints in a microwave

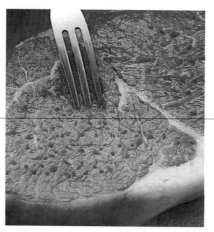

Cook's notes

Buy firm, fine-grained beef and avoid meat with a coarse-grained texture. Store the meat, covered, in the coolest part of the refrigerator and cook it as soon as possible after buying it.

Pierce *the meat deeply all over on both sides with a long-pronged fork to help ensure even cooking throughout. For extra tenderness and flavour, marinate the joint for several hours or overnight in a dish or roasting bag before microwaving.*

Place *the meat and liquid in a roasting bag or casserole. Tie the roasting bag loosely with a strip of plastic cut from the bag; cover dishes with a lid or cling film rolled back at one edge. Place the roasting bag in a baking dish.*

174

Fruity pot roast

52 mins

Standing time: 8 mins

900g-1.6kg / 2-3½lb topside of beef, trimmed of excess fat and cut into 2×4cm / 1½in thick slices
75ml / 3fl oz orange juice
30ml / 2tbls barbecue sauce
15ml / 1tbls soy sauce
5ml / 1tsp finely grated orange zest
salt and pepper
210g / 7½oz can sliced mushrooms, drained
1 onion, sliced
65ml / 2½fl oz water
22.5ml / 1½tbls cornflour
15g / 1tbls light brown sugar
1 orange, thinly sliced
parsley sprigs, to garnish

SERVES 4-8

1 Calculate the meat cooking time at 25-30 minutes per 450g / 1lb. Prick both sides of the meat slices thoroughly with a fork. Place in a 2.5-2.8L / 4½-5pt casserole dish.
2 Combine orange juice, barbecue and soy sauces, orange zest and seasoning. Pour over the meat, then add mushrooms and onion.
3 Cover with the lid or cling film, rolling back one edge a little, and microwave at 50% (Medium) for calculated time, or until meat is tender. Turn the meat over half-way through the cooking time.
4 Combine the water, cornflour and sugar in a measuring jug and pour in enough of the cooking juices to measure 300ml / 11fl oz.
5 Place the orange slices on top of meat, cover loosely with foil and leave to stand for 8 minutes.
6 Meanwhile, microwave the sauce at 100% (High) for 2-3 minutes to thicken, stirring once. Stir into remaining meat juices.
7 Slice meat thinly. Garnish with parsley sprigs and serve with the sauce and boiled potatoes.

VARIATION
Substitute lemon zest for the orange zest, 125ml / 4fl oz water and 15ml / 1tbls lemon juice for the orange juice and 2 sliced lemons for the sliced orange.

Microwave *at 50% (Medium) for half the time given in the recipe. Turn the joint over in the casserole **or** turn the roasting bag, and add the vegetables when specified in the recipe. Cover again or re-tie the roasting bag and finish microwaving.*

Leave *the joint to stand, covered, in the roasting bag or casserole for the time specified in the recipe. This is essential to complete the cooking and improve the flavour. It also makes it easier to carve the joint when serving as the meat has tenderized.*

175

Swedish pot roast

66½ mins

Standing time: 10 mins

To microwave at 30% (Low), increase the cooking time to 40-50 minutes per 450g / 1lb.

1.1-1.6kg / 2½-3½lb silverside of beef, trimmed of excess fat
2 onions, sliced
30ml/2tbls cider vinegar
30ml/2tbls golden syrup
2 bay leaves
salt and pepper
2.5ml / ½tsp ground allspice
75ml / 3fl oz water
25g / 1oz plain flour
150ml / ¼pt whipping cream

SERVES 6-8

1 Calculate meat cooking time at 25-30 minutes per 450g / 1lb. Prick the meat all over.
2 Place meat with the remaining ingredients, except the water, flour and cream, in a 2.5-2.8L / 4½-5pt casserole. Cover.
3 Microwave at 50% (Medium) for the calculated time, turning the joint over halfway through.
4 Remove the meat from the casserole, cover loosely with foil and leave to stand for 10 minutes. Skim fat from the meat juices.
5 Blend the water and flour together and stir into the meat juices. Microwave at 100% (High) for 3-4 minutes; stir twice.
6 Stir in the cream and microwave at 50% (Medium) for 1-2 minutes.
7 Serve the meat with gravy.

Barbecued beef

55 mins

Standing time: 10 mins

To microwave at 30% (Low), increase the cooking time to 35-40 minutes per 450g / 1lb.

1.1-1.6kg / 2½-3½lb silverside of beef, trimmed of excess fat
425ml / ¾pt barbecue sauce

SERVES 6-8

Above: *Swedish Pot Roast*
Below: *Barbecued Beef*

1 Calculate meat cooking time at 25-30 minutes per 450g / 1lb. Prick the meat all over.
2 Place in a roasting bag and add the sauce. Close the bag with a strip of plastic or an elastic band and leave to marinate at room temperature for 3-4 hours or overnight in the refrigerator.
3 Place the bag in a shallow dish and microwave at 50% (Medium) for the calculated time, or until the meat is tender. Turn the meat over halfway through the time.
4 Leave to stand in the bag for 10 minutes before serving.
5 Slice thinly and serve with cooking juices and mashed potatoes.

Braised topside

70 mins

Standing time: 10 mins

To microwave at 30% (Low), increase the cooking time to 60 minutes and 60-70 minutes.

1.4-1.8kg / 3-4lb topside of beef, trimmed of excess fat
1 beef stock cube
125ml / 4fl oz hot water
15ml / 1tbls Worcestershire sauce
2 large celery stalks, sliced
1 onion, cut into 8 wedges

SERVES 6-8

1 Prick meat thoroughly on both sides and place in a roasting bag.
2 Mix the stock cube with the hot water and Worcestershire sauce and add to the bag. Close the bag loosely with a strip of plastic or an elastic band, leaving space for steam to escape. Microwave at 50% (Medium) for 35 minutes.
3 Turn the meat over, add the vegetables and re-close the bag. Microwave for 35-45 minutes. Leave to stand in the bag for 10 minutes before serving.
4 Slice the meat thinly and serve with the cooking juices.

Microtip

Remove the joint from the cooker when the microwave thermometer reads 65°C / 150°F.

Fresh mince

As well as being one of our most useful convenience foods, mince also lends itself to all sorts of tasty and unusual dishes — from a substantial Dutch Omelette to spicy Middle Eastern Meatballs.

Mince cooks quickly and remarkably well in the microwave. The loose texture of the meat means the microwaves penetrate easily, so that it takes little time to cook yet still retains its flavour. Saving time in cooking means extra time for more adventurous recipes. Try enclosing mince in cabbage leaves, after softening the leaves in the microwave, then cook these little parcels in a tasty piquant sauce.

Beef and lamb mince cook equally well by microwave. Lamb mince is particularly suitable for dishes with a Middle Eastern flavour — where lamb is the principal meat. Season the meat with mint, cinnamon and cumin for Middle Eastern Meatballs.

When casseroling mince, microwave at 100% (High), stirring and breaking up the meat once or twice during cooking. Once cooked, mince should have lost its pinky colour and be an even, pale brown.

Taco Salad

Taco salad

14½ mins

Standing time: none

450g / 1lb minced beef
1 onion, chopped
432g / 15.2oz can red kidney
    beans, drained
125ml / 4fl oz water
25-40g / 1-1½oz taco seasoning
1 small lettuce, shredded
2 tomatoes, cut into chunks
½ green pepper, chopped
50g / 2oz Cheddar cheese, grated
50g / 2oz Red Leicester, grated
small packet corn chips, broken

SERVES 4

Meatballs with tangy sauce

13½ mins

Standing time: 2-3 mins

450g / 1lb minced beef
1 egg, beaten
1 carrot, grated
salt and pepper

SAUCE
15ml / 1tbls oil
½ onion, chopped
4 tomatoes, skinned, chopped
½ green pepper, in strips
2.5ml / ½tsp dried basil
15ml / 1tbls tomato purée
salt and pepper

How to microwave Taco salad

Crumble *meat into a casserole. Add onion and microwave at 100% (High) for 4½-6½ minutes. Stir once. Add beans, water and seasoning. Microwave, at 50% (Medium) for 10-13 minutes, stirring twice.*

Combine *lettuce, tomatoes and green pepper in a salad bowl. Spoon the mince and kidney bean mixture over salad and top with the grated Cheddar and Red Leicester cheese and corn chips. Serve at once.*

5ml / 1tsp cornflour blended
    with 30ml / 2tbls water

SERVES 4

1 Microwave oil and onion in a bowl at 100% (High) for 2½-3 minutes until onion is tender.
2 Add remaining sauce ingredients. Microwave covered at 100% (High) for 3-4 minutes. Stir twice.
3 Combine beef, egg, carrot and seasoning and form into 12 meatballs. Arrange on roasting rack, cover with absorbent paper and microwave at 100% (High) for 6-9 minutes. Cover, stand for 2-3 minutes. Heat sauce at 100% (High) for 2-3 minutes. Serve together.

Meatballs with Tangy Sauce

Cook's notes

Taco seasoning, a blend of various Mexican herbs and spices, is available from most supermarkets. It is normally sold in approximately 40g / 1½oz packets, which the makers recommend to use with 450g / 1lb minced beef. However, if you prefer food less spicy, cut this down a little. Alternatively, make taco seasoning by mixing together 2.5ml / ½tsp chilli powder, 5ml / 1tsp cumin, 5ml / 1tsp paprika, 5ml / 1tsp garlic powder 5ml / 1tsp oregano, salt and pepper. If wished, make up a quantity and store in an airtight container.

Cabbage rolls

23 mins

Standing time: 5 mins

8 large white cabbage leaves
450g / 1lb minced beef
1 onion, chopped
60g / 2½oz long-grain rice, cooked
1 egg
pinch of salt

SAUCE
400g / 14oz can sieved Italian tomatoes
10ml / 2tsp soft brown sugar
good pinch of dried basil

SERVES 4

Microtips

Use the microwave to help you remove whole cabbage leaves. First break off any broken or damaged leaves and trim base. Then microwave the whole cabbage at 100% (High) for 2-4 minutes or until eight outer leaves can be removed easily. Remove each outer leaf from the cabbage as soon as it is soft enough. Refrigerate the remaining cabbage for further use.

How to microwave Cabbage rolls

Cut *out hard centre rib from each cabbage leaf. Place leaves in a shallow dish, cover with cling film rolled back at one edge and microwave at 100% (High) for 3-4 minutes until the leaves are pliable.*

Combine *sauce ingredients and set aside. Then combine mince, onion, cooked rice, egg and salt and shape into 8 small loaves. Overlap cut edges of cabbage leaves and place a meat 'loaf' at base of each leaf. Roll up.*

Place *rolls, seam-side down around the edge of shallow dish. Add sauce, cover and microwave at 100% (High) for 8 minutes. Baste with sauce, turn dish and cook for 12 minutes. Stand for 5 minutes.*

179

Beef mince Stroganoff

12½ mins

Standing time: none

450g / 1lb lean minced beef
225g / 8oz mushrooms, sliced
3 spring onions, trimmed and
   roughly chopped
15ml / 1tbls tomato purée or paste
2.5ml / ½tsp mustard powder
salt and pepper
150ml / 5fl oz soured cream

SERVES 4

1 Crumble mince into a large casserole. Cover and microwave at 100% (High) for 5-6 minutes or until meat loses pink colour, stirring once.
2 Add mushrooms, spring onions, tomato purée, mustard and seasoning, stir and microwave, covered, at 100% (High) for 6-8 minutes, stirring halfway through cooking.
3 Add soured cream and microwave at 100% (High) for 1½-3 minutes until hot, stirring once.

Beef bean pot

15½ mins

Standing time: none

4 rashers streaky bacon, rinds
   removed, chopped
450g / 1lb lean minced beef
1 onion, chopped
1 apple, peeled and diced
2 × 450g / 1lb cans baked beans
   with pork sausage
15ml / 1tbls black treacle
5ml / 1tsp Hoisin barbecue sauce

SERVES 4

1 Place bacon in large casserole. Cover with absorbent paper and microwave at 100% (High) for 4½-6½ minutes or until crisp. Add minced beef, onion and apple and mix well.
2 Microwave at 100% (High) for 4-6 minutes, stirring once.
3 Add remaining ingredients. Microwave at 100% (High) for 7-9 minutes until hot, stirring once. Serve at once.

Dutch Omelette

180

Dutch omelette

13½ mins

Standing time: 3 mins

350g / 12oz pork sausagemeat
1 small onion, chopped
15ml / 1tbls soy sauce
25g / 1oz butter
350g / 12oz potatoes, grated
5 eggs
50ml / 2fl oz milk
2.5ml / ½tsp paprika

SERVES 4

Stuffed peppers

28 mins

Standing time: 5 mins

4 large green peppers

STUFFING
350g / 12oz lean minced lamb
400g / 14oz can whole tomatoes
100g / 4oz easy-cook rice
100g / 4oz can sweetcorn
45ml / 3tbls grated Parmesan cheese
1 small onion, finely chopped

1 garlic clove, crushed
salt and pepper

SERVES 4

1 Cut off tops of green peppers, remove core and seeds and cut away a little of the base so they stand upright.
2 Mix stuffing ingredients, spoon into peppers and arrange in a large square baking dish. Replace tops.
3 Microwave at 70% (Medium-High) for 28-35 minutes, or until stuffing is set, rearranging two or three times. Stand for 5 minutes.

How to microwave Dutch omelette

Place *sausagemeat and onion in a round casserole. Microwave, uncovered, at 100% (High) for 4-5 minutes, stirring twice.*

Stir *in soy sauce. Drain the meat mixture on absorbent paper. Discard any fat from dish and dot base of dish with the butter.*

Add *potatoes to casserole. Cover with vented cling film. Microwave at 100% (High) for 2½-3 minutes or until tender, stirring once.*

Combine *remaining ingredients and add to dish. Microwave, uncovered, at 100% (High) for 1 minute. Stir; spoon on sausagemeat.*

Reduce *to 50% (Medium) and cook for 1 minute. Lift edges of omelette carefully with a spatula so uncooked egg spreads evenly.*

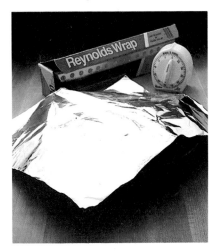

Microwave *at 50% (Medium) for a further 5-6 minutes until eggs are just set. Stand, covered with foil, for 3 minutes.*

181

Middle Eastern meatballs

11 mins

Standing time: 5 mins

450g / 1lb lean minced lamb
1 small onion, finely chopped
2.5ml / ½tsp chopped fresh mint
   or 1.5ml / ¼tsp dried
5ml / 1tsp chopped parsley
pinch of ground cinnamon
pinch of ground cumin
salt and pepper

SAUCE
4 tomatoes, skinned and chopped
1 small onion, finely chopped
1 green pepper, seeded and
   chopped
10ml / 2tsp olive oil
15ml / 1tbls chopped parsley
salt
garlic powder (optional)

SERVES 4

Microtips

Middle Eastern Meatballs or beef meatballs can be brushed with 15ml / 1tbls soy or Worcestershire sauce before cooking to give an attractive brown colour.

How to microwave Middle Eastern meatballs

Mix *together minced lamb, onion, herbs and spices. Season. Form into 12 meatballs. Place the meatballs on a roasting rack and cover with greaseproof paper.*

Microwave *at 100% (High) for 3 minutes. Rearrange meatballs and microwave for a further 2-3 minutes or until meat is no longer pink. Cover and stand for 5 minutes.*

Mix *sauce ingredients in dish. Cover and microwave at 100% (High) for 5-7 minutes. Add meatballs, cover and microwave at 100% (High) for 1-2 minutes.*

182

Prime steaks

Succulent, tender and tasty, prime steaks make wonderful meals. Cooked simply and quickly in a microwave, they are just as delicious as ever, especially served with Garlic Butter or Béarnaise Sauce.

Prime steaks — whether fillet, sirloin, T-bone or rump — are a great treat and it is natural to want the best possible result from cooking. Steaks cooked by microwave are just as tender as those cooked conventionally.

Although they can be cooked successfully without a browning dish by brushing the meat with a browning agent, if you plan to microwave steak frequently, a browning dish is a good investment, since it helps sear the meat.

Follow the timings in the charts on page 184 and use the guide below to test for doneness. With a browning dish, stand meat for 1-2 minutes; otherwise stand for 3 minutes for rare/medium-rare steak; 5 minutes for medium/well done meat.

Rare: surface of meat should look cooked but have traces of red meat juices over parts of surface.

Medium-rare: red meat juices should come to the surface when steak is pressed firmly with a knife.

Medium: centre of meat should be slightly pink if pierced.

Well done: meat should be evenly brown and meat juices run clear when pierced with a knife.

Béarnaise sauce

$1\frac{1}{4}$ mins

Standing time: none

3 egg yolks
15ml / 1tbls tarragon or wine vinegar
10ml / 2tsp chopped tarragon leaves or 5ml / 1tsp dried
salt and pepper
100g / 4oz well chilled unsalted butter
15ml / 1tbls grated onion

SERVES 4

1 Whisk egg yolks, vinegar, tarragon and seasoning together in a bowl until blended.

2 Place 15g / $\frac{1}{2}$oz of the butter in a bowl with the onion and microwave at 100% (High) for 1-1$\frac{1}{2}$ minutes or until onion is softened. Beat into egg yolk mixture.

3 Cut remaining butter into six pieces and microwave at 100% (High) for 15 seconds or until butter is softened but not melted.

4 Gradually beat into egg yolk mixture until thickened and pale. Serve at once, spooned over the steak.

Fillet steak with Béarnaise Sauce

183

How to microwave Fillet steak

Dry steak thoroughly on absorbent paper, then brush with 10ml / 2tsp soy sauce. Grease a shallow dish with 15g / $^{1}/_{2}oz$ melted butter or 10ml / 2tsp oil.

Add steaks and microwave at 100% (High) for $1^{1}/_{2}$-$3^{1}/_{2}$ minutes, according to taste (see chart below). Drain juices; turn steaks over.

Microwave at 100% (High) for $2^{1}/_{2}$-4 minutes (see chart). Stand, covered with foil for 3 minutes for rare/medium rare; 5 minutes for medium/well done.

How to microwave T-bone steak in a browning dish

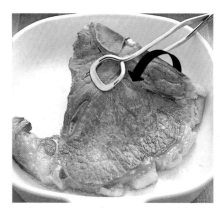

Make small cuts in fat of steak at 2.5cm / 1in intervals to prevent curling during cooking. Heat browning dish for 5 minutes or follow manufacturer's instructions.

When hot, add 10ml / 2tsp oil and tilt the dish to coat the base. Add steak, pressing down well for maximum contact and wait until sizzling dies down.

Microwave at 100% (High) for $1^{3}/_{4}$-$4^{1}/_{2}$ minutes (see chart below — a 450g / 1lb T-bone steak is equivalent to 2 x 225g / 8oz steaks). Turn once. Stand for 1-2 minutes.

Microwave times for steaks

STEAK COOKED WITHOUT A BROWNING DISH			STEAK COOKED IN A BROWNING DISH		
		2 x 225g / 8oz steaks or 1 x 450g / 1lb T-bone	4 x 225g / 8oz steaks	2 x 225g / 8oz steaks or 1 x 450g / 1lb T-bone	4 x 225g / 8oz steaks
RARE	1st side	$1^{1}/_{2}$ mins	3-$3^{1}/_{2}$ mins	$^{3}/_{4}$ min	1 min
	2nd side	$2^{1}/_{2}$ mins	$3^{1}/_{2}$-4 mins	1 min	$1^{3}/_{4}$-2 mins
MEDIUM-RARE	1st side	2-$2^{1}/_{2}$ mins	$3^{1}/_{2}$-4 mins	1 min	$1^{1}/_{2}$ mins
	2nd side	3 mins	4-$4^{1}/_{2}$ mins	$1^{1}/_{4}$-$1^{1}/_{2}$ mins	2-$2^{1}/_{2}$ mins
MEDIUM	1st side	$2^{1}/_{2}$-3 mins	$4^{1}/_{2}$-5 mins	$1^{1}/_{2}$ mins	2 mins
	2nd side	3-$3^{1}/_{2}$ mins	$4^{1}/_{2}$-5 mins	$1^{1}/_{2}$-2 mins	$2^{1}/_{2}$-3 mins
WELL DONE	1st side	$3^{1}/_{2}$ mins	5-6 mins	2 mins	$2^{1}/_{2}$ mins
	2nd side	4-5 mins	6-7 mins	$2^{1}/_{2}$-3 mins	$4^{1}/_{2}$-5 mins

Garlic butter

$\frac{1}{4}$ min

Standing time: none

100g / 4oz butter
2 cloves garlic, crushed
1.5ml / ¼tsp French mustard
salt and pepper

SERVES 4

1 Cut butter into quarters and place in a small bowl.
2 Microwave, covered, at 100% (High) for 20 seconds or until just softened.
3 Beat in garlic, mustard and seasoning and serve.

VARIATIONS
Chilli Butter: substitute ½ small red pepper and 1 chilli, seeded and finely chopped, for the garlic and mustard.
Blue Cheese and Watercress: substitute 50g / 2oz blue Stilton, mashed, plus 45ml / 3tbls chopped watercress for the garlic and mustard.

Rump Steak with Garlic Butter

Microtips

Low-fat spreads, which tend to separate when heated conventionally, work perfectly in a microwave and make a calorie-saving alternative to butter for weight-watchers. Simply halve the microwave time.

Rump steak with coriander

$4\frac{1}{2}$ mins

Standing time: 1-2 mins

2 x 450g / 1lb rump steaks, halved with excess fat removed
15ml / 1tbls oil

MARINADE
1 clove garlic, crushed
grated zest and juice of 1 lemon
5ml / 1tsp ground coriander
30ml / 2tbls vegetable oil

SERVES 4

1 Mix together garlic, lemon zest and juice, coriander and oil for the marinade.
2 Place steaks in a large shallow dish, add marinade, cover and refrigerate for 6-8 hours. Drain well and dry thoroughly.
3 Heat browning dish for 5 minutes or according to manufacturer's instructions. Add oil, tilting dish to coat the base.
4 Add steak, pressing down well. When sizzling dies down, microwave at 100% (High) for 2¾-7 minutes (see chart page 184), turning once. Stand for 1-2 minutes.

Microtips

This recipe can be made without a browning dish. Follow the steps for How to microwave Fillet steak (on page 184), omitting soy sauce. During microwaving, excess juices will collect in dish. A quick sauce can be made with these: add 45ml / 3tbls natural yoghurt, 2.5ml / ½tsp sugar, seasoning and leftover marinade to 45ml / 3tbls meat juices. Microwave at 100% (High) for 15 seconds and serve with the steaks.

Microtips

T-bone steak is the largest steak of all — a 2.5cm / 1in thick piece weighs around 450g / 1lb. Cook one at a time, following timings for 2 x 225g / 8oz steaks. Cut from the bone into two small steaks after cooking to serve two.

Cook's notes

Always dry steak thoroughly before searing in a browning dish, otherwise meat will 'steam' and not develop a rich, appetizing colour. For extra browning, flash under hot grill for 1 minute.

Sirloin steak with oysters

7 mins

Standing time: 1-2 mins

4 x 225g / 8oz sirloin steaks, each about 2.5cm / 1in thick
2 rashers streaky bacon, rinds removed, and chopped
105g / 4oz can smoked oysters, drained
grated zest of 1 lemon
45ml / 3tbls chopped parsley
salt and pepper
15ml / 1tbls oil

SERVES 4

1 Place bacon and onion in small bowl and microwave at 100% (High) for 2½-3 minutes until onion is soft.
2 Stir oysters, lemon zest, parsley and seasoning into onions and bacon mixture.
3 Using a sharp knife, make horizontal cuts into steak to form pockets for oyster mixture. Divide mixture among steak cavities.
4 Heat browning dish for 5 minutes or follow manufacturer's instructions. When hot, add oil, tilting dish to coat the base. Add steak and press down.
5 When sizzling dies down, microwave at 100% (High) for 2¾-7 minutes (see chart page 184), turning once. Stand for 1-2 minutes.

Fillet steak with ginger wine

7¾ mins

Standing time: 5 mins

2 x 4cm / 1½in thick fillet steaks, about 175g / 6oz each
10ml / 2tsp soy sauce
6mm / ¼in fresh root ginger, peeled and finely chopped
25g / 1oz cream cheese
salt and pepper
15g / ½oz butter
10ml / 2tsp oil
2 large mushrooms
2 slices bread, cut into 9cm / 3½in rounds
60ml / 4tbls ginger wine

SERVES 2

1 Coat steaks thoroughly with soy sauce. Mix root ginger, cheese and seasoning in a small bowl.
2 Place butter and oil in a shallow baking dish. Microwave, covered, at 100% (High) for 1 minute.
3 Brush mushrooms with a little of the butter and set aside. Add

Fillet Steak with Ginger Wine

bread to baking dish, coating well. Microwave at 100% (High) for 1½ minutes. Turn over and cook for 1 minute or until turning crisp. Drain on absorbent paper, then spread with cheese mixture.
4 Add steaks to dish and cook at 100% (High) for 2 minutes. Turn and cook for a further 2 minutes.
5 Place steaks on prepared bread rounds, return to baking dish and spoon over the ginger wine.
6 Top each steak with a mushroom and microwave at 100% (High) for 15 seconds or until heated through. Stand, covered, for 5 minutes.

Microtips

Cooking times in all recipes are for 'medium' steak. In this recipe, allow 1 minute on each side for rare steak; 3 minutes on each side for well done meat.

Beef olives

34 mins

Standing time: 10 mins

700g / 1½lb rump steak, cut into 4, with excess fat removed
75g / 3oz button mushrooms, sliced
1 small onion, chopped
1 celery stalk, sliced
3 rashers streaky bacon, rinds removed, chopped
25g / 1oz butter
30ml / 2tbls chopped parsley
5ml / 1tsp dried sage
3 slices white bread, diced
pepper

SAUCE
25g / 1oz plain flour
275ml / ½pt beef stock
15ml / 1tbls tomato purée
5ml / 1tsp Worcestershire sauce

SERVES 4

Cook's notes

The sauce and stuffing in this recipe means that the steak cooks more slowly than it would if microwaved by itself — it takes longer for the microwaves to penetrate through the rolled meat and into the stuffing. The sauce also acts as a shield for the food, keeping the meat tender and moist preventing it from drying out.

How to microwave Beef olives

Place *steaks on a board or other flat surface and pound to 6mm / ¼in thickness with the edge of a saucer or a meat mallet. This tenderizes the meat as well as flattening it out.*

Place *mushrooms, onion, celery, bacon and butter in a bowl and microwave uncovered at 100% (High) for 3-4 minutes, stirring once. Add parsley, sage, bread and seasoning.*

Spoon *stuffing on to steak. Roll up and secure with wooden cocktail sticks. Make sauce by blending flour with a little beef stock, then whisk in remaining ingredients.*

Microwave *sauce uncovered at 100% (High) for 1-2 minutes until thickened, stirring once. Arrange beef olives in a shallow dish. Spoon over sauce and cover.*

Microwave *at 50% (Medium) for 20 minutes. Re-arrange beef olives and microwave for a further 10 minutes. Allow to stand, covered, for 10 minutes before serving.*

187

Pork casseroles

Sliced, diced or cubed, pork makes marvellous casseroles. Combining deliciously with other flavours, it is also quick and easy to microwave. So make the most of pork whenever you need a substantial, tasty meal.

A choice of cuts of fresh pork can be used for casseroling. Prime cuts, such as fillet or tenderloin or boneless loin chops are ideal for the quick and easy recipes. They have a very good flavour and tend to shrink less than the cheaper cuts. Cuts such as shoulder steaks or leg, on the other hand, do casserole well but require a little more cooking, so choose these cuts for recipes with the longer microwaving time.

Cut the meat into strips against the grain when pork slices are required. When dicing, make sure the cubes are neat and of equal size to encourage even cooking. The sauces and vegetables in the recipes add flavour and colour to the meat, so there is no need to use a browning dish or any browning agent. Be sure to stir casseroles two or three times during microwaving; so that the meat cooks evenly.

De luxe pork casserole

| 10 mins |

Standing time: none

1 onion, chopped
350g / 12oz boneless pork, cut into 12mm / ½in strips
100g / 4oz button mushrooms, sliced
340g / 12oz can asparagus, chopped and drained
15ml / 3tsp cornflour
15ml / 1tbls lemon juice
150ml / ¼pt milk
1.5ml / ¼tsp dried thyme
salt and pepper

SERVES 4

1 Place onion in a large casserole, cover and microwave at 100% (High) for 2 minutes until soft.
2 Stir in pork, mushrooms and asparagus. Cover and microwave at 100% (High) for 5-7 minutes, or until pork is no longer pink, stirring twice. Drain off the cooking liquid, reserving 150ml / ¼pt.
3 Blend cornflour and lemon juice in a large jug. Add remaining sauce ingredients with reserved liquid and microwave at 100% (High) for 2 minutes, or until sauce thickens, stirring every minute.
4 Stir the sauce into the pork and vegetables. Microwave at 100% (High) for 1 minute to heat through. Serve immediately.

Left: *De Luxe Pork Casserole*
Above: *Pork and Vegetable Pot*

Pork and vegetable pot

| 32 mins |

Standing time: 5 mins

450g / 1lb boneless pork, cut into 2.5cm / 1in cubes
½ onion, finely chopped
4 carrots, sliced diagonally
3 celery stalks, sliced diagonally
150ml / ¼pt dry white wine or chicken stock
2 strips pared lemon rind
5ml / 1tsp dried marjoram
1 bay leaf
2.5ml / ½tsp garlic salt
1 green pepper, seeded and sliced
15ml / 1tbls plain flour

SERVES 4

1 Place pork and onion in a large casserole. Microwave at 100% (High) for 5 minutes, stirring once. Add carrots, celery, wine, lemon rind, herbs and garlic salt. Stir well.
2 Cover and microwave at 50% (Medium) for 23-25 minutes, or until meat and vegetables are tender, stirring three times. Add green pepper for last 5 minutes.
3 Blend the flour with a little cooking liquid. Remove lemon rind and bay leaf, then stir in the flour mixture. Increase power to 100% (High) and microwave for 4 minutes or until bubbling and thickened, stirring every minute. Cover and stand for 5 minutes.
4 Serve with plain boiled rice or noodles, cooked conventionally, and an apple and cabbage salad.

Pork stew

| 14 mins |

Standing time: 5 mins

350g / 12oz boneless pork, cut into 12mm / ½in cubes
1 small onion, finely chopped
1 sweet potato (about 175g / 6oz), cut into 6mm / ¼in cubes
1 carrot, thinly sliced
2 celery stalks, thinly sliced
25g / 1oz butter
1 courgette, cut into 12mm × 5cm / ½ × 2in strips
400g / 14oz can tomatoes
1.5ml / ¼tsp dried rosemary
30ml / 2tbls chopped parsley
salt and pepper
30ml / 2tbls plain flour
75ml / 3fl oz white wine

SERVES 4

1 Microwave pork and onion in a large covered casserole at 100% (High) for 5-7 minutes until meat is no longer pink; stir twice.
2 Add potato, carrot, celery and butter; cover and microwave at 100% (High) for 4 minutes, or until the vegetables are tender-crisp, stirring once.
3 Mix in courgette, tomatoes, rosemary, parsley and seasoning, microwave, covered for 2 minutes.
4 Blend flour with wine. Add a few tablespoons of the casserole juices to make a smooth sauce, then stir into casserole. Microwave at 100% (High) for 3 minutes, stirring every minute. Cover and stand for 5 minutes.

189

Tomato pork casserole

20 mins

Standing time: 5 mins

Serve this well-flavoured casserole with green tagliatelle, or with hunks of French bread.

100g / 4oz button mushrooms, sliced
1 onion, thinly sliced
30ml / 2tbls olive oil
1 garlic clove, crushed
450g / 1lb boneless pork, cut into 2.5cm / 1in cubes
400g / 14oz can tomatoes
60ml / 4tbls tomato purée or paste
75ml / 3fl oz dry white wine
1 small bay leaf
5ml / 1tsp dried basil
salt and pepper
15ml / 3tsp cornflour
15ml / 1tbls water

SERVES 4

1 Place mushrooms, onion, oil and garlic in a large casserole. Stir, then cover and microwave at 100% (High) for 4-5 minutes, or until onion is tender, stirring once.
2 Stir in pork together with tomatoes, tomato purée, wine, herbs and seasoning. Cover and microwave at 100% (High) for 13 minutes or until pork is no longer pink, stirring well, two or three times.
3 Blend cornflour with water and stir into casserole. Microwave for a further 3 minutes, until slightly thickened, stirring once. Stand, covered, for 5 minutes.

Tomato Pork Casserole

Freezer notes

Pork freezes very successfully and Pork Stew can be microwaved and then frozen for up to 3 months. Make up to step 3, turn into microwave freezer dish, cover and freeze. To thaw, cover with vented cling film and microwave at 20-30% (Defrost) for 16-18 minutes, break up and stir every 2 minutes after the first 5 minutes. Follow step 4 to finish recipe.

Mexican pork casserole

15¼ mins

Standing time: 10 mins

8 canned tortillas, or small pancakes

FILLING
1 small onion, chopped
10ml / 2tsp vegetable oil
225g / 8oz boneless pork, cut into 6mm / ¼in cubes
100g / 4oz canned tomatoes
pinch of black pepper
225g / 8oz canned baked beans with chilli
1.5ml / ¼tsp Tabasco sauce

SAUCE
25g / 1oz butter
5ml / 1tsp plain flour
pinch of mustard powder
175ml / 6fl oz milk
salt and pepper

TOPPING
50g / 2oz Cheddar cheese, mixed red and white if possible, grated
paprika for dusting

SERVES 4

1 Place onion and oil in a large casserole. Cover and microwave at 100% (High) for 2-3 minutes. Add pork, tomatoes and season with pepper. Cover and microwave at 100% (High) for a further 3-4 minutes, or until pork is no longer pink, stirring twice.
2 Add remaining filling ingredients and microwave for 3 minutes. Stand for 10 minutes.
3 Melt butter at 100% (High) 15-30 seconds, stir in flour and mustard and then blend in milk. Microwave for 3 minutes or until thick, stir three times; season.
4 Assemble and microwave the casserole as shown below.

Mexican Pork Casserole

How to assemble Mexican pork casserole

Dip *each tortilla in cold water to soften. Divide the filling equally between the tortillas. Roll up each one and arrange in a row, seam side down, in a large rectangular casserole which takes tortillas in a single layer.*

Pour *the white sauce over the tortillas while still hot, coating them evenly. Spread the sauce to the edges of the tortillas using the back of a spoon, so that the sauce just runs over the edges and covers tortillas completely.*

Sprinkle *the top of the coated tortillas evenly with the grated cheese. Microwave at 100% (High) for 4-5 minutes or until the cheese melts and the sauce is well heated. Dust with paprika and serve hot.*

191

Caribbean casserole

19 mins

Standing time: 10 mins

350g / 12oz boneless pork, cut in
    12mm / ½in strips
1 red pepper, seeded and sliced
175g / 6oz long-grain rice
376g / 13.3oz can crushed
    pineapple
5ml / 1tsp grated orange zest
15ml / 1tbls soy sauce
575ml / 1pt boiling water
salt and pepper

SERVES 4

1 Combine pork and pepper strips in a large casserole, cover and microwave at 100% (High) for 6 minutes.

2 Add all the remaining ingredients and stir thoroughly. Cover and microwave at 100% (High) for 13-15 minutes, or until rice is tender; stir twice. Stand 10 minutes.

Creamy pork casserole

20½ mins

Standing time: none

1 large onion, thinly sliced
450g / 1lb boneless pork, cut in
    2.5cm / 1in cubes
1 large cooking apple, peeled,
    cored and sliced
425ml / 15fl oz strong dry cider
5ml / 1tsp ground allspice
15ml / 1tbls plain flour
75ml / 3fl oz single cream
salt and pepper

SERVES 4

1 Microwave the onion in a covered casserole at 100% (High) for 5 minutes, or until tender. Add pork, apple, cider and allspice. Cover and microwave at 100% (High) 12-14 minutes, stir twice.

2 Blend the flour and cream with enough casserole liquid to make 275ml / ½pt. Microwave at 100% (High) for 1½ minutes, stirring twice. Stir into the casserole and season. Microwave at 100% (High) for 2 minutes to heat.

Caribbean Casserole

Pork chops

Pork chops are a versatile cut of meat which combine well with all sorts of other textures and flavours. Cooking them in a microwave ensures they cook through without drying out.

Pork chops are available in four types: rib, spare rib, loin and chump. Rib and spare rib chops have a long bone down one side of the meat; loin chops are larger and have a bone down the centre, and chump chops are boneless. Any type can be used for the recipes here.

Don't trim all the fat from the meat until after cooking; it will help to keep the pork tender and juicy. Standing time is particularly necessary for pork. It allows it to cook through, without drying out. Alternatively a stuffing or bread crumb coating will also help to keep the meat moist.

Saucy pork chops

| 16 mins |

Standing time: 5-10 mins

4 pork chops, 1cm / ½in thick
295g / 10.4oz can condensed mushroom soup

SERVES 4

Calculate the cooking time, allowing 16 minutes per 450g / 1lb at 50% (Medium); use chops cut to a width of 1cm / ½in to ensure accurate timing.
Leave a small amount of fat at the edges to prevent drying out.

1 Arrange the chops in a shallow dish with the meaty portions to the outside. Spread over the soup.
2 Cover with cling film. Microwave at 50% (Medium) for the calculated time, turning once. Let stand for 5-10 minutes. Serve with vegetables of your choice.

Microtips

If you prefer chops without fat, it is best to cook them in a liquid such as the soup used here, to seal in the juices. A coating of bread crumbs also retains moisture well.

Honey-glazed chops

6 mins

Standing time: 3-5 mins

4 lean pork chops, 1cm / ½in thick
45ml / 3tbls barbecue sauce
5ml / 1tsp dark soy sauce
15ml / 1tbls clear honey

SERVES 4

1 Trim the fat from the chops and place them in a shallow dish.
2 In a small bowl, mix together the sauces and honey. Brush the sauce over the chops and leave to marinate as directed (right).
3 Arrange chops on a roasting rack. Microwave at 100% (High) for 6-8 minutes, turning as directed (right); stand for 3-5 minutes.

How to microwave Honey-glazed chops

Brush *the sauce over the chops to cover and leave to marinate for 20 minutes. This improves the flavour and colour. Brush with the sauce again before microwaving.*

Turn *the roasting rack 180° three times during the cooking. The chops should be turned over after half the cooking time. Leave to stand for 3-5 minutes.*

194

Stuffed pork chops

27 mins

Standing time: 5-10 mins

4 pork chops, about 2.5cm / 1in thick
30ml / 2tbls dried breadcrumbs

MUSHROOM STUFFING
50g / 2oz mushrooms, chopped
½ onion, finely chopped
15g / ½oz butter or margarine
40g / 1½oz parsley, thyme and lemon stuffing mix
120ml / 8tbls cold water

SERVES 4

1 Make pockets in the chops following the step-by-step instructions (right). Set aside while preparing the mushroom stuffing.
2 To make the stuffing, combine the mushrooms, onion and butter in a measuring jug. Microwave at 100% (High) for 2 minutes until the onions are just tender, then remove from the cooker.
3 Add the stuffing mix and cold water and stir well.
4 To fill each pocket of the chops, spoon in the stuffing, then press the edges together and secure with wooden cocktail sticks.
5 Press the chops in the dried breadcrumbs until coated, then arrange in a 20 x 30cm / 8 x 12in shallow dish with the thickest parts to the outside.
6 Cover the dish with greaseproof paper, then microwave at 50% (Medium) for 15 minutes.
7 Turn and rearrange the chops so they cook evenly and continue to cook for a further 10-15 minutes. Let stand for 5-10 minutes. Serve with tomato wedges and parsley, accompanied with beetroot in white sauce and a wholewheat pasta, if liked.

Microtips

Read the stuffing mix instructions and, if hot water is called for, measure out the water in a cup, place in the cooker and heat the water for about 45 seconds before adding to the other ingredients.

How to stuff pork chops

Slit *horizontally through the pork chops up to the bone with a sharp knife, leaving a 2.5cm / 1in border at the sides, to make pockets.*

Spoon *the stuffing into the pockets. Insert a wooden cocktail stick diagonally across the open end to hold the stuffing inside the cavity.*

195

Normandy pork

31 mins

Standing time: 8 mins

2 x 350g / 12oz pork tenderloins
salt and pepper
2.5ml / ½tsp dried thyme
2.5ml / ½tsp dried sage
2.5ml / ½tsp crumbled dried bay
    leaf
75ml / 3fl oz dry cider or calvados
3 garlic cloves, each cut into 10
    slivers
30 tiny sprigs fresh rosemary or
    30 dried leaves
15g / ½oz butter
75ml / 3fl oz chicken stock
30ml / 2tbls finely chopped
    parsley
15-30ml / 1-2tbls lemon juice

SERVES 4

1 Slice horizontally three-quarters of the way through each tenderloin to make a pocket.
2 Season the inside of each pocket with salt, pepper and a sprinkling of dried herbs. Sprinkle about 30ml / 2tbls of the cider or calvados over each tenderloin and secure with wooden cocktail sticks to make a neat roll.
3 With a small sharp knife, make 15 small incisions in each joint. Push a sliver of garlic and rosemary into each one.
4 Heat a large browning dish for 5 minutes at 100% (High) or according to the manufacturer's instructions. Add the butter and press the pork firmly on to the surface. Microwave at 100% (High) for 1½ minutes.
5 Turn the joints over and microwave at 100% (High) for a further 1½ minutes. Cover the dish and microwave at 50% (Medium) for 20-25 minutes or until the meat is tender. Remove the pork from the browning dish, discard the cocktail sticks. Stand, covered for about 8 minutes.
6 Add the stock to the juices in the browning dish and microwave for 3 minutes at 100% (High). Correct the seasoning and add the parsley and lemon juice to taste. Pour into a heated sauce boat.
7 In a large ladle, gently heat the remaining cider or calvados over a very low flame. Ignite and pour over the pork, standing well back. Allow the flames to die down: serve with the sauce.

Microtips

When using a browning dish, never pre-heat the dish longer than the recommended time as this can damage the glass turntable or glass plate cooker base. Some manufacturers recommend placing the browning dish on an upturned heatproof glass plate or special microwave trivet.

Cook's notes

Calvados is a fiery, apple-flavoured brandy distilled in Normandy from the local cider. It is drunk after meals and used in cooking. Dry cider is a good substitute. Or use apple juice and do not flambé.

For a very simple pork and apple dish, microwave plain pork tenderloin as in the steps below but spread softened apple chunks over the pork for the last 6-9 minutes of cooking.

Microwave times for tenderloin

WEIGHT	TIME AT 100% (HIGH)	TIME AT 50% (MEDIUM)
For average 350g / 12oz tenderloin	3 mins	10-15 mins
Per 450g / 1lb	3 mins	14-18 mins

How to microwave pork tenderloin

Shield *ends with well secured foil. Insert the temperature probe into the centre at the thickest part. Estimate the cooking time (see chart).*

Place *the meat on a roasting rack in a dish. Microwave at 100% (High) for 3 minutes. Reduce to 50% (Medium) and microwave for half the time.*

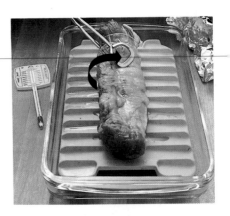

Remove *foil, turn meat and cook until temperature reaches 74°C / 165°F. Stand, covered, for about 8 minutes until it reaches 78°C /170°F.*

Vegetable-stuffed pork

18 mins

Standing time: 8 mins

275ml / ½pt dry white wine
45ml / 3tbls apple sauce
1 small onion, chopped
2 lemon slices
3 whole cloves
1 garlic clove, finely chopped
large pinch of dried tarragon
350g / 12oz pork tenderloin
3 rashers streaky bacon, rinded
15g / ½oz butter or margarine
1 carrot, cut into long thin strips
2 spring onions, each quartered
   lengthways

SERVES 2

1 In a large shallow dish, mix the wine, apple sauce, onion, lemon slices, cloves, garlic and tarragon. Microwave at 100% (High) for 2-3 minutes until heated.
2 Cut the tenderloin in half horizontally, without cutting through the opposite long side. Open out and place in the dish with the wine marinade. Cover and leave to marinate in the refrigerator for 2 hours.
3 Place the bacon on absorbent paper and cover with another sheet. Microwave at 100% (High) for 1½ minutes or until lightly brown but not crisp.
4 Place the butter, carrot strips and onion in a shallow casserole. Cover and microwave at 100% (High) for 1½-2½ minutes until tender. Stir half way through cooking.
5 Remove the meat from the marinade, place the vegetables in the centre of the tenderloin, close up and secure with wooden cocktail sticks. Wrap bacon rashers round the pork and secure with more cocktail sticks.
6 Place the joint on a roasting rack. Insert a thermometer at an angle into the meat; not touching the stuffing. Microwave at 100% (High) for 3 minutes, reduce power to 50% (Medium) and microwave for 10-15 minutes or until temperature reaches 74°C / 165°F, turning dish two or three times. Stand, covered, for 8 minutes before carving.

Gooseberry tenderloin

30 mins

Standing time: 8 mins

2 x 350g / 12oz pork tenderloins
100g / 4oz cooking gooseberries
15g / ½oz butter or margarine
1 onion, finely chopped
50g / 2oz fresh wholemeal
   breadcrumbs
10ml / 2tsp chopped parsley
10ml / 2tsp chopped marjoram or
   5ml / 1tsp dried
pinch of ground cloves
150ml / ¼pt dry white wine
150ml / ¼pt ham or chicken
   stock
30ml / 2tbls honey

SERVES 4

1 Slit through each tenderloin horizontally, leaving it uncut along one long side. Open each tenderloin out flat like a book. Beat with a meat bat or rolling pin until the meat has approximately doubled in size and is only about 6mm / ¼in thick.
2 Top and tail the gooseberries and finely chop half of them. Cut each of the remaining gooseberries

Vegetable-Stuffed Pork

in half and reserve.
3 Put the butter and onion in a small dish. Microwave, covered, at 100% (High) for 2 minutes. Stir in the finely chopped gooseberries and microwave, uncovered, at 50% (Medium) for a further 5 minutes. Stir in the breadcrumbs, herbs and cloves and 15ml / 1tbls wine or stock.
4 Spread the mixture on the open pork tenderloins, then roll up from a long edge, tie at intervals with strong thread or string.
5 Place in a shallow casserole dish and spoon the honey on top. Microwave, covered, at 100% (High) for 3 minutes. Reduce power and microwave for 10 minutes at 50% (Medium).
6 Add the reserved gooseberries, and the remaining wine and stock. Cover and microwave at 50% (Medium) for a further 10-15 minutes or until tender, turning the joints over several times during cooking.
7 Let stand for 8 minutes. Remove string, top the pork with the gooseberries and serve with the sauce from the dish.

199

Lamb chops

Microwave lamb chops in a browning dish for an extra speedy supper that will look and taste good. Or combine them with traditional mint sauce or a savoury stuffing for a variety of microwave meals.

Lamb chops can be quickly and successfully cooked in the microwave. For a speedy family supper for two or four people, just pop the lamb chops onto a preheated browning dish and they will be cooked in a maximum of 10 minutes, and will look and taste most appetizing.

The chart (see page 201) gives timings for cooking loin and chump chops, lamb steaks and best end of neck cutlets. Flexibility of final timings is given to allow for personal taste, depending on whether you like chops rare, medium or well done.

Weight and thickness of chops are given in the chart, but they can vary greatly; the size of individual best end of neck cutlets, for instance, will depend on the size of the back bone.

Microwave lamb chops with herbs and other flavourings to make a variety of meals. Cook at 50% (Medium) for tender meat.

Below: *Orange-glazed Lamb Chops*
Below right: *Lamb Amandine*

Microwave times for lamb chops in a browning dish

TYPE AND THICKNESS	QUANTITY	WEIGHT PER CHOP	MICROWAVE COOKING TIME AT 100% (HIGH)	FIRST SIDE	SECOND SIDE
Loin 2-2.5cm / ¾-1in	2	100-175g / 4-6oz	6-7 mins	3 mins	3-4 mins
	4	100-175g / 4-6oz	8–9 mins	3 mins	5-6 mins
Chump 2-2.5cm / ¾-1in	2	100-175g / 4-6oz	6-8 mins	3 mins	3-5 mins
	4	100-175g / 4-6oz	8–10 mins	4 mins	4-6 mins
Lamb steaks 12mm-2cm / ½-¾in	2	100-175g / 4-6oz	5½-6½ mins	3 mins	2½-3½ mins
	4	100-175g / 4-6oz	6½–8 mins	3 mins	3½-5 mins
Best end of neck cutlets about 12mm-2cm /½-¾in	2	50-75g / 2-3oz	3½-5 mins	2 mins	1½-3 mins
	4	50-75g / 2-3oz	5–6 mins	2 mins	3-4 mins

How to microwave lamb chops

Preheat *a browning dish at 100% (High) for 5 minutes or according to the manufacturer's instructions.*

Place *the chops in the dish, pressing down well. Microwave the first side, uncovered, following chart times.*

Turn *the chops and cook, uncovered, following the chart times for the second side. Leave to stand for 3-5 minutes.*

Lamb steaks with onions

16¼ mins

Standing time: 3-5 mins

25g / 1oz butter or margarine
10ml / 2tsp chopped parsley
5ml / 1tsp dried marjoram
5ml / 1tsp dried rosemary
salt
4 lamb leg chops, total weight
    about 700-900g / 1½-2lb
2 onions, sliced into thin rings

SERVES 4

1 Melt the butter in a large, cover-ed casserole at 100% (High) for 15-30 seconds.
2 Stir in the herbs and salt.
3 Add the chops, turning to coat with the seasoned butter.
4 Sprinkle the onions over, cover and microwave at 100% (High) for 5 minutes. Reduce the power to 50% (Medium) and microwave for 11-16 minutes. Turn steaks over and rearrange halfway through cooking. Stand, loosely covered, for 3-5 minutes.

Mushroom lamb chops

14¼ mins

Standing time: 3-5 mins

25g / 1oz butter or margarine
30ml / 2tbls plain flour
5ml / 1tsp ground ginger
salt and pepper
good pinch of garlic powder
5ml / 1tsp soy sauce
8 loin lamb chops, 12mm-2.5cm /
    ½-1in thick
225g / 8oz button mushrooms,
    sliced

SERVES 4

1 Melt the butter in a large, shal-low, covered casserole at 100% (High) for 15-30 seconds.
2 Stir in the flour, seasonings and soy sauce. Mix until smooth.
3 Arrange the chops in the cas-serole with the meaty portions to the outside of the dish.
4 Add the mushrooms, cover and microwave at 100% (High) for 5 minutes. Reduce to 50% (Medium) and microwave for 9-14 minutes. Halfway through, remove chops

DON LAST

and stir sauce. Replace chops and turn. Cook for remaining time. Stand for 3-5 minutes, serve with the sauce.

Bacon-wrapped chops

9¾ mins

Standing time: 3-5 mins

15g / ½oz butter or margarine
100g / 4oz canned sliced mush-rooms, drained, chopped
60ml / 4tbls fresh breadcrumbs
1.5ml / ¼tsp dried parsley
good pinch of salt
1.5ml / ¼tsp dried marjoram
1.5ml / ¼tsp garlic powder
4 loin lamb chops, 12mm-2.5cm /
    ½-1in thick
4 bacon rashers

SERVES 2

1 Melt the butter in a covered

Bacon-wrapped Chops

bowl at 100% (High) for 10-15 seconds. Stir in the mushrooms, breadcrumbs, parsley, salt, mar-joram and garlic powder.
2 Make a slit in the meaty side of each chop and stuff each with one-quarter of the mushroom mixture. Press in firmly, then secure with wooden cocktail sticks.
3 Place bacon on absorbent paper and microwave at 100% (High) for 2½-3 minutes, until cooked but not crisp.
4 Wrap one bacon slice around meaty portion of each chop and secure with a cocktail stick.
5 Arrange the chops on a roasting rack, meaty portions to the out-side. Microwave, uncovered, at 100% (High) for 7-10 minutes. Turn chops over halfway through cooking. Stand the chops, covered, for 3-5 minutes before serving.

202

Orange-glazed lamb chops

23½ mins

Standing time: 3-5 mins

4 loin lamb chops, 2.5cm / 1in thick
5ml / 1tsp cornflour

GLAZE
75g / 3oz marmalade
45ml / 3tbls clear honey
15ml / 1tbls made English mustard
10ml / 2tsp lemon juice
5ml / 1tsp Worcestershire sauce

SERVES 4

1 Combine glaze ingredients in a 1.1L / 2pt casserole. Microwave at 100% (High) for 30-45 seconds until marmalade has melted. Stir.
2 Arrange the chops on a roasting rack with the meatiest portions to the outside.
3 Spoon half of the glaze over the chops. Cover with cling film rolled back at one edge and microwave at 100% (High) for 6 minutes.
4 Reduce the power to 50% (Medium) and microwave for a further 5 minutes. Turn the chops over and rearrange. Spoon the remaining glaze over the chops.
5 Re-cover and microwave for 10-15 minutes at 50% (Medium), until chops are cooked to your liking.
6 Remove the chops, cover and stand for 3-5 minutes. Stir the cornflour into the juices and microwave at 100% (High) for 2 minutes. Spoon over chops.

Lamb amandine

24 mins

Standing time: 5-6½ mins

10ml / 2tsp plain flour
10ml / 2tsp dried parsley
1.5ml / ¼tsp salt
generous sprinkling of pepper
90ml / 6tbls sherry
2 lamb leg chops, about 225g / 8oz each, 12mm / ½in thick
30ml / 2tbls flaked almonds
15g / ½oz butter or margarine
60ml / 4tbls soured cream

SERVES 2

Minty lamb chops

15 mins

Standing time: 3-5 mins

4 loin lamb chops, about 2.5cm / 1in thick

MINT SAUCE
150ml / ¼pt water
7.5ml / 1½tsp red wine vinegar
10ml / 2tsp malt vinegar
60ml / 4tbls chopped mint
7.5ml / 1½tsp sugar
salt (optional)

SERVES 4

1 Combine all the ingredients for the mint sauce in a 1.1L / 2pt bowl.

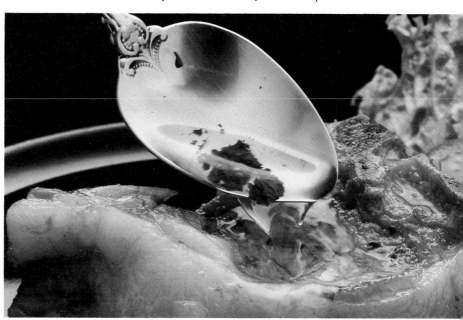

Minty Lamb Chops

2 Cover and microwave at 100% (High) for 2-3 minutes or until boiling.
3 Reduce the power to 50% (Medium) and microwave for 5 minutes.
4 Preheat a browning dish and add the chops, pressing down well. Cook, uncovered, at 100% (High) for 3 minutes.
5 Turn the chops over and rearrange; spoon 5ml / 1tsp mint sauce over each chop. Microwave for another 5-6 minutes. Cover and leave the chops to stand for 3-5 minutes.
6 Transfer remaining sauce to a sauce boat and serve. Store left-over sauce in the refrigerator.

1 In a small shallow casserole mix together the flour, parsley, salt, pepper and sherry until they form a smooth paste.
2 Place the chops in the casserole and turn several times to coat in the sherry mixture.
3 Cover the casserole and microwave at 50% (Medium) for 20-25 minutes or until tender. Turn the chops over and rotate the dish 2-3 times. Remove chops, cover and stand for 5-6½ minutes.
4 Meanwhile, place the almonds and butter in a small dish. Microwave at 100% (High) for 2-3 minutes or until light brown. Stir the almonds every minute.

5 Stir the almonds and soured cream into the casserole. Reduce the power to 50% (Medium) and microwave for 2-3½ minutes or until hot. Stir well before pouring over the meat and serving.

VARIATION
To make a single serving of Lamb Amandine simply halve all the ingredients. Prepare as above, then microwave the lamb chop at 50% (Medium) for 11-15 minutes or until tender. Microwave the almonds for the same length of time but reduce the power to 50% (Medium) and cook the sauce for only 1-2 minutes.

Roasting and braising lamb

A nicely browned roast of lamb can be cooked quickly and successfully in your microwave cooker. Alternatively, braise it and use the cooking liquid to make a tasty sauce.

Lamb is an economical and versatile meat which will go down well with the family or with dinner party guests. Roasting lamb in the microwave cuts down radically on cooking time and produces a tasty and attractive joint which browns quite successfully during microwaving.

Lamb comes from animals up to a year old, after that it is generally known as mutton. The main producers are Europe, North America and New Zealand and supplies are fairly constant throughout the year. It is a meat which freezes well. When buying joints remember that a neat and uniform piece of meat will do best in the microwave — bone with little meat on it will burn before the rest of the meat is cooked.

A small leg of lamb will roast well in the microwave, otherwise choose half a large leg. Boned and rolled shoulder is ideal for microwaving, but shoulder with bone will also microwave well.

Marinated Leg of Lamb

Roasting lamb

Weigh the joint, then place the meat on a rack in a baking dish so it does not cook in its own juices. Shield any thinly covered bone with a small, smooth piece of foil and insert a microwave thermometer, or probe, from the start of cooking.

Estimate the cooking time using the chart overleaf and microwave at 100% (High) for the first 5 minutes. Reduce the power to 50% (Medium) and microwave for the rest of the first half of the calculated cooking time.

Remove from the microwave, turn the joint over and remove any foil shielding. Continue to microwave until the meat reaches the desired temperature (see chart). A conventional meat thermometer cannot be used in a microwave, but you can remove the joint from the oven to check temperatures. All recipe timings are for medium cooked meat. Use them as a guide but always ensure that correct internal temperatures have been reached.

Standing time

When the meat is removed from the microwave it should be loosely covered with foil and left to stand. The temperature will continue to rise during this standing time, (see chart). Carve after 15 minutes.

Pot roasting and braising

These two methods of cooking suit both lamb joints and the microwave cooker. A pot roast is cooked at 50% (Medium) in a covered dish. Very little liquid is added to the meat, the moisture from the meat being sufficient. Braised lamb is also cooked slowly in a covered dish but with a little more added liquid. Cook in a casserole covered with a lid, or cling film.

Using marinades

Lamb is a very tender meat so methods of cooking are concentrated on bringing out the full flavour rather than tenderizing the joint. Marinades are a useful method of giving added flavour to a dish, especially when traditional slow cooking methods are speeded up in the microwave.

How to insert a thermometer or probe

Leg with bone: *Insert thermometer at start of cooking so the tip is in the centre of meaty area and does not touch the bone.*

Boned and rolled shoulder: *Insert the thermometer at start of cooking in the centre of end or side meat, but not touching the fat.*

Boned and rolled leg: *Insert the microwave probe at start of cooking, making sure the tip of the probe is not touching the fat.*

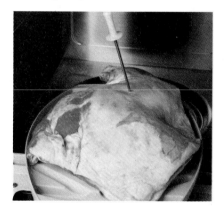

Shoulder with bone: *Insert the microwave probe at start of cooking into the meatiest areas near the joint of bone, but not touching bone.*

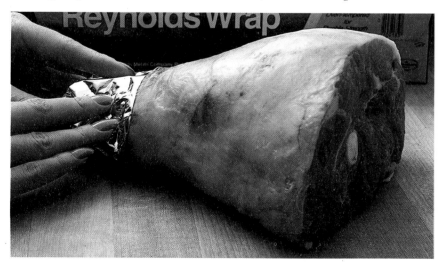

Shield *the end of a full leg with a small piece of smooth foil; this will prevent the thinnest area of meat around the bone end from cooking too quickly and burning or drying out before the rest of the meat is cooked.*

Honey braised lamb

41 mins

Standing time: 10-15 mins

1.4kg / 3lb boned and rolled
    shoulder of lamb
30ml / 2tbls cider vinegar
15ml / 1tbls olive oil
15ml / 1tbls clear honey
2.5ml / ½tsp dried marjoram
65ml / 2½ fl oz dry cider
30ml / 2tbls soy sauce
15ml / 1tbls butter
1 onion, chopped
2 carrots, sliced
salt
pepper
25g / 1oz plain flour

SERVES 4

How to microwave Honey braised lamb

Place *the lamb in the casserole and surround it with the onion and carrots, pour over the cider and season.*

Make *a paste from the flour and a little cooking liquid. Stir into the remaining liquid to make the sauce.*

1 Combine the vinegar, oil, honey, marjoram, cider and soy sauce. Stir well. Place the lamb in a shallow dish and pour the mixture over it. Baste the lamb thoroughly and marinate for at least 5 hours or overnight. Baste occasionally.

2 Put the butter in a casserole, cover with cling film rolled back at one edge, and melt it at 100% (High) for 2 minutes. Place shoulder of lamb and marinade in the casserole with the onion and carrots. Season.

3 Calculate the cooking time from the chart and microwave the lamb at 100% (High) for 5 minutes, then reduce to 50% (Medium) for the remaining time.

Honey Braised Lamb

Turn the meat over half way through cooking. Stand covered for 15 minutes.

4 Add a little of the cooking liquid to the flour and stir to a smooth paste. Stir back into the casserole and microwave the sauce at 100% (High) for 4 minutes to thicken it, stirring twice during microwaving. Strain the sauce and serve with the lamb, cooked green beans, sliced carrots and onions. Garnish with a rosemary sprig.

Microtips

Standing time also allows the meat to settle after cooking; this makes it much easier to carve.

206

Microwave roasting and standing times

MINUTES PER 450g / 1lb	PROCEDURE	DEGREE OF DONENESS	REMOVE AT INTERNAL TEMP	TEMP AFTER 10 MINS	TEMP AFTER 15 MINS
Leg with bone 8-10 10-12 12-14		Rare Medium Well done	54°C / 129°F 64°C / 147°F 70°C / 158°F	64°C / 147°F 74°C / 165°F 80°C / 176°F	66°C / 150°F 76°C / 168°F 82°C / 180°F
Shoulder 7-9 9-11 11-13	Cook at 100% (High) 5 mins continue at 50% (Medium)	Rare Medium Well done	54°C / 129°F 64°C / 147°F 70°C / 158°F	64°C / 147°F 74°C / 165°F 80°C / 176°F	66°C / 150°F 76°C / 168°F 82°C / 180°F
Boned joints 10-12 13-15 16-18		Rare Medium Well done	54°C / 129°F 64°C / 147°F 70°C / 158°F	64°C / 147°F 74°C / 165°F 80°C / 176°F	66°C / 150°F 76°C / 168°F 82°C / 180°F

Marinated leg of lamb

39 mins

Standing time: 10-15 mins

1.4kg / 3lb boned and rolled leg of lamb
5-10ml / 1-2tsp cornflour

MARINADE
150ml / ¼pt barbecue sauce
1 small onion, finely chopped
15ml / 1tbls finely chopped mint
salt and pepper

SERVES 6

1 Combine marinade ingredients.
2 Place lamb in a shallow dish and score meat all over. Pour the marinade over the meat, cover and chill for 8 hours or overnight, turning the meat occasionally.
3 Place the meat on a roasting rack and calculate the cooking time from the chart above. Microwave at 100% (High) for the first 5 minutes, then reduce the power to 50% (Medium) for the remaining time. Turn meat over halfway through and baste occasionally with the marinade.
4 Cover the meat loosely with foil and stand for 15 minutes.
5 Bring the marinade juices to the boil, stir in the cornflour and cook for 1-2 minutes.
6 Slice the lamb, pour over a little sauce and serve with carrots and peas. Garnish with mint sprigs.

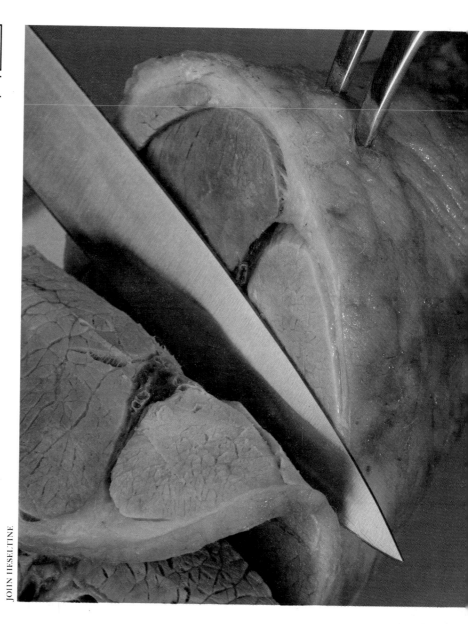

JOHN HESELTINE

207

Spicy Indian Raan

36 mins

Standing time: 10 mins

Raan is a spicy Indian lamb dish; serve it with rice and courgettes or sliced aubergine.

2kg / 4½lb leg of lamb, trimmed of fat
2 garlic cloves, crushed
2 onions
juice and zest of 1 lemon
5cm / 2in piece fresh ginger root, sliced
5ml / 1tsp cumin seeds
5ml / 1tsp cardamom seeds
5ml / 1tsp turmeric
2.5ml / ½tsp ground cloves
5ml / 1tsp salt
50g / 2oz ground almonds
15ml / 1tbls dark brown sugar
150ml / 5fl oz natural yoghurt

SERVES 6

1 Pierce the leg of lamb all over with the point of a knife. Put the garlic, onions, lemon juice and zest, ginger root, spices and salt into an electric blender and grind to a paste. Alternatively use a mortar and pestle. Spread the paste all over the lamb until it is completely covered, then place on a shallow dish and set aside for at least 1 hour.

2 Beat together the almonds, sugar and yoghurt. Spread the mixture over the lamb, cover the dish loosely with foil, and leave in the refrigerator for several hours or overnight.

3 Place the lamb in a deep casserole and microwave at 100% (High) for 5 minutes, turning the meat once during the time. Reduce the power to 50% (Medium) and microwave for the remainder of the calculated cooking time (see chart), or until the lamb reaches the desired internal temperature and is tender and done to taste. Turn the meat 2 or 3 times during cooking. Leave to stand, covered loosely with foil, for 15 minutes. Garnish the lamb with watercress and serve with boiled rice and courgettes.

Spicy Indian Raan

How to microwave Raan

Grind *to a paste the garlic, onions, lemon juice and zest, ginger root, spices and salt in a blender; or use a mortar and pestle. Spread over the lamb.*

Beat *together the almonds, sugar and yoghurt and spread the mixture over the lamb. Leave to marinate in a cold place for several hours.*

Veal escalopes

Microwaved veal escalopes make dinner party meals in a matter of minutes. Tender veal steaks cooked in a sumptuous soured cream sauce or with a tasty Mozzarella cheese topping are just two of the alternatives.

Veal is naturally tender and fine grained and has little or no marbling of fat. Because of this it must be shielded during cooking in the microwave by covering the meat with a sauce or by coating the meat in breadcrumbs.

A veal escalope is a lean, boneless piece of meat cut across the grain, from the leg. Before cooking, it is usually placed between two sheets of cling film or wet greaseproof paper and beaten out to a 6mm / ¼in thickness with a rolling pin or meat bat as shown in the steps on page 210. The meat will then be thin enough to cook quickly and retain its moisture.

If veal escalopes are not readily available, boneless steak cutlets can be used instead. Beat them out to the right thickness or, if they are too thick, cut them across the width and then beat out.

Add seasonings to bring out the delicate flavour of the veal or cook in a tasty sauce.

Hungarian Veal Paprika

Preparing veal escalopes

Beat *out veal escalopes to a 6mm / ¼in thickness for extra fast cooking. Place between 2 sheets of wet grease-proof paper or cling film and beat with a meat bat or rolling pin.*

Use *veal steak cutlets if escalopes are hard to obtain. Cut them in half through the width if they are too thick, trim away fat and beat out in the same way as an escalope.*

Cut *strips of veal from escalopes or cutlets, after they have been beaten out to a 6mm / ¼in thickness. Cut the meat across the grain into even, 12mm / ½in strips.*

Veal and vegetable bake

| 14 mins |

Standing time: none

4 veal escalopes or steaks, about
   100g / 4oz each
1 onion, thinly sliced and
   separated into rings
175g / 6oz tomato purée
15ml / 1tbls plain flour
2.5ml / ½tsp dried basil
2.5ml / ½tsp dried oregano
10ml / 2tsp dried parsley
1.5ml / ¼tsp garlic powder
1.5ml / ¼tsp salt
1.5ml / ¼tsp black pepper
2 large tomatoes, skinned and
   chopped
2 small courgettes, thinly
   sliced
1 green pepper, cored, seeded
   and cut into thin strips

SERVES 4

1 Beat out the veal with a rolling pin or meat bat (see steps).
2 Place the veal in a 30×20cm / 12×8in baking dish and top with the onion rings. Beat together the tomato, flour, basil, oregano, parsley, garlic powder, salt and pepper to form a smooth paste. Stir in the tomatoes, courgettes and green pepper. Spread the mixture over the veal and onions.
3 Cover with cling film rolled back at one edge and microwave at 100% (High) for 14-15 minutes, or until the veal is no longer pink and the vegetables are tender. Re-arrange the veal in the dish after 8 minutes cooking time.

210

Lemony veal with carrots

14 mins

Standing time: none

A refreshing summer lunch: easy to make in the microwave.

550g / 1¼lb veal escalopes
4 carrots, cut into matchsticks
30ml / 2tbls plain flour
5ml / 1tsp paprika
5ml / 1tsp dried parsley
2.5ml / ½tsp dried rosemary
1.5ml / ¼tsp pepper
125ml / 4fl oz white wine
45ml / 3tbls lemon juice
½ beef stock cube dissolved in
    60ml / 4tbls hot water

SERVES 4

1 Beat out the veal with a rolling pin or meat bat (see steps). Cut into 2.5cm / 1in pieces.
2 Place the carrots in a 1.7L / 3pt casserole. Mix together the flour, paprika, parsley, rosemary and pepper and toss the meat in the mixture, to coat. Add to carrots.
3 Combine the wine, lemon juice and stock and stir into the meat and carrots. Cover with cling film rolled back at one edge and microwave at 70% (Medium-High) for 14-15 minutes, or until the meat and carrots are tender. Stir 2-3 times during cooking. Serve with boiled rice.

Hungarian veal paprika

21½ mins

Standing time: none

4 veal escalopes, about
    100g / 4oz each
25g / 1oz pkt cheese or white
    sauce mix
425ml / 15fl oz hot water
25g / 1oz butter or margarine
175g / 6oz tagliatelle
150ml / 5fl oz soured cream
30ml / 2tbls plain flour
2.5ml / ½tsp salt
large pinch of pepper
paprika
6-8 pepper rings, to garnish

SERVES 4

1 In a 30 × 20cm / 12 × 8in baking dish, combine the sauce mix, water and butter, stirring until the sauce mix is dissolved. Add the tagliatelle, cover and microwave at 100% (High) for 5 minutes.
2 Stir in the soured cream, reduce the power to 50% (Medium) and cook for 5-7 minutes, until the noodles are tender. Stir.
3 Meanwhile combine the flour, salt and pepper. Beat out the escalopes with a meat bat or rolling pin to a thickness of 6mm / ¼in and dip in the flour to coat. Place on top of the pasta and cover with greaseproof paper.
4 Microwave at 50% (Medium) for 8-10 minutes, until the veal is tender. Turn escalopes over and sprinkle pasta with paprika. Microwave, uncovered, for 3 minutes.
5 Microwave 6-8 pepper rings at 100% (High) for 30-45 seconds. Spoon some of the sauce over the escalopes if wished, garnish and serve.

Veal Mozzarella

15 mins

Standing time: none

4 veal escalopes, about
    100g / 4oz each
75g / 3oz Mozzarella cheese,
    grated
15ml / 1tbls chopped parsley

SAUCE
225g / 8oz tomato purée
1.5ml / ¼tsp dried oregano
2.5ml / ½tsp dried basil
1.5ml / ¼tsp garlic powder
salt and pepper
1.5ml / ¼tsp sugar
chopped parsley, to garnish

SERVES 4

1 Combine all the sauce ingredients, cover and microwave at 100% (High) for 1 minute. Reduce to 50% (Medium) and microwave for 3 minutes. Set aside.
2 Place the veal in a 30 × 20cm / 12 × 8in dish. Cover with cling film and microwave at 50% (Medium) for 8-10 minutes until veal is no longer pink, turning over and rearranging once. Drain.
3 Pour the sauce over the veal then sprinkle with Mozzarella cheese and parsley. Microwave at 50% (Medium) for 3-4 minutes, or until the sauce is hot and the cheese has melted. Rotate the dish halfway through cooking. Garnish with chopped parsley.

Veal Mozzarella

Veal rolls with ham and cheese

7¾ mins

Standing time: 5 mins

4 veal steak cutlets, about
   100g / 4oz each
2 ham slices, each cut in half
20ml / 4tsp grated Parmesan
   cheese
1.5ml / ¼tsp pepper
2.5ml / ½tsp ground ginger
45ml / 3tbls cornflake crumbs
10ml / 2tsp dried parsley
20ml / 4tsp butter or margarine
20ml / 4tsp plain flour
2.5ml / ½tsp salt
150ml / ¼pt milk
60ml / 4tbls grated Edam or low
   fat Cheddar cheese,
chopped parsley, to garnish

SERVES 4

1 Beat out the veal cutlets with a meat bat or rolling pin (see steps). Place a piece of ham on each veal cutlet and sprinkle with Parmesan cheese, pepper and a small pinch of the ginger.

2 Roll each cutlet up tightly, secure with a wooden cocktail stick.

3 Mix the cornflake crumbs with 2.5ml / ½tsp dried parsley, then roll the meat in the crumb mixture.

4 Put the coated rolls in a 30 × 20cm/12 × 8in baking dish and cover with cling film rolled back at one edge. Microwave at 50% (Medium) for 6-7 minutes, or until the meat is no longer pink, turning the rolls over twice. Drain, then cover and leave to stand for 5 minutes.

5 Increase the power to 100% (High) and microwave the butter in a covered 575ml / 1pt bowl for 45-60 seconds, until melted. Stir in the flour, salt, remaining ginger and dried parsley. Blend in the milk. Microwave at 100% (High) for 1-1½ minutes, or until thickened, stirring once. Stir in the cheese until it melts. Pour the sauce over the veal rolls and garnish with fresh parsley.

VARIATION
Use 45ml / 3tbls bread crumbs instead of the cornflakes crumbs.

212

Veal with dumplings

21 mins

Standing time: none

4 veal escalopes, about
  100g / 4oz each
30ml / 2tbls plain flour
5ml / 1tsp paprika
2.5ml / ½tsp salt
1.5ml / ¼tsp dried thyme
pinch of pepper
25g / 1oz butter or margarine
2 onions, quartered
295g / 10.4oz can condensed
  cream of chicken soup
150g / 5oz can sliced mushrooms,
  undrained

DUMPLINGS
175g / 6oz plain flour
10ml / 2tsp baking powder
1.5ml / ¼tsp salt
10ml / 2tsp poppy seeds
5ml / 1tsp dried chives
1.5ml / ¼tsp dried thyme
125ml / 4fl oz milk
1 egg, beaten
25g / 1oz butter or margarine,
  melted at 100% (High) for 30-
  45 seconds
45ml / 3tbls seasoned
  breadcrumbs

SERVES 4

VARIATION
Instead of the breadcrumbs, substitute any dried stuffing mix of
your choice to coat the dumplings.
Use fresh instead of the dried
herbs, doubling given quantities.

How to microwave Veal with dumplings

Combine *flour and seasoning; coat escalopes. Place butter in a 30 × 20cm / 12 × 8in baking dish. Cover, microwave at 100% (High) for 1½ minutes. Add escalopes and onions.*

Cover *and microwave at 100% (High) for 2 minutes. Reduce the power to 50% (Medium), then cook for 8 minutes, until the veal is tender. Turn halfway through. Leave to stand.*

Combine *the flour, baking powder and seasonings for the dumplings in a bowl. In a jug, combine milk, egg and melted butter. Blend the liquid into the flour mixture.*

Drop *rounded tablespoonfuls of dough into the seasoned breadcrumbs. Roll to coat on all sides. Reserve. Combine the soup, mushrooms and their juice and mix well.*

Pour *soup mixture over veal. Cover and microwave at 100% (High) for 4 minutes, until hot. Top with dumplings. Microwave, uncovered, for 5 minutes, until dumplings are firm.*

213

RAY DUNS

Escalopes in soured cream

9 mins

Standing time: none

4 veal escalopes, about
   100g / 4oz each
60ml / 4tbls plain flour
15ml / 1tbls butter or margarine,
15ml / 1tbls vegetable oil
275ml / 10fl oz soured cream
5ml / 1tsp plain flour
salt and pepper
chopped parsley, to garnish

SERVES 4

1 Heat a large browning dish for 5 minutes, or according to the manufacturer's instructions.
2 Meanwhile, beat out the escalopes with a meat bat or rolling pin to a thickness of 6mm / ¼in (see steps). Cut them in half and dip in the 60ml / 4tbls flour to coat.
3 Place the escalopes, butter and oil in the preheated dish, cover and microwave at 100% (High) for 1 minute on each side.

4 In a medium-sized bowl, mix together all the remaining ingredients except the parsley and stir until smooth. Pour the sauce over the escalopes.
5 Cover with cling film rolled back at one edge, reduce the power to 50% (Medium) and microwave for 7-8 minutes, or until the veal is tender, stirring the sauce twice during cooking. Sprinkle with parsley just before serving.

Cheesy veal noodles

18 mins

Standing time: 3-4 mins

1 large onion, chopped
25g / 1oz butter or margarine
60ml / 4tbls plain flour
2.5ml / ½tsp mustard powder
2.5ml / ½tsp mixed dried herbs
2.5ml / ½tsp pepper
450g / 1lb veal escalopes, cut into
   12mm / ½in strips (see steps)
500ml / 18fl oz hot beef stock
100g / 4oz tagliatelle

Escalopes in Soured Cream

175g / 6oz mushrooms, sliced
15ml / 1tbls dry vermouth
100g / 4oz Cheddar cheese, grated

SERVES 4

1 In a 2.8L / 5pt casserole combine the onion and butter. Cover and microwave at 100% (High) for 2-3 minutes, or until the onion is soft, stirring once.
2 Put the flour, mustard, mixed herbs and pepper in a plastic bag. Add the meat and shake to coat.
3 Add the floured meat to the casserole and stir in the stock and noodles. Cover with cling film.
4 Microwave at 50% (Medium) for 13-15 minutes, or until the meat and noodles are tender. Stir halfway through cooking.
5 Stir in the mushrooms and vermouth, cover and microwave at 50% (Medium) for 3-4 minutes, or until heated. Stir once.
6 Stir in the cheese until it melts, then cover and leave to stand for 3-4 minutes.

Turkey pieces

Cranberry-pineapple turkey drumsticks or rolled turkey breast with ham and cheese are just two of the tasty recipes made with ease in your microwave using this economical meat.

Turkey drumsticks and boneless breast portions can be cooked quickly and remarkably easily in the microwave. Don't just save this tasty, versatile meat for special occasions. These useful meal-sized portions make great mid-week suppers and with a little dressing up with a sauce or a coating, make elegant meals too.

Turkey drumsticks and breast portions should be available, chilled or frozen from most good supermarkets or butchers. They are good value, so are well worth shopping around for. Turkey drumsticks are large and meaty, so one portion is normally ample for two servings. Turkey breasts can range between 75-225g / 3-8oz, and will make one or two servings according to size (allow about 100g / 4oz per person).

Turkey breasts or fillets come ready skinned and boned and are a boon for everyday and entertaining, since they are so simple and versatile. They are delicious roasted — brushed with melted butter and a sauce of your choice, or they can be rolled, coated or casseroled to make a whole range of mouthwatering dishes.

Drumsticks also are popular and tasty roasted in the microwave. Use a soy or Worcestershire sauce browning mixture to give them a more appealing finish.

Stand turkey breasts for 2 minutes and drumsticks for 5 minutes to complete cooking and further tenderize the meat.

Individual Turkey Rolls

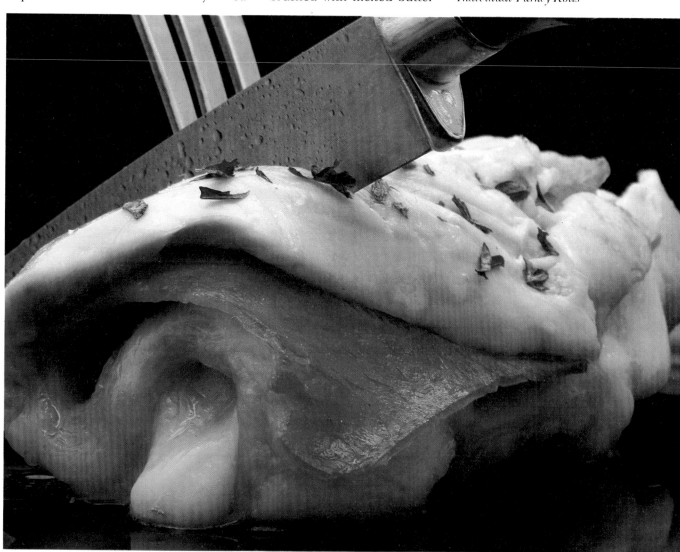

215

Individual turkey rolls

11 mins

Standing time: 5 mins

4 thin slices cooked ham
4 slices processed cheese
4 turkey breasts, 75g-100g / 3-4oz
  each, beaten out to 6mm / ¼in
  thickness
2.5ml / ½tsp dried parsley or
  5ml / 1tsp chopped parsley

SERVES 4

1 Trim the ham and cheese to fit turkey breasts. Place one slice of ham and cheese on each breast.
2 Starting at the narrow end, roll up each breast and secure with a wooden cocktail stick.
3 Arrange, seam up, in a 20cm / 8in square dish. Cover with greaseproof paper.
4 Microwave at 50% (Medium) for 6 minutes. Turn rolls over and sprinkle with parsley. Re-cover and microwave for 5-6 minutes or until the turkey is no longer pink. Stand for 5 minutes.

Cook's notes

Beat out turkey breasts to a thin, even thickness so that this delicate cut of poultry cooks quickly and retains its moisture.

Place breasts between two sheets of cling film or greaseproof paper, dampening the paper first so that it does not stick to the meat. Then use a meat bat or rolling pin to beat out the meat.

How to microwave turkey breasts

Place *each turkey breast between two sheets of cling film or dampened greaseproof paper and beat out to an even 6mm / ¼in thickness with a rolling pin or meat bat.*

Combine *15ml / 1tbls each of melted butter and Worcestershire sauce and brush half over the meat. Place in dish and microwave at 50% (Medium) (see chart on page 217 for timings).*

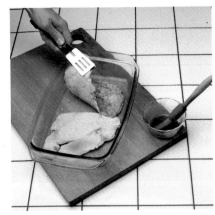

Turn *breasts over halfway through cooking and brush with remaining sauce mixture. Cook for remaining time until flesh is white and juices run clear. Stand for 2 minutes.*

How to microwave turkey drumsticks

Place *turkey drumsticks on a rack, with the meaty parts downwards. Mix together 15ml / 1tbls each oil and soy sauce and brush half the mixture over turkey joints.*

Cover *with greaseproof paper and microwave at 100% (High) for 5 or 8 minutes (see chart on page 217). Reduce to 50% (Medium) and cook for remaining first half of cooking time.*

Turn *the drumsticks over, with meatiest parts placed to the outside. Brush with remaining coating and cook for the rest of the time until the juices run clear. Stand for 5 minutes.*

216

Cranberry Turkey Drumsticks

Creamed turkey

18½ mins

Standing time: 5 mins

50g / 2oz butter or margarine
50g / 2oz plain flour
salt and pepper
250ml / 9fl oz milk
4 bacon rashers, chopped
450g / 1lb turkey breasts, cut
  into thin strips
1 garlic clove, crushed
2.5ml / ½tsp dried basil
100g / 4oz Mozzarella cheese,
  grated

SERVES 4

1 Melt the butter in a large covered jug at 100% (High) for 30-60 seconds. Stir in flour and seasonings and blend in milk.
2 Microwave for 3-4 minutes or until thickened, whisking every minute. Set aside.
3 Microwave bacon in a large covered casserole at 100% (High) for 3-4 minutes until crisp. Drain away surplus fat.
4 Add turkey, white sauce, garlic and basil to casserole. Cover and microwave at 50% (Medium) for 12-15 minutes, until turkey is no longer pink, stirring twice.
5 Add cheese, cover and stand for 5 minutes. Serve with tagliatelle, cooked conventionally.

Cranberry turkey drumsticks

33¼ mins

Standing time: 5 mins

225g / 8oz cranberry sauce
225g / 8oz can crushed pineapple,
  drained

10ml / 2tsp finely grated
  orange zest
10 drops red food colouring
25g / 1oz butter or margarine
30ml / 2tbls Worcestershire
  sauce
4 turkey drumsticks, about
  350g-400g / 12-14oz each

SERVES 4-6

1 In a bowl combine the cranberry sauce, pineapple, orange zest and food colouring.
2 In a small, covered bowl, melt the butter at 100% (High) for 15-30 seconds. Stir in Worcestershire sauce.
3 Place drumsticks on a microwave roasting rack with the meatiest parts upwards and brush with half of both the butter and cranberry mixture. Cover with greaseproof paper.
4 Microwave at 100% (High) for the first 8 minutes of cooking time, then reduce to 50% (Medium) and cook for 25-31 minutes (as calculated in chart left) until juices run clear.
5 Halfway through, turn over and brush with remaining butter and cranberry mixture. Re-cover.
6 Stand, covered with foil, for 5 minutes. Serve whole, or carve meat into slices.

Microwave times for turkey portions

TURKEY PORTION	QUANTITY	START AT 100% (HIGH)	TOTAL COOKING TIME PER 450g / 1lb FINISHING AT 50% (MEDIUM)
Drumsticks	2	5 mins	11-13 mins per lb
	4	8 mins	11-13 mins per lb
Breasts	2	none	8-10 mins per lb
	4	none	8-10 mins per lb

Turkey divan

15 mins

Standing time: 5 mins

250g / 9oz pkt frozen broccoli
290g / 10.6oz can cream of
    chicken soup
30ml / 2tbls sherry
2.5ml / ½tsp salt
4 turkey breasts, about
    100g / 4oz each, beaten out to
    6mm / ¼in thickness
60ml / 4tbls grated Parmesan
    cheese
45ml / 3tbls cornflake crumbs
10ml / 2tsp dried parsley

SERVES 4

1 Microwave broccoli in the packet at 100% (High) for 3-4 minutes, or until thawed. Drain well and chop.

2 Combine the broccoli, chicken soup, sherry and salt in a 30 × 20cm / 12 × 8in dish, spreading the mixture over the base. Cover with cling film and microwave at 100% (High) for 3-5 minutes.
3 Stir and then top with turkey breasts. Cover with greaseproof paper and microwave at 50% (Medium) for 8-10 minutes until meat juices run clear, turning turkey halfway through cooking.
4 Combine the cheese, crumbs and parsley in a small mixing bowl and sprinkle evenly over the turkey breasts.
5 Microwave, uncovered, at 100% (High) for 1-2 minutes until cheese melts. Stand for 5 minutes.

Vegetable braised turkey

25 mins

Standing time: 5 mins

4 turkey drumsticks, about 250g /
    9oz each
1 large tomato, coarsely
    chopped
1 large onion, sliced and
    separated into rings
1 large green pepper, cut into
    thin strips
1 chicken stock cube
65ml / 2½fl oz hot water
1.5ml / ¼tsp salt, optional
2.5ml / ½tsp red wine vinegar

SERVES 4

1 Skin and bone turkey drumsticks and cut meat into 2.5cm / 1in cubes. A 250g / 9oz drumstick yields approximately 150g / 5oz meat.
2 Combine the tomato, onion rings and pepper strips in a 20cm / 8in square dish.
3 Arrange turkey meat over the vegetables.
4 Combine the remaining ingredients and pour over the turkey and vegetables. Cover.
5 Microwave at 100% (High) for 5 minutes. Rotate the dish and rearrange turkey pieces. Reduce the power to 50% (Medium) and microwave for 20-24 minutes or until the meat is no longer pink and juices run clear, rotating the dish twice during cooking.
6 Stand for 5 minutes.

Orange turkey drumsticks

<table><tr><td>24
mins</td></tr></table>

Standing time: 5 mins

2 turkey drumsticks, weighing
about 450-500g / 16-18oz
each, skinned
onion salt
pepper
75ml / 3fl oz orange juice
5ml / 1tsp soy sauce
5ml / 1tsp grated orange zest
2.5ml / ½tsp ground coriander

SAUCE
125ml / 4fl oz orange juice
5ml / 1tsp soy sauce
5ml / 1tsp cornflour

SERVES 4

1 Sprinkle both sides of drumsticks with a little onion salt and pepper. Arrange, bone side up, in a 30 × 20cm / 12 × 8in dish.
2 Combine orange juice, soy sauce, orange zest and coriander. Pour over turkey. Cover with greaseproof paper.
3 Microwave at 100% (High) for 5 minutes. Reduce to 50% (Medium) and microwave for 17-21 minutes (according to chart, page 217) until juices run clear.
4 Halfway through cooking, turn drumsticks over, basting with sauce. Re-cover.
5 When cooked, remove from dish and cover loosely with foil.

Orange Turkey Drumsticks

DAVE KING

Leave to stand for 5 minutes.
6 Mix together the sauce ingredients. Stir into meat juices and microwave at 100% (High) for 2 minutes until sauce thickens slightly.
7 Cut the meat from the bone and serve with the sauce poured over or served separately.

Honey-glazed drumsticks

<table><tr><td>45
mins</td></tr></table>

Standing time: 5 mins

4 turkey drumsticks, about
450-700g / 1lb-1½lb each

GLAZE
125ml / 4fl oz honey

Honey-glazed Drumsticks

grated zest of 1 lemon
10ml / 2tsp lemon juice
1.5ml / ½tsp Worcestershire
sauce

SERVES 6-8

1 Combine the glaze ingredients in a bowl and microwave at 100% (High) for 1 minute, until warm.
2 Place turkey on rack, meaty part down. Brush with half the glaze.
3 Microwave at 100% (High) for the first 8 minutes, then at 50% (Medium) for 36-46 minutes (see chart, page 217).
4 Turn drumsticks over once and brush with remaining glaze. Stand, covered, for 5 minutes, then carve meat from the bone and serve.

Microwaving whole turkey

Cooking turkey the conventional way can be a daunting experience — even for the experienced cook. However, the microwave makes the job easy and the turkey cooks beautifully in under half the conventional time.

By using the microwave to cook a whole turkey, the problem of accurate timing (so critical for moist, succulent results) is easily solved and the cooking is completed in under half the time it would take conventionally.

There should be about 5cm / 2in clear space between the turkey and the cooker walls, so bear this in mind before buying the turkey. As a guide an average-sized microwave with a cooker capacity about 35.5cm / 14in (deep), 35.5cm / 14in (wide) and 28cm / 11in

(high), holds a 5.4-5.9kg / 12-13lb whole turkey comfortably. The maximum size turkey most larger de-luxe microwaves can take is a 6.3-6.8kg / 14-15lb bird.

Buying and storing
Turkeys are available either fresh, chilled or frozen, in a range of sizes. Whichever you buy, the breast should be plump and white (with no dark bruising), and the drumsticks firm and rounded. For a fresh, oven-ready bird, check for a pliable breastbone as this indicates a young, tender bird. Chilled turkeys are prewrapped, with the giblets packed separately inside them, and are available from butchers and supermarkets. Frozen turkeys are sold oven-ready and are the cheapest to buy. Complete thawing is essential before cooking to ensure the bird will be tender and safe to eat.

A fresh turkey, loosely covered on a plate, will keep for up to two days in the refrigerator.

Glazing the turkey
To help keep the turkey flesh juicy and appetizing and give the skin its golden brown appearance it is necessary to glaze the turkey before cooking. There are several glazes to choose from (see recipe and variations page 222).

Stuffing the turkey
Although a stuffing is not essential, it is always a popular addition to a turkey meal. In the microwave a stuffed turkey cooks in the same time as an unstuffed bird, provided that the neck cavity — **not** the body cavity — is stuffed. Alternatively make the stuffing into balls and cook these while the turkey is completing its standing time (see recipes page 224).

Accompaniments
To complete the meal, don't forget the trimmings. Serve the turkey with traditional accompaniments like Brussels sprouts, carrots and potatoes, plus Bread Sauce, Cranberry Sauce (page 308) and Rich Giblet Gravy (page 223).

Glazed turkey on a bed of endive, garnished with maraschino cherries

221

How to microwave whole turkey

Stuff *the neck cavity of the oven-ready turkey, if liked (see recipes page 224). Truss the bird if necessary to keep shape during cooking and secure the loose neck skin with a wooden cocktail stick. Weigh the turkey and calculate the cooking time (see the chart page 223); divide the cooking time into quarters. Place the turkey, breast-side down, in a large shallow dish.*

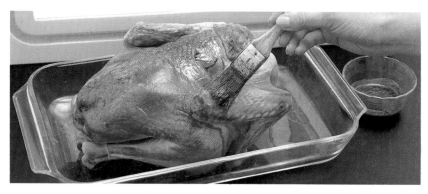

Brush *with a glaze (see recipe, above right). Microwave at 100% (High) for one quarter of calculated cooking time. Turn turkey on one side, brush with glaze and juices in dish. Cook at 100% (High) for another quarter of calculated time. Turn on to other side, baste again and cook for the third quarter calculated time. (If some areas begin to overbrown, shield with well secured small pieces of smooth foil.)*

Turn *the turkey breast-side up and baste well. Microwave at 100% (High) for remaining cooking time; baste turkey every 10-15 minutes. Drain off juices and reserve for making gravy (see recipe opposite). Cover turkey with foil and stand (see chart page 223).*

To test *if the turkey is cooked: drumsticks will move freely at the joints; flesh will feel very soft when pressed. The juices should run clear when fleshy part under leg is pierced with a fine skewer. If juices appear pink, cook a further few minutes.*

Basic turkey glaze

½ min

Standing time: none

50g / 2oz butter
15ml / 1tbls soy sauce

SUFFICIENT FOR GLAZING A
5.4kg / 12lb TURKEY

1 Put the butter in a bowl, cover and microwave at 100% (High) for 30-60 seconds until melted.
2 Stir in the soy sauce.

VARIATIONS
Spiced glaze: omit the soy sauce and add 2.5ml / ½tsp turmeric to the melted butter.
Tangy glaze: add the finely grated zest of ½ lemon to the Basic Turkey Glaze.
Herb glaze: add 5ml / 1tsp dried oregano to the Basic Turkey Glaze.

Cook's notes

Once the standing time is completed, an additional check (when testing turkey is cooked) can be carried out using a conventional meat thermometer. Insert the thermometer into the joint between the thigh and breast, rotate it two or three times and allow 1 minute for an accurate reading. If the turkey is cooked it will register 85°C / 185°F; if not, remove the thermometer and cook for a further few minutes before testing again. Do not use the meat thermometer when microwaving the turkey in the cooker; a microwave thermometer, however, can be used — follow the manufacturer's instructions.

222

Rich giblet gravy

13 mins

Standing time: none

turkey giblets, defrosted if frozen
575ml / 1pt boiling water
1 large onion, cut into quarters
salt and pepper
15ml / 3tsp cornflour
30ml / 2tbls cold water
a few drops of gravy browning
meat juices from cooked turkey
10ml / 2tsp sherry

SERVES 8

1 Put the giblets into a bowl with the boiling water, onion and seasoning. Cover and microwave at 100% (High) for 10-12 minutes, stirring twice during cooking.
2 Blend the cornflour with the cold water in a separate bowl. Strain the giblet stock into bowl, stirring well all the time. Add a few drops gravy browning. Skim off any fat from surface of reserved turkey juices; add juices to the bowl. Stir in sherry.
3 Microwave at 100% (High) for 3-4 minutes, stirring twice until smooth and thickened. Taste and adjust seasoning if necessary.

Freezer notes

If using frozen giblets: put giblets into a bowl, cover and microwave at 20-30% (Defrost) for 2-3 minutes until thawed.

Cook's notes

You may like to remove the liver from the giblets before making the stock as it can sometimes give a rather strong flavour.

Freezer notes

If using a frozen turkey: unwrap and weigh the turkey and calculate the thawing time, allowing 3½-5½ minutes per 450g / 1lb. Place turkey, breast side down, in a shallow dish and microwave at 50% (Medium) for quarter of calculated thawing time. Shield warm areas with well secured small, smooth pieces of foil, turn turkey breast side up and microwave for a further quarter of the time. Check for warm or brown spots and shield with smooth pieces of foil, if necessary. Shield legs and wing tips; turn turkey over, rotate dish and microwave for half the remaining time. Turn turkey over and microwave for the remaining thawing time. Make sure the body cavity of turkey is cool but not icy before cooking.

Microtips

Giblets should always be cooked on the day of purchase. Use giblets for stock, if not making Rich Giblet Gravy. Add 275ml / ½pt of boiling water to giblets, sliced carrot, onion, celery and season. Microwave at 100% (High) for 7-10 minutes. Strain.

Microwave times* for whole turkey

TURKEY SIZE	COOKING TIME (with or without stuffing)	STANDING TIME (tented with foil)	NUMBER OF SERVINGS
2.7kg / 6lb	42 mins	10 mins	6-8
4kg / 9lb	1 hr 3 mins	15 mins	10-12
5.4-5.9kg / 12-13lb	1 hr 24 mins-1hr 31 mins	20 mins	14-16
6.8kg / 15lb	1 hr 45 mins	25 mins	18

Times are calculated at 7-8 minutes per 450g / 1lb at 100% (High)

How to carve whole turkey

Hold *the drumstick and pull away from the body. Cut between thigh and body to the leg joint. Pull leg out and back, using point of a knife to sever it. Cut off drumstick from thigh at joint. Slice the thigh and drumstick meat parallel to the bone.*

Make *a long horizontal cut above the wing joint into the body frame of the turkey. Ease the wing away from the body and cut through the gristle using the point of a knife to sever the wing joint from the body of the bird. Repeat this on other side of the bird.*

Beginning *halfway up the breast, cut thin even slices parallel with the breast bone down to a horizontal cut made above the wing joint. Continue slicing the white breast meat in this way, then carve the breast meat on other side of the bird in the same way.*

223

Artichoke nut stuffing balls

11 mins

Standing time: none

1 small onion, finely chopped
1 celery stalk, finely chopped
4 rashers streaky bacon, rinded
  and chopped
50g / 2oz butter or margarine
100g / 4oz walnuts, chopped
175g / 6oz fresh breadcrumbs
400g / 14oz can artichoke hearts,
  thoroughly drained on
  absorbent paper and chopped
10ml / 2tsp dried oregano
1 egg, beaten
salt and pepper

SERVES 8

1 Put the onion, celery, bacon and butter into a large bowl. Cover and microwave at 100% (High) for 4-5 minutes until onion and celery have softened, stirring once.
2 Add the chopped walnuts, breadcrumbs, artichoke hearts, oregano, egg and seasoning to taste; mix thoroughly. Form mixture into 16 even-sized balls, using lightly floured hands.
3 Arrange these in a circle around the edge of a large plate. (Place any remaining balls in the centre.) Microwave at 100% (High) for 7-8 minutes, until just firm.

Microtips

For convenience, make and cook the stuffing balls in advance. Reheat them at 100% (High) for 3-4 minutes while the turkey completes its standing time.

Freezer notes

Frozen cranberries can be used instead of the fresh berries. Put the cranberries on a plate and microwave at 20-30% (Defrost) for 3-4 minutes, rearranging every minute, then follow the recipe instructions. Canned cranberries, well drained, can also be substituted; follow recipe instructions from Step 2.

PAUL WEBSTER

Cranberry spice stuffing

5½ mins

Standing time: none

175g / 6oz fresh cranberries
30ml / 2tbls soft brown
  sugar
15ml / 1tbls water
25g / 1oz butter or margarine
1 onion, finely chopped
225g / 8oz pork sausagemeat

100g / 4oz fresh breadcrumbs
60ml / 4tbls chopped parsley
2.5ml / ½tsp ground
  allspice
salt and pepper

FOR A 5.4kg / 12lb TURKEY

1 Put the fresh cranberries into a bowl with the soft brown sugar and the water. Microwave, uncovered, at 100% (High) for 2½-3 minutes until the cranberries have softened slightly.

Turkey with chilli beans

<table><tr><td>8
mins</td></tr></table>

Standing time: 5 mins

When you need a tasty supper in a hurry, this Mexican-style dish using leftover turkey meat and red kidney beans should fit the bill.

1 onion, chopped
1 garlic clove, crushed
30ml / 2tbls vegetable oil
225-275g / 8-10oz cooked turkey meat, diced
227g / 8oz can tomatoes, broken up
30ml / 2tbls tomato purée or paste
425g / 15oz can red kidney beans, drained
5ml / 1tsp mild chilli seasoning
150ml / ¼pt soured cream
salt and pepper
1 ripe avocado, skinned and sliced
5ml / 1tsp lemon juice

SERVES 4

1 Put the onion, garlic and oil into a large dish and microwave at 100% (High) for 3 minutes, stirring once.
2 Stir in the turkey, tomatoes, tomato purée, beans, chilli seasoning, 30ml / 2tbls of the soured cream and season.
3 Cover and microwave at 100% (High) for 5-6 minutes until the mixture is heated through and thickened slightly, stirring once.
4 Swirl the remaining soured cream into mixture and top with slices of avocado, tossed in lemon juice. Cover; stand for 5 minutes.

Turkey with Artichoke Nut Stuffing Balls and accompaniments

Turkey and bacon kebabs

<table><tr><td>7½
mins</td></tr></table>

Standing time: 3 mins

Use up leftover cooked turkey meat in this fun recipe that is quick to make and would serve as ideal party time nibbles.

175g / 6oz streaky bacon rashers, rinded; cut in half crossways
45ml / 3tbls mango chutney
225g / 8oz cooked turkey meat, cut into 12mm / ½in chunks
1 small onion, quartered and separated into layers
1 small red pepper, seeded and cut into 12 pieces

SAUCE
1 banana, peeled and mashed
5ml / 1tsp lemon juice
150ml / 5fl oz natural yoghurt
salt and pepper

SERVES 4

1 Spread the halved bacon rashers with 30ml / 2tbls of chutney. Wrap bacon around turkey chunks, chutney-sides in.
2 Thread the turkey rolls, onion layers and pieces of red pepper alternately on to four wooden or bamboo skewers.
3 Space skewers well apart on a large plate and cover with absorbent paper. Microwave at 100% (High) for 7½-9 minutes, until bacon is cooked. Turn twice and drain off any liquid. Stand for 3 minutes.
4 Meanwhile, mix together the mashed banana, lemon juice, yoghurt, remaining chopped chutney and seasoning. Serve kebabs with yoghurt sauce.

2 Place the butter and onion in a separate bowl and microwave at 100% (High) for 3-4 minutes, until the onion has softened, stirring once.
3 Beat the cranberry and onion mixtures together, then add the sausagemeat, breadcrumbs, parsley, allspice and seasoning to taste; mix well until thoroughly combined.
4 Use to stuff the neck cavity of the turkey.

Cook's notes

Although leftover cooked turkey is ideal for this dish, fresh turkey fillets, diced, can also be used. Add to the garlic and onion mixture after 3 minutes and microwave at 100% (High) for a further 4-6 minutes, stirring once. Add tomatoes, tomato purée, beans, chilli and cream; then follow recipe instructions.

Microtips

Remember that metal kebab skewers cannot be used in the microwave. Bamboo skewers are available from good food shops or oriental stores. These wooden skewers are sold in packets, containing 40-50. If you have difficulty finding them, use wooden cocktail sticks instead and allow three per person.

Stuffed roast chicken

Roast chicken with a moist, flavoursome stuffing is a favourite treat for the whole family. Use your microwave and have a satisfying dinner in under 45 minutes.

Everyone enjoys a whole roasted chicken either for a family meal or special occasion dinner. Tasty stuffings and glazes enhance the flavour of the chicken and help to keep it moist and succulent. Cook the chicken in your microwave, add accompany- ing vegetables and you have a quick satisfying meal.

The cooking time varies slightly according to the shape and size of the chicken, so it is essential to test that it is thoroughly cooked. Pierce the flesh just behind the thigh where the meat is very thick. The juices should run clear with no trace of pinkness. The legs should also move freely. If the chicken isn't done, return it to the micro- wave for 1-2 minutes more.

Since the stuffing recipes given

Chicken with Herb Stuffing

226

here are pre-cooked or cook quickly, weigh the bird before stuffing to calculate the cooking time. Otherwise you may find that the chicken is overdone. Allow 6-9 minutes per 450g / 1lb.

Do not pack the stuffing in too tightly, but allow some room for it to swell. Once the chicken is stuffed, tie the legs and wings with string. This helps it to maintain a good shape and to cook evenly. Since chicken does not brown evenly in the microwave, you may want to use a glaze or browning agent to achieve an oven-roasted appearance, such as the glazes on page 230.

Place the chicken, breast uppermost, on a roasting rack or in a large dish. Check to make sure that it is cooking evenly, particularly on the underside. A large bird may need to be turned over to

finish, and you should rotate the dish during cooking. If chicken splatters, cover loosely with greaseproof paper.

After draining, tent with foil, shiny side in, and stand for 10-12 minutes. Test and microwave for 1-2 minutes more if necessary.

Microtips

Any reserved stuffing can be microwaved in a covered bowl at 100% (High) for 5 minutes or until heated through, while chicken stands.

Microwave times for roasting chicken

WEIGHT OF CHICKEN	TIME AT 100% (HIGH)*	PROCEDURE
1kg / 2lb	12 – 16 mins	Check halfway through cooking. Turn dish. Stand 10 mins.
1.5kg / 3lb	18 – 24 mins	Check two-thirds through cooking. Turn dish. Stand 10-12 mins.
1.8kg / 4lb	25 – 36 mins	Check and turn over after 20 mins. Stand 12 mins.

*Times are a guide; test for doneness at the end of minimum recommended cooking time and again after standing. Return chicken to microwave for 1-2 minutes at 100% (High) if necessary, to finish.

Chicken with herb stuffing

| 23 mins |

Standing time: 10 mins

1.5kg / 3lb oven-ready chicken

STUFFING AND COATING
2.5ml / ½tsp grated lemon zest
5ml / 1tsp dried oregano
5ml / 1tsp dried sage
5ml / 1tsp dried marjoram
1 garlic clove, crushed
1 small onion, finely chopped
25g / 1oz butter
100g / 4oz fresh breadcrumbs
45ml / 3tbls milk
salt and pepper
15ml / 1tbls chopped parsley

SERVES 4

Cook's notes

To keep the flesh of a roasted chicken moist, do not prick the skin before cooking. Instead, prick it all over before leaving it to stand to allow any juices and fat to drain off. These juices from the chicken can be used to make a sauce or gravy.

How to microwave Chicken with herb stuffing

Mix *the lemon zest, dried herbs and garlic. Microwave onion and butter in a covered bowl at 100% (High) for 5 minutes or until soft. Combine with breadcrumbs, half the herb mixture and milk. Season to taste.*

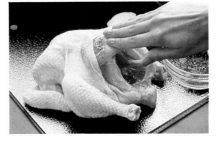

Loosen *and lift skin over breast of chicken. Rub remaining herb mixture under skin carefully to avoid tearing it. Stuff chicken loosely with breadcrumb mixture, but do not overfill it. Reserve any extra.*

Truss *chicken legs with string. Mix the parsley with pepper and sprinkle over the top. Place chicken, breast side up, on a roasting rack or in a shallow dish. Microwave at 100% (High) for 18-24 minutes; turn after 12 minutes.*

Check *underside after 15 minutes; turn over if not cooking evenly. Test leg at end of cooking time, it should move freely. Pierce thickest part of thigh: juices should run clear. Tent with foil; stand 10 minutes.*

227

Farmhouse chicken

23
mins

Standing time: 10 mins

1.5kg / 3lb oven-ready chicken

VEGETABLE STUFFING
1 small potato, peeled and diced
1 onion, chopped
2 celery stalks, chopped
1 garlic clove, crushed
5ml / 1tsp dried rosemary
25g / 1oz butter or margarine
salt and pepper
50g / 2oz fresh breadcrumbs
100g / 4oz mushrooms, chopped
1 small canned pimiento,
   chopped

SERVES 4

Festive roast chicken

23
mins

Standing time: 10 mins

1.5kg / 3lb oven-ready chicken

CHESTNUT STUFFING
1 large onion, finely chopped
25g / 1oz butter or margarine
5ml / 1tsp dried sage
salt and pepper to taste
439g / 15.5oz can unsweetened
   chestnut purée
50g / 2oz fresh breadcrumbs
60ml / 4tbls brandy or sherry

SERVES 4

1 Put onion and butter in a bowl, cover and microwave at 100% (High) for 5 minutes. Stir in the sage, salt and pepper and chestnut purée, mixing well. Add breadcrumbs and brandy.
2 Fill chicken with stuffing, reserving any extra (see Microtips, page 227). Tie legs with string. Place chicken, breast-side up, on a roasting rack or in a large dish.
3 Microwave at 100% (High) for 18-24 minutes. Turn after about 12 minutes and check underside of chicken. Turn over if it is not cooking evenly. Test for doneness at end of cooking time.
4 Cover chicken with foil; stand for 10 minutes.

VARIATION
For Crunchy nut stuffing, use 50g / 2oz ground almonds and 100g / 4oz finely-chopped mixed nuts instead of the chestnuts.

How to microwave Farmhouse chicken

Put *potato, onion and celery into a bowl with the garlic and rosemary. Add butter, cover and microwave at 100% (High) for 5-7 minutes or until all the vegetables are just tender.*

Stir *in salt and pepper, breadcrumbs, mushrooms and pimiento. Stuff chicken loosely: reserve extra stuffing. Tie chicken with string. Place on roasting rack or in large dish.*

Microwave *at 100% (High) for 18-24 minutes. Turn after 12 minutes and check underside. Turn chicken over if it is not cooking evenly. Test for doneness at end of cooking time.*

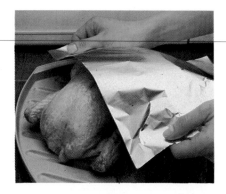

Tent *cooked chicken with foil, shiny side in. Stand 10 minutes. Microwave any reserved stuffing while chicken is standing (see Microtips, page 227). Test chicken after standing.*

228

CHRIS KNAGGS

Chicken with fruity stuffing

24 mins

Standing time: 10 mins

1.5kg / 3lb oven-ready chicken

FRUITY PORK STUFFING
225g / 8oz pork sausagemeat
1 onion, finely chopped
1 small cooking apple, peeled,
  cored and chopped
2.5ml / ½tsp ground mixed spice
30ml / 2tbls raisins
45ml / 3tbls fresh breadcrumbs
salt and pepper to taste

SERVES 4

1 Put sausagemeat in a bowl; break up. Add onion, cover and microwave at 100% (High) for 6-7 minutes. Stir once and drain.
2 Stir in apple, spice, raisins, and breadcrumbs; season. Mix well and stuff chicken loosely.
3 Tie chicken legs with string. Place on a roasting rack or dish.
4 Microwave at 100% (High) for 18-24 minutes. Turn after 12 minutes; check underside. Turn chicken over if not cooking evenly. Test.
5 Tent with foil; stand 10 minutes. Test again.

Above from left to right: *Chestnut, Crunchy Nut and Fruity Pork Stuffings* **Left:** *Farmhouse Chicken*

Bacon-stuffed roast chicken

26½ mins

Standing time: 10 mins

1.5kg / 3lb oven-ready chicken

BACON STUFFING
**5 rashers smoked bacon, rinds
removed, diced
1 onion, finely chopped
1 celery stalk, thinly sliced
30ml / 2tbls chopped parsley
50g / 2oz fresh breadcrumbs
salt and pepper**

GLAZE
**25g / 1oz butter
pinch of turmeric**

SERVES 4

1 Put bacon in a bowl, cover and microwave at 100% (High) for 4-5 minutes, or until crisp. Remove bacon with slotted spoon; drain.
2 Place onion and celery in bacon fat and microwave at 100% (High) for 4-5 minutes, or until soft. Stir in parsley, breadcrumbs and bacon; season. Mix well and use to stuff the chicken.
3 Melt butter in a covered bowl for 30 seconds at 100% (High). Stir in turmeric.
4 Tie legs with string. Place, breast side up, on a roasting rack or in a large dish; brush with butter glaze.
5 Microwave at 100% (High) for 18-24 minutes. Turn after 12 minutes; check underside. Turn it over if not cooking evenly. Test.
6 Cover with foil; stand for 10 minutes. Test again.

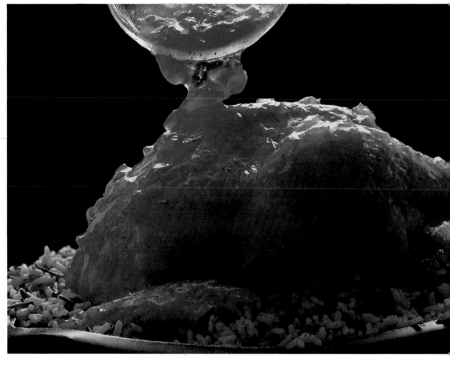

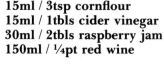

Glazed chicken with rice

41 mins

Standing time: 15 mins

1.5kg / 3lb oven-ready chicken

RICE STUFFING
**100g / 4oz long-grain rice
1 onion, finely chopped
275ml / ½pt water
30ml / 2tbls chopped fresh herbs,
mixed or 15ml / 1tbls dried
mixed herbs
salt and pepper to taste**

GLAZE
**grated zest and juice of 1
orange**

**15ml / 3tsp cornflour
15ml / 1tbls cider vinegar
30ml / 2tbls raspberry jam
150ml / ¼pt red wine**

SERVES 4

1 Put rice and onion in a large bowl. Stir in water, cover and microwave at 100% (High) for 15 minutes. Stand for 5 minutes; stir in herbs and season.
2 Stuff chicken with rice. Tie legs with string. Place chicken, breast side up, on a roasting rack or in a large, rectangular dish.
3 Microwave at 100% (High) for 18-24 minutes. Turn a half turn after 12 minutes and check underside. Turn chicken over if necessary. Test at end of cooking time.
4 Tent chicken with foil. Stand for 10 minutes, test again.
5 Make glaze. Combine orange juice and zest, cornflour, vinegar, jam and wine. Microwave at 100% (High) for 4-5 minutes or until hot; stir.
6 Pour off juices from chicken and add to glaze. Microwave for a further 3 minutes, stirring once.
7 Heat remaining stuffing at 100% (High) for 1-2 minutes. Pour hot glaze over chicken. Serve with extra stuffing.

Above: *Glazed Chicken with Rice*
Left: *Bacon-stuffed Roast Chicken*

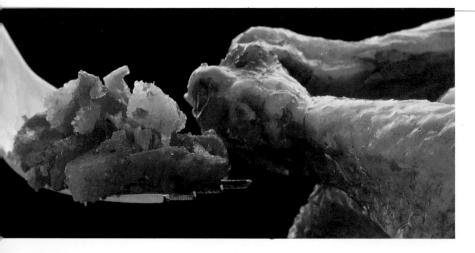

Casseroling chicken portions

Chicken cooks to perfection in the microwave, remaining moist and tender every time. Combine it with a variety of other ingredients for quick-to-produce, tasty casseroles.

Chicken is surely the most versatile of meats. Its flavour marries happily with a huge variety of ingredients, from every kind of fruit and vegetable to all sorts of herbs and spices. The fact that it can be further enhanced and enriched by flavoursome stock, wine or cream makes it possible to produce all manner of casseroles.

Use the readily available chicken portions for making casseroles, buying them as portions. Or, joint a whole chicken yourself (see recipe and steps, page 232). Chicken portions make catering for specific numbers very easy; they also cook quickly and evenly in the microwave.

When buying chicken portions, choose those that look plump and fresh. If possible, examine the pieces carefully to ensure they have no large bits of fat sticking to them. If you find they do have when you get them home, cut this off before cooking. Skin the chicken, too, if you want to reduce the amount of fat in your diet.

Herby Spring Chicken

Freezer notes

Frozen chicken portions are an ideal freezer stand-by, but must be completely thawed before cooking. To thaw, brush off any particles of ice, then arrange on a plate with the meatiest parts outwards. Cover and microwave at 20-30% (Defrost), allowing 7-8 minutes per 450g / 1lb, turning the plate a quarter turn three times; separate pieces if necessary. Stand, covered, for 8-10 minutes.

RAY DUNS

231

Herby spring chicken

38 mins

Standing time: 5 mins

1.5kg / 3lb oven-ready chicken
15ml / 1tbls vegetable oil
12-16 tiny new potatoes (total weight 350g / 12oz)
225g / 8oz baby carrots, sliced lengthways
100g / 4oz French beans
100g / 4oz button mushrooms
1 onion, cut into wedges
15ml / 1tbls plain flour
150ml / ¼pt chicken stock or half stock and half dry white wine
30ml / 2tbls chopped mixed herbs
salt and pepper

SERVES 4

Chicken curry with coconut

68 mins

Standing time: none

Serve this curry with boiled rice, poppadums, a sliced tomato and onion salad, sliced bananas and mango chutney.

4 chicken pieces (total weight about 1.6kg / 3½lb)
5cm / 2in piece fresh root ginger, finely chopped
4 garlic cloves, crushed
50g / 2oz flaked almonds
50g / 2oz sultanas
5ml / 1tsp turmeric
5ml / 1tsp chilli powder
100g / 4oz creamed coconut, broken into pieces
425ml / ¾pt water

30ml / 2tbls finely chopped coriander leaves or 5ml / 1tsp ground coriander
salt and pepper
15ml / 3tsp cornflour, blended with 30ml / 2tbls water

SERVES 4

1 Heat a browning dish at 100% (High) for 5 minutes or according to manufacturer's instructions. Skin the chicken.
2 Cook two pieces of chicken in the browning dish at 100% (High) for 2 minutes. Transfer to a 2.3L / 4pt casserole. Reheat the browning dish for 2 minutes at 100% (High) and cook the remaining chicken in the same way. Transfer to the casserole.
3 Mix the ginger and garlic together. Add to the casserole with all the remaining ingredients ex-

How to microwave Herby spring chicken

Place *chicken on a board. Using poultry shears or a sharp, strong knife, cut off parson's nose, wing tips and small end joints from the legs. Pull out and discard any fat from inside the carcass.*

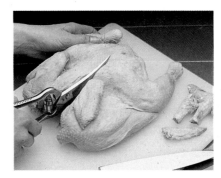

Cut *lengthways along and through the breastbone. Press open the chicken so that it lies flat, then cut through the length of the backbone so that the chicken is now in two halves.*

Cut *through between the leg and carcass of one chicken half to make two even-sized quarters. Repeat with the other half of the chicken. Pierce the portions all over with a fork.*

Pre-heat *browning dish at 100% (High) for 5 minutes or according to maker's instructions. Add oil. Add chicken skin side down. Press until sizzling stops; cover and microwave at 100% (High) for 8 minutes.*

Remove *chicken from the dish and set aside. Place the potatoes, carrots and beans in a bowl, cover and microwave at 100% (High) for 5 minutes, stirring once. Add the mushrooms and onion and cook for 5 minutes more.*

Stir *in flour; gradually add stock, half the herbs and season. Arrange chicken on top; microwave at 100% (High) for 15 minutes or until cooked. Stand 5 minutes; sprinkle with remaining herbs. Transfer to serving dish.*

232

cept for the blended cornflour. Cover and microwave at 30% (Low) for 55-57 minutes, until tender. Rearrange three times.

4 Remove the chicken from the casserole and skim any fat from the sauce. Stir in the cornflour. Microwave at 100% (High) for 2 minutes, stirring once. Return the chicken to the dish and serve.

Moroccan chicken stew

32 mins

Standing time: 5 mins

3 carrots, sliced
1 large onion, chopped
225g / 8oz swede, diced
2.5ml / ½tsp ground coriander
pinch of ground cinnamon
2.5ml / ½tsp cayenne pepper
2.5ml / ½tsp caraway seeds
salt and pepper
2 courgettes, sliced
397g / 14oz can tomatoes
50ml / 2tbls tomato purée or paste
50g / 2oz raisins
4 chicken breasts on the bone, skinned (total weight about 1.1kg / 2½lb)

SERVES 4

1 Place carrots, onion, swede, spices and seasonings in a 2.3L / 4pt casserole. Cover and microwave at 100% (High) for 12 minutes or until vegetables are tender. Stir twice during cooking.
2 Add the courgette, tomatoes, tomato purée and raisins. Arrange the chicken pieces on top.
3 Cover and microwave at 100% (High) for 20 minutes or until meat near bone is no longer pink. Rearrange chicken and stir vegetables once. Stand for 5 minutes.

Moroccan Chicken Stew

Cook's notes

Fresh herbs make all the difference to Herby Spring Chicken. A selection is usually available in the fresh vegetable section of most supermarkets or from your greengrocer. Parsley and tarragon are especially good with chicken.

Creamy tomato chicken

24 mins

Standing time: none

1 small onion, chopped
1 garlic clove, crushed
15g / ½oz butter
400g / 14oz can sieved tomatoes
5ml / 1tsp caster sugar
2.5ml / ½tsp dried basil
2.5ml / ½tsp dried marjoram
pepper
60ml / 4tbls chicken stock or
  white wine
4 chicken quarters (total weight
  about 1.1kg / 2½lb)
150ml / ¼pt soured cream
50g / 2oz grated Parmesan cheese
50g / 2oz flaked almonds

SERVES 4

Slimmer's notes

*Skin the chicken before cooking.
Substitute low-fat spread for the
butter and natural yoghurt for the
soured cream. Use only 25g / 1oz
Parmesan cheese and sprinkle with
basil instead of nuts for 255Cal /
1070kJ per portion.*

How to microwave Creamy tomato chicken

Place *the onion, garlic and butter in a
2.3L / 4pt casserole. Cover and
microwave at 100% (High) for 3
minutes, or until the onion is tender.
Add tomatoes, sugar, herbs, pepper
and stock and stir together well.*

Add *the chicken and spoon the sauce
over it. Cover and microwave at 100%
(High) for 20 minutes, or until the
chicken is done and the meat near the
bone is no longer pink. Stir well twice
during cooking.*

Place *the chicken on a serving dish.
Skim fat off the surface of the sauce,
then stir in the cream and cheese.
Reheat at 100% (High) for 1 minute
and spoon the sauce over the chicken.
Sprinkle with almonds and serve.*

Orange and Walnut Chicken

Orange and walnut chicken

| 23 mins |

Standing time: none

4 chicken quarters (total weight about 1.1kg / 2½lb)
275ml / ½pt orange juice
5ml / 1tsp chicken seasoning
30ml / 6tsp cornflour
30ml / 2tbls water
3 spring onions, chopped
50g / 2oz walnut halves

SERVES 4

1 Put chicken into a 2.3L / 4pt casserole, meaty parts to outside.
2 Mix orange juice and seasoning. Pour over chicken; cover and microwave at 100% (High) for 20 minutes, until cooked.
3 Place chicken on a serving dish.
4 Blend cornflour and water to a smooth paste. Stir into the juice. Add spring onions and walnuts.
5 Microwave at 100% (High) for 3 minutes, until thick; stir once. Pour over chicken and serve.

Stewed chicken and broth

| 20 mins |

Standing time: 5 mins

This is a 'two-in-one' casserole: reserve the cooked chicken to use cold — in a salad or diced in a risotto for example — serve the tasty, nourishing broth hot, with wholewheat rolls if liked.

4 chicken quarters (total weight about 1.1kg / 2½lb)
1 carrot, cut in chunks
1 celery stalk, cut in pieces
1 small onion, thinly sliced
225ml / 8fl oz hot chicken stock
1 bay leaf
3 whole peppercorns
pepper

SERVES 4

VARIATION
Chicken and vegetable casserole: add a 225g / 8oz can tomatoes and 100g / 4oz sliced button mushrooms with the other vegetables, plus 5ml / 1tsp dried mixed herbs. Do not reserve the chicken portions, but serve the complete casserole with rice or noodles.

Slimmer's notes

The casserole is a satisfying meal for slimmers. With 50g / 2oz rice, a portion has 225Cal / 945kJ.

Chicken with olives

| 20½ mins |

Standing time: 5 mins

25g / 1oz butter or margarine
15ml / 1tbls plain flour
225ml / 8fl oz dry white wine
1 chicken stock cube
1 garlic clove, crushed
salt and pepper
dash of Tabasco sauce
1kg / 2¼lb chicken portions
1 onion, thinly sliced
50g / 2oz pimiento-stuffed green olives, chopped
finely chopped parsley, to garnish

SERVES 4

1 Place butter in a 2.5L / 4½pt casserole, cover, and microwave at 100% (High) for 30-45 seconds, or until melted. Stir in the flour and blend in the wine until smooth. Crush the stock cube and mix it in with the garlic, seasoning and Tabasco.
2 Add the chicken portions, placing meatiest portions to the outside of the casserole. Sprinkle with onion and olives.
3 Cover and microwave at 100% (High) for 10 minutes. Turn chicken and rearrange. Spoon sauce over chicken, cover and microwave for a further 10-15 minutes, or until the meat near the bone is no longer pink.
4 Cover and stand for 5 minutes. Sprinkle with parsley and serve.

How to microwave Stewed chicken and broth

Arrange *the chicken in a 2.3L / 4pt casserole dish with the meatiest parts to the outsides of the dish. Add all the remaining ingredients, seasoning generously with pepper.*

Microwave, *covered, at 100% (High) for 20 minutes or until chicken is cooked, rearranging pieces twice. Stand, covered, for 5 minutes. Remove chicken; serve broth.*

235

Poultry rolls

Chicken and turkey breasts, stuffed and rolled, are simple to prepare and can be microwaved in minutes. Just pick a filling for an unusual and tasty treat.

The delicate white meat of chicken and turkey breasts microwaves beautifully. The meat is naturally tender, so can be cooked at the fastest setting — 100% (High) — and the moist cooking method means the breasts don't dry out or lose their flavour.

Rolling chicken and turkey breasts around a filling adds an extra dimension to a cook's repertoire. Poultry always combines well with other flavours so a whole range of fillings can be used.

Both chicken and turkey breasts are available from butchers and supermarkets, sold loose or in packs of two or three. Whole turkey breasts are quite large and should be sliced horizontally to serve two. Alternatively, buy breast slices or turkey escalopes;

Easy Chicken Kiev

236

these weigh between 175-225g / 6-8oz each.

Chicken breasts are smaller than turkey breasts, weighing about 150-175g / 5-6oz each — still ample for one serving. Chicken supreme is another name often given to chicken breasts, which sometimes include the tip of the wing bone.

Preparing poultry breasts

Place the poultry breast on a piece of greaseproof paper or between two pieces of cling film. Beat flat with a rolling pin or the flat side of a meat mallet until meat is about 6mm / ¼in thick. Season one side with a little salt and black pepper and then add filling.

Adding the filling

Place filling at the end of the flattened breast and roll breast up, tucking in sides as you go. If there is a large amount of filling, place in centre and fold meat around. Secure the rolls with wooden cocktail sticks.

Microwave the prepared rolls at 100% (High). Since the meat is rolled and stuffed, it will take longer to microwave than normal, and the more substantial the filling, the longer the cooking time needed.

Meat is cooked when no longer pink and the juices run clear when pierced with a knife. Leave the rolls to stand for 5 minutes before serving.

Easy chicken Kiev

$6\frac{3}{4}$ mins

Standing time: 5 mins

175g / 6oz butter
10ml / 2tsp dried chives
1 clove garlic, crushed
white pepper
4 chicken breasts, (about 575g / 1¼lb total weight)
60ml / 4tbls browned breadcrumbs
45ml / 3tbls grated Parmesan cheese
15ml / 1tbls chopped parsley
5ml / 1tsp paprika

SERVES 4

How to microwave Easy chicken Kiev

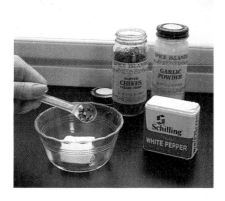

Place *100g / 4oz of the butter in a small bowl, cover and microwave at 30% (Low) for 10 seconds or until soft but not melted. Add chives, garlic and pepper and mix well.*

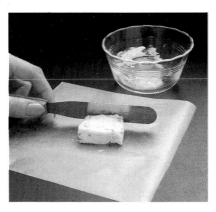

Shape *the butter into four 4 × 2.5cm / 1½ × 1in rectangles on a piece of greaseproof paper. Once shaped, place each in freezer and chill for 10 minutes until firm.*

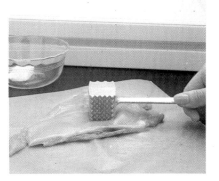

Place *chicken breasts on greaseproof paper and beat to a 6mm / ¼in thickness. Place remaining butter in small bowl, cover and microwave at 100% (High) for 30-60 seconds.*

Place *the breadcrumbs, grated Parmesan cheese, parsley and paprika in a shallow bowl or on a sheet of greaseproof paper and mix well. Set to one side.*

Place *the butter rectangles at the end of each chicken breast. Fold end over butter, then fold in sides and roll up. Secure with cocktail sticks. Brush chicken rolls with melted butter.*

Roll *in crumb mixture; place around edge of a round dish. Microwave at 100% (High) for 6-7 minutes, turning rolls and rotating dish once. Stand for 5 minutes.*

Freezer notes

To thaw asparagus spears, pierce the wrapping two to three times with a knife and then microwave at 20-30% (Defrost) for 3 minutes. Remove from packet and place on a plate. Microwave at 20-30% (Defrost) for a further 2½-3 minutes until just thawed. Stand for 2-3 minutes, then drain.

If frozen asparagus spears are not available, use canned asparagus. The turkey wrapping prevents overcooking.

Turkey Asparagus Rolls, sprinkled with Parmesan to serve

Turkey asparagus rolls

6 mins

Standing time: 5 mins

4 boneless turkey breasts (700g / 1½lb total weight) beaten to 6mm / ¼in thickness
salt and pepper
1.5ml / ¼tsp garlic powder
1.5ml / ¼tsp dried rosemary
50g / 2oz mozzarella cheese
200g / 7oz packet frozen asparagus spears, thawed
pinch of paprika
10ml / 2tsp grated Parmesan cheese

SERVES 4

1 Place turkey breasts on board, season well and sprinkle with garlic and rosemary.
2 Lay thin slices of mozzarella on top, with four asparagus spears on the mozzarella. Roll up and secure with a cocktail stick.
3 Sprinkle rolls lightly with paprika, then place, seam side down around the outside of a baking dish. Cover with grease-proof paper.
4 Microwave at 100% (High) for 3-4 minutes. Turn and rearrange rolls, sprinkle with Parmesan cheese and re-cover. Microwave at 100% (High) for a further 3-4 minutes or until turkey is tender and juices run clear. Stand for 5 minutes. Remove cocktail sticks.

Turkey roulades

11½ mins

Standing time: none

STUFFING
100g / 4oz mushrooms, chopped
1 small onion, finely chopped
1 celery stalk, finely chopped
small clove of garlic, crushed
knob of butter
30ml / 2tbls fresh breadcrumbs
salt and pepper
2 boneless turkey breasts (175-200g / 6-7oz each), beaten to about 6mm / ¼in thickness
30ml / 2tbls golden or browned breadcrumbs
5ml / 1tsp chopped parsley
15ml / 1tbls vegetable or olive oil

MUSHROOM SAUCE
100g / 4oz button mushrooms, sliced
1 small onion, chopped
25g / 1oz butter
30ml / 2tbls plain flour
salt and pepper
150ml / ¼pt single cream
45ml / 3tbls white wine

SERVES 2

1 Make the stuffing. Combine mushrooms, onion, celery, garlic and butter in a casserole. Cover and microwave at 100% (High) for 2-4 minutes or until onion is tender. Stir in the fresh breadcrumbs and season.
2 Place half the mixture on each

Freezer notes

Turkey Roulades (page 238) freeze well; they can be thawed and cooked in one simple operation. After coating in breadcrumbs, place rolls in microwave / freezer dish, cover and freeze for up to 1 month. To cook and serve: remove freezer covering and re-cover with grease-proof paper. Microwave at 100% (High) for 5 minutes. Reduce power to 50% (Medium) and microwave for 10-12 minutes or until meat is no longer pink, rearranging rolls and giving dish a half turn halfway through cooking. Make sauce, see step 4, and serve.

Turkey Roulades

of the turkey breasts. Fold sides of breast over, roll up and secure each with a wooden cocktail stick.

3 Mix golden breadcrumbs and parsley. Brush rolls with oil and roll in breadcrumb mixture. Arrange in a shallow baking dish and microwave at 100% (High) for 5-6 minutes, rearranging after 3 minutes. Cover tightly and set aside while making sauce.

4 Make sauce. Combine mushrooms, onion and butter and microwave, covered, at 100% (High) for 2 minutes or until onions are tender. Add flour and seasoning and mix well. Blend in cream.

5 Microwave at 100% (High) for 2-3 minutes or until thickened and bubbly, stirring once or twice. Stir in wine and microwave for a further 30 seconds until heated through. Pour the sauce over the turkey breasts when about to serve.

Sweet 'n' sour turkey

11 mins

Standing time: 5 mins

225g / 8oz lean minced beef
50g / 2oz finely chopped walnuts
15ml / 1tbls fresh white breadcrumbs
1 small onion, very finely chopped
30ml / 2tbls soy sauce
2.5ml / ½tsp ground ginger
1.5ml / ¼tsp ground nutmeg
4 boneless turkey breasts, about 225g / 8oz each, beaten out to 6mm / ¼in thickness
15ml / 1tbls dark rum
15ml / 1tbls runny honey
15ml / 1tbls soy sauce
225g / 8oz can sliced pineapple, drained
20ml / 4tsp sesame seeds

SERVES 4-6

1 Mix minced beef, walnuts, breadcrumbs, onion, soy sauce and spices in a bowl.

2 Place a quarter of the mixture in centre of each turkey breast. Roll up and secure with a cocktail stick. Place in a shallow baking dish.

3 Mix rum, honey and soy sauce. Brush about one third over the turkey rolls and cover with greaseproof paper.

4 Microwave at 100% (High) for 4-5 minutes. Rearrange rolls and turn over, brush with another third of the sauce.

5 Microwave at 100% (High) for a further 3-4 minutes, then rearrange again, placing a pineapple slice under each roll. Add remaining sauce and sprinkle each roll with 5ml / 1tsp sesame seeds.

6 Microwave at 100% (High) for 4-5 minutes or until turkey is tender and juices run clear. Stand for 5 minutes. Serve one per person, or cut rolls into 12mm / ½in slices to serve 6.

Sweet 'n' Sour Turkey

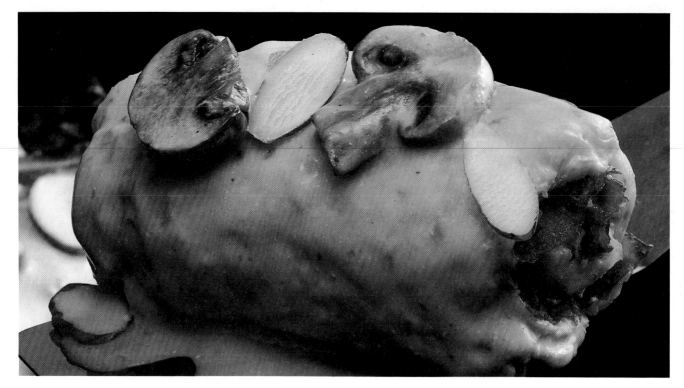

Chicken and bacon rolls

14 mins

Standing time: 5 mins

225g / 8oz smoked back bacon, rinds removed, chopped
4 boneless chicken breasts, about 575g / 1¼lb total weight) beaten out to 6mm / ¼in thickness
pepper, to taste
225g / 8oz button mushrooms, sliced
1 × 300g / 11oz can cream of mushroom soup
150ml / ¼pt soured cream
50g / 2oz flaked almonds

SERVES 4

1 Place bacon in a shallow dish. Cover with absorbent paper and microwave at 100% (High) for 5-6 minutes until crisp, stirring once.
2 Season each chicken breast with a little pepper. Place a quarter of the bacon on top, roll up and secure with a wooden cocktail stick.
3 Place mushrooms in a baking dish, arrange chicken rolls on top. Combine soup and soured cream, pour over chicken.
4 Cover with greaseproof paper and microwave at 100% (High) for 4-5 minutes. Rearrange chicken and stir sauce. Cook for a further 5-6 minutes or until chicken is no longer pink.
5 Stand for 5 minutes, then sprinkle with almonds. Serve with noodles or plain boiled rice.

Artichoke chicken rolls

9¾ mins

Standing time: 5 mins

25g / 1oz butter
30ml / 2tbls plain flour
½ chicken stock cube, crumbled
1 spring onion, finely chopped
salt and pepper
150ml / ¼pt single cream
150ml / ¼pt water
150g / 6oz canned artichoke hearts, about 6 hearts
50g / 2oz Cheddar cheese, grated
30ml / 2tbls fresh brown breadcrumbs
4 boneless chicken breasts, (about 575g / 1¼lb total weight), beaten out to 6mm / ¼in thickness

SERVES 4

1 Place butter in a bowl, cover and microwave, covered at 100% (High) for 15-30 seconds or until melted. Add flour, stock cube,

Chicken and Bacon Rolls

spring onion and seasoning and stir. Blend in cream and water.
2 Microwave at 100% (High) for 2½-3 minutes or until thickened, stirring every minute. Set aside.
3 Drain and chop artichoke hearts; mix with cheese and breadcrumbs. Place a quarter of the mixture in the centre of each chicken breast. Fold chicken over stuffing and secure with wooden cocktail sticks.
4 Place rolls, seam side up in a shallow baking dish. Microwave at 100% (High) for 4-5 minutes. Rearrange rolls and turn over. Coat evenly with sauce, then microwave for a further 3-4 minutes until chicken is tender and juices run clear. Stand for 5 minutes.

Slimmer's notes

Turkey or chicken breast rolls can be simply converted to make a low-calorie meal. For Artichoke Chicken Rolls, use skimmed milk for the cream and substitute Edam for Cheddar cheese. This works out at 300Cal / 1,260kJ per serving. A 100g / 4oz serving of new potatoes will add 75Cal / 315kJ; a 150g / 5oz jacket potato is 130Cal / 546kJ.

Drumsticks

Cheap, cheerful and convenient — chicken and turkey drumsticks are the answer when you need a tasty meal in a hurry. Your microwave cooks them quickly and keeps them juicy and tender.

Readily available chicken and turkey drumsticks are a boon when you have to provide a quick, inexpensive meal. They need little preparation, other than a wipe over with a damp cloth, and can be cooked plainly, with a brush of oil and a sprinkling of herbs, such as thyme or tarragon.

It takes just a little extra time, however, to turn this everyday meat into a special treat. Cover each plump drumstick in a crunchy coating and serve as 'finger food' or with a crisp salad, or cook in a golden lemon egg glaze or minty yoghurt sauce that becomes richer and more concentrated during cooking.

If you have a browning dish, use this to crisp the skin to a golden brown. Otherwise, remove the skin before cooking, or give it an appetizing colour and extra flavour by brushing with a browning agent, such as soy sauce, paprika pepper or yeast extract.

However you choose to cook the drumsticks, cooking times are easy — 17-20 minutes for 8 drumsticks, (the shorter time is for a 700W oven), 8-10 minutes for 4 and so on (see the chart on page 243).

Lemon-glazed Drumsticks

How to microwave Coated drumsticks

Thoroughly *mix the crushed crackers and poultry seasoning together on a large plate. Beat the egg lightly in a shallow dish. Lightly brush each drumstick with oil.*

Roll *drumsticks in coating and press on firmly. Roll in egg, press on another layer of coating. Place drumsticks on rack, bony sides down, meatiest parts to outside.*

Microwave *on 100% (High) for 8 minutes or until juices run clear. Turn the drumsticks over halfway through cooking time. Leave to stand for 2 minutes before serving.*

242

Savoury cracker coating

8 mins

Standing time: 2 mins

Crunchy, savoury coatings add variety, extra flavour and contrasting texture to succulent drumsticks. They also protect the lean flesh from becoming overcooked and dry. Be sure that the drumsticks are evenly moistened with egg or coating will not stick.

If you do not like chicken skin, you can remove it before coating.

100g / 4oz salted wheat crackers, finely crushed
10ml / 2tsp poultry seasoning
1 egg
30ml / 2tbls vegetable oil

SERVES 4

Left to right: *Wheatflake Coating, Coconut Crumb Coating, Savoury Cracker Coating, Poppy Seed Coating, Herbed Coating.*

Freezer notes

Cooked coated drumsticks freeze well for up to 4 months and the coating stays crisp when thawed in the microwave. Prepare them ahead for picnics, or for filling snacks.

Slimmer's notes

Chicken drumsticks are lean and ideal for slimmers. Most of the fat is found in the skin, so save calories by removing the skin with a knife before cooking.

Microtips

Cook coated drumsticks on a roasting rack, so they crisp on all sides. If you do not have a rack, cook on a plate, but don't turn them over during cooking — this keeps the uppermost surface crisp.

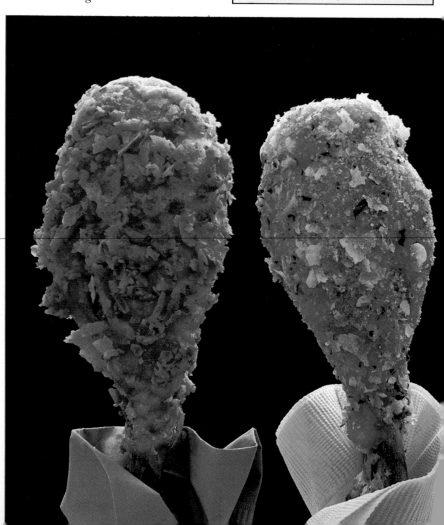

RAY DUNS

Coating variations

More crunchy coatings to ring the changes. To coat and cook, see the steps left; for cooking times, see the chart below. Except for the wheatflake variation, far right, there is no need to coat the drumsticks twice.

● **Coconut:** combine 75g / 3oz dried breadcrumbs with 75ml / 5tbls desiccated coconut and 10ml / 2tsp dried parsley. Season to taste.

● **Poppy seed:** mix 10ml / 2tsp poppy seeds with 75g / 3oz golden breadcrumbs. Sprinkle each drumstick lightly with garlic salt halfway through the cooking time.

● **Sesame seed:** mix 10ml / 2tsp sesame seeds with 75g / 3oz golden breadcrumbs. Sprinkle the coated drumsticks with celery salt.

● **Herb:** mix 100g / 4oz parsley and thyme brown breadcrumb stuffing mix, lightly crushed, with 2.5ml / ½tsp garlic salt.

● **Wheatflake:** crush 100g / 4oz wheat flakes. Brush drumsticks thoroughly with oil. Roll in coating, press on firmly. Then roll in beaten egg and press on another layer of coating.

● **Tarragon and onion:** combine 5ml / 1tsp chopped fresh tarragon (or 2.5ml / ½tsp dried), and 15ml / 1tbls minced onion with 75g / 3oz golden breadcrumbs.

Microwave times for coated drumsticks

QUANTITY	MICROWAVE TIME AT 100% (HIGH)	STANDING TIME
2 (total weight 200g / 7oz)	3-5 minutes	1 minute
4 (total weight 400g / 14oz)	8-10 minutes	2 minutes
8 (total weight 800g / 1¾lb)	17-20 minutes	5 minutes

Microtips

If you have a browning dish or griddle use it to give chicken skin a crisp golden finish. There is no need to add any extra fat when browning on a microwave griddle, but it is best to give the drumsticks a coating of oil to prevent sticking if cooking them in a browning dish.

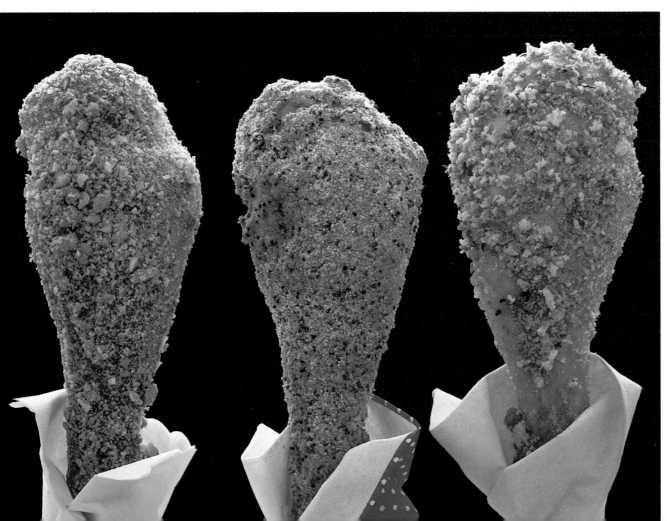

Lemon-glazed drumsticks

20 mins

Standing time: 5 mins

Remove the skins from the drumsticks so that the flavour of the lemon juice can soak right into the chicken flesh.

**8 drumsticks, about 800g / 1¾lb
total weight
1 large lemon
2 egg yolks**

SERVES 4

1 Using a sharp knife, cut the skin away from the bony end of the drumsticks. Place drumsticks in a large dish.
2 Cut eight thin slices from the lemon, squeeze juice from remaining half and pour over drumsticks. Arrange a slice of lemon on each. Cover dish with cling film and marinate for 3-4 hours.
3 Drain drumsticks, reserving the marinade, and transfer them to a roasting rack. Arrange bony side up with fleshiest parts to outside. Microwave on 100% (High) for 5 minutes.
4 Mix 10ml / 2tsp of reserved marinade with the egg yolks.
5 Remove lemon slices from drumsticks and set aside. Brush drumsticks with egg and lemon glaze. Microwave at 100% (High) for 5 minutes.

6 Turn drumsticks over and brush with glaze. Microwave at 100% (High) for 10 minutes, glazing again after 5 minutes.
7 Arrange a lemon slice over bony end of each drumstick. Leave to stand for 5 minutes before serving, garnished with parsley.

Stuffed drumsticks

20 mins

Standing time: 5 mins

**4 large chicken or small turkey
drumsticks (225g / 8oz each)**

STUFFING
**125g / 4oz Cheddar cheese, grated
50g / 2oz dried breadcrumbs
10ml / 2tsp mixed dried herbs
15ml / 1tbls finely chopped onion
salt
75ml / 5tbls oil**

SAUCE
**275ml / ½pt tomato juice
10ml / 2tsp Worcestershire sauce
15ml / 1tbls plain flour
salt and pepper
125g / 4oz button mushrooms,
sliced**

SERVES 4

1 Pull back skin over fleshiest part of each drumstick. Combine the stuffing ingredients and divide into four. Push a quarter between the skin and flesh of each drumstick. Pull the skin back over the stuffing and secure with a wooden cocktail stick.
2 Arrange the drumsticks in a large shallow dish, meatiest parts to the outside. Microwave at 100% (High) for 10 minutes.
3 Combine sauce ingredients, except mushrooms, seasoning well. Arrange mushrooms over drumsticks. Spoon sauce over and microwave at 100% (High) for 10-12 minutes, basting with sauce twice during cooking time. The drumsticks are cooked when the juices run clear.
4 Leave to stand, covered, for 5 minutes before serving.

Maryland drumsticks

20 mins

Standing time: 5 mins

**50g / 2oz salted wheat crackers,
crushed
1.5ml / ¼tsp paprika, plus extra
for dusting
150ml / ¼pt milk
1 egg, beaten
15ml / 1tbls plain flour
325g / 11½oz can sweetcorn
kernels
4 spring onions, chopped
8 drumsticks, about 800g / 1¾lb
total weight
a little oil for brushing**

SERVES 4

1 Mix 30ml / 2tbls crushed crackers with the paprika and set aside.
2 Combine remaining cracker crumbs, milk, egg, flour, sweetcorn and onions in a 30cm / 12in round dish.
3 Arrange drumsticks on top, bone side up. Microwave at 100% (High) for 10 minutes.
4 Remove drumsticks and stir sweetcorn mixture. Brush the least well done parts of the·drumsticks with oil and roll them in the reserved crumbs. Arrange on top of the corn, crumbed side up. Shake extra paprika pepper on top for colour.
5 Microwave at 100% (High) for 10 minutes, or until the juices run clear.
6 Leave to stand, covered, for 5 minutes before serving.

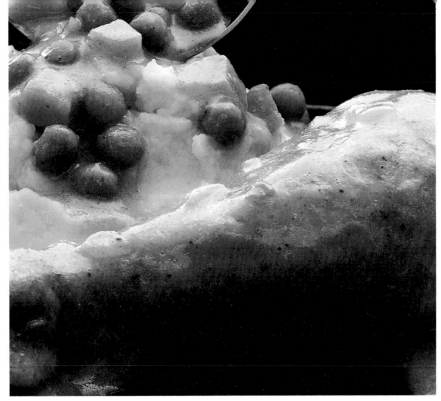

Drumsticks in wine sauce

27 mins

Standing time: 5 mins

350g / 12oz packet frozen peas and carrots
8 drumsticks, about 800g / 1¾lb total weight
285g / 10.4oz can cream of chicken soup
1 small onion, finely chopped
5ml / 1tsp poultry seasoning
salt
large pinch dry mustard
150ml / ¼pt dry white wine

SERVES 4

1 Pierce the packet of frozen vegetables. Microwave in packet, at 100% (High) for 4-5 minutes until thawed. Set aside.
2 Arrange the drumsticks, bony side up, in a large shallow dish. Combine soup, onion, seasonings and wine and pour 15ml / 1tbls over each drumstick. Microwave at 100% (High) for 5 minutes.
3 Turn drumsticks and pour over another 15ml / 1tbls wine sauce. Microwave at 100% (High) for 5 minutes. Repeat twice.
4 Remove drumsticks to serving plate, cover and leave to stand for 5 minutes.
5 Meanwhile, add peas and carrots to dish with remaining sauce.

Far left: *Stuffed Drumsticks*
Left: *Maryland Drumsticks*
Above: *Drumsticks in Wine Sauce*

Microwave at 100% (High) for 3 minutes or until vegetables are tender. Serve the vegetables in sauce with the drumsticks, together with mashed potatoes.

Herby yoghurt drumsticks

20 mins

Standing time: 5 mins

8 drumsticks, total weight 800g / 1¾lb
15ml / 3tsp finely chopped mixed fresh herbs, or 15ml / 3tsp concentrated mint sauce
150ml / ¼pt natural yoghurt

SERVES 4

1 Arrange the drumsticks on a roasting rack or large plate, bony side up and fleshiest part to the outside.
2 Mix herbs or sauce into yoghurt, then brush liberally over chicken.
3 Microwave at 100% (High) for 10 minutes. Turn drumsticks over, brush with the yoghurt mixture and microwave at 100% (High) for 10 minutes, brushing with glaze again after 5 minutes. Stand for 5 minutes before serving.

245

CHAPTER FIVE
VEGETABLES AND FRUIT

When cooked in the microwave, vegetables remain bright coloured, crisp and fresh tasting. They can be cooked quickly, using only a very little water, so that they also retain more of their nutrients than when they are cooked by conventional methods. Similarly, fruit, when cooked in a compote, for example, holds its shape much better so that its contrasting textures can be enjoyed.

Vegetables are incredibly versatile. Here you will find them used to make main dishes (ideal for vegetarians), soups and side dishes. Any number of vegetable varieties are used, including those that can be stuffed, such as peppers and aubergines, and those that combine well in decorative platters for the buffet table or a summer lunch. Salads, too, are included – not the traditional lettuce and tomato variety, but unusual, cooked salads which use crisply cooked vegetables in countless innovative ways. You will even find a section on Greens which is full of new and nutritious ideas for cooking the familiar 'good for you' vegetables.

Both dried and fresh fruits feature in the second half of the chapter. The dried fruit section includes recipes that use our familiar dried fruits in a number of unfamiliar but tempting ways, such as in sauces to serve with meat, or stuffings for poultry. Fresh fruit combinations make delicious and attractively colourful desserts or party platters, and tropical fruits always add interest to a dinner party menu or buffet spread. More and more tropical fruits are becoming available in our supermarkets; here you will find recipes using passion fruit, guavas and mangoes, amongst others.

Some of our most popular fruits are the currants and berries – available for so short a season each year. Make the most of them by trying some of the tempting recipes featured here. Don't wait for a special occasion – they are delicious any time.

Vegetable main dishes

Capture all the goodness of vegetables by cooking them in the microwave — this way you can mix and match textures, colours and flavours to make mouthwatering main course dishes.

Main courses based on vegetables are appetizing, colourful — and good for you too. Vegetarian diets are increasingly popular these days and many people are reducing the amount of meat they eat. Thinking of a main course based on vegetables, not meat, can be difficult; the recipes here are sure to fit the bill — and give you an appetite for more.

Cooking vegetables by microwave is naturally healthy, using little water and retaining every ounce of goodness. Crisp textures and bright colours are captured to make the finished dish look and taste really special. As an extra bonus, cooking times are considerably reduced.

A vegetarian diet is perfectly healthy provided you eat a wide selection of foods and choose the less processed wholefoods, such as brown rice and pasta and wholemeal bread. Very strict vegetarians (Vegans) exclude all animal products (including eggs, milk, cheese and so on) from their diets and eat only plant foods. The majority of vegetarians include dairy products and eggs for protein; other useful sources of protein are nuts, seeds (such as sesame and sunflower seeds) and beans. Many vegetables contain a degree of protein too — so there is little danger of going short. Try the recipes here — and be prepared to be converted.

Courgette Quiche

Courgette quiche

18 mins

Standing time: 5 mins

Serve this deliciously light quiche with rice salad or baked potato and salad.

23cm / 9in cooked pie case (see page 28)
2 courgettes, thinly sliced
15ml / 1tbls water

FILLING
1 courgette, grated
225g / 8oz curd cheese
50g / 2oz Cheddar cheese, grated
100g / 4oz cottage cheese
2 eggs, beaten
15ml / 1tbls plain flour
2.5ml / ½tsp dried oregano
1.5ml / ¼tsp garlic salt
pepper

SERVES 4-6

1 Combine all the filling ingredients in a large bowl and beat with a wooden spoon to blend thoroughly. Spoon into the pastry case and smooth over the top.
2 Microwave the sliced courgette and water in a covered bowl at 100% (High) for 2 minutes.
3 Arrange the slices on top of the filling. Place the pie dish on a saucer and microwave at 50% (Medium) for 16-18 minutes, or until the centre is softly set. Rotate the dish a half turn every 3 minutes. Brown under the grill after microwaving, if wished.
4 Leave to stand for 5 minutes before serving hot or let cool.

Freezer notes

Quiches freeze well and this Courgette Quiche is no exception, taking next-to-no-time to thaw in the microwave. To freeze, wrap, label and freeze for up to 3 months.

To thaw and reheat, unwrap completely and microwave, uncovered, at 50% (Medium) for 2½-3 minutes, rotating half a turn once during microwaving. Leave to stand for 30-60 seconds before serving hot.

Gingered vegetables

12 mins

Standing time: 1-2 mins

Serve this Oriental dish over conventionally cooked couscous, or plain boiled brown or white rice, if preferred.

340g / 12oz can asparagus tips and cuts, drained
450g / 1lb tofu, drained, rinsed and cut into 2cm / ¾in cubes
100g / 4oz mushrooms, sliced
225g / 8oz can sliced bamboo shoots, drained
3 spring onions, thinly sliced
45ml / 3tbls light soy sauce, or 30ml / 2tbls rich soy sauce, mixed with 15ml / 1tbls water
15ml / 3tsp cornflour
15ml / 1tbls white wine or water
1 garlic clove, crushed
10ml / 2tsp vegetable oil
1.5ml / ¼tsp ground ginger
pinch of cayenne pepper

SERVES 4

Gingered Vegetables

1 In a large casserole combine the asparagus, tofu, mushrooms, bamboo shoots and onions.
2 Blend the remaining ingredients in a small bowl and pour over the tofu and vegetable mixture, stirring to coat. Cover and microwave at 100% (High) for 12-14 minutes, or until the sauce thickens, stirring every 4 minutes. Stand for 1-2 minutes.

Cook's notes

Tofu (pronounced toe-fu) is made from soya beans and is very nutritious (high in protein, calcium and iron), but low in calories. It is sold in small blocks, loose or vacuum-packed, and only needs to be rinsed before use. Tofu is very bland; it does not need to be cooked, just reheated. Take care when stirring during microwaving not to break up the pieces of tofu as they are very soft.

Tangy topped potatoes

16 mins

Standing time: 8-9 mins

To give the potatoes a crispy skin, place under the grill after standing time until browned.

4 × 175g / 6oz baking potatoes, scrubbed and pricked
450g / 1lb broccoli florets
60ml / 4tbls water

TANGY SAUCE
100g / 4oz Feta cheese, crumbled
60ml / 4tbls natural yoghurt
1.5ml / ¼tsp lemon juice

SERVES 4

1 Arrange the potatoes around the edge of a plate, or on a piece of absorbent paper. Microwave at 100% (High) for 10-12 minutes, turning once. Wrap in foil and stand for 5 minutes.
2 Arrange the broccoli in a dish with the florets to the centre of the dish. Add the water. Cover and microwave at 100% (High) for 6-8

Tangy Topped Potatoes

Mediterranean bake

23 mins

Standing time: none

1 aubergine, halved and cut into 12mm / ½in slices
575ml / 1pt hot water
salt and pepper
1 egg
90ml / 6tbls fine breadcrumbs
2 courgettes, sliced diagonally
30ml / 2tbls grated Parmesan
1 small onion, sliced
1 green pepper, seeded and chopped
1 garlic clove, crushed
15ml / 1tbls olive oil
½ quantity Quick Tomato Sauce (see variation, page 252)
2.5ml / ½tsp dried oregano

SERVES 4

1 Put the aubergine slices and water into a large bowl. Add 10ml / 2tsp salt and stir; soak for 5 minutes. Drain, turn into a clean

Mediterranean Bake

teatowel; squeeze out moisture.
2 Beat the egg in a shallow dish. Spread 60ml / 4tbls of the crumbs on a plate. Season the aubergine slices. Dip in the egg, then coat with crumbs; arrange around the edge of a large plate. Microwave at 100% (High) for 8-9 minutes until just tender, rotating twice.
3 Generously butter a 23cm / 9in pie dish. Coat sides and base with the remaining breadcrumbs.
4 Microwave the courgettes in a covered dish at 100% (High) for 2 minutes, stirring once; drain. Arrange around sides and base of pie dish. Sprinkle with Parmesan.
5 Combine onion, pepper, garlic and oil in a bowl. Cover and microwave at 100% (High) for 5 minutes. Stir in sauce and herbs.
6 Spoon over courgettes and top with aubergine slices. Microwave at 100% (High) for 8-10 minutes; rotate twice. Stand 2 minutes; garnish with sliced black olives.

minutes until tender-crisp, rotating dish a half turn once; drain. Stand, covered, for 3-4 minutes.
3 Meanwhile, combine the cheese, yoghurt and lemon juice in a blender and purée until smooth.
4 Cut a cross in the the top of each potato. Hold each potato in turn in a clean teatowel and squeeze gently to open out the cut. Top with broccoli, then spoon over the tangy sauce.

Tangy topped potatoes for two: halve all the ingredients. Microwave the potatoes for 5-6 minutes and the broccoli for 3-4 minutes. Stand as directed in recipe, then top and spoon over sauce.

Slimmer's notes

This makes a very nourishing light lunch or supper dish, at only 245Cal / 1030kJ per potato. Serve with a tomato salad.

Rice and vegetable bake | 15 mins

Standing time: 1 min

A substantial and nutritious dish which will be a favourite with all the family.

225g / 8oz brown rice, cooked and cooled
100g / 4oz cottage cheese
100g / 4oz curd or ricotta cheese
60ml / 4tbls natural yoghurt
5ml / 1tsp dried basil
1.5ml / ¼tsp dried marjoram
pepper
2 large courgettes, thinly sliced
2 tomatoes, seeded and chopped
30ml / 2tbls grated Parmesan cheese
Quick Tomato Sauce (see recipe, page 252) to serve

SERVES 4

1 Press half the rice lightly over the base of a round 1.1L / 2pt

Rice and Vegetable Bake

casserole.
2 Combine the cheeses, yoghurt, basil, marjoram and pepper in a food processor or blender and process until smooth. Alternatively, beat together with a wooden spoon until blended.
3 Top the rice with half the courgette and tomato slices and then half the cheese mixture. Repeat rice, vegetable and cheese layers. Sprinkle with Parmesan.
4 Cover and microwave at 70% (Medium-High) for 15-17 minutes, or until the courgettes are tender crisp, rotating the dish a quarter turn twice. Let stand, covered, for 1 minute. Serve with Quick Tomato Sauce.

Rice and vegetable bake for two: halve all the ingredients except the curd cheese and layer in a 700ml / 1¼pt casserole. Microwave at 70% (Medium-High) for 8-10 minutes in stage 4.

251

Quick tomato sauce

10 mins

Standing time: none

This zippy sauce is very versatile — try it with Rice and Vegetable Bake (page 251) as well as quiches, egg and cheese dishes.

397g / 14oz can chopped tomatoes
30ml / 2tbls tomato paste or purée
1 carrot, grated
½ small onion, finely chopped
1 garlic clove, crushed
10ml / 2tsp olive oil
salt and pepper to taste

MAKES 425ml / ¾pt

1 Combine all the ingredients in a large, deep bowl.
2 Microwave at 100% (High) for 10 minutes, until the sauce boils and the flavours are well blended. Stir twice during cooking.

VARIATION
To make half the quantity of Quick Tomato Sauce, use 227g / 8oz can tomatoes and halve all the other ingredients. Break up the tomatoes, combine with the other ingredients and microwave at 100% (High) for 5-7 minutes.

Spicy vegetable curry

16½ mins

Standing time: 3-4 mins

Choose the number of chillies depending on how 'hot' you like your food. Serve with boiled rice and poppadums.

60ml / 4tbls vegetable oil
5cm / 2in piece fresh ginger, peeled and cut into slivers
2 garlic cloves, quartered
1 onion, sliced
1-3 red chillies, split, seeds removed
1 bay leaf
6 cardamom pods
5ml / 1tsp mild curry powder
1 carrot, sliced
100g / 4oz green beans, chopped
½ small cauliflower, cut into tiny florets
2 large potatoes, diced
575ml / 1pt vegetable stock
1 small aubergine, cut into 2.5cm / 1in strips
1 red pepper, seeded and chopped
salt and pepper
SERVES 6

Spicy Vegetable Curry

1 Place the oil, ginger and garlic in a large casserole. Cover and microwave at 100% (High) for 30-60 seconds. Stir in the onion and chillies. Cover and microwave at 100% (High) for 2-2½ minutes, until the onion is tender, stirring once.
2 Stir in the bay leaf and spices, then add all the vegetables except the aubergine strips and pepper, tossing to coat. Stir in the stock, cover and microwave at 100% (High) for 6 minutes.
3 Stir in the aubergine and pepper. Cover and microwave for a further 8-10 minutes, or until all the vegetables are tender, stirring once.
4 Season to taste and stand, covered, for 3-4 minutes. Remove chillies before serving and garnish with slices of lime or orange, if liked.

Microtips

The flavour of this curry is even better if made in advance. You can prepare this dish the day before and keep it in the refrigerator. Reheat at 100% (High) for 5-6 minutes, or until piping hot.

Cheesy vegetable bake

24 mins

Standing time: 3 mins

This makes a really spicy dish, which is ideally accompanied by a crisp green salad.

1 large onion, finely chopped
1 small green pepper, finely chopped
25g / 1oz butter or margarine
100g / 4oz can diced green chillies, drained (or mild fresh green chillies)
3 eggs, beaten
225g / 8oz cottage cheese, sieved
2.5ml / ½tsp dried oregano
1.5ml / ¼tsp ground cumin
salt and pepper
3 × 100g / 3.53oz packets tortilla or corn chips
225g / 8oz Emmental cheese, grated
175g / 6oz Cheddar cheese, grated
150ml / ¼pt soured cream

SERVES 6-8

VARIATION
For a milder flavour, use a 198g / 7oz can of sweetcorn kernels, drained, in place of the green chillies. Continue as in steps.

How to microwave Cheesy vegetable bake

Combine *onion, pepper and butter in a large casserole. Microwave at 100% (High) for 4 minutes; stir in chillies. Blend eggs, cottage cheese and seasoning in separate bowl. Sprinkle one-third tortilla chips over base of a deep 30 × 20cm / 12 × 8in dish.*

Spoon *over half cottage cheese mixture. Spread over half the onion and pepper mixture; sprinkle with half the grated cheeses. Repeat chips, cottage cheese and onion layers. Cook at 100% (High) 5 minutes then at 50% (Medium) 12-15 minutes.*

Rotate *dish a quarter turn twice during cooking. Mix remaining grated cheeses with soured cream. Pour over and top with remaining chips. Microwave at 100% (High) for 3-5 minutes, rotating half a turn once. Stand for 3 minutes.*

253

Stuffed vegetables

Stuffed vegetables make excellent lunch or supper-time dishes, dinner party starters or buffet snacks. They taste as good as they look when cooked by microwave.

Many vegetables are ideal for stuffing. Their centres can be simply hollowed out (see steps), leaving a natural shell for filling with combinations of delicious savoury ingredients. The stuffed vegetables cook quickly in the microwave, leaving softened shells and moist fillings.

Artichokes, aubergines, courgettes, marrow, onions, sweet peppers and tomatoes are especially popular for stuffing as they are well-shaped and a good size. Cabbage leaves can be stuffed, but a whole cabbage is especially attractive, particularly when served with a tomato sauce for extra

colour (see recipe, page 256). Choose even-sized vegetables so they will all be ready at the same time. When hollowing out the centre of a vegetable to make a shell, take care not to puncture the skin, otherwise the juices will run out during cooking and the finished dish will not be as moist as

it should be.

Vegetables with hard outer shells or centres, such as squash or onions, may need a short spell in the microwave to soften them and ease cutting and scooping out the flesh. The flesh is usually added to the stuffing ingredients, provided it does not contain seeds or pith.

Cooked rice makes a substantial base for stuffings. Because it is bland, it combines well with other ingredients. Breadcrumbs are a good alternative. A topping of grated or sliced cheese gives a colourful finish to a dish.

Courgette Boats

Courgette boats

| 5 mins |

Standing time: 2-3 mins

2 courgettes

STUFFING
50g / 2oz long-grain rice, cooked
½ onion, chopped
½ green pepper, chopped
1.5ml / ¼tsp dried basil
salt
1 small tomato, skinned, seeded and chopped

SERVES 4

1 Cut the courgettes in half lengthways. Scrape out the pulp, leaving a 6mm / ¼in shell. Chop the pulp and combine with the rice, onion, green pepper, basil and salt.
2 Place the courgette shells in a 25 × 15cm / 10 × 6in dish. Mound quarter of the vegetable mixture into each shell. Top with the chopped tomato.
3 Cover with greaseproof paper and microwave at 100% (High) for 5-7 minutes, or until the shells are tender, rotating dish half turn once. Let stand for 2-3 minutes. Serve with Herby Tomato Sauce (page 256), if liked.

How to prepare vegetables for stuffing

Slice *off the stalk end from sweet peppers, then scoop out the white seeds and pith from the centre. Use wooden cocktail sticks to hold peppers upright during microwaving, if necessary.*

Microwave *trimmed, peeled onions for half cooking time before hollowing out centres — the centres can be easily removed with a spoon when the onions are cool enough to handle.*

Halve *trimmed courgettes or aubergines lengthways. Use a spoon to hollow out centre, leaving a 12mm / ½in shell. Courgettes can also be cut into chunky slices for stuffing.*

Microwave *whole squash for half the cooking time to soften skin and flesh and ease cutting. Cut in half, then use a spoon to scrape out the seeds and membrane, and discard.*

Herby tomato sauce

4½ mins

Standing time: none

This sauce is particularly good with meat-stuffed vegetables. If stuffing sweet peppers, save the tops to use in the sauce.

30ml / 2tbls finely chopped onion
30ml / 2tbls finely chopped green or red pepper
15g / ½oz butter or margarine
142g / 5oz can tomato paste
5ml / 1tsp sugar
1.5ml / ¼tsp dried oregano
large pinch of dried basil
large pinch of garlic powder
300ml / 10fl oz tomato juice
salt and pepper

MAKES 275ml / ½pt

1 Put the onion, pepper and butter in a bowl. Cover and microwave at 100% (High) for 1½-2 minutes.
2 Mix in the remaining ingredients. Microwave, uncovered, at 100% (High) for 3-4 minutes or until bubbling hot, stirring once.

Cook's notes

Insert a few wooden cocktail sticks in the base of each stuffed pepper so that it stands upright, if needed. Remember to remove the sticks before serving, but wait until the last moment or the juices will escape through the pierced skin.

Beefy peppers

16 mins

Standing time: 2-3 mins

These peppers make an excellent lunch or supper dish — serve them with a crisp lettuce, grated carrot and celery salad.

4 large green or red peppers

STUFFING
450g / 1lb lean minced beef
1 small onion, chopped
1 tomato, skinned and chopped
75g / 3oz long-grain rice, cooked
5ml / 1tsp horseradish relish
salt and pepper
1 slice of cheese, cut into 16 thin strips

SERVES 4

Beefy Peppers

1 Slice the tops from the peppers and remove the seeds and white pith without piercing the shells.
2 Crumble the beef into a large bowl. Mix in the onion, tomato, rice, horseradish and seasoning. Fill the peppers with the mixture. Stand them on a roasting rack or in a dish, supporting them with wooden cocktail sticks if necessary (see Cook's notes, right).
3 Cover and microwave at 100% (High) for 15-17 minutes or until the shells are just tender when pressed at the base with a knife, rearranging them two or three times during cooking.
4 Place four cheese strips on top of each pepper. Microwave at 100% (High) for 1-2 minutes, or until the cheese melts. Let stand for 2-3 minutes before serving.

Stuffed cabbage

24 mins

Standing time: none

1 large white or green cabbage
150ml / ¼pt water

STUFFING
225g / 8oz lean minced beef
225g / 8oz lean minced pork
1 cooking apple, chopped
1 onion, chopped
90ml / 6tbls fresh breadcrumbs
175g / 6oz cooked rice
1 egg, beaten
10ml / 2tsp Worcestershire sauce
salt and pepper
1.5ml / ¼tsp ground allspice

SERVES 6

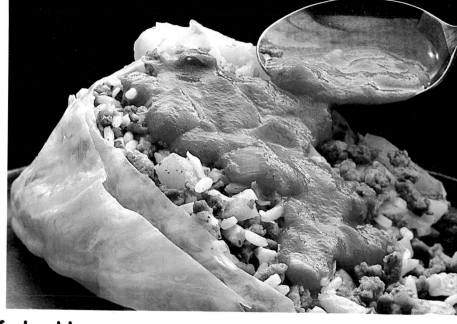

How to microwave Stuffed cabbage

Place *the cabbage and water in a deep casserole. Cover and microwave at 100% (High) for 10-12 minutes until the outer leaves are supple. Drain and leave to cool.*

Position *the cooled cabbage on two crossed sheets of cling film. Carefully peel back outer leaves. Cut out the centre heart leaving the outer leaves attached to the stem.*

Chop *the centre leaves finely with a sharp knife, discarding any tough stalk. Put into a large casserole with the minced beef and pork, the chopped apple and onion.*

Microwave *at 100% (High) for 6-7 minutes until the meat is no longer pink, stirring once. Mix in remaining stuffing ingredients. Place the cabbage leaves on the cling film in a deep bowl.*

Press *the meat mixture into the centre of the prepared cabbage leaves. Cover it with one or two leaves. Press remaining mixture round the edges, folding remaining leaves over top.*

Secure *the cling film over the cabbage. Microwave at 100% (High) for 8-9 minutes or until the cabbage is soft, turning twice; unwrap. Serve with Herby Tomato Sauce (see opposite).*

257

Piquant tomatoes

2 mins

Standing time: none

These spicy tomatoes make a moreish starter, or tasty nibble with pre-dinner drinks. Try using half green and half red pepper.

225g / 8oz curd cheese
½ onion, grated
1 egg yolk
5ml / 1tsp horseradish sauce
1 garlic clove, crushed
pepper
1 small green or red pepper, seeded and finely chopped
700g / 1½lb small, firm tomatoes

SERVES 6

1 Place the curd cheese in a large casserole together with the onion, egg yolk, horseradish sauce, crushed garlic and pepper. Beat with an electric mixer at medium speed for 1 minute until well blended and fluffy. Stir in the chopped pepper with a spoon.
2 Slice off the tomato tops. Use a teaspoon to scoop out the seeds. Fill each tomato with the cheese mixture. Arrange half the tomatoes in a ring on a plate lined with absorbent paper, placing two or three in the centre. Arrange remainder on a second plate.
3 Microwave at 50% (Medium) for 1-2 minutes, or until just warmed through, rotating the plate a quarter turn every 30 seconds. Repeat with the remaining plate.

Sausage-stuffed aubergine

17 mins

Standing time: 3-4 mins

350g / 12oz pork sausagemeat
1 large aubergine
1 onion, chopped
50g / 2oz mushrooms, chopped
90ml / 6tbls fresh breadcrumbs
5ml / 1tsp Worcestershire sauce
1.5ml / ¼tsp dried basil
salt and pepper
75ml / 3fl oz water
50g / 2oz Cheddar cheese, grated

SERVES 4

1 Break up the sausagemeat into a large casserole. Cover and microwave at 100% (High) for 4-5 minutes or until no longer pink, stirring once. Break up the meat and drain on absorbent paper.
2 Cut the aubergine in half lengthways; trim off stalk. Scoop out the flesh, leaving a 6mm / ¼in shell. Chop the flesh roughly and place in the cleaned casserole with the onion. Microwave, covered, at 100% (High) for 4-5 minutes, or until the onion is transparent, stirring twice. Stir in the sausagemeat, mushrooms, breadcrumbs, Worcestershire sauce, basil and seasoning. Use the mixture to fill the aubergine shells.
3 Pour the water into a 25 × 15cm / 10 × 6in dish. Add the filled aubergine shells. Cover and microwave at 100% (High) for 8-9 minutes, or until shells are just soft, rearranging twice.
4 Sprinkle with cheese. Microwave, uncovered, at 100% (High) for 1-1½ minutes until cheese has melted. Stand for 3-4 minutes. Cut in half and serve with a crisp salad.

Sausage-stuffed Aubergine

Crab-stuffed courgettes

<table><tr><td>6
mins</td></tr></table>

Standing time: none

Serve warm or cold as a mouth-watering snack or as a starter for a dinner party, garnished with lettuce leaves.

50g / 2oz mushrooms, chopped
15g / ½oz butter or margarine
15ml / 1tbls plain flour
large pinch of paprika
75ml / 3fl oz creamy milk
6 small spring onions, chopped
salt and pepper
15ml / 1tbls dry sherry
170g / 6oz can crabmeat, drained
   well and flaked
700g / 1½lb small courgettes, cut
   into 2cm / ¾in slices

SERVES 6-8

Slimmer's notes

These succulent morsels make an excellent dinner party starter for the weight conscious. Just use 90ml / 6tbls skimmed milk for the creamy milk and omit the sherry. It serves six as a starter, allowing about four pieces each. This gives 85Cal / 355kJ per serving.

How to microwave Crab-stuffed courgettes

Place *the mushrooms and butter in a casserole. Microwave at 100% (High) for 1-1½ minutes until mushrooms are soft. Stir in flour and paprika. Blend in the milk, then mix in the onions, salt, pepper and sherry.*

Microwave *at 100% (High) for 2-3 minutes, whisking two or three times, or until thickened. Stir in crabmeat; set aside. Scoop out centre of each courgette slice with a small spoon, leaving a 3mm / ⅛in border at sides.*

Spoon *crab mixture into courgettes. Arrange on two plates lined with absorbent paper. Sprinkle with paprika. Microwave one plate at 50% (Medium) for 1½-2 minutes, rotating twice. Repeat with second plate.*

V getable soups

Vegetable soups can be a light start to a meal or they can be a meal in themselves. However you serve them, they always make a tasty, welcome dish.

Vegetables add flavour, texture and colour to soups — as well as goodness. They can be used whole, or puréed for a velvety-smooth, thick texture.

Versatility is the key to these super soups — using seasonal fresh vegetables means there is really no limit to their content and they need never be dull and 'samey'. Use a well flavoured stock, add the herbs and flavourings and cook the vegetables until they are tender. Add rice, pasta or beans for extra bulk, if wished, or try stirring a little cream into puréed soups for extra richness. Alternatively, a simple clear vegetable soup is ideal if you are counting calories.

A home-made stock makes a vegetable soup especially tasty — and adds extra goodness too. Making stock in the microwave is not a fast process but the extra flavour it adds makes it well worthwhile (see Microtips below).

Although you don't have to be a vegetarian to enjoy these delicious soups they seem an obvious choice for a light vegetarian meal or starter. It is easy to replace chicken stock with vegetable stock, if necessary. Use any waste trimmings from vegetables, such as potato or carrot peelings, onion skins and outside leaves of greens. Season and microwave in the same way as chicken stock. Strain through a fine sieve before using.

Microtips

For chicken stock, place carcass bones in a deep casserole and just cover with water. (Less water is needed than conventionally as there is less evaporation.) Bring to the boil at 100% (High), then reduce to 50% (Medium) and microwave for about 30 minutes. Strain.

Cook's notes

Choose floury potatoes for the Creamy Potato Soup as they disintegrate to a soft purée. Do not over-process or it will be 'gluey'.

Hearty minestrone

31 mins

Standing time: none

Served with hunks of bread this soup makes a satisfying supper.

50g / 2oz brown rice
275ml / ½pt hot vegetable stock
1 onion, thinly sliced
1 garlic clove, crushed
275g / 10oz frozen mixed
  vegetables
275ml / ½pt tomato juice
397g / 14oz can tomatoes,
  chopped
400g / 14oz can cannellini beans
1 courgette, sliced
5ml / 1tsp sugar
10ml / 2tsp Italian seasoning
30ml / 2tbls tomato paste or purée
50g / 2oz wholewheat elbow
  macaroni
25g / 1oz grated Parmesan cheese

SERVES 4

1 Place the rice and half the vegetable stock in a small bowl. Cover and microwave at 100% (High) for 6 minutes. Set aside.
2 Place the onion, garlic and frozen vegetables in a 1.7L / 3pt bowl. Cover and microwave at 100% (High) for 5 minutes, until tender.
3 Add the remaining ingredients, except the rice and Parmesan cheese. Cover and microwave for 15 minutes until the courgette is tender. Stir twice.
4 Stir in rice. Cover. Microwave at 100% (High) for 5 minutes. Sprinkle with cheese to serve.

Creamy potato soup

15 mins

Standing time: 5 mins

450g / 1lb potatoes, peeled and
  thinly sliced
575ml / 1pt hot chicken or
  vegetable stock
50g / 2oz butter
1 small onion, very finely
  chopped
275ml / ½pt single cream
salt and pepper
snipped chives, to garnish

SERVES 4

1 Place the potatoes and 275ml / ½pt of the stock in a 1.7L / 3pt bowl. Cover and microwave at 100% (High) for 10-12 minutes or until tender. Stand for 5 minutes.
2 Place onion and half the butter in a small bowl. Cover; microwave at 100% (High) for 3 minutes.
3 Meanwhile, place the potatoes and their cooking liquid in a food processor or blender. Add the remaining butter and 60ml / 4tbls cream and purée until smooth. Alternatively, mash until smooth.
4 Gradually stir in the onion mixture, the remaining stock and cream. Season well.
5 To serve hot: cover and microwave at 100% (High) for 2-4 minutes, stirring twice. Or, cover and chill for 2-4 hours and serve cold. Garnish with chives.

Left: *Hearty Minestrone*
Below: *Creamy Potato Soup*

Soup in a mug

4 mins

Standing time: none

275ml / ½pt hot water
75g / 3oz frozen mixed vegetables
5ml / 1tsp beef stock granules
salt and pepper

SERVES 1

1 Put water, frozen vegetables and stock granules in a mug or jug.
2 Microwave at 100% (High) for 4 minutes, stirring once, or until heated through and the vegetables are tender. Taste and season.

VARIATION
Yeast extract makes a change from stock granules; add 2.5-5ml / ½-1tsp according to taste.

Leftover cooked vegetables can be used instead of frozen. Reduce microwave time to 2-3 minutes, just to heat through.

Soup In A Mug

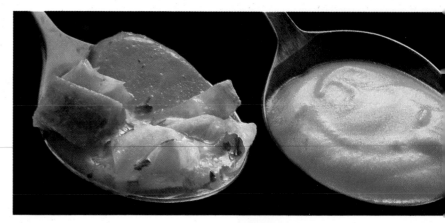

Chunky cabbage soup

22 mins

Standing time: none

1 carrot, sliced
1 onion, chopped
1 celery stalk, finely chopped·
1 garlic clove, crushed
15g / ½oz butter
1 bay leaf
5ml / 1tsp dried basil
700ml / 1¼pt hot chicken stock
350g / 12oz white cabbage, chopped
100g / 4oz chorizo sausage, thinly sliced
50g / 2oz cooked ham, diced
pepper

SERVES 4

1 Place the carrot, onion, celery, garlic, butter, bay leaf and basil in a 1.7L / 3pt bowl. Cover and microwave at 100% (High) for 3-4 minutes, or until the vegetables are softened.
2 Stir in the hot stock and cabbage. Cover and microwave at 100% (High) for 15 minutes or until the vegetables are tender.
3 Stir in the chorizo sausage and ham. Cover and microwave for 4 minutes at 100% (High) or until the meat is heated through. Season with pepper and serve hot.

Slimmer's notes

Soups in mugs are a convenient and warming way to fill-up on a cold day. At only 70 Cal / 295 kJ this soup makes an excellent alternative to conventional packet soups.

Spicy pumpkin soup

23 mins

Standing time: none

1.4kg / 3lb pumpkin, halved, seeded, skinned and chopped
1 small onion, finely chopped
15g / ½oz butter
275ml / ½pt hot chicken stock
pinch each of ground nutmeg, ginger and allspice
pepper
2.5cm / 1in piece cinnamon stick
30ml / 2tbls single cream

SERVES 4

1 Place the chopped pumpkin flesh in a 1.7L / 3pt casserole. Cover and microwave at 100% (High) for 15-17 minutes, or until tender. Stir every 5 minutes.
2 Place the pumpkin in a food processor or blender and purée until smooth. Or mash well until smooth. Return to the casserole.
3 Place the onion and butter in a small bowl. Cover and microwave at 100% (High) for 2-2½ minutes, or until the onion is tender.
4 Stir the onions and remaining ingredients into the puréed pumpkin. Cover and microwave at 50% (Medium) for 6-7 minutes, stirring twice, until the flavours have blended and the soup is piping hot. Remove and discard the cinnamon stick before serving.

VARIATION
For spicy carrot soup, use 900g / 2lb thinly sliced carrots instead of the pumpkin. Microwave in 45ml / 3tbls water for 20-25 minutes. Proceed as above, adding an extra 425ml / ¾pt hot stock.

Garlic soup

33 mins

Standing time: none

Garlic soup is popular in Spain and other Mediterranean countries. Although a lot of garlic is used, the soup has a surprisingly mellow flavour. Serve with plenty of crusty bread for a light lunch.

12 garlic cloves
1 onion, thinly sliced
15ml / 1tbls vegetable oil
300g / 10.6oz can condensed beef consommé
575ml / 1pt hot water
2.5ml / ½tsp dried mustard
2.5ml / ½tsp dried thyme
2.5ml / ½tsp dried marjoram
2 carrots, grated
60ml / 4tbls dry white wine

SERVES 4

1 Crush 2 of the garlic cloves, then place in a 1.7L / 3pt bowl with the remaining whole garlic cloves, the onion and oil. Cover and microwave at 100% (High) for 3 minutes, stirring once.
2 Add the beef consommé, hot water, mustard and herbs. Cover and microwave at 100% (High) for 20 minutes.
3 Stir in the carrots. Cover and microwave at 100% (High) for 10 minutes, or until the carrot is cooked.
4 Using a slotted spoon, remove the whole garlic cloves. Stir in the wine and serve.

Above from left to right: *Chunky Cabbage Soup, Spicy Pumpkin Soup and Garlic Soup*

Onion soup with cheese

12¼ mins

Standing time: none

450g / 1lb onions, thinly sliced
40g / 1½oz butter
2 × 300g / 10.6oz cans condensed beef consommé
275ml / ½pt hot water
5ml / 1tsp sugar
15ml / 1tbls red wine or 7.5ml / ½tbls red wine vinegar
pepper
4 slices French bread
30ml / 2tbls grated Parmesan cheese
100g / 4oz Gruyère cheese, grated

SERVES 4

1 Place the onions and 25g / 1oz butter in a 1.7L / 3pt bowl. Cover and microwave at 100% (High) for 8-9 minutes, or until the onion is tender. Stir twice.
2 Stir in the consommé, water, sugar and wine. Season to taste.
3 Melt the remaining butter in a small, covered bowl at 100% (High) for 10-20 seconds.
4 Brush one side of each slice of bread with melted butter. Sprinkle with Parmesan cheese. Toast under a hot grill until crisp.
5 Ladle the soup into four individual soup bowls. Top each bowl with a slice of toast and sprinkle with a quarter of the Gruyère.
6 Place the bowls in a circle in the microwave and cook, uncovered, at 100% (High) for 4-6 minutes until the soup is piping hot and the cheese melts. Serve at once.

Onion Soup with Cheese

Fresh tomato soup

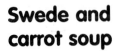

25 mins

Standing time: none

275ml / ½pt tomato juice or
   vegetable cocktail juice
350g / 12oz tomatoes, chopped
1 onion, chopped
2 celery stalks, chopped
25g / 1oz butter
10ml / 2tsp sugar
pepper, to taste
30ml / 2tbls plain flour
700ml / 1¼pt hot chicken or
   vegetable stock

watercress, to garnish

SERVES 4

1 Put the juice, tomatoes, onion, celery and butter in a 1.7L / 3pt bowl. Cover and microwave at 100% (High) for 5 minutes, until the vegetables are almost tender.
2 Whisk in the sugar, pepper and flour. Gradually stir in the stock. Cover and microwave at 100% (High) for 20-23 minutes, until the vegetables are tender and the mixture thickened. Stir three times.
3 Press the soup through a nylon sieve. Serve immediately garnished with watercress.

Swede and carrot soup

20 mins

Standing time: 5 mins

1 small swede, weighing 350g /
   12oz, peeled and diced
2-3 carrots, grated
1 onion, chopped
1 garlic clove, crushed
25g / 1oz butter
700ml / 1¼pt hot chicken stock
2.5ml / ½tsp mustard powder
15ml / 1tbls Worcestershire sauce
salt and pepper

SERVES 4

1 Place the swede, carrots, onion, garlic, butter and 275ml / ½pt of the stock in a 1.7L / 3pt bowl. Cover and microwave at 100% (High) for 15 minutes or until the vegetables are tender.
2 Place the vegetables and stock in a food processor or blender and purée for a few seconds, until almost smooth but still pulpy. Pour back into the bowl.
3 Stir in the remaining stock, mustard and Worcestershire sauce. Cover and microwave at 100% (High) for 5-6 minutes, or until hot. Season and serve.

Left: *Fresh Tomato Soup*
Below: *Swede and Carrot Soup*

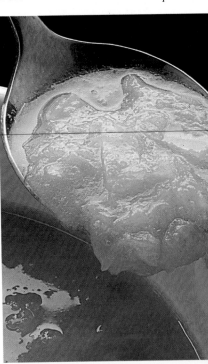

Cooked salads

Cook up a super salad in your microwave — colours stay bright and textures are crisp and appetizing. There's a cooked salad here for every occasion and it can be ready to eat in less than 15 minutes.

Whether hot or cold, as a main dish or side dish, salads are always a welcome, colourful addition to a meal. For a snack lunch with friends, a speedy mid-week supper or an accompaniment to a dinner party dish, you'll find it handy to have a few tasty salads at your fingertips.

Vegetables make a good base for a cooked salad and microwaving is the ideal method of cooking them as it retains their colour, flavour and texture beautifully. For a suc-

cessful cooked salad, it is essential that the vegetables keep their crisp crunchy texture. To avoid overcooked, flabby ingredients test at the end of the minimum microwaving time, then continue cooking, if necessary, until they are just fork-tender.

A tasty sauce or mayonnaise gives a rich creaminess to salads, and can be flavoured with herbs and seasonings to suit individual dishes. Mayonnaise is useful as it is just as good served hot or cold.

Add delicate ingredients such as grapes at the last minute to keep them at their best.

The dressing binds the salad vegetables together — and adds flavour. It can be a sauce, marinade, vinaigrette or mayonnaise. The dressing should coat the ingredients without swamping them. Add it to the salad while it's still hot so it has a good chance to soak up the flavour.

Summer Salad

265

Summer salad

7 mins

Standing time: none

This is the perfect salad for a mid-week summer supper. Serve cold with a green salad. Store any left-overs in the refrigerator.

175g / 6oz bulgar or cracked wheat
700ml / 1¼pt boiling water
2 × 175g / 6oz boneless chicken breasts, skinned
½ cucumber, seeded and chopped
1 small red onion, chopped
15ml / 1tbls chopped parsley
40g / 1½oz butter
30ml / 2tbls pine nuts
15ml / 1tbls olive oil
15ml / 1tbls white wine vinegar
2.5ml / ½tsp dried basil
pinch of garlic salt
1 tomato, seeded and chopped

SERVES 6

1 Place the bulgar or cracked wheat in a bowl and pour over the boiling water. Cover and leave to soak for 30 minutes. Drain and press out excess moisture; set aside.
2 Place the chicken breasts on a roasting rack. Cover with grease-proof paper and microwave at 100% (High) for 4-6 minutes, or until the chicken is no longer pink, turning over once. Set aside.
3 In a casserole, combine the cucumber, onion, parsley, butter, nuts, oil, vinegar, basil and garlic salt, mixing well. Cover and micro-wave at 100% (High) for 3-4 minutes, or until the cucumber is translucent, stirring once.
4 Cut the chicken into 12mm / ½in cubes and add to the casserole with the tomato, bulgar and salt to taste. Chill before serving.

Above: *Minted Potato Salad*
Right: *Courgette Salad*

Slimmer's notes

Omit the butter and this salad makes a really tasty addition to the slimmer's menu at just 215Cal / 905kJ per portion. It is perfect as a lunch or supper dish, served with a mixed green salad.

Courgette salad

6 mins

Standing time: 3-5 mins

225g / 8oz courgettes, thinly sliced
2.5ml / ½tsp dried basil
knob of butter or margarine
275g / 10oz tomatoes, chopped
salt
30ml / 2tbls grated Parmesan cheese

SERVES 4

1 In a 1.1L / 2pt casserole, combine the courgettes, basil and butter. Cover and microwave at 100% (High) for 2 minutes.
2 Stir in the tomatoes and salt. Cover and microwave at 100% (High) for 4-5 minutes, or until the courgettes are tender.
3 Sprinkle with the Parmesan cheese and let stand, covered, for 3-5 minutes, or until the cheese melts. Serve warm or cold.

266

Minted potato salad

6 mins

Standing time: 3 mins

450g / 1lb potatoes, cut into 12mm / ½in cubes
60-90ml / 4-6tbls water
125ml / 4fl oz soured cream
salt and pepper
4 spring onions, chopped
1 celery stalk, chopped
5ml / 1tsp chopped mint or 2.5ml / ½tsp dried

SERVES 4

1 Place the potatoes and water in a 1.1L / 2pt casserole. Cover and microwave at 100% (High) for 6-7 minutes, or until tender. Drain, return to the casserole and stand, covered, for 3 minutes.
2 Season the soured cream with salt and pepper and carefully stir into the potatoes with the onions, celery and mint.
3 Allow to cool, then chill. Or, microwave at 100% (High) for 1-1½ minutes to serve hot.

Broccoli and carrot salad

2⅓ mins

Standing time: 2 mins

100g / 4oz broccoli
2 carrots, cut into thin strips, 5cm / 2in long
15ml / 1tbls water
15ml / 1tbls olive oil
15ml / 1tbls chopped parsley
salt and pepper

SERVES 2

1 Cut the broccoli into small florets, each with 5cm / 2in stalk. Place the florets, carrot strips and water in a large bowl. Cover and microwave at 100% (High) for 2-2½ minutes or until the vegetables are tender-crisp, stirring once. Drain and leave to stand, covered, for 2 minutes.
2 In a small bowl, mix together the oil and parsley and season well. Cover and microwave at 100% (High) for 20-30 seconds. Pour over the vegetables and toss well. Serve at room temperature or allow to chill in the refrigerator.

Honey beets

4 mins

Standing time: none

10ml / 2tsp cornflour
salt and pepper
pinch of ground ginger
30ml / 2tbls honey
30ml / 2tbls white wine vinegar
15ml / 1tbls lemon juice
454g / 1lb jar pickled baby beetroot, drained with 45ml / 3tbls juice reserved

SERVES 4-6

1 In a small bowl, combine all the ingredients except the beetroots. Microwave at 100% (High) for 2-2½ minutes, or until thick and clear, stirring every 30 seconds.
2 Slice the beetroots into a 1.1L / 2pt casserole and pour over the hot dressing. Continue microwaving for 2-3 minutes, or until hot. Serve hot or cold.

Right: *Honey Beets*
Below: *Broccoli and Carrot Salad*

Marinated vegetables

3½ mins

Standing time: none

225g / 8oz broccoli florets
225g / 8oz cauliflower florets
1 large carrot, thinly sliced
30ml / 2tbls water
225g / 8oz button mushrooms
4 cherry tomatoes, halved

MARINADE
125ml / 4fl oz white wine or cider
  vinegar
1 garlic clove, crushed
1 small onion, sliced
45ml / 3tbls vegetable or olive oil
7.5ml / 1½tsp sugar
2.5ml / ½tsp dried basil
1.5ml / ¼tsp mustard powder
salt and pepper

SERVES 4-6

1 For the marinade: put the vinegar into a small bowl together with the garlic and onion. Microwave at 100% (High) for 30-45 seconds, or until the bowl is just warm to the touch. Cover and leave for several hours to allow the garlic to flavour the vinegar.
2 Strain the vinegar into a clean bowl and add the remaining marinade ingredients; set aside.
3 Combine the broccoli, cauliflower and carrots in a 2.3L / 4pt casserole. Add the water and cover. Microwave at 100% (High) for 3-4 minutes, or until the vegetables are just tender and colours are vibrant, stirring after 2 minutes; drain.
4 Add the mushrooms and tomatoes. Stir the marinade and pour over the vegetables. Cover and refrigerate for 3-4 hours.

Hot chicken salad

7 mins

Standing time: none

1 onion, chopped
½ green pepper, seeded and
  chopped
25g / 1oz butter or margarine
450g / 1lb cooked chicken, cut
  into 12mm / ½in cubes
50g / 2oz flaked almonds
25g / 1oz croûtons
30ml / 2tbls strong chicken stock
salt and pepper
30ml / 2tbls water
dash of chilli or Tabasco sauce
½ iceberg lettuce, shredded
small bunch of seedless green
  grapes

SERVES 6

1 Place the onion, green pepper and butter in a casserole. Microwave at 100% (High) for 4-5 minutes, or until the vegetables are tender-crisp.
2 Stir in the remaining ingredients except the lettuce and grapes. Microwave at 100% (High) for 3-5 minutes, or until heated through, stirring once.
3 Stir in the lettuce and grapes and serve hot.

Microtips

Hot Chicken Salad can be prepared in advance up to the end of stage 2. Refrigerate until needed.

To serve, microwave at 100% (High) for 5-6 minutes, then stir in the lettuce and grapes.

Vegetable side salad

$7\frac{1}{2}$ mins

Standing time: none

Yellow courgettes provide a splash of bright colour in this dish, but green courgettes can be used instead. Serve with cold meats.

275g / 10oz packet frozen green beans
225g / 8oz yellow or green courgettes, sliced
30ml / 2tbls water

DRESSING
30ml / 2tbls sunflower oil
2.5ml / ½tsp dried parsley
pinch of dried oregano
1.5ml / ¼tsp onion salt
pinch of garlic salt
pinch of pepper

SERVES 6

1 In a 1.7L / 3pt bowl or casserole, combine the beans, courgette slices and water. Cover and microwave at 100% (High) for 7-9 minutes, or until the vegetables are tender-crisp, stirring twice. Set aside.
2 In a small bowl, combine the dressing ingredients. Reduce power to 70% (Medium-High) and microwave for 30-45 seconds.
3 Drain the vegetables and pour over the flavoured dressing, stirring to coat the vegetables. Serve at room temperature.

Slimmer's notes

There are no adjustments needed to this recipe to make it a super slimmer's side salad. It provides just 45Cal/190kJ per serving.

Right: *Vegetable Mayonnaise*
Below: *Vegetable Side Salad*

Vegetable mayonnaise

12 mins

Standing time: 1-2 mins

450g / 1lb green beans, cut into 2.5cm / 1in lengths
75ml / 5tbls water
75ml / 5tbls lemon mayonnaise
150ml / ¼pt single cream
227g / 8oz can water chestnuts, drained and sliced
45ml / 3tbls milk
213g / 7½oz can sliced mushrooms, drained
15ml / 1tbls soy sauce
5ml / 1tsp vinegar
salt and pepper

SERVES 6-8

1 Place the beans and water in a casserole. Cover and microwave at 100% (High) for 9-11 minutes, or until tender, stirring once. Stand, covered, for 1-2 minutes, then drain.
2 Stir in the mayonnaise, single cream, water chestnuts, milk, mushrooms, soy sauce and vinegar. Cover and microwave at 100% (High) for 3-4 minutes, or until heated through, stirring once. Stir and check the seasoning. Serve warm.

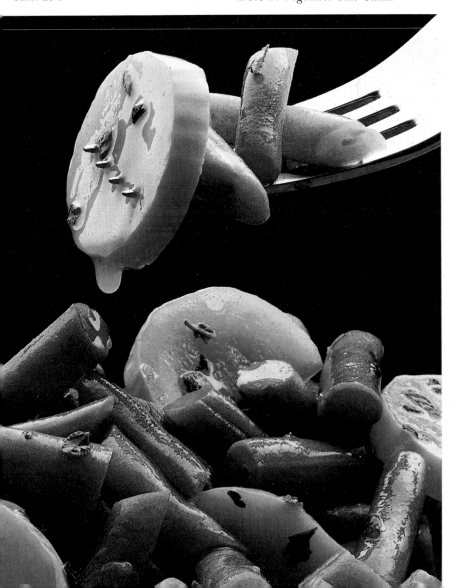

Super side dishes

Whether you're entertaining or preparing a meal for the family, make the most of your microwave and have tasty and colourful vegetables that are an exciting addition to any meal.

Vegetable side dishes enhance the main course of a meal, adding fresh, delicate flavours, colour and contrast to the main dish — and cooking vegetables in the microwave makes excellent sense. Taste and texture are retained and the goodness of the vegetables is maintained as cooking is quick and uses less water than most conventional methods.

When preparing vegetables for the microwave, cut them into even-sized pieces. This ensures even cooking. They should also be stirred thoroughly once or twice during cooking, moving food from the outside of the dish into the middle, so that all the vegetables have a chance to cook through. Cover the vegetables during cooking unless the recipe specifically says not to. This helps to retain moisture. Keep the vegetables cov-

French-style Fennel

270

ered while they are standing as well to help keep them warm and succulent. Salt should be used sparingly and only added at the end of the cooking time as it tends to toughen vegetables.

French-style fennel is a delicious and unusual dish with a subtle flavour of aniseed, impressive for a dinner party. Carrots are transformed by adding a honey glaze or by combining them with asparagus. Quick cooking helps cabbage retain its lovely, crunchy texture and the addition of caraway seeds gives a distinctive flavour. Colourful Coleslaw is another tasty dish. By serving this usually cold salad hot you bring out its full flavour.

Slimmer's notes

Herby Green Beans (page 272) have only 20Cal / 84kJ per portion, if made without oil. Use 75g / 3oz fructose to replace the sugar in Colourful Coleslaw for 80Cal / 335kJ.

Honey-glazed Carrots

French-style fennel

21 mins

Standing time: 3 mins

This rich and creamy dish, with a mild flavour of aniseed, goes well with ham or chicken. Or, you could serve it alone as a starter.

2 large heads fennel
30ml / 2tbls water
50g / 2oz butter
1 garlic clove, crushed
pepper to taste
75ml / 3fl oz double cream

SERVES 4

1 Cut the fennel bulbs in half lengthways, trim the root ends and discard. Cut away a few of the fennel fronds, chop and reserve.
2 Place the fennel halves cut side down in a shallow dish (see Microtips). Add the water, butter, garlic and pepper. Cover and microwave at 100% (High) for 10 minutes.
3 Turn the fennel over and rearrange, then microwave for a further 8-10 minutes or until very

tender. Pour over the cream and microwave for 3 minutes. Cover and leave to stand for 3 minutes.
4 Scatter the chopped fennel fronds over the fennel and serve immediately.

VARIATIONS
Fennel with Wine: use dry white wine in place of the cream.

For French-style courgettes: cut 450g / 1lb courgettes into thick diagonal slices. Add the water, butter, garlic and pepper. Cover and microwave for 7-9 minutes, stirring once and adding the cream 3 minutes before the end of cooking time. Scatter with snipped chives, if liked.

Microtips

Choose a rectangular dish and arrange the fennel halves in alternate directions so that they fit neatly together — this way they cook more evenly.

Honey-glazed carrots

7¾ mins

Standing time: none

6 carrots, total weight 450g / 1lb, cut into 6mm / ¼in slices
30ml / 2tbls water
30ml / 2tbls brown sugar
30ml / 2tbls honey
large knob of butter or margarine
2.5ml / ½tsp grated orange zest
2.5ml / ½tsp cornflour
salt and pepper

SERVES 4

1 Combine carrots and water in a 1.7L / 3pt casserole. Cover and microwave at 100% (High) for 7-8 minutes, or until just tender, stirring once during cooking time. Drain.
2 In a small bowl, mix the sugar, honey, butter, orange zest and cornflour. Microwave at 100% (High) for 45-60 seconds or until clear, thickened and bubbly. Stir once during the cooking time.
3 Pour glaze over carrots, season and toss to coat.

271

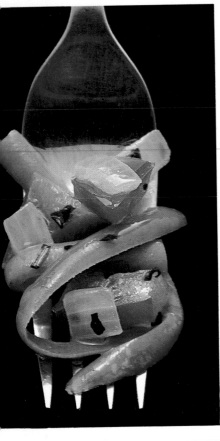

Caraway cabbage

6½ mins

Standing time: none

700g / 1½lb white cabbage, shredded
30ml / 2tbls water
25g / 1oz butter or margarine
30ml / 2tbls single cream
salt and pepper
1.5ml / ¼tsp caraway seeds

SERVES 4

1 Combine cabbage, water and butter in a 2.3L / 4pt casserole. Cover and microwave at 100% (High) for 6-7 minutes. Drain.
2 Season to taste and add cream and caraway seeds. Microwave at 100% (High) for a further 30 seconds until hot.
VARIATION
Add a splash of cider vinegar and use natural yoghurt for cream.

Left: *Herby Green Beans*
Below: *Caraway Cabbage*

Colourful Coleslaw

8 mins

Standing time: none

450g / 1lb white cabbage, shredded
225g / ½lb carrots, grated
30ml / 2tbls chopped green pepper
30ml / 2tbls chopped onion
175g / 6oz sugar
175ml / 6fl oz white wine vinegar
125ml / 4fl oz water
2.5ml / ½tsp celery seeds
pepper

SERVES 6

1 Mix cabbage, carrot, green pepper and onion in a large bowl. Microwave at 100% (High) for 4-6 minutes until tender; stir once.
2 Mix sugar, vinegar, water, celery seeds and pepper in a jug. Microwave at 100% (High) for 3-5 minutes, or until boiling; stir every minute. Microwave 1 minute.
3 Cool and pour over cabbage.

Herby green beans

8 mins

Standing time: 3 mins

250g / 9oz French beans
150ml / ¼pt water
1 green pepper, seeded and chopped
1 onion, chopped
15ml / 1tbls olive oil
2 tomatoes, peeled and chopped
salt and pepper
1.5ml / ¼tsp sugar
1.5ml / ¼tsp dried basil
pinch of dried rosemary

SERVES 4

1 Place beans in a 1.1L / 2pt bowl. Add water, cover and microwave at 100% (High) for 5-7 minutes, or until just tender, stirring once. Let stand for 3 minutes.
2 Combine green pepper, onion and oil in a small bowl. Microwave at 100% (High) for 2-3 minutes.
3 Drain beans. Add pepper mix with tomatoes, seasoning, sugar and herbs. Cover and microwave at 100% (High) for 1-2 minutes, or until heated through.

Crunchin' green beans

11½ mins

Standing time: 5 mins

450g / 1lb green beans, cut into
   2.5cm / 1in pieces
60ml / 4tbls water
30ml / 2tbls light brown sugar
10ml / 2tsp cornflour
45ml / 3tbls lemon juice
25g / 1oz butter or margarine

TOPPING
45-60ml / 3-4tbls stale
   breadcrumbs
45-60ml / 3-4tbls slivered
   almonds
15ml / 1tbls butter, softened
pinch of nutmeg

SERVES 4

1 Combine beans and water in a
2.3L / 4pt casserole. Cover and microwave at 100% (High) for 9-11
minutes, or until tender. Stir once.
Stand for 5 minutes. Drain, reserving 50ml / 2fl oz cooking liquid.
2 In a small jug, combine sugar
and cornflour. Blend in lemon
juice and reserved cooking liquid.

Microwave at 100% (High) for
1½-2 minutes, stirring once. Add
butter. Pour sauce over beans.
3 Combine topping ingredients
and sprinkle over beans. Microwave, uncovered, at 100% (High)
for 1-1½ minutes.

German potato salad

14½ mins

Standing time: 2 mins

450g / 1lb potatoes, cut into
   6mm / ¼in thick slices
30ml / 2tbls water
4 rashers back bacon, rinded and
   cut into 12mm / ½in pieces

DRESSING
275ml / ½pt milk
15ml / 3tsp cornflour
45ml / 3tbls white wine vinegar
30ml / 2tbls sugar
1.5ml / ¼tsp celery seed

SERVES 4

1 Place potatoes and water in a
large casserole. Cover and microwave at 100% (High) for 5-7
minutes, or until the potatoes are

Left: *Crunchin' Green Beans*
Above: *German Potato Salad*

just tender, stirring once. Stand,
covered, for 2 minutes, then drain.
2 Place the bacon in a large bowl
and microwave at 100% (High) for
5-6 minutes, or until crisp. Remove and drain on absorbent
paper. Drain, reserving 30ml /
2tbls bacon fat.
3 Stir milk and cornflour into the
reserved bacon fat and microwave
at 100% (High) for 2½-3½
minutes, stirring twice. Stir in
vinegar, sugar and celery seed.
4 Add the bacon and potatoes to
the dressing. Microwave at 100%
(High) for 2-3 minutes, or until
the potatoes are tender and the
mixture is heated, stirring once.

Cook's notes

*Toasted or baked breadcrumbs are a
useful standby for sprinkling over
microwaved vegetables to add
texture and a golden, toasted colour.
Alternatively, sprinkle the
vegetables with crushed crisps.*

273

Asparagus special

11 mins

Standing time: none

350g / 12oz carrots, sliced
275ml / ½pt water
350g / 12oz can asparagus cuts
  and tips, drained
75g / 3oz butter
15ml / 1tbls light soy sauce
30ml / 2tbls sunflower seeds

SERVES 4

1 Place carrots and water in a 2.3L / 4pt casserole. Cover and microwave at 100% (High) for 8-10 minutes, or until just tender. Drain and return to casserole. Gently stir in the asparagus.
2 Place butter in a small bowl. Cover and microwave at 100% (High) for 30-60 seconds, or until melted. Stir in soy sauce.
3 Pour butter mixture over vege-

tables and stir. Cover and microwave at 100% (High) for 2½-3 minutes, or until heated through.
4 Sprinkle with sunflower seeds and serve.

Creamy courgettes

6¾ mins

Standing time: none

3-4 courgettes, weighing 450g /
  1lb, cut into 6mm / ¼in slices
30ml / 2tbls water
25g / 1oz butter or margarine
50g / 2oz plain flour
2.5ml / ½tsp chopped chervil or
  parsley
salt and pepper
1.5ml / ¼tsp sugar
150ml / ¼pt half cream or top of
  milk

SERVES 4

1 Combine courgettes and water

Asparagus Special

in a 2L / 3½pt casserole. Cover and microwave at 100% (High) for 5-7 minutes or until tender, stirring once. Drain and set aside.
2 Place butter in a small bowl, cover and microwave at 100% (High) for 15-30 seconds or until melted. Stir in flour, seasonings and sugar. Blend in cream.
3 Microwave at 100% (High) for 1½-2½ minutes, or until thickened, stirring twice.
4 Pour sauce over courgettes.
5 Serve with grilled chops.

Cook's notes

You may substitute yellow courgettes to make this an especially colourful dish. They are very similar to green courgettes although not so readily available.

274

Greens

Colour, flavour and goodness are guaranteed when you cook greens in the microwave. With just a little water and a few minutes' cooking, you will have perfect vegetables every time.

Some greens are delicate in flavour while others taste more piquant. But whichever you use, they should be microwaved briefly to ensure that they retain nutrients and character.

Use your microwave as often as possible to cook greens if you want to get the maximum amount of goodness from them. The microwave makes an important contribution to healthy eating when it comes to vegetable cooking, which

is also an added bonus of cooking with your microwave.

How to select and store greens
Choose greens of any type which are clean and crisp. Avoid dry or wilted leaves, coarse stems or veins. Spinach should be deep green with either curly or flat leaves. Select kale and spring greens which are green and bright. Small, yellow leaves are edible but large ones should be

discarded. Avoid woody or flabby stems. Chard should have small, dark green leaves and firm, white stalks. Look for cabbage heads which are solid and feel heavy for their size with undamaged leaves.

Pack unwashed greens loosely in a plastic bag or covered container to prevent drying. Store in the refrigerator and use promptly.

Left to right: *Sweet-sour Spinach, Braised Cabbage, Greens with Bacon.*

Sweet-sour spinach

$11\frac{1}{2}$ mins

Standing time: none

450g / 1lb spinach
50g / 2oz rindless streaky bacon, chopped
15ml / 1tbls plain flour
15ml / 1tbls brown sugar
1.5ml / $\frac{1}{4}$tsp mustard powder
salt and pepper
125ml / 4fl oz creamy milk
15ml / 1tbls cider vinegar

SERVES 4

1 Wash the spinach well in cold water, shake out the excess water and chop or shred into pieces. Then cook the spinach as directed in the chart, right. Drain well and put to one side.
2 Microwave the bacon in a 2L/ $3\frac{1}{2}$pt covered casserole at 100% (High) for 3-4 minutes or until cooked. Drain off all but 15ml/ 1tbls of the cooking juices.
3 Blend in the flour, sugar, mustard, salt, pepper and milk, mixing until the flour is completely incorporated. Microwave at 100% (High) for $1\frac{1}{2}$-2 minutes, stirring once during the cooking time.
4 Then stir in the vinegar and spinach, and microwave at 100% (High) for 1-2 minutes.

Braised cabbage

9 mins

Standing time: 2 mins

350g / 12oz cabbage, finely shredded
65ml / $2\frac{1}{2}$fl oz boiling water
$\frac{1}{2}$ vegetable stock cube
1 carrot, coarsely grated
$\frac{1}{2}$ small onion, finely chopped
15g / $\frac{1}{2}$oz butter
2.5ml / $\frac{1}{2}$tsp dried parsley
salt and pepper

SERVES 4

1 Pour the hot water onto the stock cube in a 2L / $3\frac{1}{2}$pt casserole. Stir until the stock cube has completely dissolved.
2 Stir all the remaining ingredients into the container and cover with a lid or cling film rolled back

at one edge to allow steam to escape. Microwave at 100% (High) for 9-11 minutes, stirring once during the cooking time. Leave to stand for 2 minutes; serve.

Greens with bacon

$9\frac{1}{2}$ mins

Standing time: 2 mins

Greens and bacon are an excellent combination, which you will find even more flavourful when cooked in the microwave.

50g / 2oz rindless streaky bacon, chopped
1 small onion, finely chopped
450g / 1lb spring greens or cabbage

salt and pepper
pinch of nutmeg

SERVES 4

1 In a 2.8L / 5pt casserole, combine the bacon with the onion. Cover with cling film rolled back at one edge, and microwave at 100% (High) for 3-5 minutes, or until the bacon is cooked, stirring half way through the cooking time.
2 Discard any thick stems or stalks, then shred the greens or cabbage finely. Stir them into the onion and bacon and mix well.
3 Cover with cling film rolled back at one edge and microwave as directed in the chart below, until the greens are tender but crisp; stir once during the cooking time. Season with salt, pepper and nutmeg to taste. Let stand 2 minutes.

Microwave times for greens

TYPE	QUANTITY	MICROWAVE TIME AT 100% (HIGH)	PROCEDURE
Cabbage	450 / 1lb	9-11 minutes	Discard thick stalk; shred. Place in a 2.8L / 5pt casserole with 60ml / $2\frac{1}{2}$fl oz water; cover. Let stand 2 minutes. Serve tossed in butter and nutmeg.
Curly kale	450g / 1lb	15-17 minutes	Discard thick stalk and stems; shred. Place in a 2.8L / 5pt casserole with 150ml / 5fl oz water; cover. Stir every 5 minutes. Let stand 2 minutes. Drain; season.
Spinach Fresh	450g / 1lb	6-8 minutes	Chop or shred. Place in a covered 2.8L / 5pt casserole. Stir once. Stand 2 minutes. Drain.
Frozen (chopped or leaf)	275g / 10oz	7-9 minutes	Place in a covered 1.4L / $2\frac{1}{2}$pt casserole. Stir to break up during cooking.
Spring greens	450g / 1lb	$6\frac{1}{2}$-$8\frac{1}{2}$ minutes	Discard stalk; shred. Place in a 2.8L / 5pt casserole with 30ml / 2tbls water; cover. Stir once. Stand 2 minutes. Drain; season.
Swiss chard	450g / 1lb	$5\frac{1}{2}$-$6\frac{1}{2}$ minutes	Discard thick stalk; shred. Place in a 2.8L / 5pt casserole with 150ml / 5fl oz water; cover. Stir every 3 minutes. Let stand 2 minutes. Drain, add salt to taste.

276

Spinach soup

16 mins

Standing time: none

This is a hearty, meal-in-itself soup. The contrast of the spinach with the creamy sauce is particularly good.

275g / 10oz packet frozen chopped spinach
1 small onion, finely chopped
25g / 1oz butter or margarine
40g / 1½oz plain flour
2 chicken or vegetable stock cubes
850ml / 1½pt milk
salt and pepper
pinch of grated nutmeg
65ml / 2½fl oz soured cream (optional)
15-30ml / 1-2tbls snipped chives (optional)

SERVES 4-6

1 Make a small hole in the packet of frozen spinach and microwave at 100% (High) for 3-5 minutes. Shake once or twice during cooking. Remove the spinach from the packet and drain well.
2 In a 2L / 3½pt bowl, microwave the onion and butter together at 100% (High) for 1-1½ minutes, or until the onion is just tender.
3 Mix the flour into the onion and butter mixture until completely incorporated, then mash in the stock cubes and finally blend in the milk. Stir the mixture until smooth.
4 Stir in the spinach, then microwave at 100% (High) for 12-15 minutes until the soup is thick and creamy, stirring after the first 5 minutes and then every 2-3 minutes. Season to taste with salt, pepper and grated nutmeg.
5 If liked, when serving the soup, top each portion with soured cream and sprinkle with 5ml / 1tsp snipped chives to garnish.

VARIATION
Creamy spinach soup: If preferred, the finished dish can be puréed in a blender or food processor. Toast 2 slices of brown bread, cube and scatter over each bowl.

Swiss chard and mushrooms

9 mins

Standing time: 2 mins

450g / 1lb chard or spring greens
1 onion, finely chopped
25g / 1oz butter or margarine
295g / 10.4oz can condensed cream of mushroom soup
175g / 6oz mushrooms, sliced
65ml / 2½fl oz soured cream
2.5ml / ½tsp soy sauce (optional)
salt and pepper
25g / 1oz toasted almonds

SERVES 4-6

1 Cook the chard or spring greens as directed in the chart, page 276; drain. In a 1.1L / 2pt casserole, microwave the onion and butter at 100% (High) for 1½ minutes.
2 Stir in the drained vegetable and remaining ingredients except almonds. Microwave at 100% (High) for 2 minutes, stirring once. Leave to stand for 2 minutes. Garnish with toasted almonds.

Cook's notes

Greens are very nutritious vegetables, containing plenty of vitamins. Consequently, microwaving is the best form of cooking, as all the goodness is retained. However, the microwave cannot work wonders on tough, old vegetables, so take care when selecting greens.

Preparation is also important. Cut out thick stalks or stems and discard any damaged outside leaves. Wash the leaves in cold water and shake out the excess well. Then chop or shred the leaves coarsely before cooking as directed in the chart, opposite. Season after cooking and serve with butter.

Crustless Ricotta pie

| 12 mins |

Standing time: 5 mins

Spinach has a distinctive flavour which is perfectly complemented by the cheese and eggs in this dish. It can be served as a light starter or snack, or as an accompaniment to beef or lamb dishes.

225g / 8oz spinach
1 onion, chopped
2 eggs
225g / 8oz Ricotta cheese
1.5ml / ¼tsp salt (optional)
1.5ml / ¼tsp pepper
1.5ml / ¼sp nutmeg
10ml / 2tsp plain flour
large pinch of paprika

SERVES 6

1 Wash, then chop or shred spinach. Combine the spinach and onion in a 1.7L / 3pt casserole and cover. Microwave at 100% (High) for 5-6 minutes, stirring once. Drain well.
2 In a medium mixing bowl, beat the eggs with a fork. Stir in the Ricotta, salt, if using, pepper, nutmeg and flour. Blend in the spinach and onion. Spread the spinach mixture in a 23cm / 9in pie plate with a rubber spatula. Sprinkle over the paprika.
3 Microwave at 100% (High) for 4 minutes, rotating after 2 minutes. Reduce the power to 50% (Medium). Microwave for 3 minutes longer, or until the centre is set. Let stand for 5 minutes.

VARIATION
Substitute 275g / 10oz packet frozen chopped spinach for the fresh if preferred. Empty the spinach straight into the casserole with the onion; microwave at 100% (High) for 4-6 minutes, stirring once. Continue as directed.

Cook's notes

Vegetables cooked in a microwave retain their texture and more of their nutrients than when cooked conventionally in more water.

Cheesy spring greens

| 3½ mins |

Standing time: 2 minutes

30ml / 2tbls olive or vegetable oil
1 garlic clove, crushed
350g / 12oz spring greens, shredded, washed and well drained
5ml / 1tsp sesame seeds
25g / 1oz mature Cheddar or Parmesan cheese, grated
salt and pepper
2 slices rye or granary bread, toasted and cubed

SERVES 4

1 Combine the oil and garlic in a casserole and microwave at 100% (High) for 1 minute.

2 Quickly stir in the greens and sesame, cover and microwave at 100% (High) for 2 minutes, stirring once; let stand for 2 minutes. Drain.
3 Stir two-thirds of the cheese into the hot spring greens and season to taste. Cover and microwave at 100% (High) for 30 seconds. Sprinkle over the cubes of bread and remaining cheese.

Microtips

Substitute kale for spring greens, if preferred and microwave at 100% (High) for 7-9 minutes. Let stand for 2 minutes before serving. To make a delicious main-course snack for 2-3, simply add more cheese.

278

Microwaving dried fruit

Quick, clean and easy to use, dried fruit is an excellent store-cupboard standby. In moments it can be microwaved into some deliciously succulent sweet or savoury dishes.

Take a look along any supermarket shelf at the range of dried fruit on offer. There are far more than the familiar raisins and prunes — dried bananas, apple rings, pears are just some of those available.

Types of dried fruit
There are three types of dried fruit: the ordinary ones, which need soaking before using; the tenderized or 'no need to soak' fruit, or semi-dried fruit, none of which require soaking.
Overnight soaking: all large dried fruit such as pears, peaches or figs

requires soaking before using. Use twice as much tepid liquid as fruit to cover the fruit generously. The liquid can be water or, for more flavour, try cold black tea with brandy or sherry to flavour, or unsweetened fruit juice. Add flavourings such as a cinnamon stick or a slice of lemon, if liked. Soak for at least eight hours or overnight. Drain.
Short soaking: this is also suitable for large fruit, but is a time-saving alternative to overnight soaking. Cover the fruit in cold water, bring to boil and simmer for 10 minutes. Leave, covered, for 40 minutes

before draining and using.
Plumping: small dried fruit such as currants and raisins, which can be used without soaking, can be plumped up in the microwave if liked (see Microtips, page 280).

Storage
Use as much fruit as required from a packet, then simply transfer any unused fruit to an airtight container and store in a cool dark place. Keep unopened packets in the store cupboard. For best results, use within three months.

Dried Fruit Compote (page 283)

Muesli Bars

Muesli bars

13½ mins

Standing time: none

100g / 4oz butter or margarine
100g / 4oz soft dark brown sugar
pinch of salt
2 eggs, lightly beaten
1.5ml / ¼tsp almond flavouring
1 quantity Crunchy muesli (see
  right, but omit raisins)

MAKES 12

1 Put the butter in a bowl and microwave, covered, at 100% (High) for 1-1½ minutes or until melted.

2 In a large bowl, combine the brown sugar, salt, eggs and almond flavouring. Beat in the melted butter and stir in the Crunchy muesli until coated. Press into a greased dish, about 23 × 25cm / 9 × 10in.

3 Microwave, uncovered, at 100% (High) for 6-9 minutes, or until firm to the touch; rotate the dish a half turn and press the mixture down with a spatula every 2 minutes. Mark into 12 bars.

4 Allow to cool completely before removing from the dish. Store in an airtight container in a cool, dark place for up to one week.

Microtips

To plump dried fruit, place 100g / 4oz dried fruit in a shallow bowl, sprinkle with 45ml / 3tbls liquid. Cover and microwave at 100% (High) for 2½-3 minutes until the fruit is plump and swollen, stirring well once. Leave to stand, covered, for 2-3 minutes; drain.

Crunchy muesli

6½ mins

Standing time: none

Serve with milk or yoghurt.

200g / 7oz porridge oats
50g / 2oz desiccated coconut
50g / 2oz flaked almonds
200ml / 7fl oz clear runny honey
50g / 2oz soft dark brown sugar
50ml / 2fl oz vegetable oil
5ml / 1tsp ground cinnamon
5ml / 1tsp vanilla flavouring
75g / 3oz raisins
25g / 1oz dried apple rings,
  chopped

MAKES 700g / 1½lb

Cook's notes

If you forget to stir the muesli during cooling it sets in a solid lump. To soften and make it pliable again, microwave uncovered at 100% (High) for 45-60 seconds. Break apart with a fork and let cool completely before storing.

When cool store the muesli in an airtight container for no longer than one to two weeks.

No-bake fruit cake

4½ mins

Standing time: none

Store this cake in an airtight container in a cool place for no longer than two weeks.

225g / 8oz mixed glacé fruit, chopped
175g / 6oz raisins
100g / 4oz dates, chopped
100g / 4oz chopped nuts
100g / 4oz digestive or plain sweet biscuits
75g / 3oz butter or margarine
200g / 7oz dairy fudge, cut in small pieces
2.5ml / ½tsp rum flavouring

MAKES 24-28 SLICES

1 Line the sides and base of a 900g / 2lb loaf dish (23 × 12.5cm / 9 × 5in) with cling film.

2 In a large bowl, mix together the fruit and nuts. Stir in the biscuit crumbs, tossing to coat the fruit. Set aside.

3 In a medium-sized bowl, microwave the butter or margarine, covered, at 100% (High) for 1-1½ minutes or until melted. Add the fudge and continue to microwave at 100% (High) for 3½-5 minutes or until the fudge has melted and the mixture is smooth, stirring every minute. Stir into the fruit mixture together with the rum flavouring until the mixture is evenly blended.

4 Spoon into the prepared tin and press down firmly. Cover and chill for at least 4 hours until set.

5 To serve, run a sharp knife under cold water and use to cut the cake into slices.

No-bake Fruit Cake

How to microwave Crunchy muesli

Mix *together the rolled oats, desiccated coconut and flaked almonds in a large bowl, stirring well to combine. Set on one side while preparing the boiling syrup mixture.*

Combine *the remaining ingredients except the raisins and apples in a bowl or jug. Microwave, uncovered at 100% (High) for 2 minutes, or until boiling, stirring once.*

Pour *the boiling mixture over the oats, tossing to coat. Microwave, uncovered, at 100% (High) for 4½-6 minutes until mixture begins to stiffen and appear dry, stirring every 2 minutes.*

Microwave *for a further 30 seconds for crunchier cereal. Stir in the raisins and apple. Leave to cool for 1-1½ hours, stirring to break the muesli apart once or twice during cooling.*

Cook's notes

Dried fruit has a very high energy value as it takes between 1.8-2.7kg / 4-6lb fresh fruit to make 450g / 1lb dried, depending on the fruit. The fresh fruit is sun or air-dried to produce fruit with concentrated amounts of vitamins, minerals and sugar. This high sugar content means the fruit needs less added sugar during cooking, so either omit sugar or try using honey or syrup as sweet alternatives for extra flavour.

281

Fruity pork roast

44½ mins

Standing time: 10 mins

175g / 6oz soft dark brown sugar
100g / 4oz 'no need to soak', or
  tenderized dried apricots
75g / 3oz 'no need to soak'
  prunes, halved and stoned
175ml / 6fl oz hot water
178ml / 6¼fl oz frozen
  concentrated orange juice,
  thawed (see Microtips)
1 small onion, sliced
2.5ml / ½tsp ground ginger
salt and pepper
15g / ½oz butter or margarine
1.4kg / 3lb loin of pork, boned,
  rind removed

SERVES 6

1 In a medium-sized bowl, combine 100g / 4oz sugar, the apricots, prunes, hot water, 45ml / 3tbls orange juice, onion, ginger, salt and pepper. Microwave, uncovered, at 100% (High) for 8-12 minutes, stirring frequently.

2 Melt the butter, covered, in a small bowl at 100% (High) for 30-45 seconds, then stir in the remaining sugar and orange juice.

3 Place the pork, fat side down, on a roasting rack. Brush with the orange butter mixture. Calculate the total cooking time, allowing 12-15 minutes per 450g / 1lb. Cover the meat and microwave at 100% (High) for 5 minutes. Reduce power to 50% (Medium) for remaining first half of time.

4 Uncover meat and turn over. Spoon half fruit mixture over top. Cover and microwave at 50% (Medium) for remaining time.

5 Spoon over remaining fruit. Stand, covered, 10 minutes.

Microtips

To thaw 178ml / 6¼fl oz frozen orange juice, remove the metal lid and surround from the carton. Microwave at 20-30% (Defrost) for 2-3 minutes, stirring twice. Stand for 5 minutes.

Fruity Pork Roast

282

Dried fruit compote

	18 mins

Standing time: 2-3 mins

Use a combination of fruit, such as apples, figs, apricots, peaches, pears, prunes and raisins for this compote. Serve it warm or cold, topped with thick natural yoghurt. Remove the cinnamon sticks.

700g / 1½lb mixed dried fruit, soaked
45ml / 3tbls orange juice or brandy
3 large cinnamon sticks
60ml / 4tbls runny honey
1 orange, thinly sliced

SERVES 6-8

VARIATION
Dried fruit compote for four: halve all the ingredients. Microwave the dried fruit with the water, juice and cinnamon for 8-10 minutes. Add the remaining ingredients and microwave for a further 2 minutes. Stand for 2-3 minutes.

Microtips

It is important to stir dried fruit during microwaving — particularly if using alcohol. Otherwise, its high concentration of sugar can lead to spot burning.

Gammon with raisin sauce

	11 mins

Standing time: 3-5 mins

4 gammon steaks (each about 100g / 4oz)

SAUCE
100g / 4oz soft brown sugar
15ml / 3tsp cornflour
1.5ml / ¼tsp ground cinnamon
1.5ml / ¼tsp mustard powder
pinch of ground cloves
225ml / 8fl oz apple juice
75g / 3oz raisins
10ml / 2tsp butter or margarine

SERVES 4

1 Preheat a browning dish at 100% (High) for 5 minutes, or follow manufacturer's instructions. Add steaks and microwave for 1-2 minutes. Turn and microwave 2-3 minutes. Stand 3-5 minutes.
2 Meanwhile, mix brown sugar, cornflour, cinnamon, mustard and cloves. Blend in apple juice. Microwave, uncovered, at 100% (High) for 3-4 minutes until thickened, stirring three times. Add raisins and butter and stir until melted. Serve with gammon.

VARIATION
For a sweet raisin sauce to serve with desserts, omit the mustard powder.

Gammon with Raisin Sauce

How to microwave Dried fruit compote

Drain *the fruit; measure the liquid and make up to 575ml / 1pt with water. Place all in a large bowl with the juice or brandy and cinnamon.*

Cover *and microwave at 100% (High) for 15-18 minutes, or until the fruit is tender, stirring well three times during cooking.*

Stir *in the honey and orange slices. Cover and microwave at 100% (High) for 3-5 minutes. Let stand, covered, for 2-3 minutes before serving.*

Raisin pork with apples

22 mins

Standing time: 10 mins

This makes a delicious and very simple Sunday lunch for two. Serve with a green vegetable, microwaved while the joint is standing.

700g / 1½lb boned loin of pork, rind removed
3 small dessert apples

STUFFING
30ml / 2tbls raisins
45ml / 3tbls maple syrup
15ml / 1tbls soft brown sugar
1.5ml / ¼tsp ground cinnamon

SERVES 2

1 Core and chop one apple. To make the stuffing, combine the chopped apple, raisins, maple syrup, soft brown sugar and cinnamon in a small bowl.

2 Cut through the centre of the pork from the lean side, without cutting the joint completely in half. Open out and spread some of the stuffing over the centre of the meat. Reshape the joint and tie with string to secure. Place on a roasting rack and cover loosely.

3 Microwave at 100% (High) for 2 minutes. Reduce power to 50% (Medium) for 15 minutes, rotating the roasting rack a quarter turn twice during cooking.

4 Core the remaining apples. Cut a slit in the skin around the waist of each, then place on the rack next to the meat. Fill the centres with the remaining fruit stuffing. Baste the meat with any juices from the stuffing.

5 Microwave, covered, at 50% (Medium) for a further 5-7 minutes, or until the centre of the pork is cooked to taste. Remove

Raisin Pork with Apples

from the cooker. Cover loosely with foil and let stand for 10 minutes before serving. (The apples tenderize on standing.)

VARIATION
Apricot pork with apples: Substitute four dried apricots and one prune for the raisins; soak and chop. Assemble and microwave as directed in the recipe. For a better contrast, use small green-skinned cooking apples.

Cook's notes

Remember to score the skin of each of the apples to be stuffed. This prevents heat building up under the skin during microwaving, which would cause the apples to split open and burst in the cooker.

Tropical fruits

Colourful tropical fruits bring a taste of sunshine to your table. Whether for main courses or desserts, the microwave will make the most of their exciting textures and flavours.

It's now so easy to find a wide variety of tropical fruits to impress and delight your friends and family. The range in supermarkets is increasing all the time, and if yours doesn't stock what you want — ask for it. Once you know how to choose, store and prepare these fruits, you can include them with confidence in your menus.

Guava can be pear-shaped with tough yellow skins and pale green flesh, or round with purple skins and red flesh. They have a strong, musky aroma but the flavour is delicate. When ripe they have a strong smell and are slightly soft when pressed. To prepare: peel and slice.

Kiwifruit are oval with thin and hairy brown skins. The flesh is bright green with edible black seeds — a very attractive fruit when sliced, though rather tart. To prepare: thinly peel away the skin and cut across into 6-8 slices.

Mangoes can be round or kidney-shaped and they vary in size. The fruit contains a large stone and has a bright yellow, juicy flesh when ripe. The tough skin softens and changes from green to reddish-orange when it is ready to eat.

Calypso Fruit Compote

285

Passion fruit are plum-sized fruits with tough purple-brown skins. When ripe, the skin becomes wrinkled. The flesh is juicy, sweet and yellow with small edible black seeds. To prepare: halve and scoop out the flesh. Eat raw or make into a sauce.

Pawpaw (or papaya) is a large pear-shaped fruit with a tough green skin which turns yellow as it ripens. The flesh is pinky-orange with small black inedible seeds in the centre. To prepare: cut in half, remove the seeds and peel. Use in fruit salads and in sorbets.

To store: keep these fruits at room temperature until ripe. Then store in the refrigerator and use within 1-2 days for kiwifruit and 2-3 days for passion fruit, guava, mango and pawpaw.

Calypso fruit compote

| 3 mins |

Standing time: none

75ml / 3fl oz exotic pure fruit or mango juice
75ml / 3fl oz white wine
50g / 2oz caster sugar
good pinch of ground cinnamon
1 mango, peeled, stoned, diced
1 pawpaw, peeled, seeded, diced
1 guava, peeled and thinly sliced
2 passion fruit, cut in half and flesh scooped out
1 kiwifruit, peeled and sliced
1 slice fresh pineapple, peeled, cored and cut into wedges

SERVES 6

1 In a 2.3L / 4pt bowl, combine the fruit juice, wine (if using), sugar and cinnamon. Microwave at 100% (High) for 2-2½ minutes to dissolve the sugar, stirring once.
2 Stir the fruit into the hot syrup. Microwave at 100% (High) for 1 minute to heat the fruit. Serve hot or chilled.

Cook's notes

For perfectly round slices of kiwi fruit, cut the fruit horizontally before peeling. Then use a knife to remove the skin from each slice.

Tropical plaice rolls

| 9¾ mins |

Standing time: 5 mins

15g / ½oz butter
1 small onion, finely chopped
50g / 2oz fresh breadcrumbs
10ml / 2tsp fresh parsley
1 kiwi fruit, peeled and finely chopped
grated zest of ½ orange
15ml / 1tbls orange juice
50g / 2oz frozen prawns, thawed and chopped (see Microtips)
salt and pepper
4 × 100-150g / 4-6oz plaice fillets, skinned

SAUCE
15ml / 3tsp cornflour
about 50ml / 2fl oz fish stock
about 50ml / 2fl oz white wine
45ml / 3tbls single cream

GARNISH
1 kiwifruit, peeled and sliced
8 orange slices

SERVES 4

1 Place the butter and onion in a 1.1L / 2pt bowl. Cover and microwave at 100% (High) for 2-3 minutes or until the onion is soft.
2 Mix in breadcrumbs, parsley, kiwifruit, half the orange zest, orange juice and prawns. Season.
3 Lay the fillets, skinned side up on a board and spread the stuffing

Tropical Plaice Rolls

over. Roll up and secure with wooden cocktail sticks. Arrange, join side down, in a large, shallow, buttered dish.
4 Cover the dish with cling film, and microwave at 100% (High) for 5-7 minutes or until the fish flakes easily, rotating the dish once during cooking. Leave to stand for 5 minutes, then remove the cocktail sticks.
5 Place the cornflour in a jug and mix to a smooth paste with a little of the drained juices from the fish. Add the remaining juices and make up to 150ml / ¼pt with fish stock and white wine. Add the remaining orange zest and stir well.
6 Microwave, uncovered, at 100% (High) for 2-2½ minutes, or until boiling, stirring after every minute. Taste and adjust the seasoning, then stir in the cream. Pour the sauce over the fillets. Place two slices of kiwifruit on each roll. Microwave at 70% (Medium-High) for 45-60 seconds. Garnish with orange twists.

Microtips

Place frozen prawns in a single layer in a shallow dish. Cover and microwave at 20-30% (Defrost) for 1-2 minutes. Drain and use.

286

Pawpaw fiesta

3 mins

Standing time: none

An elegant as well as exotic dessert for your next dinner party.

2 pawpaw
5-10ml / 1-2tsp lime juice
vanilla ice cream or thick natural yoghurt, to serve
chopped unsalted pistachio nuts or ground cinnamon, to decorate
lime slices and mint sprigs to decorate

SERVES 4

1 Cut the pawpaw in half and scoop out the seeds. Arrange the pawpaw on a large plate with the stem ends to the outside and sprinkle evenly with lime juice. Microwave at 100% (High) for 3 minutes, giving the dish a quarter turn every minute.

2 Fill the centre of each pawpaw with scoops of ice cream or yoghurt. Sprinkle with nuts or dust with cinnamon. Serve at once.

VARIATION
For a boozy alternative, sprinkle the pawpaw with orange liqueur, instead of lime juice.

Above: *Pawpaw Fiesta*
Below: *Guava Exotica*

Slimmer's notes

Use low-fat natural yoghurt to fill the pawpaws and a sprinkling of cinnamon. This gives a dessert at just 60Cal / 250kJ per portion.

Guava exotica

2 mins

Standing time: none

8 drained canned guava halves
50g / 2oz macaroons, crushed
50g / 2oz finely chopped Brazil nuts
25g / 1oz butter, softened
soft brown sugar to sprinkle

SERVES 4

1 Remove the pulpy centre flesh and pips from the guava halves and press through a sieve into a bowl. Add the macaroons, finely chopped Brazil nuts and softened butter and mix together until well blended.

2 Place the guava halves on a large flat plate, fill the centre of each fruit half with the mixture and sprinkle the top of each with a little sugar.

3 Microwave at 100% (High) for 2-3 minutes, until warmed through. Serve with pouring cream or Greek yoghurt.

RAY DUNS

To prepare mangoes

Stand *mango, on its side, on a plate to catch the juice. Make two lengthways cuts, either side of the flat stone. Peel skin from central section; cut remaining flesh from stone.*

Using *a sharp knife, criss-cross flesh through to skin. Push from underneath, so the cubed flesh pops up; cut flesh away from the skin, or scoop out the flesh with a spoon.*

Jamaican chicken

21 mins

Standing time: 5 mins

40g / 1½oz butter, cut in pieces
1 large onion, chopped
1 garlic clove, crushed
2-3 fresh red chillies, cored, seeded and finely chopped
10ml / 2tsp curry powder
2.5ml / ½tsp ground ginger
2.5ml / ½tsp ground cinnamon
1 chicken stock cube
425ml / ¾pt exotic pure fruit or mango juice
4 × 175g / 6oz chicken breasts, on the bone, skinned
1 large ripe mango, peeled, stoned and diced
15ml / 3tsp cornflour
little cold water to mix
salt
juice of 1 lime
banana slices, to garnish

SERVES 4

1 Place the butter, onion, garlic and chillies in a 2.5L / 4½pt deep dish. Cover and microwave at 100% (High) for 4-5 minutes or until the onion is soft, stirring halfway through cooking.

Jamaican Chicken

2 Stir in the curry, ginger and cinnamon powders, crumbled stock cube and fruit juice. Stir well. Add the chicken, placing the thicker parts to the outside of the dish, spoon over sauce to coat.
3 Cover and microwave at 100% (High) for 12 minutes. Add the mango and microwave, covered, for a further 3-5 minutes or until the chicken is tender.
4 Arrange the chicken on a warm serving dish, cover and leave to stand for 5 minutes. Mix the cornflour with a little water to form a smooth paste and stir into the sauce with salt to taste and the lime juice. Microwave, uncovered, for a further 2-2½ minutes or until boiling, stirring after every 30 seconds. Pour over the chicken. Serve with rice and banana slices.

Cook's notes

Red chillies are hotter than green ones. Removing the core and seeds gives a milder taste. Remember to wash your hands after preparing the chillies.

Microtips

Mangoes make a speedy sweet sauce to serve with ice cream, sponge puddings or meringues. To make 425ml / ¾pt sauce microwave the chopped flesh of two mangoes with 60ml / 4tbls frozen concentrated orange juice at 100% (High) for 2-2½ minutes, or until the orange juice has melted. Stir twice. Purée in a blender, then sweeten the sauce to taste and reheat at 100% (High) for 1-1½ minutes, until the sauce is hot but not boiling. Stir twice during microwaving.

Party platters

The microwave gives vegetables and fruit a marvellous colour and texture — put this to good use and prepare impressive platters as a centrepiece for entertaining or for tasty individual suppers.

Microwaving brings out the best in vegetables and fruit — they retain their vibrant colours and lose none of their flavour into cooking liquids. What better way to enjoy them?

The microwave also provides a unique facility for cooking vegetables together, but without mixing them, in attractive platter arrangements. This would not be possible conventionally, as the vegetables would need to be in liquid in order to cook. The microwave also enables you to add to a platter as it cooks: start with the vegetables or fruit which need the longest cooking and add more in order of density — thickest first — finishing with any which need only brief cooking or heating.

Use fresh and / or frozen vegetables. If mixing the two, take into consideration the time needed for thawing the frozen ones, and add a little more time for the whole dish to cook.

When assembling a whole platter of vegetables or fruit which have slightly different cooking times, arrange them so that the tenderest are in the centre, graduating to the ones needing the most cooking at the outside. (Microwave energy penetrates more at the outside, cooking this area more quickly.) The pieces of food can be rearranged and turned without disturbing the appearance of the platter.

Platters for one and two

The individual vegetable gratin recipes serve one as a substantial supper dish, or two as an accompaniment for a main dish. The crunchy topping adds a good finishing touch — and the appearance is enhanced by browning under a hot grill. Heat the toppings through by microwaving at 100% (High) for 1 minute.

Vegetable Bouquet

Vegetable bouquet

35 mins

Standing time: none

100g / 4oz frozen sweetcorn
15g / ½oz butter
100g / 4oz frozen peas
100g / 4oz frozen button onions
100g / 4oz frozen Brussels
sprouts
100ml / 3½fl oz water
100g / 4oz green beans, sliced
100g / 4oz cauliflower florets
100g / 4oz carrots, sliced
100g / 4oz asparagus spears
1 artichoke, trimmed
50g / 2oz mushrooms, sliced
5ml / 1tsp lemon juice

SERVES 4

1 Place the sweetcorn in a small bowl with half the butter. Place the peas, onions and sprouts in separate bowls with 15ml / 1tbls water each. Microwave the four bowls at 100% (High) for 8-10 minutes to heat, stirring twice.
2 Place the beans, cauliflower, carrots and asparagus in separate small bowls, each with 15ml / 1tbls water. Microwave, covered, at 100% (High) for 11-12 minutes, or until tender, stirring twice.
3 Place the artichoke on a saucer and sprinkle with the remaining water. Cover and microwave at 100% (High) for 10 minutes, or until outer leaves are loose.
4 Place the mushrooms in a small bowl with the remaining butter and the lemon juice. Cover and microwave at 50% (Medium) for 3-4 minutes, until tender; stir once.
5 To assemble, place the artichoke at the side of a large round platter. Drain the other vegetables well and arrange them radiating from the artichoke in sections.
6 Cover the platter loosely and microwave at 100% (High) for 3-5 minutes to reheat the vegetables.

Cook's notes

When assembling any vegetable or fruit platter, make sure that the plate you use will fit into the microwave or on the turntable.

Cauli and broccoli crisp

4¾ mins

Standing time: 2-3 mins

75g / 3oz broccoli, broken into
small florets
75g / 3oz cauliflower, broken into
small florets
60ml / 4tbls water
25g / 1oz unsalted cashew nuts,
chopped
25g / 1oz butter
30ml / 2tbls granary or
wholewheat breadcrumbs

SERVES 1-2

1 Place the broccoli and cauliflower florets in a shallow dish and add the water. Cover and microwave at 100% (High) for 4-5 minutes, or until just tender, rearranging once. Stand, covered, for 2-3 minutes.
2 Combine the nuts and butter in a bowl and microwave, uncovered, at 100% (High) for 45-60 seconds, or until the butter has melted. Stir in the crumbs.
3 Drain the florets, then arrange broccoli and cauliflower in circles, alternating them to reform a cauliflower head on a plate. Scatter with the crumb mixture. Toast quickly under a hot grill.

Cabbage tricolour

14 mins

Standing time: 3-5 mins

25g / 1oz margarine
1 onion, finely chopped
3 celery stalks, finely chopped
175g / 6oz red cabbage, shredded
175g / 6oz white cabbage, finely
shredded
175g / 6oz green cabbage, finely
shredded
5ml / 1tsp wine vinegar
150ml / ¼pt chicken stock
50g / 2oz walnuts, chopped
30-45ml / 2-3tbls natural yoghurt
chopped parsley to garnish

SERVES 4-6

1 Place the margarine in a large shallow rectangular dish and add the onion and celery. Cover and microwave at 100% (High) for 4-5 minutes, or until tender, stirring twice.
2 Keeping the types of cabbage separate, toss each with a little vinegar. Arrange two-thirds of each type of cabbage in rows in the dish on top of the celery. Hollow out the centre of each row and pour over the stock. Cover and

Cauli and Broccoli Crisp

PAUL GRATER

290

microwave at 100% (High) for 6-7 minutes, or until tender-crisp, giving the dish a quarter turn and stirring the rows twice, taking care to keep them separate.

3 Stir the cabbage to mix with the celery mixture, still keeping the rows separate. Top each row with the remaining cabbage, cover and microwave at 100% (High) for 4-5 minutes, or until tender. Stand, covered, for 3-5 minutes.

4 Sprinkle the chopped nuts between the rows and spoon yoghurt or soured cream across the rows. Sprinkle with chopped parsley.

Hot salad platter

8½ mins

Standing time: none

100g / 4oz finger carrots
100g / 4oz baby sweetcorn
90ml / 6tbls water
100g / 4oz French beans, trimmed and cut in 5-7.5cm / 2-3in pieces
100g / 4oz courgettes, cut in 5-7.5cm / 2-3in strips
100g / 4oz mange tout peas, topped and tailed
8 spring onions, cut in 5-7.5cm / 2-3in pieces
15g / ½oz butter

PAUL GRATER

MAYONNAISE SAUCE
125ml / 4fl oz mayonnaise
5ml / 1tsp snipped chives
2.5ml / ½tsp capers, finely chopped
2.5ml / ½tsp chopped parsley
1.5ml / ¼tsp finely grated lemon zest

SERVES 4

1 Place the carrots and sweetcorn in a small bowl with 30ml / 2tbls of the water. Cover and microwave at 100% (High) for 3-4 minutes, or until tender-crisp, stirring once. Drain and set aside.

2 Mix the French beans and courgette strips in a bowl. Add 30ml / 2tbls of the water, cover and microwave at 100% (High) for 3-4 minutes, or until tender-crisp, stirring once. Drain and set aside.

3 Combine the mange tout and spring onions in a bowl with the rest of the water. Cover and mic-

Hot Salad Platter

rowave at 100% (High) for 1-2 minutes, stirring once, until the onions are tender. Drain and set aside.

4 Divide each type of vegetable into two bundles and arrange in alternate colours around the edge of a large platter, like the spokes of a wheel.

5 Mix the mayonnaise ingredients together and spoon into a small bowl. Place in the centre of the platter.

6 Place the butter in a cup, cover and microwave at 100% (High) for 30-45 seconds to melt. Brush the butter over the vegetables, cover the whole platter with vented cling film and microwave at 100% (High) for 1-2 minutes, or until the vegetables and mayonnaise are warm. Serve immediately with the sauce as a dip.

291

Fresh fruit flapjack

8¾ mins

Standing time: none

115g / 4½oz butter
100g / 4oz dark soft brown sugar
175g / 6oz porridge oats
50g / 2oz walnuts or pecans, chopped

TOPPING
100g / 4oz large strawberries, hulled and sliced
100g / 4oz black grapes, halved and seeded
425g / 15oz can apricots in fruit juice, drained, juice reserved
2 kiwifruit, peeled, halved and sliced
10ml / 2tsp cornflour
5ml / 1tsp lemon juice

SERVES 6

1 Place the butter in a 1.1L / 2pt bowl, cover and microwave at 100% (High) for 1-1½ minutes, or until melted. Stir in the sugar, oats and nuts.

2 Pat the mixture firmly over the base of a 25cm / 10in flat platter. Microwave at 100% (High) for 4 minutes, giving a quarter turn once, until almost set; cool.

3 Arrange the strawberry slices in a thick overlapping band across the centre of the cooled flapjack base. Microwave, uncovered, at 100% (High) for 15-30 seconds, or until the fruit is just warm.

4 Place a row of apricot halves on either side of the rows of grapes. Microwave, uncovered, at 100% (High) for 15-30 seconds or until just warm.

5 Add overlapping slices of kiwifruit on either side of the apricots and microwave, uncovered, at 100% (High) for 15-30 seconds.

6 Mix 45ml / 3tbls of reserved juice with the cornflour and lemon juice. Add remaining juice and microwave, covered, at 100% (High) for 3-4 minutes, or until thick and glossy, stirring twice. Spoon over the fruit. Serve the flapjack warm or cold.

Fresh Fruit Flapjack

PAUL GRATER

Pineapple and melon platter

7 mins

Standing time: none

90ml / 6tbls lemon juice
90ml / 6tbls demerara sugar
3 pieces of preserved stem ginger, finely chopped
1 small pineapple, about 700g / 1½lb
1 ogen melon, about 700g / 1½lb

SERVES 4

1 Mix the lemon juice, sugar and ginger in a bowl. Microwave, uncovered, at 100% (High) for 3-4 minutes, or until the sugar has dissolved, stirring once. Set aside in a small serving bowl.

2 Halve the pineapple lengthways through the woody base and leafy crown. Halve each half lengthways, then trim off the leafy crown pieces and reserve. Run a sharp knife between the flesh and the skin, then cut in 12mm / ½in slices, crossways. Push alternate pieces to the right and left to overlap the skin.

PETER REILLY

292

Pineapple and Melon Platter

3 Halve the melon lengthways and scoop out the seeds. Quarter and slice in the same way as the pineapple, sliding slices sideways.

4 Place the pineapple wedges on a 35.5cm / 14in platter like the spokes of a wheel. Cover and microwave at 100% (High) for 2-2½ minutes, or until just hot.

5 Arrange the melon slices between the pineapple pieces and stand the bowl of sauce in the centre of the platter. Microwave, covered, at 100% (High) for 2-2½ minutes, or until the fruit is hot and the sauce is quite warm.

6 Decorate with the reserved pineapple leaves and serve at once.

Apple and blackberry platters $\boxed{\begin{array}{c} \textbf{12} \\ \text{mins} \end{array}}$

Standing time: none

4 red-skinned apples, cored and thickly sliced
225g / 8oz fresh blackberries, hulled

SYRUP
60ml / 4tbls sugar
125ml / 4fl oz water

SERVES 4

1 For the syrup, mix the sugar and water in a 1.1L / 2pt heat-proof bowl. Microwave, covered, at 100% (High) for 2 minutes, stirring once to dissolve the sugar.
2 Arrange the apple slices in an overlapping ring round the edge of four individual serving plates. Pour a little of the syrup over each plate. Microwave plates separately, covered, at 100% (High) for 1½-2 minutes each, or until almost tender, turning twice.
3 Divide the blackberries between the plates and pile into the centre space. Spoon on remaining syrup and microwave, uncovered, for 1-1½ minutes, or until the blackberries are heated through, giving the plate a quarter turn every 30 seconds. Serve at once with yoghurt or cream spooned over each plate.

Apple and Blackberry Platter

Warm sunset salad $\boxed{\begin{array}{c} \textbf{45} \\ \text{secs} \end{array}}$

Standing time: none

1 large orange
1 small grapefruit
2 tomatoes, skinned and sliced
10ml / 2tsp demerara sugar
sprigs of mint, to garnish

SERVES 4

1 Peel the orange and the grapefruit using a sharp knife and taking care to remove all the white pith. Cut the fruit in slices across the segments.
2 Arrange the orange, grapefruit and tomato slices on four individual plates, overlapping and alternating them to give a striped ring on each plate. Sprinkle each with 2.5ml / ½tsp sugar.
3 Arrange the plates in a circle in the cooker and microwave, uncovered, at 100% (High) for 45-60 seconds, or until fruit is warmed through, rearranging once. Garnish with a sprig of mint on each.

PETER REILLY

293

Fruit combinations

Use fresh fruit to add a tang to salads, or make a mouthwatering finale to a meal. Fresh fruit combinations offer a wealth of colours, textures and flavours to excite and delight your taste buds.

The microwave is ideal for cooking fruit. Baked, poached or simply heated through, microwaved fruits retain their vibrant colours and firm textures. With care, even delicate fruits can be warmed through without losing their shape.

Modern methods of processing and preserving have made a great variety of fruit available all year round. Now you can mix and match fresh, frozen and canned fruits to create a host of colourful desserts.

Flavour and colour are not the

French Fruit Flan

only advantages of the recipes here. Fruit (especially fresh fruit) is rich in vitamins, and, provided you use fruit canned in natural juice — not syrup — and don't add extra sugar, it makes a slimmer's pudding as well.

Start by choosing fruit in peak condition. Store carefully, and spend a little time preparing it for microwaving. Cut into even-sized pieces to ensure even cooking. Microwave soft fruit in the minimum amount of water to retain all their goodness and flavour.

French fruit flan

| 6 mins |

Standing time: none

25cm / 10in sponge flan case
700-900g / 1½-2lb mixed fruits, prepared

ALMOND CREAM
2 egg yolks
50g / 2oz caster sugar
52.5ml / 3½tbls plain flour
150ml / ¼pt milk
67.5ml / 4½tbls ground almonds
1 drop of almond flavouring

GLAZE
275ml / ½pt sparkling or still white wine
22.5ml / 4½tsp arrowroot
30ml / 2tbls caster sugar

SERVES 6

1 Make the almond cream: mix the egg yolks, sugar and flour to a paste in a bowl. Microwave the milk at 100% (High) for 2-2½ minutes, and stir into the egg mixture. Microwave at 50% (Medium) for 1-2 minutes. Stir in the almonds and flavouring and cover surface with cling film. Leave to cool.
2 Make the glaze: blend 45ml / 3tbls of the wine with the arrowroot and the sugar. Microwave the remaining wine at 100% (High) for 1½-2 minutes until hot, whisk into the blended mixture. Microwave, uncovered, at 100% (High) for 1½-2 minutes, until thickened and boiling, whisking twice. Allow to cool.
3 Pour the cooled almond cream

into the flan case and spread evenly.
4 Arrange the fruits decoratively in the flan case.
5 Spoon the glaze carefully over the fruits, making sure they are all covered. Chill until ready to serve.

VARIATIONS
Instead of wine, use the same quantity of reserved syrup from the canned fruit, and omit the sugar if preferred.

Unusual fruits such as canned guava halves or figs, melon cubes, or blackberries, can be used.

Baked ambrosia

| 2½ mins |

Standing time: none

2 large oranges
340g / 12oz can pineapple cubes, drained
22ml / 1½tbls soft light brown sugar
15ml / 1tbls runny honey
30ml / 2tbls desiccated coconut
4 maraschino cherries

SERVES 4

Baked Ambrosia

1 Halve the oranges horizontally. Remove the segments using a grapefruit knife, remove and discard the pith and pips. Place the segments in a bowl. Stir in the pineapple cubes, sugar, honey and coconut.
2 Divide the mixture equally between the orange shells and top each with a cherry. Put on individual serving dishes and microwave, uncovered, at 100% (High) for 2½-3 minutes or until warmed through. Rotate the oranges a half turn, once. Serve immediately.

VARIATION
Grapefruit gives a tarter flavour.

Savoury fruit salad

1 min

Standing time: none

This salad dressing stores in the refrigerator for a week.

2 × 298g / 10½oz cans mandarin segments, drained
225g / 8oz green grapes, halved and seeded
lettuce leaves, to serve

DRESSING
50ml / 2fl oz wine vinegar
5ml / 1tsp chopped mint or 2.5ml / ½tsp dried
finely grated zest of 1 orange
pinch of celery salt
15ml / 1tbls runny honey
150ml / ¼pt sunflower oil

SERVES 4

Left: *Savoury Fruit Salad*
Below: *Nutty Fruit Slaw*

1 For the dressing, put the vinegar into a small bowl with the mint. Microwave, uncovered, at 100% (High) for 1 minute. Leave until cold, then strain.
2 Put the remaining dressing ingredients in a screw top jar, add the mint-flavoured vinegar and mix well.
3 Assemble the salad just before serving. Arrange the fruit on a bed of lettuce leaves and spoon over the dressing.

VARIATION
Instead of canned, use fresh mandarin segments with all the white pith removed. Allow 2-4 fruit, depending on size.

Microtips

If you only have thick honey, measure into a small cup and microwave for 15 seconds at 100% (High) until runny before using.

Nutty fruit slaw

Standing time: none

This crunchy salad keeps for up to two days in the refrigerator. It goes well with cold or hot meats, such as chicken or ham.

350g / 12oz white or green cabbage, shredded and chopped
376g / 13¾oz can crushed pineapple, well drained
2 × 298g / 10½oz cans mandarin orange segments, drained
50g / 2oz walnuts, chopped

DRESSING
25g / 1oz butter or margarine
60ml / 4tbls plain flour
30ml / 2tbls caster sugar
2.5ml / ½tsp mustard powder
salt and pepper
225ml / 8fl oz creamy milk
60ml / 4tbls apple juice
15ml / 1tbls white wine or cider vinegar
2 egg yolks, beaten

SERVES 4-6

1 First make the dressing. Microwave the butter in a large covered jug or bowl at 100% (High) for 15-30 seconds, until melted.
2 Stir in the flour, then blend in the remaining dressing ingredients, except the egg yolks. Microwave, uncovered, at 100% (High) for 2½-3½ minutes, or until thickened; stir after 1½ minutes, then every 30 seconds.
3 Stir a small amount of the dressing into the beaten yolks, then stir thoroughly into the hot mixture.
4 In a large bowl, combine the salad ingredients. Pour over the dressing and toss until the salad ingredients are well coated. Chill for at least 2 hours before serving.

Cook's notes

Make sure to remove bitter pith from grapefruit segments. Microwaving releases the juice but segments keep their shape.

Sherried fruit salad

Standing time: none

1 grapefruit, segmented
2 peaches, skinned, stoned and sliced
60ml / 4tbls grapefruit juice
30ml / 2tbls sweet sherry
225g / 8oz strawberries, hulled and halved
100g / 4oz seedless green grapes

SAUCE
65ml / 2½fl oz double cream
22.5ml / 4½tsp sugar
7.5ml / 1½tsp plain flour
7g / ¼oz butter
SERVES 4

Sherried Fruit Salad

1 Remove all the white pith from the grapefruit segments then place in a bowl with the peach slices, fruit juice and sherry. Cover and microwave at 100% (High) for 3-4 minutes, until slightly softened.
2 Allow the mixture to cool, then carefully stir in the remaining fruit. Cover and chill.
3 Make the sauce: combine all the ingredients in a round bowl or jug. Microwave at 100% (High) for 1½ minutes, whisk after every 30 seconds. Cool, then transfer to the refrigerator to chill.
4 To serve, transfer the fruit salad to four individual serving bowls and spoon over the sauce just before serving.

Fruit pudding

5½ mins

Standing time: none

340g / 12oz can pineapple cubes in syrup or natural juice, drained, juice reserved
411g / 14½oz can peach slices in syrup, drained, syrup reserved
425g / 15oz can cherries in syrup, stoned, drained, syrup reserved
33g / 1¼oz packet vanilla blancmange powder, or 60ml / 4tbls custard powder and 15ml / 1tbls sugar
5ml / 1tsp vanilla flavouring (with custard powder only)
1 banana, sliced

SERVES 5-6

1 Make the reserved juice from the pineapple and peaches up to 575ml / 1pt with cherry juice.
2 Blend the blancmange powder or custard powder and sugar with 60ml / 4tbls of the fruit juices.
3 Microwave the remaining juices at 100% (High) for 3½-4 minutes, or until hot. Whisk the hot juice in to the blended mixture.
4 Microwave, uncovered, at 100% (High) for 2-2½ minutes whisking twice, or until thickened. Stir in the vanilla flavouring if using.
5 Cover the surface with cling film, cool, then chill for 1 hour. Mix in the pineapple, peach slices and cherries. Chill again. Add banana just before serving.

Gingered peach parfait

7 mins

Standing time: none

33g / 1¼oz packet vanilla blancmange powder, or 60ml / 4tbls custard powder and 50g / 2oz sugar
575ml / 1pt milk
5ml / 1tsp vanilla flavouring (with custard powder mix only)
225g / 8oz canned peach slices in syrup, drained and chopped
298g / 10½oz can mandarin segments, drained
1.5ml / ¼tsp ground cinnamon

Fruit Pudding

1.5ml / ¼tsp ground ginger
1.5ml / ¼tsp grated nutmeg
150ml / ¼pt sweetened, whipped cream

SERVES 4

1 In a large bowl, blend blanc-mange powder or custard powder and sugar with 60ml / 4tbls milk.
2 Microwave remaining milk in a tall jug at 100% (High) for 4-4½ minutes, until almost boiling. Whisk the hot milk into blended blancmange or custard mixture. Microwave, uncovered, at 100% (High) for 3-3½ minutes, whisking three times, or until thickened and boiled. Stir in vanilla flavouring, if using.
3 Add the peaches and mandarins mixing well. Lay cling film on surface to prevent a skin forming. Cool, then chill for 2 hours.
4 Blend the spices and cream.
5 Fill four sundae glasses with layers of peach mixture and cream, finishing with cream. Cover, chill before serving.

Easy fruit salad

2 mins

Standing time: none

30ml / 2tbls caster sugar
410g / 14½oz can peach slices in natural juice, drained, 150ml / ¼pt juice reserved
75g / 3oz green grapes, seeded
75g / 3oz black grapes, seeded
175g / 6oz fresh or frozen raspberries

SERVES 4

1 Make the syrup: place the sugar and reserved peach juice in a tall jug; microwave at 100% (High) for 2-2½ minutes or until the sugar is dissolved and the mixture is boiling, stirring after one minute.
2 If using frozen raspberries, add to the syrup and set aside to cool.
3 Combine the peaches and grapes in a serving bowl. Add the fresh raspberries, if using. Pour over the syrup. Stir gently to mix, then cover and chill for 2 hours before serving.

Above: *Easy Fruit Salad*
Left: *Gingered Peach Parfait*

299

Vegetable combinations

A dish of brightly coloured mixed vegetables is simply stunning — yet so easy in the microwave; just put everything into one container, or arrange on a serving plate, and cook.

Once you have mastered basic vegetable cookery in the microwave, try your hand at some creative combinations. Mixing and matching vegetables provides scope for all sorts of appetizing new dishes.

The secret is to select vegetables that have similar cooking times, so they can be microwaved together. If using vegetables that vary in their cooking time, start the slower vegetables in the microwave first and add the speedier ones as necessary. Or arrange all the vegetables in circles on a plate with the denser, more time-consuming ones to the edges, as in the Seasoned Vegetable Tray (see page 302). There is less microwave energy in the centre so the vegetables take longer to cook.

To start with, try a vegetable stir-fry (see page 303), which is always a popular choice. For a really colourful dish, try the Celery Corn Medley (opposite), or the Marinated Vegetables (see page 302). As you gain experience and confidence you will enjoy selecting your own mixtures.

Seasoned Vegetable Tray

Celery corn medley

9½ mins

Standing time: none

396g / 14oz can tomatoes, well
  drained
1.5ml / ¼tsp dried mixed herbs
15ml / 1tbls grated onion
1 garlic clove, crushed
2 celery stalks, sliced
½ small green pepper, seeded
  and chopped
10ml / 2tsp vegetable oil
5ml / 1tsp brown sugar
10ml / 2tsp tomato ketchup
salt and pepper
340g / 12oz can sweetcorn
  kernels, drained
100g / 4oz mushrooms, sliced
  with stems

SERVES 4

1 Put the tomatoes into a large

Below: *Celery Corn Medley*
Above left: *Okra Creole*

Okra creole

13½ mins

Standing time: none

350g / 12oz fresh okra
65ml / 2½fl oz water
15ml / 3tsp cornflour
396g / 14oz can tomatoes
30ml / 2tbls red wine or reserved
  cooking liquid from the okra
2.5ml / ½tsp paprika
2.5ml / ½tsp sugar
good pinch of cayenne pepper
1 garlic clove, crushed
15ml / 1tbls chopped fresh
  parsley or 5ml / 1tsp dried
salt and pepper

SERVES 4

1 Trim and wash the okra and
place in a large bowl with the
water. Cover and microwave at
100% (High) for 7-8 minutes, until
tender-crisp; stir once. Drain and
set aside, reserving liquid if using.
2 In the same bowl, blend cornflour, a little juice from the tomatoes, the wine or okra liquid, paprika, sugar and cayenne. Mix in
the tomatoes and the remaining
juice, garlic and parsley. Season.
3 Cover and microwave at 100%
(High) for 5-6 minutes until thickened, stirring 1-2 times. Stir in
the okra, cover and microwave at
100% (High) for 1½-2 minutes.

bowl with the herbs, onion and
garlic. Cover and microwave at
100% (High) for 5-6 minutes, until
thick and pulpy, stirring twice.
2 Combine the celery, pepper and
oil in a medium bowl. Cover and
microwave at 100% (High) for
2½-3 minutes, or until the vegetables are just tender, stirring
once. Strain off the liquid.
3 Stir the sugar, ketchup, seasoning and all the vegetables, including the sweetcorn and
mushrooms, into the tomato
sauce. Cover and microwave at
100% (High) for 2-2½ minutes
until hot, stirring once.

Microtips

*Cooked fresh corn can be used in
place of canned. Scrape the
kernels off the cob and cook with the
celery and pepper in Step 2, adding
30ml / 2tbls water. Continue as
directed in the recipe.*

Seasoned vegetable tray

7½ mins

Standing time: 3-4 mins

Serve this appetizing array of vegetables either hot or cold, as an accompaniment to a main course or a tempting appetizer.

2 carrots, sliced diagonally
150g / 5oz cauliflower florets
150g / 5oz broccoli florets
1 small swede, cut into 12mm / ½in pieces
1 small courgette, sliced
1 tomato, cut into 6 wedges
30ml / 2tbls water

SAUCE
25g / 1oz butter or margarine
15ml / 1tbls grated Parmesan cheese
2.5ml / ½tsp onion salt
pepper

SERVES 4

1 Arrange the vegetables on a 25-30cm / 10-12in plate. Place the carrots around the outside, then make a ring of cauliflower florets, followed by a ring of broccoli. Add the swede, followed by the courgette in the centre, as they require the least cooking time. Sprinkle with the water and cover.
2 Microwave at 100% (High) for 6-8 minutes until all the vegetables are tender-crisp, rotating the plate 2-3 times.
3 Arrange the tomato wedges at intervals on the cauliflower or broccoli ring, cover and microwave at 100% (High) for 1-1½ minutes. Leave to stand, covered, for 3-4 minutes, while preparing the sauce.
4 Microwave butter in a small jug, covered, at 100% (High) for 30-45 seconds until melted and hot. Stir in cheese, onion salt and pepper.
5 Drain the vegetables carefully, then pour the sauce over them.

VARIATION
Use fresh pumpkin, squash or turnips in place of the swede, or another vegetable in season. Remember to cut the vegetables into evenly thick slices to ensure even cooking.

Marinated vegetables

9 mins

Standing time: none

425ml / 15fl oz white wine vinegar
65g / 2½oz sugar
5ml / 1tsp salt
5 carrots, peeled and cut into matchstick strips, about 5cm / 2in long and 6mm / ¼in thick
100g / 4oz cauliflower florets
100g / 4oz broccoli florets
2 rings of green pepper, about 12mm / ½in wide
150ml / ¼pt water
2 garlic cloves

MAKES 2 x 575ml / 1pt JARS

1 Pour the vinegar into a 1L / 1¾pt jug; add the sugar and salt. Cover with cling film rolled back and microwave at 100% (High) for 4-5 minutes until boiling, then

Marinated Vegetables

continue boiling for 1 minute.
2 Uncover and leave until cold. Place the carrots, cauliflower, broccoli, pepper rings and water in a large bowl. Cover and microwave at 100% (High) for 4-5 minutes until the vegetables are tender-crisp and brightly coloured; stir once. Drain and rinse under cold water to retain crispness and colour. Drain on absorbent paper.
3 Arrange the carrot strips in two 450g / 1lb glass jars, standing them upright. Add the pepper rings, then cauliflower and broccoli florets. Put a garlic clove into each jar, then pour in the cooled vinegar to cover the vegetables.
4 Cover and leave in the refrigerator for 4 days to marinate before serving. Serve with cold meats or bread and cheese and store in the refrigerator up to 4 weeks.

302

Stir-fried vegetables

5 mins

Standing time: 2-3 mins

45ml / 3tbls soy sauce
5ml / 1tsp cornflour
1.5ml / ¼tsp sugar
275g / 10oz cauliflower florets
225g / 8oz mushrooms, sliced,
  with stalks
a bunch of spring onions, sliced
  (including green tops)
45ml / 3tbls flaked almonds
15g / ½oz butter or margarine

SERVES 4

Cook's notes

Browning the butter first gives a nutty flavour to the cauliflower and almonds. However, if preferred, add the butter to the browning dish after it has been heated.

Soy sauce gives the vegetables spice; it also colours the cauliflower quite brown. For less colour, dip the florets briefly in the sauce before cooking and add less of the sauce during cooking. Soy sauce is salty; do not add extra salt.

How to microwave Stir-fried vegetables

Combine *the soy sauce, cornflour and sugar in a large bowl. Stir in the cauliflower, mushrooms, onions and almonds. Set aside while preheating a browning dish in the cooker.*

Preheat *the browning dish at 100% (High) for 5 minutes, or according to the manufacturer's instructions. Add butter for the last 30 seconds. Stir in vegetables and sauce.*

Cover *and microwave at 100% (High) for 5-7 minutes, or until the cauliflower is tender but crisp; stir once during the cooking time. Let stand for 2-3 minutes before serving.*

303

Currants and berries

Currants and berries have a short season so make the most of them while they are available. Cooked in the microwave they keep every ounce of their fresh, tangy flavour.

Fresh currants and berries should be plump and firm, with a good flush on their skins. When buying punnets, check that the berries at the bottom are not wet or crushed as they will soon go mouldy. If buying loose or picking your own, keep the fruit in small punnets to avoid the berries being crushed by their own weight. Store in the refrigerator and use within a few days.

Currants are available in three varieties, black, red and white. White currants are the sweetest and relatively scarce. You can use them instead of black or red currants and adjust the amount of sugar in the recipe accordingly. Using them together with black and redcurrants, in a compote for example, helps balance flavours because they are less tart. Black and redcurrants are perfect in tansies and whips, giving an irresistibly rich colour to these desserts. However, they are equally good poached and left whole for pies and cobblers.

Cranberries are large, hard berries, with a sour taste. They are particularly good made into sauces and preserves or cakes.

Blueberries are blue-black in colour, with a purple bloom. Blueberry pie is a favourite American recipe, but the berries can also be poached and used to decorate cheesecakes, or soaked in port and served with sugar.

Prepare the fruit just before using. Place it in a colander and rinse under cold running water, then drain on absorbent paper. Cranberries and blueberries need no further preparation, but strip currants from their stalks (see steps, opposite).

PAUL WEBSTER

Blackcurrant and sherry trifle

13½ mins

Standing time: none

**8 trifle sponges, or sponge cakes
45ml / 3tbls blackcurrant jam
275g / 10oz raspberries
225g / 8oz blackcurrants, stripped
from their stalks
65g / 2½oz caster sugar
30ml / 2tbls water
75ml / 5tbls sherry or rum
1 egg
40g / 1½oz cornflour
30ml / 2tbls soft brown sugar
grated zest and juice of 1 orange
1.5ml / ¼tsp vanilla flavouring
575ml / 1pt milk
225ml / ½pt whipping cream
ratafias to decorate**

SERVES 6

1 Halve the sponges and sand-

wich together with jam. Arrange in the base of the dish and top with most of the berries.
2 Place the blackcurrants in a large bowl. Stir in the sugar and water and cover. Microwave at 100% (High) for 3½-4 minutes, stirring once. Stir in sherry or rum and pour over sponge.
3 Beat together, the egg, cornflour, sugar, orange zest and juice and flavouring. Microwave the milk at 100% (High) for 3-4 minutes. Whisk into the egg, then strain back into the bowl.
4 Microwave at 50% (Medium) for 7 minutes, whisking every 2 minutes until thickened. Cool slightly, pour over trifle. Chill.
5 Decorate with whipped cream, ratafias and raspberries just before serving.

Redcurrant and peach pie

15 mins

Standing time: none

**450g / 1lb redcurrants, stripped
from their stalks
30ml / 2tbls sugar
275ml / ½pt water
20ml / 4tsp arrowroot
3 peaches, skinned, halved,
stoned and sliced, or
425g / 15oz can sliced peaches,
well drained
23cm / 9in cooked pastry case
(see page 28)
45ml / 3tbls redcurrant jelly**

SERVES 6

1 Place the redcurrants in a large bowl, stir in the sugar and water; cover. Microwave at 100% (High) for 5-6 minutes; stir twice.
2 Blend the arrowroot with 15ml / 1tbls water and stir into the currants. Microwave at 100% (High) for 4 minutes; stir once. Cool.
3 Spoon into the pastry case; top with the peach slices.
4 To glaze the pie, place the redcurrant jelly in a small bowl and microwave at 100% (High) for 1 minute, stirring once. Brush over the fruit and allow to set.

Left to right: *Redcurrant Tansy,
Blackcurrant and Sherry Trifle,
Redcurrant and Peach Pie*

How to microwave currants

Pick over *450g / 1lb currants. Hold the stalk at one end and strip the currants from the stalk into a bowl using the prongs of a fork.*

Stir *in caster sugar, if using, and 30ml / 2tbls water. Cover with cling film rolled back at one edge and place in the microwave cooker.*

Microwave *at 100% (High) for 5 minutes, or until the fruit is tender, stirring once during cooking. Let stand for 5 minutes before serving.*

RAY DUNS

305

Redcurrant tansy

| 13 |
| mins |

Standing time: none

450g / 1lb redcurrants, stripped
  from their stalks
100g / 4oz sugar
15ml / 1tbls caster sugar
10ml / 2tsp cornflour
1 egg, lightly beaten
2 egg yolks
275ml / ½pt milk
2-3 drops vanilla flavouring
150ml / ¼pt double cream
extra redcurrants to decorate

SERVES 6

1 Place the prepared currants in a large bowl. Stir in the sugar and cover. Microwave at 100% (High) for 6 minutes, or until tender, stirring twice. Crush the fruit with a fork and set aside.
2 Mix the caster sugar with the cornflour. Gradually blend in beaten egg and egg yolks. Place the milk in a large bowl and microwave at 100% (High) for 2-2½ minutes. Whisk into egg mixture, strain back into bowl; stir in flavouring.
3 Microwave the custard at 50% (Medium) for 5-7 minutes, whisking after 2 minutes, then every 30 seconds. Cool, then chill.
4 Whisk the cream until it forms soft peaks. Fold the custard into the redcurrants, then lightly fold in cream. Serve in small dishes.

Blackcurrant cobbler

| 11 |
| mins |

Standing time: 3 mins

675g / 1½lb blackcurrants,
  stripped from their stalks
45ml / 3tbls juice plus zest of
  1 orange
100g / 4oz soft light brown sugar
100g / 4oz self-raising flour
100g / 4oz wholemeal flour
large pinch of salt
2.5ml / ½tsp baking powder
50g / 2oz butter or margarine
25g / 1oz caster sugar
150ml / ¼pt milk
15ml / 1tbls demerara sugar

SERVES 4

RAY DUNS

Left: Blackcurrant Whip
Right: Blackcurrant Cobbler

1 Put the fruit and juice into a 20cm / 8in dish. Stir in the sugar.
2 Microwave, covered, at 100% (High) for 6 minutes; stir once.
3 Sift the flours with the salt and baking powder. Add the bran from the sieve. Rub in the butter then stir in the sugar and orange zest. Add enough milk to mix to a soft but not sticky dough.
4 Roll out the dough to a thickness of 12mm / ½in. Cut into 5cm / 2in rounds. Arrange the rounds around the edge of the dish. Brush with milk and sprinkle with sugar.
5 Microwave at 100% (High) for 5-6 minutes until the topping is set; turn the dish once. Stand for 3 minutes. Brown under the grill.

Blackcurrant whip

| 4¼ |
| mins |

Standing time: none

225g / 8oz blackcurrants,
  stripped from their stalks
30ml / 2tbls water
272ml / ½pt low-fat natural
  yoghurt
10ml / 2tsp powdered gelatine
30ml / 2tbls sugar
2 egg whites
20g / ¾oz blanched almonds

SERVES 4

1 Purée the blackcurrants with the water. Sieve into a bowl and stir in the yoghurt.
2 Sprinkle the gelatine over 30ml / 2tbls water in a bowl; soak for 5 minutes. Microwave at 100%

Blueberry pie

10 mins

Standing time: none

23cm / 9in cooked pastry case
  (see page 28)
450g / 1lb blueberries
100g / 4oz sugar
50g / 2oz plain flour
2.5ml / ½tsp finely grated lemon
  zest
1.5ml / ¼tsp ground cinnamon
1.5ml / ¼tsp ground nutmeg

TOPPING
50g / 2oz quick-cook rolled oats
30ml / 2tbls brown sugar
2.5ml / ½tsp ground cinnamon
50g / 2oz butter or margarine,
  diced

SERVES 6

1 Combine the blueberries with the sugar, flour, lemon zest and spices. Turn into the pastry case.
2 Put the oats, sugar and cinnamon into a bowl and rub in the butter until the mixture is crumbly. Sprinkle over the fruit.
3 Place the pie on a piece of greaseproof paper and microwave at 100% (High) for 5 minutes, rotating the dish ¼ turn once.
4 Microwave at 50% (Medium) for 5-10 minutes until the filling is thickened and bubbling, rotating the dish ¼ turn every 2 minutes.

Currant compote

8 mins

Standing time: none

450g / 1lb redcurrants,
  stripped from their stalks
450g / 1lb blackcurrants,
  stripped from their stalks
225g / ½lb whitecurrants,
  stripped from their stalks
90-120ml / 6-8tbls sugar
30ml / 2tbls orange juice
30ml / 2tbls rum

SERVES 4-6

1 Place all the berries in a large bowl and add the sugar and orange juice.
2 Microwave, covered, at 100% (High) for 8-10 minutes, stirring carefully two or three times during cooking.
3 Stir the rum into the fruit and serve hot.

Blueberry Pie

Freezer notes

Frozen blueberries can be used. To thaw 450g / 1lb frozen blueberries, place in a bowl and microwave at 20-30% (Defrost) for 8-12 minutes or until a few berries feel warm, stirring twice. Let stand for 10-15 minutes.

(High) for 20-30 seconds.
3 Pour the gelatine on to the purée, stirring constantly. Add sugar to taste.
4 Whisk the egg whites until standing in soft peaks, then fold evenly into the purée. Spoon in to a serving dish or glasses. Cover and chill until set.
5 To decorate, microwave the almonds on a plate at 100% (High) for 4-4½ minutes, stirring once. Allow to cool, then sprinkle over whip. Or top with extra yoghurt and cooked blackcurrants.

Slimmer's notes

Omit the almonds for a perfect slimmer's dessert at only 90 Cal / 380kJ per portion.

Sweet cranberry loaf

21 mins

Standing time: 15 mins

175g / 6oz plain flour, sifted
5ml / 1tsp baking powder
175g / 6oz soft brown sugar
75g / 3oz butter or margarine, softened
15ml / 1tbls vegetable oil
2 large eggs
50g / 2oz walnut halves, chopped
50g / 2oz desiccated coconut
5ml / 1tsp vanilla flavouring
225g / 8oz cranberries
376g / 13¼oz can crushed pineapple, drained, with 30ml / 2tbls juice reserved

DECORATION
30ml / 2tbls icing sugar
50g / 2oz desiccated coconut

SERVES 6-8

1 Line the base of 1.7L / 3pt loaf dish with greaseproof paper. Beat together all the cake ingredients in a large bowl until blended. Turn the mixture into the dish, level the surface; place on an upturned plate.
2 Microwave at 50% (Medium) for 9 minutes, rotating ¼ turn every 2 minutes. Increase power to 100% (High) for 12-14 minutes, or until well risen, rotating ¼ turn every 2 minutes.
3 Allow to stand in the container, covered loosely with absorbent paper for 15 minutes.
4 Cover a cooling rack with two sheets of absorbent paper and sift over a little icing sugar. Turn the cake out on the rack. Sprinkle top with sieved icing sugar and desiccated coconut.

Freezer notes

Use frozen cranberries if they are easier to obtain. To thaw, microwave on a plate at 20-30% (Defrost) for 3-4 minutes, rearranging every minute. Leave the cranberries to stand for 10-15 minutes before using them in recipes.

Cranberry sauce

16 mins

Standing time: none

This ruby red sauce makes an excellent accompaniment to roast chicken and turkey, pork and gammon. It can be served warm or cold.

350g / 12oz cranberries
150ml / ¼pt water
175g / 6oz sugar
grated zest of 1 lemon

Sweet Cranberry Loaf

5ml / 1tsp lemon juice
½ stick of cinnamon

MAKES 575ml / 1pt

1 Place the cranberries in a large bowl and stir in the remaining ingredients.
2 Cover and microwave at 100% (High) for 8 minutes, stirring and crushing the berries twice. Reduce power to 20-30% (Defrost) for 8 minutes; stir twice.
3 Cover and leave to cool. The sauce thickens on cooling.

Fruit in syrup

Give fruit a really special treatment and poach it in a light sugar syrup. Serve hot or cold as a delicious dessert or a fruity accompaniment to meat and poultry.

Fresh fruit microwaved in a simple sugar syrup is mouth-wateringly tender and juicy. It can be served immediately, hot or cold, or stored in the refrigerator for up to four days, ready to turn into all sorts of delicious desserts.

Choose fruit that is fresh, sound and perfectly ripe — neither too hard nor too soft. For combinations, choose fruit of a similar size and ripeness — this will ensure even cooking.

Make the syrup in a heatproof jug or bowl large enough to ensure that the syrup will not boil over. Similarly, make sure the bowl in which you microwave the fruit is large enough, too.

For a speedy dessert serve fruit in syrup on its own or topped with ice cream, cream or yoghurt. Alternatively, turn it into a family pudding (see Serving suggestions, page 312). Some fruit in syrup can be served as a chutney or relish. Citrus fruits are best for this.

Rosy Plums

RAY DUNS

309

Light sugar syrup

| 4 mins |

Standing time: none

This syrup is suitable for poaching most fruit. If you have a sweet tooth or for tart fruit such as gooseberries or rhubarb, you may prefer to use a stronger sugar syrup which is thicker and sweeter (see Variations).

100g / 4oz sugar
275ml / ½pt cold water

MAKES 275ml / ½pt

To prepare syrup: *microwave the sugar and liquid in a heatproof jug at 100% (High) for 4-5 minutes or until boiling, stirring three times.*

VARIATIONS
Red wine syrup: prepare as Light Sugar Syrup but use red wine instead of the water.
Honey syrup: replace 50g / 2oz of the sugar with 50ml / 3½tbls clear honey.
Boozy syrup: use 30ml / 2tbls fruit liqueur made up to 275ml / ½pt with an appropriate fruit juice, such as apple or pineapple.
Spiced syrup: add 1 cinnamon stick, 4-6 whole cloves or 2-3 allspice berries and strain the syrup before using. This is particularly good with apples.
Strong sugar syrup: increase the sugar to 175g / 6oz.

Microwave times for poaching fruit in syrup

FRUIT	QUANTITY	TIME AT 100% HIGH	STANDING TIME	PROCEDURE
Apples (cooking) sliced	900g / 2lb	6 mins	5 mins	Peel, core, cut into 6mm / ¼in slices
Apples (eating) quartered	450g / 1lb	5 mins	5 mins	Peel and core, then quarter
Apples (tart eating) sliced	450g / 1lb	3 mins	5 mins	Peel and core, then cut into 6mm / ¼in slices
Blackberries	450g / 1lb	2 mins	5 mins	Pick over. Rinse, drain and pat dry with absorbent paper
Nectarines	8	6 mins	5 mins	Skin. Prick to the stone with skewer. Add lemon juice to syrup
Oranges sliced	4	3 mins	5 mins	Scrub well, dry. Slice into 6mm / ¼in pieces
Peaches whole	4 large (approx 700g / 1½lb)	4 mins	5 mins	Skin. Prick to the stone with skewer
Peaches halved	4 large (approx 700g / 1½lb)	3 mins	5 mins	Skin, then cut in half and remove stones
Pears whole	900g / 2lb	5 mins	5 mins	Peel. Prick to core with a skewer
Pears halved	900g / 2lb	3 mins	5 mins	Peel. Cut in half and remove cores
Pears (cooking) whole	900g / 2lb	10 mins	5 mins	Peel. Prick to core with skewer
Pineapple cut into bite-sized pieces	900g / 2lb	5 mins	5 mins	Peel, quarter and core. Cut into bite-sized pieces
Plums whole	450g / 1lb	3 mins	5 mins	Prick to the stone with a fork
Plums halved	450g / 1lb	2 mins	5 mins	Cut in half and remove stones
Raspberries	450g / 1lb	1 min	5 mins	Pick over. Wash and pat dry with absorbent paper
Rhubarb	450g / 1lb	4 mins	5 mins	Trim. Cut into 5cm / 2in lengths

How to microwave fruit in syrup

Prepare fruit *(see chart) and arrange in a large, heatproof bowl. Pour the hot syrup over the prepared fruit. Cover bowl with cling film rolled back at one edge.*

Microwave *for recommended time (see chart) until tender, stir once. Serve hot or cold. To store: cool, then refrigerate, covered, for up to four days.*

Rosy plums

14½ mins

Standing time: 5 mins

550g / 1¼lb whole firm plums

SYRUP
100g / 4oz sugar
225ml / 8fl oz red grape juice
30ml / 2tbls kirsch
toasted flaked almonds

SERVES 4-6

1 Prick each plum two or three times with a fork. Place in a large heatproof bowl.

2 Place the sugar and grape juice in a bowl and microwave at 100% (High) for 5 minutes, until boiling; stir three times to ensure the sugar dissolves.
3 Pour the syrup and kirsch over the plums, cover and microwave at 100% (High) for 5 minutes. Stir then reduce the power to 50% (Medium) and microwave for a further 4½-5 minutes. Stand, covered, for 5 minutes.
4 Serve hot or cold, sprinkling over the almonds before serving.

VARIATION
Stir 1-2 sliced bananas into the plums just before serving.

Microtips

When you need just a few almonds to decorate a dish, toast them conventionally. (The quantity is too small to absorb the microwaves.) Sprinkle over just before serving.

Spiced oranges

14 mins

Standing time: 5 mins

This makes a delicious accompaniment to meat, especially rich meats like ham.

6 thin-skinned oranges
1 cinnamon stick
4 cloves
275ml / ½pt hot Light Sugar Syrup (see recipe page 310)

MAKES 900g-1.4kg / 2-3lb

1 Scrub the oranges and slice into 6mm / ¼in thick rings. Place in a large heatproof bowl with the cinnamon stick and cloves.
2 Pour over the sugar syrup. Cover and microwave at 100% (High) for 10 minutes, stirring once. Leave to stand, covered, for 5 minutes.

Spiced Oranges

TONY HURLEY

311

Microtips

Cooking time depends on the variety and ripeness of the fruit. Check for doneness at the end of microwaving time. The fruit should be just tender when tested with a sharp knife. Remember it continues to cook during standing.

Cook's notes

Sugar dissolves much faster if it is warmed before being added to liquid. Heat 100g / 4oz sugar in the microwave at 100% (High) for 2½ minutes, 175g / 6oz for 3½ minutes stirring twice. Take extra care not to overheat the sugar or it may burn — watch carefully toward the end of microwaving.

Tropical Kiwi and Pineapple

TONY HURLEY

Tropical kiwi and pineapple

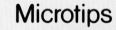

9 mins

Standing time: 5 mins

7 firm kiwi fruit
1 pineapple (about 900g / 2lb)
275ml / ½pt hot Light Sugar Syrup (see recipe page 310)

SERVES 4

1 Peel the kiwi fruit, cut into thick slices and place in a large heatproof bowl. Remove the peel and the core from the pineapple and remove any brown 'eyes'. Cut into bite-sized pieces and add to the bowl.
2 Pour the hot syrup over the fruit, making sure the fruit is well submerged. Cover and microwave at 100% (High) for 3 minutes. Stir, then reduce the power setting to 50% (Medium) and microwave for a further 2 minutes. Stand, covered, for 5 minutes.

Microtips

Use a wooden cocktail stick or fine skewer to prick fruit with smooth, shiny skin, such as plums, gooseberries and apples, if cooking them whole. Otherwise, the build-up of steam within the fruit during microwaving will cause the skins to burst. Cover the bowl of fruit in syrup with cling film or a lid to prevent splattering. Roll cling film back enough at one edge to make stirring or turning the fruit during microwaving easier.

Serving suggestions for fruit in syrup

● Spoon the hot or cold fruit in syrup over ice cream, frozen yoghurt or sorbet for a speedy dessert.

● Use for a fruit pie or crumble filling but thicken the syrup with a little arrowroot. Allow 20ml / 4tsp arrowroot to each 275ml / ½pt syrup and blend with 15-30ml / 1-2tbls cold water first. Remember to use a deep dish for cooking crumbles to avoid the fruit filling boiling over.

● Drain the fruit and arrange neatly in a cooked pastry case or sponge flan case. Thicken a little of the syrup with arrowroot and brush over the fruit to glaze.

● Include in fruit salads with fresh seasonal fruit. Serve with whipped cream, ice cream, soured cream or yoghurt.

● Purée in a blender to make a fruit mousse or a sweet soufflé or fool.

● Serve as an unusual garnish for roast meat, or as an accompaniment to cold cuts. Kumquats are delicious with glazed ham or duck. Plums complement roast poultry, spiced oranges are a good foil for fatty meat like pork or rich game birds.

312

Italian peaches

9 mins

Standing time: 5 mins

4 large ripe peaches, pricked and skinned (see chart, page 310)
50g / 2oz sugar
50ml / 2fl oz water
12.5ml / 2½tsp arrowroot
250ml / 9fl oz medium sweet semi-sparkling red wine
whipped double cream to serve

SERVES 4

1 Arrange peaches in a fairly deep bowl. Place the sugar and water in a jug. Stir until the sugar dissolves. Microwave at 100% (High) for 3 minutes, stirring twice to make sure the sugar has completely dissolved before the syrup boils.
2 Cover peaches with boiling syrup. Cover and microwave at 100% (High) for 4 minutes, stirring once during cooking. Turn peaches over, cover and stand for 5 minutes.
3 Strain off the syrup and allow to cool slightly. Blend arrowroot with 15ml / 1tbls wine. Add 30ml / 2tbls of the warm reserved syrup, stir well, then stir in remaining syrup. Cook on 100% (High) for 2 minutes, until thickened and clear, stirring after 1 minute.
4 Pour thickened syrup over peaches, allow to cool, cover, then chill in the refrigerator for several hours. Put the remaining wine to chill in the refrigerator.
5 Stir in the remaining chilled wine just before serving. This will make the syrup froth and sparkle. Serve the peaches immediately with whipped cream while the syrup is still frothing.

Cook's notes

Some fruits, particularly peaches, nectarines and pears, tend to discolour after poaching. Adding a little lemon juice to the syrup, and turning the fruit over frequently during cooking so that it is well coated with syrup, helps keep it a good colour.

Liqueur-laced kumquats

11 mins

Standing time: 5 mins

These tiny citrus fruit are eaten whole — rind and all. Serve them with roast duck or ham. They also make a welcome gift: when cold, transfer kumquats to a wide-necked jar using a slotted spoon pack down tightly, then pour in the syrup to cover. Cover jars securely and store in refrigerator.

700g / 1½lb kumquats
1 cinnamon stick
6 whole cloves
275ml / ½pt hot Light Sugar Syrup (see recipe page 310)
30ml / 2tbls orange liqueur

MAKES 700g / 1½lb

1 Prick each kumquat three or

Liqueur-laced Kumquats

CHRIS KNAGGS

four times with a fine skewer or needle. Place in a large heatproof bowl with the cinnamon stick and cloves.
2 Pour over the hot sugar syrup. Add the orange liqueur. Cover and microwave at 100% (High) for 4 minutes. Stir, then reduce the power to 50% (Medium) and microwave for a further 3 minutes. Leave to stand, covered, for 5 minutes.

Cook's notes

Most fruit cooked in syrup keeps for up to four days, tightly covered, in the refrigerator, but peaches and nectarines are best eaten at once. Make sure the fruit stays submerged in the syrup. If necessary, lay a piece of cling film directly over the top of the fruit before covering the container, or weight it down with a plate.

CHAPTER SIX
DESSERTS AND BAKING

When planning a meal, especially if entertaining, the dessert is often the last thing you think about and your choice may depend very much on the time available. With your microwave cooker to help, however, you can prepare a dessert in advance in double-quick time, or you can even cook it between courses while your guests wait at the table!

Baking, too, can be done much faster in the microwave. For some breads and cakes, the lack of browning can be a problem but you will find plenty of advice on how to overcome this here. Many of the recipes, for Gingerbreads or Teabreads, for example, have a brown-coloured appearance anyway, and many others use wholemeal flour or dark sugar in order to achieve this. For cakes that are to be iced or frosted, of course, the colour of the cooked cake is unimportant.

Amongst the desserts are cheesecakes, summer desserts, creams and custards that are ideal for entertaining, but you will also find some old family favourites, such as sponge puddings, grain puddings and fruit crumbles. For something a little bit different, try one of the recipes from the International Desserts section, such as Russian Pudding or Swedish Apple Torte.

Home-made ice cream is always popular and can obviously be made well in advance and stored in the freezer until required. You can prepare a delicious hot chocolate sauce to pour over ice cream literally seconds before serving. Other desserts need nothing more than fresh cream or yoghurt to accompany them. Smooth and creamy Greek yoghurt makes a particularly good healthy substitute for cream.

The microwave cooker is also very useful for batch baking as you can cook cakes in half the time that it takes in a conventional oven. Many of the recipes here, such as plain sponge cakes or cookies, can easily be doubled up and some frozen for a later date.

Sponge puddings

Sponge puddings are one of the microwave's great success stories: speed and ease of cooking combined with super-light results make these warming traditional puddings even more tempting.

Upside-down puddings, fruity sponges or packet mix dishes — all make the very best use of speedy microwave energy to produce light, moist sponges. Fruit combinations are ideal for adding flavour and texture and an upside-down topping is the answer to the drawback of mixtures which do not brown during cooking.

Microwaved sponge puddings have a very moist, springy texture and are noticeably more spongy than conventionally-cooked ones. (Leftovers dry out more quickly than conventionally-baked or steamed sponge puddings, too, although they can be refreshed once).

The puddings here are made using one of two basic methods — creaming and 'all-in-one'. Creaming is the traditional way and microwaving can speed up the process

Orange and Ginger Pudding

by softening the butter. Adding the eggs and flour after creaming is sometimes thought to give a lighter texture but the all-in-one method, using baking powder for extra lightness, is just as successful — and is certainly faster.

Almost any shape dish can be used for microwaved sponge puddings, from rectangular loaf dishes to conventional pudding basins. If using a boilable non-stick pudding basin, there is no need to grease the sides. Greasing would be necessary, however, if you want to improve the appearance of a plain sponge by a coating of crumbs on the sides of the bowl.

There are other ways in which the colour of sponge puddings can be made more attractive — adding chocolate, spices, fruit or a colourful topping will help, as will a few drops of yellow food colouring in a plain recipe.

While most sponges are a one hundred per cent success, it is worth noting that puddings with a layer of syrup or honey in the base are not recommended for microwave cooking: microwave energy is attracted to fats and sugars and their high sugar content will make the puddings more liable to burn. Similarly, energy concentrated at the bottom of the basin might make it crack or burn if it is not heatproof.

As a rule, to prevent overcooking of fruits, microwave fresh fruit puddings at a low power. While most plain puddings cook well at 100% power, those with a high proportion of fat and sugar are better cooked at medium power.

Traditional sponge pudding

9 mins

Standing time: 2 mins

1-2 digestive or plain sweet biscuits, crushed
175g / 6oz butter
175g / 6oz caster sugar
3 eggs, beaten
few drops of vanilla flavouring
175g / 6oz self-raising flour
60ml / 4tbls milk

SERVES 6

How to microwave Traditional sponge pudding

Lightly *grease the base and sides of a 1.1L / 2pt pudding basin and coat the sides evenly with biscuit crumbs. If necessary, soften the butter by microwave (see Microtips below).*

Cream *the butter and sugar together until pale and fluffy. Beat eggs with vanilla flavouring then gradually beat into the creamed mixture. Sift and fold in flour. Stir in the milk.*

Spoon *the mixture into the prepared dish and spread evenly. Microwave at 70% (Medium-High) for 9 minutes, turning the dish every 2-3 minutes for even cooking.*

Test *pudding is cooked by inserting a cocktail stick; it should come out clean when pushed into centre. Remove from the cooker using oven gloves. Stand for 2 minutes, then turn out.*

Cook's notes

The flavour of the basic sponge pudding can be altered by the addition of any of the following: grated zest of an orange or a lemon, 2.5ml / ½tsp ground ginger, 15ml / 1tbls ground almonds with a few drops of almond flavouring, 2.5ml / ½tsp ground cardamom, or 50g / 2oz finely chopped hazelnuts or walnuts.

An assortment of dessert sauces can be used to add the finishing touch to a plain pudding — see recipes from pages 23-26 or try the fruit sauce as given in Microtips, right.

Microtips

To soften butter, microwave 175g / 6oz at 30% (Low) for 15 seconds.

The steps above show how to microwave a traditional sponge pudding in a basin. To make a loaf-shaped pudding (as illustrated on page 319), use a 900g / 2lb loaf dish and follow the same timings as for the basic recipe. Serve with blackcurrant sauce made with a 385g / 13½oz can blackcurrant pie filling and the grated zest and juice of an orange. Microwave the pie filling with the orange juice and zest at 100% (High) for 2-3 minutes, stirring twice.

317

Eve's pudding

8
mins

Standing time: 3 mins

350g / 12oz cooking apples
grated zest and juice of ½ lemon
45ml / 3tbls sugar
1 packet lemon sponge pudding
   mix
1 egg, beaten
15ml / 1tbls water

SERVES 4

1 Peel the apples and cut into thick slices. Lightly grease the base and sides of an 850ml / 1½pt pie dish. Arrange the apple slices in the base of the dish and sprinkle with the lemon zest and juice. Add the sugar, sprinkling evenly over the top.
2 Place the pudding mix in a bowl. Beat in the egg and water until smooth. Spoon the mixture over the apples and microwave at 50% (Medium) for 8 minutes. Leave to stand for 3 minutes.
3 For an appetizing appearance, brown quickly under the grill.

Microtips

When cooking sponge mixtures with a fresh fruit base, avoid using full power, as this tends to draw moisture from the fruit and makes the sponge soggy.

Saucy sponge pudding

11
mins

Standing time: 2 mins

1 quantity Traditional Sponge
   Pudding (see page 317)

SAUCE
385g / 13½oz can blackcurrant
   pie filling
grated zest and juice of 1 orange

SERVES 6

1 Prepare a 10 x 20cm / 4 x 8in dish by greasing and lining with crumbs, as in the recipe, page 317.
2 Prepare the Traditional sponge pudding mixture and spread evenly in the dish.
3 Microwave according to the recipe, turning every minute. Leave to stand for 2 minutes.
4 While the sponge is standing, mix the pie filling with the orange zest and juice and microwave at 100% (High) for 2-3 minutes, until hot through, stirring twice.
5 Turn the sponge out on to a warm serving dish and pour the sauce over the top.

VARIATION
Use another flavoured pie filling such as cherry, for the sauce.

Below: *Eve's Pudding and Saucy Sponge Pudding*

Primrose puddings

3¾
mins

Standing time: 2 mins

40ml / 8tsp lemon curd
50g / 2oz butter or margarine,
   softened
60ml / 4tbls caster sugar
grated zest of ½ lemon
1 egg, beaten
2-3 drops yellow food colouring
60ml / 4tbls self-raising flour,
   sifted
45ml / 3tbls lemon curd
juice of ½ lemon, strained

SERVES 4

DON LAST

318

1 Lightly grease the sides of four 200ml / 7fl oz paper cups. Put 10ml / 2tsp lemon curd into each one.

2 Place the butter or margarine in a bowl, and beat with the sugar and lemon zest until light and fluffy.

3 Beat in the egg and colouring, then fold in the flour. Divide the mixture evenly between the cups.

4 Cover each one with vented cling film and microwave at 100% (High) for 3 minutes.

5 Remove from the cooker and leave to stand for 2 minutes. Meanwhile, mix the lemon curd and juice and microwave at 100% (High) for 45 seconds.

6 Turn the puddings out of the cups, loosening the edges with a palette knife if necessary, and spoon the sauce over the tops. Serve immediately.

Orange and ginger pudding

9¼ mins

Standing time: 3 mins

25g / 1oz butter
30ml / 2tbls demerara sugar
1 large orange
60ml / 4tbls fresh brown bread crumbs
50g / 2oz drained ginger in syrup, chopped

SPONGE
100g / 4oz butter or margarine, softened
100g / 4oz caster sugar
grated zest of ½ orange
2 eggs
100g / 4oz self-raising flour

SAUCE
15ml / 3tsp cornflour
275ml / ½pt orange juice
juice of ½ lemon
15-30ml / 1-2tbls sugar

SERVES 4-6

1 Lightly grease the sides of an 18cm / 7in soufflé dish. Place the butter in the dish and microwave at 100% (High) for 15-30 seconds to melt. Stir in the demerara sugar and spread to coat the base.

2 Finely grate the zest from half of the orange and set aside. Cut the top and the base from the orange and slice off the rind and the pith. Slice the orange into 6mm / ¼in rounds and remove the pips. Arrange the slices over the coated base.

3 Sprinkle the breadcrumbs over the base and press down lightly. Scatter the chopped ginger evenly over the top.

4 To make the sponge, beat the butter or margarine with the sugar and reserved orange zest until light and fluffy. Beat in the eggs then fold in the flour.

5 Spoon the mixture into the soufflé dish and spread evenly. Cover and microwave at 100% (High) for 6 minutes, turning twice. Leave to stand while making the sauce.

6 Mix the cornflour with the orange and lemon juices in a bowl. Microwave at 100% (High) for 3 minutes, stirring twice. Add sugar to taste. Turn out the pudding and serve hot with the sauce.

Microtips

Store leftover sponge pudding wrapped in cling film in the refrigerator when cold. To freshen up one serving, unwrap and microwave at 100% (High) for 30 seconds. Serve immediately while still warm.

319

Layer pudding

Standing time: 2 mins

175g / 6oz self-raising flour
2.5ml / ½tsp baking powder
pinch of salt
100g / 4oz caster sugar
100g / 4oz butter or margarine, softened
2 eggs, beaten
1.5ml / ¼tsp vanilla flavouring
few drops green food colouring
few drops peppermint flavouring
22.5ml / 1½tbls cocoa powder
15ml / 1tbls milk

SAUCE
25g / 1oz butter
30ml / 2tbls plain flour
30ml / 2tbls sugar
1.5ml / ¼tsp vanilla flavouring
425ml / 15fl oz milk

SERVES 4-6

1 Lightly grease a 1.1L / 2pt pudding basin. Reserve 30ml / 2tbls of the flour, then sift the rest into a mixing bowl with the baking powder and salt. Add the butter or margarine, sugar and eggs. Beat together using an electric mixer for 1 minute, or by hand for 2 minutes.
2 Divide the mixture between three small mixing bowls. (Spoon the mixture so that the quantity is the same in each bowl). Beat the vanilla flavouring into the first and the green colouring and flavouring into the second.
3 Sift the cocoa powder and the reserved flour into the third bowl. Stir in the milk until smooth.
4 Spoon the vanilla mixture into the pudding basin and smooth the top. Add the peppermint mixture and level the top, then add the chocolate mixture.
5 Cover and microwave at 100% (High) for 5-6 minutes, turning twice during cooking. Leave to stand for 2 minutes.
6 Meanwhile, mix all the sauce ingredients in a heatproof jug. Microwave at 100% (High) for 2½-3½ minutes until boiling and thickened, stirring twice.
7 Turn the pudding out on to a warm dish. Serve with the sauce.

Chocolate pudding

Standing time: 2 mins

100g / 4oz self-raising flour
2.5ml / ½tsp baking powder
45ml / 3tbls cocoa powder
100g / 4oz caster sugar
100g / 4oz soft margarine
few drops of vanilla flavouring
2 eggs, beaten
75ml / 5tbls milk

MOCHA SAUCE
50g / 2oz plain chocolate
150ml / ¼pt hot black coffee
150ml / ¼pt milk
15ml / 3tsp cornflour
30-45ml / 2-3tbls sugar

SERVES 4-6

1 Lightly grease a 1.1L / 2pt pudding basin. Sift the flour, baking powder and cocoa into a bowl and add the sugar, margarine, vanilla, egg and milk. Beat using an electric whisk for 1 minute or by hand for 2 minutes.
2 Spoon the mixture into the prepared basin, cover and microwave at 100% (High) for 6 minutes, turning twice. Stand for 2 minutes.
3 To make the sauce, break the chocolate into pieces and place in a bowl. Microwave at 50% (Medium) for 2 minutes to melt.
4 Stir in the coffee. Gradually blend the milk into the cornflour then stir into the sauce. Microwave at 100% (High) for 2½-3 minutes until boiling. Stir twice during cooking. Stir in sugar to taste.
5 Turn out the pudding and serve hot with the mocha sauce.

Microtips

Cover fruit or liquid mixtures in the base of sponge puddings with a layer of fresh breadcrumbs before adding the sponge mixture. This absorbs any excess moisture in the fruit and helps to prevent the sponge from becoming too moist and soggy during microwaving.

Pastry and sweet flans

Microwave cooking is perfect for unfilled shortcrust pastry cases. It takes only 5 minutes to cook crisp pastry for sweet flans and savoury quiches.

Shortcrust pastry cooked without a filling becomes crisp and has just as good a flavour as pastry cooked in a conventional oven, but it does not become brown. Other types of pastry cannot be cooked successfully as the pastry will not become crisp in the microwave cooker.

A cooked pastry case can be filled and eaten cold or filled and reheated in the microwave.

Uncooked filled pastry cases or double crust pies are not successful as the water content in the filling turns to steam in the microwave cooker and makes the pastry wet and soggy. With a double crust pie, the filling cooks more rapidly than the pastry and is ready long before the pastry has a chance to cook through.

For perfect, even cooking, prick the bottom and sides of the pastry case with a fork and rotate the plate every minute when microwaving.

To ensure crisp pastry, the base should be covered with absorbent paper. This soaks up the moisture as it is driven to the surface.

Strawberry Glacé Pie

Shortcrust pastry case

5 mins

Standing time: none

A shortcrust pastry case for sweet or savoury pies and flans cooks perfectly in the microwave. Follow the step-by-step guide below.

75g / 3oz butter or margarine
175g / 6oz plain flour
2.5ml / ½tsp salt
45ml / 3tbls cold water

MAKES A 23cm / 9in CASE

DO
● Cook pastry cases unfilled, then fill and reheat as necessary.

● Use a mixture of plain and wholemeal flour for colour.

● Add drops of yellow food colouring for stronger colour.

● Add cold water very slowly to the fat and flour mixture.

● Prick base of pastry case very thoroughly for even cooking.

● Cover base with double layer of absorbent paper to absorb steam and produce crisp pastry.

DON'T
● Microwave raw pastry with a filling as the steam from the filling makes the pastry soggy.

● Make double crust pies for the same reason. The filling will also cook before the pastry.

● Cook choux or puff pastry as they will not become crisp.

● Add sugar to pastry when it is going to be cooked in a microwave, it causes pastry to burn.

● Use baking beans to weight down the pastry as you would normally when baking blind.

How to make shortcrust pastry

Cut *the butter or margarine and lard into the flour and salt in a bowl or large jug until the mixture resembles fine breadcrumbs. Use the lowest speed on a mixer, or use a pastry blender to do this, if preferred.*

Sprinkle *over the cold water, stirring lightly with a fork, until the mixture clings together and forms a ball. (Add the water a little at a time, you may not need to use all of it and once added it is too late to remove any.)*

Add *just the right amount of water. Too little makes a dry dough which is hard to roll out and cracks around the edge. Too much makes a very sticky dough. Either will result in an unpleasantly tough pastry.*

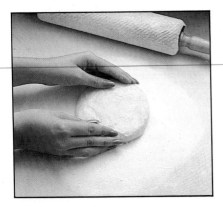

Form *into a ball on a floured surface. Flatten to a thickness of 1cm / ½in. Roll out to a circle 3mm / ⅛in thick and 5cm / 2in larger than the top of the dish.*

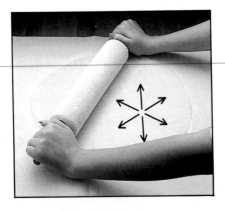

To *maintain the pastry dough in a circular shape and keep it an even thickness, roll only from the centre out towards the edge all the way round the pastry circle.*

Transfer *the rolled out pastry circle to the pie dish by folding it in half and then in half again. Placing both hands underneath it, carefully lift on to the dish without tearing.*

322

How to line a pie dish

  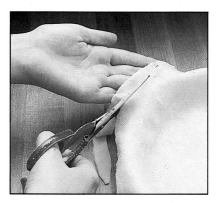

Unfold the pastry and fit it loosely into the dish. Pat out any air pockets on the bottom. Lift the sides and let them fall gently into the dish. Do not stretch the dough or it will shrink during cooking.

Leave the pastry to relax in a cool place or in the refrigerator for 10 minutes to prevent it shrinking while cooking. If put in the refrigerator, it will take a little longer to cook.

Trim the pastry overhang, using kitchen scissors, to a generous 1cm / ½in to allow for a high rim. Using fingers, fold the pastry to form a high standing rim all around the top.

  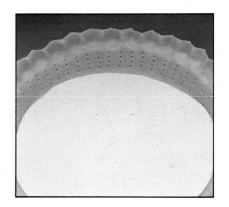

Place the left index finger inside the rim and the right thumb and index finger on the outside of the rim. Push the pastry into a 'V' shape every 1cm / ½in. Pinch to make sharp edges.

Prick the pastry case continuously at the bend of the dish with a fork, then make pricks on the bottom and sides of the pastry, 1cm / ½in apart to ensure even cooking in the microwave.

Cover the base of the pastry case with 2 layers of absorbent paper, cut to size. These will absorb the steam produced during cooking and help to make the pastry crisp.

How to microwave a pastry case

Place the dish on an upturned plate in the microwave cooker. Microwave at 100% (High) for 3 minutes, rotating the dish ¼ turn every minute.

Remove the paper; microwave for 2-3 minutes. Check readiness before minimum time by looking through the base. It should appear opaque.

Microtip

Brown spots may appear on the surface of the pastry after the first part of the cooking. You will discover these when the absorbent paper on the base is removed. They occur in 'hot spots' in the oven where microwaves continuously bounce off the same spot, causing over-cooking. They will also occur where butter has not been well incorporated during the preparation stage and so attracts a concentration of microwaves. Placing the pie dish on an upturned plate will ensure a more even distribution of the microwaves.

Strawberry glacé pie

$\boxed{\text{8 mins}}$

Standing time: none

450g / 1lb fresh strawberries,
   wiped
23cm / 9in cooked Shortcrust
   Pastry Case (see page 322)
50g / 2oz sugar
15g / ½oz cornflour
225g / 8oz frozen strawberries,
   thawed with juice reserved
15ml / 1tbls lemon juice
few drops red food colouring
   (optional)

SERVES 6

1 Pat the fresh strawberries dry and place in the pastry case.
2 In a small bowl, combine the sugar and cornflour. Stir in the frozen strawberries and reserved juice. Microwave at 100% (High) for 3-4 minutes, or until thickened and clear, stirring every minute.
3 Add lemon juice and colouring, if wished. Cool. Spoon over the strawberries to cover.
4 Chill for 2-3 hours.

Wheatmeal crumb case

$\boxed{\text{2 mins}}$

Standing time: none

75g / 3oz butter or margarine
225g / 8oz wheatmeal or digestive
   biscuits, crushed
30ml / 2tbls demerara or
   granulated sugar

MAKES A 23cm / 9in CRUMB CASE

1 Melt the butter in a 23cm / 9in pie plate at 100% (High) for 45-60 seconds.
2 Stir in the crumbs and sugar, reserving 30ml / 2tbls crumbs for decoration when filled, if wished (see How to microwave Meringue topping, opposite).
3 Press crumbs firmly and evenly against bottom and sides of plate, using a smaller plate or spoon.
4 Stand the pie dish on an upturned plate and microwave at 100% (High) for 30 seconds. Rotate the dish ½ turn and microwave for a further 45-60 seconds. Allow to cool before filling as desired.

VARIATION
For a stronger-flavoured base, try using the same amount of crushed ginger biscuits instead of digestive.

Glazed peach pie

$\boxed{\text{4 mins}}$

Standing time: none

23cm / 9in cooked Wheatmeal
   Crumb Case
5 large peaches, peeled, stoned
   and sliced
65g / 2½oz sugar
30ml / 2tbls cornflour
100ml / 3½fl oz water
30ml / 2tbls lemon juice

SERVES 6

1 Mash one fifth of the peach slices.
2 In a small bowl, mix the sugar and cornflour. Stir in the water, lemon juice and mashed peaches.
3 Microwave at 100% (High) for 2-3 minutes, or until thickened and clear, stirring every minute.
4 Place remaining peach slices into the crumb case; spoon over the glaze, spreading carefully to cover.
5 Chill for 2-3 hours. To serve, top with whipped cream or ice cream.

Pineapple lemon pie

15 mins

Standing time: none

225g / 8oz caster sugar
50g / 2oz cornflour
1.5ml / ¼tsp salt
225ml / 8fl oz cold water
225g / 8oz can crushed pineapple
3 egg yolks
juice and zest of 2 lemons
20g / ¾oz butter, diced
23cm / 9in cooked Shortcrust
   Pastry Case (see page 322)

SERVES 6

1 In a small mixing bowl, combine the sugar, cornflour, salt and 50ml / 2floz water. Stir in the remaining water and pineapple.
2 Microwave, uncovered, at 100% (High) for 6-8 minutes, or until thickened and clear, stirring every 2-3 minutes.
3 Mix a little of the hot mixture into the egg yolks in a small bowl, then stir into the pineapple mixture. Microwave at 100% (High) for 1 minute.
4 Stir in the lemon zest and juice and the butter. Cool slightly, then pour into the cooked pastry case. Top with meringue (see below) and microwave as directed.

VARIATION
Lemon Meringue Pie: omit the crushed pineapple and increase the cold water to 400ml / 14floz.

Meringue Topping

3 egg whites
5ml / 1tsp cornflour
1.5ml / ¼ tsp cream of tartar
90ml / 6tbls caster sugar
30ml / 2tbls wheatmeal biscuit
   crumbs (optional)

Microtip
An egg white at room temperature will whisk to a greater volume than a cold egg. To bring a refrigerated egg to room temperature, microwave the whole egg at 100% (High) for 5 seconds only. Do not microwave for longer or the egg may explode.

How to microwave Meringue topping

Beat *the egg whites, cornflour and cream of tartar in a bowl or jug until standing in soft peaks. Add the sugar, 15ml / 1tbls at a time, beating until straight peaks form when the beaters are raised. Spread over the filling, taking it to the pastry edge. Sprinkle over the biscuit crumbs if using.*

Microwave *at 50% (Medium) for 3-6 minutes until the meringue has set, rotating the dish ½ turn after half the cooking time. If browned meringue is preferred, microwave for only 3-4 minutes, then place under a pre-heated grill for 2-4 minutes. Watch the meringue closely to make sure it does not burn.*

Fruit crumbles

Crisp, golden fruit crumbles have always been a traditional favourite — as tasty as a pie, but so much simpler. Microwaving makes them even quicker and easier — a really special pudding in no time.

While pastry-topped pies do not number among the microwave's success stories, crumble toppings cook particularly well. Use them to make a 'pastry' base and a crumble-style pie crust and turn simple stewed fruit into something special.

A basic crumble can be flavoured with mixed spice, cinnamon or nutmeg, or be given added texture with chopped nuts, rolled oats or shredded coconut. Crumble the mixture lightly for a smooth, fine covering, or add water to the crumbled ingredients to produce a coarser texture.

Deep Dish Crumble made with rhubarb and raspberries

326

Where the raw fruit is quite fibrous (rhubarb, for example), it may need preliminary cooking before adding the crumble. Do not add too much liquid to the fruit, or the crumble will sink into it.

The crumble pastry mixture (see Quick Cherry Crumble Pie, page 329) fulfils a dual purpose. Crumble one half with water to make a rich topping, and knead the other to a smooth dough to make a pastry case.

Choose a deep dish for crumbles, and do not fill it right to the top. This ensures that the juice from the cooking fruit does not bubble over the top of the dish.

As with most microwave bakes, overcooking will make the centre of the crumble dry and hard.

Freezer notes

Fruit crumbles freeze well, so it is worth making double amounts while you're cooking.

Freeze assembled crumbles, either cooked or uncooked, for up to three months. To cook crumbles from frozen: microwave at 20-30% (Defrost) for 15 minutes, to thaw completely, then at 100% (High) for 5 minutes to heat a ready-cooked one, or for 10-14 minutes to cook a raw one, turning several times.

Microtips

Crumble toppings do colour a little during microwaving. If you want to give a more appetizing, golden appearance to the finished pudding, flash the topping under a hot grill after microwaving, turning dish frequently, until evenly browned. Alternatively, use whole-wheat flour in place of white in the basic mixture, or substitute dark soft brown sugar for light. (Cooking times remain the same.)

Crispy apple pudding

14¾ mins

Standing time: 5 mins

900g / 2lb cooking apples, peeled and sliced
15ml / 1tbls lemon juice
60ml / 4tbls caster sugar

TOPPING
75g / 3oz butter, diced
60ml / 4tbls demerara sugar
75g / 3oz quick-cooking rolled oats
75g / 3oz plain flour
5ml / 1tsp ground cinnamon

SERVES 6

How to microwave Crispy apple pudding

Mix *the apples, lemon juice and sugar and spread in a deep 20cm / 8in dish. Place the butter in a large bowl, cover and microwave at 100% (High) for 45-60 seconds, or until melted.*

Stir *the topping ingredients into the butter, mixing until an even, crumbly texture is reached. Sprinkle evenly over the apples and microwave at 100% (High) for 14-16 minutes until tender.*

Give *the dish a quarter turn after 7 minutes, then stop microwaving when the apples are just tender. Remove from the cooker and stand for 5 minutes. Serve hot with cream.*

Deep dish apple crumble

10 mins

Standing time: 10 mins

900g / 2lb cooking apples, peeled,
  cored and sliced
50g / 2oz sultanas
75-100g / 3-4oz light soft brown
  sugar
30ml / 2tbls plain flour
2.5ml / ½tsp ground cinnamon
1.5ml / ¼tsp grated nutmeg

TOPPING
225g / 8oz plain flour
pinch of salt
175g / 6oz butter, diced
60ml / 4tbls demerara sugar

SERVES 6-8

1 Combine the apples, sultanas,
sugar, flour and spices in a large
bowl. Mix well and turn into a
deep buttered 25cm / 10in pie
dish.
2 To make the topping, sift the
flour and salt into a bowl and rub
in the butter, using the fingertips,
until the mixture resembles fine
breadcrumbs. Add the sugar and
mix until evenly blended.
3 Spread the topping evenly
over the apple mixture. Microwave, uncovered, at 100% (High)
for 10-14 minutes, or until the
apples are tender, giving the dish a
quarter turn every 4 minutes. Remove from the cooker and leave to
stand for 10 minutes to complete
cooking. Serve warm with cream
or custard.

VARIATION
Rhubarb and raspberry crumble:
use two 450g / 1lb cans rhubarb,
drained. Mix with 275g / 10oz defrosted frozen raspberries, 60ml /
4tbls sugar and 30ml / 2tbls flour.
Omit the nutmeg.
  Microwave the filling on its own,
covered, at 100% (High) for 3-3½
minutes, stirring after 3 minutes.
Uncover, stir again, then sprinkle
the topping over it. Microwave at
100% (High) for 10-14 minutes, as
for the apple crumble. Leave to
stand for 10 minutes to finish
cooking.

Deep Dish Apple Crumble

Quick cherry crumble pie

11 mins

Standing time: 3 mins

400g / 14oz cherry pie filling

CRUMBLE PASTRY AND
TOPPING
225g / 8oz plain flour
100g / 4oz butter, diced
50g / 2oz lard or cooking
  margarine, diced
60-75ml / 4-5tbls cold water

SERVES 6

VARIATION
Use 425g / 15oz can apple pie
filling in place of cherry. For
a browner topping, use wholemeal
flour instead of white, or brown
under the grill before serving.

How to microwave Quick crumble pie

Make *the crumble topping: sift the flour into a bowl. Rub or cut in the butter and lard until the mixture resembles coarse breadcrumbs.*

Transfer *half of the crumble mixture to a lightly-greased shallow dish and sprinkle over 30ml / 2tbls of water, tossing with a fork to mix.*

Spread *the crumble mixture evenly in the dish and microwave at 100% (High) for 4-5 minutes, or until crisp and crumbly. Set aside.*

Make *the crumble pastry: sprinkle the remaining water over the raw crumble and cut it in with a knife. Form into a dough and roll out to line a 23cm / 9in pie dish. Prick the base all over with a fork.*

Line *with absorbent paper and microwave at 100% (High) for 3 minutes, giving a quarter turn every minute. Remove paper and microwave for 2-3 minutes. Cool and fill with the chosen fruit filling.*

Sprinkle *the cooled crumble evenly over the fruit. Place the dish on an upturned plate, then microwave at 100% (High) for 2-2½ minutes, or until the filling is warm. Leave to stand for 3 minutes.*

Grain puddings

Rice and grain puddings have been popular for centuries. Bring them right up to date with the help of your microwave. Embellish them with a few extra ingredients for a special occasion dessert.

For inexpensive desserts with almost endless versatility, it's hard to beat a traditional grain and milk pudding.

Rice is the most commonly used pudding grain. Round or short-grain Carolina rice is the most suitable. Generally white rice will produce a creamier result than brown, as the grains swell more and stick together. (Brown rice needs much longer cooking and produces a more grainy pudding.)

Flaked and ground rice make more closely textured puddings, suitable for serving hot or cold.

Semolina, which is made from durum wheat, and cornmeal both make thick, close-textured puddings suitable for moulding.

In spite of their 'school lunches' reputation, tapioca and sago both make delicious desserts.

Milk can be used in all kinds of blends — enrich pasteurized milk by replacing up to half the amount with thin cream (but never use all cream, as this will make a sticky pudding). Evaporated milk is used combined with milk and water in some of the recipes here as it gives a rich texture and has a slightly sweet flavour. Condensed milk needs no extra sugar added to it when diluted, as it is already sweetened.

If using reconstituted skimmed milk, add 50g / 2oz butter to 575ml / 1pt milk for a richer texture. Sterilized and ultra heat-treated milk produce a creamy-textured pudding when used on their own. To give a refreshing

Italian Semolina Pudding

fruity flavour, replace up to a quarter of the total liquid with fruit juice. (Adjust the amount of sugar used if the fruit juice is sweetened.)

Unlike conventionally-cooked grain puddings, these microwaved desserts will not have a golden skin. The method of cooking also requires that the pudding be stirred regularly in most cases, so the mixture is evenly cooked. A similar pudding would have to be cooked for about 1¾ hours, and stirred frequently on a conventional cooker, while a microwaved version will take only 30-40 minutes. Also, there is no danger of the milk burning or sticking but make sure your bowl is large enough to avoid the pudding boiling over.

Cook's notes

For a really creamy pudding, soak the rice for the pudding in the cooking liquid for 6 hours or overnight. This allows the grains to slowly absorb the liquid.

Microtips

To give extra flavour to a grain pudding, infuse a few strips of orange or lemon zest or a vanilla pod in the milk for 20 minutes. Microwave at 100% (High) for 4-5 minutes until almost boiling. Stand for 20 minutes, then proceed with the recipe.

Traditional rice pudding

36 mins

Standing time: 5 mins

225ml / 8fl oz milk
170g / 6oz can evaporated milk
175ml / 6fl oz water
1.5-2ml / ¼-¾tsp ground cinnamon or mixed spice (optional)
75ml / 5tbls round-grain rice
30ml / 2tbls caster sugar
grated nutmeg or jam to serve

SERVES 4

VARIATIONS
Chocolate rice pudding: omit the cinnamon or spice from the basic recipe and add 30ml / 2tbls cocoa powder, blended with a little of the milk. Microwave as before.
Brown rice pudding: omit the spice from the basic recipe and replace the round-grain rice with brown rice. This will take much longer to microwave, so allow 56 minutes in all, stirring frequently to separate the grains.
Fruited brown rice pudding: add 45ml / 3tbls chopped dried apricots and 30ml / 2tbls sultanas to the brown rice pudding halfway through the cooking time. Stir well to separate the grains and the pieces of fruit.
Nutty brown rice pudding: add 45ml / 3tbls chopped almonds, hazelnuts or mixed nuts to the pudding 20 minutes before the end of the cooking time. Stir well and microwave as before.

How to microwave Traditional rice pudding

Pour *the milk, evaporated milk and water into a 2.8L / 5pt bowl. Stir in the spice (if used), the rice and the sugar and mix thoroughly.*

Cover *the pudding and microwave at 100% (High) for 6-8 minutes, or until the mixture is boiling, stirring after 2-3 minutes.*

Reduce *the power to 50% (Medium) and microwave for a further 30 minutes, or until the pudding is thick and creamy, stirring every 15 minutes.*

Leave *the cooked pudding to stand for 5 minutes before serving in individual dishes. If liked, serve sprinkled with nutmeg, or topped with jam.*

Microtips

As a general rule, you can use 50g / 2oz of any grain with 575ml / 1pt liquid, adding 30ml / 2tbls sugar. Cook as for the Traditional rice pudding, for about 36 minutes.

As they need stirring, microwaved grain puddings tend to lose some of their liquid by evaporation. This makes them thicker than a conventionally cooked pudding, so you may like to stir in a little extra milk or cream at the end of cooking time.

Italian semolina pudding

33½ mins

Standing time: none

50g / 2oz butter
100g / 4oz semolina
grated zest of ½ lemon
50g / 2oz flaked almonds
575ml / 1pt milk
60ml / 4tbls caster sugar
2 eggs, separated
420g / 14.8oz can apricots, drained

SERVES 6-8

1 Place the butter in a large bowl. Cover and microwave at 100% (High) for 30-60 seconds until melted. Stir in the semolina, lemon zest and flaked almonds.
2 Pour 425ml / 15fl oz of the milk into a large jug; stir in sugar. Cover and microwave at 100% (High) for 6-8 minutes, to boil.
3 Pour the hot milk over the semolina, stirring continuously. Microwave at 50% (Medium) for 5 minutes, stirring three times during cooking. Allow to cool.
4 Lightly beat the egg yolks with the remaining milk and stir into the pudding. Whisk the egg whites to soft peaks, then fold them into the semolina.

5 Arrange the apricots, round side down, over the base of a buttered 2.3L / 4pt round dish. Pour the semolina pudding over the apricots and cover. Microwave at 50% (Medium) for 20 minutes, or until the pudding is firm in the centre.
6 Turn the pudding out on to a warmed serving plate and microwave at 50% (Medium) for 2 minutes before serving.

Flaked rice pudding

21 mins

Standing time: 5 mins

575ml / 1pt full cream milk
75ml / 5tbls flaked rice
30ml / 2tbls sugar
1.5ml / ¼tsp grated nutmeg
15g / ½oz butter

SERVES 4

1 Pour the milk into a 2.8L / 5pt bowl. Cover and microwave at 100% (High) for 6 minutes, to boil.
2 Stir in the rice, sugar, nutmeg and butter. Cover and microwave at 50% (Medium) for 15 minutes.
3 Leave the pudding to stand for 5 minutes before serving.

Greek-style Pudding

VARIATIONS
Greek-style pudding: use 30ml / 2tbls honey in place of the sugar, and omit the nutmeg. Stir in the grated zest of half a lemon and 30ml / 2tbls sultanas with the rice. Microwave as above. Dust with ground cinnamon if liked.
Danish-style pudding: add 50g / 2oz blanched almonds and omit the nutmeg. Sprinkle the cooked pudding with 30ml / 2tbls demerara sugar and microwave at 100% (High) for 1 minute to melt.

Indian corn pudding

10 mins

Standing time: 2-3 mins

50g / 2oz margarine, softened
60ml / 4tbls caster sugar
1 egg, beaten
75g / 3oz self-raising flour
5ml / 1tsp baking powder
45ml / 3tbls cornmeal
100ml / 3½fl oz milk
125ml / 4fl oz maple syrup

SERVES 4-6

1 Mix the margarine, caster sugar, egg, flour, baking powder and cornmeal. Stir in the milk.
2 Grease a 1.1L / 2pt pudding basin. Add 30ml / 2tbls of the maple syrup, then the pudding.
3 Cover loosely and microwave at 30% (Low) for 10 minutes. Stand for 2-3 minutes.
4 Turn out on to a warmed serving dish. Serve the maple syrup.

Microtips

Because of the sugar content of the syrup, this pudding needs to be cooked at a lower power than other grain puddings. This will prevent the syrup burning.

Cook's notes

Cornmeal is a pale yellow, starchy meal. It is sold in healthfood shops, some supermarkets and Italian delicatessens, where it is called polenta.

RAY DUNS

332

Peach condé

38 mins

Standing time: 5 mins

1 quantity Traditional rice
  pudding
2 large egg yolks
60ml / 4tbls double cream,
  whipped
15-30ml / 1-2tbls orange liqueur
2 small peaches, peeled, halved
  and stoned
100g / 4oz raspberries, defrosted
  if frozen
30ml / 2tbls sugar

SERVES 4

1 Microwave the Traditional rice pudding. Remove from the cooker and quickly beat in the egg yolks. Stand for 5 minutes.
2 Cool completely, then mix in the cream and liqueur.
3 Lightly oil an 850ml / 1½pt soufflé dish or straight-sided mould. Turn the rice mixture into the dish and chill for 1-2 hours.
4 Turn the chilled dessert out on to a serving dish and decorate the top with the peach halves.
5 Microwave the berries and sugar together at 100% (High) for 2 minutes. Purée, then sieve. Serve with the pudding.

Strawberry and tapioca sundae

36 mins

Standing time: none

60ml / 4tbls tapioca
575ml / 1pt milk
30ml / 2tbls caster sugar
few drops of vanilla flavouring
150ml / ¼pt double cream,
  whipped
225g / 8oz fresh strawberries

SERVES 4

1 Rinse and drain the tapioca. Pour the milk into a 2.8L / 5pt bowl. Cover and microwave at 100% (High) for 6-8 minutes, to boil.
2 Stir in the tapioca, sugar and vanilla. Cover and microwave at 50% (Medium) for 30 minutes, stirring twice during cooking. Leave until completely cold.
3 Reserve four strawberries for decoration. Hull the remaining fruit and slice each one in half.
4 Layer the tapioca, sliced strawberries and whipped cream in four sundae glasses, finishing with a layer of cream. Top each with a strawberry and serve.

Below: *Peach Condé* **Right:** *Strawberry and Tapioca Sundae*

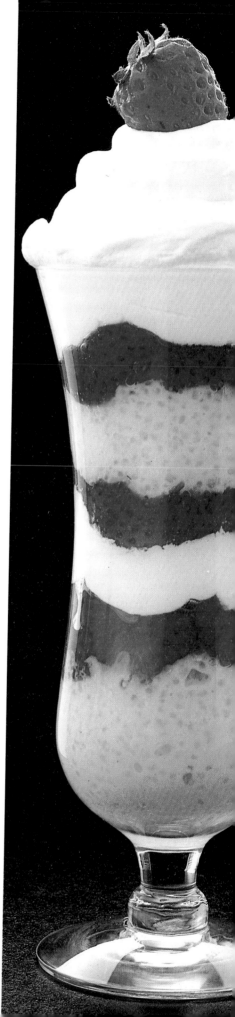

RAY DUNS

Cheesecakes

Cooked or refrigerator-style, cheesecakes are delicious as a dessert or a special tea-time dish, and microwaving makes professional results so easy. Try this mouthwatering selection, and see!

For perfect cheesecakes every time, microwaving is ideal — bear these important pointers in mind for the best results.

When microwaving whole cheesecakes, frequent turning is essential — every 3 minutes in some cases. The mixtures are quite thick and cannot be stirred, so it is vital to turn the dish for even cooking. Place the dish on an inverted saucer or bowl to use the microwaves to the best effect.

Standing time is an integral part of the cooking process. Cheesecakes will go on cooking after they are removed from the cooker, so take them out when the edges are firm, but the centre is still not set. During standing the centre will finish cooking perfectly.

Refrigerated cheesecakes set with gelatine make use of the non-direct heat from the microwave for dissolving and melting, but whichever type of cheesecake you prefer, the microwave will make all the stages easier and quicker.

Valentine Cheesecake

Valentine cheesecake

<table><tr><td>2½
mins</td></tr></table>

Standing time: none

100g / 4oz butter
175g / 6oz wheatmeal biscuits, crushed
30ml / 2tbls soft brown sugar

FILLING
20ml / 4tsp powdered gelatine
juice of 1 lemon
225g / 8oz cream cheese
225g / 8oz curd cheese
75g / 3oz caster sugar
2 eggs, separated
150ml / ¼pt natural yoghurt

PAUL WEBSTER

225g / 8oz fresh or frozen raspberries (see Microtips)
150ml / ¼pt whipping cream

SERVES 6-8

1 Place the butter in a large bowl, cover and microwave at 100% (High) for 1 minute. Stir in the crumbs and sugar.
2 Line the base of a 21.5cm / 8½in heart-shaped cake tin with greaseproof paper and grease thoroughly. Using the back of a spoon, press the mixture firmly and evenly over base of tin. Refrigerate for up to 1 hour. .
3 Put the lemon juice into a small bowl and sprinkle on the gelatine. Mix and soak until spongy. Microwave at 50% (Medium) for 1½ minutes, stirring every 30 seconds until the gelatine is dissolved. Leave to cool slightly.
4 Beat together the cheeses, sugar, egg yolks and yoghurt.
5 Purée the raspberries in a blender or food processor, then press through a fine nylon sieve. Stir into the cheese mixture.
6 Beat the egg whites until they form stiff peaks. Stir the dissolved gelatine into the cheese mixture, then fold in the egg whites.
7 Pour into the cake tin, and refrigerate for at least 4 hours to set. Loosen the edges with a knife dipped into hot water, then invert on cling film then back on to a plate. Whip the cream and use to decorate.

Microtips

If using frozen raspberries, thaw them by microwaving at 20-30% (Defrost) 3-4 minutes. Stir the raspberries to loosen them and rearrange once during thawing time.

Cook's notes

For a more special presentation, make individual cheesecakes, dividing the base and filling between 6-8 small heart-shaped moulds. Top with rosettes of whipped cream.

Low-cal lime cheesecake

<table><tr><td>2½
mins</td></tr></table>

Standing time: none

75g / 3oz low-calorie margarine
150g / 5oz wheatmeal biscuits, crushed

FILLING
20ml / 4tsp powdered gelatine
45ml / 3tbls water
450g / 1lb curd cheese
60ml / 4tbls caster sugar
juice of 1½ limes
150ml / ¼pt natural yoghurt
few drops of green food colouring

TOPPING
2 kiwi fruit, peeled and thinly sliced
5 green grapes, halved and pips removed

SERVES 8-10

1 To make the base, place the margarine in a mixing bowl, cover and microwave at 100% (High) for 1 minute. Add the biscuit crumbs.
2 Using the back of a spoon, press the mixture into the base of a 20cm / 8in loose-bottomed cake tin. Refrigerate for about 1 hour.
3 Sprinkle the gelatine over the water in a small bowl. Mix and leave to soak until spongy. Microwave at 50% (Medium) for 1½ minutes, stirring every 30 seconds until the gelatine is dissolved.
4 Let the gelatine cool slightly. In a large bowl, beat the curd cheese and sugar together using a wooden spoon. Mix in the lime juice, yoghurt and a few drops of green colouring. Mix well, then stir in the dissolved gelatine.
5 Pour the mixture into the cake tin and return it to the refrigerator for 2-3 hours until set.
6 Transfer the cheesecake to a serving plate and arrange the sliced kiwi fruit and halved grapes on the top.

VARIATION
Lemon cheesecake: Substitute lemon juice for the lime, yellow colouring for green and use fruit such as pineapple slices, orange segments or apricot halves.

335

White chocolate cheesecake

21½ mins

Standing time: 30-45 mins

75g / 3oz butter
225g / 8oz chocolate wheatmeal
  biscuits, crushed

FILLING
700g / 1½lb cream cheese
2 eggs plus 1 egg yolk
30ml / 6tsps cornflour
225g / 8oz white chocolate
30ml / 2tbls crème de cacao
50g / 2oz chocolate, grated

SERVES 12-16

Almond ricotta cheesecakes

15½ mins

Standing time: 30-45 mins

50g / 2oz ratafia biscuits
30ml / 2tbls toasted almonds
40g / 1½oz unsalted butter

FILLING
450g / 1lb Ricotta cheese
100g / 4oz caster sugar
30ml / 6tsps cornflour
2 eggs, beaten
312g / 7oz can mandarin oranges,
  drained

SERVES 6

1 Crush the biscuits with the almonds in a food processor, or add finely-chopped almonds to biscuits crushed with a rolling pin.
2 Melt the butter by microwaving in a covered bowl at 100% (High) for 30-40 seconds. Stir the butter into the biscuit crumbs and mix well. Divide the mixture between 6 individual ramekin dishes, pressing it over the base and half way up the sides. Chill well.
3 Beat together the Ricotta, sugar and cornflour, then add the eggs gradually, mixing well.
4 Chop 75g / 3oz of the mandarins lightly and add to the cheese filling mixture.
5 Divide the filling between the

How to microwave White chocolate cheesecake

Line *a 23cm / 9in dish with two wide strips of greaseproof paper to enable you to lift the cheesecake out when set. Cross the strips in the middle and leave enough paper above the rim to be able to hold ends firmly.*

Place *the butter in a bowl , cover and microwave at 100% (High) for 1-2 minutes to melt. Stir in the biscuit crumbs and mix well. Press the crumbs mixture onto the base of the lined dish, on top of the paper strips.*

Place *the cream cheese in a large bowl and microwave at 50% (Medium) for 2 minutes until soft. Beat well. Add the eggs, egg yolk and cornflour and mix thoroughly, beating until smooth and thick.*

Place *white chocolate in a bowl and microwave at 50% (Medium) for 3½-4 minutes, stirring after 2 minutes, until melted. Stir all but 30ml / 2tbls into the the cheese mixture with the crème de cacao. Spread on crumb base.*

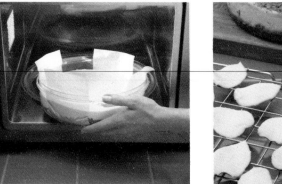

Microwave *at 50% (Medium) for 15-20 minutes, or until the edges are set and the centre is beginning to cook. Turn every 3-4 minutes. Leave to stand for 30-45 minutes. Chill for at least 8 hours or overnight.*

Decorate *with grated chocolate. Coat perfect rose leaves from the garden with the remaining melted white chocolate on the underside and leave to set. Peel off the leaves and use the chocolate ones to decorate.*

RAY DUNS

336

ramekins. Arrange in a circle on the base of the microwave.

6 Microwave at 20-30% (Defrost) for 15-20 minutes, rearranging them every 5 minutes, even if your microwave has a turntable.

7 Leave the cheesecakes to stand for 30-45 minutes and allow to cool. Refrigerate overnight, then decorate the tops with the remaining mandarins.

White Chocolate Cheesecake

Microtips

To brown almonds, microwave at 100% (High) for 5-6 minutes, stirring well after every minute. Allow to cool before using in recipes. The same method can be used to brown the nuts for the Hazelnut Cheesecake. Flake away the dry skin from the nuts after half the microwaving time.

Rosé glazed cheesecake

Standing time: 30-45 mins

25g / 1oz butter
150g / 5oz ginger biscuits, crushed
30ml / 2tbls caster sugar

FILLING
2 eggs, separated
75g / 3oz caster sugar
400g / 14oz fromage blanc or cream cheese
15ml / 1tbls lime juice
finely grated zest of 1 lemon

TOPPING
30ml / 2tbls lime marmalade
125ml / 4fl oz rosé wine
225g / 8oz strawberries, hulled and sliced

SERVES 4-6

1 Place the butter in a large bowl and cover. Microwave at 100% (High) for 15-30 seconds, then stir in the biscuit crumbs and the caster sugar.

2 Press the mixture into the base of an 18cm / 7in flan dish. Put in a cool place to set.

3 To make the filling, beat the yolks with the sugar in a large bowl until pale and creamy. Add the cheese, lime juice and lemon zest and beat well.

4 In a separate bowl, whisk the egg whites until they stand in soft peaks, then fold into the cheese mixture. Turn into the prepared flan case and smooth the top.

5 Microwave at 100% (High) for 2 minutes then at 20-30% (Defrost) for 7-8 minutes. Cook until the edges are firm and the centre is just starting to set. Stand for 30-45 minutes; leave until cold.

6 Put the marmalade into a small bowl with the wine. Microwave at 100% (High) for 5 minutes or until the liquid is syrupy, then cool.

7 Arrange the strawberry slices in rings all over the cheesecake, then spoon over the cooled glaze. Chill for at least 15 minutes before you attempt to cut the cheesecake so that the glaze has set properly. The cheesecake is best chilled before serving.

RAY DUNS

337

Hazelnut cheesecake

22 mins

Standing time: 30-45 mins

175g / 6oz plain flour
100g / 4oz unsalted butter
75g / 3oz light brown sugar

FILLING
350g / 12oz quark
150g / 5oz caster sugar
75g / 3oz hazelnuts
3 eggs
5ml / 1tsp lemon juice
30ml / 6tsp cornflour
225g / 8oz whipping cream

TOPPING
75g / 3oz plain flour
100g / 4oz light soft brown sugar
50g / 2oz unsalted butter
30ml / 2tbls icing sugar

SERVES 8

1 To make the base, sift the flour into a large bowl and rub in the butter until the mixture resembles fine breadcrumbs.

2 Stir in the sugar and work the mixture together to form a dough. Press this into the base of a 25cm / 10in flan dish. Prick the base all over with a fork. Microwave base at 70% (Medium-High) for 7 minutes, turning several times. It should be fairly dry on the surface when removed from the microwave. Leave to stand for 30-45 minutes.

3 Beat together the quark and the sugar. Stir in the nuts, eggs and lemon juice.

4 In a separate bowl, add the cornflour to the cream and whisk until it forms soft peaks. Fold into the cheese mixture.

5 Pour the filling into the prepared dish. Microwave at 50% (Medium) for 15-20 minutes, turning several times during cooking.

6 Remove when the edges are cooked and the centre is beginning to cook. (Cooking continues during standing time — about 30-45 minutes). Once set, chill lightly in the refrigerator.

7 To make the topping, rub the flour, sugar and butter together to a crumbly mixture. Sprinkle over the top of the cheesecake and grill quickly at a medium heat until the topping is brown and crisp. Cool then chill well. Lay strips of paper over the top, then sift with icing sugar to form a lattice pattern. Remove the paper strips.

Cook's notes

As the cheesecake needs the topping to be grilled until brown and crisp, remember to use a dish which is non-metallic and suitable for the microwave, but flameproof too.

PAUL WEBSTER

Summer desserts

The soft fruits of summer need only the gentlest microwaving to make delicious, fresh desserts with light textures and melt-in-the mouth flavours. These light puddings make an irresistible finale to a meal.

Microwave your summer desserts and you avoid heat in the kitchen, stay cool and cut down cooking time.

This assortment of recipes offers a choice for any occasion, from an everyday, spur-of-the-moment pudding, to a special dinner party dish.

Gentle cooking is important for fruit desserts — microwaving is therefore ideal for softening marshmallows, setting cream custards, melting chocolate and heating fruit (all of which might be spoiled by direct heating).

In some recipes, the main fruit ingredient can be replaced by

another similar one — except the Summer Pudding, which is traditionally made with red fruits. Similarly, if the fresh fruit is not available, the frozen variety can be used. Thaw by microwave and use according to the recipe.

Summer Pudding

Summer pudding

50 secs

Standing time: 1 hour

225g / 8oz raspberries
100g / 4oz blackcurrants, stalks removed
100g / 4oz redcurrants, stalks removed
225g / 8oz black cherries, pitted
175g / 6oz caster sugar
225g / 8oz strawberries, hulled
6-8 slices of white sandwich loaf, cut medium-thick

SERVES 6

1 Combine all the prepared fruit except the strawberries, in a bowl and stir in the caster sugar and 15ml / 1tbls water.
2 Cover and microwave at 100% (High) for 50-60 seconds, stirring twice. Leave the fruit to stand for 1 hour.
3 Remove the crusts from the bread and cut across diagonally, just offset from opposite corners to make wedge shapes.
4 Arrange the bread so the slices just overlap around the sides of a 1.1L / 2pt pudding bowl, with the thicker end of the wedges to the top. Cut a small piece of bread for the base and one to fit the top.
5 Cut the strawberries in half and add to the fruit mixture. Stir well and turn into the bread-lined bowl. Cover with a bread 'lid'.
6 Cover the bowl with a small plate or saucer which just fits snugly inside the top of the rim. Weight it down and leave to chill overnight.
7 Just before serving, run a knife around the inside of the bowl, then invert the pudding onto a serving dish.
8 Serve pudding with whipped cream. This is best served on individual helpings as it will become pink if piped straight onto the pudding.

Cook's notes

Factory-baked bread tends to become soggy when steeped in fruit juice, so it is best to use 'baker-made' bread.

Microtips

Stale bread absorbs the juices better than if it is absolutely fresh, so if your bread is very fresh, place slices on a cardboard egg box for support in the cooker and microwave at 100% (High) for 50-90 seconds, then leave until cold before using. This method also makes bread easier to make into crumbs.

Summer fruit yoghurt mallow

6½ mins

Standing time: 5 mins

225g / 8oz raspberries
225g / 8oz rhubarb, cut in 2.5cm / 1in pieces
60ml / 4tbls sugar
128g / 4oz marshmallows
150ml / ¼pt yoghurt
150ml / ¼pt double cream

SERVES 4-6

1 Place all but 4-6 of the raspberries in a bowl and mix with

Summer Fruit Yoghurt Mallow

the rhubarb and sugar. Cover and microwave at 100% (High) for 5-6 minutes until the fruit is tender, stirring every 2 minutes. Stand for 5 minutes, then sieve well.
2 Spoon the purée into a bowl with the marshmallows. Microwave at 100% (High) for 1½-2 minutes until puffy.
3 Stir well to make a smooth mixture. Allow to cool, then fold in the yoghurt.
4 Divide the mixture between 4-6 individual dishes. Chill for about 1 hour. Whip the cream and use to fill a piping bag fitted with a large star nozzle. Pipe rosettes on the tops and add a raspberry on each.

VARIATION
This pudding could also be made using other summer fruit, to make about 450g / 1lb purée.

Cook's notes

When sieving the fruit for the purée, it is best to use a nylon sieve, as metal ones tend to make the fruit discolour and can affect the flavour of the dessert.

DON LAST

340

Mango mousse

$1\frac{1}{2}$ mins

Standing time: none

135g / 4½oz packet orange jelly
225ml / 8fl oz water
30ml / 2tbls sugar
1 fresh ripe mango
juice of 1 lemon
150ml / ¼pt double cream
2 egg whites
pared zest of 1 orange to decorate

SERVES 6

1 Break the jelly into pieces and place in a measuring jug with the water. Cover with cling film, rolled back at one edge, and microwave at 100% (High) for 1½ minutes. Stir well to dissolve the jelly, then stir in the sugar. Set aside to cool.

2 Slice the mango in half, cutting to one side of the flat stone. Scoop the flesh into a food processor or blender and purée. (Alternatively it can be pressed through a sieve

with a wooden spoon.)

3 Add the purée to the measuring jug, and make the level up to 575ml / 1pt with water if necessary.

4 Pour the jelly mixture into a bowl and stir in the lemon juice.

5 Refrigerate until starting to set, so that it is the consistency of softly-whipped cream.

6 Lightly whip the cream and fold two-thirds of it into the jelly until smoothly blended.

7 Whisk the egg whites until stiff, then gently fold into the fruit cream. Either turn into a 1.1L / 2pt serving bowl, or divide between 6 individual glasses or sundae bowls.

8 Pipe the remaining cream onto the top as a decoration.

9 Slice the pared orange zest into very fine strips and scatter over the mousse either around the edge or in rosettes on small individual bowls.

341

Tropical lemon gateau

9½ mins

Standing time: 5 mins

100g / 4oz soft margarine
100g / 4oz caster sugar
100g / 4oz plain flour
2 eggs
45ml / 3tbls milk
2 lemons
150g / 5oz sugar
100ml / 3½fl oz water
1 small fresh pineapple, (or a
    425g / 15oz can of slices in
    natural juice, drained)
275ml / ½pt double cream
15ml / 1tbls icing sugar
few green grapes, to decorate

SERVES 8

How to microwave Tropical lemon gateau

Line *the base and sides of a 1.1L / 2pt round pudding or rectangular loaf dish with cling film, making sure that it fits closely all round and leaves no pockets of air.*

Combine *the margarine, caster sugar, flour, eggs and milk in a bowl. Beat well for about 3 minutes until light and creamy. When smooth, stir in zest grated from the lemons.*

Pour *the mixture into the prepared dish and stand on an upturned plate in the cooker. Microwave at 50% (Medium) for 8-9 minutes, turning the dish every 2 minutes, until just dry.*

Allow *the cake to stand, in the dish, for 5 minutes. Meanwhile, cut the lemons in half and squeeze the juice. Mix the juice with the sugar and water in a jug.*

Cover *and microwave at 100% (High for 1½-2 minutes, then stir to dissolve the sugar. Prick the cake, still in the dish, all over with a cocktail stick and slowly pour on the syrup.*

Cover *the dish and refrigerate overnight. Cut the crown from the pineapple and set aside. Remove the skin from the pineapple and cut into slices. Reserve 2-3 and chop the rest.*

Whip *the cream and icing sugar until thick. Set aside three-quarters of cream and fold the chopped pineapple into rest. Turn out cake and slice in half horizontally.*

Sandwich *the halves together with the cream and pineapple mixture. Coat with remaining cream and decorate with the pineapple, the grapes and the crown. Serve same day.*

342

DON LAST

Tropical Lemon Gateau

Gooseberry fool

$7\frac{1}{2}$ mins

Standing time: 5 mins

Gooseberry fool is a classic dessert in which the sharp flavour of the fruit is complemented by the sweetness of a creamy custard mixture. It is important for the texture that, even if the fruit is puréed by blender, it should be sieved to remove all the pips.

450g / 1lb gooseberries, topped and tailed
30ml / 2tbls water
15ml / 3tsp cornflour
150ml / ¼pt milk
1 egg, beaten
150ml / ¼pt double cream
60ml / 4tbls sugar
6 ratafia biscuits to decorate (optional)

SERVES 6

1 Place the gooseberries in a bowl with the water. Cover and microwave at 100% (High) for 6 minutes, stirring every 2 minutes until the fruit is soft.
2 Leave to stand for 5 minutes, then press through a sieve to make a purée.
3 Mix the cornflour with the milk in a small bowl. Microwave, uncovered, at 100% (High) for 1½-2 minutes until thick, stirring after 1 minute, beating well when cooked.
4 Mix the hot sauce with the purée, then stir the beaten egg into the hot mixture. Allow to cool.
5 Whip the cream with the sugar until thick, then fold it gently into the fruit custard.
6 Spoon the fool into six tall glasses, then leave to chill in the refrigerator for 2 hours.
7 Serve with ratafia biscuits.

VARIATION
Fruit fools: A fool is particularly refreshing made with tart fruit such as gooseberries, but any sharp flavoured fruit can be cooked in the same way to make 275ml / ½pt purée. If the flavour is too bland, add a little lemon juice according to taste.

Freezer notes

If using frozen gooseberries, place them in a bowl and microwave, uncovered, at 20-30% (Defrost) for 8-10 minutes, then allow to stand for 5 minutes. The cooked purée could be frozen, but cream should only be added after it has been thawed, as cream may separate after thawing.

DON LAST

Blackcurrant crème brûlée

10 mins

Standing time: none

100g / 4oz blackcurrants, stalks removed
15ml / 3tsp cornflour
30ml / 2tbls sugar
100ml / 3½fl oz water
4 egg yolks
275ml / ½pt single cream
45-60ml / 3-4tbls caster sugar

SERVES 6

1 Combine the blackcurrants, cornflour, sugar and water in a small bowl. Cover and microwave at 100% (High) for 3-3½ minutes until thick, stirring once.
2 Divide the blackcurrant mixture between 6 small ramekins, allow to cool then refrigerate.
3 Beat the egg yolks with the cream, then pour gently over the cold blackcurrant sauce.
4 Arrange the ramekins in a large circle in the cooker and microwave at 20-30% (Defrost) for 7-8 minutes until the topping is not quite set, but is no longer runny. Move the dishes around in the cooker and turn them every 2 minutes to ensure even cooking. Cool, then refrigerate overnight.
5 About 3 hours before serving, sprinkle the tops with the caster sugar, covering them completely.
6 Cook under a hot grill until the sugar melts. Chill thoroughly before serving so that the sugar sets to form a brittle layer.

Chocolate orange layers

3 mins

Standing time: none

This dessert can be made using any fresh fruit in season.

312g / 11oz can mandarin oranges
150ml / ¼pt double cream
15ml / 1tbls icing sugar
100g / 4oz plain cooking chocolate
2 eggs, separated

SERVES 6

1 Drain the mandarins, reserve the juice and 6 whole segments and set aside. Chop the remainder coarsely.
2 Whip the cream with the sugar until thick. Fold in the chopped

Chocolate Orange Layers

mandarins.
3 Break the chocolate into pieces in a bowl. Microwave, uncovered, at 50% (Medium) for 3 minutes, stirring after 1 minute.
4 Stir the egg yolks with 30ml / 2tbls of the reserved mandarin juice, then mix gently into the melted chocolate.
5 Whisk the egg whites until stiff and meringue-like, then fold in the chocolate mixture using a metal spoon, until smooth.
6 Starting with chocolate mousse, layer the 2 mixtures in six 100ml / 3½fl oz glasses. Finish each one off with a layer of chocolate.
7 Refrigerate for at least 1 hour, then serve topped with a mandarin. (Save remaining mandarin juice for a jelly or sauce.)

Freezer notes

If using frozen blackcurrants, thaw them at 20-30% (Defrost) for 2 minutes for 100g / 4oz fruit then use as in the recipe.

344

Making ice cream

For party desserts or a kiddies treat, home-made ice cream is everyone's favourite. The microwave will also be your favourite when you see the creamy smooth and subtly flavoured ice creams you can produce with it.

The secret of a smooth ice cream lies in the fat content, as this prevents large ice crystals forming during the freezing process. Double cream, whipped and flavoured, is a popular form of fat to use for ice creams, or, if you wish to reduce

the quantity of cream, try using a custard base. The recipe for basic vanilla ice cream given here has a custard base, made with milk and egg yolks.

The microwave is perfect for cooking custards. Conventionally made egg custards are notoriously

difficult: they stick and burn easily, and can overcook in seconds if you place the saucepan over direct heat. The microwave solves all those problems, however,

Left to right: *Chocolate, Vanilla and Strawberry Ice Cream*

since the food is heated rather than the container. You will also be able to achieve a smooth custard with comparatively little stirring.

For a smooth ice cream it is important to dissolve the sugar before freezing. So whisk the egg and sugar together until frothy, heat the milk and stir it in carefully to blend thoroughly. Then microwave the mixture until thick and creamy.

Try flavouring ice creams as suggested here, or experiment with your own ideas. Flavourings such as vanilla and peppermint are simple to add, while fruit purées can give you endless subtle variations as the seasons change. Alcohol can be used to dress up an ice cream, but be wary of adding too much — in large quantities it will prevent the mixture freezing; rum or brandy flavourings give good results and are less expensive. Add texture with nuts or chocolate drops or bits.

Freeze ice cream in shallow containers as the mixture will freeze more quickly. When it starts to harden around the edges, beat it well to add lightness and smoothness. Return it to the freezer to harden completely. To serve, remove from the freezer a little before time so it has time to soften, or thaw slightly in the microwave. Both flavour and texture are better when the ice is not totally frozen.

Vanilla ice cream

$\boxed{\textbf{5}\\ \text{mins}}$

Standing time: none

Serve this ice cream in scoops or blocks with wafers or biscuits. For other desserts, add sauces or fruits, or use to fill pancakes, sponge flans or meringue shells.

275ml / ½pt milk
2 eggs
100g / 4oz caster sugar
10ml / 2tsp vanilla flavouring
275ml / ½pt double or whipping cream

SERVES 6-8

How to microwave ice cream

Heat *the milk in a jug at 100% (High) for 2 minutes until hot but not boiling. Meanwhile, break the eggs into a large freezer/microwave container, add the sugar and whisk.*

Whisk *the hot milk gradually into the eggs. Microwave at 100% (High) for 3-3½ minutes, whisking after 2 minutes, then every 30 seconds until it has a coating consistency.*

Stir *in the flavouring and place cling film on the custard so it is touching the surface to prevent skin forming. Allow to cool, then leave to chill thoroughly in the refrigerator.*

RAY DUNS

Whip *the cream until just thick and standing in soft peaks; fold into the cold custard. Cover and freeze about 1 hour until frozen at the edges and slushy in the centre.*

Whisk *the partially frozen ice cream with an electric mixer or food processor until the mixture is quite smooth. Cover and freeze for a further 3-4 hours until the ice cream is quite firm.*

To serve, *soften the ice cream for 30-45 minutes in the refrigerator, or 20-30 minutes at room temperature; or microwave at 20-30% (Defrost) for 30-40 seconds just before serving.*

346

Chocolate ice cream balls

9½ mins

Standing time: none

½ quantity Vanilla Ice Cream
(see opposite)
225g / 8oz plain chocolate cake
covering, or plain chocolate

MAKES 30

1 Put a baking tray in the freezer to chill.
2 Microwave the ice cream at 20-30% (Defrost) for 30-40 seconds to soften slightly. Use a melon baller to scoop the ice cream into balls. Place on the chilled baking tray, insert a cocktail stick into each. Return to the freezer to harden.
3 Break the chocolate into a small bowl and microwave at 50% (Medium) for 4 minutes until melted and smooth, stirring once or twice.
4 Quickly dip each ball in the chocolate, coating evenly. Return the chocolate to the microwave to soften if necessary. Place the dipped balls on the tray, remove the cocktail sticks and freeze until needed. Serve with rolled wafers.

VARIATION
While the coating chocolate is still moist, dip the balls quickly in finely chopped walnuts, crumbled cereals or hundreds and thousands.

Strawberry ice cream

5 mins

Standing time: none

2 × 400g / 14.1oz cans
strawberries or 450g / 1lb fresh
strawberries
275ml / ½pt milk
2 eggs
100g / 4oz caster sugar
275ml / ½pt double or whipping
cream

SERVES 6-8

1 Drain the canned strawberries thoroughly and chop (reserve the syrup for another dish). If using fresh strawberries, hull and mash them. Put the strawberries in a dish and chill in the refrigerator

RAY DUNS

until ready to use.
2 Prepare the custard as directed in Steps 1-3 for Vanilla Ice Cream, opposite.
3 Whip the cream until thick and standing in soft peaks, then fold into the cold custard together with the chopped or mashed strawberries. Mix well.
4 Cover and freeze for about 1 hour until frozen around the edges and slushy in the centre. Remove from the freezer and whisk until completely smooth.
5 Cover and freeze for 3-4 hours until firm. Soften to serve, see Step 6, opposite.

Cook's notes

For a smooth ice cream, blend, then sieve the strawberries. Add a few drops of colouring with the cream for a deeper colour. Adding 50g / 2oz crumbled meringues after whisking the partially frozen ice cream also gives a crunchy texture.

Chocolate Ice Cream Balls

Chocolate ice cream

7½ mins

Standing time: none

275ml / ½pt milk
2 eggs
75g / 3oz caster sugar
100g / 4oz plain chocolate
2.5ml / ½tsp vanilla flavouring
275ml / ½pt double or whipping
cream

SERVES 6-8

1 Microwave the milk as directed in Step 1 for Vanilla Ice Cream, opposite, and combine the eggs and sugar as directed. Gradually whisk in the milk.
2 Break the chocolate into a small bowl; microwave at 100% (High) for 2½-3 minutes until melted. Whisk into the egg mixture.
3 Continue to microwave and freeze as directed in Steps 2-6, opposite.

347

Coffee ice cream

5 mins

Standing time: none

275ml / ½pt milk
30ml / 2tbls instant coffee
  granules
2 eggs
100g / 4oz caster sugar
125ml / 5fl oz double or whipping
  cream
125ml / 5fl oz natural yoghurt
grated plain chocolate, to serve

SERVES 6-8

1 Pour the milk into a jug and sprinkle over the coffee granules. Heat the milk and continue to prepare and microwave the custard as directed in Steps 1-3 for Vanilla Ice Cream, page 346.
2 Whip the cream and fold into the cold custard with the yoghurt. Cover and freeze for about 1 hour until frozen at the edges.
3 Whisk, freeze and serve as directed in Steps 5-6 for Vanilla Ice Cream, page 346. Sprinkle with grated chocolate, if wished.

Almond ice cream

5 mins

Standing time: none

275ml / ½pt milk
2 eggs
75g / 3oz caster sugar
5ml / 1tsp almond flavouring
275ml / ½pt double or whipping
  cream
50g / 2oz ratafias or macaroons,
  crumbled
golden syrup, to serve

SERVES 6-8

1 Prepare and microwave the custard as directed in Steps 1-4 for Vanilla Ice Cream, page 346.
2 Whisk the partially frozen ice cream until smooth and stir in the crumbled ratafias or macaroons.
3 Cover and freeze for 3-4 hours until firm and serve as directed in Step 6 on page 346. Drizzle with golden syrup just before serving.

Above: *Coffee Ice Cream*
Below: *Almond Ice Cream*

RAY DUNS

Pineapple ice cream

3½ mins

Standing time: none

1 large pineapple
caster sugar for sprinkling
finely grated rind and juice of 1
    small lemon
15ml / 1tbls icing sugar
125ml / 5fl oz milk
1 egg
50g / 2oz caster sugar
125ml / 5fl oz double cream
30ml / 2tbls kirsch or rum

SERVES 6

1 Cut the pineapple in half lengthways, including the leaves. Scoop out the flesh, taking care not to pierce the skin. Drain and reserve the juice; sprinkle each pineapple half with caster sugar, cover and chill until serving.
2 Remove the pineapple core and finely chop or process the flesh. Put into a container, stir in the lemon rind, juice and icing sugar. Cover and freeze until slushy.
3 Microwave the milk in a jug at 100% (High) for 1½ minutes until hot. Break the egg into a freezer / microwave container and whisk in the sugar. Continue to prepare the custard as directed in Steps 2-4 for the Vanilla Ice Cream, page 346, microwaving the egg and milk mixture for only 2-2½ minutes. The first freezing need only be 45 minutes.
4 Whisk the ice cream until smooth, stir in the frozen pineapple and kirsch or rum. Cover and freeze for 2-3 hours until firm.
5 To serve, scoop or spoon the ice cream into the pineapple shells and serve immediately.

Cook's notes

The Pineapple Ice Cream softens more quickly than the other flavoured ice creams because of the high proportion of pineapple and juice in it. For this reason, the ice cream does not need softening in the microwave or refrigerator before serving.

Walnut Spice Pie

Walnut spice pie

9½ mins

Standing time: none

23cm / 9in cooked Wheatmeal
    Crumb Case (see page 324)
275ml / ½pt milk
2.5ml / ½tsp grated nutmeg
2.5ml / ½tsp ground cinnamon
2 eggs
100g / 4oz caster sugar
275ml / ½pt double or whipping
    cream
50g / 2oz crystallized or
    preserved ginger, chopped
75g / 3oz walnuts, finely chopped
50g / 2oz plain chocolate

SERVES 6-8

1 Pour the milk into a jug, sprinkle over the nutmeg and cinnamon, stir well, then continue as directed in Steps 1-4 for Vanilla Ice Cream, page 346.
2 Remove from the freezer and whisk until smooth. Stir in the chopped ginger and walnuts. Spoon the mixture into the prepared crumb case, smooth the surface and freeze for 2-3 hours.
3 To serve, transfer the pie to the refrigerator for about 20 minutes to soften. Microwave the chocolate in a small bowl at 50% (Medium) for 2½-3 minutes; stir once or twice. Drizzle over the pie.

Apricot brandy ice cream

25 mins

Standing time: none

225g / 8oz pre-soaked dried
    apricots
575ml / 1pt water
30ml / 2tbls icing sugar
30ml / 2tbls brandy or Drambuie
275ml / ½pt milk
2 eggs
100g / 4oz caster sugar
275ml / ½pt double or whipping
    cream

SERVES 6-8

1 Put the apricots and water in a bowl, cover and microwave at 100% (High) for 20 minutes, stirring several times until the apricots are soft and the liquid mostly absorbed. Cool, then purée in a blender or food processor. Stir in the icing sugar and brandy or Drambuie. Cover and chill in the refrigerator.
2 Prepare and microwave the custard as directed in Steps 1-3 for Vanilla Ice Cream, page 346.
3 Whip the cream until just thick and standing in soft peaks, then fold into the cold custard with the apricot purée. Freeze for 1 hour.
4 Whisk the ice cream until smooth. Cover and freeze for 3-4 hours. Soften as directed in Step 6 on page 346 before serving with wafer biscuits, if wished.

Creams and custards

Use your microwave to make smooth, silky creams or custards for the family. Then with the addition of more sophisticated flavourings you can transform them into elegant party desserts.

On a conventional cooker, cream desserts can turn lumpy, curdle or stick to the bottom of the saucepan. Cooking them in a microwave eliminates these problems; they don't need to be stirred continuously and will not stick to the dish.

To make a successful custard in the microwave you need slightly less liquid than you would normally use because there is less evaporation. Make sure the cornflour is blended thoroughly with the cold liquid before heating and, if eggs are added, blend them in carefully before cooking.

Vanilla custard cream

8 mins

Standing time: none

50g / 2oz caster sugar
30ml / 2tbls cornflour
15ml / 1tbls plain flour
500ml / 18fl oz milk
3-4 egg yolks
25g / 1oz butter
2.5ml / ½tsp vanilla flavouring

SERVES 6-8

1 Blend the caster sugar, cornflour, plain flour and milk together in a 1.4-1.7L / 2½-3pt bowl mixing well with a whisk.
2 Microwave at 100% (High) for 7-7½ minutes until thick, stirring vigorously with a hand whisk every 2 minutes.
3 Lightly beat the yolks in a separate bowl and mix in 90ml / 6tbls of the hot custard. Blend thoroughly, then stir the yolk mixture into the remaining custard.
4 Microwave for a further 1-2 minutes or until thick.
5 Beat in the butter and vanilla flavouring, then cover with cling film or greaseproof paper. Leave to cool.

Flavoured creams

Chocolate cream: omit the sugar and butter and add 100g / 4oz plain dark chocolate, broken into small pieces, to the blended flour and milk mixture before microwaving. Stir vigorously every 2 minutes until the mixture is thick.

Banana cream: fold 2 sliced bananas into the custard with the vanilla flavouring. Serve in individual long glasses, and top each serving with a banana slice.

Coffee walnut cream: use half brown sugar and add 10ml / 2tsp instant coffee to the mixture before microwaving. Stir in 25g / 1oz chopped walnuts with the vanilla if preferred. Top each serving with 5ml / 1tsp of whipped cream and a walnut.

Butterscotch cream: substitute light soft brown sugar for the caster sugar. If wished, stir in 25g / 1oz chopped walnuts with the vanilla for extra flavour. Pipe a swirl of whipped cream on top.

Eggnog cream: make the Vanilla Cream with 4 egg yolks. Stir 5ml / 1tsp rum flavouring and 1.5ml / $\frac{1}{4}$tsp ground nutmeg in with the vanilla flavouring. Spoon into tall stemmed glasses. Serve topped with whipped cream (125ml / 4fl oz is sufficient for 6 glasses) and sprinkle with grated nutmeg.

Strawberry cream: make the Vanilla Cream with 4 egg yolks. When cold, fold in 125ml / 4fl oz whipping cream, whipped. Layer the custard with the strawberries (see below) and a little of their juice in individual sundae dishes or long-stemmed glasses. Top with a slice of strawberry.

For the strawberry layer: microwave 450g / 1lb frozen strawberries in a large mixing bowl at 25% (Low) for 6 minutes, stirring carefully with a spatula every 2 minutes. Halve the strawberries, which will still be firm, reserving 6 slices for decoration. Keep these 6 slices frozen. Return the remaining strawberries to the bowl and sprinkle over 15ml / 1tbls caster sugar and 15ml / 1tbls brandy (optional). Microwave at 25% (Low) for 2½-3 minutes until just thawed, stirring every minute.

Coconut cream: stir about 50g / 2oz unsweetened desiccated coconut into the mixture before microwaving. Add 2.5ml / ½tsp almond flavouring with the vanilla.

From left to right: *Banana Cream, Butterscotch Cream, Chocolate Cream, Strawberry Cream, Coffee Walnut Cream, Eggnog Cream.*

Brandy Alexander

3 mins

Standing time: none

30ml / 2tbls caster sugar
10ml / 2tsp cornflour
275ml / ½pt whipping cream

50g / 2oz plain chocolate
30ml / 2tbls crème de cacao
    liqueur
15ml / 1tbls brandy

TO DECORATE
15ml / 1tbls hazelnuts, toasted
dark chocolate, chopped
SERVES 4

Microtip

Toast the hazelnuts in the microwave: spread them out in a dish and microwave at 100% (High) for 5 minutes, stirring every minute to prevent burning.

How to microwave Brandy Alexander

Mix *together the caster sugar, cornflour and half the whipping cream in a 1.4L / 2½pt mixing bowl. Break the plain chocolate into small pieces and stir them into the cream mixture with a wooden spoon, making sure everything is thoroughly mixed.*

Microwave *at 50% (Medium) for 3 minutes or until very thick, stirring after 1 minute, then every 30 seconds. Stir in the crème de cacao liqueur, leave to cool, then chill for 1 hour. Whisk together the brandy and remaining cream.*

Fold *the brandy cream into the chilled chocolate mixture carefully until evenly mixed. Spoon the mixture into 4 individual serving dishes. Decorate with chopped hazelnuts and pieces of dark bitter chocolate and chill in the refrigerator for 1-2 hours.*

Crème au chocolat

3 mins

Standing time: none

225ml / 8fl oz single cream
45ml / 3tbls caster sugar
150g / 5oz plain chocolate
3 egg yolks
5ml / 1tsp vanilla flavouring
SERVES 6

1 Mix the cream, sugar and chococolate in a 1.4L / 2½pt bowl.
2 Microwave at 100% (High) for 3 minutes or until thick and well blended, stirring vigorously every minute. Do not allow to boil.
3 Beat the egg yolks and vanilla until well blended and pale in colour. Gradually beat the chocolate mixture into the yolks and pour into 75ml / 3fl oz ramekin dishes or small wine glasses. Chill for at least 2 hours.

Crème au Chocolat

International desserts

Make a fitting finale to any meal with one of these classic international desserts. The microwave can help you to create authentic and delicious dishes in less than half the time of conventional cooking.

This tempting selection of desserts from places as far-flung as Florida and Sweden will show off the versatility of your microwave to the best advantage and you will find the fast, clean efficiency of your microwave invaluable.

Baked sponge puddings and cake desserts are light and moist cooked by microwave – irresistible when fresh. The Plum Duff should be eaten hot, or be refreshed by microwaving at 100% (High) for 30 seconds per portion if necessary. The Devil's Food cake

stays moist because of the frosting and the almonds in the mixture, so it will keep for 1-2 days in the refrigerator. Lemon Zabaglione starts to lose volume after a few minutes, so serve immediately.

Florida Orange Mousse (page 357)

353

Brown bread ice cream

6 mins

Standing time: none

2 eggs plus 2 egg whites
425ml / ¾pt milk
175g / 6oz sugar
15ml / 1tbls dark rum
275ml / ½pt double cream
100g / 4oz brown breadcrumbs,
   toasted
crisp biscuits to serve

SERVES 4-6

1 Place the whole eggs, milk and sugar in a bowl and mix well. Microwave at 100% (High) for 6 minutes, stirring every 3 minutes, until smooth and slightly thickened. Cool.
2 Mix in the rum and cream. Pour into a large freezer container and freeze until almost firm.
3 Remove the half-frozen ice cream from the freezer and turn into a bowl. Whisk until smooth and free from large ice crystals.
4 Using clean beaters, whisk the egg whites until they hold stiff peaks. Fold into the ice cream with the breadcrumbs, using a large spoon. Return to the container and freeze for 3-4 hours. Serve in chilled glasses with crisp biscuits.

Jamaican South Seas Bubble

Russian pudding

13 mins

Standing time: 5 mins

450g / 1lb cooking apples, peeled,
   cored and cubed
75g / 3oz soft brown sugar
25g / 1oz butter
grated zest and juice of 1 lemon
60ml / 12tsp cornflour
575ml / 1pt milk
30ml / 2tbls sugar
1 egg, beaten
grated nutmeg to sprinkle

SERVES 4

1 Place the apples in a large pie dish with the soft brown sugar, butter, lemon zest and juice and mix well. Cover and microwave at 100% (High) for 3 minutes, stirring once.
2 Blend the cornflour with the milk, adding a little at a time and stirring well. Microwave at 100% (High) for 4-5 minutes, stirring three times until smooth and thickened.
3 Stir in the sugar and egg and mix well. Pour this custard over the fruit mixture, then mix thoroughly. Sprinkle grated nutmeg to taste over the top.
4 Microwave at 30% (Low) for 6 minutes, turning the dish twice. Leave to stand for 5 minutes.

Jamaican South Seas bubble

6 mins

Standing time: none

50g / 2oz butter
100g / 4oz demerara sugar
45ml / 3tbls lime juice
2.5ml / ½tsp ground mixed spice
1 small pineapple, peeled, cored
   and cubed
2 papaya, peeled, seeded and
   sliced
1 mango or guava, peeled, stoned
   and sliced
2 bananas, peeled and sliced
50g / 2oz dried figs, peeled and
   quartered
60ml / 4tbls dark rum or coconut
   liqueur
45ml / 3tbls shelled Brazil nuts,
   coarsely chopped
ice cream or soured cream to
   serve

SERVES 4

1 Put the butter into a large heat-proof dish, cover and microwave at 100% (High) for 1 minute until half melted.
2 Add the sugar, lime juice and spice and mix thoroughly. Microwave at 100% (High) for 2 minutes, covered, stirring once during cooking.
3 Add the pineapple, papaya, mango or guava, bananas and figs. Toss gently to coat in the spiced butter. Cover and microwave at 100% (High) for 2-3 minutes, stirring gently once, until the fruit has softened a little, but still holds its shape firmly.
4 Add the rum or coconut liqueur and stir well to blend.
5 Cover again and microwave at 100% (High) for a further 1 minute.
6 Sprinkle with the Brazil nuts and serve warm with ice cream or soured cream.

Microtips

Drained canned tropical fruits can be used; as they are softer than the fresh ones, reduce the microwaving time by 30-60 seconds before adding liqueur.

RAY DUNS

Swedish apple torte

18 mins

Standing time: none

25ml / 5tsp sugar
1.25ml / ¼tsp ground cinnamon
350g / 12oz plain flour
large pinch of salt
100g / 4oz butter or margarine, diced
100g / 4oz lard or shortening, diced
1 egg, beaten
45ml / 3tbls whipping cream
5 drops of yellow food colouring
385g / 13½oz can apple pie filling
125ml / 4fl oz whipping cream

SERVES 8

How to microwave Swedish apple torte

Mix *the sugar with the cinnamon. Sift the flour and salt into a bowl. Rub in the diced fats, using fingertips or a mixer, until the mixture resembles fine breadcrumbs.*

Combine *the egg, cream and food colouring. Stir into the crumb mixture and mix with a fork to make a firm but pliable dough. Knead on a lightly floured board until smooth.*

Cut *the dough into quarters. Roll out each on a lightly floured board or greaseproof paper and cut into a 25cm / 10in round using an inverted dish as a guide.*

Sprinkle *each circle with a quarter of the cinnamon sugar mixture. Using a plain 7.5cm / 3in cutter, cut a circle of dough from the centre of each of the pastry rounds. Halve and set aside to use later as decoration.*

Microwave *each ring on double absorbent paper at 100% (High) for 4-6 minutes; turn every minute. Cool. Microwave reserved rounds on absorbent paper at 100% (High) for 2-3 minutes, turning twice.*

Place *one ring on a serving dish. Top with a third of the apple filling. Repeat twice, ending with a plain ring, then chill for 30 minutes. Top with whipped cream and pastry semi-circles. Store unfilled layers for 1-2 days.*

355

French apricot tart

13 mins

Standing time: none

100g / 4oz sugar
150ml / ¼pt water
700g / 1½lb apricots, halved and
    stoned
2 egg yolks
60ml / 4tbls caster sugar
grated zest of 1 orange
25ml / 5tsp cornflour
20ml / 4tsp plain flour
275ml / ½pt milk
1 egg white
23cm / 9in cooked pastry case
    (see page 28)
30ml / 2tbls flaked almonds,
    toasted

SERVES 6

1 Mix the sugar with the water in a bowl. Microwave at 100% (High) for 2 minutes to dissolve the sugar. Mix in the apricots.
2 Cover and microwave at 100% (High) for 4-6 minutes, stirring once, until apricots are just cooked.
3 Remove the apricots using a slotted spoon and set aside to cool.
4 Microwave the remaining syrup at 100% (High) for 3-4 minutes until thick and syrupy, then cool.
5 Whisk the egg yolks with half the caster sugar until thick. Add the orange zest, cornflour and flour, whisking thoroughly.
6 Pour the milk into a jug and microwave at 100% (High) for 2 minutes. Slowly pour the milk on to the egg mixture, stirring continuously. Microwave at 100% (High) for a further 2-2½ minutes, stirring three times, until smooth and thick. Set aside to cool.
7 Whisk the egg white until it stands in stiff peaks. Whisk in the remaining caster sugar until thick and glossy. Fold into the custard using a large metal spoon.
8 Spoon the custard mixture into the prepared pastry case, rounding it slightly in the centre. Arrange the apricots on the top, cut side down.
9 Brush or spoon the cooled syrup glaze over the top and scatter with the almonds. Chill lightly. Best eaten the same day.

Lemon zabaglione

3 mins

Standing time: none

1 large egg
2 large egg yolks
60ml / 4tbls caster sugar
150ml / ¼pt Marsala, sweet
    sherry or sweet white wine
finely grated zest of 1 lemon
sponge finger biscuits or langues
    de chat, to serve

SERVES 4

1 Put the egg and egg yolks into a large bowl and whisk until smooth and creamy. Add the sugar and continue whisking until beginning to thicken.
2 Pour the Marsala, sherry or wine into a jug. Add the lemon zest and microwave at 100% (High) for 1½ minutes until just boiling.
3 Pour the lemon liquid on to the egg mixture and whisk until slightly thickened. Microwave at 30% (Low) for 1½ minutes.
4 Whisk the mixture again until very thick and frothy — about 4-5 minutes.
5 Pour the zabaglione into warmed dessert glasses and serve at once with the sponge finger biscuits or langues de chat.

Plum duff

10 mins

Standing time: 5-10 mins

60ml / 4tbls currants
60ml / 4tbls raisins
60ml / 4tbls sultanas
30ml / 2tbls sweet sherry
30ml / 2tbls orange juice
100g / 4oz self-raising flour
5ml / 1tsp ground cinnamon
5ml / 1tsp ground mixed spice
100g / 4oz shredded suet
100g / 4oz brown breadcrumbs
75g / 3oz dark brown sugar
1 egg, beaten
75ml / 5tbls milk
custard, to serve

SERVES 4-6

1 Mix currants, raisins, sultanas, sherry and orange juice in a bowl. Cover and microwave at 100% (High) for 2 minutes. Cool.
2 Sift flour, cinnamon and mixed spice. Stir in all the other ingredients and beat thoroughly.
3 Turn into a lightly greased 1.1L / 2pt bowl and level the top. Cover with pleated cling film to allow for rising and microwave at 100% (High) for 8 minutes.
4 Stand for 5-10 minutes, then turn out onto a warmed dish. Serve with pouring custard.

356

Florida orange mousse

2½ mins

Standing time: 5 mins

Microwaving is an ideal way to thaw frozen orange juice concentrate, whether you intend to use it for a dessert or for a drink.

178ml / 6¼fl oz carton frozen orange juice concentrate
3 eggs, separated
75g / 3oz caster sugar
15ml / 1tbls orange-flavoured liqueur (optional)
15ml / 1tbls lemon juice
10ml / 2tsp powdered gelatine
45ml / 3tbls water
150ml / ¼pt double cream

DECORATION
150ml / ¼pt whipping cream
1 small orange, thinly sliced
30ml / 2tbls chopped nuts

SERVES 4-6

1 Remove any metal lid or surround from the carton of orange juice and microwave at 20% (Defrost) for 2-3 minutes, stirring twice. Allow to stand for 5 minutes.
2 Put the egg yolks and sugar into a bowl and whisk until thick and creamy. Whisk in half of the orange juice concentrate. (The rest can be diluted according to the manufacturer's instructions, and served as a drink.)
3 Whisk in the liqueur and lemon juice.
4 Sprinkle the gelatine over the water in a small bowl and soak until spongy. Microwave at 100% (High) for 30 seconds until the liquid is clear and the gelatine has dissolved. Allow to cool slightly.
5 Whisk the egg whites until they stand in soft peaks. Whip the cream until it holds soft peaks. Stir the gelatine into the orange mixture, then fold in the cream and egg whites using a large metal spoon.
6 Pour into a serving dish and chill for 2-4 hours until set.
7 Whip the cream and use to pipe rosettes around the edge of the mousse. Decorate with slices of orange and chopped nuts.

Devil's food cake

10 mins

Standing time: 10 mins

100g / 4oz butter, softened
100g / 4oz caster sugar
2 eggs, beaten
100g / 4oz self-raising flour, sifted
90ml / 6tbls cocoa powder, sifted
30ml / 2tbls ground almonds
125ml / 4fl oz milk
60ml / 4tbls golden syrup

FROSTING
50g / 2oz plain chocolate
50g / 2oz butter
90ml / 6tbls milk
450g / 1lb icing sugar, sifted
5ml / 1tsp vanilla flavouring

SERVES 8-10

1 Line a 1.1L / 2pt straight-sided deep cake or soufflé dish with cling film or line the base with greaseproof paper.
2 Cream the butter and sugar together until light and fluffy. Add the eggs, a little at a time, beating well.

Devil's Food Cake

3 Fold in the flour, cocoa and ground almonds using a large metal spoon. Add the milk and golden syrup and mix thoroughly.
4 Spoon the mixture into the prepared dish and microwave at 100% (High) for 6-7 minutes, turning every 1½ minutes. When cooked, the top of the cake will still look slightly wet. It will dry out while the cake stands for 10 minutes in the dish. Turn out on to a wire rack, remove the cling film or paper and leave to cool.
5 To make the frosting, break the chocolate into a bowl. Add the butter and milk and microwave at 50% (Medium) for 4-5 minutes, stirring once, until smooth.
6 Add the icing sugar and vanilla and mix well. Leave to cool for 10 minutes, then beat until smooth, thick and glossy.
7 Split the cool cake in half horizontally. Use a quarter of the frosting to sandwich the two halves together, then use the rest to cover the top and sides of the cake. Swirl the frosting decoratively using a palette knife.

357

Make and frost a sponge cake

Cakes can be cooked very quickly in the microwave. As they do not brown like conventional cakes, give them a touch of colour with one of the exciting frostings shown here.

One of the simplest and most versatile cakes to make in your microwave is a basic Victoria sponge, made with an 'all in one' mixture. A microwaved sponge feels heavier than a conventionally cooked cake, but the taste and texture are beautifully moist. However, microwave sponges dry out quickly, so serve on the day of making.

Because plain sponge cakes do not brown when cooked by microwave, they do look much more attractive when decorated with a complementary frosting.

Victoria sponge cake

| 5½ mins |

Standing time: 10 mins

175g / 6oz butter or margarine, softened
175g / 6oz self-raising flour
2.5ml / ½tsp baking powder
175g / 6oz caster sugar
3 eggs
30-45ml / 2-3tbls milk
frosting (see page 360)

MAKES A 20cm / 8in ROUND CAKE OR A 22 x 22cm / 8½ x 8½in SQUARE CAKE

This cake has been tested on all four standard wattages. See the times below (in minutes).

Wattage	Round	Square
700	5-6	6-7
650	5½-6½	7-8
600	6-7	7½-8½
500	7-8	8-9

Frostings *pictured left to right*
Top row: *Chocolate Hazelnut, Buttercream, Maple* **2nd row:** *Lemon, Butterscotch, Orange* **3rd row:** *Peanut Butter, Chocolate, Browned Butter* **Bottom row:** *Coffee, Cherry nut, Butternut.*

How to microwave a Victoria sponge cake

Grease *a 20cm / 8in soufflé dish or microwave-safe 22 x 22cm / 8½ x 8½in square dish and line the base with greased greaseproof paper.*

Beat *together the butter, flour, baking powder, sugar, eggs and milk for 1-2 minutes until blended. Spoon into the cake dish.*

Microwave *round cake at 100% (High) for 5½-6½ minutes, until edges are shrunken from sides of dish — top will still be moist in the centre. Rotate dish ¼ turn every 2 minutes.*

Microwave *square cake at 100% (High) for 6½-8 minutes, or until edges have shrunk from sides of dish and centre begins to dome. Rotate dish ¼ turn every minute for even cooking.*

Leave *the cake to stand in the dish for 10 minutes, then turn out onto a wire rack. Remove paper and let cool.*

Split *in half and sandwich with jam when the cake is cold. Sieve icing sugar over the top or frost as desired.*

359

Fancy frostings

Make your microwaved sponge cakes really interesting with a variety of frostings. The quantities given in our recipes will frost the top and sides of one round- or square-shaped cake.

Buttercream frosting

[30 secs]

Standing time: none

15g / ½oz butter or margarine
15ml / 1tbls cream or milk
pinch of salt
225g / 8oz icing sugar
1.5ml / ¼tsp vanilla or rum
   flavouring

1 Combine the butter, cream and salt in a mixing bowl. Microwave at 50% (Medium) for 30-40 seconds or until bubbling.
2 Add the icing sugar and flavouring and beat until the frosting is smooth and of a spreading consistency, adding a few more drops of cream or milk to thin the mixture a little if necessary.

VARIATIONS
Coffee Frosting: Add 1.5ml / ¼tsp instant coffee powder to the butter mixture and mix in well before microwaving.
Maple Frosting: Beat in 10ml / 2tsp maple syrup or flavouring with the sugar.
Peanut Butter Frosting: Add 15ml / 1tbls peanut butter to the mixture before microwaving.
Butternut Frosting: Increase butter to 25g / 1oz and add 25g / 1oz finely chopped nuts before microwaving.

Butterscotch frosting

[1½ mins]

Standing time: none

25g / 1oz butter or margarine
15ml / 1tbls milk
45ml / 3tbls soft dark brown sugar
225g / 8oz icing sugar

1 Combine butter, milk and brown sugar in a bowl. Microwave at 100% (High) for 1-2 minutes, until mixture boils, stirring halfway through. Boil for 30 seconds.
2 Add the icing sugar, and beat until of a spreading consistency.

VARIATION
Browned Butter: Microwave butter at 100% (High) for 1-3 minutes, until brown, then continue as above.

How to make and use Buttercream frosting

Combine *butter, cream and salt in a mixing bowl. Microwave at 50% (Medium) for 30-40 seconds until bubbling, to give a good cooked flavour.*

Add *the sugar and flavouring. Beat until smooth and of a spreading consistency. Add more sugar to thicken the mixture, add liquid to thin.*

Make *the frosting stiff enough to hold deep swirls, but soft enough to look moist. Warm frosting may need thinning as it cools.*

Spread *a thin layer of frosting over the sides of the cake with a palette knife; repeat with a heavier coating using about two thirds of the frosting.*

Frost *the top of the cake in the same way using the remaining frosting. If freezing the cake, freeze before decorating, then frost when thawed.*

Make *swirls, using a palette knife or the back of a teaspoon. Decorate the top of the frosting with a sprinkling of coconut or chopped nuts, if wished.*

360

Chocolate frosting

| 2 mins |

Standing time: 3-5 mins

30ml / 2tbls cocoa powder
25g / 1oz butter or margarine
30ml / 1fl oz milk
225g / 8oz icing sugar
2.5ml / ½tsp mint flavouring

1 In a bowl, combine the cocoa, butter and milk. Microwave at 50% (Medium) for 2 minutes, stirring after 1½ minutes.
2 Stir in remaining ingredients. Leave to stand for 3-5 minutes. Beat frosting until smooth and of spreading consistency.

VARIATION
Chocolate Hazelnut: Add 25g / 1oz hazelnuts to the chocolate mixture before microwaving. Omit the mint.

Lemon frosting

| ½ min |

Standing time: none

15g / ½oz butter or margarine
7.5ml / 1½tsp cream or milk
7.5ml / 1½tsp lemon juice
2.5ml / ½tsp grated lemon zest
pinch of salt
225g / 8oz icing sugar
1.5ml / ¼tsp vanilla flavouring
1-2 drops yellow food colouring

1 In a mixing bowl, combine the butter, cream or milk, lemon juice, grated zest and salt. Microwave at 50% (Medium) for 30-40 seconds, or until the mixture has started bubbling.
2 Add the sugar, vanilla and colouring. Beat until smooth and of a spreading consistency; thin with a few drops of cream or milk if the frosting is too thick.

VARIATIONS
Orange: Substitute 30ml / 2tbls orange juice for the cream and lemon juice and 10ml / 2tsp orange zest for the lemon.
Cherry Nut: For more colour, use 15ml / 1tbls bottled cherry juice for the lemon juice and omit the zest. After microwaving, stir in 30ml / 2tbls each chopped maraschino cherries and walnuts, together with the sugar. Omit food colouring.

Microtips

Leftover frosting can be stored in the refrigerator. Soften cold frosting by microwaving at 100% (High) for a few seconds.

Luscious, moist sponge cake is coated with lemon frosting and filled with lemon curd.

361

Savoury crackers

Microwaving savoury crackers is really simple, whether you are making them to serve with cheese or as cocktail snacks. The savoury flavours and nutty textures will make this selection firm family favourites.

The flavour of cheese, herbs and spices will make these assorted crackers quite irresistible. Although microwaving will not brown the tops, the use of coatings such as sesame seeds will add colour, as will paprika, wholemeal flour, or a few drops of food colouring in the mixture.

These crackers are simple to make, and look quite plain; but they can be made to look more attractive by using fluted cutters or a fluted pastry wheel for stamping out or cutting, or by crimping the edges of the shortbread-style biscuits which are cut in wedges.

Ten minutes should be enough

for preparing and microwaving a batch of crackers, so make sure you have a good stock of basic dry ingredients (flour, herbs, oats, seasonings and toppings), and you will be able to conjure them up at the last minute for any occasion.

Wholewheat and Rye Crackers

Rye crackers

6¾ mins

Standing time: none

60ml / 4tbls plain flour
60ml / 4tbls rye flour
1.5ml / ¼tsp salt
5ml / 1tsp caraway seeds
75g / 3oz butter or margarine
30-45ml / 2-3tbls cold water

MAKES 42

Wholewheat crackers

6¾ mins

Standing time: none

100g / 4oz plain wholewheat flour
1.5ml / ¼tsp salt
10ml / 2tsp sesame seeds
75g / 3oz butter or margarine
30-45ml / 2-3tbls cold water

MAKES 42

Cheese sticks

9 mins

Standing time: none

100g / 4oz plain flour
1.5ml / ¼tsp salt
10ml / 2tsp caraway or dill seeds (optional)
60g / 2½oz lard or white vegetable fat
100g / 4oz Cheddar or Edam cheese, grated
45ml / 3tbls water
3-4 drops yellow food colouring

MAKES 42

1 Mix the flour with the salt and caraway or dill seeds if used.
2 Rub in the fat, using the fingertips, until the mixture resembles fine breadcrumbs.
3 Stir in the cheese, mixing well.
4 Mix the water with the food colouring. Sprinkle it over the rubbed-in mixture and bind together using a fork to make a firm but pliable dough. Knead lightly until smooth.
5 Roll out on a lightly floured surface to a rectangle 38 × 23cm / 15 × 9in. Trim the edges neatly with a sharp knife. Sprinkle lightly with extra salt if liked.
6 Using a sharp knife, cut into 7.5 × 2.5cm / 3 × 1in sticks.
7 Arrange 14 sticks on a greased microwave baking tray or large flat plate. Microwave at 100% (High) for 3 minutes (for 500 watt, 3½ minutes), turning after 2 minutes, checking constantly.
8 Remove at once with a palette knife and transfer to a wire rack to cool. Repeat with two more batches of sticks.

Microtips

Microwaved crackers are not crisp when just cooked, so care should be taken when moving them to the wire rack to cool.

How to microwave Rye crackers and Wholewheat crackers

Combine *the flour(s), salt and seeds in a bowl. Cut in the butter with a whisk at low speed, or by rubbing in with the fingertips.*

Sprinkle *the water over the crumble mixture. Bind together with a fork to make a firm but pliable dough. Knead lightly until smooth.*

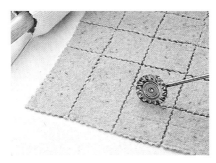

Roll *out on a lightly floured surface to a rectangle 35 × 30cm / 14 × 12in. Trim edges and cut into 5cm / 2in squares with a fluted pastry wheel.*

Arrange *11-14 crackers on a lightly greased microwave baking tray or large plate, spacing them evenly so that all receive similar energy.*

Microwave *at 100% (High) for 2¼-2½ minutes (500 watt, 3-3½ minutes), turning the crackers once. They should be dry and firm to touch.*

Transfer *to a rack to cool using a metal spatula. The crackers will become crisp as they cool. Store in an airtight tin for up to 2 weeks.*

363

Savoury oaties

13 mins

Standing time: 5 mins

75ml / 5tbls water
25g / 1oz butter
225g / 8oz medium oatmeal
1.5ml / ¼tsp bicarbonate of soda
1.5ml / ¼tsp salt
5ml / 1tsp chopped sage or thyme

MAKES 8

1 Put the water and fat in a small bowl. Microwave at 100% (High) for 1 minute to melt the fat. Allow to cool slightly.
2 Mix the oatmeal with the bicarbonate of soda, salt and sage or thyme in a bowl.
3 Stir in the cooled liquid and mix to form a smooth dough. Form this into a ball and place on a microwave baking tray or large flat plate. Pat out using your hand to make a 23cm / 9in round. Pinch and flute the edges decoratively. Mark into eight wedges with a knife.
4 Microwave at 50% (Medium) for 12 minutes (500 watt, 7-9 minutes), giving the tray ¼ turn every 3 minutes. Allow to stand for 5 minutes.
5 Re-mark the wedges with a sharp knife and transfer to a wire rack to cool.
6 Serve warm or cold with soup or cheese.

Poppy seed cheese layers

10 mins

Standing time: none

125g / 4½oz plain flour
1.5ml / ¼tsp baking powder
2.5ml / ½tsp paprika
1.5ml / ¼tsp salt
65g / 2½oz butter
75g / 3oz Emmental cheese, grated
45ml / 3tbls single cream
poppy seeds or sesame seeds, to sprinkle
85g / 3½oz packet full fat soft cheese with chives or with garlic and herbs

MAKES 22

PAUL WEBSTER

1 Sift the flour with the baking powder, paprika and salt.
2 Rub in the butter until the mixture resembles fine breadcrumbs.
3 Add cheese and cream and mix to a firm, pliable dough.
4 Roll out on a slightly floured surface and stamp out 44 rounds using a 5cm / 2in fluted cutter.
5 Arrange a quarter of the rounds in a circle on a microwave baking tray. Microwave at 100% (High) for 2½ minutes, (500 watt, 3½-4 minutes) turning once. Cool on a wire rack.
6 Arrange remaining rounds in two batches. Sprinkle with poppy seeds. Microwave as before.
7 Sandwich plain and coated biscuits together with the cream cheese.

Cheesy digestives

10 mins

Standing time: none

175g / 6oz plain wholewheat flour
2.5ml / ½tsp salt
45ml / 3tbls medium oatmeal
75g / 3oz lard or white vegetable fat

Poppy Seed Cheese Layers

40g / 1½oz Cotswold or Cheddar cheese with walnuts, grated
15ml / 1tbls demerara sugar
1 egg, beaten
30ml / 2tbls water

MAKES 20

1 Sift the flour and salt into a bowl and add the oatmeal. Mix in any bran which remains in the sieve.
2 Rub in the fat, using the fingertips, until the mixture resembles fine breadcrumbs.
3 Stir in the cheese and sugar, mixing well.
4 Add the egg and water and mix to make a firm but pliable dough.
5 Roll out on a lightly floured surface and cut out about 20 rounds using a 7.5cm / 3in cutter. Re-roll the dough if necessary.
6 Arrange five biscuits in a ring on a double layer of absorbent paper. Microwave at 100% (High) for 2½-3 minutes (500 watt, 3½-4 minutes), turning once.
7 Remove with a palette knife and transfer to a wire rack to cool and become crisp. Repeat the microwaving for three more batches.
8 Serve with cheese and pickles.

364

Cheesy chive shortbread

2 mins

Standing time: 5 mins

65g / 2½oz plain flour
15ml / 1tbls ground rice
pinch of grated nutmeg
pinch of mustard powder
pinch of salt
50g / 2oz butter or margarine
50g / 2oz Cheddar cheese, grated
5ml / 1tsp snipped chives
10ml / 2tsp single cream
grated Parmesan cheese, to sprinkle
stuffed olives, sliced, to garnish

MAKES 8

1 Line an 18cm / 7in fluted flan dish with cling film.
2 Sift the flour, ground rice, nutmeg, mustard and salt into a bowl. Rub in the butter or margarine, until the mixture resembles fine breadcrumbs. Stir in the cheese and chives. Bind with cream to a firm dough.
3 Press into the flan dish and level. Mark into eight wedges with a knife and prick with a fork.
4 Microwave at 100% (High) for 2-3 minutes (for 500 watt, 4 minutes), giving the dish ¼ turn every minute.
5 Re-mark the wedges with a sharp knife. Stand for 5 minutes.
6 Cut into wedges and cool on a wire rack. Sprinkle with cheese and garnish with olives.

Mustard cheese snacks

7 mins

Standing time: none

225g / 8oz plain flour
salt and pepper
2.5ml / ½tsp mustard powder
50g / 2oz butter or margarine
50g / 2oz lard or white vegetable fat
40g / 1½oz mature Cheddar cheese, grated
15ml / 1tbls grated Parmesan cheese
5ml / 1tsp wholegrain mustard
60ml / 4tbls water
paprika, to sprinkle

MAKES 24

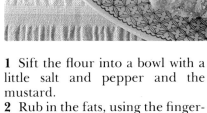

1 Sift the flour into a bowl with a little salt and pepper and the mustard.
2 Rub in the fats, using the fingertips, until the mixture resembles fine breadcrumbs.
3 Add the cheeses and mix well.
4 Mix the wholegrain mustard with the water and sprinkle over the rubbed-in mixture. Bind together using a fork to make a firm but pliable dough.
5 Form the mixture into 24 small balls, each a little smaller than a walnut.
6 Place four at a time on a double

Above: *Mustard Cheese Snacks*
Below: *Cheesy Chive Shortbread*

layer of absorbent paper on a microwave baking tray or large flat plate and sprinkle the tops evenly with paprika to improve the colour. Microwave at 100% (High) for 1¾-2¼ minutes (for 500 watt, 4 minutes), turning once during cooking.
7 Remove from the baking tray with a palette knife and leave on a wire rack to cool.
8 Serve the biscuits with cheese or as a snack with dips.

365

Cookies

More substantial than a biscuit, but less filling than a cake, crunchy cookies are always tempting — whether as a teatime favourite or a quick, any-time snack.

In minutes you can work miracles with every-day store-cupboard ingredients. There's no need for rolling out, the dough mixtures are quick to prepare and microwaving times are very short.

Several of the recipes give quantities to make large numbers of cookies. They will keep for two to three weeks in an airtight container, but it is easy to store the dough in the refrigerator and use it as you want more fresh cookies.

Mixtures containing bicarbonate of soda will keep for up to one week; those with baking powder for three to four days.

As with all microwave-baked goods, cookies will not brown during cooking; conveniently, the mixtures here include spices, chocolate or treacle to add colour.

Although it is possible to freeze microwaved cookies for 2-3 weeks, it is just as quick to make up a batch as it is to defrost them.

Microwaving times for 500 watt machines are given as these can vary a great deal, particularly as many of these do not have variable power. If your 500 watt machine has variable power, cook biscuits at 100% (High).

Clockwise from top left: *Swedish Cookies; plain and decorated Peanut Butter Cookies; Chocolate Peanut Poles; Swedish Butter Balls; Swedish Pole Cookies.*

Swedish cookies

7½ mins

Standing time: 15 mins

225g / 8oz plain flour
65g / 2½oz sugar
2.5ml / ½tsp cream of tartar
2.5ml / ½tsp bicarbonate of soda
good pinch of salt
2.5ml / ½tsp almond flavouring
2.5ml / ½tsp vanilla flavouring
175g / 6oz butter, softened
36 unblanched almonds
sifted icing sugar to dust

MAKES 36

VARIATIONS
Swedish pole cookies: omit the almonds. Make a deep furrow down the centre of each strip using the handle of a knife. Microwave as for the Swedish Cookies. Remove from the cooker and spoon 30ml / 2tbls jam down the centre of each strip. Dust with icing sugar. Cut into 2.5cm / 1in diagonal strips when cool.

Swedish butter balls: form the mixture into 2.5cm / 1in balls. Place six in a large ring on greaseproof paper or freezer tissue on the base of the cooker. Press an almond on top of each one and microwave at 50% (Medium) for 3-4½ minutes (500 watts, 3-4 minutes), turning every 30 seconds. Remove the paper with the cookies on it, leave for 3 minutes to crisp, then transfer to a wire rack using a palette knife. Leave to cool. Repeat with the remaining cookies.

How to microwave Swedish cookies

Place *all the ingredients except the almonds and extra icing sugar in a mixing bowl. Beat with an electric whisk at low speed to form a light dough. Divide into 5 equal parts.*

Shape *each piece into a 23cm / 9in strip on a 10cm / 4in wide piece of greaseproof paper. Place the strip on the paper on the turntable or floor of the microwave, or on a baking sheet.*

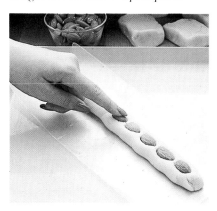

Press *eight or nine almonds firmly on to the strip of dough at 3mm / ⅛in intervals, forming a line down the centre. Try not to let the dough spread out sideways.*

Microwave *at 50% (Medium) for 1½-3 minutes (500 watts, 2-3 minutes) or until the surface is dry, turning every 30 seconds. Remove from the oven on the paper.*

Sprinkle *the icing sugar over the dough while still warm. Leave for 3 minutes to crisp. Cut into 2.5cm / 1in pieces between nuts when almost cool. Repeat with remaining dough.*

Guidelines for microwaving cookies

● *If you have time, wrap and refrigerate the dough for at least 1 hour before use. This gives the best results, as the cookies do not spread as much during cooking.*
● *Arrange the cookies in a circle on the greaseproof paper or freezer tissue for the most efficient use of the microwave energy.*
● *Turn the paper with the cookies on it every 30 seconds during microwaving for even cooking.*
● *Remember to check the cookies after the shortest time, as microwaves vary from one model to another.*

● *Remove the cookies as soon as the surface looks dry. Further cooking will burn them.*
● *Allow 3-5 minutes standing time on the paper, according to the recipe, for the cookies to become crisp. Do not move the cookies from the paper until crisp.*
● *Remove the cookies from the paper immediately after the standing time and transfer to a wire rack using a palette knife. The bases will be unpleasantly greasy and less appetizing if the cookies are left on the paper to cool.*

Ginger cookies

10 mins

Standing time: 15 mins

100g / 4oz butter
15ml / 1tbls black treacle
175g / 6oz self-raising flour
5ml / 1tsp ground ginger
75g / 3oz caster sugar
pinch of bicarbonate of soda

MAKES 18-22

1 Place the butter and black treacle in a bowl and microwave at 100% (High) for 1 minute (500 watts, 1½ minutes). Stir in all the remaining ingredients.

Salted Peanut Cookies

Salted peanut cookies

15 mins

Standing time: 15 mins

40g / 1½oz butter or margarine
100g / 4oz soft brown sugar
1 egg, beaten
2.5ml / ½tsp vanilla flavouring
1.5ml / ¼tsp bicarbonate of soda
1.5ml / ¼tsp baking powder
pinch of salt
100g / 4oz plain flour
75g / 3oz rolled oats
105ml / 7tbls puffed rice cereal
50g / 2oz salted peanuts

MAKES 30

1 Mix the butter or margarine, sugar, egg, vanilla flavouring, bicarbonate of soda, baking powder and salt and beat until light and fluffy.
2 Stir in the flour and all the remaining ingredients.
3 Drop six round teaspoons of the mixture on to greaseproof paper or freezer tissue in a large ring.
4 Microwave at 50% (Medium) for 3-4 minutes (500 watts, 2½-3½ minutes) or until the surface of the cookies is dry. Turn the paper every 30 seconds.
5 Remove the paper from the cooker with cookies on it. Leave for 3 minutes for the cookies to crisp, then transfer to a wire rack using a palette knife, and leave to cool. Repeat with the remaining mixture.

2 Knead together to make a firm dough. Wrap in cling film and refrigerate for 1 hour.
3 Form the mixture into 2.5cm / 1in balls. Place six to eight balls in a large circle on a piece of greaseproof paper or freezer tissue on the turntable or floor of cooker.
4 Microwave at 50% (Medium) for 3-4 minutes (500 watts, 2-3 minutes), turning every 30 seconds.
5 Leave to stand on the paper for 5 minutes. Transfer the cookies to a wire rack to cool, using a palette knife.
6 Repeat the procedure with the remaining mixture.

Peanut butter cookies

18 mins

Standing time: 18 mins

75g / 3oz margarine, softened
225g / 8oz peanut butter
225g / 8oz soft brown sugar
2 eggs
2.5ml / ½tsp bicarbonate of soda
pinch of salt
2.5ml / ½tsp vanilla flavouring
250g / 9oz plain flour, sifted
peanut butter or jam for topping
  (optional)

MAKES 48

1 Mix all the ingredients except the flour and topping to a light fluffy consistency. Fold in the flour.
2 Shape the dough into 2.5cm / 1in balls. Place six to eight balls on a piece of greaseproof paper or freezer tissue on the floor of the cooker.
3 Microwave at 50% (Medium) for 3-4½ minutes (500 watts, 3-4 minutes). Turn every 30 seconds.
4 Remove the paper with the cookies on it. Stand for 3 minutes, then transfer to a wire rack to cool, using a palette knife.
5 Repeat the procedure with the remaining mixture. Decorate with jam or peanut butter.

VARIATIONS
Peanut butter poles: divide the dough into eight equal parts. Shape each piece into a 23 × 4cm / 9 × 1½in strip on greaseproof

paper, on turntable or floor of the cooker. Flatten the top lightly with a fork. Microwave at 50% (Medium) for 1½-3 minutes (500 watts, 2½-4 minutes), turning every 30 seconds, until just dry. Allow to stand for 3 minutes. When almost cool, cut diagonally into 2.5cm / 1in strips. Repeat the procedure with the remaining seven pieces of dough.
Chocolate peanut poles: add 75g / 3oz chocolate chips to the mixture with the flour. Microwave as for the Peanut Butter Poles.

Syrupy oat wedges

6 mins

Standing time: 4 mins

45ml / 3tbls golden syrup
100g / 4oz soft brown sugar
100g / 4oz butter or margarine
225g / 8oz rolled oats
pinch of salt
MAKES 8

Ginger Cookies (drizzled with glacé icing) and Syrupy Oat Wedges

1 Line the base of a shallow 23cm / 9in round dish with greaseproof paper or freezer tissue. Grease lightly.
2 Mix the syrup, sugar and butter or margarine in a 1L / 1¾pt bowl until lightly blended.
3 Microwave at 100% (High) for 2-2½ minutes (500 watts, 2½-3 minutes). Stir well until the sugar has dissolved and the mixture is smooth.
4 Stir in the oats and salt and spread evenly in the dish.
5 Microwave the mixture at 100% (High) for 4-5 minutes (500 watts, 5-7 minutes), turning the dish every 30 seconds.
6 Remove from the cooker and leave to stand for 4 minutes to become firm.
7 Mark the warm biscuit into eight wedges, then leave to cool. Cut into eight pieces as marked to remove from dish.

Spiced puffs

23 mins

Standing time: 18 mins

100g / 4oz sugar
75g / 3oz margarine
100g / 4oz golden syrup
60ml / 4tbls water
2.5ml / ½tsp instant coffee
  powder (optional)
3 eggs
5ml / 1tsp bicarbonate of soda
5ml / 1tsp ground cinnamon
pinch of salt
2.5ml / ½tsp ground ginger
450g / 1lb plain flour
icing sugar to dust or Orange
  Frosting (recipe page 361)

MAKES 48

1 In a mixing bowl, combine the sugar, margarine, syrup, water and coffee. Microwave at 100% (High) for 5 minutes (500 watts, 2-3 minutes), stirring after 2 minutes. Cool for 10 minutes.
2 Add all the remaining ingredients except the icing sugar or frosting and mix well. Wrap in cling film and refrigerate for 6 hours or overnight to prevent spreading when cooked.
3 Shape the dough into 2.5cm / 1in balls.
4 Place six to eight balls in a ring on greaseproof paper or freezer tissue on the floor or turntable of the cooker.
5 Microwave at 50% (Medium) for 3-4 minutes (500 watts, 3-4 minutes), or until the surface is just dry, turning every 30 seconds. Remove the paper with the cookies on it. Leave for 3 minutes until the

cookies become crisp, then transfer to a wire rack using a palette knife and leave to cool.
6 Repeat the procedure with the remaining mixture in five or six more batches.
7 Let cool, sprinkle with icing sugar or top with orange frosting.

Chocolate cookies

20 mins

Standing time: 18 mins

40g / 1½oz butter
50g / 2oz plain chocolate
225g / 8oz sugar
2 eggs
10ml / 2tsp baking powder
5ml / 1tsp vanilla flavouring
pinch of salt
225g / 8oz plain flour, sifted
50g / 2oz chopped nuts
icing sugar

MAKES 36

1 Place the butter and chocolate in a mixing bowl and microwave at 50% (Medium) for 2-4 minutes until melted. Mix thoroughly until smooth.
2 Beat in the sugar, eggs, baking powder, vanilla flavouring and salt. Stir in the flour and nuts.
3 Wrap the mixture in cling film and refrigerate for 6 hours or overnight.
4 Shape the dough into 2.5cm / 1in balls and coat each one all over in icing sugar (see Cook's notes).
5 Place six to eight balls in a large circle on a piece of greaseproof paper or freezer tissue on the floor or turntable of the cooker. Microwave at 100% (High) for 2-4 min-

Left: *Chocolate Cookies*
Right: *Spiced Puffs*

utes (500 watts, 2-3 minutes), or until the surface is just dry. Turn the cookies on the paper every 30 seconds.
6 Remove the paper with the cookies on it. Leave to stand for 3 minutes to crisp, then transfer them to a wire rack using a palette knife. Leave the cookies to cool completely.
7 Repeat the prodecure with the remaining cookies in five or six more batches.

Cook's notes

To coat the dough, first shape into 2.5cm / 1in balls, then roll in icing sugar to cover all over. It is important to refrigerate the dough overnight before shaping and using, otherwise the cookies will spread too much. If necessary, chill shaped and coated dough again before microwaving.

370

Teabreads

No longer a time-consuming exercise, you can make a rich-textured, spicy teabread in less than half an hour using your microwave. There's an added bonus — teabreads freeze well too.

Teabreads from the microwave are rich-tasting, moist and make a filling teatime treat. Like any microwave 'baking', you achieve results much faster than with a conventional oven, so you can beat up a mixture and microwave the centre piece for an impromptu tea in just 25 minutes.

Apart from being quick and easy to make, teabreads freeze well, and can also be kept in the refrigerator, wrapped in cling film or foil. With a microwave, you can thaw in minutes teabreads which have been made in advance and stored frozen, so it is well worth preparing them in advance.

Choose straight-sided loaf dishes or soufflé-style round dishes (each recipe recommends a size of dish). If you have transparent microwave cookware, it is easy to check that the teabread is cooked by looking through the base.

Apple Spice Loaf

371

How to microwave teabreads

Chop up large pieces of fruit or nuts into small pieces before mixing them into a teabread mixture. Before they cook, microwave batters become more liquid, so large lumps will sink.

Avoid using shallow dishes or one with sloping sides for cooking teabreads. For most of the recipes given, a dish measuring $19 \times 12.5cm$ / $7\frac{1}{2} \times 5in$ or a round $18cm$ / $7in$ dish is ideal.

Grease or line dish with greased greaseproof paper or cling film. Spread the mixture evenly in the dish. If using a rectangular dish, protect ends with $5cm$ / $2in$ wide strips of foil.

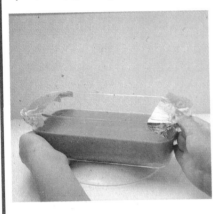

Place the loaf in its dish on an inverted saucer in the centre of the cooker, microwave at 50% (Medium) for the recommended time, giving the dish $\frac{1}{4}$ turn every 3 minutes for the first part of the cooking time.

Remove any foil protection if used, and increase the power to 100% (High), then microwave for 2-8 minutes more, as directed in the recipe, until the teabread is cooked and shrinks from sides.

Check the teabread to see if it is cooked by looking through the base. It is cooked when no unbaked mixture is visible on the bottom of the loaf in the centre. If using a plastic dish, or paper lining, tip out the loaf and press to test.

Avoid overcooking teabread. It is best to keep checking the base, rather than let it cook too much. This occurs on the inside of the loaf where it is not immediately visible.

Remove the teabread from the cooker and leave to stand for 10 minutes. Loosen the edges, then turn the cooked teabread out onto a wire rack to cool completely.

Remove the lining piece of cling film or paper from the teabread. Allow it to cool completely before cutting in thin slices for serving. (Freeze or store once cool).

372

Apple spice loaf

12 mins

Standing time: 5-10 mins

150g / 5oz plain flour
175g / 6oz caster sugar
5ml / 1tsp bicarbonate of soda
5ml / 1tsp salt
5ml / 1tsp ground cinnamon
1.5ml / ¼tsp grated nutmeg
1.5ml / ¼tsp ground cloves
50ml / 2fl oz vegetable oil
175g / 6oz sweetened apple purée
100g / 4oz raisins (optional)
2 eggs
50ml / 2tsp lemon juice
apple slices dipped in lemon
  juice to decorate

MAKES A 19 × 12.5cm / 7½ × 5in LOAF

1 Mix all the ingredients in a large mixing bowl using an electric mixer at low speed until smooth.
2 Line the base of the dish with greased greaseproof paper or cling film and spread the mixture evenly over it. Protect the ends of the loaf with foil (see opposite) so that the ends of the loaf do not overcook.
3 Place the dish on an inverted saucer in the centre of the cooker and microwave at 50% (Medium) for 9 minutes, giving the dish ¼ turn every 2 minutes.
4 Increase the power to 100% (High) and microwave for 3-5 minutes. Remove the foil after 2 minutes and give the dish ¼ turn every 2 minutes until it is cooked.
5 The teabread is cooked when no uncooked mixture is visible through the bottom of the dish.
6 Leave to stand for 5-10 minutes. Loosen the sides of the teabread before turning out onto a wire rack to cool. Top with apple slices before serving.

Microtips

If the loaf seems to be uncooked in the centre, return it to the dish and place on an inverted saucer in the cooker. Microwave at 100% (High) for 1-2 minutes. It is always easier to remedy an undercooked dish, rather than spoil it through overcooking.

Date nut teabread

10 mins

Standing time: 5-10 mins

175g / 6oz dates, halved
5ml / 1tsp bicarbonate of soda
175g / 6oz soft brown sugar
grated zest of 1 large orange
50ml / 2fl oz vegetable oil
1 egg
175g / 6oz plain flour
5ml / 1tsp salt
50g / 2oz chopped nuts

MAKES AN 18cm / 7in ROUND LOAF

1 Mix the dates, bicarbonate of soda and 175ml / 6fl oz boiling water in a bowl and leave to stand for 10 minutes.
2 Mix the sugar, orange zest, oil and egg together until smooth and add the date mixture. Gradually stir in the flour, salt and nuts.
3 Line the base of the dish with

Apple Spice Loaf (top) and Date Nut Teabread

greased greaseproof paper or cling film and spread the mixture evenly over it.
4 Place the dish on an inverted saucer in the centre of the cooker and microwave at 50% (Medium) for 8 minutes, giving the dish a ¼ turn every 2 minutes. Increase the power to 100% (High). Microwave for 2-6 minutes. The loaf is cooked when no uncooked mixture is visible through the base of the dish.
5 Leave to stand for 5-10 minutes. Loosen the sides of the teabread before turning out onto a wire rack to cool.

Note: If preferred cook this in a 19 × 12.5cm / 7½ × 5in dish but remember to protect the ends of the loaf with foil at first.

Carrot loaf

11 mins

Standing time: 5-10 mins

85g / 3½oz plain flour
175g / 6oz caster sugar
5ml / 1tsp baking powder
5ml / 1tsp bicarbonate of soda
5ml / 1tsp salt
10ml / 2tsp ground cinnamon
125ml / 4fl oz vegetable oil
2 eggs
50g / 2oz chopped nuts (optional)
175g / 6oz carrot, finely grated

MAKES A 19 × 12.5cm / 7½ × 5in LOAF

1 Mix all the ingredients together in a large bowl using an electric mixer at low speed, then beat at medium speed until smooth.
2 Line the base of the loaf dish with greased greaseproof paper or cling film and spread the mixture evenly in the dish. Protect the ends of the loaf with 5cm / 2in wide strips of foil, so that 2.5cm / 1in each end is covered and the rest is moulded around the end of the dish.
3 Place the dish on an inverted saucer in the middle of the cooker and microwave at 50% (Medium) for 9 minutes, giving the dish ¼ turn every 3 minutes.
4 Remove the foil and increase the power to 100% (High). Microwave for 2-3 minutes. If using a clear glass dish, check to see if the teabread is cooked by looking through the bottom. It is done when no uncooked mixture is visible on the bottom. Leave to stand for 5-10 minutes, then turn out to cool on a wire rack.

Left: *Carrot Loaf*
Middle top: *Country Raisin Bread*
Middle bottom: *Brown Crumb Loaf*
Right: *Wholewheat Banana Bread*

Microtips

When making teabreads, it is easier to tell if the loaf is cooked if you use a glass dish. If using a non-transparent dish, tip the loaf out and press to check if it is cooked underneath. Return to the cooker if necessary.

Country raisin bread

10 mins

Standing time: 5-10 mins

75g / 3oz raisins
5ml / 1tsp bicarbonate of soda
175g / 6oz soft light brown sugar
grated zest of 1 large orange
50ml / 2fl oz vegetable oil
1 egg
175g / 6oz plain flour
salt
5ml / 1tsp ground cinnamon
2.5ml / ½tsp grated nutmeg
pinch of ground cloves

MAKES AN 18cm / 7in ROUND LOAF

1 Mix the raisins, bicarbonate of soda and 175ml / 6fl oz boiling water in a bowl and leave to stand for 10 minutes until the raisins have plumped up.
2 Mix the sugar, orange zest, oil and egg together until smooth and add the raisin mixture. Gradually stir in the remaining ingredients.
3 Line base of dish with a circle of greased greaseproof paper or cling film to fit, then spread the mixture evenly over it.
4 Place the dish on an inverted saucer in the centre of the cooker and microwave at 50% (Medium) for 8 minutes, giving the dish ¼ turn every 2 minutes. Increase the power to 100% (High) and microwave for 2-6 minutes or until it is cooked.
5 The loaf is cooked when no uncooked mixture is visible through the base of the dish.
6 Leave to stand for 5-10 minutes before turning out onto a wire rack to cool.

RAY DUNS

374

Brown crumb loaf

5 mins

Standing time: 5-10 mins

75g / 3oz plain flour
75g / 3oz wheatmeal biscuit
  crumbs
5ml / 1tsp bicarbonate of soda
salt
175ml / 6fl oz milk
50ml / 2fl oz black treacle
50ml / 2fl oz oil
75g / 3oz raisins

MAKES AN 18cm / 7in ROUND LOAF

1 Place all ingredients but the raisins in a mixing bowl and blend using an electric mixer until smooth. Stir in raisins.
2 Line the base of a 18cm / 7in round dish with a circle of greased greaseproof paper or cling film.

Pour the loaf mixture into the prepared dish and cover with a piece of cling film rolled back at one edge.
3 Microwave at 50% (Medium) for 5-7 minutes, or until the top springs back when pressed lightly and no unbaked mixture is visible at the bottom. Give the loaf ½ turn every 3 minutes during cooking.
4 Leave the teabread to stand for 5-10 minutes in the dish before turning onto wire rack to cool.
5 To serve the loaf warm, reheat slices on a plate, covered loosely with cling film. Microwave at 100% (High) for 30-60 seconds, then serve at once.

Wholewheat banana bread

12 mins

Standing time: 5-10 mins

75g / 3oz wholewheat flour
75g / 3oz plain flour
175g / 6oz caster sugar
75ml / 5tbls vegetable oil
30ml / 2tbls milk
2 eggs
2 very ripe bananas, sliced
15ml / 1tbls lemon juice
2.5ml / ½tsp bicarbonate of soda
salt
50g / 2oz chopped nuts

STREUSEL TOPPING
50g / 2oz flour
50g / 2oz soft light brown sugar
generous pinch of ground
  cinnamon
25g / 1oz butter

MAKES A 19 × 12.5cm / 7½ × 5in LOAF

1 First prepare the topping. Mix all the ingredients together and rub into fine breadcrumbs using the fingertips. Set aside.
2 Place the teabread ingredients in a large mixing bowl and beat at low speed using an electric mixer for about 15 seconds until smooth.
3 Line the base of the baking dish with greased greaseproof paper or cling film. Spread the mixture evenly in the dish and sprinkle the streusel mixture over the top. Protect the ends of the teabread with two 5cm / 2in wide strips of foil. Mould 2.5cm / 1in around the rim of the dish, leaving 2.5cm / 1in of

Microtips

You can decorate any teabread with a layer of chopped glacé fruit and nuts. Make a glaze by mixing 100g / 4oz sugar with the juice of 1 lemon, made up to 150ml / ¼pt with water, in a bowl. Microwave at 100% (High) for 4-6 minutes, until the mixture makes a syrup. While the syrup is still hot, pour it evenly over the fruit mixture on the teabread, then leave to stand for about 30 minutes until cool. (It will also mean the teabread can be stored for 4-5 days.)

the loaf protected at each end with foil.
4 Place the dish on an inverted saucer in the centre of the cooker. Microwave at 50% (Medium) for 9 minutes. Increase the power to 100% (High) and microwave for 3-5 minutes. Remove the foil after 2 minutes and give the dish ¼ turn every 2 minutes.
5 If using a clear glass dish, test to see if the teabread is cooked by looking at the bottom of the loaf. It is cooked when no uncooked mixture is visible on the base.
6 Remove from the cooker and leave to stand for 5-10 minutes before turning out onto a wire rack and removing the paper.

VARIATIONS
Basic banana bread: substitute plain white flour for the wholewheat flour.

Holiday banana bread: stir 100g / 4oz chopped mixed peel into the mixture before putting it into the dish. Microwave at 100% (High) for 1-3 minutes longer.

Freezer notes

To freeze teabreads, wrap them thoroughly in foil or cling film. It is a good idea to freeze individual slices of teabread for use in packed lunches — take them straight from the freezer in the morning, and they will thaw of their own accord by the time you are ready to eat them.

Gingerbreads

Generous squares or slices of dark, sticky gingerbread have long been a tea-time favourite. Now you can cook this spicy, moist cake in a fraction of the time needed for conventional cooking.

Gingerbread is a 'natural' for the microwave because the ingredients — spices, dark sugar and black treacle — give a good, rich colour, so avoiding a pallid cake; a perennial problem when baking in the microwave. Gingerbread is also naturally moist and this, together with its high proportion of sugary ingredients, also makes it a good candidate for microwaving.

But these natural assets don't prevent you from varying the basic recipe — try adding a sweet topping or a cool, lemony icing.

Traditional Gingerbread

376

Lining the dish

Gingerbread is traditionally cooked in a rectangular, square or loaf shape. To prepare the dish, cut a strip of greaseproof paper the same width as the dish but long enough to stand above the rim at either side. Lightly oil the dish and line it with the paper, so that a 'handle' of paper is left at either end. This enables you to lift the cooked gingerbread cleanly and easily out of the dish.

Remove the lining paper very carefully while the gingerbread is still warm.

Storing gingerbread

Most of the cakes here keep for a few days. Traditional Gingerbread and Iced Treacle Cake have excellent keeping qualities — they stay moist for three to four weeks if closely wrapped.

Traditional gingerbread

15 mins

Standing time: 10 mins

This gingerbread has a moist, spongy texture. Serve it plain or buttered or — as they do in the north of England — with a slice of Cheddar cheese.

225g / 8oz self-raising flour
pinch of salt
7.5ml / 1½tsp ground ginger
75g / 3oz soft brown sugar
75g / 3oz golden syrup
75g / 3oz treacle
75g / 3oz white cooking fat or cooking margarine
150ml / ¼pt milk
1 egg, lightly beaten

MAKES 12 PIECES

Microtips

Gingerbread has a high proportion of sugary ingredients, so watch the mixture closely during microwaving to make sure it does not overcook — if the top starts to look dry, remove immediately.

Freezer notes

Traditional Gingerbread and Banana Gingerbread can be frozen for up to three months.

To thaw, unwrap the cake, place on a plate and microwave at 20-30% (Defrost) for 4½ minutes, or until the top is soft and springy to the touch. Allow to stand for 10 minutes before cutting.

How to microwave Traditional gingerbread

Sift *the flour, salt and ginger into a medium-sized mixing bowl and make a shallow well in the centre of the dry ingredients.*

Put *the sugar, syrup, treacle and fat in a 575ml / 1pt bowl. Microwave at 50% (Medium) for 3 minutes, or until melted.*

Allow *to cool until the bowl is no more than hot, then beat in the milk, then the beaten egg. Pour into the well in the flour mixture.*

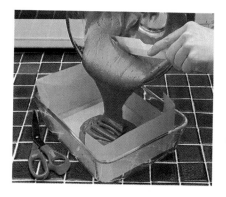

Beat *together with a wooden spoon, to make a thick, smooth batter. Pour into an oiled and lined 25 × 15cm / 10 × 6in dish, 6cm / 2½in deep.*

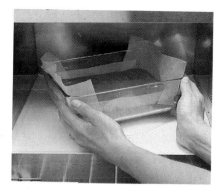

Place *on a trivet or upturned plate and microwave at 50% (Medium) for 12 minutes, or until cooked, giving dish a quarter turn every 3 minutes.*

Test *for doneness by pressing with a fingertip — it should be springy. Allow to stand for 10 minutes and lift out on to a wire rack to cool.*

Banana gingerbread

13 mins

Standing time: 10 mins

Serve this cake hot as a pudding with pouring cream or Butterscotch Sauce (page 26); or leave the gingerbread to cool and serve sliced and buttered.

2 bananas
5ml / 1tsp lemon juice
50g / 2oz white cooking fat or cooking margarine
175g / 6oz soft dark brown sugar
1 egg, lightly beaten
30ml / 2tbls milk
175g / 6oz self-raising flour
2.5ml / ½tsp bicarbonate of soda
pinch of salt
2.5ml / ½tsp ground cinnamon
5ml / 1tsp ground ginger

MAKES 8 PIECES

1 Mash the bananas with the lemon juice.
2 Melt the fat in a small bowl at 50% (Medium) for 3 minutes. Stir in the sugar, egg and milk.
3 Sift the flour, bicarbonate of soda, salt, cinnamon and ginger into a mixing bowl. Make a well in the centre.
4 Add the banana to the well and pour in the liquid. Beat until smooth.
5 Spoon the mixture into an oiled and lined 900g / 2lb loaf dish. Shield the ends with small, smooth pieces of foil, well secured. Place on an upturned plate or a microwave trivet at 50% (Medium) for 10 minutes, or until the top is springy. Give the dish a quarter turn three times during cooking. Remove the foil after 5 minutes.
6 Allow to stand for 10 minutes. Serve at once for a hot pudding, or lift out on to a wire rack to cool. To store, keep well wrapped.

Hot-topped gingerbread

25 mins

Standing time: 20 mins

100g / 4oz sugar
150ml / ¼pt water
thinly pared zest of ½ lemon
3 whole cloves
2.5cm / 1in stick cinnamon
3 eating apples, peeled, cored and sliced
40g / 1½oz raisins
1 quantity Traditional Gingerbread mixture (see recipe page 377)

SERVES 8

1 Put the sugar and water in a large bowl and microwave at 100% (High) for 1½ minutes. Stir until sugar has completely dissolved.
2 Add the lemon zest, cloves and cinnamon. Microwave at 100% (High) for a further 4 minutes, to make a thick syrup. Remove zest, cloves and cinnamon.

Hot-topped Gingerbread

3 Add the sliced apples and raisins. Cover and microwave at 100% (High) for 3 minutes. Remove and leave the apple mixture to stand for 10 minutes.
4 Meanwhile, prepare and microwave the Traditional Gingerbread following the steps on page 377. Once cooked, allow to stand for 10 minutes.
5 Spoon the apple topping evenly over the top of the gingerbread. Microwave at 100% (High) for 1½ minutes, or until the apple is heated through. Serve hot, straight from the dish.

Cook's notes

Hot-topped Gingerbread does not keep well once assembled, but you can make the Traditional Gingerbread in advance and add the topping when you serve it.

Microtips

Provided they are in glass or plastic jars, treacle and syrup can be warmed in the microwave. Remove the lid and microwave the jar at 100% (High) for 1½-2 minutes.

Gingerbread house

8¾ mins

Standing time: none

150g / 5oz plain flour
150g / 5oz self-raising flour
2.5ml / ½tsp ground ginger
2.5ml / ½tsp ground cinnamon
65g / 2½oz soft tub margarine
50g / 2oz caster sugar
1 egg
100g / 4oz treacle
25g / 1oz plain chocolate

ICING
100g / 4oz icing sugar, sifted
about 15ml / 1tbls warm water
food colourings

MAKES 1 × 18cm / 7in HOUSE

How to microwave a Gingerbread house

Sift *the flours, ginger and cinnamon into a mixing bowl. In a 575ml /1pt bowl, beat the margarine and sugar until pale and fluffy. Add the egg and the treacle and stir with a wooden spoon, until smooth.*

Place *the chocolate on a saucer and microwave at 100% (High) for 45 seconds, then beat into the treacle mixture. Pour the mixture into the spiced flour and stir well until evenly combined.*

Knead *until soft, shape into a ball, wrap and chill for 4 hours. Unwrap and roll between sheets of greaseproof paper to 3mm / ⅛in thick. Trim edges to make a 20cm / 8in square. Reserve trimmings for biscuits.*

Score *shapes for a house, door, two windows, hedges and steps with a serrated knife. Microwave on cardboard at 50% (Medium) for 8-10 minutes, or until firm, making a quarter turn every 2-3 minutes.*

Cool *the gingerbread on a wire rack. When cool, cut through the score marks to separate the house from the chimney, roof, hedges and steps. Discard trimmings unless wanted for extra windows or features.*

Mix *the icing sugar with the warm water to make a smooth paste. Divide between three small bowls; stir a different food colouring into each bowl. Use to assemble and decorate the completed house.*

379

Iced treacle cake

15 mins

Standing time: 10 mins

225g / 8oz self-raising flour
pinch of salt
5ml / 1tsp ground ginger
5ml / 1tsp bicarbonate of soda
50g / 2oz drained stem ginger
50g / 2oz walnuts, chopped
100g / 4oz caster sugar
175g / 6oz treacle
75g / 3oz white cooking fat or
    margarine
1 egg
150ml / ¼pt milk
5ml / 1tsp lemon juice

ICING
50g / 2oz cream cheese
25g / 1oz soft tub margarine
25g / 1oz icing sugar, sifted
5ml / 1tsp lemon juice

MAKES 8 PIECES

1 Sift the flour, salt, ginger and bicarbonate of soda into a mixing bowl. Rinse the stem ginger under cold water to remove the syrup and dry on absorbent paper. Chop finely and add to the flour, with the chopped walnuts. Make a well in the centre.
2 Place the sugar, treacle and fat in a 575ml / 1pt bowl and microwave at 50% (Medium) for 3 minutes. Leave to cool until the bottom of the bowl is hand-hot, then beat in the egg.
3 In a separate bowl or jug, mix the milk with the lemon juice. Pour the treacle mixture and milk into the well in the flour.
4 Beat the flour into the liquid ingredients with a wooden spoon until blended. Pour into an oiled and lined 25 × 15cm / 10 × 6in dish, about 6cm / 2½in deep.
5 Place on an upturned plate or a trivet and microwave at 50% (Medium) for 12-14 minutes, or until the surface is dry and springy

to the touch. Give the dish a quarter turn every 4 minutes.
6 Stand for 10 minutes, then lift out on to a wire rack to cool. When the cake is cool, remove the lining paper.
7 Mix all the icing ingredients together in a bowl and beat until smooth. Spread over the top of the cold cake.

Cook's notes

Measuring treacle or syrup can be a sticky business! A fuss-free method you can use for the Traditional Gingerbread and Iced treacle cake is to weigh the sugar first, spreading it out across the base of the weighing pan, and pour the treacle or syrup on to the sugar, until the combined weights are correct. If the treacle will not pour readily, you can melt it in the microwave provided it is in a plastic or glass container.

380

Quick-mix cakes

Use the easy all-in-one method for mixing cakes instead of creaming or rubbing in to make microwaving cakes for a crowd or a family tea speedier than ever.

If you're going to cook quickly, why spend time over laborious mixing? Beat everything together in one easy stage.

To make the mixing easier, all the ingredients should be in a 'mixable' condition. If you are using butter or margarine straight from the refrigerator, soften it by microwaving at 30% (Low) for 10 seconds per 100g / 4oz. This will make it easy to beat and, therefore, ideal for all-in-one cakes. For mixing, use an electric mixer or beat by hand with a wooden spoon. In either case, take care not to overbeat — the mixture should be just evenly blended — otherwise the cake will be tough and heavy. If using an electric mixer, add ingredients such as chopped dates or raisins after the main mixing, and beat them in using a wooden spoon to avoid their being broken up between the mixer blades.

These recipes produce 'slab' cakes — not loaves. This form is more suited to the texture of the mixture and to microwave cooking. The mixtures are generally moister than for conventional cooking; if using a see-through container, a reliable way to check if the cakes are cooked is to look through the base of the dish and stop cooking when no moist, uncooked patches are visible.

Wait until cakes are cool to add the frosting. This is best done while the cake is still in its dish, from which it can be served.

Rose marble cake

11 mins

Standing time: 5 mins

Distilled rose water is available from Asian food stores, health-food shops and delicatessens.

225g / 8oz self-raising flour
10ml / 2tsp baking powder
225g / 8oz butter or margarine, softened
175g / 6oz caster sugar
4 eggs, beaten
60ml / 4tbls water
10ml / 2tsp rose water
few drops of pink food colouring
2.5ml / ½tsp vanilla flavouring
60ml / 4tbls jam

ICING
350g / 12oz icing sugar, sifted
5ml / 1tsp rose water
water to mix
2 drops of pink food colouring

SERVES 12

1 Lightly grease a 2.5L / 4½pt ring dish. Sift the flour and baking powder and add the butter, sugar, eggs, water and rose water.
2 Beat using an electric mixer at medium speed for 2 minutes, or by hand for 3 minutes.
3 Divide mixture in half. Beat the colouring into one part and vanilla into the other.
4 Drop alternate spoonfuls of the mixtures into the dish. Draw a knife around once in each direction to marble the mixtures.
5 Place on an inverted saucer and microwave at 50% (Medium) for 11-12 minutes, or until just firm to the touch, turning once.
6 Stand in the dish for 5 minutes, then turn out on to a wire rack to

cool. Split horizontally and fill with the jam when cold.
7 Sift the icing sugar; add the rose water and cold water to make a coating consistency. Reserve 45ml / 3tbls and colour it pink. Pour the plain icing over the cake. Leave to set, then pipe pink icing in a zig-zag pattern over the top.

Gingerbread squares

14 mins

Standing time: 5 mins

175g / 6oz plain flour
pinch of salt
5ml / 1tsp baking powder
2.5ml / ½tsp bicarbonate of soda
5ml / 1tsp ground cinnamon
7.5ml / 1½tsp ground ginger
75g / 3oz margarine or butter
60ml / 4tbls soft brown sugar
30ml / 2tbls golden syrup
30ml / 2tbls black treacle
1 egg, beaten

30ml / 2tbls milk

MAKES 16 PIECES

1 Lightly grease a 20cm / 8in square dish. Sift the flour with the salt, baking powder, bicarbonate of soda, cinnamon and ginger. Make a well in the centre.
2 Place the margarine, sugar, syrup and treacle in a bowl. Cover and microwave at 50% (Medium) for 3 minutes until melted and hot.
3 Pour the hot liquid into the dry ingredients, with the egg and milk. Beat until smooth.
4 Spread the mixture evenly in the prepared dish and shield the edges with small, smooth pieces of foil. Place the dish on an inverted saucer and microwave at 30% (Low) for 10-12 minutes, or until still slightly moist but almost set in the centre. Give a quarter turn every 2-3 minutes.
5 Remove the foil and microwave at 100% (High) for 1 minute. Leave to stand 5 minutes; then turn out and cool on a wire rack.

Quick ginger bars

13½ mins

Standing time: 5 mins

100g / 4oz plain flour
100g / 4oz self-raising flour
pinch of salt
5ml / 1tsp ground ginger
2.5ml / ½tsp ground cinnamon
2.5ml / ½tsp grated nutmeg
2.5ml / ½tsp ground cloves
175g / 6oz margarine, softened
175g / 6oz soft brown sugar
3 eggs, beaten
45ml / 3tbls milk
frosting (see pages 359-361)

MAKES 12-14

1 Lightly grease a 25 × 15cm / 10 × 6in rectangular dish. Sift the flours with the salt, ginger, cinnamon, nutmeg and cloves.
2 Add margarine, sugar, eggs and milk and beat, using an electric mixer at medium speed for 1-2 minutes, or by hand for 2-3 minutes.

Gingerbread Squares

382

3 Spread the mixture evenly in the prepared dish. Shield the corners with small, smooth pieces of foil. Place on an inverted saucer and microwave at 30% (Low) for 12-14 minutes, giving a quarter turn every 3-4 minutes.

4 Remove the foil and microwave at 100% (High) for 1½-2 minutes to finish the cooking. The cake should feel just springy to the touch in the centre. Stand for 5 minutes, then cool in the dish on a wire rack. Top the cooled cake with the frosting of your choice.

Nifty almond slices

14 mins

Standing time: 5 mins

200g / 7oz plain flour
60ml / 12tsp cornflour
5ml / 1tsp baking powder
100g / 4oz butter or margarine, softened
100g / 4oz caster sugar
2 eggs, beaten
30ml / 2tbls milk
5ml / 1tsp vanilla flavouring
100g / 4oz pressed dates, chopped
50g / 2oz blanched almonds, chopped

Above: Quick Ginger Bars
Right: Nifty Almond Slices

frosting (see pages 359-361)

MAKES ABOUT 12 PIECES

1 Lightly grease a 25 × 15cm / 10 × 6in rectangular dish. Sift the flour, cornflour and baking powder together several times.

2 Add the butter, sugar, eggs, milk and vanilla and beat using an electric mixer at medium speed for 1 minute, or by hand for 2 minutes. When smooth, stir in the dates, almonds and soured cream.

3 Spread the mixture evenly in the prepared dish. Shield the corners with small, smooth pieces of well-secured foil.

4 Place on an inverted saucer and microwave at 30% (Low) for 13-14 minutes, giving a quarter turn every 2-3 minutes. Remove the foil; microwave at 100% (High) for a further 1-2 minutes, or until no moist patches are visible through the base of the dish.

5 Stand to complete cooking for 5 minutes, then cool completely. Top with the frosting of your choice. Cut into 12 pieces.

383

Date and nut cake

	10 mins

Standing time: 5 mins

350g / 12oz self-raising flour
2.5ml / ½tsp baking powder
pinch of salt
2.5ml / ½tsp ground cinnamon
75g / 3oz butter or margarine,
  softened
75g / 3oz soft brown sugar
3 eggs, beaten
150ml / ¼pt milk
100g / 4oz pressed dates, chopped
50g / 2oz blanched almonds,
  chopped
**Lemon or Orange Frosting (see
page 361)**

MAKES 10-12 PIECES

1 Lightly grease a 25 × 15cm /
10 × 6in rectangular dish. Sift the
flour, baking powder, salt and
cinnamon into a bowl. Add the
butter, sugar, eggs and milk and
beat, using an electric mixer for 1-
2 minutes or by hand for 2-3 minutes, to produce a soft dropping
consistency. Stir in the dates and
almonds.

Left: *Speedy Spiced Square*
Below: *Date and Nut Cake*

Speedy spiced squares

	12½ mins

Standing time: 5 mins

225g / 8oz plain flour
pinch of salt
2.5ml / ½tsp baking powder
pinch of bicarbonate of soda
5ml / 1tsp ground mixed spice
  or cinnamon
75g / 3oz margarine
60ml / 4tbls dark soft brown
  sugar or muscovado
15ml / 1tbls runny honey
22½ml / 1½tbls black treacle
3 eggs
grated zest of 1 small lemon
45ml / 3tbls milk

SERVES 6-8

1 Grease an 18cm / 7in square or
20cm / 8in round cake dish and
line the base with greased greaseproof paper.

2 Sift the flour, salt, baking powder, bicarbonate of soda and spice
into a bowl and make a well in the
centre.

3 Place the margarine, sugar,
honey and treacle in a bowl, cover
and microwave at 50% (Medium)
for about 2½-3 minutes, or until
melted. Add the eggs, lemon zest,
and the melted mixture to the
flour and beat using an electric
mixer at medium speed for 2 minutes, or by hand using a wooden
spoon for 3 minutes.

4 Spread the mixture evenly in
the prepared dish and place on an
inverted saucer. Microwave at 30%
(Low) for 9-10 minutes, then at
100% (High) for 1-2 minutes, or
until just springy to the touch in
the centre. Give the dish a quarter
turn every 2-3 minutes.

5 Stand for 5 minutes, then turn
out and cool on a wire rack. Serve
warm with whipped cream or a hot
jam or lemon sauce.

2 Spread the mixture evenly in the prepared dish and shield the corners with small, smooth pieces of foil.

3 Stand on an inverted saucer and microwave at 50% (Medium) for 10-12 minutes, turning occasionally, until quite springy to the touch and no longer damp on top. Stand for 5 minutes. Transfer the dish to a wire rack and cool.

4 Frost the top of the cold cake and serve from the dish.

Banana nut cake

20 mins

Standing time: 5 mins

225g / 8oz self-raising flour
pinch of salt
5ml / 1tsp baking powder
pinch of bicarbonate of soda
100g / 4oz butter or margarine, softened
2 ripe bananas
10ml / 2tsp lemon juice
100g / 4oz caster sugar
75g / 3oz walnuts, chopped
1 egg, beaten
15ml / 1tbls milk

ICING
15g / ½oz butter or margarine
15ml / 1tbls single cream
175g / 6oz icing sugar, sifted
10ml / 2tsp maple or golden syrup

MAKES 15 PIECES

1 Lightly grease a 25 × 15cm / 10 × 6in rectangular dish. Sift the flour with the salt, baking powder and bicarbonate of soda several times to mix evenly.

2 Add all the remaining cake ingredients and beat using an electric mixer at medium speed for 2 minutes, or by hand for 3 minutes, until smooth and light.

3 Spread the mixture evenly in the prepared dish and shield the corners with small pieces of smooth foil. Place on an inverted saucer and make sure that the foil cannot touch the sides of the cooker.

4 Microwave at 30% (Low) for 17-19 minutes, giving the dish a quarter turn twice during cooking. Remove the foil and increase the power to 100% (High). Microwave for a further 2-3 minutes, or until no uncooked mixture is visible through the base of the dish, or the cake is just springy to the touch.

5 Stand for 5 minutes to complete cooking. Leave to cool.

6 To make the icing, place the butter and cream in a bowl and microwave at 50% (Medium) for 60-80 seconds, or until bubbling. Stir in the sugar and syrup and mix until smooth. Spread evenly over the cooled cake. Cut into 15 pieces and serve from the dish.

Microtips

When cooking in square or rectangular dishes, shield the corners with small, smooth pieces of foil. Stand the dish on an inverted saucer so that microwave energy can reach the base, making sure that the foil cannot touch the sides of the cooker.

Banana Nut Cake

Scones

Scones are part of the great home-baking tradition — an old favourite on the teatime table. Speedy mixing and cooking, however, were never among the scone's advantages, until the advent of the microwave.

Left: *Rolled Spice Scones, Cheese Scones, and Academy Oat Scone.*

Made in the microwave, scones are not only particularly light and airy, but they are simple to make in a matter of minutes, to cater for impromptu visitors.

As microwaving will not produce a browned top, a number of tricks can be used to give an attractive appearance. Place them under a hot grill to brown; alternatively, they can be sprinkled with a crunchy, golden topping before cooking. It is a good idea to keep a choice of toppings in screw-topped jars — toasted bran, wheatgerm, sesame seeds or rolled oats; or biscuit crumbs, crushed cornflakes or crisps.

Use this delicious selection as a guide for adapting your own favourite scone recipes too. Remember that the heavier doughs, particularly those made with wholemeal flour, will require slightly longer cooking and should be raised from the floor of the cooker on the base of an inverted plate or flan dish. This makes sure that they cook evenly.

Scones may be frozen, but as they take about 4 minutes to thaw by microwaving at 20-30% (Defrost), which is roughly the same time they take to cook, it is better to eat them the same day.

Generally, the timings given will suit 600, 650 and 700 watt machines. Check the scones after the shortest recommended time if you are using a powerful model. A 500 watt microwave will take longer to complete cooking, so times are given with each recipe.

Loaves and scone rounds will continue to cook after microwaving — stop cooking as soon as they are springy, then leave to stand.

Yoghurt scone loaf

3 mins

Standing time: 4 mins

225g / 8oz self-raising flour
1.5ml / ¼tsp salt
5ml / 1tsp bicarbonate of soda
50g / 2oz butter or margarine
15-30ml / 1-2tbls caster sugar
30ml / 2tbls raisins (optional)
150ml / ¼pt yoghurt
30ml / 2tbls toasted bran

MAKES 9 SCONES OR 1 LOAF

1 Sift the flour, salt and bicarbonate of soda into a bowl. Cut in the butter, then rub in until it resembles fine breadcrumbs.
2 Stir in the sugar and raisins and add enough yoghurt to make a soft, but not sticky dough.
3 Knead lightly in the bowl, then turn out onto a lightly floured surface. Either form into a 2cm / ¾in thick round and cut out 9 scones with a 5cm / 2in cutter or make into a large roll to fit an oiled 575ml / 1pt loaf dish. Mark slits 12mm / ½in deep at 2cm / ¾in intervals across the loaf.
4 Invert a large plate or flan dish in the microwave. Arrange scones in a ring on non-stick paper on the base of the plate or stand the dish on the plate.
5 Sprinkle the toasted bran over the top of the scones or the loaf. Microwave the scones at 100% (High) for 3-4 minutes and the loaf for 4-5 minutes, until well risen and springy to the touch. (For 500 watt, allow 4½ minutes for scones, 5 minutes for a loaf). Turn the scones after 3 minutes and the loaf after 4.
6 Allow the loaf to stand in the dish for 4 minutes then cool on a rack after the standing time.

Below: *Five-minute Scones*

Microtips

Scones cooked by microwave are best eaten fresh from the cooker, while they are light in texture and moist.

While it is not recommended to freeze scones for defrosting and reheating at a later date, it is possible to refresh scones for immediate consumption. If keeping scones overnight, wrap closely in cling film or store in an air-tight container. Microwave the scones at 100% (High) for 20-30 seconds each to restore freshness and heat them through. Scones can only be refreshed once in this way, and they should be eaten immediately.

Five-minute scones

3½ mins

Standing time: none

50g / 2oz butter or margarine
125ml / 4fl oz mixed milk and
  water
225g / 8oz self-raising flour
5ml / 1tsp baking powder
1.5ml / ¼tsp salt
30ml / 2tbls caster sugar
  (optional)

MAKES 9 SCONES

1 Place the butter in a bowl and cover. Microwave at 100% (High) for 30-60 seconds until melted.
2 Stir in half the liquid, then sift in the dry ingredients. Mix to a soft, but not sticky dough, adding liquid as necessary.
3 Turn the dough out onto a floured board and knead lightly.
4 Pat the dough into 12.5cm / 5in square and cut across twice each way to make 9 scones.
5 Arrange the scones in a large ring on a piece of non-stick paper and brush tops with milk. Microwave at 100% (High) for 3-4 minutes (5 minutes for 500 watt) until light and well risen. Turn after 2 minutes.
6 If liked, brown quickly under a conventional grill.

Cheese scones

4 mins

Standing time: none

225g / 8oz self-raising flour
1.5ml / ¼tsp salt
25g / 1oz butter or margarine
50g / 2oz Cheddar cheese, finely grated
1 egg, beaten
75-105ml / 5-7tbls milk or water
15ml / 1tbls grated Parmesan cheese
15ml / 1tbls toasted breadcrumbs
1.5ml / ¼tsp dried parsley

MAKES 12 SCONES

1 Sift the flour and salt into a bowl and rub in the butter or margarine until the mixture resembles fine breadcrumbs.
2 Stir in the Cheddar cheese, egg and enough liquid to make a soft, but not sticky dough. Knead lightly in the bowl.
3 Turn the dough onto a lightly floured surface and pat it into a round 12mm / ½in thick. Cut out 12 rounds using a 5cm / 2in cutter.

4 Invert a large plate or flan dish in the microwave. Arrange 6 scones in a circle on a piece of non-stick paper on the base of the upturned plate.
5 Mix the Parmesan cheese with the crumbs and parsley and sprinkle evenly over the top.
6 Microwave at 100% (High) for 2-3 minutes (4 minutes for 500 watt) until risen. Repeat with the remaining scones. Brown lightly under the grill.

Academy oat scone

4 mins

Standing time: 1 min

50g / 2oz butter or margarine
15ml / 1tbls golden syrup
150ml / ¼pt mixed milk and water
225g / 8oz 81% self-raising flour
1.5 ml / ¼tsp salt
5ml / 1tsp baking powder
45ml / 3tbls rolled oats
15ml / 1 tbls rolled oats, toasted

MAKES 6 LARGE PIECES

Academy Oat Scone and Cheese Scones

1 Mix the butter and syrup in a bowl and microwave at 100% (High) for 1 minute to melt. Stir in half the milk and water mixture.
2 Sift in the flour, salt and baking powder, then add the rolled oats and stir into the liquid. Mix to form a soft, but not sticky dough, adding more of the milk and water mixture as necessary.
3 Invert a large plate or flan dish in the microwave. Pat the dough into a 15cm / 6in round then mark it into 6 wedges with a knife. Place on a piece of non-stick paper on base of inverted plate. Sprinkle the surface of the scone evenly with the toasted oats.
4 Microwave at 100% (High) for 3-4 minutes (5 minutes for 500 watt) until well risen and no longer doughy in the centre. Give the scone ½ turn after 3 minutes. Leave to stand for 1 minute.
5 If liked, lightly brown the top of the round under a hot grill just before serving hot with butter and jam, or leave to cool and serve with cheese for a picnic.

388

Beech farm scones

| 4 mins |

Standing time: none

200g / 7oz self-raising flour
30ml / 2tbls caster sugar
50g / 2oz butter or margarine
50g / 2oz bran
30ml / 2tbls finely-chopped
    walnuts (optional)
30ml / 2tbls raisins
150ml / ¼pt mixed milk and
    water
toasted bran for coating

MAKES 9-10 SCONES

1 Sift the flour into a mixing bowl and add the sugar. Cut in the butter or margarine with a knife, then rub in with the fingertips until the mixture resembles fine breadcrumbs.
2 Stir in the bran, nuts and raisins, then mix in sufficient liquid to make a soft, but not sticky, dough. Knead lightly in the bowl.
3 Turn the scone dough out onto a surface which has been dusted generously with toasted bran. Pat the dough out to a round shape, about 2cm / ¾in thick. Using a 5cm / 2in cutter, cut out 9 or 10 rounds, re-rolling the dough if necessary. Coat the rolls all over with bran.
4 Invert a large plate or flan dish in the microwave and arrange the scones in a circle on a piece of non-stick paper on the base of the upturned plate.
5 Microwave at 100% (High) for 4-5 minutes (6 minutes for 500 watt) until springy and no longer doughy. Give them a ½ turn every 2 minutes and turn over after 6 minutes. Leave to cool on a wire rack before serving.

Rolled spice scones

| 4¼ mins |

Standing time: 4 mins

25g / 1oz butter
90ml / 6tbls fresh brown
    bread crumbs
10ml / 2tsp ground cinnamon
60ml / 4tbls soft brown sugar

SCONES
225g / 8oz self-raising flour
1.5ml / ¼tsp salt
25g / 1oz butter or margarine
30ml / 2tbls caster sugar
1 egg, beaten
60-90ml / 4-6 tbls milk

MAKES 9 SCONES

1 Place the butter in a bowl, cover and microwave at 100% (High) for 15-30 seconds to melt. Stir in the breadcrumbs, cinnamon and soft brown sugar. Set aside.
2 Sift the flour and salt into a bowl and rub in the butter to resemble fine breadcrumbs.
3 Mix in the sugar, egg and sufficient milk to make a soft, but not sticky dough. Knead in the bowl.

Beech Farm Scones

4 Turn the dough onto a lightly floured board and roll to a 15 × 23cm / 6 × 9in rectangle.
5 Scatter the cinnamon crumb mixture over the dough then, starting at a long edge, roll it up like a Swiss roll, sealing the edge with the milk. Cut into slices.
6 Arrange the slices, spiral pattern uppermost, in an oiled 20-23cm / 8-9in flan dish, placing 8 around edge and 1 in middle.
7 Microwave the scones at 100% (High) for 4-5 minutes (6 minutes for 500 watt) until well risen and no longer doughy, turning every 2 minutes. Stand 4 minutes. Brown under a hot grill if wished.

389

CHAPTER SEVEN
ENTERTAINING

Here are all your entertaining problems solved. With the help of your microwave cooker, this chapter makes it possible for you to prepare and serve delicious meals quickly and easily. It is full of ideas for whole menus, or you can pick and choose from among them to put together the meal of your choice.

Menus range from something simple for an easy weekend lunch or informal supper to an elegant dinner party or even a sophisticated summer buffet. Amongst others, you will find a traditional Sunday lunch, a vegetarian menu and an exotic meal for four. For spontaneous entertaining, when friends or family arrive unannounced, the freezer meal is ideal. It can be prepared completely in advance and be ready and waiting in the freezer until required.

As always when entertaining, it is important to be organized and to plan ahead as much as possible. All the recipes in this chapter give detailed and precise instructions, and cooking and standing times are given for each one. A helpful 'countdown' plan is also provided for each menu, advising on which recipes can be cooked in advance, and telling you the best order in which to prepare and cook dishes so that they are ready to serve at exactly the right time. The colour photographs throughout provide hints on attractive ways to garnish or decorate foods for entertaining. As in the preceding chapters, any difficult or unusual techniques are also illustrated in colour. You will even find advice on what wine to serve with each meal!

No matter what the occasion, you will be sure to find a menu to serve in this chapter, together with all the help and advice needed to guarantee success. With all the hard work done in advance and only the last-minute cooking to do in your microwave, you can relax and enjoy entertaining as you should.

Informal supper party

All the courses for this simple but delicious menu of traditional dishes with a difference are given a special touch and are all the easier to prepare with your microwave.

The rich flavour of beef braised in red wine makes a delicious centrepiece for a 'not-too-formal' dinner party for six to eight people. The starter, a rich mushroom soup with cream, can be prepared in advance and is easy to reheat and serve to fit in with your time schedule. The braised beef can be kept hot wrapped in foil, and the vegetables take very little time to cook when they are required, so the whole dinner party can adapt to fit in with a flexible, leisurely timetable. You can microwave the vegetables and sauce while the beef is standing. Even when it has been carved, the beef can be reheated briefly in the microwave, provided it is covered with cling film.

The quantities given for the soup, vegetables and cream pie will serve up to eight, but the amount of meat should be increased according to appetites and for numbers over six.

For the purposes of presentation, you may choose to cook the beans and broccoli so that they can be arranged separately in a serving dish. If you do this, make sure the beans are to the outside of the cooking dish and the broccoli in the centre, as the slower-cooking food needs to be subjected to the most microwave energy.

When serving the main course, all the vegetables and sliced meat can be arranged on a large serving platter. The combination of colours makes an attractive presentation, making the food even more appetising.

The Grasshopper Pie should be pale green — so a few drops of green colouring help to offset the pink of the marshmallows.

When choosing wine for the supper, a hearty red such as Valpolicella complements the dishes.

MENU

Mushroom Soup
Enriched with cream and wine

Vineyard Beef Braise
Topside in a rich wine sauce

Potatoes and Carrots
Fresh vegetables cooked for flavour

Green Beans and Broccoli
A blend of delicious fresh textures

Grasshopper Pie
An unusual cream filling in a biscuit crust

SERVES 6

Countdown

The day before
Prepare and microwave the crumb case for the Grasshopper Pie; allow it to cool then refrigerate overnight. Microwave the soup (but do not stir in the full amount of cream). Cover and refrigerate until just before serving.

Early on the day
Prepare the filling for the Grasshopper Pie and pour it into the crumb case. Leave to set and chill (this must be done at least six hours before the pie is to be served). Prepare the vegetables and refrigerate in separate plastic bags to keep crisp and fresh.

2 hours before serving
Start microwaving the beef. If cooking a larger joint than stated in the recipe, calculate the cooking time, allowing 20-25 minutes per 450g / 1lb, and time it so that you take standing time into consideration. Microwave the vegetables and the sauce while the meat is standing.

Just before serving
Reheat the soup by microwaving at 100% (High) for 10 minutes, stirring several times. Reheat vegetables for a few minutes at 100% (High) if necessary. Serve and add the cream and parsley.

ANDREW WHITTUCK

Vineyard beef braise

82 mins

Standing time: 15 mins

1.6kg / 3½lb topside of beef
30ml / 2tbls vegetable oil
2 celery stalks, thinly sliced
1 onion, thinly sliced
2 carrots, thinly sliced
150ml / ¼pt red wine
salt and pepper
2 garlic cloves, crushed
1 bouquet garni
watercress, to garnish

SAUCE
1 beef stock cube
150ml / ¼pt water
150ml / ¼pt red wine
15ml / 1tbls soy sauce
10ml / 2tsp tomato purée
10ml / 2tsp cornflour

SERVES 6

1 Put the oil, celery, onion and carrots in a 2.3L / 4pt casserole. Cover and microwave at 100% (High) for 8 minutes, until tender, stirring once.
2 Arrange the beef on top of the vegetables. Add the wine, salt, pepper, garlic and the bouquet garni. Cover and microwave at 50% (Medium) for 35 minutes.
3 Turn the meat over, cover and microwave at 50% (Medium) for a further 35 minutes. Turn again, cover; stand for 15 minutes.
4 Remove meat from casserole and wrap it in foil to keep warm.
5 Remove the vegetables using a slotted spoon and discard. Reserve the cooking juices.
6 Pour off any excess, then add the stock cube to the remaining liquid. Stir in the water, wine, soy sauce and tomato purée. Microwave at 100% (High) for 2-3 minutes, stirring once.
7 Mix the cornflour with a little water until smooth, then stir it into the sauce. Cover and microwave at 100% (High) for 2 minutes, stirring once or twice until smooth and thick.
8 Arrange the cooked vegetables on a heated serving dish. Arrange sliced meat with a little sauce. Garnish with watercress. Serve the rest of the sauce separately.

393

Mushroom soup

12 mins

Standing time: 1 min

1 large onion, finely chopped
40g / 1½oz butter
350g / 12oz mushrooms, finely
   chopped
2.5ml / ½tsp ground coriander
15ml / 1tbls plain flour
1L / 1¾pt chicken stock
150ml / ¼pt dry white wine
150ml / ¼pt single cream
salt and pepper
chopped parsley, to garnish

SERVES 6-8

1 Place the onion and butter in a large bowl and cover. Microwave at 100% (High) for 3-4 minutes, or until the onion is tender.
2 Stir in the mushrooms and coriander. Cover and microwave at 100% (High) for 2 minutes.
3 Stir in the flour and gradually add the stock, then microwave, uncovered, at 100% (High) for 5 minutes. Stir in wine and microwave at 100% (High) for 2 minutes. Purée in a blender.
4 Stir in half the cream, season to taste and stand for 1 minute.
5 Pour into bowls, add a swirl of cream and sprinkle with chopped parsley.

Green beans and broccoli

10 mins

Standing time: 5 mins

700g / 1½lb broccoli, cut into
   florets
225g / 8oz whole green beans
salt and pepper
25g / 1oz butter

SERVES 6-8

1 Place the broccoli and beans in a large casserole with 30ml / 2tbls water. Cover.
2 Microwave at 100% (High) for 10-13 minutes until tender, stirring once half way through the time. Season with the salt and pepper.
3 Dot with butter. Cover and leave to stand for 5 minutes.

ANDREW WHITTUCK

394

Potatoes and carrots

18 mins

Standing time: 5-10 mins

700g / 1½lb small new potatoes, scrubbed
6 carrots
30ml / 2tbls water
15ml / 1tbls butter

SERVES 6-8

1 Prick the potatoes with a fork several times. Cut the carrots in half crossways, then into quarters lengthways.
2 Place the potatoes and carrots in a 2.3L / 4pt casserole with the water and butter. Cover with cling film rolled back at one edge.
3 Microwave at 100% (High) for 18-20 minutes, stirring once or twice during cooking. Leave to stand for 5-10 minutes.
4 Serve the vegetables arranged on a carving dish around the cooked meat.

Grasshopper pie

4½ mins

Standing time: none

100g / 4oz butter or margarine
275g / 10oz plain chocolate digestive biscuit crumbs
275g / 10oz marshmallows
75ml / 3fl oz milk
75ml / 3fl oz green crème de menthe
350ml / 12fl oz whipping cream
few drops of green food colouring
angelica, to decorate

MAKES A 23cm / 9in PIE

1 Place the butter in a 23cm / 9in flan dish. Cover and microwave at 100% (High) for 30-60 seconds until melted. Mix in the biscuit crumbs and press the mixture into the base and sides of the dish.
2 Microwave at 100% (High) for 1-3 minutes, or until hot, turning once or twice. Set aside to cool.

3 In a 2.8L / 5pt casserole or large bowl, combine the marshmallows and milk. Microwave at 100% (High) for 3-5 minutes, or until the marshmallows are melted, stirring frequently. Mix in the crème de menthe. Refrigerate for 1-2 hours, stirring occasionally.
4 Whisk the cream, and fold three-quarters into the marshmallow mixture. Pour into the case and chill for at least 3 hours. Decorate with cream and angelica.

Cook's notes

Although the Grasshopper Pie is traditionally meant to be green coloured, a variety of other flavours could be achieved by using orange or mandarin liqueur and using plain biscuit crumbs for the base. If liked, a little orange food colouring could be added, or pink marshallows used instead of white to give the pie a rosy colour.

Easy weekend lunch

If you dream of having a lie-in on Sunday morning, but still want a traditional, substantial lunch, your microwave can make it come true — and the Countdown makes it even easier.

With a little careful pre-planning, using the Countdown and some help from the microwave, even a late riser can conjure up an impressive Sunday lunch.

The courses balance well — the light soup is followed by rich glazed pork and parsnips with fresh-tasting tomatoes and creamy mashed potato. Round the meal off with a creamy raspberry fool.

Prepare the vegetables for the soup in advance, but do not shred the lettuce, as it will become limp overnight. Trim the pork, but leave a thin layer of fat around the roll to moisten and flavour the meat. (not too much, as this attracts microwaves from the meat).

As there is a double quantity of biscuits, store leftovers in an airtight tin for 2-3 days.

Glazed Pork with Parsnips

Lettuce soup

Standing time: none

[7 mins]

2 celery stalks, finely chopped
1 small green pepper, seeded and finely chopped
2 spring onions, chopped
25g / 1oz butter, cut in small pieces
1.1L / 2pt hot vegetable or chicken stock
¼ crisp lettuce, shredded
100g / 4oz cooked long-grain rice
2 carrots, thinly sliced
salt and pepper
4 thin lemon slices

SERVES 6

1 Place the celery, green pepper, onion and butter in a large casserole dish. Cover and microwave at 100% (High) for 4-5 minutes, or until the vegetables are just tender, stirring after 2 minutes to ensure even cooking.
2 Add all the remaining ingredients except the lemon slices, stirring thoroughly.
3 Cover the dish and microwave at 100% (High) for 3-4 minutes, or until thoroughly heated. Stir well, then ladle straight into heated serving bowls and serve each one with a slice of lemon floated on top.

Cook's notes

To make thin slices of carrot, use a vegetable peeler to pare thin curls down the length of the carrots. These curls also make a pretty decoration for cold dishes and cocktail savouries.

Countdown

The previous day
Microwave the biscuits, cool on a wire rack, then store in an airtight container. Prepare the vegetables for the soup, but do not shred the lettuce. Store in individual polythene bags in the refrigerator. Peel the potatoes and parsnips, cover with cold water and refrigerate.

Microwave the raspberries until just soft and make the fool. Cover the surface with cling film and refrigerate.

During the morning
Remove all the vegetables from the refrigerator. Shred the lettuce and microwave the soup. Cover and set aside. Prepare the tomatoes and arrange in a dish. Divide the fool between six dessert glasses, decorate and return to the refrigerator. Microwave the potatoes, mash thoroughly, then place in a serving dish. Cover and set aside. Microwave the glaze for the meat and parsnips.

An hour and a half before
Baste the meat and microwave for the calculated time. Cover with foil and leave to stand while you microwave the parsnips. Reheat the soup at 100% (High) for 6-8 minutes. Serve immediately.

Between courses
Reheat the potato by microwaving at 100% (High) for 4-5 minutes. Microwave the tomatoes, then serve the main course.

MENU

Lettuce Soup
A fresh-tasting, light vegetable mixture

Glazed Pork with Parsnips
Easy-to-carve joint with a fruity glaze

Creamy Mashed Potato
A hot family favourite

Hot Herb Tomatoes
Seasoned and heated but not cooked

Raspberry Yoghurt Fool
Lightly crushed fruit in creamy thick yoghurt

Hazelnut Biscuits
A perfect sweet complement to fruit fool

SERVES 6

Glazed pork with parsnips

51 mins

Standing time: 20 mins

1.4kg / 3lb boned and rolled loin
  of pork
700g / 1½lb parsnips, cut in
  5cm / 2in wedges
parsley sprigs to garnish

GLAZE

100g / 4oz demerara sugar
10ml / 2tsp cornflour
150ml / ¼pt orange juice
100g / 4oz pineapple or apricot
  jam

SERVES 6

1 First make the glaze. Combine all the ingredients in a 1.1L / 2pt bowl and microwave, covered, at 100% (High) for 3 minutes, or until thickened, stirring every minute. Set aside, covered.

2 Trim any excess fat from the pork loin and weigh it. Calculate the cooking time allowing 11 minutes per 450g / 1lb. Brush the pork all over with the glaze and place it on a roasting rack, set in a shallow dish, seam side up. Insert a microwave thermometer. Cover and microwave at 70% (Medium-High) for 33 minutes (or the calculated cooking time), or until the internal temperature of the meat reaches 82°C / 180°F. After 20 minutes cooking time, turn the meat over; baste with more glaze

3 Remove from the cooker and leave to stand, covered in foil, for 15 minutes.

4 Meanwhile, cook the parsnips. Mix the parsnips with the remaining glaze in a 1.7L / 3pt bowl. Toss well to coat, then cover and microwave at 100% (High) for 15-20 minutes, or until the par-snips are tender, turning them over after half the cooking time. Leave to stand for 5 minutes. Arrange on a heated carving dish with the parsnips. Garnish.

Microtips

Drain away any excess juices which run out of the meat during cooking. These detract microwave energy from the meat and slow down the cooking process.

Cook's notes

If you do not have a roasting rack, stand the joint on an upturned saucer in a shallow dish so that it does not rest in the fat or juices while it is cooking.

Creamy mashed potatoes

20 mins

Standing time: 5 mins

1.4kg / 3lb floury potatoes,
  quartered
100ml / 3½fl oz water
salt and pepper
75ml / 5tbls milk or milk and
  cream mixed
50g / 2oz butter

SERVES 6

1 Arrange the potato quarters in a large casserole. Mix the water with salt to taste and pour over the potatoes. Cover and microwave at 100% (High) for 20-25 minutes, stirring the potato pieces at 5-minute intervals.

2 When all the pieces are tender, remove the dish from the cooker and leave to stand for 5 minutes. Drain thoroughly.

3 Add the milk and butter with pepper to taste, and mash thoroughly, either using a fork or a potato masher.

4 If liked, pipe through a large star nozzle for a decorative finish; or, fork the top of the potato into peaks and serve from the dish.

Lettuce Soup

Hot herb tomatoes

<table><tr><td>3
mins</td></tr></table>

Standing time: none

**6 firm tomatoes, about 65g /
2½oz each
salt and pepper
5ml / 1tsp dried sage or thyme**

SERVES 6

1 Cut the tomatoes in half horizontally. Arrange the bottom halves on a large plate in a circle and sprinkle with salt, pepper and sage or thyme.
2 Replace the top halves and microwave at 100% (High) for 3-3½ minutes, or until hot but not cooked. Serve with the loin of pork, glazed parsnips and creamy mashed potato.

Raspberry yoghurt fool

<table><tr><td>2½
mins</td></tr></table>

Standing time: none

**350g / 12oz frozen raspberries
850ml / 1½pt thick Greek-style
  yoghurt
30-45ml / 2-3tbls caster sugar
mint leaves to decorate**

SERVES 6

1 Break the raspberries up slightly and spread in the base of a 1.1L / 2pt dish. Cover and microwave at 100% (High) for 2½-3 minutes, or until just warm, arranging and breaking up after every minute. Reserve twelve whole raspberries in a covered container in the refrigerator to use for decoration. Break up and lightly mash remaining berries.
2 Pour the yoghurt into a bowl and mix in the sugar to taste. Add the mashed raspberries, folding them into the yoghurt to leave a marbled effect. Spoon into six dessert glasses and chill until ready to serve.
3 Decorate with the reserved raspberries and mint leaves. Serve with hazelnut biscuits (see right).

VARIATION
Use 350g / 12oz frozen strawberries, defrosted and drained.

CHRIS KNAGGS

Hazelnut biscuits

<table><tr><td>3
mins</td></tr></table>

Standing time: none

**90ml / 6tbls plain flour
pinch of salt
30ml / 2tbls caster sugar
40g / 1½oz butter
50g / 2oz toasted hazelnuts,
  coarsely ground
15ml / 1tbls water**

MAKES 24

1 Sift the flour, salt and sugar into a bowl. Add the butter and rub in until the mixture resembles fine breadcrumbs.

Raspberry Yoghurt Fool and Hazelnut Biscuits

2 Stir in the nuts, then add the water, working into a firm dough. Knead lightly on a floured surface until smooth.
3 Roll the mixture out thinly into a rectangle 15 × 25cm / 6 × 10in and cut into 24 even fingers.
4 Arrange 12 biscuits at a time on a greased microwave baking tray. Microwave at 100% (High) for 1½-2 minutes, (500 watt, 3½ minutes, turning after 2 minutes).
5 Remove carefully with a palette knife and leave to cool on a wire rack. Repeat with the remaining 12 fingers.

399

Midweek supper for 4

Give a new look to a classic 'meat and three vegetables' theme with this handy turkey roast, served up with three colourful vegetable combinations; it's quick, clean and simple by microwave.

Boned turkey roasts are a good-value, no-waste way to serve up a solid, meaty meal — and they're simple to carve and economical, too.

The microwave makes quick work of these boneless joints, cooking them speedily and evenly without drying. The sharp-sweet cranberry sauce and marmalade baste keeps the joint moist during cooking and provides a tangy sauce which can be served hot with the finished dish.

Vegetables cook so well by microwave, and it's easy to create colourful mixtures with complementing flavours and textures.

When microwaving vegetables of different textures together, start with the harder, thicker of the two and then add the second when the first is almost tender. Remember that some vegetables, such as tomatoes, scarcely need cooking, merely heating, to be ready to serve, so these can be stirred in

with cooked vegetables.

Individual crème caramels cook more evenly than a large single dessert and are more attractive to serve for entertaining. Make sure that the egg mixture never boils, or it will scramble and curdle. Use 50% (Medium) power and check frequently to see that it does not overheat. Serve the crème caramels on their own, with fresh fruit such as strawberries or raspberries, or with a fruit compote (see pages 286 or 307).

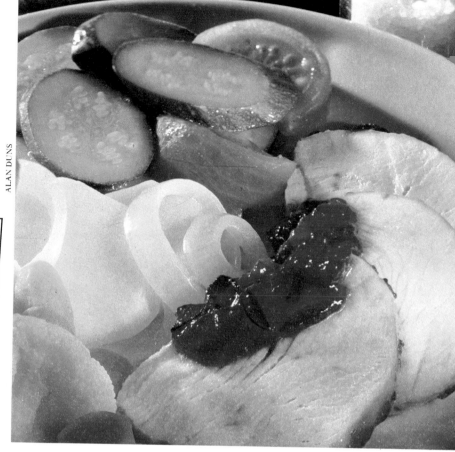

ALAN DUNS

MENU

Cranberry Turkey Roast
A juicy, easy-carve roast in a tangy baste

Cauliflower with Carrots
Crunchy florets and strips combined

Courgette Tomato Medley
A delicious Italian partnership

Potato with Onion
A buttery blend of sharp and mild flavours

Crème Caramels
Lightly set custard in bitter-sweet caramel

Assorted Fresh Fruit
An accompaniment for crème caramels

SERVES 4

Cranberry turkey roast

| 19 mins |

Standing time: 10 mins

576g / 1¼lb turkey breast roast
175g / 6oz cranberry sauce
30ml / 2tbls marmalade
lettuce leaves to garnish

SERVES 4

1 Remove the outer wrapper from the turkey roast. Place the joint in a shallow dish and microwave at 70% (Medium-High) for 7 minutes. Take off inner wrapping and turn the joint.
2 Place the cranberry sauce and marmalade in a small bowl, mix well and microwave at 100% (High) for 2 minutes. Spread half evenly over the turkey roast.
3 Microwave at 70% (Medium-High) for a further 10 minutes. Cover with foil and allow to stand for 10 minutes. Arrange on a bed of lettuce. Serve with the rest of the sauce handed separately.

Countdown

In the morning
Prepare all the vegetables for the mixtures and refrigerate them separately in polythene bags.
Microwave the Crème Caramels, allow to cool, then chill.

An hour before the meal
Take the vegetables from the refrigerator so that they can come to room temperature.
Microwave the turkey roast and leave to stand, keeping it warm by wrapping it in foil, for 10 minutes. Meanwhile, microwave the Potato with Onion and Cauliflower with Carrots. While they are standing, microwave the Courgette Tomato Medley. Turn out the Crème Caramels and return to the refrigerator. Serve the roast and vegetables hot, passing the remaining baste in a separate serving dish as a sauce.

Microtips

The remainder of the cranberry and marmalade sauce may become cold while the turkey roast is still cooking. Microwave it at 100% (High) for about 30 seconds, or until hot. Make sure the sauceboat has no metal trim. If it has, microwave in a bowl and transfer to sauceboat.

401

Potato with onion

10 mins

Standing time: 3 mins

**550g / 1¼lb potatoes, sliced
 in 6mm / ¼in rounds
25g / 1oz butter
1 onion, cut in 6mm / ¼in
 slices and separated into rings
salt and pepper**

SERVES 4

1 Place the potatoes in a 1.1L / 2pt casserole, add the butter and cover. Microwave at 100% (High) for 7 minutes, stirring twice to rearrange the slices.
2 Stir in the sliced onion and cover. Microwave at 100% (High) for 3 minutes; season to taste. Keep covered and stand for 3 minutes.

Courgette tomato medley

5 mins

Standing time: none

The tomatoes in this medley scarcely need cooking, just heating, to serve.

**4 courgettes, (about 225g / 8oz)
 cut in 6mm / ¼in slices
25g / 1oz butter
4 tomatoes, cut in wedges
salt and pepper**

SERVES 4

1 Place the courgettes in a 1.1L / 2pt casserole with the butter. Cover and microwave at 100% (High) for 3 minutes.
2 Stir in the tomato wedges, cover and microwave at 100% (High) for a further 2-3 minutes. Season to taste with salt and pepper.

Potato with Onion, Courgette Tomato Medley, Cauliflower with Carrots

Microtips

Always season vegetables after cooking, as the salt can toughen them if it is added before microwaving.

Cauliflower with carrots

8 mins

Standing time: 3 mins

1 cauliflower, weighing about
    275g / 10oz, cut in florets
60ml / 4tbls water
2 large carrots, cut in 6mm / $\frac{1}{4}$in
    slices
salt and pepper

SERVES 4

1 Place the cauliflower in a 1.1L / 2pt casserole and add the water. Cover and microwave at 100% (High) for 3 minutes, stirring the pieces once to ensure even cooking.
2 Mix carrots into cauliflower and cover. Microwave at 100% (High) for a further 5 minutes, until vegetables are just tender but still crisp, stirring once during the cooking time.
3 Allow to stand for 3 minutes, then drain thoroughly and season to taste with salt and pepper. Place in a heated serving dish and leave covered until served.

Crème caramels

13½ mins

Standing time: none

When turning out the crème caramels, dip the bases into a bowl of boiling water until just hot to the touch. This will loosen the caramel layer.

100g / 4oz caster sugar
75ml / 3fl oz cold water
15ml / 1tbls boiling water
3 large eggs
150ml / $\frac{1}{4}$pt double cream
150ml / $\frac{1}{4}$pt milk
few drops of vanilla flavouring

SERVES 4

1 Place 75g / 3oz of the sugar in a large, heatproof bowl with the cold water. Microwave at 100% (High) for 3 minutes, then stir to dissolve the sugar. Microwave at 100% (High) for a further 6-10 minutes, or until the mixture turns a golden brown colour.
2 Stir in the boiling water and set aside to cool slightly. Divide be-

Crème Caramels with fresh fruit

tween four individual ramekin dishes.
3 Beat the eggs, sugar, cream, milk and flavouring together lightly, then strain into the ramekins.
4 Arrange the filled dishes in a circle in the cooker and microwave at 50% (Medium) for 4½-7 minutes, or until the mixture is just starting to set in the centre, giving the dishes a quarter turn every 2-3 minutes.
5 Remove the dishes from the cooker and allow to cool. Keep in the refrigerator until firm and set.
6 To serve, turn out on to a serving dish, letting the caramel sauce run around the desserts.

Cook's notes

Use a bowl which will withstand very high temperatures for heating the sugar. It should be deep enough to allow enough room for the syrup to expand without boiling over on to the cooker floor.

Sunday supper for 6

What better way to enjoy a relaxed Sunday evening than lingering over a delicious meal with good friends? The microwave makes the cooking easy — and leaves you more time to enjoy yourself.

This menu is designed to be enjoyed at leisure. There is no fussy starter — just a satisfying, meaty one-pot main course, a crunchy salad accompaniment and individual chilled desserts. Hot black coffee laced with rum rounds off the meal in a suitably indulgent style.

Warm, home-made Horseradish Sauce complements the pot roast beautifully. Mustard goes well with beef — for extra interest, offer a choice of interesting types, like wholegrain, Dijon and Meaux, and let your guests make their own selection.

The potatoes and carrots are hot vegetables cooked with the beef, so the cold crunchy slaw served with a warm, creamy dressing makes a lively accompaniment to the main dish.

For dessert, serve pretty striped Blackberry Bombes. These individual frozen moulds have a good creamy texture without being rich or cloying. They are decorated with whole blackberries and mint sprigs and served with crisp biscuits such as langues du chat or shortbread fingers. The slaw and dessert can be made well ahead, leaving just the main course and Horseradish Sauce to be cooked. This presents no problem as the pot roast needs very little attention and the sauce takes just a few minutes to make.

A special coffee makes a lovely ending to an enjoyable meal and this variation on Irish coffee should make a satisfying finish to this Sunday supper.

Serve either chilled lager or a medium-bodied red wine such as a St Emilion or Côtes-du-Rhône with the beef.

Countdown

The day before
Soak the salt beef in a bowl of cold water overnight as in Stage 1. Microwave bombes and freeze.

In the morning
Prepare the Green and White Slaw to the end of Stage 3, but do not garnish. Cover and refrigerate. Scrub the carrots and potatoes for the Salt Beef Pot Roast.

1¼ hours before the meal
Drain and rinse the salt beef and proceed with the recipe from Stage 2, cutting up the vegetables before adding them to the casserole in Stage 4. Microwave the Salt Beef from Stage 2 to the end of Stage 6. Set the table.

15 minutes before the meal
Take the slaw out of the refrigerator and garnish. Empty the mustards into small pots and put on the table. Grate the horseradish and measure the remaining ingredients for the sauce.

Just before the meal
Microwave the Horseradish Sauce. Dish up the Salt Beef Pot Roast and serve with the warm sauce. While clearing the dishes soften the Blackberry Bombes in the microwave at 20-30% (Defrost) for about 30 seconds, then turn out and decorate. Serve with crisp biscuits. Just after the dessert microwave the Coffee with Rum and serve.

MENU

Salt Beef Pot Roast
A tasty, satisfying beef and vegetable dish

Horseradish Sauce
The perfect partner for beef

Green and White Slaw
A crunchy salad with a creamy dressing

Blackberry Bombes
Individual blackberry and ice cream moulds

Coffee with Rum
Rum-laced coffee topped with cream

SERVES 6

Salt beef pot roast

60 mins

Standing time: 15 mins

- **2.7-3.2kg / 3-3½lb joint rolled salted brisket of beef**
- **1.1L / 2pt boiling water**
- **8 potatoes, scrubbed and cut into three**
- **6 large carrots, cut into chunks**
- **1 small onion, sliced into thick rings**

SERVES 6

1 Soak the beef in a bowl of cold water for 8-12 hours or overnight.
2 Next day, drain and rinse the beef and place in a 2.7L / 5pt casserole. Add 575ml / 1pt boiling water. Cover and microwave at 50% (Medium) for 30 minutes, turning the meat over after 15 minutes. Pour off the cooking liquid and discard. Take the meat out of the casserole and set aside. Rinse out the dish.
3 Put the meat back in the dish, surround with potatoes, carrots and onion rings and pour over 575ml / 1pt boiling water. Cover

405

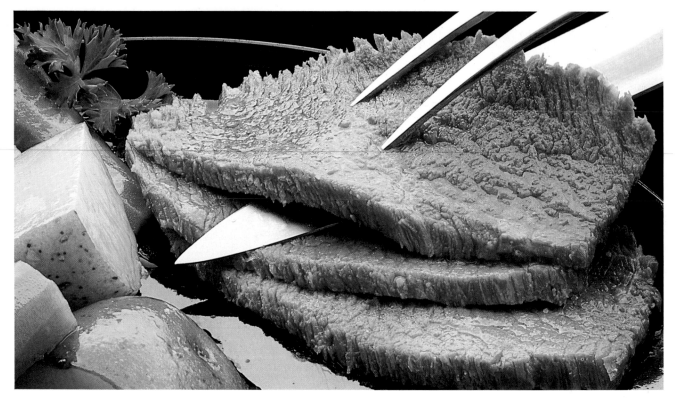

Salt Beef Pot Roast

and microwave at 50% (Medium) for 20 minutes. Stir the vegetables.
4 Increase the power to 100% (High). Cover and microwave for 10 minutes, until all the vegetables are just tender when pierced with a sharp knife. Leave to stand for 15 minutes.
5 Drain the meat and vegetables from the cooking liquid.
6 Arrange the meat on a large serving plate, surround with the vegetables. Carve the meat into thick slices and serve with the warm Horseradish Sauce.

Horseradish sauce

2½ mins

Standing time: none

15g / ½oz butter or margarine
15g / ½oz plain flour
150ml / ¼pt milk
salt and pepper
15-30ml / 1-2tbls grated horseradish
15ml / 1tbls malt vinegar
60ml / 4tbls fresh breadcrumbs
15ml / 1tbls single cream

SERVES 6

1 Place the fat in a 575ml / 1pt jug. Cover and microwave at 100% (High) for about 30 seconds, or until just melted.
2 Stir in the flour, then blend in the milk until smooth. Microwave at 100% (High) for for 2-2½ minutes, or until the sauce is thick and smooth, stirring after 1 minute.
3 Season to taste, then stir in the vinegar, breadcrumbs and cream.

Green and white slaw

1 min

Standing time: none

700g / 1½lb white cabbage, shredded
1 small green pepper, chopped
½ cucumber, coarsely chopped
2 celery stalks, chopped
1 green eating apple, chopped
15ml / 1tbls vinegar
1 onion, sliced
1 garlic clove, crushed
2 tomatoes, halved to garnish

DRESSING
90ml / 6tbls mayonnaise
150ml / ¼pt soured cream
salt and pepper

SERVES 6

PAUL GRATER

406

1 In a large bowl, combine the cabbage, green pepper, cucumber, celery and apple, vinegar, onion and garlic.
2 Combine the mayonnaise and soured cream with the salt and pepper in a small bowl. Cover and microwave at 70% (Medium) for 1 minute, until the dressing is warm but not hot.
3 Stir, then pour over the prepared vegetables and mix well to coat. Cover and chill for at least 2 hours. Garnish with tomato halves just before serving with the Salt Beef Pot Roast, vegetables and Horseradish Sauce.

Blackberry bombes

8
mins

Standing time: none

500g / 1lb blackberries, thawed and drained if frozen

45ml / 3tbls water
2.5ml / ½tsp vanilla flavouring
275ml / ½pt double cream, lightly whipped
15ml / 1tbls lemon juice
30ml / 2tbls Cassis
extra blackberries, and mint sprigs to decorate

ICE CREAM BASE
275ml / ½pt milk
2 eggs
100g / 4oz caster sugar

SERVES 6

1 First prepare the ice cream base. Heat the milk by microwaving in a large jug at 100% (High) for 2-2½ minutes, until hot but not boiling.
2 Whisk the eggs and sugar together in a 1.1L / 2pt bowl until frothy. Gradually whisk in the hot milk. Microwave at 100% (High) for 3-3½ minutes, whisking after 2 minutes, then every 30 seconds, until the mixture will coat the back of a spoon.
3 Cool the mixture, then cover closely and chill thoroughly.
4 Place the blackberries in a bowl with the water, cover and microwave at 100% (High) for 3-4 minutes, or until tender, stirring once. Purée in a blender until smooth and sieve to remove pips. Leave to cool completely.
5 Mix the vanilla flavouring with one-third of the chilled ice cream base. Mix the remaining ice cream base with the blackberry purée, lemon juice and Cassis.
6 Fold one-third of the whipped cream into the vanilla mixture and the rest into the blackberry mixture.
7 Divide half of the blackberry mixture between six chilled individual ramekins or freezer / microwave moulds. Spoon the vanilla mixture on top, spreading it smoothly. Carefully top with the remaining blackberry mixture so that it does not sink. Cover with greaseproof paper and foil and freeze for 4 hours, or until firm.
8 To serve, arrange the ramekins or moulds in a circle in the cooker and microwave at 20-30% (Defrost) for 30 seconds. Turn out and decorate. Serve with biscuits.

Left: *Blackberry Bombes*

PAUL GRATER

Coffee with rum

5
mins

Standing time: none

850ml / 1½pt strong black coffee
30ml / 6tsp light brown sugar
175ml / 6fl oz dark rum
150ml / ¼pt double cream, whipped
grated chocolate to decorate

SERVES 6

1 Pour the coffee into six heatproof glass coffee mugs and add 5ml / 1tsp sugar to each one.
2 Arrange three mugs in a triangle in the cooker, with space between each. Microwave at 100% (High) for 2½-3½ minutes or until hot. Pour 25ml / 1fl oz rum into each glass, top with 15ml / 1tbls whipped cream and sprinkle with grated chocolate. Serve at once.
3 Repeat with the remaining mugs.

407

Vegetarian menu for four

Use the microwave to show off some all-important features of vegetarian cuisine — flavour, appearance and texture — for a meatless menu to tempt non-vegetarian friends as well.

Microwaving is the perfect way to cook vegetables and meatless dishes; all the goodness is captured in the food and not dissolved in large quantities of cooking liquid or destroyed by overcooking. Colours stay appetizing and bright and vegetables keep a good shape and texture.

This vegetarian menu makes the best possible use of all the advantages. The mushroom pâté, which includes cannellini beans for their protein, fibre and deliciously 'mealy' texture, can be served as a dip if preferred with the addition of a little more lemon juice or some yoghurt. In the main course, the aubergines are cleverly used to

line the dish and hold a satisfying pasta mixture. Unlike conventionally cooked aubergines, they keep a fresh, light colour when microwaved to give the dish an appetizing appearance. Finally, the slightly tart taste of puréed apricots combined with almond macaroons produces an irresistible dessert.

408

Countdown

The day before
Soak the apricots for the dessert in the morning. Microwave and assemble the dessert later in the day, and leave to chill overnight. Prepare the Mushroom Pâté and cover closely with cling film. Chill.

During the day
Prepare all the vegetables for the main course and keep crisp in individual polythene bags in the refrigerator. Assemble the Aubergine Bake and set aside, covered.

Half an hour before serving
Turn out the dessert and return to the refrigerator. Microwave the turnips and French beans. Set aside. Microwave the Aubergine Bake at 100% (High) for 10-15 minutes and leave to stand for 5 minutes while the Mushroom Pâté is served. Reheat the sauce, turnips and beans at 100% (High) for 3-4 minutes. Add butter to the beans and parsley to the potatoes. Turn the Aubergine Bake out and serve with the sauce.

MENU

Mushroom Pâté
A light spreading pâté served with crisp wholemeal rolls

Aubergine Bake
Fresh vegetables, cheese and pasta in an aubergine case

Glazed Turnips
Whole baby turnips served in a buttery glaze

French Beans
Crisp green beans

Apricot Almond Pudding
Chilled layers of custard, fruit and almond biscuits

SERVES 4

Mushroom pâté

13 mins

Standing time: none

1 onion, chopped
30ml / 2tbls olive oil
225g / 8oz button mushrooms, chopped
150g / 5oz cannellini beans, rinsed and drained
30ml / 2tbls lemon juice
salt and pepper
sliced mushrooms, to garnish
few sprigs of parsley

SERVES 4

1 Place the onion and olive oil in a medium-sized dish. Cover and microwave at 70% (Medium-High) for 5 minutes until onion is transparent.

2 Add the mushrooms and microwave at 70% (Medium-High) for a further 5 minutes.

3 Stir in the beans and lemon juice and microwave covered at 100% (High) for 3 minutes. Allow to cool slightly.

4 Purée in a blender and add salt and pepper to taste. Turn into a

409

serving dish and leave, covered, in the refrigerator, to chill thoroughly.

5 Stir gently, then garnish with sliced mushrooms and parsley. Serve with crisp wholemeal rolls.

Aubergine bake

| 28 mins |

Standing time: 13 mins

A vegetarian Cheddar cheese, made without rennet, is available from health food stores and some large supermarkets.

175g / 6oz wholemeal pasta shells or macaroni
salt and pepper
1 garlic clove, crushed
1 large onion, finely chopped
1 carrot, finely chopped
1 celery stalk, finely chopped
30ml / 2tbls olive oil
700g / 1½lb aubergines
2 × 425g / 15oz cans tomatoes
2.5ml / ½tsp dried oregano
1 small green pepper, seeded and chopped
100g / 4oz mushrooms
2 courgettes, thinly sliced
75g / 3oz Cheddar cheese, grated
finely chopped parsley (optional)

SERVES 4

1 Cook the pasta conventionally in boiling salted water until just tender — about 12-15 minutes. Drain and set aside, covered with cling film over the surface.

2 Mix the garlic, onion, carrot, celery and olive oil together in a large bowl. Cover and microwave at 100% (High) for 8-10 minutes until the vegetables are tender.

3 Prick the aubergines all over with a fork and cut off the stalks. Microwave at 100% (High) for 3-4 minutes. Set aside to stand for 5 minutes, then slice thinly in rounds.

4 Stir the tomatoes and oregano into the cooked vegetable mixture. Cover and microwave at 100% (High) for 5 minutes. Purée in a blender. Reserve half the puréed sauce and season to taste.

5 Add the peppers, mushrooms and courgettes to the remaining sauce. Cover and microwave at

PAUL WEBSTER

Mushroom Pâté

100% (High) for 5 minutes, or until the vegetables are just tender. Allow to stand for 3 minutes.

6 Lightly grease a 2.3L / 4pt dish and line with aubergine slices (see right), reserving enough to make a 'lid'.

7 Stir the cheese and cooked pasta into the vegetable mixture. Season to taste and spread evenly in the lined dish. Cover with the remaining aubergine slices. Cover and microwave at 100% (High) for 5 minutes. Stand for 5 minutes, then invert on to a serving dish.

8 Reheat the reserved sauce at 100% (High) for 2-3 minutes, if necessary. Spread some of the sauce over the aubergine bake. Garnish with a border of parsley. Serve remaining sauce separately.

VARIATION
Use any selection of cooked vegetables for the filling, such as broccoli, carrots or corn.

How to line a dish with aubergines

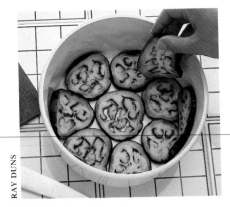

RAY DUNS

Arrange *a ring of overlapping slices of aubergines in the base, so that the slices just turn up the sides of the dish. Fill the centre of the ring with more slices. Line the sides of the dish with more rounds, so that the bottom of each one rests over those in the base. Add spoonfuls of the pasta filling in a ring around the edge of the base to keep the slices upright as you work.*

410

Glazed turnips

12½ mins

Standing time: none

450g / 1lb baby turnips
125ml / 4fl oz water
5ml / 1tsp lemon juice
25g / 1oz butter
10ml / 2tsp caster sugar
salt and pepper
2.5ml / ½tsp grated nutmeg

SERVES 4

1 Place the turnips in a shallow dish and add the water and lemon juice. Cover and microwave at 100% (High) for 10-15 minutes (small tender turnips should only take 10 minutes). Stir several times during cooking.
2 Drain the turnips and set aside. Place the butter in a small bowl, cover and microwave at 100% (High) for 30 seconds, until melted and hot. Stir in the sugar, seasoning and nutmeg. Spoon over the turnips to coat.
3 Cover and microwave at 100% (High) for 2 minutes. Arrange with the beans around the Aubergine Bake.

French beans

12 mins

Standing time: none

450g / 1lb thin French beans, trimmed
60ml / 4tbls water

SERVES 4

1 Place the beans in a large casserole with the water.
2 Cover and microwave at 100% (High) for 12-15 minutes. Stir five times during cooking.
3 Drain and arrange around the Aubergine Bake with the turnips.

Apricot almond pudding

12 mins

Standing time: none

225g / 8oz dried apricots
275ml / ½pt orange juice
30ml / 2tbls lemon juice
30-45ml / 2-3tbls plain flour
3 eggs
45ml / 3tbls sugar
grated zest of 1 orange
275ml / ½pt milk
30-45ml / 2-3tbls orange liqueur (optional)
50g / 2oz blanched almonds, toasted, to decorate
100g / 4oz small almond macaroons

SERVES 4

1 Soak the apricots for 6 hours in the orange and lemon juices.
2 Microwave the apricots in the soaking liquid, covered, at 100% (High) for 10 minutes, stirring twice. Leave to cool. In a large bowl, whisk together the flour, eggs, sugar, orange zest and milk, until smooth. Microwave at 100% (High) for 2-3 minutes, stirring after 1 minute, then whisking every 30 seconds, until smooth and thick.
3 Stir liqueur into the apricot mixture and purée in a blender.
4 Line the base and sides of a 1.1L / 2pt bowl with cling film, making sure that there are no air pockets. Arrange a ring of toasted almonds over the base.
5 Add a quarter of the custard, spreading it carefully over the almonds. Add a layer of apricot purée (about one-third of the quantity). Add a layer of macaroons, pressed into the purée, close together.
6 Continue in layers, adding three more custard layers, interspersed with two each of apricots and macaroons. Chill for about six hours or overnight.
7 Turn the dessert out on to a serving dish and peel off the cling film. Smooth the sides and return to the refrigerator. Remove from refrigerator about 5 minutes before serving.

Apricot Almond Pudding

411

Fork supper for 6

**Put on a spread that's sure to impress — an attractive buffet
is an easy to way to cater for a crowd, and this menu allows
you plenty of time to mingle with your guests.**

This menu is ideal for entertaining a small crowd — it gives you plenty of scope to prepare in advance and use the microwave for the final touches and for last-minute quick cooking. After the last dish has been served and when everyone can help themselves you can enjoy the occasion even more.

When preparing the prawns, first remove the head, then remove the soft shell, pulling it away with the legs, working from the head end to the tail on each side. Leave the tails on the prawns for easier finger eating.

Put the dip, vegetables and prawns on the table at the same time. After this first course, the only job remaining for the host is to heat the main dish and serve it — then you're free to enjoy the appreciative comments of your friends.

The unusual Savoury Fruit Salad makes a delicious flavour

contrast to the rice dish, while the Broccoli and Mushrooms add a more conventional touch.

To drink, serve a chilled white wine or a light punch — a white Glühwein punch would be ideal.

MENU

Spiced Prawns
Jumbo prawns coated in an aromatic sauce

Onion Dip
A creamy dip served with crisp raw vegetables

Chicken with Rice
Bite-sized pieces of chicken in a tasty risotto

Broccoli and Mushrooms
A medley of vegetables with a herby flavour

Savoury Fruit Salad
A refreshing salad with a difference

Coffee Ring Cake
A moist cake with a rich coffee icing

SERVES 6

Spiced prawns

6 mins

Standing time: none

50g / 2oz butter
15ml / 1tbls plain flour
10ml / 2tsp chopped parsley
2.5ml / ½tsp ground coriander
2.5ml / ½tsp ground cumin
1.5ml / ¼tsp grated nutmeg
1.5ml / ¼tsp pepper
pinch of salt
pinch of ground cloves
275ml / ½pt milk
900g / 2lb cooked king-sized prawns, peeled except for tails
sprigs of parsley to garnish

SERVES 6

1 Place the butter in a bowl, cover and microwave at 100% (High) for 1 minute, until bubbling.
2 Blend in the flour, parsley, coriander, cumin, nutmeg, pepper, salt and cloves. Gradually stir in milk. Microwave at 100% (High) for 4-6 minutes, whisking three times, until thick.
3 Place prawns in a dish. Cover and microwave at 100% (High) for 1 minute. Coat with sauce.
4 Garnish with parsley and serve with cocktail sticks.

Onion dip

1 min

Standing time: none

Serve a selection of the best fresh vegetables as dunks. Cut carrots, courgettes and celery into finger-length strips; break cauliflower and broccoli into florets.

225g / 8oz cream cheese
30ml / 2tbls milk
5ml / 1tsp onion powder
2.5ml / ½tsp garlic salt
225ml / 8fl oz soured cream
5ml / 1tsp chopped parsley
1kg / 2¼lb raw vegetables

SERVES 6

1 Place the cream cheese in a bowl. Microwave at 100% (High) for 30-45 seconds, until softened.
2 Beat in the milk, onion powder and garlic salt, blending well.
3 Microwave at 100% (High) for 30-60 seconds until warm. Beat well to blend, then stir in the soured cream. Cover and chill.
4 To serve, turn the dip into a bowl, sprinkle with the parsley and surround with the vegetables.

Spiced Prawns

Countdown

The day before
Microwave the Onion Dip and leave, covered, in the refrigerator. Microwave the Chicken with Rice. Cover and store overnight in the refrigerator. Chill the wine.

Early on the day
Microwave the Broccoli and Mushrooms and leave to marinate in the dressing in the refrigerator. (Turn the vegetables occasionally during the day.) Prepare the raw vegetables to serve with the Onion Dip and store in separate polythene bags in the refrigerator. Prepare the fruit for the salad; microwave the dressing and mix into the fruit. Cover and refrigerate. (If using bananas, do not add these to the mixture until just before serving.)

In the afternoon
Microwave the cake and allow to cool. Make the glaze and pour over the cake. Decorate.

Just before the meal
Remove the Broccoli and Mushrooms, Onion Dip and Savoury Fruit Salad from the refrigerator an hour before serving. Arrange the raw vegetables around the dip. Prepare the punch if serving.

Microwave the Spiced Prawns and serve hot with the Onion Dip. During the first course, while the guests are eating the prawns, reheat the Chicken with Rice, by microwaving at 100% (High) for 15-20 minutes. Serve with the Broccoli and Mushrooms and the Savoury Fruit Salad buffet.

413

Savoury fruit salad

4 mins

Standing time: none

Although this salad uses fruits which are conventionally used for dessert, the sharp lemon and ginger salad dressing makes it an interesting and unusual accompaniment to all sorts of light savoury dishes.

175g / 6oz sugar
15ml / 3tsp cornflour
175ml / 6fl oz water
grated zest of 1 large lemon
30ml / 2tbls lemon juice
2.5cm / 1in piece fresh ginger
  root, peeled and grated
1kg / 2¼lb mixed apples, pears,
  apricots, pineapple and
  bananas, peeled and chopped

SERVES 6

1 Place the sugar and cornflour in a bowl. Gradually add the water, lemon zest, juice and ginger, mixing well. Microwave at 100% (High) for 4-6 minutes, stirring three times during cooking, until thick and clear.
2 Place the prepared fruit in a serving dish. Pour over the lemon-ginger syrup and mix well to coat all the fruit. Keep the salad, closely covered, in the refrigerator until ready to serve.

Chicken with rice

48 mins

Standing time: 10 mins

1.6kg / 3½lb boneless chicken
  breasts, skinned
90ml / 6tbls white wine
450g / 1lb long-grain rice
4 spring onions, finely chopped
30ml / 2tbls instant rich gravy
  granules or powder
2.5ml / ½tsp pepper
100g / 4oz salted roasted peanuts,
  coarsely chopped

SERVES 6

1 Place the chicken breasts in a single layer in a large shallow dish. Pour over the wine, cover and microwave at 100% (High) for 15-

Broccoli and mushrooms

2 mins

Standing time: none

450g / 1lb broccoli, cut into
  florets
45ml / 3tbls water
450g / 1lb button mushrooms
225ml / 8fl oz bottled Italian
  dressing

SERVES 6

1 Place the broccoli in a bowl and pour over the water. Cover and

Broccoli and Mushrooms

18 minutes, rearranging twice, until just cooked.
2 Remove the chicken with a slotted spoon and chop into bite-sized pieces.
3 Drain the cooking juices into a measuring jug and make up to 1.1L / 2pt with hot water.
4 Place the rice, cooking liquid, spring onions, gravy granules and pepper in a large bowl, mixing well. Cover and microwave at 100% (High) for 8 minutes.
5 Reduce the power to 50% (Medium) and microwave for a further 25-30 minutes, or until the rice is tender and all the liquid has been absorbed.
6 Stir in the chicken and peanuts, mixing well. Cover and leave to stand for 10 minutes to complete cooking. Serve hot.

microwave at 100% (High) for 2 minutes. Drain and rinse in cold water to stop the broccoli from cooking any further.
2 Mix the broccoli and mushrooms in a bowl. Pour the dressing over and toss to coat. Cover and chill for at least 8 hours, stirring occasionally to keep the pieces coated in the marinade.
3 To serve, transfer the vegetables from the dressing with a slotted spoon to a serving dish, draining off excess liquid.

VARIATION
Turkey with rice: this is ideal for using up any left-over cooked turkey. Remove the meat from the bones and cut into bite-sized pieces. Use in place of the chicken breast. The dish can be frozen for up to three months; defrost by microwaving at 100% (High) for 13-17 minutes, breaking up and stirring twice.

Cook's notes

If you want to prepare this dish in advance, allow it to cool, then cover and refrigerate. Remove from the refrigerator 1 hour before serving time. To serve, reheat at 100% (High) for 15-20 minutes.

DON LAST

Coffee ring cake

13 mins

Standing time: 5-10 mins

1½ digestive or plain sweet biscuits, crushed
225g / 8oz plain flour, sifted
275g / 10oz caster sugar
10ml / 2tsp baking powder
pinch of salt
4 eggs
150g / 5oz margarine, softened
135ml / 4½fl oz milk
5ml / 1tsp vanilla flavouring

DECORATE
**Coffee glaze (see recipe right)
silver and gold dragees**

SERVES 6

1 Grease a 2L / 3½pt ring mould. Coat the mould thoroughly with the biscuit crumbs.
2 Place the flour, sugar, baking powder, salt, eggs, margarine, milk and vanilla flavouring in a bowl. Beat with an electric whisk for 1 minute, or with a wooden spoon for 2 minutes, until smooth and creamy.
3 Spread the mixture evenly in the dish. Microwave at 50% (Medium) for 8 minutes, giving the dish a quarter turn every 2 minutes.
4 Increase the power to 100% (High) and microwave for 5-8 minutes, giving the dish a quarter turn two or three times, until the cake is cooked. Test by pushing a cocktail stick into the centre — it should come out clean.

Coffee Ring Cake

5 Leave to stand in the dish for 5-10 minutes, then turn out on to a serving plate. Drizzle the glaze over the top and decorate with the silver and gold dragees.

Coffee glaze

200g / 7oz icing sugar
15ml / 1tbls strong coffee flavouring
45-60ml / 3-4tbls water

MAKES ENOUGH FOR 1 RING CAKE

1 Sift the icing sugar into a large bowl. Mix all the ingredients together gradually, to give a thick pouring consistency.

Romantic dinner for two

Celebrate a birthday or impress a very special friend with a romantic dinner for two. This delicious meal is simply and quickly prepared with the help of a microwave.

When there are just two of you for dinner, you want to spend as much time as possible together. This is when the microwave really comes into its own, both for advance preparation of food and last minute cooking and re-heating.

Most of the preparation for this menu can be done well ahead. The Creamy Veal takes only a few minutes to make and tastes even better if made the day before and left, covered, in the refrigerator, to allow the flavours to blend.

Veal has very little fat so it is best cooked in a liquid such as the sauce used in this menu. The creamy sauce complements the flavour of the veal as well as helping to prevent it drying out. Pasta is the perfect accompaniment.

All the vegetable, salad and fruit preparation for the meal can be done early in the day and they can then be kept cool in the refrigerator until required.

Then, with the meal well under control, you can focus your attention on the table and set the scene to suit the occasion.

Use a sparkling white table cloth or a pale-coloured one with a lace cloth over the top. Decorate the table with a pair of coloured candles and arrange an attractive centrepiece of flowers.

By the time your guest arrives, everything will be well in hand and you will be able to enjoy a pre-dinner aperitif while the microwave is gently reheating the veal. The broccoli needs only a few minutes cooking and the delicious, liqueur-flavoured cappuccino provides a flourish for the end of the meal and a final excuse to linger at the dinner table.

MENU

Lettuce Cups
Lettuce with bacon dressing

Broccoli Spears
Fresh-tasting vegetable accompaniment

Creamy Veal
Tender veal served on a bed of tagliatelle

Grapes and Italian Cheeseboard
The perfect complement to a delicious meal

Cappuccino for two
Dessert coffee with orange liqueur

Countdown

The day before
Cook the veal, omitting the fresh parsley. Cover and refrigerate until required. Remove from the refrigerator 1 hour before it needs reheating to allow to come to room temperature.

Early in the day
Prepare the salad for the Lettuce Cups; cover and refrigerate. Fry the bread cubes. Wash and drain the grapes and arrange in fruit bowl; trim the broccoli. Cover and refrigerate grapes and broccoli.

1 hour before serving
Fry the bacon for the Lettuce Cups and cut into 1cm / ½in pieces with kitchen scissors. Remove the salad from the refrigerator and fill with the chopped tomato, egg, bacon and the croûtons. Prepare the dressing, but do not spoon it over the salad until just before serving.

Remove the grapes from the refrigerator to allow them to come to room temperature before the meal.

About 20-25 minutes before serving
Cook pasta conventionally. Rinse broccoli and microwave. Leave to stand. Add the parsley to veal, cover and microwave at 50% (Medium) for 7-8 minutes, stirring once during microwaving.

Between the first course and main course
Dot the broccoli with some butter and microwave for 30-45 seconds to reheat. Spoon veal over pasta.

After the main course
Serve black grapes and cheeses. Microwave and serve cappuccino.

Sprinkle *the measured quantities of sugar and coffee over the hot water and stir in until dissolved.*

Lettuce cups

Standing time: none

SALAD
**2 bacon rashers, rinds removed
1 small head round lettuce
2 tomatoes, chopped
2 hard-boiled eggs, chopped
1 medium slice bread, cut into
   1cm / ½in cubes and fried**

DRESSING
**90ml / 6tbls olive oil
30ml / 2tbls red wine vinegar
salt and pepper
large pinch of mustard powder**

GARNISH
**2.5ml / ½tsp chopped parsley
2.5ml / ½tsp grated Parmesan
   cheese**

SERVES 2

1 Place bacon between 2 pieces of absorbent paper and microwave at 100% (High) for 2-2½ minutes. Cut into 1cm / ½in pieces.
2 Use 12 or 16 lettuce leaves and arrange on 2 small plates to form cups. Chop or tear the remaining lettuce and use to fill the cups.
3 Sprinkle the lettuce with chopped tomato, egg, croûtons and bacon.
4 Combine the oil and vinegar. Then mix in the remaining dressing ingredients. Spoon over the salad. Sprinkle with garnishes.

How to prepare Lettuce cups

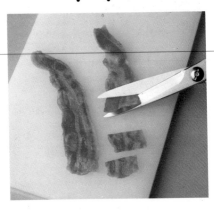

Microwave *the bacon between 2 pieces of absorbent paper, then cut into 1cm / ½in pieces. Use 6 to 8 lettuce leaves to form each cup.*

Fill *the cups with the salad ingredients; do not press down too firmly. Spoon the dressing over the cups; sprinkle with parsley and cheese.*

Broccoli spears

When cooking fresh broccoli, remember that the cooking time will be affected by the thickness and tenderness of the stalks. Select heads approximately the same size with even-sized stalks. Position the stalks towards the outside of the dish, as the heads are less dense than the stalks and cook more quickly. Pierce the stalks with a fork to test when cooked.

The broccoli should be covered with cling film, rolled back at one edge for the steam to escape, so that the stalks remain full and do not shrivel during cooking. It should come out crisp and bright green.

Fresh broccoli: Trim and prepare 225g / 8oz broccoli spears. Arrange them in a shallow dish and add 60ml / 4tbls water. Cover with cling film rolled back at one edge. Microwave at 100% (High) for 8-10 minutes, turning once. Serve hot with melted butter.

Frozen broccoli: Remove 225g / 8oz frozen spears from the packet. Place in a shallow dish with 30ml / 2tbls water. Cover with cling film rolled back at one edge and microwave at 100% (High) for 2 minutes, separate spears, then continue cooking for 3-4 minutes. Serve hot with melted butter.

Creamy veal

| 9 mins |

Standing time: 3-5 mins (optional)

20ml / 4tsp plain flour
large pinch of salt
large pinch of pepper
350g / 12oz lean, boneless veal loin, cut into 2cm / ¾in cubes
40g / 1½oz butter
75ml / 5tbls half cream or milk
30ml / 2tbls dry white wine
10ml / 2tsp chopped fresh parsley
100-150g / 4-5oz tagliatelle

SERVES 2

1 Combine 15ml / 1tbls flour with the salt and pepper in a plastic bag. Add the meat and shake until the meat is completely coated
2 Melt the butter in a 1.1L / 2pt casserole at 100% (High) for about 1 minute or until melted.
3 Stir the meat and remaining flour into the butter. Mix in the cream or milk, white wine and chopped fresh parsley.
4 Cover and cook at 50% (Medium) for about 8-9 minutes or until the meat feels tender when pierced with a fork. Stir well once during the cooking and at the end of the cooking time. Leave to stand for 3-5 minutes if you need extra time for other preparation.
5 Meanwhile, cook the tagliatelle conventionally.
6 Drain the pasta and arrange on a serving dish. Spoon over the veal and sauce to cover.

Grapes and Italian cheeseboard

100g / 4oz Fontina or smoked Emmental
100g / 4oz Dolcelatte
100g / 4oz Bel Paese
selection of cheese biscuits
225g / 8oz black grapes

1 Unwrap the cheeses and slice the Fontina or smoked Emmental into about 4 pieces. Arrange these in an overlapping row on a cheeseboard or dish, together with the Dolcelatte, Bel Paese and cheese biscuits.
2 Wash the grapes and place in a glass bowl.

Cappuccino for two

| 3 mins |

Standing time: none

275ml / ½pt cold water
10ml / 2tsp light brown soft sugar
10ml / 2tsp coffee granules
60ml / 4tbls orange-liqueur
30ml / 2tbls sweetened cream

1 Microwave the water in a jug at 100% (High) for about 2 minutes.
2 Stir in sugar and coffee. Heat at 100% (High) for 1 minute; then stir well adding the liqueur.
3 Pour the cappuccino into 2 cups and top with the cream, whipped.

Freezer dinner for 4

Make the most of the microwave's talent for thawing and heating foods. Keep the whole meal ready in the freezer and you will always be prepared for instant entertaining.

Many dishes freeze well — and microwaving is the fastest, most efficient way to thaw and heat them without damaging their flavour. This sophisticated menu can be ready from frozen in just under an hour.

Prepare and freeze the dishes any time that you are free, but remember that to enjoy the food at its best, do not store longer than the recommended times. Except for the pizza bases and casserole, no standing time is necessary.

Take care when microwaving the Seafood Starter and the vegetable towers not to heat longer than is necessary or they will toughen. Cook the pasta conventionally in boiling salted water, leaving the microwave free for other jobs.

ALAN DUNS

Seafood starter

8 mins

Thawing and heating time: 15 mins

Standing after thawing: none

These delicious individual starters make a good combination with crisp Melba toast or crusty bread. Use ocean sticks or fresh, cooked prawns, shrimps, crabmeat or mussels for more luxury.

Beef and Celery Casserole and Cauliflower and Carrot Towers

15g / ½oz butter or margarine
1 small onion, finely chopped
30ml / 2tbls plain flour
salt and pepper
pinch of cayenne pepper
150ml / 5fl oz whipping cream
15ml / 1tbls white wine
50g / 2oz mushrooms, chopped
175g / 6oz ocean or seafood sticks chopped
50g / 2oz Gruyère cheese, grated

SERVES 4

1 Place the butter and onion in a bowl. Cover and microwave at 100% (High) for 2-3 minutes.
2 Add the flour, salt, pepper, cayenne, cream, wine and mushrooms.
3 Reduce the power to 50% (Medium) and microwave for 3-4 minutes, stirring once, until thick.
4 Stir in the ocean sticks and half the cheese. Divide between four ceramic baking shells. Sprinkle remaining cheese on top and microwave at 50% (Medium) for 3-4 minutes, or until the cheese melts. Cool, then wrap and freeze in the dishes for up to 1 month. Thaw according to the Countdown.

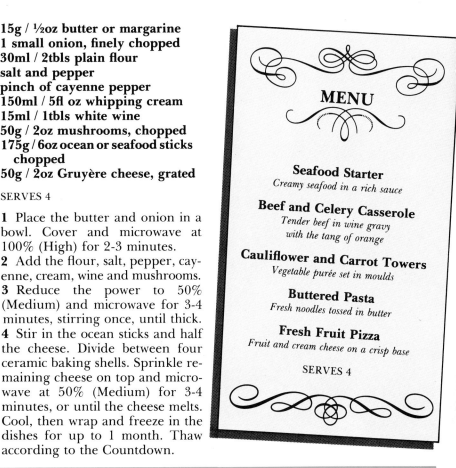

MENU

Seafood Starter
Creamy seafood in a rich sauce

Beef and Celery Casserole
Tender beef in wine gravy with the tang of orange

Cauliflower and Carrot Towers
Vegetable purée set in moulds

Buttered Pasta
Fresh noodles tossed in butter

Fresh Fruit Pizza
Fruit and cream cheese on a crisp base

SERVES 4

Countdown

As soon as you come in
Remove all the dishes from the freezer. Microwave the pizza base at 100% (High) for 1 minute, then stand for 5 minutes. Soften the cream cheese by microwaving at 30% (Low) for 10-15 seconds. Thaw the casserole by microwaving, covered at 20-30% (Defrost) for 40 minutes; break up the pieces and stir them regularly.

While the casserole thaws
Spread the cream cheese evenly over the pizza base. Prepare the fruit for the base, and arrange on cream cheese. Cook 700g / 1½lb fresh green tagliatelle conventionally in boiling salted water for 3-4 minutes (12-15 minutes if dried). Drain and add 50g / 2oz butter. Toss to coat. Season.

When the casserole has thawed
Microwave the glaze and spoon over the pizza when cool. Set aside

in a cool place (this allows the base to soften before cutting). To thaw the vegetable towers, arrange the covered ramekins in a ring on the floor of the cooker and microwave at 20-30% (Defrost) for 12-13 minutes, until the towers are just soft.

Just before the meal
Arrange the Seafood Starters in a ring in the cooker and microwave at 20-30% (Defrost) for 10-15 minutes, or until well thawed. Increase the power to 100% (High) and microwave for a further 5 minutes, or until hot. Serve with crusty bread and butter.

While the first course is served
Microwave the casserole at 100% (High) for 8-10 minutes, or until heated through. Allow to stand while microwaving the vegetable towers at 100% (High) for 2½-3½ minutes, or until hot. Turn out and serve immediately.

421

4 carrots, sliced in 12mm / ½in pieces

SERVES 4

1 Trim the meat and cut into 2.5cm / 1in cubes. Sift the flour with salt and pepper to taste and place in a polythene bag with the meat. Shake well to coat the meat.

2 Pour the oil into a large casserole dish and add the onion. Cover and microwave at 100% (High) for 2 minutes, or until the onions are soft and transparent.

3 Stir in the meat and microwave at 100% (High) for 4 minutes, stirring after 2 minutes. Add wine and stock. Cover and microwave at 70% (Medium-High) for 30-35 minutes, until meat is just tender.

4 Pare the orange rind finely and cut into very fine strips. Squeeze the juice from the fruit.

5 Add the rind and juice to the casserole with the celery and carrots. Stir well and cover. Microwave at 70% (Medium-High) for 20 minutes, or until celery is just tender. Cool completely. Pour into a rigid polythene container leaving 12mm / ½in headspace. Cover, label and freeze for up to 2 months. Thaw according to the instructions in the Countdown.

Microtips

If you want to make this satisfying casserole dish to serve straight away, allow it to stand for 5 minutes after microwaving time to complete cooking.

Beef and celery casserole | 56 mins

Thawing and heating time: 48 mins

Standing after thawing: 2-3½ mins

1.1kg / 2½lb braising steak
60ml / 4tbls plain flour
salt and pepper
60ml / 4tbls oil
1 large onion, sliced
350ml / 12fl oz red wine
1 beef stock cube
1 orange
4 celery stalks, cut in 2.5cm / 1in pieces

CARROT TOWERS
450g / 1lb carrots, thinly sliced
25g / 1oz butter
60ml / 4tbls chicken stock
salt and pepper
2 eggs
flat-leaved parsley to garnish

SERVES 4

1 To make the cauliflower towers, place the cauliflower in a dish with the milk, butter and potato. Cover and microwave at 100% (High) for 5 minutes until the vegetables are just tender, stirring several times.

2 Purée in a blender, adding the eggs when the mixture is smooth. Add salt and pepper to taste and mix in the grated nutmeg. Divide between four small greased ramekins.

3 To make the carrot towers place the carrot in a dish with the butter and stock. Cover and microwave at 100% (High) for 6 minutes, or until tender. Purée in a blender and season to taste. Beat in the eggs and spoon into four small greased ramekins.

4 Cover all eight ramekins with cling film and arrange in a ring in the cooker. Microwave at 100% (High) for 4-5 minutes, rearranging once and giving a quarter turn once every two minutes, until just firm to the touch on top.

5 Cool completely, then wrap, label and freeze for up to 3 months. Thaw following the instructions in the Countdown. Turn out on to a serving dish and garnish with sprigs of flat-leaved parsley.

Cauliflower and carrot towers | 15 mins

Thawing and heating time: 14½ mins

Standing after thawing: none

CAULIFLOWER TOWERS
450g / 1lb cauliflower, chopped
60ml / 4tbls milk
25g / 1oz butter
50g / 2oz potato, grated
salt and pepper
2 eggs
grated nutmeg

Fresh fruit pizza | 17½ mins

Thawing and heating time: 1 min

Standing after thawing: 5 mins

125ml / 4fl oz milk
20ml / 4tsp dried yeast
large pinch of sugar
50g / 2oz butter
2 eggs, beaten
400g / 14oz plain flour
large pinch of salt
Cheese 'n' fruit topping (see right)

MAKES 2 PIZZA BASES

1 Microwave the milk in a jug at 100% (High) for 1 minute, until warm. Sprinkle the yeast on top and stir in the sugar. Leave in a warm place until frothy.
2 Microwave the butter, covered, at 100% (High) for 30-60 seconds to melt. Mix into the yeast mixture with the egg. Beat well.
3 Sift the flour and salt, add the liquid and mix well to a pliable dough. Knead until elastic. Place in a lightly greased bowl, cover and microwave at 10% (Warm) for 4 minutes. Remove and stand for 10-15 minutes. Repeat procedure until doubled in size.
4 Knock back dough and knead lightly on a floured surface. Halve the dough and roll out half to fit a 25-30cm / 10-12in pizza dish, turning the edges up slightly.
5 Microwave at 100% (High) for 2 minutes, giving a quarter turn after 1 minute. Repeat with the second half. Brown under a hot grill for a golden crust. Freeze, separately wrapped, for up to 6 months. Thaw one base according to the instructions in the Countdown. Add the cheese 'n' fruit topping.

Cheese 'n' fruit topping

| 2¼ mins |

Standing time: none

225g / 8oz cream cheese
15ml / 1tbls caster sugar
grated zest of 1 lemon
350g / 12oz prepared fresh fruit

GLAZE
175ml / 6fl oz apple juice
10ml / 2tsp arrowroot

MAKES ENOUGH FOR 1 BASE

1 Soften the cream cheese by microwaving at 30% (Low) for 10-15 seconds. Beat with the sugar and lemon zest, then spread over pizza base to within 12mm / ½in of the edge.
2 Arrange the fruit slices decoratively on the cream cheese. Mix the apple juice and arrowroot and microwave at 100% (High) for 2-2½ minutes, or until clear and thick, stirring several times. Cool slightly, then spoon over the fruit.

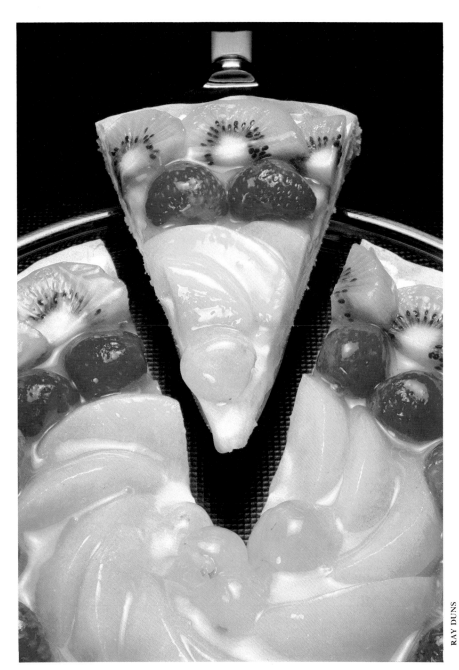

RAY DUNS

How to freeze and thaw Pizza bases

To freeze: *Wrap each base closely in foil, freezer cling film or a polythene bag; seal, label and freeze for up to one month.*

To thaw: *unwrap one base and place on a microwave roasting rack. Microwave at 100% (High) for 1 minute, then stand for 5 minutes.*

423

Three-course meal for 6

Prepare this special-occasion roast and its accompaniments with no last-minute fuss. The secret is in the timing. Here are the Countdown and tips to show you how.

Dishing up a three-course meal is easy with the microwave. You can cook foods, even delicately textured vegetables, in advance, and reheat them just before serving with no loss of texture, colour or flavour. With a little organization — see the Countdown — you can build your preparation into the day, spread the work and not be rushed immediately before the meal.

The early stages of preparation can see the cold desserts safely chilling in the refrigerator, the soup cooked and the vegetables peeled, cut and ready to microwave. In the middle stage, microwave the vegetables in advance, leaving the meat and reheating until the final stage. Then serve your meal, fuss-free.

Tomato and orange soup

24 mins

Standing time: none

2 celery stalks, chopped
1 onion, chopped
10ml / 2tsp vegetable oil
3 × 397g / 14oz cans chopped tomatoes
2.5ml / ½tsp caster sugar
finely grated zest of 1 orange
salt to taste
150ml / ¼pt chicken or vegetable stock

SERVES 6

1 Place the celery, onion and oil in a casserole, cover with cling film rolled back at one edge and microwave at 100% (High) for 3 minutes, stirring once after half the cooking time.
2 Stir in the tomatoes, then cover and microwave at 100% (High) for a further 5 minutes, stirring once.
3 Stir in the sugar, orange zest, salt and stock. Cover again and microwave at 100% (High) for 10 minutes, until all the vegetables are tender.
4 Pour the mixture into a blender and purée thoroughly until smooth. Pour through a sieve to remove the tomato seeds, then into a serving tureen, ready to heat through.
5 Microwave the soup at 100% (High) for 6-8 minutes, stirring once. If liked, swirl a little cream through the soup and sprinkle with a little extra orange zest before serving.

MENU

Tomato and Orange Soup
A smooth soup with a hint of orange

Apricot-stuffed Pork
Rolled loin with apricot stuffing

Sprouts with Almonds
Buttery young sprouts with toasted nuts

Hedgehog Potatoes
Whole potatoes dusted with paprika

Cauliflower with Sweetcorn
Crisp florets with baby corn cobs

Marbled Raspberry Tarts
Creamy individual tarts with a biscuit shell

SERVES 6

Countdown

Early in the day
Prepare the crumb shells for the dessert and leave to cool while preparing the cream filling. Add the filling and microwave the Marbled Raspberry Tarts. Cool, then chill until ready to serve. Prepare the sprouts and store in a polythene bag in the refrigerator. Toast the almonds and set aside. Trim the cauliflower and cut into florets. Refrigerate in a sealed polythene bag. Microwave the soup and allow to cool. Refrigerate in a covered tureen. Prepare the stuffing for the pork.

In the afternoon
Prepare the potatoes, dust with paprika and microwave according to the recipe. Microwave the cauliflower, drain and mix in the sweetcorn. Microwave the sprouts and drain. Arrange the sprouts, cauliflower and potatoes in a large sectioned serving dish or three smaller ones. Keep in a cool place until ready to reheat.

An hour before the meal
Remove the soup from the refrigerator. Brush or sprinkle the pork with paprika; microwave according to recipe. Prepare the apricots. Set the table. Slice the pork and fill with the stuffing. Arrange on a serving dish with the apricots and microwave to heat through. Remove and cover with foil. Stand for 10-20 minutes. Meanwhile microwave the soup at 100% (High) for 3-4 minutes, stirring several times, until hot. Prepare and microwave the gravy. Sprinkle the almonds over the sprouts. Serve the soup while microwaving the vegetables at 100% (High) for 15-20 minutes. Microwave gravy at 100% (High) until hot through.

Apricot stuffed pork

30 mins

Standing time: 10-20 mins

1.4kg / 3lb boned loin of pork
5ml / 1tsp paprika
18 canned apricot halves, drained
36 whole cloves (optional)
chopped parsley, to garnish

STUFFING
50g / 2oz fresh breadcrumbs
50g / 2oz no-need-to-soak dried
    apricots, chopped
4 spring onions, chopped
5ml / 1tsp dried sage
2 egg whites
salt and pepper

SERVES 6

How to microwave Apricot stuffed pork

Trim *the skin and most of the fat from the meat, leaving a thin layer of fat all round. Form the meat into a roll and tie neatly. Slash the fat at 6mm / ¼in intervals across the roll.*

Sprinkle *or brush the paprika over fat. Place the pork on a roasting rack and microwave at 100% (High) for 15 minutes. Reduce the power to 70% (Medium-High) for 5 more minutes.*

Mix *all the stuffing ingredients together in a large bowl while the pork is cooking. The stuffing should not be too moist, as it needs to stay in place in the sliced meat.*

Cut *the pork in 12mm / ½in slices, cutting almost to the base of the joint. Spoon stuffing between the slices. Arrange the stuffed pork on a serving dish.*

Prepare *the spiced apricots by studding each half with two whole cloves, if liked. Arrange the apricot halves, rounded side up, around the sides of the pork on the dish.*

Microwave *the pork, uncovered, at 70% (Medium-High) for 10 minutes, until no longer pink. Cover loosely with foil, stand for 10-20 minutes, then sprinkle with parsley.*

426

Pork gravy

| | 2 mins |

Standing time: none

collected juices from the meat
15ml / 3tsp arrowroot
275ml / ½pt vegetable stock
salt and pepper

SERVES 6

1 Skim any fat from the meat juices. Mix 30ml / 2tbls of the juice with the arrowroot until smooth. Stir in remaining juice.
2 Add the stock and microwave at 100% (High) for 2-3 minutes, stirring twice, until hot and thick. Season to taste, pour into a hot gravy boat and serve hot with the loin of pork and vegetables.

Cauliflower with sweetcorn

| | 10 mins |

Standing time: 2 mins

450g / 1lb cauliflower, cut into
   even florets
45ml / 3tbls water
425g / 15oz can baby sweetcorn,
   drained
15g / ½oz butter
salt and pepper

SERVES 6

1 Place the cauliflower in a large dish. Cover and microwave at 100% (High) for 8 minutes, rearranging the pieces once.
2 Meanwhile, slice the baby sweetcorn cobs in half crossways. Add to the partially cooked cauliflower, cover and microwave at 100% (High) for 2-4 minutes, or until the cauliflower is cooked and the corn is hot.
3 Stand, covered, for 2 minutes. Drain well, then add the butter. Season to taste and toss to mix.

Cook's notes

Keep the meat hot while it is standing by tenting it loosely with foil. Make sure the foil is shiny side in, so that the heat is reflected back on to the meat.

Brussels sprouts with almonds

| | 12 mins |

Standing time: 3 mins

700g / 1½lb Brussels sprouts
60ml / 4tbls water
25g / 1oz butter
25g / 1oz flaked almonds, toasted

SERVES 6

1 Place the sprouts in a large dish and add the water. Cover and microwave at 100% (High) for 12-15 minutes, stirring twice during cooking, until just tender.
2 Stand, still covered, for 3 minutes, then drain off any water. Toss well with the butter. Sprinkle the toasted flaked almonds over the top to serve.

Hedgehog potatoes

| | 15 mins |

Standing time: 3 mins

900g / 2lb even-sized potatoes
45ml / 3tbls water
30ml / 2tbls vegetable oil
paprika-for dusting
salt

SERVES 6

1 Make vertical cuts in each potato, slicing about halfway, at 6mm / ¼in intervals. Turn the

Top to bottom: Brussels Sprouts with Almonds, Hedgehog Potatoes and Cauliflower with Sweetcorn

potatoes at right angles and make another series of parallel cuts, without cutting right through.
2 Place the potatoes in a large shallow dish. Add the water. Cover and microwave at 100% (High) for 10 minutes, rearranging two or three times, until almost tender.
3 Drain the potatoes, then brush all over with oil and dust with paprika. Add salt to taste. Cover again and microwave at 100% (High) for a further 5-10 minutes, or until tender. Stand, covered, for 3 minutes, then serve.

Microtips

Cooking vegetables together: if you prefer to cook the sprouts and cauliflower together, choose baby sprouts or cut large ones in half. Arrange sprouts around outside of dish and cauliflower in the centre. Add 100ml / 3½fl oz water. Microwave, covered, at 100% (High) for 8-10 minutes, shaking dish three times. Add sweetcorn to cauliflower and microwave for 2 minutes more. Stand, still covered, for 3 minutes, then drain. Add several knobs of butter and season to taste. Toss to mix and serve.

Marbled raspberry tarts

$10\frac{1}{2}$ mins

Standing time: none

100g / 4oz butter
350g / 12oz chocolate digestive or
  plain sweet biscuits, crushed

FILLING
75g / 3oz frozen raspberries,
  thawed (see Microtips below
  for thawing raspberries)
175g / 6oz cream cheese
2 eggs, beaten
75g / 3oz caster sugar
grated zest of $\frac{1}{2}$ lemon
juice of 1 lemon
90ml / 6tbls whipping cream

SERVES 6

VARIATION
Use 225g / 8oz shortbread in place
of the chocolate digestive biscuits
and 175g / 6oz butter for a lighter
crust.

Microtips

*Use your microwave to thaw the
raspberries quickly. Place 175g /
6oz frozen raspberries in a bowl,
cover with vented cling film and
microwave at 20-30% (Defrost) for
1-2 minutes. Stir and break up
berries gently several times during
microwaving, taking care not to
break them. Drain off any surplus
liquid before using the fruit.*

How to microwave Marbled raspberry tarts

Place *the thawed raspberries in a
blender and reduce to a pulp, or mash
lightly, then press through a nylon
sieve, using a spoon, to prevent the
purée from discolouring.*

Microwave *the butter, covered, at
100% (High) for 30-60 seconds, to
melt. Stir into the biscuit crumbs, mix
well and press over the base and sides
of six 10cm / 4in ceramic tartlet dishes.*

Whisk *all filling ingredients except the
raspberry purée together in a large
bowl until smooth, using an electric
mixer for 1 minute, or beating by hand
for 2 minutes.*

Divide *the filling between the crumb
cases. Do not overfill. Drizzle the
raspberry purée in wavy lines over the
tops and marble by drawing a cocktail
stick through in lines or swirls.*

Microwave *three tartlets, in a ring at
30% (Low) for 5-6 minutes, turning
every minute, until just firm. Repeat
with the remaining three and then cool.
Chill until needed.*

428

Summer buffet

A summer buffet party for eight needn't be a daunting prospect with careful planning and your microwave helping you to cook everything to perfection. Set out the food, relax and enjoy the company of friends.

Hot lazy summer days cry out for party spreads of delicately flavoured cold food. This summer menu starts with a chilled soup which can be prepared in advance.

Trout is the centrepiece of the meal. Individual fish make the serving easy but if you prefer to cook large trout, buy two 1.1-1.6kg / 2½-3½lb fish. Microwave in the poaching liquor, one at a time, at 100% (High) for 7-9 minutes. Wrap the head and tail in a little foil for the first half of the cooking time to prevent overcooking. Colourful cooked salads complement the main course.

Strawberries and cream sandwiched in a moist shortcake, make a mouthwatering dessert.

ANDREW WHITTUCK

Countdown

The day before
Cook trout; cool in liquor. Cover when cold and store in the refrigerator.

Make the soup, strain and store covered in the refrigerator. Prepare the pasta salad dressing and store in the refrigerator.

Early on the day
Skin the fish and prepare the cucumber and lemon slices for garnishing; store covered. Prepare and cook the Bean and Cauliflower salad; leave coated in dressing. Cook pasta, blanch peppers. Cook shortcake; leave to cool.

Just before the guests arrive
Arrange salads, lay out fish, finish cake, stir lemon juice into the soup and top with lemon slices.

into a large shallow dish (big enough to hold four of the trout).
2 Cover and microwave at 100% (High) for 5 minutes. Add four fish, cover and microwave for 7-9 minutes at 100% (High).
3 Remove from the cooker and leave to cool. Stir several times.
4 Repeat this with the remaining fish and fresh poaching liquor.
5 To serve the fish, remove from liquor and remove skin. Garnish with cucumber and lemon.
6 Serve with green mayonnaise. (see recipe, below).

Iced beetroot soup

45 mins

Standing time: none

1.4kg / 3lb raw beetroot, peeled and diced
2.3L / 4pt boiling water
3 chicken stock cubes
2 large onions, peeled and halved
6 cloves
3 garlic cloves, crushed
1 bouquet garni

15ml / 1tbls sugar
salt and pepper
30ml / 2tbls orange juice
orange slices, to garnish

SERVES 8

1 Put the beetroot, water, stock cubes, onions, cloves, garlic, bouquet garni and sugar into a 3.4L / 6pt bowl.
2 Microwave, uncovered, for 20 minutes at 100% (High), stir once.
3 Reduce power to 50% (Medium) and cook for a further 25 minutes.
4 Strain the soup through a fine sieve. Season to taste and chill.
5 Just before serving, stir in orange juice and garnish.

Poached trout

26 mins

Standing time: none

The quantity of poaching liquor will cook 2 large trout or two batches of 4 small trout.

8 trout, about 175g-225g / 6-8oz each
cucumber and lemon slices, to garnish

POACHING LIQUOR
150ml / ¼pt white wine
2.5ml / ½tsp salt
1 sprig parsley
1 bay leaf
2 peppercorns
275ml / ½pt water

SERVES 8

1 Put half poaching ingredients

Green mayonnaise

4 mins

Standing time: none

1 bunch watercress
small bunch of parsley
575ml / 1pt mayonnaise

SERVES 8

1 Remove the tough stalks from the watercress and the parsley.
2 Rinse the parsley and watercress under cold running water. Place in a bowl with 30ml / 2tbls water.
3 Microwave, covered, at 100% (High) for 4 minutes.
4 Drain off all the water and chop finely by hand or in a processor.
5 Wrap the watercress and parsley in a teatowel and gently squeeze until all the moisture has been removed.
6 Mix the parsley and watercress into the mayonnaise. Chill before serving with the trout.

Bean and cauliflower salad

19½ mins

Standing time: 10 mins

450g / 1lb baby green beans
1 cauliflower, broken into florets
1 egg

DRESSING
2.5ml / ½tsp salt
15ml / 1tbls made mustard
3-4 drops of Tabasco
90ml / 6tbls red wine vinegar
120ml / 8tbls olive oil
150ml / ¼pt vegetable oil
30ml / 2tbls chopped chervil

MENU

Iced Beetroot Soup
A delicate-flavoured clear soup

Poached Trout
Served with Green Mayonnaise

Bean and Cauliflower Salad
With egg garnish

Pasta Salad
With lemony dressing

Strawberry Shortcake
Sandwiched with whipped cream

SERVES 8

430

1 Cook beans, covered, with 60ml / 4tbls water at 100% (High) for 13-15 minutes, stirring 3-4 times. Cook cauliflower with 75ml / 3fl oz water for 6-7 minutes, stirring once. Stand both for 5 minutes.
2 Break the egg into a small dish and prick yolk. Add 15ml / 1 tbls hot water. Microwave at 50% (Medium) for $1\frac{1}{2}$-2 minutes. Drain and stand until cold.
3 Mix dressing ingredients together. Chop the egg white and mix into the dressing.
4 Drain beans and cauliflower and pour half of the dressing over each. Toss, cover and chill.
5 Just before serving, toss vegetables again and arrange on a large platter in a decorative pattern. Sieve the egg yolk over the top.

Pasta salad | 19 mins

Standing time: 5 mins

450g / 1lb pasta spirals
1.4L / $2\frac{1}{2}$pt boiling water, salted
1 yellow pepper, cut into rings
1 red pepper, cut into thin strips
1 green pepper, cut into squares

DRESSING
2.5ml / $\frac{1}{2}$tsp salt
15ml / 1tbls made mustard
90ml / 6tbls lemon juice
120ml / 8tbls olive oil
150ml / $\frac{1}{4}$pt vegetable oil
30ml / 2tbls chopped basil

SERVES 8

1 Place the pasta in a large bowl with boiling salted water.
2 Microwave covered at 100% (High) for 14-16 minutes, until just tender.
3 Rinse well and set aside.
4 Place the seeded and cut peppers in a bowl with 90ml / 6tbls water. Microwave, covered, for 5 minutes at 100% (High). Stand for 5 minutes, then rinse in cold water.
5 To make dressing, combine all the ingredients and mix well.
6 To serve, combine pasta, peppers and dressing. Toss well.

ANDREW WHITTUCK

Strawberry shortcake | 7 mins

Standing time: none

Cook this cake the same day you wish to serve it and fill just before serving time.

275g / 10oz self-raising flour
2.5ml / $\frac{1}{2}$tsp salt
100g / 4oz butter, diced
90g / $3\frac{1}{2}$oz soft brown sugar
grated zest of 1 orange
1 egg, beaten
30-45ml / 2-3tbls milk
450g / 1lb strawberries
425ml / $\frac{3}{4}$pt whipping cream

SERVES 8

1 Sift flour and salt. Rub in the butter until the mixture resembles fine crumbs. Stir in the sugar and the orange zest. Using a round-bladed knife, stir in the egg, a little at a time.

2 Stir in the milk and knead lightly into a smooth dough.
3 Press dough into a prepared 25cm / 10in flan dish. Place dish on an inverted saucer and microwave for 7-9 minutes at 100% (High).
4 Turn out onto a cooling tray and leave until cold before slicing in half horizontally.
5 Thinly slice half the strawberries; cut the rest in half. Whip the cream.
6 Fill the shortcake with sliced strawberries and half the whipped cream. Top with the remaining cream and strawberries.

Cook's notes

To ensure that the shortcake comes easily out of the dish, grease the dish lightly and line with greaseproof paper. Let paper stand above the edges so the cake can be lifted out.

Elegant dinner for four

Prepare a meal to satisfy sophisticated tastes — and do the bulk of the work in advance. All the dishes can be reheated successfully, so you can relax and enjoy the meal with your guests.

This simple but elegant meal is easy to cook and reheat by microwave. The delicate flavour of the main dish, Pork with Artichokes, is retained far more efficiently than by conventional direct reheating, which could congeal the sauce and dry the piped potato. In fact, the same applies to all the dishes — cook them in advance, then reheat them in sequence — this way you can spend more time with your guests. (Your microwave is a great secret to have up your sleeve when it comes to carefree dinner party catering!)

Once you have served the soup you can start to reheat the meat — make sure the pork and artichokes are evenly spread in the potato ring for thorough reheating.

As a special decoration for the oranges, remove the zest of one orange, omitting the pith, and cut it into thin strips. Microwave at 100% (High) with 150ml / ¼pt water for 5 minutes. Drain off and discard the water, then sprinkle the strips on the caramel oranges before serving.

If wished, some of the dishes can be prepared well in advance and frozen. The soup, pork with artichokes and courgettes can be frozen (courgettes should only be frozen for a short time or they will become soft). Mashed potato can be frozen, but for best results pipe a border of freshly cooked potato for this dish.

Use a clear, heatproof bowl for microwaving the dessert syrup so that you can see it colouring. Take it from the cooker as soon as it starts to brown — it will continue to darken afterwards. Be careful not to overcook the syrup.

MENU

Fresh Lettuce Soup
A subtle-flavoured, creamy hot soup

Pork with Artichoke Hearts
A rich casserole in a piped potato border

Courgettes with Tomatoes
A lightly cooked vegetable combination

Caramel Oranges
Whole fresh fruit laced with Grand Marnier

SERVES 4

Countdown

The day before
Prepare, microwave and refrigerate the Caramel Oranges. Peel the oranges on a board, using a knife to remove the pith. Turn them several times in the syrup. Microwave and chill the soup.

Early on the day
Clean the potatoes and courgettes and cut up, then leave in water. Prepare and slice the meat. Leave covered in the refrigerator.

1¼ hours before serving
Microwave the potatoes. Allow to cool slightly after mashing, then pipe around the edge of the main serving dish, If the dish is suitable, brown under the grill. Cook the courgettes and leave to stand, covered. Microwave the pork and artichokes and arrange in the centre of the mashed potato border. Sprinkle a little paprika over each potato rosette.

10-15 minutes before serving
Heat the soup through for 10-12 minutes. Stir once during heating and again on removal from the cooker. Serve at once.

While soup is served
Microwave the Pork with Artichoke Hearts at 100% (High) for 10 minutes. Leave to stand for 3 minutes. Reheat the courgettes by microwaving at 100% (High) for 3 minutes while clearing the soup plates. Sprinkle with chopped parsley before serving.

Fresh lettuce soup

35½ mins

Standing time: none

2 lettuces, cleaned and shredded
100g / 4oz frozen leaf spinach
25g / 1oz butter
1 small onion, finely chopped
30ml / 2tbls plain flour
575ml / 1pt chicken stock
salt and pepper
150ml / ¼pt single cream
15ml / 1tbls chopped parsley
15ml / 1tbls chopped chervil

SERVES 4

1 Mix the lettuce and spinach in a large bowl. Cover with cling film rolled back at one edge and microwave at 70% (Medium-High) for 8 minutes, stirring once. Set aside, covered.
2 Place the butter in a 2.3L / 4pt bowl, cover and microwave at 100% (High) for 30-60 seconds until melted. Add the onion and microwave, covered, at 50% (Medium) for 5 minutes.
3 Stir in the flour, then add the stock. Microwave at 100% (High) for 5 minutes, stirring after 3 minutes.
4 Add the lettuce, spinach and seasoning, then cover and microwave at 100% (High) for 12 minutes, stirring several times.
5 Allow the soup to cool slightly, then purée it in a blender or by pressing through a sieve. Stir in the cream and herbs.
6 Microwave the soup at 100% (High) for 5 minutes to heat through, stirring, before serving.

Freezer notes

If you are going to freeze the soup, do not add the cream. Thaw and reheat the soup, stir in the cream and warm through.

Pork with artichoke hearts

28 mins

Standing time: 5 mins

700g / 1½lb pork tenderloin
30ml / 2tbls vegetable oil
100g / 4oz shallots or small
  onions, left whole
45ml / 3tbls plain flour
200ml / 7fl oz chicken stock
salt and pepper
397g / 14oz can artichoke hearts,
  drained and halved
75ml / 3fl oz double cream
30ml / 2tbls chopped
  parsley

POTATO BORDER
700g / 1½lb potatoes, cut into
  12mm / ½in cubes
125ml / 4fl oz water
25g / 1oz butter
salt and pepper
milk to mix
paprika to sprinkle

SERVES 4

1 First prepare the potato border. Place the potatoes and water in a 1.4L / 2½pt dish or casserole, cover and microwave at 100% (High) for 9 minutes or until the potatoes are tender and easy to pierce with a knife.
2 Drain thoroughly, then leave to stand, covered, for 5 minutes.
3 Mash the potatoes with the butter, salt and pepper using a fork or potato masher, adding just enough milk to produce a soft piping consistency.

PAUL WEBSTER

4 Fit a large piping bag with a star-shaped nozzle; fill with potato, pressing down firmly.

5 Pipe a border of potato rosettes around the edge of a large serving dish.

6 Sprinkle a little paprika over the border, or if preferred, brown quickly under the grill.

7 Remove any sinew or fat from the pork and cut the meat into 12mm / ½in-thick slices.

8 Preheat a browning dish at 100% (High) for 5 minutes or according to manufacturer's instructions. Add the oil, meat and shallots to the dish and press down firmly onto the base of the browning dish.

9 Microwave at 100% (High) for 3 minutes, then turn the meat and shallots over. Sprinkle with the flour, then microwave at 100% (High) for 3 minutes.

10 Stir in the stock and seasoning, then cover with a lid or with cling film and microwave at 100% (High) for 8 minutes.

11 Add the artichokes and cream, stir well then microwave at 100% (High) for 5 minutes to heat.

12 Stir, then arrange the pork and artichokes in the piped border.

13 Sprinkle chopped parsley over the dish before serving.

PAUL WEBSTER

Cook's notes

If you do not have a browning dish, pre-seal the pork and shallots by frying briefly in a little oil in a conventional frying pan. Transfer the meat and shallots to a dish which is suitable for the microwave, and proceed from the stage where the flour is added, using 70% (Medium-High) throughout the recipe but keeping the timings the same.

Microtips

A heated browning dish will act in much the same way as a hot frying pan when meat is added, so it is advisable to dry off any excess dampness before adding the pork to the dish.

Courgettes with tomatoes

| 8 mins |

Standing time: 5 mins

450g / 1lb courgettes
397g / 14oz can chopped tomatoes
salt and pepper

SERVES 4

1 Trim the courgettes and cut into 4cm / 1½in chunks. Cut each piece into quarters lengthways.

2 Place the courgettes in a 1.4L / 2½pt casserole with the tomatoes and toss to coat.

3 Cover and microwave at 100% (High) for 8-10 minutes, stirring halfway through the time to distribute the heat evenly.

4 Stir in the seasoning. Cover and leave to stand for 5 minutes before serving.

Caramel oranges

| 17 mins |

Standing time: none

4 large or 8 small oranges
150g / 5oz sugar
200ml / 7fl oz hot water
15ml / 1tbls Grand Marnier
SERVES 4

Caramel Oranges

1 Cut all the zest and pith from the oranges. Place the oranges in a serving dish or suitable fruit bowl.

2 Place 150ml / ¼pt of the water in a 1.4L / 2½pt ovenproof bowl with the sugar.

3 Microwave, uncovered, at 100% (High) for 4 minutes.

4 Stir well to dissolve the sugar, then microwave at 100% (High) for 13-16 minutes until the syrup is starting to turn a rich caramel colour.

5 Cool the syrup slightly, then stir in the remaining hot water and the Grand Marnier.

6 Pour the syrup over the orange and leave to marinate overnight in the refrigerator, turning occasionally before serving.

7 Serve the caramel oranges chilled with whipped cream, or a thick yoghurt for a flavour contrast.

Microtips

Do not let the sugar boil until it has all dissolved. Avoid stirring during cooking and watch carefully — if burning occurs in some areas, move the dish around gently holding it with an oven glove.

435

Exotic meal for 4

This exciting menu is a rich feast of colours and flavours. Each dish is a work of art, yet surprisingly simple to prepare, and the Countdown helps you put them together with ease.

A microwave cuts down the cooking time needed for your ingredients, so that you can produce a wonderful meal in minutes.

This menu, however, requires a certain amount of attention between courses, which is why the Countdown is extremely useful.

You can plan your entries and exits from the kitchen so that the exotic dishes appear with the minimum of fuss. This meal is best served at an informal gathering.

The benefit of advance planning is that you can use recipes that call for a marinade, as in the kebabs here. Cubes of sirloin steak are immersed in a mixture of lemon and tomato juices, with Worcestershire, soy and hot pepper sauces for extra 'kick'.

Prepare several batches of pancakes for freezing, so that you have a supply for impromptu entertaining.

The final dish of poached fruits is a stunning swirl of orange, green and yellow; it can be prepared during the day and chilled.

Party Beef Kebabs and Fruits with Apricot Sauce

Spicy brown rice

28 mins

Standing time: 5 mins

225g / 8oz brown rice
30ml / 2tbls sesame or vegetable oil
1 onion, finely chopped
1 garlic clove, crushed
2.5ml / ½tsp ground cumin
2.5ml / ½tsp ground coriander
2.5ml / ½tsp ground mace
5ml / 1tsp salt
50g / 2oz unsalted cashew nuts
500ml / 18fl oz boiling water
1 hard-boiled egg, sliced

SERVES 4

1 Place the rice, oil, onion and garlic in a 2.3L / 4pt casserole dish. Cover and microwave at 100% (High) for 3 minutes. Stir in the spices, salt and nuts.
2 Pour in the boiling water, cover and microwave at 50% (Medium) for 25 minutes, or until the rice is tender and the liquid absorbed, stirring twice. Leave to stand, covered, for 5 minutes.
3 Fluff rice, garnish with egg and serve.

RAY DUNS

MENU

Parsley Pancakes
Herby pancakes with julienne vegetables

Party Beef Kebabs
Succulent cubes of steak with crisp salad

Spicy Brown rice
Tender grains with cumin, coriander and mace

Fruits with Apricot Sauce
Lightly cooked fruits with a tangy purée

SERVES 4

Countdown

The day before
Prepare the Parsley Pancakes, interleaving them with greaseproof paper. Wrap the pancake stack in vented cling film and store in the refrigerator.

In the morning
Cut the vegetables for the Vegetable Medley into julienne strips. Place the peppers and the carrots and beans in separate polythene bags and refrigerate. Hard boil the eggs for the Spicy Brown Rice, but do not shell them. Microwave the apricot sauce and chill. Microwave fruits; allow to cool and then chill.

One hour before the meal
Marinate the beef for 30 minutes. Meanwhile, prepare the Spicy Brown Rice to the end of stage 2. Make up the kebabs, threading the skewers with beef and chestnuts.

Just before the first course
Microwave the Vegetable Medley. Then place the pancake stack on a plate and microwave at 100% (High) for 1¼-1¾ minutes. Assemble the pancakes with the filling and serve. Place the rice in the microwave and re-heat, covered, at 100% (High) for 5-6 minutes.

During the first course
Microwave the kebabs, turning them halfway through. Meanwhile, garnish the rice with the sliced egg. Leave the kebabs to stand.

Just before the second course
Microwave the sauce and serve hot, with the rice, kebabs and a crisp green salad.

Parsley pancakes

ANDREW WHITTUCK

$6\frac{1}{4}$ mins

Standing time: 3 mins

100g / 4oz wholewheat flour
pinch of salt
1 egg, lightly beaten
275ml / ½pt skimmed milk
30ml / 2tbls chopped parsley
vegetable oil for cooking
Vegetable Medley (see recipe)
  to fill

MAKES 8

1 Sift the flour and salt into a bowl, adding any bran caught in the sieve. Stir in the egg and half the milk and beat with a wooden spoon until smooth. Cover and refrigerate for 30 minutes. Stir in enough of the remaining milk to give the batter the consistency of single cream. Mix in the parsley.
2 Grease the base of a 15cm / 6in crêpe or frying pan with a thin film of oil. Heat the pan on a conventional cooker. Add about 30ml / 2tbls batter and swirl around to evenly coat the base of the pan. Cook over a medium to high heat until underside of the pancake has set. Turn over and cook until the other side is golden.
3 Transfer to a plate or clean working surface to cool, and re-peat the process until all the batter has been used. Then stack the cooked and cooled pancakes on top of each other, with a strip of greaseproof paper between each one. You should make 8 pancakes. Prepare the filling.
4 Cover the stack of pancakes with vented cling film and mic-rowave at 100% (High) for 45-60 seconds. Fold each in four to make a triangle, fill and serve at once.

Freezer notes

The batch of pancakes can be frozen and stored for up to three months. Prepare the pancakes, interleaving them with strips of greaseproof paper. Place the stack in a freezer bag and freeze. To thaw, microwave at 100% (High) for 1¼-1¾ minutes.

Vegetable medley

$5\frac{1}{2}$ mins

Standing time: 3 mins

100g / 4oz carrots, cut into strips
100g / 4oz French beans, cut into
  5cm / 2in lengths
30ml / 2tbls white wine vinegar
½ yellow pepper, seeded and cut
  into thin 5cm / 2in strips
½ red pepper, seeded and cut
  into thin 5cm / 2in strips
5cm / 2in piece cucumber, cut
  lengthways into thin 5cm / 2in
  strips
75ml / 5tbls natural yoghurt
5ml / 1tsp wholegrain mustard
pepper

MAKES 8 PANCAKES

1 To prepare the filling, place the carrots and beans in a bowl with the vinegar. Cover with vented cling film and microwave at 100% (High) for 3 minutes. Add the yellow and red peppers, stir to mix, then microwave for a further 2½-3½ minutes or until the vegetables are just tender.
2 Add the cucumber, yoghurt, mustard and pepper, stir thoroughly and leave to stand, covered, for 3 minutes. Cover and leave to one side until needed.

Party beef kebabs

7 mins

Standing time: 3-4 mins

450g / 1lb sirloin steak, cut into
  20 bite-sized cubes
4 × 25g / 1oz slices ham
225g / 8oz water chestnuts,
  drained
30ml / 2tbls tomato purée or paste

MARINADE
30ml / 2tbls lemon juice
60ml / 4tbls tomato juice
10ml / 2tsp Worcestershire sauce
10ml / 2tsp soy sauce
1 garlic clove, crushed

Fruits with apricot sauce

12 mins

Standing time: none

2 pears, peeled, cored and
  quartered
2 peaches or nectarines, halved,
  stoned and sliced
30ml / 2tbls lemon juice
2 kiwi fruits, peeled and sliced
2 oranges, peeled and thickly
  sliced, pips removed

SAUCE
100g / 4oz dried apricots
425ml / ¾pt unsweetened orange
  juice
15-30ml / 1-2tbls lemon juice

SERVES 4

1 Place the apricots for the sauce in a 2.3L / 4pt bowl with half the orange juice. Cover and microwave at 50% (Medium) for 10 minutes, stirring twice.
2 Cool, then purée in a food processor or blender until smooth. Stir in the remaining orange juice

Left: *Parsley Pancakes*
Below: *Fruit with Apricot Sauce*

and add the lemon juice to taste. Pour into a serving jug or bowl, cover and chill until needed.
3 Sprinkle the pears and peaches or nectarines with the lemon juice to prevent them discolouring.
4 Arrange all the prepared fruit on a large shallow plate: place the kiwi fruit in the centre, with the orange slices, overlapping, around them. Drain the pears and peaches, reserving the lemon juice for later. Arrange them in a circle around the outside of the serving dish.
5 Cover the fruit with vented cling film and microwave at 100% (High) for 2-4 minutes, or until just tender. Baste the pears and peaches with lemon juice and rotate the dish twice.
6 Leave to cool, then chill in the refrigerator. Serve with the apricot sauce.

Cook's notes

Use a serrated knife to peel the oranges, and cut them with a sawing movement; take care to remove the bitter white pith.

few drops Tabasco sauce

SERVES 4

1 In a bowl, combine the lemon juice, tomato juice, Worcestershire sauce, soy sauce, garlic and Tabasco to make the marinade. Add the cubes of beef and marinate for at least 30 minutes.
2 Cut each ham slice into four strips and wrap each strip round a water chestnut. Thread five cubes of beef and four water chestnuts alternately on to each skewer.
3 Place the kebabs on a microwave roasting rack, cover with greaseproof paper and microwave at 100% (High) for 5-7 minutes, turning the kebabs after half the cooking time.
4 Wrap the kebabs in foil and stand for 3-4 minutes. Meanwhile, add the cooking juices to the marinade with the tomato purée. Part-cover and microwave at 100% (High) for 2-3 minutes, until boiled and slightly thickened. Serve hot with the kebabs.

RAY DUNS

439

A meal to impress

It is easy, using your microwave, to produce an impressive meal with that extra-special flair. Colours, textures and flavours stay bright and crisp, so you can present all the food at its very best.

Your guests will be convinced that you have spent hours over this elegant (but oh-so-simple) three-course meal! Make the dessert the day before so you don't have to worry about it on the day — you're free to deal with the starter and main course.

Reheating is ideal for the rice, but delicate vegetables should be served immediately after cooking for best results. Artichokes cook well by microwave — they retain their goodness and are ready in minutes! Serve them stylishly with two dips, one cold and creamy, the other warm and buttery, to make an unusual and delicious starter to the meal.

Serve a crisp, light white wine to complement the flavours of the meal really well, or for warm summer days serve a sparkling one. Any of these wines should be chilled for 1-2 hours to enjoy them at their best.

Artichokes with dips

$17\frac{1}{2}$ mins

Standing time: 7 mins

4 globe artichokes
150ml / ¼pt vegetable stock
30ml / 2tbls lemon juice

MUSTARD DIP
1 small onion, finely chopped
1 garlic clove, crushed
10ml / 2tsp lemon juice
60ml / 4tbls natural yoghurt
60ml / 4tbls mayonnaise
5ml / 1tsp French mustard

HERBY BUTTER DIP
100g / 4oz butter
15ml / 1tbls chopped parsley
15ml / 1tbls snipped chives
15ml / 1tbls lime juice
pepper

SERVES 4

1 Trim artichoke stems to the base. Cut the top 2.5cm / 1in from the artichokes. Shake off excess water.
2 Stand the artichokes upright in a deep 23cm / 9in round dish. Pour the stock and lemon juice over them and cover. Microwave at 100% (High) for 15-18 minutes, or until the bases are tender and a leaf from close to the base pulls out easily. Baste and rearrange twice during cooking.
3 Stand, covered, for 5 minutes. Meanwhile, make the dips.
4 Mix the onion, garlic and lemon juice. Cover and microwave at 100% (High) for 1½-2 minutes, or until onion is tender. Add remaining ingredients; stand for 2-3 minutes.
5 Mix the butter and herbs, cover and microwave at 100% (High) for 1-1½ minutes. Whisk in the lime juice and pepper and serve warm with the artichokes.

MENU

Artichokes with Dips
Tender artichokes with two contrasting dips

Poussins Veronique
Baby chickens on a bed of rice with a wine and grape sauce

Red Vegetable Kebabs
Carrots, peppers and tomatoes on skewers

Pineapple Ginger Tortoni
Refreshing ice cream with crisp biscuit

SERVES 4

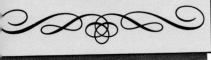

Countdown

The day before
Make the ice cream and freeze until almost solid, then assemble the tortoni. Return to the freezer.

Early on the day
Prepare both dips for the artichokes and refrigerate.

In the afternoon
Cook 150g / 5oz long grain rice with 2.5ml / ½tsp salt, 5ml / 1tsp butter and 350ml / 12fl oz boiling water at 100% (High) for 3 minutes. Reduce to 50% (Medium) and cook for 12 minutes, stirring 2-3 times. Cool. Prepare the Red Vegetable Kebabs and set aside ready to microwave. Turn out the Pineapple Ginger Tortoni and return to the freezer.

An hour before serving
Remove the dips from the refrigerator. Microwave the poussins and the sauce. Leave the poussins covered with foil while microwaving the artichokes. Transfer the tortoni to the refrigerator. Microwave the butter dip at 100% (High) for 60 seconds or until melted and warm. Serve the artichokes with the dips.

During the first course
Microwave the vegetable kebabs, then reheat the rice at 100% (High) for 2-3 minutes. If necessary, reheat the sauce for the poussins while clearing the starter away. Serve the poussins on a bed of rice, with the sauce poured over, accompanied by the kebabs.

Poussins Veronique

25½ mins

Standing time: 10 mins

10ml / 2tsp paprika
30ml / 2tbls soy sauce
60ml / 4tbls runny honey
85g / 3½oz butter
4 poussins (about 450-
　　550g / 1-1¼lb each)

SAUCE
60ml / 4tbls plain flour
60ml / 4tbls chicken stock
150ml / ¼pt dry white wine
150ml / ¼pt milk
275g / 10oz seedless white grapes
60ml / 4tbls single cream

SERVES 4

1 Mix the paprika, soy sauce, honey and 40g / 1½oz of the butter in a bowl. Cover and microwave at 100% (High) for 30-45 seconds, or until melted.
2 Truss the legs of the poussins

Poussin Veronique with rice

neatly and place, breast-side down, on a roasting rack. Brush with half the melted butter mixture.
3 Microwave at 100% (High) for 22-26 minutes, turning over and basting with the remaining mixture after half the cooking time. When cooked, the juices should no longer run pink. Cover and stand for 10 minutes.
4 To make the sauce, place the remaining butter in a bowl, cover and microwave at 100% (High) for 30-60 seconds, or until melted. Stir in the flour, stock, wine and milk. Microwave at 100% (High) for 2½-3 minutes, whisking every 15 seconds, until thick and smooth. Stir in the grapes and cream.
5 Serve the poussins on a bed of boiled rice with the sauce poured over the top.

Microtips

Make sure the poussins are well dusted with paprika and brushed with soy to ensure a good colour.

RAY DUNS

Red vegetable kebabs

7 mins

Standing time: none

12 baby carrots (or thin carrots
　　cut in 5cm / 2in lengths)
15ml / 1tbls water
2 red peppers, seeded and cut in
　　18 pieces
18 cherry tomatoes (or 9 small
　　tomatoes, halved)
12 bay leaves
50g / 2oz butter
chopped parsley, to garnish
lemon wedges, to serve

SERVES 4

1 Place the carrots in a dish with the water. Cover and microwave at 100% (High) for 2½-3½ minutes, or until almost tender, stirring once.
2 Thread on to each of six small wooden skewers two tomatoes, one carrot, a piece of pepper and a bay leaf. Thread on to each of another six small wooden skewers two pieces of pepper, one carrot, one tomato and a bay leaf.

442

Pineapple ginger tortoni

3½ mins

Standing time: none

175g / 6oz ginger biscuits, crushed
lime slices to decorate
pineapple pieces, to decorate

ICE CREAM
1 large pineapple
finely grated zest and juice of 1 lime
15ml / 1tbls icing sugar
125ml / 4fl oz milk
1 egg
45ml / 3tbls caster sugar
150ml / ¼pt double cream
30ml / 2tbls rum or kirsch

SERVES 6-8

1 Halve the pineapple lengthways and scoop out the flesh, discarding any woody core. Finely chop the flesh and mix with the lime zest, juice and icing sugar.
2 Cover and freeze until slushy.
3 Microwave the milk at 100% (High) for 1½ minutes, or until hot. Beat the egg with the caster sugar and gradually whisk in the hot milk. Microwave at 100% (High) for 2-2½ minutes and stirring every 30 seconds until the custard is smooth and thickened.
4 Stir in the cream, allow to cool with a layer of cling film over the top to prevent skin from forming. Freeze until almost solid.
5 Whisk the frozen mixture until smooth then stir in the frozen pineapple and rum or kirsch. Cover and freeze for 2-3 hours or until almost firm.
6 Line the base of a 900g / 2lb loaf dish with foil and sprinkle with 50g / 2oz of the biscuit crumbs.
7 Beat 75g / 3oz of the biscuit crumbs into the ice cream and spread evenly in the prepared dish. Top with the remaining crumbs and freeze until solid.
8 Run a palette knife around the edges of the ice cream to loosen, then turn out on to an oblong freezer-proof dish. Decorate with lime and pineapple. Return to the freezer.

Above: *Red Vegetable Kebabs*
Right: *Pineapple Ginger Tortoni*

3 Arrange the kebabs on a dish, making sure they do not overlap. Place the butter in a bowl, cover and microwave at 100% (High) for 30-60 seconds, or until melted. Brush over kebabs, then microwave at 100% (High) for 4-5 minutes, until the tomatoes are hot. Rearrange the kebabs after 2 minutes and brush with more butter. Arrange the kebabs on a serving dish, sprinkle with parsley and serve hot with lemon wedges.

Cook's notes

Kebabs of vegetables of a similar colour make an attractive accompaniment. For a main course in a red or tomato sauce, combine a selection of green vegetables: pieces of small courgettes, green pepper slices, bay leaves and small crisp broccoli spears. Part-cook the broccoli as for the carrots, then continue as in the recipe.

RAY DUNS

Budget buffet for 10

When you've a crowd to cater for but don't want to break the bank, this stylish, yet economical buffet menu will fit the bill — and it's simple and straightforward to prepare with the microwave.

This generous spread, can for the most part, be prepared in advance — and quickly, too — with the help of the microwave. The Glazed Ham is microwaved a day in advance, to cook the delicious sugary crust, and is then chilled until required; it is microwaved again on the day, to serve hot. The Coffee and Almond Gâteau can be made and decorated up to two days beforehand.

Serve a medium-dry sherry with the Florentine Canapés. With the main course, a dry white wine or — for more of a party atmosphere — a chilled rosé is suitable. Offer coffee with the Coffee and Almond Gâteau.

Florentine canapés

$\boxed{\textbf{3}\ \textbf{mins}}$

Standing time: none

These canapés have a distinctly Italian taste due to the combinations of Parmesan with spinach — the ingredient that gives them the name 'Florentine'.

250g / 9oz packet frozen leaf spinach
45ml / 3tbls grated Parmesan
60ml / 4tbls dried breadcrumbs
1 small tomato, seeded and chopped
10ml / 2tsp grated onion
2.5ml / ½tsp grated nutmeg
salt and pepper
24 round 5cm / 2in light crisp crackers

MAKES 24 CANAPÉS

1 Place spinach in a bowl and microwave at 100% (High) for 3-4 minutes, or until thawed, stirring once. Drain and chop coarsely.
2 Stir in cheese, breadcrumbs, tomato, grated onion and nutmeg. Mix well and season to taste. Allow to cool, then cover and refrigerate until needed.
3 Up to two hours before serving, spread the chilled spinach mixture on the crackers. Return to the refrigerator until required.
4 Serve the canapés cold. Or, arrange in a ring on a plate lined with absorbent paper; microwave at 100% (High) for 1¼-1¾ minutes, or until hot, turning the plate once.

Countdown

The previous day
Microwave the Florentine Canapés to the end of stage 2. Microwave the Glazed Ham to the end of stage 3. Microwave the Black-eyed Bean Casserole and refrigerate. Microwave the Coffee and Almond Gâteau, ice and decorate it and store in an airtight container in a cool place until required.

In the morning
Slice the Glazed Ham and arrange on a serving plate with the pineapple slices. Cover with vented cling film and set aside. Microwave the lemon butter for the Lemon Brussels Sprouts, then cover and refrigerate.

45 minutes before the meal
Assemble the Florentine Canapés. Remove the bay leaf from the Black-eyed Bean Casserole, season and reheat at 100% (High) for 10-12 minutes, or until heated through. Cover and leave to stand;

this casserole will keep hot for up to an hour. Microwave the Glazed Ham with the pineapple at 100% (High) for 3-4 minutes, or until hot. Keep warm. Microwave the Brussels sprouts at 100% (High) for 12-15 minutes, or until tender. Reheat the lemon butter at 100% (High) for 30 seconds, or until melted. Toss the sprouts in the butter and serve as soon as possible.

When your guests arrive
Serve the Florentine Canapés cold, or microwave 12 at a time at 100% (High) for 1¼-1¾ minutes, or until hot, turning plate once. Set out the hot food on the table.

Before serving the dessert
Set the coffee tray ready and place the Coffee and Almond Gâteau on a serving plate. Slice it into individual serving-sized wedges. Serve with the freshly brewed strong black coffee.

MENU

Florentine Canapés
Cheesy spinach spread mounded on crisp crackers

Glazed Ham
Tender ham with a pineapple garnish

Black-eyed Bean Casserole
Tasty beans cooked with garlic and bay

Lemon Brussels Sprouts
Crisp sprouts in a tangy, buttery sauce

Coffee and Almond Gâteau
A stunning finale, decorated to suit the occasion

SERVES 10-12

Glazed ham

8 mins

Standing time: none

1.1-1.2kg / 2½-2¾lb cooked boneless ham
822g / 1lb 13oz can pineapple rings in juice, drained
parsley sprig, to garnish

GLAZE
50g / 2oz soft light brown sugar
15ml / 1tbls Dijon mustard

SERVES 10-12

1 In a small bowl, mix the sugar and mustard to a smooth paste.
2 Score the ham fat in a diamond pattern, making cuts 6mm / ¼in deep. Place the ham in a 23cm / 9in round dish and coat with the mustard and sugar glaze.
3 Microwave at 100% (High) for 8-10 minutes, or until the glaze has set to a caramel-like crust. Turn the dish and baste every 2-3 minutes. Allow to cool.
4 Slice the cold ham and arrange on a serving platter with the pineapple slices, cut in half. Cover and microwave at 100% (High) for 3-4 minutes, or until hot. Garnish with parsley and serve.

Black-eyed bean casserole

40 mins

Standing time: 10 mins

450g / 1lb black-eyed beans
2.3L / 4pt boiling water
100g / 4oz gammon or bacon, cut in 12mm / ½in cubes
1 onion, chopped
1 garlic clove, crushed
2 bay leaves
salt and black pepper

SERVES 10-12

Glazed Ham and Black-eyed Bean Casserole

1 Place beans in a 4L / 7pt casserole and pour on 1.1L / 2pt boiling water. Microwave at 100% (High) for 20 minutes. Allow to stand for 10 minutes, then drain.
2 Add 1.1L / 2pt boiling water to the casserole, then the gammon, onion, garlic and bay leaves. Cover and microwave at 100% (High) for 20-25 minutes, or until beans are tender, stirring every 5 minutes.
3 Remove the bay leaves, season to taste and serve.

Cook's notes

The flavour of the Black-eyed Bean Casserole is improved if the dish is made the day before serving, giving time for the flavours to blend.

446

Lemon Brussels sprouts

12½ mins

Standing time: none

900g / 2lb frozen Brussels sprouts
60ml / 4tbls hot water

LEMON BUTTER
40g / 1½oz butter
grated zest of 2 lemons
15ml / 1tbls lemon juice
salt and pepper

SERVES 10-12

1 First, make the lemon butter: melt the butter in a small, covered bowl at 100% (High) for 30-45 seconds. Stir in the lemon zest and juice, and season to taste.
2 Put the sprouts and water in a 1.7L / 3pt casserole. Cover and microwave at 100% (High) for 12-15 minutes, or until tender.
3 Add the lemon butter to the sprouts, toss to mix and serve.

Coffee and almond gâteau

13 mins

Standing time: 5 mins

350g / 12oz butter, softened
350g / 12oz caster sugar
6 eggs, beaten
225g / 8oz self-raising flour, sifted
100g / 4oz ground almonds
45ml / 3tbls instant coffee dissolved in 30ml / 2tbls hot water

ICING AND DECORATION
40g / 1½oz butter
75ml / 5tbls single cream or milk
400-450g / 14-16oz icing sugar
5ml / 1tsp instant coffee powder
dragées, to decorate

SERVES 10-12

1 Grease and base-line a 26cm / 10½in square cake dish; grease the lining paper. Place all the cake ingredients, except for the icing and dragées, in a large bowl and beat with an electric mixer for 2-3 minutes, until blended. Turn the mixture into the prepared dish.
2 Place the dish on an upturned plate and microwave at 70% (Medium) for 5 minutes. Increase the power to 100% (High) and continue cooking for 7-8 minutes more, or until springy to the touch and still slightly moist on top. Give the dish a quarter turn every 2-3 minutes.
3 Stand for 5 minutes and then cool on a wire rack.
4 Make the icing; combine the butter, cream and coffee in a large bowl. Microwave at 50% (Medium) for 1-1½ minutes, or until hot and bubbling.
5 Gradually beat in the icing sugar, until the icing has a smooth spreading consistency. If the icing is too thick, add a little more cream or milk, 15ml / 1tbls at a time.
6 Slice the cold cake horizontally in half. Sandwich the layers back together with one-third of the icing. Use the remaining icing to coat sides and top, marking it decoratively with a palette knife. Decorate with the dragées.

VARIATION
If you prefer a more formal effect, spread the icing into a smooth layer, using a warm palette knife. Break 75g / 3oz plain chocolate into pieces. Place it in a jug and microwave at 70% (Medium-High) for 2 minutes, or until soft and shiny. Stir until smooth. Spoon the chocolate into a piping bag and pipe a message or design over the top of the cake. Instead of a piping bag try a greaseproof paper bag; simply snip off one corner.

Coffee and Almond Gâteau

RAY DUNS

447

Traditional Sunday lunch

Relax and at the same time present an impressive display with this traditional Sunday lunch. The microwave countdown provides a detailed plan for all the courses.

A Sunday lunch for eight is a lovely idea, but often involves a lot of hard work. It generally takes a good slice out of the weekend to prepare and cook, leaving you feeling exhausted and ready for another weekend. With the microwave, however, the idea can actually become reality in half the time it takes with a conventional oven.

Roast lamb is a traditional Sunday dish, which can be cooked to perfection in the microwave. The best method of cooking it is to keep the power on 50% (Medium) for the majority of the time. This will ensure that the meat stays tender and succulent. Taken out of the microwave to complete its required standing time, it will keep warm for an additional 30 minutes

if kept covered. The heat continues to spread by conduction inside the meat for some time, unlike conventionally cooked roasts, which rapidly lose their heat once out of the oven.

Fresh green asparagus is an excellent appetizer for a mid-day meal and the tangy lemon sauce enhances its flavour. New potatoes, served with plenty of butter and teamed with baby carrots and beans, can all be cooked ahead,

kept covered then briefly reheated just before serving. Warmed up in the microwave, they will taste freshly cooked. Then arrange them separately or with the meat. Finish off with a tempting Chocolate Almond Flan.

The timing for this meal depends on how well cooked you like your lamb. If you prefer it well-done begin the roast about 1¾ hours before serving time; with rare meat, allow about 1¼ hours.

MENU

Lemony Asparagus
Fresh asparagus served with lemon butter

Lamb Roast
Flavoured with a bouquet of herbs

Vegetable Medley
A trio of new potatoes, baby carrots and green beans

Chocolate Almond Flan
A sweet almond pastry filled with rich chocolate custard

SERVES 8

Countdown

The day before
Microwave the flan case. Cool and store in an airtight container. Make the custard filling and cover closely with cling film to prevent a skin forming. Store in the refrigerator until needed.

Early on the day
Prepare the vegetables. Microwave the potatoes and set aside. Microwave the carrots and set aside. Microwave the beans and set aside. Arrange all three vegetables on a large platter and cover with cling film. Set aside in the refrigerator or cool place until required.

1¼-1¾ hours before serving
Prepare and microwave the lamb until internal temperature reaches desired reading. Cover the lamb loosely with foil and leave to stand to finish cooking for 10 minutes, then cover tightly with the foil; it will hold its heat for 40 minutes.

While the lamb is cooking
Assemble and finish the Chocolate Almond Flan. Prepare the lemon butter for serving with the fresh asparagus appetizer.

20 minutes before the meal
Microwave the asparagus as directed. Set aside, covered. Microwave the lemon butter sauce and pour over the cooked asparagus when ready to eat.

Before the main course
Reheat the vegetable platter at 100% (High) for 2-3 minutes. While the lamb is being carved, quickly microwave the juices and cornflour to make gravy. Serve with the lamb.

Beat the chilled custard for the Chocolate Almond Flan until smooth, then spoon it into the pastry case.

449

Lemony asparagus

17 mins

Standing time: 5 mins

1kg / 2¼lb fresh asparagus spears
125ml / 4fl oz hot water
100g / 4oz butter
30ml / 1½tbls lemon juice
salt and pepper
lemon slices, to garnish

SERVES 8

1 Cut off the tough ends of the asparagus. Place the asparagus in a $30 \times 20cm$ / $12 \times 8in$ dish with the spears pointing inwards. Add the water and cover with cling film rolled back at one edge to allow steam to escape.
2 Microwave at 100% (High) for 16-18 minutes or until tender, rearranging the spears and turning the dish 2-3 times during cooking. Leave to stand for 5 minutes, then drain.

3 Place the butter and lemon juice in a small bowl. Microwave at 100% (High) for 1-1½ minutes or until the butter is melted. Add salt and pepper to taste, stir, then pour over the asparagus spears and serve at once, garnished with lemon slices. Alternatively, serve the butter separately.

Baby carrots

12 mins

Standing time: 3 mins

900g / 2lb whole baby carrots
60ml / 3tbls water
salt and pepper

SERVES 8

1 Scrub or peel the carrots.
2 Arrange the carrots in a 1.1L / 2pt casserole dish and add the water.
3 Cover and microwave at 100% (High) for 12-15 minutes, stirring

twice during the cooking time.
4 Leave to stand, covered, for 3 minutes, then drain thoroughly before serving. Season to taste.

Green beans

15 mins

Standing time: 2-3 mins

900g / 2lb French beans
60ml / 3tbls water
salt and pepper

SERVES 8

1 Trim the beans and cut into approximately 5cm / 2in lengths.
2 Put the beans in a 1.7L / 3pt casserole dish and add the water.
3 Cover and microwave at 100% (High) for 15-18 minutes, until tender but still crisp. Stir once during cooking.
4 Leave to stand, still covered, for 2-3 minutes, then drain thoroughly before serving. Season to taste.

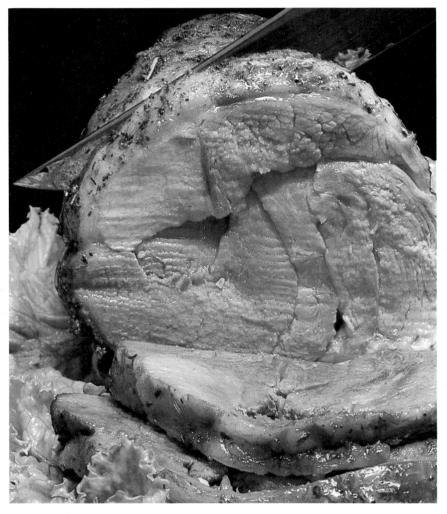

Microtips

You start with an advantage when you microwave lamb: lamb is a tender meat. However, factors such as size, how well done you like your lamb, and whether the meat is at room temperature or has come from the refrigerator all affect timing. Shield thinner areas of meat and/or bone with small pieces of smooth foil, shiny side innermost.

If you use a microwave thermometer or a probe it can be left in while the meat cooks. Alternatively, the meat can be taken from the cooker, tested with a conventional oven thermometer, then returned without the thermometer, should further cooking be necessary. Do not put a conventional thermometer in the microwave as the mercury affects the microwaves.

Microwaving the meat at 50% (Medium) gives a much more succulent joint and prevents fat spitting.

To enjoy hot, leftover, roast meat that has been in the refrigerator without cooking it further, simply slice, cover with cling film and microwave at 100% (High); 225g / 8oz will take about 3 minutes.

Lamb roast

45 mins

Standing time: 10 mins

1.8kg / 4lb boneless rolled leg of lamb
2 garlic cloves, cut in thin slivers
2.5ml / ½tsp dried thyme
2.5ml / ½tsp dried rosemary
2.5ml / ½tsp dried chervil
salt and pepper

GRAVY
5ml / 1tsp cornflour
about 150ml / ¼pt stock or water

SERVES 8

1 Cut small slits in the lamb and insert a garlic sliver into each.
2 Combine the seasonings and rub all over the joint.
3 Place the roast, fat side down, on a roasting rack and insert a meat thermometer or a probe into the thickest part. Calculate the total roasting time from the chart

below. Microwave the lamb at 100% (High) for 5 minutes. Reduce the power to 50% (Medium) and microwave for the remaining part of first half of cooking time.
4 Turn the joint over. Microwave at 50% (Medium) for the second half of the cooking time or until it reaches the required temperature. Leave to stand, covered loosely with foil, for 10 minutes.
5 Stir the cornflour into the meat juice and stir in the stock. Bring to the boil and cook for 1-2 minutes.

Microwaving times for roast lamb

Desired doneness	Time per 450g / 1lb	Standing times	Removal Temperature
Rare	10-12 mins	10 mins	54°C / 129°F
Medium	13-15 mins	10 mins	64°C / 147°F
Well done	16-18 mins	10 mins	70°C / 158°F

New potatoes

15 mins

Standing time: 10 mins

1.1kg / 2½lb small new potatoes
275ml / ½pt hot water
2.5ml / ½tsp salt
butter, to serve
watercress sprigs, to garnish

SERVES 8

1 Wash the potatoes thoroughly, then peel a narrow strip from the centre of each, or pierce.
2 Pour the hot water into a large casserole and add the salt. Stir well until dissolved. Add the potatoes and cover.
3 Microwave at 100% (High) for about 15 minutes or until the potatoes are tender. Leave to stand for at least 10 minutes, drain and add a knob of butter to serve. Garnish with watercress sprigs before serving.

Chocolate almond flan

11½ mins

Standing time: none

50g / 2oz caster sugar
75g / 3oz butter, plus extra for greasing
2 egg yolks
150g / 5oz plain flour
50g / 2oz ground almonds

FILLING
30ml / 6tsps cornflour
15ml / 1tbls plain flour
500ml / 18fl oz milk
10ml / 2tsp instant coffee powder or granules
175g / 6oz plain chocolate, broken into pieces
2 eggs
30ml / 2tbls orange-flavoured liqueur

TO FINISH
150ml / ¼pt double cream
25g / 1oz flaked almonds, toasted

SERVES 8

1 To make the pastry, cream the sugar and butter until light and fluffy. Beat in the egg yolks one at a time, then gradually work in the flour and ground almonds to form a soft, smooth dough. Knead lightly on a floured surface.
2 Lightly grease a 23cm / 9in round flan dish, then roll out the pastry to fit the dish. Chill for half an hour. Prick very thoroughly to help crisp the pastry case and stop it from puffing up. Microwave at 100% (High) for about 5 minutes until the pastry begins to colour; allow to cool.
3 Blend the cornflour, flour, milk and instant coffee together in a 2L / 3½pt bowl. Add chocolate.
4 Microwave at 100% (High) for 5½-6 minutes or until thick, stirring vigorously every 2 minutes.
5 Lightly beat the eggs in a separate bowl and mix in 90ml / 6tbls of the hot custard. Blend, then stir into the remaining custard.
6 Microwave at 100% (High) for about 1 minute until thick. Beat in the liqueur. Cover and chill.
7 About 1½ hours before serving, beat the custard until smooth and spoon into the pastry case.
8 Whip the cream until thick then pipe rosettes over the custard. Decorate the rosettes with toasted almonds, then chill for at least 1 hour before serving.

CHRIS CROFTON

INDEX